THE BAVARIAN
COMMENTARY AND OVID

The Bavarian Commentary and Ovid

Clm 4610, The Earliest Documented Commentary on the Metamorphoses

Robin Wahlsten Böckerman

https://www.openbookpublishers.com

© 2020 Robin Wahlsten Böckerman

ISBN Paperback: 978-1-78374-575-3
ISBN Hardback: 978-1-78374-576-0
ISBN Digital (PDF): 978-1-78374-577-7
DOI: 10.11647/OBP.0154

Cover image: Bayerische Staatsbibliothek München, Munich, clm4610 61v. All rights reserved.
Cover design: Anna Gatti.

Contents

Acknowledgements

This book stems from my PhD thesis and I continue to be grateful to everyone who contributed to that text. Before being transformed into this book the thesis also benefitted from two external examiners who contributed valuable insights and critique, Marek Thue Kretschmer and Mariken Teeuwen. The work on this book was started with the help of the generous Claudio Leonardi stipend from the Zeno Karl Schindler Foundation. The book was finished as a part of a project financed by the Swedish Research Council.

I am deeply grateful to all the people at Open Book Publishers for their invaluable support and aid in the entire process from accepted proposal to published book.

While putting the finishing touches to this book I heard the sad news that Peter Dronke had left us. I never had the pleasure of meeting him, but I would nevertheless like to dedicate this book to him. His scholarship has been a great inspiration for me and many others.

1. Introduction

In noua fert animus mutatas dicere formas
corpora; di, coeptis (nam uos mutastis et illa)
aspirate meis primaque ab origine mundi
ad mea perpetuum deducite tempora carmen.

My mind is bent to tell of bodies changed into new form. Ye
gods, for you yourselves have wrought the changes, breathe
on these my undertakings, and bring down my song in
unbroken strains from the world's very beginning even unto
the present time.[1]
(*Metamorphoses* 1:1-4)

So begins Ovid's *Metamorphoses*, today one of the most well-known
works of literature from ancient Rome. In these first four lines, out of
more than 12,000 in the longest of the Latin epics, Ovid announces his
subject matter—bodies transformed by the acts of the gods—and asks
the gods to support his work. The stories of transformation in the
Metamorphoses, numbering more than 250, have proven to be
tremendously popular throughout history, inspiring authors and
artists in the ancient world, and later famous authors such as Chaucer
and Shakespeare, as well as readers and writers today.

Ovid asks that his poem should be brought to us through history 'in
unbroken strains' and in the very last lines he also wishes for fame for
himself:

Ore legar populi, perque omnia saecula fama,
siquid habent veri vatum praesagia, vivam.

I shall have mention on men's lips, and, if the prophecies of
bards have any truth, through all the ages shall I live in
fame.
(*Metamorphoses* 15:878-79)

We may perhaps agree that among the ancient authors known and
discussed today, Ovid does indeed 'live in fame'. However, the
Metamorphoses has not been brought to us through history 'in
unbroken strains'. With a slow beginning in the eleventh and early

---

[1] All Latin quotations are from *Metamorphoses*, ed. Richard J. Tarrant, (Oxford, 2004). All
translated passages from the *Metamorphoses*, if not otherwise stated, are from
Metamorphoses: Books 1-8 and *vol. 2 Books 9-15*. Transl. Frank Justus Miller (revised by
G.P. Goold) (Cambridge MA, 1977).

twelfth centuries, it was only in the late twelfth century that Ovid entered the medieval mainstream. For several centuries after antiquity Ovid's works seem to have been little read, and they arrived on the medieval literary scene surprisingly late compared to many other ancient authors. Until the 1100s we have only a handful of preserved manuscripts containing the text of the *Metamorphoses*, occasional mention of, and quotation from Ovid by intellectuals, and from around the year 1100 the earliest preserved commentary on the work, known as the Munich Bayerische Staatsbibliothek clm 4610.[2] This commentary is the first systematic study of the *Metamorphoses* and represents the beginning of a tradition.

As the twelfth century progressed, Ovid's work was increasingly copied and more commentaries began to appear. There were at least four families of commentaries in circulation during this century. Two or three of them may stem from the German lands, while the most famous is by Arnulf of Orléans, who made use of the earlier commentaries but added his own inventive dimension. The school milieu in Orléans also produced other commentaries on Ovid's works during the early thirteenth century. Over the next hundred years a noticeable shift in interpretative technique occurred, at least as far as Ovid was concerned; the allegorical interpretation gained ground. This approach can be found here and there in the earlier commentaries; it was consistently used by Arnulf but it was developed and finally used as the dominant form of interpretation in the thirteenth and fourteenth centuries. Representative for the thirteenth century are the later generations of the Orléans school, for example the *Bursarii* by William of Orléans; the work of John of Garland, active at Paris and Oxford; and the anonymous so-called Vulgate commentary, which, judging from the number of manuscripts it has been transmitted in, exerted a strong influence for several centuries. John of Garland offered the most obscure, allegorical, almost mystical interpretation of the *Metamorphoses*, while the Vulgate commentary was more eclectic and easy to use, and could be taken up by subsequent generations to better understand the basic meaning of the text. During the following century the most voluminous commentaries and reworkings of the *Metamorphoses* were created, most famous of which is the *Ovidius Moralizatus* by Pierre Bersuire and the French *Ovide Moralisé*, a moralising translation of the *Metamorphoses* more than three times longer than the original. Giovanni del Virgilio, a Bolognese scholar and

---

[2] From here on clm 4610. The manuscript consists of two codicological units. The first codicological unit is a commentary on Lucan and the second the commentary on the *Metamorphoses*. In this book I use clm 4610 to signify only the *Metamorphoses* commentary.

correspondent with Dante, also wrote an allegorical commentary on the *Metamorphoses* during this century.

Parallel to the commentaries, Ovid's poem was taken up by contemporary culture in many other ways. It was translated into several languages, the earliest of which appears to be Albrecht von Halberstadt's translation into German around 1200; in the east, Maximus Planudes translated the *Metamorphoses* into Greek in the late thirteenth century; the *Ovide Moralisé* gave the *Metamorphoses* shape in French, and during the fourteenth and fifteenth centuries the text was translated into several other languages, such as Italian, Catalan, and English.[3] From the twelfth century onwards Ovid also began to exert a strong influence on literature, both in Latin and in the vernacular languages and in both poetry and prose, as well as on other art forms.

The end of the fifteenth century witnessed the first printed editions of the *Metamorphoses*, which also contained a commentary based on material from the preceding centuries.[4] From this point on, the text of Ovid's work stabilises somewhat, but every new century saw several new editions, together with a multitude of commentaries. Ovid became almost synonymous with Greco-Roman mythology. This continues to the present day: the latest edition of the *Metamorphoses* was produced sixteen years ago by Richard Tarrant and the latest commentary, line-by-line and very much in the spirit of its medieval predecessors, was published as late as 2018.[5]

This is significant not only because it demonstrates the continued interest in engaging with Ovid and his texts, but also the accumulation and reuse of the knowledge and ideas of previous generations. This is where clm 4610 is important. Although there is no reason to believe that clm 4610 was the first *Metamorphoses* commentary ever created, it is the earliest preserved document belonging to the commentary tradition and as such it is significant.

This book is a close study of this single document, the manuscript clm 4610, which stands for *codex latinus monacensis* number 4610. This manuscript is today at the Bayerische Staatsbibliothek, the Bavarian state library in Munich, but was originally one of several hundred manuscripts that came to the library from the Benedictine monastery Benediktbeuern during the *Säkularisation* in the early nineteenth

---

[3] Albrecht von Halberstadt's translation is only preserved in fragments. Giovanni Bonsignori, *Ovidio Methamorphoseos vulgare*, 1375-77; Francesc Alegre, *Transformacions*, between 1472-1482; William Caxton, *The Booke of Ovyde Named Methamorphose*, 1480.

[4] *Metamorphoses*, ed. Raphael Regius, (Venice, 1497).

[5] Tarrant 2004; Luis Rivero García, *Book XIII of Ovid's Metamorphoses: A Textual Commentary*, Sammlung Wissenschaftlicher Commentare (Berlin: De Gruyter, 2018), https://doi.org/10.1515/9783110612493.

century. During this time, Napoleon raised the duchy of Bavaria to a kingdom and, in the process, confiscated the holdings of the monasteries in the region and transferred the books from their libraries to what was then known as Bibliotheca Regia Monacensis.

The manuscript consists of two different codicological units that have been bound together at some point during the middle ages and it carries owner marks from the monastery in a gothic script. The script used in the commentary would suggest a south-German, late-eleventh- or early-twelfth-century hand. The commentary contains copy errors and must therefore be based on one or several pieces of earlier text. There are also some signs of clm 4610 having influenced the other twelfth-century commentaries when it comes to individual explanations, but as far as we know there exists only one single copy of this text. We have no further details available to shed light on the fate of the manuscript from its creation until it attracted the interest of two German scholars at the end of the nineteenth century.

In 1873 the commentary was first noticed by M. Haupt, who included a transcription of a small section of it in his article 'Coniectanea'; less than ten years later, Karl Meiser made a more thorough study of the text in his article 'Ueber einen Commentar zu den Metamorphosen des Ovid'. [6] Here he identifies which passages from the *Metamorphoses* are commented upon and also includes transcriptions of some extracts, as well as a discussion on, among other things, some of its sources. This forty-two-page article from almost a century and a half ago about an obscure commentary on Ovid has had a remarkable impact. It has been cited by almost every scholar dealing with the reception of Ovid, but also by scholars interested in medieval philosophy and theology. This is partly because Meiser highlighted the few Christianising explanations that exist in the commentary and because he, following Haupt, identified the name Manogaldus, which appears a few times in the commentary, with Manegold of Lautenbach. Several scholars, such as Paule Demats and Michael Herren, have followed the tracks laid out by Meiser, often with the purpose of examining Christian-Platonic ideas in the commentary. [7]

[6] M. Haupt, 'Coniectanea', *Hermes: Zeitschrift Für Klassische Philologie*, 1873.7 (1873); Karl Meiser, 'Ueber Einen Commentar Zu Den Metamorphosen Des Ovid', *SitzungsBerichte Der Königlich Bayerischen Akademie Der Wissenschaften. Philosophisch-Philologische Und Historische Klasse*, 1885 (1885), 47–117.

[7] Paule Demats, *Fabula: Trois Études de Mythographie Antique et Médiévale*, Publications Romanes et Françaises, (Genève: Droz, 1973); Michael Herren, 'Manegold of Lautenbach's Scholia on the Metamorphoses - Are There More?', *Notes and Queries*, 2004.5 (2004), 218–22, https://doi.org/10.1093/nq/510218.

More recently Peter Dronke has treated facets of clm 4610 in two separate books.[8]

Although these scholars achieved good results with the help of Meiser's extracts, it is my belief that the entire commentary should be made available and studied. It is relatively short, but still deals with all fifteen books of the *Metamorphoses*: clm 4610 thus offers a unique opportunity to understand how an entire commentary, rather than selected parts of it, functions as a hermeneutic device on its own and in relationship to its target text.

There is an intrinsic value to clm 4610 as the earliest known commentary on the *Metamorphoses*. When it comes to editing, it presents both challenges and opportunities. It is a reasonably short commentary and only exists in one manuscript, which saves the editor from the problematic textual situation of, for example, Arnulf's commentary or the Vulgate commentary, or the sheer temporal or logistical challenge of trying to edit a text as long as the *Ovide Moralisé*. However, only having access to one manuscript also presents a challenge. The text in clm 4610 contains many errors and problematic readings, all of which can be solved by the editor's judgement alone. For this reason, I have strived to be as transparent as possible as far as editorial decisions are concerned, so that the reader may critically engage with my version of the text

Clm 4610 presents other challenges: it is the first of its kind, and it is anonymous, both of which cause some difficulties in providing context. However, it is certainly not the last of its kind, and it must be regarded in the context of all the other *Metamorphoses* commentaries. Some of these commentaries are the objects of ongoing research projects, while many others are still unedited, or only partially edited, or in some cases virtually unknown to the research community. The latter problem will be remedied by Frank Coulson's forthcoming article on Ovid in *Catalogus Translationum et Commentatorium*, which will prove an invaluable aid when it comes to finding the relevant manuscripts for research, among other things. The work on the remaining twelfth-century commentaries is divided between myself and David Gura, University of Notre Dame, who is soon to publish a

---

[8] Peter Dronke, *The Spell of Calcidius: Platonic Concepts and Images in the Medieval West* (Firenze: SISMEL edizioni del Galluzzo, 2008); Peter Dronke, *Sacred and Profane Thought in the Early Middle Ages* (Firenze: SISMEL edizioni del Galluzzo, 2016).

critical edition of Arnulf's commentary with Brepols.[9] This is a long-awaited work as it will be the first edition of the text since the transcriptions of Fausto Ghisalberti and the partial edition in Gura's PhD dissertation.[10] The work of another member of the Orléans school, William of Orléans (c. 1200) and his *Bursarii super Ovidios*, a lengthy and dense commentary on all of Ovid's works, has been edited by Wilken Engelbrecht, Palacký University Olomouc.[11] Frank Coulson has long been working on the Vulgate commentary, which is important because of its lasting popularity and difficult because of its expansive textual tradition. Coulson first published a part of the text with the Toronto Medieval Latin Texts series, and recently translated Book 1 from this commentary. In cooperation with Piero Andrea Martina (Universität Zurich) he is now contracted to produce an edition of the entire commentary with Classiques Garnier.[12] At the Institut für Klassische Philologie at Universität Bern, work on a new edition of Giovanni del Virgilio's *Expositio* is being done by Gerlinde Huber-Rebenich.[13] The dauting task of working on the *Ovide Moralisé* is being approached as a group effort by a team of researchers gathered in various projects in France, Switzerland and Germany, such as the project *Ovide en français* (2014-2017) directed by Marylène Possamaï

[9] The edition will be published in Brepols' *Corpus Christianorum Continuatio Mediaevalis* series. Gura has also published articles on Arnulf of Orléans and related material: David T. Gura, 'Living with Ovid: The Founding of Arnulf of Orléans' Thebes' in *Manuscripts of the Latin Classics 800-1200*, ed. Erik Kwakkel, 131-66. Leiden University Press, 2015; 'The Ovidian Allegorical Schoolbook: Arnulf of Orléans and John of Garland Take Over a Thirteenth-Century Manuscript', *Pecia* 20 (2018), 7-43.

[10] Fausto Ghisalberti, 'Arnolfo d'Orleans: Un Cultore Di Ovidio Nel Secolo XII', *Memorie Del R. Istituto Lombardo, Classe Lettere*, 1932.24 (1932), 157–234; David T. Gura, *A critical edition and study of Arnulf of Orléans' philological commentary to Ovid's Metamorphoses*. (Unpublished doctoral dissertation, Ohio State University, 2010).

[11] Wilken Engelbrecht, *Filologie in de Dertiende Eeuw: de Bursarii super Ovidios van Magister Willem van Orléans. Editie, inleiding en commentaar.* (Olomouc: Vydavatelství Univerzity Palackého, 2003).

[12] Frank T. Coulson, *The 'Vulgate' Commentary on Ovid's Metamorphoses: The Creation Myth and the Story of Orpheus*, Toronto Medieval Latin Texts, 0082-5050; 20 (Toronto: Centre for Medieval Studies: 1991); Frank T. Coulson, *The Vulgate Commentary on Ovid's Metamorphoses Book 1* (Kalamazoo: Medieval institute publications, 2015).

[13] At the time of writing I have no information on when this edition is due for print. Previously the only available edition has been: F. Ghisalberti, *Giovanni del Virgilio epositori delle* Metamorfosi (Firenze: Olschki, 1933).

(Université de Lyon 2) and Richard Trachsler (Universität Zürich).[14] Trachsler is currently continuing with the project *Les Sources de l'Ovide Moralisé* (2018-2020), which involves several other researchers. Marek Thue Kretschmer (Norwegian University of Science and Technology) and PhD student Pablo Piqueras (Universidad de Murcia) are investigating the relationship between the French *Ovide Moralisé* and the Latin *Ovidius moralizatus* by Pierre Bersuire (c. 1350-1360), as well as the complex textual transmission of the latter work.[15] Piqueras is also working on the first complete Castilian translation of the *Ovidius Moralizatus*. A translation by Frank Coulson of *Ovidius moralizatus* is also forthcoming with Dumbarton Oaks Medieval Library.

Currently there is also a surge of interest in the reception of Ovid in other languages. With regard to the Romance context, Irene Salvo Garcia (CIHAM, Lyon) has recently finished the project 'Romaine: Ovid as Historian. The reception of classical mythology in medieval France and Spain', which investigates the connection between Ovidian material and the Castilian *General estoria* of Alfonso X.[16] Where the Celtic world is concerned, Paul Russell (University of Cambridge) has recently published the book *Reading Ovid in Medieval Wales*.[17]

---

[14] Marylène Possamaï-Pérez, *L'Ovide moralisé, essai d'interprétation*, (Paris: Honoré Champion, 2006).

C. Baker, M. Possamaï-Pérez, M. Besseyre, M. Cavagna, S. Cerrito, O. Collet, M. Gaggero, Y. Greub, J.-B. Guillaumin, V. Rouchon, I. Salvo García, T. Städtler, R. Trachsler (ed.) *Ovide moralisé, Livre I, édition collective*, (Paris: SATF, 2018).

M. Possamaï-Pérez, S. Biancardi, P. Deleville, F. Montorsi, *Ovidius explanatus: Traduire et commenter les 'Métamorphoses' au Moyen Âge*, (Paris: Classiques Garnier, 2018).

Irene Salvo García 'Les sources de l'*Ovide moralisé* I: types et traitement', *Le Moyen Âge*. *Revue d'histoire et de philologie*, 2018/2, tome CXXIV, 307-336.

[15] Marek Thue Kretschmer 'L'*Ovidius moralizatus* de Pierre Bersuire: essai de mise au point', *Interfaces: A Journal of Medieval European Literatures* 3 (2016), 221-244; 'L'*Ovide moralisé* comme source principale de la version parisienne de l'*Ovidius moralizatus* de Pierre Bersuire', in C. Gaullier-Bougassas et M. Possamaï-Pérez (ed.), *Réécritures et adaptations de l'*Ovide moralisé *(XIVe - XVIIe siècle)*, Brepols (forthcoming).

[16] Irene Salvo García, 'Ovidio en la 'General estoria' de Alfonso X' (Unpublished doctoral dissertation, Madrid-Lyon 2012).

[17] Paul Russell, *Reading Ovid in Medieval Wales*, Text and Context (Columbus: The Ohio State University Press, 2017).

These are only the ongoing projects known to me and mainly those related to the *Metamorphoses*.[18]

This book is structured in the following way: The core is the edition of clm 4610 presented in Part II. The rest of the book serves the purpose of providing the reader with different aids to better understand the text. **Chapter 1** is this introduction. **Chapter 2** contains a brief survey of the reception of Ovid leading up to the twelfth century. **Chapter 3** consists of a contextual discussion around the question of where and when the commentary was produced and used. **Chapter 4** seeks to answer the question of what the commentary is and how it was used by carefully analysing the function of the commentary. **Chapter 5** examines clm 4610 in relationship to eleventh- and twelfth-century marginal commentary as well as the other freestanding commentaries of the twelfth century. **Part II** consists of the edition of the entire commentary together with a facing-page translation. The edition is introduced by a manuscript description and editorial principles. The **appendix** contains an edition and translation of Book 1 of the near contemporary commentary found in the manuscript clm 14482.

A note on the text and translations

If nothing else is stated all translations are by the author. Translations of Ovid are taken from the Loeb Classical Library's six volumes of Ovid. Passages in the *Metamorphoses* are referred to by book and line, and when necessary by an abbreviated form of the title (e.g. Met. 1:555 is line 555 in Book 1 of the *Metamorphoses*). Passages in the edition of

---

[18] For different perspectives and a good overview of the field see: Birger Munk Olsen, *L'étude Des Auteurs Classiques Latins Aux XIe et XIIe Siècles. T. 2, Catalogue Des Manuscrits Classiques Latins Copiés Du IXe Au XIIe Siècle: Livius - Vitruvius: Florilèges - Essais de Plume* (Paris: Éd. du CNRS, 1985). As far as Ovid's other works are concerned there are some manuscripts, or fragments of manuscripts, of the other works of Ovid dated to the ninth through to the eleventh century, and some of them carry marginal glosses. However, no substantial commentary on Ovid's work predating clm 4610 seems to exist, but there are some glosses on the *Ibis*, which Alan Cameron argues may also represent an ancient commentary. For a study of this and other commentaries on Ovid's other work see: Ralph J. Hexter, *Ovid and Medieval Schooling: Studies in Medieval School Commentaries on Ovid's Ars Amatoria, Epistulae Ex Ponto, and Epistulae Heroidum*, Münchener Beiträge Zur Mediävistik Und Renaissance-Forschung (München: Arbeo-Gesellschaft, 1986).
See also Alan Cameron, *Greek Mythography in the Roman World*, American Classical Studies, v. 48 (Oxford; New York: Oxford University Press, 2004), p. 181. Birger Munk Olsen, *L'étude Des Auteurs Classiques Latins Aux XIe et XIIe Siècles. T. 4. P. 1, La Réception de La Littérature Classique*, (Paris: CNRS éd., 2009), pp. 88-95.

the commentary are also usually referred to by the book and line in the *Metamorphoses* to which they are related (e.g. 2:15 refers to the commentary on line 15 in Book 2). This information is located in the left margin of the edition and is the most convenient way of referencing entire passages. When more precision is needed, specific lines in the edition are referenced (e.g. edition 1. 147). Medieval manuscripts and transcriptions of these are referred to by a short form of the modern manuscript name and manuscript folio (e.g. clm 14809, 29r refers to München Bayerische Staastbibliothek clm 14809, folio 29 recto).

Part I
2. The Fate of Ovid Until the Twelfth Century

When and how did the *Metamorphoses* make its entrance onto the literary and scholarly scene of the Middle Ages? The general consensus regarding the *Metamorphoses* is that it was not widely read from Late Antiquity until the eleventh century, from which point we have more substantial material evidence. The following is a survey of the material evidence of the reception of Ovid from the Carolingian period until the twelfth century.

The Material Evidence

We will start by considering the material evidence in the form of the surviving *Metamorphoses* manuscripts from the ninth to the twelfth centuries, as illustrated by the following table:

Table 1. Number of preserved manuscripts for the *Metamorphoses* over four centuries[19]

Century:	9th	10th	11th	12th	Total
Germany	1	1	5	15	22
Italy	-	1	4	14	19
France	1	-	3	8	12
England	-	1	-	1	2
Spain	-	-	-	1	1
Total	2	3	12	39	56

Of all of Ovid's works, the *Metamorphoses* survives in the largest number of copies. At the other end of the scale, we find the spurious *Halieutica* with only one copy from the ninth century, *De medicamine* with one copy from the eleventh century, and the *Ibis* with two copies from the twelfth century. As for the *Metamorphoses*, these numbers show a clear increment as the centuries pass, with four times as many

---

[19] This table is a translation of Jean-Yves Tilliette's table in 'Savant et poètes du moyen âge face à Ovide: les débuts de l'*aetas Ovidiana* (v. 1050-v. 1200)' in *Ovidius Redivivus: Von Ovid zu Dante*, ed. M. Picone, B. Zimmerman (Freiburg: Rombach, 2014), p. 70. Tilliette's table is based on the information in Birger Munk Olsen, *L'étude Des Auteurs Classiques Latins Aux XIe et XIIe Siècles. T. 2, Catalogue Des Manuscrits Classiques Latins Copiés Du IXe Au XIIe Siècle: Livius - Vitruvius: Florilèges - Essais de Plume* (Paris: Éd. du CNRS, 1985).

preserved manuscripts from the twelfth century compared to the eleventh.

To get a clearer idea of what these figures entail we will add some comparative material from the other curriculum authors:[20]

Century:	9th	10th	11th	12th	Total
Virgil, *Aeneis*	37	25	47	85	194
Cicero, *De inventione*	5	9	33	128	175
Lucan, *Bellum civile*	10	14	32	118	174
Horace, *Epistulae*	6	15	37	95	153
Sallust, *Bellum Iugurth.*	2	7	37	94	140
Juvenal, *Saturae*	7	23	36	52	118
Terence, *Comoediae*	6	18	34	50	108
Statius, *Thebais*	3	11	20	70	104
Persius, *Satirae*	4	16	30	22	72

Virgil's *Aeneid* is at the top of this league with a total of 194 preserved manuscripts, while Persius's *Satirae* comes last with seventy-two manuscripts—still almost twenty more than for the *Metamorphoses*.

All works show the same pattern of a steady, almost exponential, increase from century to century (except for the *Aeneid* with regard to the ninth and the tenth centuries and Persius with regard to the eleventh and twelfth). These numbers tell us that, even though we are looking at preserved manuscripts and not the actual number of manuscripts available at the time, the pattern is the same for all authors. This means that it is unlikely that there was a large quantity

---

[20] This table is created from the information in Birger Munk Olsen, *L'Étude des Auteurs Classiques Latins aux XIe et XIIe Siécles* vol. 4:2 (Paris: CNRS Éditions, 2014), pp. 24-30. Munk Olsen also has the following numbers for the *Metamorphoses*:

Century:	9th	10th	11th	12th	Total
Metamorphoses	1	2	10	40	53

The number of manuscripts in relation to century does not completely match the information in Munk Olsen 1985. The reason seems to be that Munk Olsen has classified some of the *Metamorphoses* fragments as excerpts, and thus removed them from numbers illustrated in the table above. I have chosen to use Tilliette's table because it has regional division, but it should be noted that the table for the other authors might contain a few more manuscripts if fragments/excerpts were included.

of Ovid's work in circulation during, for example, the ninth century, which has subsequently been destroyed or lost.[21]

While comparing Ovid to the other ancient authors, it should also be mentioned that there are, of course, several other writers who are well known today, but were much less read than Ovid or the other authors I have mentioned during the ninth to the twelfth centuries: for example, Apuleius (a total of two surviving manuscripts for his *Metamorphoses*), Caesar (sixteen in total for *De bello Gallico*) and Plautus (six in total for his *Comoediae*).

We can also compare the number of manuscripts to the number of occurrences of the *Metamorphoses* in medieval inventories from before the thirteenth century. In the case of the *Metamorphoses*, the number of mentions is twenty-nine (compared to fifty-three surviving manuscripts).[22] This can be compared to the case of Persius, who is mentioned eighty-nine times in the inventories, but with only seventy-two surviving manuscripts from this period.[23] A thorough examination of, for example, medieval German library catalogues, could probably also add to the inventory information (unspecific as to time and place) listed by Munk Olson, but that falls outside the scope of this study.[24]

We can pinpoint the *Metamorphoses* manuscripts more precisely in time and space. Of the twelve oldest manuscripts listed in Tarrant's edition of the *Metamorphoses*, eight are from the latter part of the eleventh century or from the end of the eleventh/beginning of the twelfth century.[25] Two are dated as twelfth century only, and two as tenth century. As far as space is concerned, the information in the table above indicates that Germany, followed by Italy, dominate as far as provenance of the manuscripts is concerned.

Also worth mentioning in this context are the florilegia, in which there are some traces of Ovid's works preserved. Among the oldest are a ninth-century florilegium from St Gall and the *Opus prosodiacum* by

---

[21] Munk Olsen has limited his catalogue to cover the period from the ninth to the twelfth century. If we consult *Texts and Transmission*, we can add to this that the only authors that seem to have an older tradition than the ninth century are Persius, Terence and Virgil, whose texts are extant in manuscripts from the fourth century onwards. *Texts and Transmission: A Survey of the Latin Classics*, ed. L. D. Reynolds (Oxford: Clarendon Press, 1983), pp. 293-295, 412-420 and 433-437.

[22] Munk Olsen 2014, p. 86. Munk Olsen does not give any more specific information in regard to time and place than '*antérieurs au début du xiiie siécle*' (p. 82).

[23] Munk Olsen 2014, p. 83.

[24] A few mentions of Ovid are to be found in Günther Glauche, *Schullektüre im Mittelalter: Entstehung und Wandlungen des Lektürekanons bis 1200 nach den Quellen dargestellt* (München: Arbeo-Gesellschaft, 1970) pp. 82, 86-87, 93, 95, 102.

[25] Tarrant 2004, pp. viii-xiv.

Micon Centulensis, which has survived in many copies, the oldest of which stems from the ninth century.[26] Since only a fragment of the *Metamorphoses* and a few of Ovid's other texts are extant in copies from this period, these florilegia are important witnesses to the fact that Ovid was being read alongside other ancient authors at this time, albeit in the form of short extracts. However, the absolute majority of the florilegia as well as the manuscripts of the complete works stem from the twelfth century, and the evidence from the florilegia seems to accord with that of the manuscripts in regard to establishing a growing interest in Ovid towards the end of the eleventh century.

Ovid and the Medieval Authors

Thus far, the material evidence of Ovid's work, which, together with the preserved commentaries, is the direct evidence of the Ovidian tradition. In the following, we will take a look at the indirect evidence in the form of the slightly more nebulous witness consisting of mentions and quotations of Ovid among scribes and scholars. In general, it is difficult to tell if the types of allusions, mentions, and quotations to be discussed here are the result of direct contact with and use of Ovid's texts by the medieval scholars, or whether they stem from second-hand sources of some sort. In addition, many of the authors mentioned below may have a complicated textual tradition of their own, which may contribute to complicating the picture. The end point of this short survey is the late twelfth and thirteenth centuries, which were famously named the *Aetas Ovidiana* by Ludwig Traube on account of the influence Ovid's verse (mainly his elegiac couplets) had on the poets of that period, an influence that is, by now, well researched, and not the topic of this study.[27]

To begin the discussion of the medieval familiarity with Ovid we will look at a type of indirect familiarity, namely how Ovid was known through Virgil. Virgil was always the most popular poet among scholars of this period, with a manuscript and commentary tradition that eclipses those of all other ancient authors. There exists a

---

[26] Sankt Gallen, Stiftsbibliothek, 870; Brussels, Bibliothèque royale, 10470-10473. For more on the florilegia see Birger Munk Olsen, *L'étude Des Auteurs Classiques Latins Aux XIe et XIIe Siècles. T. 3. P. 1, Les Classiques Dans Les Bibliothèques Médiévales* (Paris: Éd. du CNRS, 1987)., pp. 837-883; Munk Olsen 2014, pp. 300-328.

[27] Ludwig Traube, *Vorlesungen und Abhandlungen 2, Einleitung in die lateinische Philologie des Mittelalters* (Munich, 1911), p. 113. For a discussion of the concept, see Hexter 1986, p. 2. A good starting point for exploring this period is *Ovid in the Middle Ages*, ed. James G. Clark, Frank T. Coulson, Kathryn L. McKinley (Cambridge: Cambridge University Press, 2011).

curious connection between Virgil and Ovid: the so-called pseudo-Ovidian *Argumenta Aeneidis*. These verses introduce each new book of the *Aeneid* and are found in several Virgil manuscripts, one dating as far back as the fifth century.[28] In these verses, Ovid is juxtaposed with Virgil and the younger poet often confesses his lower status, as in the following:

> *Vergilius magno quantum concessit Homero,*
> *   tantum ego Vergilio, Naso poeta, meo.*
> *Nec me praelatum cupio tibi ferre, poeta;*
> *   ingenio si te subsequor, hoc satis est.*

> 'As much as Virgil yielded to mighty Homer, / so much do I, the poet Ovid, [yield] to my Virgil. / Nor is it my wish to relate that I am preferred to you, O poet. / If my talent is second to yours, this is sufficient.' [29]

These verses, when encountered by the medieval reader, must have established or strengthened the subordinate position of Ovid compared to Virgil, but also teased the reader with a glimpse of an unknown or little-known poet during a time when Ovid's works were not in circulation.[30] As a side note, when considering the relationship between Virgil and Ovid even during the high middle ages, the fascinating manuscript Ottob. lat. 3313 in the Vatican library is illustrative. In this large eleventh- or twelfth-century manuscript containing all of Virgil's texts, the *Metamorphoses* has been copied into the margins. On fol. 9ᵛ, in which the main text is *Eclogue* 7, a few lines from *Tristia* introduced by the title *Epythapion ouidii* function as a brief introduction to the *Metamorphoses*, which begins after these lines and continues in the margin until fol. 65ʳ where it stops at *Met.* 6:294. The *Metamorphoses* text does not seem to be written by the same hand as the main text and there may have been more than one hand involved in this work.[31] This is, of course, a unique occurrence, but the very idea of writing the *Metamorphoses* in the margins of Virgil's work tells us

---

[28] Vatican City, Biblioteca Apostolica Vaticana: Vat. lat. 3867.

[29] Jan M. Ziolkowski, Michael Putnam (ed.), *The Virgilian Tradition: The First Fifteen Hundred Years* (New Haven: Yale University Press, 2008), p. 22. Translation M. Putnam.

[30] Hugo of Trimberg brings up these verses in his thirteenth century *Registrium multorum auctorum: Antequam Virgilius Eneados tangatur,* | *Titulus Ovidii sibi preponatur.* | *Hic enim libris singulis titulos prefixit,* | *In laudem tanti operis unde scribens dixit. Das Registrum multorum auctorum des Hugo von Trimberg: ein Quellenbuch zur lateinischen Literaturgeschichte des Mittelalters*, ed. J. Huemer (Wien: F. Tempsky, 1888)]., l. 44-47.

[31] The manuscript was examined on location by me in November 2015.

something about the connection between these two authors that was made by the medieval reader.

As far as its initial medieval reception is concerned, the locus classicus for early familiarity with Ovid is the eighth-century bishop, Theodulf of Orléans and his friend Modoin, bishop of Autun. The latter added the nickname Naso to his given name, and wrote poetry inspired by his namesake. However, only two of Modoin's poems composed in elegiac couplets survive.[32] In the case of Theodulf, far more texts are preserved. His most famous poem related to Ovid is named *De libris quos legere solebam et qualiter fabulae poetarum a philosophis mystice pertractentur*, in which Ovid appears on line 18:

> *Et modo Pompeium, modo te, Donate, legebam,*
> *Et modo Virgilium, te modo, Naso loquax.*
> *In quorum dictis quamquam sint frivola multa,*
> *Plurima sub falso tegmine vera latent.*[33]

> At one time I read Pompeius, at another you, Donatus, / At one time Virgil, at another you, talkative Naso. / Although there are many frivolous things in these authors' sayings, / There is a great truth hidden under a false covering.

However, Theodulf and Modoin are far from the only ones who mention or draw inspiration from Ovid at this time. In fact, Ovid is referenced by several of the most well-known names of the period. The most famous of all the Carolingian scholars, Alcuin, uses Ovid in a few places, such as in this extract from a letter to Angilbert, who is also known by the nickname Homer:

> *'Si nihil adtuleris, ibis, Homere, foras'.*
> *Hoc de te tuoque itinere prophetatum esse, quis dubitat? Si Christum Sibilla*
> *eiusque labores praedixit venturum, cur non Naso Homerum eiusque itinera praececinit?*[34]

> 'if you bring nothing, Homer, out you go!' Why do you doubt that this was foretold about you and your trip? If the Sybil foretold the coming of Christ and his work, why would Naso not prophesise about Homer and his travels?

[32] E. H. Alton, 'Ovid in the Medieval Schoolroom' in *Hermathena* 94 (1960), p. 24.
[33] *Monumenta Germaniae Historica* (MGH) Poetae Latini aevi Carolini, vol. 1, p. 543, l. 17-20.
[34] MGH *Epistolae Karolini aevi* vol. 2, p. 141.

The quotations here is from *Ars amatoria* 2:280. Alcuin uses Book 2 of this work at least twice more, once in prose form in letter and the same passage (*Ars amat.* 2:670) is then also used in a piece of poetry in another letter.[35] Angilbert, the addressee of Alcuin's letter, also uses many Ovid allusions in his poems.[36]

In general, Ovid seems often to be juxtaposed with other ancient authors or placed last in a list of authorities, as can be seen here in a part of a poem listed as one of the *carmina dubia* of Paul the Deacon:

> *Teudulfus rutilat mire de arte Iuvenci*
> *Atque Angelpertus, divini ambo poetae,*
> *Quos Flaccus Varro Lucanus Nasoque honorant;*
>
> Theodulf glows with wonder at Iuvencus's art, as does Angilbert, both divine poets, whom Flaccus, Varro, Lucan and Naso honour;[37]

Here the ancient poets are described as taking second place to the Christian poets. The same theme is picked up during the ninth century, in a letter from the monk Otfridus to archbishop Moguntinus from 865, where Ovid is mentioned among the *gentilium vates* (pagan poets) and then again contrasted with the virtues of the Christian poets Arator, Juvencus, and Prudentius.[38] Around the same time, Ermenrich

---

[35] MGH *Epistolae Karolini aevi* vol. 2, p. 369 and 481. In addition to this, in a poem Alcuin paraphrases Virgil's Corydon and ends the poem with:

Virgilius quondam: 'Rusticus es Corydon'.

Dixerat ast alter, melius sed, Naso poeta:

'Presbyter est Corydon', sit cui semper ave. MGH Poetae Latini aevi Carolini, vol .1, p. 250.

[36] MGH Poetae Latini aevi Carolini, vol .1, pp. 358-380.

[37] MGH Poetae Latini aevi Carolini, vol .1, p 77, l. 15-22.

[38] *Dum rerum quondam sonus inutilium pulsaret aures quorundam probatissimorum virorum eorumque sanctitatem laicorum cantus inquietaret obscenus, a quibusdam memoriae dignis fratribus rogatus, maximeque cuiusdam venerandae matronae verbis, nimium flagitantis, nomine Iudith, partem evangeliorum eis Theotisce conscriberem, ut aliquantulum huius cantus lectionis ludum secularium vocum deleret et in evangeliorum propria lingua occupati dulcedine sonum inutilium rerum noverint declinare (petitioni quoque iungentes queremoniam, quod gentilium vates, ut Virgilius Lucanus Ovidius caeterique quam plurimi, suorum facta decorarent lingua nativa – quorum iam voluminum dictis fluctuare cognoscimus mundum, nostrae etiam a sectae probatissimorum virorum facta laudabant, Iuvenci Aratoris Prudentii caeterorumque multorum, qui sua lingua dicta et miracula Christi decenter ornabant, nos vero, quamvis eadem fide eademque gratia instructi, divinorum verborum splendorem clarissimum proferre propria lingua dicebant pigrescere) – hoc dum eorum caritati importune mihi instanti negare nequivi, feci, non quasi peritus, sed fraterna petitione coactus.* MGH Epistolae Karolini aevi vol. 4, p. 166–67.

of Ellwangen (died 874), monk at the monastery in Ellwangen, who was then a student of Rabanus Maurus and eventually became bishop of Passau, quotes a passages from Ovid in a long letter to Grimaldus, abbot of St Gall:

> *Item nomina, quę in penultimis naturaliter sunt longa, postquam*
> *in obliquis casibus additur quęlibet liquida, permanent longa: ut*
> *'salûber salûbris',*
> *'lugûber lugûbris'. Ut Ovidius in libro Metamorphoseon. 'Phoebe*
> *salûber, ades'.*[39]

Nouns, which naturally have a long penultimate, remain long after a liquid is added to the oblique cases, as in *'salûber salûbris', 'lugûber lugûbris'*. As Ovid in the Metamorphoses: Salubrious Phoebus, be present.

This passage is noteworthy because it explicitly mentions the *Metamorphoses*. However, the quotation is from *Remedia amoris*, verse 704, and may be at least partially derived from Prisican.[40] Later on in the same letter Ermenricus quotes the *Metamorphoses* again:

> *Productum: ut Ovidius in I Metamorphoseon:*
> *'Iussit et ambite, circumdare litora terrę'.*[41]

Lengthened, as Ovid in Book 1 of the *Metamorphoses*: He commanded the waters to surround the edge of the earth.

This is an explicit mention of the work and a quotation from *Metamorphoses* 1:37, but again via Priscian, which highlights the importance of intermediaries.[42]

There are not many traces of Ovid to be found in the tenth century. E. H. Alton, in his published lecture 'Ovid in the Medieval Schoolroom,' claims that there is 'considerable evidence' that Ovid was studied in the schoolroom during this period, but he never supplies any sources to support this claim.[43] I have, however, managed to find a few traces of Ovid. First and foremost, by Ratherius of Verona, who

---

[39] MGH Epistolae Karolini aevi vol 3, p. 544.

[40] *Ovidius tamen 'saluber' dixit et 'celeber' in IIII || fastorum: Phoebe saluber ades et: Circus erit pompa celeber numero que deorum. Grammatici Latini. Vol. 2, Prisciani : Institutionum grammaticarum libri I-XII,* ed. Heinrich Keil, Martin Julius Hertz, (Teubner: Leipzig, 1855-1880), 3:96:15.

[41] MGH Epistolae Karolini aevi vol 3, p. 551.

[42] *Grammatici Latini. Vol. 2,* 10:547:2.

[43] Alton 1960, p. 26.

mentions Ovid in the prologue to his *Phrenesis* written sometime between 955-56. Ovid is mentioned at the end of a list of authors and is listed among the satirists.[44] Ratherius also quotes from *Ars amatoria* (3:49) in a letter to count Nanno of Verona from 968 and paraphrases *Ex Ponto* in a letter to bishop Hubert of Parma from 963.[45] Around the same time, Gerbert of Reims or Aurillac, later pope Sylvester II, makes an allusion to both Ovid and Virgil in one sentence in a letter, which may imply thorough familiarity with their work.[46] The particular scene alluded to in the *Metamorphoses* is where Io is being tortured by Juno and chased by the Erinys.

Moving into the eleventh century there is clear evidence of Ovid's growing popularity. The letters from this period shows how Ovid is both mentioned by name and portions of his work used in paraphrases and allusions.[47] The most prolific Ovid reader in the German lands seems to have been Meinhard of Bamberg (died in 1088). In a letter to the bishop of Bamberg from c. 1060, Meinhard quotes from *Tristia* (5:14:44):

> *Quę omnia etsi vos ipsos penitus nosse non ambigimus, nos tamen*
> *ad promptius excitandam memoriam capitulatim ea descripsimus,*
> *et ut ille ait,*
> Vela damus, quamvis remige navis eat.

---

[44] *satyrographus omnibus praeferendum Flaccum Horatium, in libris quoque, qui praetitulantur Ex ponto, Nasonem Ovidium.* MGH *Die Briefe des Bischofs Rather von Verona*, p. 63.

[45] *Tolerabilius nam fuerat vestrum sic ferre dominium, ut, quem timerem, eundem diligerem ipsum, ut facere inchoaveram illum, de quo mihi congruere illud feci Nasonicum:* Probra Teraphneae qui dixerat ante marite, Mox cecinit laudes prosperiore lyra. MGH *Die Briefe des Bischofs Rather von Verona*, p. 182; for the paraphrase see the same volume, p. 97.

[46] *Laudo igitur et glorifico misericordias et miserationes eius cum in vobis tum in me, quem peregrinum,* totoque, *ut ita dicam,* orbe profugum *quandoque requiescere iussit certaque* consistere terra. MGH *Die Briefsammlung Gerberts von Reims*, p. 247. The allusion is to *Met.* 1:727 and *Aen.* 1:629.

[47] For examples see MGH *Die ältere Wormser Briefsammlung*, p. 43 and 49. Here Ovid's stories of Hercules and Busiris, and of Icarus are used. MGH *Briefsammlungen der Zeit Heinrichs IV*, the index lists nine passages, but besides this Ovid is mentioned by name several times in the Hildesheim collection in this volume. MGH *Poetae Latinii medii aevi* vol. 5.1-2, p. 764. The index of quotations notes 15 parallels to the *Metamorphoses.*, e.g. Walter of Speyer's poetry, or the epitaph for the abbess Hathawiga of Essen. MGH *Scriptores rerum Germanicarum in usum scholarum separatim editi* vol. 24. The eleventh-century allegorical animal fable *Ecbasis cuiusdam captivi per tropologiam* contains several parallels or allusions to Ovid (5 to the Met., and 3 to other works).

> Even if I do not doubt that you know all of this thoroughly, I
> will still describe these things summarily to refresh your
> memory, and as he says: 'I am but giving sails to a ship that
> is already using the oars.'[48]

Interestingly Meinhard reuses this quotation in two more letters, one
from 1075 and one written sometime between 1057-1085.[49] In the first
(lengthy) letter, the quotation appears near the beginning, while in the
latter two cases it is used at the end just before the farewell phrase. The
quotation seems to function as a type of tagline for Meinhard and, if
these were the only words from Ovid he quoted, it would be tempting
to assume he used a florilegium or some other type of second-hand
source for Ovid's poetry. However, there are more examples of Ovid
in Meinhard's writings. In 1064, he writes to the bishop and quotes
both Ovid and Virgil.[50] In the previous letters Meinhard had
introduced Ovid with just a 'as he/that one says' (*ut ille ait*), but here
Ovid is introduced by name, which is followed by a quotation from
the *Metamorphoses* (7:740). Meinhard uses the 'as he says' phrase for
Virgil instead (Aen. 1:671). Ovid is referred to as 'the best interpreter of
female ease' (*muliebris facilitatis optimus interpres*). In the same letter,
which is peppered with quotations and allusion to Ovid, Virgil, Cicero,
and Horace, Meinhard again quotes from the *Metamorphoses* (9:523):

> *Modo enim volo deplorare discessum tuum, sed hoc ociosum est;*
> *modo que apud nos gerantur digerere, sed hoc ineptum est; modo*
> *hortatorium aliquid tibi instillare, sed hoc mihi triste et luctuosum*
> *est. Denique illud Ovidianum patior:*
> Incipit et dubitat, scribit dampnatque tabellas.
> Et notat et delet, mutat culpatque probatque,
> Quid velit ignorat, quicquid factura videtur,
> Displicet.
>
> One moment I want to lament your departure, but this is
> useless; one moment I want to digest all of these things that
> happened between us, but this is senseless; and then one

---

[48] MGH *Briefsammlungen der Zeit Heinrichs IV*, p. 108.

[49] MGH *Briefsammlungen der Zeit Heinrichs IV*, p. 131 and 228. N.B. The latter letter also
contains an uncommon Martial quotation: *denique ut Marcialis tuus ait: facis o omnia belle.*

[50] MGH *Briefsammlungen der Zeit Heinrichs IV*, p. 218: *Ipse quidem in primis hanc molem
oppido recusare idque inceptum eorum mirabunda adversari, sed tamen, ut mos est feminis, immo
ut Ovidius muliebris facilitatis optimus interpres ait:* tandem dubitare coacta est. *Igitur
dilatum est usque Radasponem; ibi quod suorum fidelium deliberatio statuerit, se executuram
spopondit. Et certe, ut ille ait:* vereor, quo se Iunonia vertant hospicia.

moment I want to instil you with something encouraging, but this makes me sad and full of sorrow. Finally, I experience this Ovidian sensation:

'She begins, then hesitates and stops; writes on and hates what she has written; writes and erases; changes, condemns, approves; by turns she lays her tablets down and takes them up again. What she would do she knows not; on the point of action, she decides against it.'[51]

Meinhard shows a thorough familiarity with many of the ancient authors. He favours Virgil, Horace and Cicero most of all, but also Ovid, which was still a fairly rare thing at this point in time. Through Meinhard we can identify a certain Ovidian discourse (as part of a larger ancient-authors-discourse) in southern Germany in the eleventh century, which has its counterpart in the Loire valley. For it is here we find a group of churchmen and intellectuals who are probably most famous for being influenced by Ovid: a group commonly referred to as the Loire valley poets or the Loire circle. The group consists of Baudri (Baldric) of Bourgeuil (c. 1050-1130) abbot of Bourgeuil, later bishop of Dol; Marbode (Marbodus, Marbod) of Rennes (c. 1035-1123) first schoolmaster and possibly Baudri's teacher, then bishop of Rennes; and Hildebert of Lavardin (c. 1055-1133) bishop of Tours.[52] These men were active in the late eleventh and early twelfth centuries. They were all men of the church, schoolmasters and monks earlier in life, and all three later became bishops.

This group of poets is known for writing verse inspired by Ovid. We know that Marbode is the author of ten poems modelled on the *Amores*.[53] However, it is Baudri who seems to have been the foremost champion of Ovid. Baudri wrote many Ovidian-influenced poems and even had Ovid himself appear in two of them, in which he corresponds with his fictional friend Florus (poem 97-98). Another pair consists of an imitation of *Heroides* wherein Paris writes to Helen on

[51] MGH *Briefsammlungen der Zeit Heinrichs IV*, p 219.

[52] Max Manitius, *Geschichte der Lateinischen Literatur des Mittelalters. Vol. 3, Vom Ausbruch des Kirchenstreites bis zum Ende des zwölften Jahrhunderts*, (München: C: H. Beck,1931), p. 883–898 (Baudri), 719-730 (Marbode), 853-865 (Hildebert). For a thorough study of Baudri and the ovidian influence see Gerald A. Bond ''Iocus amoris': The Poetry of Baudri of Bourgueil and the Formation of the Ovidian Subculture' in *Traditio* vol. 42 (Fordham University, 1986), pp. 143-193.

[53] Walther Bulst, 'Liebesbriefgedichte Marbods' in *Liber Floridus: Mittellateinische Studien Paul Lehmann zum 65. Geburtstag gewidmet*, ed. B. Bischoff and S. Brechter (St. Ottilien: Eos Verlag der Erzabtei, 1950), pp. 287-301.

300 lines of distichs and receives a 370-line reply from Helen (poem 7-8). Baudri went on to compose his own letter modelled on the *Heroides*, to a lady named Constance, to which the lady replied (poem 200-201).[54]

These are three educated men, firmly established in the hierarchy of the church. They correspond with each other and pepper their poetry and letters with themes from Ovid (as well as many other sources), which invites the question: from where did their knowledge of, and fondness for, Ovid originate? Had their schoolmasters introduced them to Ovid at some point in the middle of the eleventh century, or had they picked him up later in life?[55] Whatever the answer to those questions might be, this little group seems to be of crucial importance for the establishment of a learned Ovidian discourse around 1100. This discourse has, by some scholars, been seen as a witness to a new 'turn' in medieval literature, one towards fictionality and, to use the words of Wim Verbaal, 'the emancipation of the poetical/textual world.'[56] This is not the place to explore such a turn, but merely to point out the possibility that Ovid was associated with, or perhaps even conducive to, a new development of the literature of this period.

Most of the authors mentioned above use Ovid as an authority and generally refer to him in a positive way. This, however, was not always the case:

> Interea cum versificandi studio ulta omnem modum meum animum immersissem, ita ut universa divinae paginae seria pro tam ridicula vanitate seponerem, ad hoc ipsum, duce mea levitate, jam veneram, ut ovidiana et bucolicorum dicta praesumerem, et

[54] *Baudri de Bourgueil vol. 1-3*, ed. J.-Y. Tilliette (Paris: Les Belles Lettres, 1998, 2002, 2013).

[55] The question of the Loire school and Ovid is a subject for a book of its own and much has already been written on the topic. For a recent article with a good bibliography on the subject, see Jean-Yves Tilliette, 'Savant et poètes du moyen âge face à Ovide: les débuts de l'*aetas Ovidiana* (v. 1050- v. 1200)', in *Ovidius Redivivus: Von Ovid zu Dante*, ed. M. Picone and B. Zimmerman (Freiburg: Rombach, 2014), pp. 63-105; Marek T. Kretschmer, 'The love elegy in medieval Latin literature (pseudo-Ovidiana and Ovidian imitations)' in *The Cambridge Companion to Latin Love Elegy*, ed. T. S. Thorsen (Cambridge: Camebridge University Press, 2013), pp. 271-89, https://doi.org/10.1017/CCO9781139028288.024.

[56] Wim Verbaal, 'How the West was Won by Fiction: The Appearance of Fictional Narrative and Leisurely Reading in Western Literature (11th and 12th century)', in *True Lies Worldwide: Fictionality in Global Contexts*, ed. A. Cullhed, L. Rydholm (Berlin: de Gruyter, 2014), pp. 189-200, https://doi.org/10.1515/9783110303209.189. See also Jean-Yves Tilliette, 'Le retour du grand Pan: remarques sur une adaptation en vers des Mitologiae de Fulgence à la fin du XIe siècle (Baudri de Bourgueil, c. 154)', *Studi Medievali 38* (1996), p. 92.

lepores amatorios in specierum distributionibus epistolisque nexilibus affectarem.[57]

I had, however, plunged my spirit beyond all limits into writing poetry, and I set aside every single page of scripture in favor of such pointless vanity. My inconstancy had already led me to mimic verses of Ovid and the bucolic poets, and the way I made a show of arranging the material into epistolary exchanges was an affectation of their erotic elegance.

These are the words of Guibert of Nogent (1055-1124), who is sharing his experience of writing poetry in his youth and includes Ovid in the context of an earlier sinful life. However, Herbert of Losinga (1054-1119) seems merely to find Ovid annoying:

taediosa est mihi ouidianarum fabularum prolixitas.[58]

the great length of Ovid's stories is tedious to me.

Conrad of Hirsau (ca 1070-1150) has far more than this to say about Ovid. In his *Dialogus super auctores*, a master and a student discuss different aspects of both classical and Christian authors. When it comes to discussing Ovid, the student asks whether it is really wise to read Ovid when doing so may harm or taint the reader. The master responds that it is probably wise to stay away from Ovid, even though there may be some small merit to his *Fasti*, *Epistulae ex Ponto* and *Nux*. The one work absolutely to be avoided is the *Metamorphoses*, because here Ovid wrote about transformations that are contrary to Christian dogma. Conrad then continues with a long quotation from the Epistle to the Romans to prove his point.[59]

This focus on transformations seems to touch upon a concern of the period. Caroline Walker Bynum has investigated different expressions of transformations during the twelfth and thirteenth centuries. She has identified a tendency in the early twelfth century to think of transformation in terms of evolution, while in the latter part of the century, a shift in paradigm occurred and people became interested in change through replacement (i.e. a new thing/being is created). The

---

[57] Guibert de Nogent, *Autobiographie*, ed. E. R. Labande (Paris: Les Belles Lettres, 1981), p. 134. Translation Jay Rubenstein, *Guibert of Nogent: Portrait of a Medieval Mind* (New York: Routledge, 2002), p. 53.

[58] Munk Olsen 2014, p. 429.

[59] *Dialogus super auctores*, ed. Robert B. C. Huygens (Berchem-Bruxelles: Latomus, 1955), p. 51.

first model of transformation is represented in theology with the idea that only God can create from nothing; the second model is represented by, for instance, the interest in alchemy and stories of metamorphosis, not least the Ovidian ones.[60]

In the Bavarian B family of *Metamorphoses* commentaries, the *accessus* offers a detailed taxonomy of transformations, starting with a tripartite division into magical, spiritual and natural. These three categories are then modified with five sets of binaries: body/quality, natural/non-natural, living/non-living, sensate/insensate and magical/spiritual. Lycaon being transformed into a wolf is an example of a magical, non-natural transformation with regard to the body of a living creature with senses to another living creature with senses.[61] This detailed analysis of transformations is not used explicitly in the commentary text itself, a fact that seems to hold true for other commentaries as well.[62] The Bavarian B commentary, however, brings up the topic of transformations again in the commentary itself:

> *Sunt quidam, qui hic faciunt casuum mutationem dicentes corpora m<utata> in uarias formas, ideo quia dicunt corpus non mutari, nisi formas tantum. Contra quos nos dicimus c<orpora> et f<ormas> equaliter mutari.*

> There are those who here change the cases saying that bodies are transformed into various shapes, since they say that a body does not transform, lest in shape only. Against these we say that bodies and shapes transform equally. (clm 14482, 28ʳ)

This seems to be one of those rare witnesses to a contemporary debate where one group (*quidam*) holds the position that a body can transform in shape only (i.e. not its essence), while another group (*nos*) holds the position that transformations affect both body (essence) and shape.

Clm 4610 does not contain this list of transformations or any longer discussions of them. Instead, it contains laconic commentaries like the following:

---

[60] Caroline W. Bynum, *Metamorphosis and Identity* (New York: Zone Books, 2001), pp. 22-26. It is also tempting to speculate about the possible influence of the debate concerning transubstantiation in the eleventh and twelfth century, but that is too broad and deep a subject for this chapter.

[61] See Appendix 1, l. 3-25.

[62] Bynum has identified the same phenomenon in the commentaries of Arnulf and John of Garland. Bynum 2001, pp. 98-99.

FIT LVPVS. Ista mutatio propinqua est ueritati, quia si umquam posset fieri, taliter mutaretur.

HE BECOMES A WOLF. This transformation is close to the truth, since if ever it could happen, he would have transformed in such a way. (1:237)

This type of explanation is closer to an allegorising explanation. It does not discuss the type of transformation, suggesting instead that it is fictional, but still a fitting example.

With these instances we enter the twelfth century, which marks the end of this survey. During the twelfth century, the use of Ovid seems to become more diverse. In the following we will look to some examples of the seemingly fruitful combination of Ovid and philosophy. Winthrop Wetherbee has pointed out that the implicit context for medieval mythography is Plato's *Timaeus* and its cosmology, where the ancient poets' myths could mix with philosophical concepts such as *noys* and *hyle*.[63] Many of the sources for the commentaries seem to be different sorts of mythographic compendia, and indeed the *Metamorphoses* itself could be regarded as mythography. The Neoplatonist worldview was available to the medieval reader via Calcidius's translation and commentary on Plato's text, but also via authors such as Boethius, Macrobius and Martianus Capella, and of course through Augustine's interpretation. As the popularity of the *Metamorphoses* increased from the eleventh and twelfth centuries onwards, so did the study of Calcidius's *Timaeus*. From the period 850-1000, a total of seven manuscripts survive, while from the eleventh century we have twenty-nine manuscripts, the majority of them from Germany.[64] The neoplatonic stream gave rise to several famous philosophical poems and works of prose centred around Plato's cosmology, e.g. William of Conches' *Dragmaticon Philosphia*, Bernardus Silvestris's *Cosmographia* and Alains de Lille's *Anticlaudianus* and *De Planctu Naturae*.

During our period, several authors seem to have made a connection between the *Metamorphoses* and Plato. Otto of Freising, writing around

---

[63] Winthrop Wetherbee, 'Learned Mythography: Plato and Martianus Capella', in *Oxford Handbook of Medieval Latin Literature*, ed. Ralph J. Hexter and David Townsend (Oxford: Oxford University Press, 2012), p. 335.

[64] Stephen Jaeger, *The Envy of Angels: Cathedral Schools and Social Ideas in Medieval Europe, 950-1200* (Philadelphia: University of Pennsylvania Press, 1994), p. 174. For a more recent study see A. Somfai 'The Eleventh-Century Shift in the Reception of Plato's "Timaeus" and Calcidius's "Commentary"', Journal of the Warburg and Courtauld Institutes, Vol. 65 (2002), 1-21, https://doi.org/10.2307/4135103.

the middle of the twelfth century, pairs Ovid together with Plato in Book 8 of *his De duabus civitatis,* where he refers to Ovid as 'one of the poets', but he cites Book 1 of the *Metamorphoses* (1:256) and clearly associates him with 'the first of the philosophers, Plato'.[65] In poetry, we also find the connection between Ovid and Plato. The following example is from a late-twelfth-century anonymous poem from Tegernsee addressed to some cloistered women. The poem in question is called *Profuit ignaris* and consists of 191 lines of leonine hexameter. Its subject is love (or courtly love, as Dronke argues), love poetry and the moral aspects of these two. In the following two samples, the poet first gives a type of moral explanation or justification for Ovid's scandalous stories and then, in the second sample, he describes a practical application of this poetry.

> *Miror cur vates*   *tot feda, tot improbitates*
> *Dicturus demum,*   *voluit primordia rerum,*
> *Celi vel terre,*   *subtiliter ante referre.*
> *Iuxta Platonem*   *Nature condicionem,*
> *Post res mutatas,*   *rerum species variatas,*
> *Et mutatorum scelus,*   *impia stupra deorum*
> *Explicat–et quare?*   *Vult nobis significare*
> *Quantum Natura,*   *quondam sine crimine pura*
> *Nunc degravata,*   *corrupta sit et viciata.*
> *... (l. 137-145)*
> *Hec de virtute,*   *de vera verba salute*
> *Quando tractamus,*   *ad sidera mente volamus:*
> *Sic celum petimus,*   *non ut ferat Ossan Olimpus.*
> *Hunc habitum mentis*   *tum rursus ad impia sentis*
> *Prave mutari,*   *scortari, luxuriari.*
> *Mortales actus*   *Iovis implet ad infima tractus,*
> *Mens vitio victa*   *peccat virtute relicta.*

---

[65] *Ottonis episcopi Frisingensis Chronica sive Historia de duabus civitatibus,* ed. Adolf Hofmeister, MGH - Scriptores Rerum Germanicarum in Usum Scholarum Separatim Editi, 45 (München: Monumenta Germaniae Historica, 1912), p. 401, book 8:8: *Cum* iuxta apostolum *pax et securitas dixerint, repentinus interitus supervenit,* terribilisque ignis virtute cuncta cremabantur. Quam seculi per ignem exterminationem non solum nostri prophetico spiritu veridice predixerunt, sed et quidam ex gentibus humana subnixi ratione phisicis opinionibus somniaverunt. Unde precipuus philosophorum Plato mundum abditis naturae rationibus, aqua prius, post igne purgandum in Tymeo suo asserit, et quidam poetarum de eadem re sic ait:
...... reminiscitur affore tempus,
Quo mare, quo tellus inmensaque regia caeli
Ardeat et mundi moles inmensa laboret.

Est quod in illorum   discas deitate deorum,
Nec sine doctrina   migrare feruntur ad ima.[66]
(l. 155-163)

'I wonder why the poet about to tell of so many monstrous
and shameful things wished first to relate the beginnings of
heaven and earth. Like Plato he gives a cosmology, and then
explains the things that were changed, the varied species, the
flaw in what is mutable, the unholy lewdness of the gods.
Why does he do this? He wants to show us how much
Natura, once guiltlessly pure, has been dragged down,
seduced and defiled. [...] When we expound such things
about virtue and true salvation, in spirit we are flying to the
stars. Thus do we (truly) seek heaven – this is not to pile
Ossa on Olympus! Then again you feel this state of mind
changing, turning to impiety, wantonness, and luxury. Jove,
drawn deep down, fills human action, the mind sins,
overcome by vice, casting virtue aside. Yet there is
something you can learn from the nature of these gods: it is
not without significance that they are said to make their way
to the depths.'

This poem combines several topics discussed thus far: The poetic
imitation of Ovid, critique of Ovid and now also the association of
Ovid with Plato.[67]

In clm 4610, Ovid himself is twice referred to as a philosopher
(*philosophus*). Paule Demats explored this *Ovidius Philosophus* and the
commentary tradition in her *Fabula: Trois études de mythographie antique
et médiévale*.[68] She explores three different aspects of Ovid: the ethical,
philosophical and theological. The first aspect is principally related to
the medieval interpretation of Ovid's shorter works as ethical, in the

---

[66] Translation Peter Dronke. The poem is found in the manuscript Munich, Bayerische
Staatsbibliothek, clm 19488. It is from Tegernsee and can be dated to the end of twelfth
century. An edition and translation of the poem can be found in Peter Dronke, *Medieval
Latin and the Rise of European Love-Lyric*, vol 2 (Oxford: Clarendon Press, 1968), pp. 452-
463.

[67] Another much shorter poem from twelfth-century Metz that also combines courtly
love with mentions of both Ovid and Plato can be found in the manuscripts Berlin,
Staatsbibliothek zu Berlin, Phillipps 1694. An edition and translation can be found in
Geralrd Bond, *The Loving Subject: Desire, Eloquence, and Power in Romanesque France*
(Philadelphia: University of Pennsylvania Press, 1995), pp. 146-47.

[68] Paule Demats, *Fabula: Trois études de mythographie antique et médiévale* (Geneve: Librarie
Droz, 1973), pp. 107-177.

sense that they were meant to illustrate bad behaviour and thus warn the reader. The theological aspect is related to the later allegorical tradition of interpreting Ovid. The philosophical aspect is the connection between the *Metamorphoses* and *Timaeus* as well as the work of Boethius. The commentary in clm 4610, which she had available only through the excerpts in Meiser's article, is discussed briefly by Demats and mainly to juxtapose it with the later commentary tradition.[69]

In clm 4610, the first reference to Ovid as a philosopher is in the *accessus*, where three kinds of philosophers and their views on God are described.[70] The first group believes that God created the world from nothing, the second that God created it from atoms and emptiness, and the third that there have always existed three things: God, the four elements and the pure ideas or essential properties existing in the mind of God. Ovid is said to be a philosopher belonging to the last group. This section of the *accessus* was of particular interest to Karl Young, who also transcribed four *accessus* in the Bavarian B family. Young believed that this passage was evidence of a medieval association between platonic ideas and the *Metamorphoses*, which might then in turn have inspired Chaucer.[71] More recently, Michael Herren has proved that the vocabulary[72] and general ideas used in the *accessus* to clm 4610 at this point is derived from two different parts of Macrobius's commentary on *Somnum Scipionis*.[73]

The second reference to the philosopher Ovid is implicit in one of the rare Christianising passages of the commentary where he is spoken of in the context of the 'other philosophers' (*alii philosophi*).[74] However, just as in the case with the transformations discussed above, there are not many passages in the actual commentary that reflect any specific Platonic interest. There are a few explanations of a cosmographical nature, most of which are found in the commentary to Book 1, where the creation of the world is treated.[75] Regarded as a whole, the

---

[69] Demats first mentions clm 4610 on p. 114 and then returns to it several times in this chapter.

[70] For more on the *accessus* see chapter Form and Function.

[71] Karl Young, 'Chaucer's Appeal to the Platonic Deity' in *Speculum* Vol. 19:1 (1944), p. 11.

[72] I.e. words such as *togaton, nous* and *anima mundi*.

[73] Michael Herren 'Manegold of Lautenbach's Scholia on the *Metamorphoses* - Are There More?' in *Notes and Queries* (2004), p. 222.

[74] Clm 4610, 2:850. For more on this explanation see chapter The Commentary and its Focus on the *Metamorphoses*.

[75] For more on these see chapter Form and Function, sub-section Function of the Commentary: Categories of Explanation.

Bavarian commentaries cannot be said to be cosmographical or otherwise neoplatonic. Instead, they must be regarded as products from a period where neoplatonic ideas gained centre stage. As such, they could be interpreted as reflecting an ongoing dialogue in the schoolroom at the time when new ideas were gaining ground and the *Metamorphoses* was being carefully introduced into the curriculum.

The philosophical aspect of the reception of Ovid is only one of the facets of his use during the twelfth century and onwards. When his popularity starts to grow, it becomes more difficult to give a brief description of his readers. Another sign of Ovid's increased renown is the fact that he can be found referenced in different chronicles from the twelfth century and onwards (but not, to my knowledge, before this).[76]

This chapter has surveyed Ovid from the Carolingian period to the twelfth century, with a focus on material as well as indirect evidence. The material evidence has been shown to go hand in hand with the indirect evidence as the number of preserved manuscripts, as well as mentions and quotations of Ovid, have increased century by century. Ovid was evidently known already in the Carolingian period, although usually placed towards the bottom of a list over which Virgil would usually preside. During the eleventh century, a distinct increase in Ovid's popularity is evident, and a type of Ovid discourse seem to have existed in both the German lands and France. During the twelfth century, Ovid's renown grew further and contemporary intellectuals seemed to find new uses for him in everything from philosophical texts to chronicles, all of which would also increase the need for commentaries explaining his works.

---

[76] MGH SS 16, p. 549-550. In the *Annales Cameracenses* (Cambrai in the Hauts-de-France region), in a passage about the year 1169 Ovid is mentioned and quoted:
Immittitur a Domino nobis correptio febrium saepius ob salutem animarum, aliquando datur in medicinam, quibusdam initia fiunt tormentorum subsequentia. Ovidius sic dicit:
Temporibus medicina valet, data tempore prodest.
This seems to refer to an alternate reading in Remedia amoris l. 131.
MGH SS 10, p. 157: The chronicler quotes *Ponticus Ovidius* (Ex Ponto 4:7:49).
MGH SS 24, p. 558: *Lamberti Ardensis Historia comitum ghisnensium*. Written in the 1190s. In the prologue an advanced discussion of Ovid can be found, and the author also seems to quote him in several other places.

3. Situating the Commentary

The previous chapter examined the fate of Ovid leading up to the period relevant for clm 4610. In the following chapter we will turn to the commentaries and seek to provide some context to give the anonymous text some flesh. We know for a fact that the commentaries were later kept at the Bavarian monastery Benediktbeuern, and on paleographical grounds it also seems likely that the commentary was written somewhere in southern Germany. With this in mind, the following section will expand on Bavaria as a setting and its educational institutions.

Bavaria and the Holy Roman Empire[77]

In the context of cultural history, we are at the beginning of 'the long twelfth century,' which is an extension of the concept of the renaissance of the twelfth century first famously formulated by C. H. Haskins in the first part of the last century.[78] The long twelfth century extends this renaissance a few decades on both sides of the century (e.g. 1095-1229 by Cotts and 1050-1215 by Noble and Van Engen).[79] Much of the research on the twelfth century focuses on France and Norman England, but as far as the German lands and the renaissance are concerned, Rodney Thomson points out that it is not so much a new renaissance as an intensifying of the Ottonian renaissance of the late tenth century, which, among other things, entailed the continued copying and studying of the ancient authors, while the early

---

[77] A good overview of the period is found in Hanna Vollrath, 'The Western Empire Under the Salians' and Benjamin Arnold, 'The Western Empire, 1125-1197', in *The New Cambridge Medieval History Volume 4:2 c.1024–c.1198*, ed. D. Luscombe and J. Riley-Smith. (Cambridge: Cambridge University Press, 2004), https://doi.org/10.1017/CHOL9780521414104. See also A. Haverkamp, *Medieval Germany, 1056-1273* (translated by H. Braun and R. Mortimer), (Oxford: Oxford University Press, 1990).

[78] Charles H. Haskins, *The Renaissance of the Twelfth Century* (Harvard University Press, 1927).

[79] John D. Cotts, *Europe's Long Twelfth Century: Order, Anxiety, and Adaptation, 1095-1229* (New York: Palgrave Macmillan, 2013); Thomas F. X. Noble, John Van Engen (ed.), *European Transformations: The Long Twelfth Century* (Notre Dame: University of Notre Dame Press, 2012).

scholasticism that was gaining momentum in France did not attract attention in many places in the German lands.[80]

The Holy Roman Empire provides the macro setting. The empire was not one centrally controlled kingdom, but rather a conglomerate of duchies and bishoprics, all of which struggled for power in relationship to their neighbours, the emperor and the pope; armed conflicts and sometimes all-out civil war were frequent results. In the period studied here, the empire consisted of three large units: the kingdoms of Germany, Burgundy and Italy. The German king and emperor (the first title was given through election by the German dukes, the second by the pope) had no fixed residence, but instead travelled the empire and held court in different locations, such as Cologne, Worms and Regensburg, where the lords gathered and gave council.

The Duchy of Bavaria had many different rulers during the eleventh century but was, for most of the twelfth century, controlled by the Welf family. The secular ruler of Bavaria had his equals in the mighty bishops and abbots of the many cathedrals and monasteries that existed in the duchy, many of which date back to the time of Charlemagne. The most important cities in Bavaria at this time were Regensburg, Freising, Passau and Salzburg (then part of Bavaria). All of these cities were bishoprics (Salzburg was the seat of the archbishop) and thus housed cathedrals, which, in turn, housed cathedral schools and libraries. Besides the cathedrals, both the cities and the countryside that surrounded them housed many monasteries, which usually adhered to the rule of Benedict. At this point in time and all over Europe, the Benedictine monasteries, by far the most numerous among the different religious communities that existed, made up a network of independent units. However, other orders, for instance the Carthusians (founded in 1084), were also present throughout the empire.[81]

The monasteries and cathedrals were not the only institutions influencing cultural development at this time. The itinerant royal court had a well-functioning chancery, which was staffed by clerics and supervised by a chancellor, who was formally under obedience to the

---

[80] Rodney Thomson, 'The Place of Germany in the Twelft-Century Renaissanc', in *Manuscripts and Monastic Culture: Reform and Renewal in Twelfth-Century Germany* (Turnhout: Brepols, 2007), p. 22, https://doi.org/10.1484/M.MCS-EB.3.3543.

[81] For an overview of religious life during this period see Giles Constable, 'Religious communities, 1024–1215' in *The New Cambridge Medieval History Volume 4:1 c.1024–c.1198*, ed. D. Luscombe, J.Riley-Smith (Cambridge: Cambridge University Press, 2004), , pp. 335-368.

archbishop of Mainz.[82] We do not know if there was any room for literature or formal schooling at the itinerant court, but we do know that there was a dynamic interaction between court, cathedral and monastery, which affected the intellectual life of the period.[83]

Monasteries and Cathedrals

In this section we will look closer at the cathedrals and monasteries of Bavaria, many of which date from Carolingian times, and many of which suffered during the Hungarian raids in the tenth century and were then re-established. In order to get a picture of what went on in these institutions of learning, some information can be gleaned from contemporary or near-contemporary library lists, letters and other such documents.

In general, it seems like both books and lists of books from monasteries have been much better preserved than those from cathedrals—in fact, it is difficult to track down information from any of the Bavarian cathedrals. In those cases where there is some evidence, there do not seem to be many traces of the pagan authors. The cathedral library in Würzburg serves as an example. Here we have a book list from the year 1000 in which not a single pagan author appears on a list that stretches to almost four printed pages.[84] It seems unlikely that such a library would not at least contain a copy of Virgil, which makes it possible that the list does not include the 'school-authors'. Another list has been preserved from the Augustinerchorherrenstift, St Nikolau in Passau; this fairly long document from the middle of the twelfth century again contains no pagan authors.[85] However, from the cathedral in eleventh-century Freising two short notes survive, one of which mentions Terence and the other Ovid. The one that mentions Ovid is phrased in such a way

---

[82] Luscombe 2004, p. 399.

[83] For more on court and school during the Carolingian and Ottonian period see Jaeger 1994, pp. 21-53.

[84] Bernhard Bischoff, Günter Glauche, and Hermann Knaus, *Mittelalterliche Bibliothekskataloge Deutschlands Und Der Schweiz. Bd 4, Bistümer Passau, Regensburg, Freising, Würzburg* (München, 1979), pp. 985-88. None of the other lists for this library mentions pagan authors either, cf. pp. 977-994.

[85] Bernhard Bischoff and Elizabeth Ineichen-Eder, *Mittelalterliche Bibliothekskataloge Deutschlands Und Der Schweiz. Bd 4, Bistümer Passau, Regensburg, Freising, Würzburg* (München, 1977), pp. 53-55.

that it might imply a list of donations or a lending list.[86] Finally, in this short discussion of cathedral libraries it may benefit us to look at an eleventh-century list from an unknown library, but which may stem from either the cathedral or the Michelsberg monastery in Bamberg. This list, in contrast to the first two mentioned above, consists entirely of pagan authors and philosophy. It does not mention Ovid, but is still relevant since it mentions many commentaries, some of them by known authors, as for example 'Donatus's commentary on Virgil' (*commentum Donati super Virgilium*).[87]

We will now turn to four monasteries connected to the revival of Ovid: Benediktbeuern and Tegernsee, close to the modern border to Austria, St Emmeram in Regensburg and St Peter's Abbey in Salzburg. Neither clm 4610 nor any of the manuscripts from the Bavarian B family carries a contemporary library or owner's mark. We know, however, that they were, at a later date, stored in Benediktbeuern (clm 4610), St Emmeram (clm 14482 and clm 14809 from the Bavarian B family) and Salzburg (Salzburg AV4 from the Bavarian B family). Even though none of the commentaries can conclusively be tied to Tegernsee, this monastery is nevertheless included in the survey since we know that it was an important centre of text production and associated with the three other monasteries mentioned here. It is also the location where one of the earliest *Metamorphoses* manuscripts is believed to have been copied.[88]

St Emmeram, Regensburg

St Emmeram, founded in the eight century, had been an Imperial abbey since 972. It was originally located outside of the city of Regensburg, but by the tenth century the city had grown to surround the monastery. St Emmeram was also the Bavarian centre for the Gorze reform, which, like the Cluny reform, strived for a stronger adherence to the rule of St Benedict, although in contrast to Cluny, it was not associated with centralised authority. It was under the influence of this reform that the library at St Emmeram was built in the

---

[86] Gustav Becker, *Catalogi Bibliothecarum Antiqui: Collegit Gustavus Becker. 1. Catalogi Sæculo 13. Vetustiores. 2. Catalogus Catalogorum Posterioris Ætatis* (Bonnæ, 1885), p. 148: *Chunradus Ovidium & Salustium* (Chonradus [has borrowed/donated] Ovid and Sallust.)

[87] Becker 1885, p. 147. This list is found in the philosophical miscellanea manuscript Munich Bayerische Staastsbibliothek clm 14436, 61v, and has been digitised: https://daten.digitalesammlungen.de/0003/bsb00033074/images/index.html?id=00033074 &groesser=&fip=ewqeayaxdsydenqrsqrsxdsydewqfsdr&no=13&seite=126

[88] The fragments Harley 2610 (London, British Library) and clm 29208 (Munich, Bayerische Staatsbibliothek).

late tenth century and later became the most important library in the area during the next century.[89] All three monasteries mentioned below were reformed during the eleventh century by monks from St Emmeram.[90] William of Hirsau had his training in St Emmeram before he left for the monastery he is named after in 1079, and where he instituted the Hirsau reform. This reform was then quickly established back in St Emmeram.[91] The Hirsau reform has itself been associated with a huge increase in book production and also with the copying of the classical authors.[92]

As far as manuscripts are concerned, we seem to have quite a large production in the monastery around the year 1000. A list from that time primarily contains Christian authors, but also several different grammars, two commentaries by Remigius (on Martianus and on Sedulius) and a gloss on Virgil.[93]

Together with Cologne, Regensburg had been one of the biggest cities in the German lands ever since the Carolingian period, and was also an important and renowned place for scholarship, as illustrated here by an exclamation by an excited eleventh-century writer:[94]

> *Ratispona vere secunda Athene, aeque studiis florida, sed verioris philosophiae fructibus cumulata.*[95]
>
> Regensburg is truly a second Athens, equally blooming with learning, but [in Regensburg] there has also been gathered the fruits of the truer philosophy.

Regensburg is one of the oldest bishoprics in Bavaria and the See was connected with St Emmeran in such a way that the bishop was chosen

[89] Jospeh D. Kyle, 'The Monastery Library at St. Emmeram (Regensburg)', *The Journal of Library History*, 1980.15:1 (1980), 1–21, pp. 6-13.

[90] Kyle 1980, p. 13.

[91] Martin Schubert, *Schreiborte Des Deutschen Mittelalters* (Berlin: De Gruyter, 2013)., p. 463, https://doi.org/10.1515/9783110217933.

[92] Alison Beach, *Women as Scribes: Book Production and Monastic Reform in Twelfth-Century Bavaria* (Cambridge: Cambridge University Press, 2004), p. 128.

[93] *Mittelalterliche Bibliothekskataloge Deutschlands Und Der Schweiz. Bd 4, Bistümer Passau, Regensburg, Freising, Würzburg,* ed. Bernhard Bischoff and Elizabeth Ineichen-Eder (München, 1977), p. 146-147, l. 72-81.

[94] Schubert 2013, p. 459.

[95] David Sheffler, *Schools and Schooling in Late Medieval Germany: Regensburg, 1250-1500,* Education and Society in the Middle Ages and Renaissance, v. 33 (Leiden; Boston: Brill, 2008), p. 16, https://doi.org/10.1163/ej.9789004166646.i-417.

alternately from the ranks of the Canon Regulars and from the monks.[96]

In addition to St Emmeran there were several other monasteries in the city and its vicinity, among them an important Irish *Schottenkloster* (founded in the late eleventh century), where Honorius Augustodunensis was active during the first part of the twelfth century.[97] Besides the monasteries, the city also contained canonical houses (though most seem to be of a later date), most notably St Peter. Regensburg had a curious system where the bishop was chosen alternately from the monks and the canon regulars. This speaks to the power wielded by the monastery. In addition, there were three houses for women founded in the ninth and tenth centuries (Ober-, Nieder- and Mittelmünster). These institutions, together with the other orders that arrived in the city during later centuries, handled all schooling in the city until the beginning of the sixteenth century.[98] The book production in these monasteries also made Regensburg, together with Salzburg, the most important scribal centres in the south-eastern German lands during the twelfth century.[99]

Tegernsee

Tegernsee, founded in the middle of the eighth century, holds a place of pre-eminence among the Bavarian monasteries where the production of manuscripts is concerned. The majority of the earliest surviving witnesses to the texts of many of the ancient authors seem to stem from this monastery. Abbots were chosen from far and wide, as were schoolmasters, which would have created a dynamic environment. Monks were also sent out to establish and re-establish monasteries.[100]

During the early eleventh century, brother Froumund was active at the monastery, teaching, copying and writing both letters and poems. His letter collection gives us a glimpse of the intellectual life of the time (although it is limited where teaching is concerned) and it also shows the connections between Tegernsee, Cologne, Regensburg and Augsburg. Christine Eder has investigated the scribal activity at the monastery during the tenth and eleventh centuries and, through her research, it is clear that the production volume in the scriptorium was

---

[96] Bischoff and Ineichen-Eder 1977, p. 99.

[97] Schubert 2013, p. 464.

[98] Sheffler 2008, pp. 18-21.

[99] Schubert 2013, p. 472.

[100] C. E. Eder, *Die Schule Des Klosters Tegernsee in Frühen Mittelalter Im Spiegel Der Tegernseer Handschriften* (München: Arbeo-Gesellschaft, 1972), p. 52.

high and that many grammatical texts and classical authors were copied (although still a minority compared to the religious texts).

Not all manuscripts were produced in Tegernsee. Eder has identified different groups of manuscripts in the Tegernsee collection with other origins. These manuscripts from the tenth and eleventh centuries are often school texts and among them are authors such as Cicero, Sallust, Virgil and Fulgentius, as well as commentaries on Terence and Statius. The provenance is, in many cases, other parts of the German realm, but often unknown.[101]

When we turn to the twelfth century, one of the most important historical sources for this period is the Tegernsee letter collection, which, among other things, gives us a glimpse of how manuscripts were passed around between monasteries. In the following extract from a letter, the monk B writes to his friend and relative W in Tegernsee and asks for a copy of two commentaries:

> *Quapropter obsecratione efflagito, karissime, ut glosas super Macrobium mihi per aliquem fidelem transmittere non graveris et, si que super Georgica apud vos sint, cognatum meum O., quatenus mihi transmittat, rogo, depreceris.*[102]

> My dear friend, I beseech you that you will not be reluctant to send me the commentary on Macrobius with a loyal servant, and, if you have any commentaries on the Georgica, that you would please send them to me with my relative O.

In addition to letters, book inventories and lists of book donations are other important sources of information about the intellectual life at the monasteries. A list from the second part of the eleventh century mentions that a brother Reginfrid has donated almost forty books to Tegernsee. Among the ancient Roman authors, we notice Virgil, Horace, Ovid and Martianus Capella. The list also mentions Calcidius's commentary on Plato's *Timaeus* and a commentary on Lucan, as well as Fulgentius' commentary on Virgil, Boethius on Cicero's *Topics* and many other grammatical, philosophical and

---

[101] Eder 1972, p. 132–148.

[102] *Die Tegernseer Briefsammlung des 12. Jahrhunderts*, ed. H. Plechl (Hannover: Hahn, 2002), p. 221.

mythological texts.[103] The list gives us a glimpse into the type of texts to which the monks had access, and, since it is a list of donations, it is all the more interesting as it invites us to speculate about the motives behind this large donation. Did it perhaps stem from a request to supplant the library's existing texts with new or newly needed texts? We notice, for instance, that this list includes a commentary on Lucan, but no text of Lucan, which probably indicates that the library already contained a copy of Lucan. The list also includes three texts by Ovid, which is more than any other author on the list.

Benediktbeuern

Benediktbeuern was founded around 750 and had been an Imperial Abbey since Carolingian times, with a large scriptorium and library that has produced large amounts of glossed manuscripts.[104] The monastery was destroyed by the Hungarians at the end of the tenth century, but the books were saved from destruction and the monastery was rebuilt, repopulated and restocked with monks and books from the monastery of Tegernsee in 1031.[105] Although there is no documented evidence of a school at Benediktbeuern in the early centuries, there must have been some kind of institutionalised teaching as the monastery accepted oblates: boys as young as six or seven who needed to be taught and trained. Abbot Ellinger, who was sent from Tegernsee to renew the monastery after the Hungarian destruction,

---

[103] *Mittelalterliche Bibliothekskataloge Deutschlands und der Schweiz, 4:2 Bistum Freising & Bistum Würzburg*, ed. G. Glauche, H. Knaus (München 1979), p. 750: *Hos libros quidam frater Reginfridus Deo ac sancto Quiryno Tegirinse tradidit.*

Bibliothecam. Librum christiani. Librum Virgilii. Librum Oratii. Librum Platonis cum Calcidio. Commentum in Lucanum. Librum in Donati. Librum Aratoris. Rethoricam cum Victorino et Grillio. Librum Smaraddi abbatis. Librum Egesippi. Librum Sybille. Commentum in perhieramias. Librum Ovidii metamorfoseos. Librum Ovidii de remedio et de amore. Librum Martiani. Librum de computo. Duo psalteria, unum glosatum et alterum cum ymnario et officiale. Dicta Alexandri cum quodam Dindimo. Librum Virgiliane continentie. Vitas quorundam sanctorum in duobus corporibus. Sermones Chrisostomi. Librum gradalem cum sequentiis et tropis. Topica Tullii cum commentis Boetii et librum differentiarum et divisionum et multa de rethorica et de sillogismis in uno corpore. Duas mappas mundi. Librum super donatum. Librum centimeter. Librum Daretis de excidio Troie. Gesta Alexandri Magni. Librum fabularum. Librum de abaco et de minutiis. De divisione et coacervatione numerorum. De partibus loice. Unum librum evangeliorum et unum librum epistolarum.

[104] Schubert 2013, p. 22.

[105] *Mittelalterliche Bibliothekskataloge Deutschland und der Schweiz, 3:1 Bistum Augsburg*, ed. P. Ruf (München: Beck, 1932), p. 63–64; *Das Bistum Augsburg.1, Die Benediktinerabtei Benediktbeuern*, ed. J. Hemmerle (Berlin: de Gruyter, 1991), p. 270.

had been taught by the abovementioned brother Froumund and that is probably also true for his successor, Gotahelm, who modelled the Benediktbeuern system for schooling on that of Tegernsee. The teaching in Benediktbeuern, as in most monasteries at this time, was closely connected to the copying activities in the library.[106]

This first stock of library books consisted of only the Rule of St Benedict and some books of hymns and other books related to the sacral needs of the monastery.[107] From 1052, we have another brief list with mostly sacral books. However, the last sentence mentions: 'Books of the authors Boethius, Sedulius, Prosper [of Aquitaine] and another sixty.'[108]

What these other sixty books contained, we cannot know, but we notice that the library has grown and that it now includes poetry, philosophy and theology.

The next inventory is from the thirteenth century. It is a long list of books that contains many of the classical authors and a significant number of grammatical works, commentaries and glosses. As far as Ovid is concerned, the list mentions two manuscripts that each contain *Heroides*, *Epistulae ex Ponto*, *Ars amandi*, and besides this a 'part of glosses on the *Ovidius magnus*' is also mentioned, but not the *Metamorphoses* itself.[109] In comparison many of the other classical authors are mentioned with glosses, e.g. 'A glossed Horace. A very old Virgil [...] glosses on Lucan'.[110]

At this point in time, we see that the library contains many of Ovid's works, but it is unclear if they had an actual copy of the *Ovidius magnus*, i.e. the *Metamorphoses*. It is also interesting to note that the phrase 'part of glosses on the *Ovidius magnus*' suggests an unfinished commentary or a fragment.

St Peter, Salzburg

The Benedictine monastery of St Peter in Salzburg was founded around year 700. Here, as in St Emmeram, the monks and canons formed one congregation. Salzburg was the See of the Archbishop of Bavaria. Both the city and the monastery appear in letters and chronicles from our period, but there does not seem to be much

---

[106] Hemmerle 1991, pp. 265–266 and 436–438.

[107] Ruf 1932, p. 73.

[108] Ruf 1932, p. 73: *Libri poetarum Boetii, Sedulii, Prosperii [sic] et alii LX.*

[109] Ruf 1932, p. 76, l. 19–27: *Ovidius epistolarum. Ovidius de Ponto. ... Ovidius epistolarum. ... Ovidius de ar<t>e amandi. ... Pars glosarum Ovidii magni.*

[110] Ruf 1932, p. 76, l. 17-18: *Oracius glosatus. Vir<g>ilius valde vetustus. ... Item glose super Lucanum.*

modern research on the monastery. St Peter is the oldest continuously active monastery in Europe and still houses its own library, which may be the reason why there are not many modern catalogues available on its collection and also one reason for the lack of modern research.

When it comes to medieval catalogues, we have a long list from the twelfth century that begins *Hic est numerus librorum qui continentur in bibliothaeca Salzpurgensis eccelsie ad s. Petrum.*[111]

The first two pages of the transcription contain only Christian authors, but the third page (the last section of the list) shows us the collection of secular literature in the monastery. It is a solid collection of school authors and we immediately notice their collection of Ovid texts: *Metamorphoses, Heroides, De remedio* and in one volume *Amores, De remedio, Sine titulo* (*Amores*) and *Epistula ex Ponto*. Besides Ovid, the monastery is also stocked with Sallust, Juvenal (with commentary), Horace (with commentary), Terence, Martianus Capella (with commentary), Cicero's *De amicitia, De senectute* and the *Orationes in Catilinam* in one volume, two volumes with the works of Persius, two with Avianus's, three with Lucan's and three with Virgil's. Servius's commentary is listed as a separate work as are three further texts important for the readers and commentators on ancient literature (especially Ovid): Isidore, *Fabularius* (perhaps the work of Hyginus) and Homer (probably the epic Illiad themed poem *Ilias Latina*). The only author missing to make the list of school authors complete is Statius. Besides these, there are many philosophical and grammatical works (no less than six copies of Donatus) and Christian poetry.[112]

---

[111] *Mittelalterliche Bibliothekskataloge Österreichs, vol. 4 Salzburg,* ed. G. Möser-Mersky and M. Mihaliuk (Wien 1966), p. 67.

[112] Möser-Mersky and Mihaliuk 1966, pp. 71-72: *Hii sunt scolares libri istius ecclesie. Boecii commentum super kathegorias. Gisilbertus super Boetium de s. trinitate. / Priscianus m. Boetius de s. trinitate. Boetius de consolatione.*

Ovidius m(agnus). Ovidius epistolarum. Salustius. Iuvenalis et commentum super ipsum in uno volumine. Priscianus constructionem. Pergemenie Aristotilis et commentum supra, in uno volumine. Hortius et commentum super ipsum Terentii. Prudentius ymnorum et historiarum et siccomachie et contra Symachum in uno volumine. Duo Persii. Tres Lucani. Tres Virgiliani. Expositio super Donatum et Alzismus in uno volumine. Beda de arte metrica. Ars Foci grammatici. Prosper. Experimenta Ypocratis. Galienus. Duo Porphirii. Oviidus de remedio amoris. Tres Sedulios. Geometria Euclidis. Heremannus Contractus super astrolabium. Abecedarium. Marcianus et commentum super ipsum. Ovidius de amore et de remedio amoris et sine titulo et de Ponto in uno volumine. Theodulus. Libellus de Vii planetis. Tullius de amicitia et de senectute et invectivarum in uno volumine. Expositio super artem Euclidis. Servius. Ysidorus ethimologiarum. Homerus. Duo Aviani. Plato. Metaphisica et topica Aristotilis. Fabularius. Donati VI. Erchenbertus magister super Donatum. Dialectica Augustini. Tragedia. Grammatica

Both the presence of a broad selection of literature and the presence of commentaries and multiple copies of texts are, in all probability, a sign of a large and active school in the monastery.

Finally, to end this discussion of medieval libraries and book lists, a word of warning may be in order. We know, of course, that the information available to us today is extremely limited due to the ravages of time and man, but it is important to remember that the human factor played as important a role in the high middle ages as it does now, as can be witnessed by this final phrase from a twelfth-century book list from another important monastery, Hirsau:

> ...varii libri chronici et historici. et in summa valde multi libri, quorum titulos et auctores nolui huc scribere.
>
> (...various chronicles and books of history, and finally, a great number of books, whose titles and authors I do not care to write down here.)[113]

This little quotation reminds us that we can only get a glimpse, never the whole picture, of the historical context of the Ovid commentaries.

The School Context

> Commentum Terentii, si sperare id liceat, velim, ut saltem per partes mihi transmittere dignemini. Non est, quod plura vobis pollicear vel de diligentia servandi vel de fide remittendi; id operam dabo, ne vos benignitatis vestrę peniteat.
>
> If it is permitted to wish for this, I would like the commentary on Terence, if you at least deem it worthy to send it to me in parts. It is not the case that I promise too much regarding my care in preserving it or my trustworthiness in returning it. I will take great care so that you do not regret your kindness.[114]

These words are written by Meinhard of Bamberg to his former teacher in the mid-eleventh century. It is not easy to find traces of the commentaries in use, but there are a few scattered mentions like the one above that show that commentaries were precious commodities to

---

Euticentis. Plato. Scansiones metrorum. Alchorismus. Dialogus super Priscianum. Libellus de dialectica, qui sic incipit, 'Primo considerandum est in hac arte'.

[113] Becker 1885, 220.

[114] MGH *Briefsammlungen der Zeit Heinrichs IV*, p. 112.

be asked for, and not necessarily lent out without restrictions. The 'in parts' (*per partes*) in the quotation above may be taken to be either just a modest restriction of the favour asked, or, more technically, that the commentary should be sent a quire at a time to minimise risk of loss of the complete work.

Ideally, we would like to have detailed letters like this describing the movement and use of individual Ovid commentaries. Sadly, that is not the case. This section will instead discuss the environment in which the commentaries may have been produced and used, starting with a brief bibliographical sketch.

The topic of schools and education during this period has recently seen a surge in publications, with a complete volume dedicated to the twelfth-century schools and another entire volume about the abbey of Saint Victor in Paris having been published within the last few years.[115] In addition, new perspectives are also being added to the established ones, as can, for example, be seen in Laura Cleaver's recent work *Education in Twelfth-Century Art and Architecture*, where the usual focus on the written sources gives way to the rich material to be found in images and architecture.[116] A classic in the field is Pierre Riché's *Écoles et enseignement dans le Haut Moyen Age*, which covers the period up to the eleventh century.[117] Riché covers large parts of Europe, while much research often only covers France. For the German realm, Anna Grotan's *Reading in Medieval St. Gall* is important, especially for the English speaking/reading audience.[118] For Italy, Robert Black's *Humanism and Education in Medieval and Renaissance Italy* together with Ronald Witt's *The Two Latin Cultures of Medieval Italy* provide an

---

[115] *A Companion to Twelfth-Century Schools*, ed. Cédric Giraud and Ignacio Durán, Brill's Companions to the Christian Tradition, volume 88 (Leiden; Boston: Brill, 2020); *A Companion to the Abbey of Saint Victor in Paris*, ed. Hugh Feiss and Juliet Mousseau (Leiden; Boston: Brill, 2018), https://doi.org/10.1163/9789004351691.

[116] Laura Cleaver, *Education in Twelfth-Century Art and Architecture: Images of Learning in Europe, c.1100-1220*, Boydell Studies in Medieval Art and Architecture (Woodbridge, Suffolk, UK; Rochester, NY, USA: The Boydell Press, 2016).

[117] Pierre Riché, *Écoles et enseignement dans le Haut Moyen Age: fin du Ve siècle - milieu du XIe siècle*, 3. éd (Paris: Picard, 1999).

[118] A. Grotans, *Reading in Medieval St. Gall* (Cambridge: Cambridge University Press, 2006), https://doi.org/10.1017/CBO9780511483301.

excellent overview and analysis.[119] These are only a few of the most important names that have contributed important research to the field. Where commentaries and Ovid are concerned, Ralph Hexter's *Ovid and Medieval Schooling* and Suzanne Reynold's *Medieval Reading: Grammar, Rhetoric and the Classical Text* must also be mentioned.[120]

The Trivium and Quadrivium: The Foundations of the Medieval School

The framework for education during the Middle Ages was formed by the seven liberal arts, divided into the language-based *trivium* (grammar, dialectic and rhetoric), and the number-based *quadrivium* (arithmetic, geometry, astronomy and music). The liberal arts were described and enshrined in the works of the Late Antique and Early Medieval authors Martianus Capella, Boethius and Isidore of Seville, as well as in Cassiodorus's *Institutiones*.[121] As Anna Grotans observes, grammar often intersects with the other two members of the *trivium*, rhetoric and dialectics. The connection between grammar and rhetoric is quite easy to imagine. The third art, dialectic, intersects with grammar by providing a tool for syntax and general language analysis, which were not present in the ancient grammatical texts in a way that satisfied the needs of the medieval users.[122] Thus, all the arts of the *trivium* are applied when studying literature, or perhaps the other way around, literature is studied to learn the *trivium*.

Ever since Antiquity, elementary Latin education has started with the students learning the letters, then the syllables and, from there, moving on to words and phrases, which was usually accomplished by the student learning a text by heart. During Late Antiquity this first text was the aphorism collection *Disticha Catonis*, which in the Christian context, then gave way to the Psalter as the preferred first text (although the *Disticha Catonis* were still popular and widely

---

[119] R. Black, *Humanism and Education in Medieval and Renaissance Italy: Tradition and Innovation in Latin Schools from the Twelfth to the Fifteenth Century* (Cambridge: Cambridge University Press, 2001), https://doi.org/10.1017/CBO9780511496684. Ronald G. Witt, *The Two Latin Cultures and the Foundation of Renaissance Humanism in Medieval Italy* (Cambridge; New York: Cambridge University Press, 2012), https://doi.org/10.1017/CBO9780511779299.

[120] Suzanne Reynolds, *Medieval Reading: Grammar, Rhetoric and the Classical Text* (Cambridge: Cambridge University Press, 2004), https://doi.org/10.1017/CBO9780511470356.

[121] Luscombe 2004, p. 470.

[122] Grotans 2006, pp. 84-92.

disseminated).[123] After the students had mastered elementary reading, they moved on to grammar. The first step was to memorise Donatus's *Ars Minor*, which provided the students with a simple, but effective morphological knowledge of the Latin parts of speech.[124] Works of Latin grammar written when Latin was still a native tongue do not seem to concern themselve much with syntax. Instead, advanced grammars, e.g. Donatus's *Ars Maior*, deals with phonetics and figures of speech. For syntax, it was the grammatical works of Prisican, written in the Greek-speaking east that would come to be used. However, Prisican's work is extremely dense, which meant that it was often used as a reference work by schoolmasters who composed their own grammars.[125]

Besides the direct study of grammar in the works of different grammarians, the principle way of acquiring good Latin was for the student to immerse themselves in the ancient authors and to learn advanced vocabulary, grammar and style through them.[126] This means that the study of grammar after the elementary level is the study of ancient literature. This is repeated time and again in the *accessus* to the ancient authors, for instance in the following from the *accessus* to clm 4610:

> *Prodest nobis et ad ostendendam pulchram dictionum compositionem.*
>
> Ovid also benefits us by showing beautiful composition.

This manner of teaching and learning seems to have been in place for as long as Latinity, and was the privilege of only a small minority of the population, mainly in the monasteries and cathedrals.[127] Later on, with the advent of the universities, village schools and other institutions of teaching, the curriculum changed.

It should also be remembered that, although learning at this time made great use of ancient literature, both monastic and cathedral schools had at their core the study of the Bible and liturgical practice, for which the liberal arts worked as a supporting aid.[128] This is made perfectly clear in the following brief definition from an *accessus* to

---

[123] Black 2001, p. 37.

[124] Black 2001, p. 64.

[125] Black 2001, pp. 65-66.

[126] Black 2001, p. 67.

[127] Black 2001, p. 67.

[128] Luscombe 2004, p. 467.

Horace in Susanne Reynold's important study on glossing and reading in the Middle Ages:

> *Quedam enim sciuntur ut sciantur sicut evangelia, quedam propter aliud, ut auctores.*[129]

> 'Moreover some things, like the Gospels, are known for their own sake, [whereas] others, like the authors, [are known] for the sake of something else.'

The *Auctores*/the School Authors[130]

As stated, the study of the authors was the main method of grammar study, and grammar study was the first of the *trivium*, the entrance to learning. However, the selection of authors who were studied changed over time and a general fluctuation between the number of Christian authors compared to ancient authors can also be observed. During the Carolingian period, Christian authors were primarily read in schools, with only a few ancient authors like Virgil and Martianus Capella included, but by the eleventh and twelfth centuries this had changed, so that a great many of the ancients were now included.[131]

One of the most famous voices from this time is that of Conrad of Hirsau (c. 1070-1150) who divides the authors into minor and major in his *Dialogus super auctores*.[132] The minor authors, intended for elementary training, include Donatus, *Disticha Catonis* and the fables of Avianus and Aesop, as well as the Christian authors Sedulius, Juvencus, Prosper of Aquitaine and Theodulus. The major authors principally include the ancient Roman authors, for poetry: Virgil, Horace, Lucan, Persius, Juvenal, Statius and Ovid, as well as the Iliad-themed poem *Ilias Latina*, and for prose: Cicero and Sallust. Also included are Boethius and the Christian poets Prudentius and Arator.

The twelfth-century Tegernsee collection of prologues to the authors, known as *Accessus ad auctores,* gives us further insight into how the authors were studied just by the fact that this collection was constructed and disseminated as a collection with a particular selection of authors and a particular order in which they were arranged.[133]

---

[129] Reynolds 1996, p. 12. Translation S. Reynolds.

[130] For a thorough study of the authors in Medieval Italy and elsewhere, see Black 2001, pp. 173-273.

[131] Glauche 1970, pp. 83-101.

[132] Glauche 1970, pp. 108-109.

[133] Stephen Michael Wheeler, *Accessus Ad Auctores: Medieval Introductions to the Authors (Codex Latinus Monacensis 19475)* (Kalamazoo: Medieval institute publications, 2015).

The School Institutions – Monastic and Cathedral Schools

When discussing schools and schooling during this time, we will focus on formal education in a monastery or cathedral school, between which there often existed a connection. This connection was usually the master or the student. Very few of the famous masters seem to have spent time in only one place. They were often from powerful families and moved between the realms of politics, religion and culture. There also existed a strong international tendency, where, for example, Southern Germany had a strong tie to Italy, but also a connection between Bavaria and France.[134]

This was a privilege that belonged to the few. There was, however, schooling in other settings and many ways in which informal education might have manifested itself. An example of the latter can be found in the childhood of the nobleman Guibert of Nogent who, as a boy, was sent to a grammarian employed in a nearby castle.[135] As far as teachers are concerned, many famous men of letters from this time were employed as instructors to wealthy men, for instance Adelard of Bath and William of Conches (both c. 1080-1150) were instructors to sons of the nobility.[136] The schools were, in turn, tied to wealthy patrons, especially the cathedral schools, which were often a pathway to employment at a court.[137]

In the case of St Gall, and possibly also the Bavarian monasteries, both oblates and future clerics, and possibly also laymen, were taught. However, it is uncertain if these 'interns' and 'externs' were taught by the same teachers or lived in the same building.[138] A synod in the ninth century prescribed that only future monks be taught in a monastery. If this were the case later on, the future clerics would have had their rudimentary training in an external school at the monastery and then had to move on to a cathedral school for advanced training.[139]

---

[134] Joachim Ehlers, 'Deutsche Scholaren in Frankreich während des 12. Jahrhunderts', *Vorträge und Forschungen*, 30 (1986), 97–120, https://doi.org/10.11588/vuf.1986.0.15809; *Schwaben und Italien im Hochmittelalter*, ed. Helmut Maurer and others, Vorträge und Forschungen, Bd. 52 (Stuttgart: Thorbecke, 2001).

[135] Luscombe 2004, p. 462.

[136] Luscombe 2004, p. 463.

[137] Luscombe 2004, p. 464.

[138] Grotans 2006, pp. 53-54.

[139] Grotans 2006, p. 58. However, in the late tenth century several noble boys, sons of beneficiaries, were accepted to the school in St Gall. These boys practiced falconry and other noble pursuits and did not appear to be meant to become monks. Cf. Grotans 2006, p. 59.

The primary education in St Gall was three years, from age seven to ten, after which the student was expected to know how to read Latin, perhaps write, and to have grasped some other skills. After this came secondary education for four to five years, which was dedicated to the liberal arts and to theology.[140] In the cathedral schools, the students started when they were nine or ten and could ask to leave when they were fifteen.[141]

Not only did the type of student change over time, but also the number of students. In the latter part of the eleventh century, the cathedral schools became more powerful and the Investiture controversy caused many monasteries to be stricter with whom they accepted as students; for example: Cluny, one of the biggest monasteries of the period, only accepted six oblates in its school during this time.[142] All of these circumstances can be interpreted as though the schools were, at least for some periods, mixed with regard to type of student and filled different roles for different types of students, which is important to keep in mind when trying to envisage the users of the commentary text in clm 4610.

To illustrate school life during this period we have, for example, an idyllic description of eleventh-century life in Paderborn in the *Vita Meinwerci Episcopi*: we learn that both youths and boys studied with the aim of taking monastic vows or the vows of the canon regulars (*claustralis disciplina*) as well as instruction in the arts. The church seems to have been non-monastic (*ecclesia publica*) and had a school, where music, dialectics, rhetoric and grammar were studied, as well as mathematics, astronomy, physics and geometry. The ancient authors the student came into contact with were Horace, Virgil, Sallust, and Statius. Everyone laboured over verses, composition, and song. This description is then contrasted with earlier days, when bishop Imadus tells of the stern upbringing he had at the monastery, where he was not allowed to see or even talk to his father.[143]

---

[140] Grotans 2006, pp. 71-76.

[141] Riché 1979, p. 202. For more information regarding the students and their studies, see pp. 221-280.

[142] Riché 1979, p. 197.

[143] MGH SS 11, p. 140: *Studiorum multiplicia sub eo floruerunt exercitia; et bonae indolis iuvenes et pueri strennue instituebantur norma regulari, proficientes haud segniter in claustrali disciplina omniumque litterarum doctrina. Claruit hoc sub ipsius sororio Imado episcopo, sub quo in Patherbrunnensi ecclesia publica floruerunt studia; quando ibi musici fuerunt et dialectici, enituerunt rhetorici clarique grammatici; quando magistri artium exercebant trivium, quibus omne studium erat circa quadruvium; ubi mathematici claruerunt et astronomici; habebantur phisici atque geometrici; viguit Oratius magnus et Virgilius, Crispus ac Salustius, et Urbanus Statius; ludusque fuit omnibus insudare versibus, et dictaminibus, iocundisque cantibus.*

So much for the students. When we turn to the masters, Riché informs us that an appointment as a teacher was normally a life-long assignment for a monk who was supposed to be at least twenty-five years old. The teacher would cover some or all of the liberal arts and also theology, depending on his skill. There existed also a lower-level teacher called a *semi-magister*, who could be younger than twenty-five and who took care of the more elementary instruction. Besides these, the cantor also filled an important role in teaching the students to sing the liturgy. The *magister* also often served as librarian and was responsible for the scriptorium, which seems to have been the case in Benediktbeuern.[144]

Where the cathedral schools, which rose to fame during this period, are concerned, the locus classicus is John of Salisbury and his report from his school days in Paris in the 1130s. Here a large number of masters, some of them freelance and some of them attached to a cathedral, provided instruction in the liberal arts. In this environment, both teachers and students moved around looking for the best offer. John describes, with many superlatives, Bernard of Chartres' teaching of grammar, rhetoric, and theology. What is even more interesting is that we learn something about the methods employed. Bernard expects his students to memorise material daily (a type of homework) to discuss (presumably with their fellow students) and to practice both prose and verse composition.[145] Besides the important information about teaching methods, what stands out in John's description is his explicit adoration for his teachers. We see here a (former) student with opinions on what good-quality teaching is, and, through his eyes, we also receive a picture of a superstar academic of the day. Stephen Jaeger defines this type of teaching as charisma-driven, where the highest goal is the *cultus virtutum* (the cultivation of virtues) so as to become a 'well-tuned, well-composed man'.[146] To achieve this goal, the study of letters, i.e. grammar, the first in the *trivium*, was prioritised before all others.

Quorum in scriptura et pictura iugis instantia claret multipliciter hodierna experientia, dum studium nobilium clericorum usu perpenditur utilium librorum. Praefatus quoque Imadus episcopus tempore suae pueritiae tanto disciplinae claustralis rigore ibidem est nutritus, ut numquam patrem suum videre extra conventum specialiter vel ei colloqui fuerit permissus, dicente episcopo, pueros et adolescentes cum districtione debere erudiri, et non nocivis blandimentis deliniri; quoniam audaciae et ferociae nutrimenta eis ministrarent blandimenta. Adolescebant quoque se cum in tirones miliciae celestis Anno archiepiscopus Coloniensis, Frithericus Monasterienis, et perplures alii strennui postmodum in vinea Domini operarii.

[144] Hemmerle 1991, p. 265.

[145] Luscombe 2004, p.469.

[146] Jaeger 1994, pp. 180–181.

However, not all students were as impressed by their teachers. For a decidedly more acerbic description we need only turn to Abelard and his account of his former teacher William of Champeaux.[147]

Monasteries and cathedral schools should not be regarded as isolated from each other, or as opposites. For, even though they might at times have been in competition with each other, the people involved would often move from one institution to another. There are many examples that could be cited here, Abelard being perhaps the most famous, and Manegold of Lautenbach also worthy of mention. In addition to these men, during the eleventh century there is Otloh of St Emmeram, who was first a student at Tegernsee, then at Hersfeld, after which he took up a position at the cathedral in Würzburg but disliked the people there and thus ended up becoming a monk at St Emmeram monastery in Regensburg.[148] During the twelfth century Adalbert II, later archbishop of Mainz (1138-1141), is worthy of mention. As a nephew of Adalbert I he was raised and received his early education in Mainz; he then went on to Hildesheim for schooling in the trivium. From there he went to Reims to continue studying the artes/trivium and also higher exegetics. Finally, Adalbert went to Paris to study rhetoric and dialectic with Theodoric, better known as Thierry of Chartres.[149]

This chapter has situated the commentary, based on its presumed provenance, in the teaching environment in a Bavarian cathedral or monastery. Bavaria has been shown to house a plenitude of institutions relevant to a commentary such as clm 4610, all of which have been proven to have had significant libraries and often also scriptoria. As far as the educational context is concerned, the commentary fits into a curriculum that focused on the trivium in general, and grammar in particular, which was often based on reading the ancient authors. However, the commentary need not necessarily have been used in the schoolroom itself, but in all likelihood, it is at least from the schoolroom. There were many masters and students who travelled between different people and institutions, crossing from one country to another while collecting knowledge. Judging by the later proliferation of the *Metamorphoses* commentaries, at some point in the twelfth century the commentaries started to travel around the German lands and France.

---

[147] Peter Abelard, *Historia calamitatum: consolation to a friend*, ed. A. Andrée (Toronto: PIMS, 2015), pp. 28-34.

[148] Riché 1979, p. 209.

[149] Ehlers 1986, p. 51.

4. Form and Function

This chapter focuses on clm 4610 itself, first at a more general level with a discussion about the genre of commentaries, then more specifically about the different aspects of the function of the commentary.

Short Conceptual History of Medieval Commentary Terminology

The preferred word during Antiquity was *commentarius* (sometimes *commentarium*), which originally signified a notebook and then came to mean a treatise or commentary. Examples of the earlier use can be found in Cicero and Suetonius, who both refer to Caesar's works as *commentarii*. Cicero also refers to *commentarii* in his work *De officiis*:

> *Quamquam hi tibi tres libri inter Cratippi commentarios tamquam hospites erunt recipiendi.*[150]

> And yet you must welcome these three books as fellow-guests, so to speak, along with your notes on Cratippus's lectures.

The more specialised meaning *commentarius/commentarium* as a commentary or exposition on a literary work is found later in Gellius, who mentions *commentaria in Virgilium*.[151] Another term for commentary, *commentum*, is derived from the verb *comminiscor* (to devise something by careful thought).[152] This word originally had a negative meaning, signifying an invention or a falsehood, as can be seen in the following line from *Metamorphoses* where it is used almost as an antithesis to truth:

> *mixtaque cum veris passim commenta vagantur.* (*Met.* 12:54)

---

[150] Cicero, *Brutus* 262:80, ed. E. Malcovati (1970); Suetonius *Caesar* 56, ed. M. Ihm (1908); *De officiis*, 3:33, ed. C. Atzert (1963). Translation Walter Miller, *Cicero On Duties* Loeb Classical Library 30, Cambridge, MA: Harvard University Press, 1913.

[151] *Nonnulli grammatici aetatis superioris, in quibus est Cornutus Annaeus, haut sane indocti necque ignobiles, qui commentaria in Virgilium composuerunt.* Gellius, *Noctes Atticae* 2:6:1, ed. F. Serra (1993).

[152] *commentarius* is thought to be derived from *commentor*, which has virtually the same meaning as *comminiscor*.

> Fictions/falsehood (*commenta*) mixed with truths roam at random.

Later, the meaning of the word changed to become one of the two most common words to signify a commentary, the other being *glossa*. Isidore, in his *Etymologiae*, explains that *glossa* is essentially an explanation by means of a synonym, while a *commentaria* or *commenta* is an interpretation.[153]

By the time of the High Middle Ages, the meaning of *commentum* and *glossa* had been modified and developed by the philosophers and grammarians, as has been shown by Rita Copeland in this quotation from William of Conches:

> *Ut ait Priscianus in Preexercitaminibus puerorum, comminisci est plura, studio vel doctrina in mente habita, in unum colligere. Unde commentum dicitur plurium studio vel doctrina in mente habitorum in unum collectio. Et quamvis, secundum hanc diffinitionem, commentum possit dici quislibet liber, tamen non hodie vocamus commentum nisi alterius libri expositorium. Quod differt a glosa. Commentum enim, solam sententiam exequens, de continuatione vel expositione litere nichil agi. Glosa vero omnia illa exequitur. Unde dicitur glosa, id est lingua. Ita enim aperte debet exponere ac si lingua doctoris videatur docere.*[154]

> As Priscian says in his *Praeexercitamina* for boys, *comminisci* (to devise) is to collect together many things that are held in the mind by study or teaching. Whence a collection of many things held together in the mind by study or teaching is called a *commentum*. While according to this definition any book can be called a *commentum*, nevertheless today we do

---

[153] *Glossa Graeca interpretatione linguae sortitur nomen. Hanc philosophi adverbium dicunt, quia vocem illam, de cuius requiritur, uno et singulari verbo designat. Quid enim illud sit in uno verbo positum declarat, ut: 'conticescere est tacere'. Etymologiae* 1:30, ed. W. M. Lindsay (1911); *Commentaria dicta, quasi cum mente. Sunt enim interpretationes, ut commenta iuris, commenta Evangelii. (Etymologiae* 6:8:5); Isidore also gives us the meaning of *scholia*, which, although a frequently used term in modern research, does not seem to be much in use during the period that concerns us. He defines *scholia* as a brief explanation of something obscure or difficult. *Primum genus excerpta sunt, quae Graece scholia nuncupantur; in quibus ea quae videntur obscura vel difficilia summatim ac breviter praestringuntur. (Etymologiae* 6:8:1).

[154] Text and translation from Rita Copeland, 'Gloss and Commentary', in *Oxford Handbook of Medieval Latin Literature*, ed. R. Hexter and D. Townsend (Oxford: 2012), https://doi.org/10.1484/M.SA-EB.3.4872.

not call it a *commentum* unless it is an exposition of another book. This is the difference between *commentum* and *glosa*: a *commentum* only pursues the sense, but is not at all concerned with the context (*continuatio*) or with exposition of the letter. A *glosa* deals with all these matters. Whence it is called *glosa*, that is, tongue. For truly a gloss ought to expound clearly, as if seeming to teach from the speech of the scholar.

In this instance, the two terms would seem to have the opposite meaning to that in Isidore, where *commentum* is the term signifying interpretation, while in this case it is *glossa*. However, in drawing conclusions from how commentary texts were actually labelled during the period, Munk Olsen has shown that there was no strict or consistent distinction in the use of the terms. The plural *glosse* is used most frequently (with the diminutive *glossule* modestly used for longer commentaries), while *commentum* is generally reserved for supposedly ancient commentary texts, for instance Servius's commentary on Virgil.[155] Many other less frequent and more specialised terms were also in use, e.g. *expositio, interpretationes* or *tractatus*.[156]

The prologue to a commentary, in modern scholarship commonly referred to as *accessus*, was often not labelled as such. The word *accessus* is rare and is found in only a few manuscripts.[157] One such manuscript is the *Metamorphoses* commentary in the manuscript Prague VIII H32, which is discussed further in the next chapter.[158]

When discussing the medieval terminology, it should be noted that, with one single exception, neither clm 4610 nor any of the texts belonging to the Bavarian B family, or any other twelfth-century *Metamorphoses* commentary I have examined, carry a contemporary title with a genre designation. The exception is the manuscript Salzburg AV4 where a rubric, which seems to be written by the same or a contemporary hand, designates the commentary as *glosse*. Where

---

[155] Munk Olsen 2009, pp. 6-7.

[156] For a thorough survey of the medieval usage, see Munk Olsen vol 2009, pp. 3-9. Munk Olsen discusses the usage and definition of different commentary terminology by different medieval authors, both famous and anonymous. He also conducts a survey of what terms the medieval library catalogues use. See also Copeland 2012. To this I can add my observation that if one searches through the collections in DMGH, the digital version of Monumenta Germaniae Historica, *commentarius*, usually in the accusative plural *commentarios*, seems to be more common than *commentum*.

[157] Munk Olsen 2009, p. 7.

[158] Prague, Národní Knihovna Ceské Republiky VIII H32. The word appears as the final word of the *accessus* on 78va.

the other commentaries are concerned, in the few instances where they do carry a title, these have all been added by a later medieval hand. Thus, with regard to the *Metamorphoses* commentaries, we mainly have access to later terminology.[159]

Terminology Used in This Book

The terminology I employ when discussing the commentary encompasses the following:

When discussing different formats of commentaries, *catena* commentary is used to signify a freestanding commentary. The other type of commentary found in the margins of the commented-upon text is referred to as just that, marginal commentary (with the added term 'interlinear gloss' used when needed). The term *catena* was first developed to describe Biblical commentary, but seems to have been transposed to the description of commentaries on ancient authors by John Ward in 1996.[160] It is possible, perhaps even preferable, to instead speak of 'freestanding lemmatic commentary', but I have chosen to use *catena* commentary since it is the term used by other Ovid scholars.[161] It is also preferable to be able to distinguish between different types of freestanding commentaries, such as the lemmatic commentary and a commentary with a freer relationship to the target text (for instance Fulgentius's *Expositio Virgilianae continentiae secundum philosophos moralis*). This is another reason why *catena* serves a purpose as far as terminology is concerned. Other scholars have chosen different terminology; James Zetzel, for instance, uses simply 'commentary' for *catena*, and *scholia* and *glosses* for marginal and interlinear commentary.[162]

When I speak of the text itself 'commentary' denotes the whole text, in this case clm 4610. The commentary consists of smaller parts, namely:

lemma: word/-s from the commented upon text

[159] Later medieval hands have labelled clm 4610 as *commentum*.

[160] J. O. Ward 'From marginal gloss to *catena* commentary: the eleventh-century origins of a rhetorical teaching tradition in the medieval West' in *Parergon*, vol 13:2 (1996), 109-120. For a brief survey of the biblical *catena* see Nigel G. Wilson 'A Chapter in the History of Scholia' in *The Classical Quarterly*, vol .17:2 (1967), pp. 252-254.

[161] Particularly in Frank T. Coulson's work on later Ovid commentaries, for a list of such see bibliography.

[162] James E. G. Zetzel, *Marginal Scholarship and Textual Deviance: The Commentum Cornuti and the Early Scholia on Persius*, Bulletin of the Institute of Classical Studies Supplement, 84 (London: Institute of Classical Studies, School of Advanced Study, University of London, 2005), p. 4-8.

explanation: the main text in the commentary, which usually follows directly after the lemma. In circa seventy-five percent of the commentary, each lemma is provided with one explanation, which may be either short or long. In the remaining twenty-five percent, the lemma is provided with more than one explanation, which sometimes take the appearance of a string of explanations not always necessarily related to the original lemma.

While lemma is an established term, there does not seem to be a generally agreed upon term for the text that follows the lemma. Mariken Teeuwen, among others, uses the Latin term *interpretamentum*.[163] This term, however, does not seem to be in widespread usage in English-speaking literature on commentaries. Birger Munk Olsen prefers to use 'glosses' (*gloses*) instead of 'explanations', while I have chosen to use 'gloss' only when referring to marginal or interlinear commentaries.[164] In this book 'explanation' is thus to be understood as a technical term denoting the different units that, together with the lemma, make up the commentary. As a term it is convenient in being immediately understandable, but also inconvenient since it can be confused with other uses of 'explanation'. I have not, however, found a better word for a part of the text I most often need to refer to.

The Nature of the Commentary: What is clm 4610?

What does the text preserved in manuscript clm 4610 represent? This question leads to further questions, such as whether it is an original or a copy; whether it descends from a marginal commentary; or whether perhaps it has generated a marginal commentary instead? Or simply: who made the text and for what purpose?

To delve deeper into the question of the origin of a commentary, one must look closer at what could be termed the commentary technology itself, which presents itself in the form of the freestanding commentary and the marginal commentary or scholia. These two formats have always existed in a state of flux, where freestanding commentary can be contracted, abridged and chopped up to marginal commentary, then to be reassembled at a later point into a freestanding commentary with new ingredients. James Zetzel, who has made the sharpest analysis of this process in his work on the *Commentum Cornuti* on Persius, describes the historical process as having three steps. Due

---

[163] Mariken Teeuwen 'Carolingian Scholarship on Classical Authors: Practice of Reading and Writing' in *Studies in Medieval and Renaissance Book Culture: Manuscripts of the Latin Classics 800-1200*, ed. Erik Kwakkel (Leiden University Press 2015).
[164] Munk Olsen 2014, pp. 9-10.

to the technological restraint of the papyrus roll, the oldest commentaries are believed to have been freestanding. These freestanding commentaries were then transformed into marginal commentaries in late antiquity. During the Carolingian period, with its surge in manuscript production, the marginal commentaries were again copied into freestanding form. After this period, the commentaries could be copied either as a freestanding or a marginal commentary.[165] This is only a rough sketch of a complicated process, regarding which Zetzel formulates some important restrictions: for example, when considering a freestanding commentary, we cannot assume that the marginalia and other types of texts used to create the new text travelled from margin to commentary via the simple process of excerpting, nor that marginalia in its turn derived from a single ancient commentary.[166]

Even if it is in a commentary's nature to be constantly adopted and changed, a commentary can, for different reasons, become stabilised, and from a certain point in time more or less only copied in its stable form. Whether or not this is the case with clm 4610 is difficult to say, since we only have access to this one copy. The other families, discussed further in the next chapter, show some signs of being stable, but there always seems to be room for additions.

When speculating about the origin of clm 4610 we can turn to older commentaries on Ovid, older commentaries on other authors, and/or other types of texts. Sources used in the commentary will be discussed in the last section of this chapter, and the relationship to the material found in the margins of older *Metamorphoses* manuscripts is the subject of the next chapter. Besides these there only exists one older commentary-like text, the so-called Pseudo-Lactantian *Narrationes*, which does not seem to have had any greater impact on clm 4610. This text has been ascribed to many different authors, of which Lactantius Placidus is the name most commonly used, for example in Hugo Magnus's edition of the *Metamorphoses*, which also includes an edition of the *Narrationes*.[167] The attribution to Lactantius cannot be found in any of the medieval manuscripts and is today considered spurious, which has led some scholars to rename this text. For example, instead

---

[165] Zetzel 2005, p. 6-8. Zetzel also makes a valid point as to why there are several manuscripts with marginalia preserved from late antiquity and not freestanding commentaries. This is because the preserved manuscripts are big and expensive showpieces, which have been preserved because of their value, while simpler texts, although perhaps more representative, have not.

[166] Zetzel 2005, p. 86.

[167] *P. Ovidi Nasonis Metamorphoseon libri XV: Lactanti Placidi qui dicitur Narrationes fabularum Ovidianarum*, ed. Hugo Magnus (Berlin: Weidmann, 1914).

of using Pseudo-Lactantius as a placeholder name, Alan Cameron uses *Narrator* to refer to the compiler of the *Narrationes*.[168] The *Narrationes* has come down to us either as marginal text in *Metamorphoses* manuscripts, as text interspersed in the *Metamorphoses* text or as a separate text. The *Narrationes* has been dated to no earlier than the sixth century and is considered to be derived from a lost Late Antique commentary; however, Cameron argues that the *Narrationes* is, in fact, a mythographic companion to the *Metamorphoses* composed around 150-250 A.D.[169] Regardless of whether the *Narrationes* was composed in the second to third century or in the sixth century, it is the only text of a commentary nature we have on the *Metamorphoses* before around 1100 and clm 4610. As can be seen in the manuscript description in the next chapter, the *Narrationes* can be found in many of the older *Metamorphoses* manuscripts and it is highly likely that the person or persons compiling clm 4610 would have had access to it. Perhaps it is for this very reason there are no significant traces of the *Narrationes* in clm 4610.

Another aspect of clm 4610 that needs considering is who might have made and used the commentary. There is no explicit voice of the author, scribe or other person available in clm 4610 to tell us who created the commentary and to what end. This holds true for all the twelfth-century *Metamorphoses* commentaries except for Arnulf of Orléans's commentary. In this case the author makes himself visible and claims authorship at the very end of the commentary by incorporating the last line of the *Metamorphoses* in a type colophon where he also gives his name paired with Ovid's.[170] A text such as clm 4610 opens itself up to being interpreted in several different ways, such as:

1. A student's notes taken from a master's teaching and/or private reading.
2. A schoolmaster's lecture notes.
3. A schoolmaster's or other intellectual's private study notes.
4. An archival document compiled in order to preserve information from one or several sources.

---

[168] Alan Cameron *Greek mythography in the Roman world* (New York: Oxford University Press, 2004), pp. 3-33.

[169] Cameron 2004, p. 311. For a discussion of alterative dating of the *Narrationes* see R. J. Tarrant 'The Narrationes of 'Lactantius' and the Transmission of Ovid's *Metamorphoses*' in *Formative Stages of Classical Traditions: Latin Texts from Antiquity to the Renaissance*, ed. O. Pecere and M. D. Reeve (Spoleto 1995), pp. 83-115.

[170] Clm 7205, 58v. For more on this see Engelbrecht 2008.

The first three alternatives can be summarised as commentary for the schoolroom or for private use. The question of which it was led to a series of articles in the 1980s, where Michael Lapidge, on the one hand, argued for private use, and A.G. Rigg and G.R. Wieland, on the other hand, argued for schoolroom use.[171] This debate has been analysed by Malcolm Godden in a chapter in the 2011 volume *Rethinking and Recontextualizing Glosses* and he concisely sums up the debate like this:[172]

> Lapidge argued that such glosses had nothing to do with the activities of the Anglo-Saxon classroom, whether as the responses of the students or as aids to the teacher, but if they had any contemporary function at all, which he doubted, were aids for private reading, while Wieland argued that they were records of, and aids for, the activities and concerns of the Anglo-Saxon teacher.[173]

Godden then proceeds to show some proofs for scholarly use of glossed Boethius manuscripts. He shows how four different scholars from the tenth and eleventh centuries used glosses from specific Boethius manuscripts in their own texts, which proves that the glosses were not necessarily used to explain Boethius' text but to produce new knowledge; in short, it proves they were not used only for teaching. These arguments allow for a new way of seeing the commentary, which allows for more leeway than only regarding it as a schoolroom document.

However, Godden and the others are all discussing a very specific type of commentary: the glossed text. The freestanding commentary is quite a different thing, especially if we keep the fact about Arnulf the

---

[171] Michael Lapidge 'The Study of Latin Texts in Late Anglo-Saxon England, I. The Evidence of Latin Glosses', N. Brooks, ed., *Latin and the Vernacular Languages in Early Medieval Britain* (Leicester: University Press 1982), pp. 99-140. (Reprinted in Lapidge, Anglo-Latin Literature 600-899, (Hambledon Press, 1996), pp. 455-498).
A.G. Rigg and G.R. Wieland, 'A Canterbury Classbook of the Mid-Eleventh Century', Anglo Saxon England 4 (1975), p. 113-130. A. G. Wieland 'The Glossed Manuscript: Classbook or Library Book?', Anglo Saxon England 14 (1985), pp. 153-173.
[172] Malcolm Godden 'Glosses to the *Consolation of Philosophy* in Late Anglo-Saxon England: Their Origins and their Uses' in *Rethinking and Recontextualizing Glosses: New Perspectives in the Study of Late Anglo-Saxon Glossography*, ed. Patrizia Lendinara, Textes et Études Du Moyen Âge, 54 (Porto: Fédération Internationale des Institus d'Études Médiévales, 2011), pp. 67-93, https://doi.org/10.1484/M.TEMA-EB.4.00835. Many of the chapters in this volume can be said to be strong contributions to this debate.
[173] Godden, p. 68.

schoolmaster in mind. If we also consider the material aspect, the high cost of parchment makes it highly unlikely that a commentary text is a student notebook, even though the *Metamorphoses* commentaries are only little booklets. The equivalent to today's student notes would have been made on wax tablets or, at most, parchment scraps. The students were also often left to simply memorise everything the masters expounded to them. As for the teachers, Pierre Riché points out that the schoolmasters often travelled with their own books and continuously sought new books to use in their teaching.[174] In preparation for their lessons, the masters took down their own notes (or had a student copy them) and in so doing they also reused previous masters' material in their own work.[175]

However, the teacher-student dichotomy need not be so sharp. We could also imagine a more mature student, a junior intellectual, who has recorded some new findings, perhaps while travelling from one master to another, or when visiting a particular monastery or cathedral. In this scenario the commentary could have belonged to a type of student.

We must also realise that memory and oral culture are essential in understanding the interaction between master and student, between written text and spoken word. Mary Carruthers has shown us the vast amount of information that could, and was, memorised during the medieval period.[176] To this we must add the supposition that, just as today, the majority of the 'teaching actions' in the schoolroom were oral rather than textual (even though the final goal might have been to foster competent Latin composition). This means that we can never use the commentary as anything more than an incomplete record of the actions in the schoolroom, if it was ever used there.

---

[174] Riché 1979, pp. 216-219.

[175] As a short digression, it may be worth mentioning that one of the few authors who discusses the actual composing of a commentary during this time is Guibert of Nogent. When he composed his commentary, 1083-1086, he did so as a monk with acknowledged intellectual capabilities, but not as a schoolmaster. He did not write a commentary on the Roman authors, but on the first books of Genesis. He writes of how he first composed a prologue of sorts and then wrote his analysis in a tropological mode, from beginning to end directly on the parchment page, without first writing drafts. This manner of composing a commentary, writing without a draft, must not be taken completely seriously, or at least not as representative of the standard way of composing a commentary. See Guibert de Nogent, *Autobiographie*, ed. E.-R. Labande (Paris: Les Belles Lettres, 1981), pp. 142-146.

[176] Mary Carruthers, *The Book of Memory: A Study of Memory in Medieval Culture* (Cambridge: Cambridge University Press, 1990).

The fourth option, the archival document, is analytically quite sterile, since it presents an end to a discussion rather than a beginning. However, we must still keep in mind the possibility that all knowledge was not necessarily gathered to be used in a calculated way, but could also be gathered for the sake of gathering.

The Language of the Commentary

In this chapter, I will make a brief overview of the language of the commentary in terms of vocabulary and grammatical structure, which will serve as a basis for the discussion of the function of the commentary.

The explanations are usually given in a short, compact language, not displaying any particular attempts at style. The explanations are either very short or work as a chain in which detail after detail is linked to the preceding with the help of attributes or dependant clauses. One and the same lemma can also be elucidated by a string of explanations, with words signifying alternatives. In a few cases, the explanations are longer and take a more narrative form.

The commentary is transmitted as an anonymous work and the voice in the commentary is usually an impersonal third-person form, but every now and then an 'I' appears. However, this form is a part of standard commentary style and not indicative of an author's voice or anything similar. This 'I' appears five times in the shape of a first-person verb.[177] In these cases the first-person form of the verb functions as an emphasis when the syntax is explained, e.g. VENERIS, *dico*, PROSPICIENTIS. Here *dico* signals that these two forms belong together and it also serves the function of referring back to an earlier part of the explanation where *veneris* is discussed, but not in relation to the word *prospicientis*. There are also several other first-person forms appearing in the commentary, but these are all used in the paraphrasing explanations, which will be discussed below under Function of the commentary.

Vocabulary

The vocabulary in the commentary is, usually, not complicated. It employs standard expressions most of the time, e.g. *interficio* is almost always used for 'to kill', *colo* for 'to venerate'. Intercourse (the explanations often triggered by the 'adventures' of Jupiter) is denoted by either *rem habere* or *concumbere*.

The vocabulary can get technical when cosmographical matters are discussed, as well as in some other cases. In the *accessus*, for instance,

---

[177] *dico*: edition l. 214, 335, 859, 1731; *puto*: edition l. 1514.

we have the following words: *naturalis – artificalis, literalis – inliteralis*
(natural – artificial, literal – non-literal), *dragmatice, exagematice,
cinomitice* (dramatic, explanatory and mixed style) taken from the
philosophical and aesthetical realm. In Book 1, we have *intellegibilis*
(hypothetical) and in Book 2 *dimidium signum* (astrological half sign).

In Book 9, we have the rare *werra* for the more common *guerra* (war)
and the even rarer *inventicius* (foundling). Besides these, the
commentary contains three words that are not found in any of the
dictionaries. In Book 2 *lavilis* (probably meaning 'ability to clean'), in
Book 9 *inethos* (which seems to mean 'unethical') and in Book 11 *sigere*,
a word which is not found anywhere else, although the explanation
makes it clear that it is formed from the place name Sigeum and is
meant to be a synonym for *latere* (to hide/lurk). This word is probably
a misunderstanding, because, in Servius, we read that the place was
named after *sige*, which Servius claims is the Greek word for
'silence'.[178] Silence has then been confused with 'to hide/lurk', which is
what was done at Sigeum.

There are a few examples of specific Christian Latin words being
used, such as *capellas* (chapels) in Book 1 and *reliquiis* (relics) in Book
13.

In Books 4 and 8, we have two instances of what might be signs of
native German speakers' mistakes or variants, namely *fas* for *vas* and
fatem for *vatem*. F for v is usually associated with German, but
according to Peter Stotz, the use was not limited to the German lands
but can, for example, also be observed in manuscripts from England.[179]
Another possible indication of German speakers could be the
abovementioned word *werra*. It is Old High German, which in other
texts has then been Latinised to *guerra*.[180]

In Book 6, we have the rare form *faxanum* for *phasianus*. This form,
according to Du Cange, is only reported in a charter without
provenance from 1345.

Language on Sentence Level

The first example illustrates the simplest possible language in an
explanation:

---

[178] Servius *in Aen.* 2:312, ed. Thilo-Hagen (1881-1902).

[179] Peter Stotz *Handbuch zur lateinischen Sprache des Mittelalters. Bd. 3, Lautlehre.*
(München: Beck, 1996) pp. 272-273.

[180] Stotz 1996, p. 152.

> *DENSIOR H<IS> T<ELLVS> ELEMENTA G<RANDIA>*
> *T<RAXIT>, scilicet truncos, lapides et cetera, que sunt partes*
> *terre.* (1:29)[181]

> The earth heavier than these dragged the larger elements
> along, that is to say: tree trunks, stones and other things that
> are parts of the earth.

The explanation is signalled by *scilicet* (that is to say) and then *elementa grandia* (larger elements) is explained by adding concrete examples (tree trunks, stones and other things). These are then further explained with a relative clause (that are parts of the earth).

The following sentence is an example of the use of prepositional phrases in the commentary:

> *Ipolitus fuit acusatus Theso patri suo a nouerca Phedra, quia, cum*
> *ipse, puer, rogatus esset ab ea, ut iaceret secum, et nollet, illa dixit*
> *Theso, quod ex hoc rogata esset ab illo, sed abiecit eum.* (2:646)

> Hippolytos was accused by his mother-in-law Phaedra in
> front of his father Theseus, since when as a boy he was asked
> by Phaedra to sleep with her and he refused, she told
> Theseus that he had asked her about this, but that she had
> rejected him.

This sentence may look clumsy, but it is constructed to achieve maximal precision. The names, as so often, have epithets (*Theso patri suo*), which makes the sentence seem crowded. Here he is asked by her (*rogatus esset ab ea*) to sleep with her (*ut iaceret secum*) and when he refuses, she turns it around and claims that she was asked by him (*rogata esset ab illo*) regarding this thing (*ex hoc*). The use of the same prepositional construction might not look very elegant, but it makes the order of events and the players involved unequivocally clear to the reader.

The last example is of a longer and slightly more complex passage (I have arranged each sentence on a new line for maximum clarity):

> *PHRIXEAQVE VELLERA.*
> *Athemas de quadam marina dea habuit Frixum et Hellem.*
> *Qui secum manere nequerunt pro afflictione nouerce I[u]nonis.*
> *Et cum recedendo uenirent ad mare, mater eorum dedit eis arietem*
> *habentem aureum uellus et ualentem tam ire per mare quam per*

---

[181] When entire passages from the edition are quoted, reference is given to the lemma by book and line in the *Metamorphoses* (listed in the left margin in the edition).

terram, ut in eo sedentes transirent mare, predicens illum esse submersurum, qui retro aspiceret.

Et quia Helle retro axpexit, submersa est, unde mare, in quo cecidit, Hellespontiacum dicitur.

Phrixus transiens per mare, quod est inter Sexton et Abidon, ad Cholcon insulam iuit et ibi arietem Marti consecrauit uel sacrificauit.

Et <eo> sacrificato translatus est signum celeste.

Vellus uero positum in sumitate cuiusdam arboris costoditur a dracone in ea inuoluto, ne uellus inde auferatur, quia, si aufereretur, non esset ibi caput mundi, sed locus ille, in quo fuerit uellus. (7:7)

THE PHRIXEAN FLEECE.

Athamas had Phrixus and Helle from a sea goddess.

They could not stay with him because of oppression from their step-mother, Ino.

And when they were departing and came to the sea, their mother gave them a ram that had a golden fleece and could walk on water as well as on land, so that they might cross the sea sitting on it and she warned them that the one who looked back would be drowned.

Since Helle looked back, she was drowned, wherefore the sea into which she fell is called the Hellespont.

Phrixus crossed the sea between Sestos and Abydus and came to the island of Colchis and there he consecrated or sacrificed the ram to Mars.

When the ram had been sacrificed it was transformed into a heavenly sign.

The fleece was placed in the top of a tree and is guarded by a serpent wrapped around it, so that the fleece cannot be carried away, because, if it were to be carried away, then the centre of the world would not be there, but in the place where the fleece would be.

This explanation is around eleven lines long and consists of seven complete sentences in the edition. The subordinate clauses used are relative, temporal with *cum*, final *ut*-clause and final *ne*-clause, causal clause with *quia*, and a conditional clause. This example also contains an ablative absolute, several participles and one gerund.

The explanation is not linked to the lemma with any words, but consists of reactions to the words in the lemma. *Phrixeaque* in the lemma is explained with the differently spelled *Frixum* in the first sentence, and *vellera* is picked up in the third sentence.

The language is not sophisticated, but correct and precise. It aims at including a maximum amount of detail with a minimum of ambiguity. There are not really any unusual or irregular words or phrases, except perhaps for *recedendeo* in the third sentence, which I interpret as a modal ablative, but this form is otherwise rarely used in the commentary. The *uel* connecting the last two verbs in the fifth sentence, *consecrauit uel sacrificauit*, tells us that this might have originally been a marginal gloss introducing an alternative synonym, but its inclusion in the running text does not affect the grammar. The last sentence contains four subordinate clauses and is fairly complex.

The examples above describe what the sentences used in explanations to the lemma in the commentary look like. Where the connection between the lemma and the explanations is concerned, this is done by either the use of a *id est* or a *quia* and a subsequent explanation, or simply by starting the explanation without any specific connectors in the beginning, but the explanation may then instead pick up one or several words from the lemma.

Sometimes pronouns, nouns or verbs can also be added directly to the lemma and are used as a very compact type of explanation. This will be described further in the next section.

Function

The commentary in clm 4610 fills twenty-three folios and numbers, in total, circa 16,500 words, which comment on around 460 passages from all fifteen books of the *Metamorphoses*. The following sections aim to investigate the form and function of the entire commentary. The first thing to be discussed is the prologue to the commentary, the *accessus*, which has a distinct character compared to the rest of the commentary and is therefore best treated separately. After this the function and, finally, its use of sources will be discussed.

The *accessus*

The *accessus* is a general introduction to the work in question and can function as a separate text with its own transmission history. The *accessus* in general is short and more discursive than the commentary text it precedes, so it has received far more scholarly attention than the long, difficult commentary texts. A significant amount of research has therefore been conducted on the *accessus*, which, in turn, attracts further research, while the commentary texts themselves are neglected: this has created an imbalance in the research on, for instance, the reception of Ovid. [182] The *accessus* provides good material for the study of the medieval theory of interpreting text, but to study the practice of interpreting the text more editions of commentary texts are needed.

The *accessus* in clm 4610 spans over circa fifty lines in the manuscript and two pages in the edition. It consists of a short introduction and then eight different parts, which are not linked to each other in any particular manner. The *accessus* is never followed up in the commentary itself, which seems to be typical for most *accessus* and the texts they introduce. However, it is important to note that the *accessus* is an integrated part of the commentary in this manuscript; it is written by the same hand and there is no division between the end of the *accessus* and the beginning of Book 1.

It most closely follows the schemes for the so-called philosophical and the modern type of *accessus*.[183] The philosophical type, thought to be derived from Boethius, applies the following topics when analysing a work: intention of the author; utility and order of the work; name of the author; title and part of philosophy under which it is classified. The modern type adopts intention, utility and part of philosophy from the philosophical type and adds to them the topic of subject matter.

The *accessus* in clm 4610 begins with acknowledging the different traditions for composing an *accessus* by mentioning that many things can be investigated regarding any book, but that 'the moderns' prescribe three topics only: subject matter (*materia*), intention (*intentio*) and to which part of philosophy the work belongs to (*cui parti philisophiae*).[184] Of these three, subject matter is never treated, but intention and 'part of philosophy' as well as the unannounced topics utility (*utilitas*) and title (*titulus*) are discussed.

Intention is treated twice. The first time the *accessus* echoes Horace, claiming that Ovid's intention is, just as any other author's, to entertain and by so doing also to give some moral instructions.[185] This

[182] For more on the medieval theory of interpretation see *The Cambridge History of Literary Criticism, volume 2 The Middle Ages*, ed. Alastair J. Minnis and I. Johnson (Cambridge: Cambrige University Press, 2005).

[183] The following is based on Wheeler's introduction to *Accessus ad auctores* (p. 2). Wheeler gives ample references to previous research, of which the most commonly referred to works are: R. W. Hunt 'The Introduction to the 'Artes' in the Twelfth Century' in *Studia Mediaevalia in Honorem Admodum Reverendi Patris Raymundi Josephi Martin* (Bruge: De Tempel, 1948); and Alastair J. Minnis *Medieval Theory of Authorship: Scholastic Literary Attitudes in the Later Middle Ages*, Middle Ages Series (Philadelphia: University of Pennsylvania Press, 1988). I use Wheeler's translation of the Latin terms in the following.

[184] Edition l. 1-3.

[185] Horace, *Ars poetica* l. 333, ed. D. R. Shackleton Bailey (1995).

is then combined with the topic 'part of philosophy' by stating that most authors lean towards ethics.[186] The second time intention is treated it does not concern Ovid specifically. Instead, it is said that poets, in general, are *correptores* (stern correctors) and *immitatores* (imitators) of the Latin language.[187] This is a somewhat strange expression. It could be an error, and is indeed treated as such by Meiser, who emendated it to *correctores* and *emendatores* (correctors and emendators), which is easier to understand.[188] *Correptores* as a scribal error for *correctores* is, of course, easily understandable, but it is nevertheless possible to make a sensible reading out of *correptores* and *immitatores* in the sense of authors imitating and handing down good classical Latin to new generations.[189]

The utility of the work is said to be twofold: Ovid brings to light forgotten stories and he helps the reader with Latin composition.[190]

The last paragraph brings up the topic 'title of the work'.[191] The fact that it states the title as *Incipit liber Ouidii Metamorphoseos* has led previous researchers to mistake it for a sign that the commentary actually starts here, but this is simply a reference to the title of the work as written in the manuscript the commentator used.[192] This is then followed by an etymological explanation of the title, which is typical for this topic.

The main body of the *accessus* does not concern Ovid, but is rather a short, general treaty on what philosophy is, triggered by the phrase *cui parti philosophie* in the introduction. The *accessus* continues by carefully describing these parts, along with an etymology for *philosophus*, which ascribes the word to Pythagoras.[193] This etymology seems to have been immensely popular during the Middle Ages and is used by, among others, Roger Bacon, who ascribes it to Augustinus.[194] Then follows a description of the different parts of philosophy and the etymology of these different parts.

The division of philosophy according to the *accessus* is as follows:

---

[186] Edition l. 53.

[187] Edition l. 58.

[188] Meiser 1885, p. 51.

[189] I have thus chosen not to correct this phrase in the edition.

[190] Edition l. 54.

[191] Edition l. 59-62.

[192] For examples of medieval titles, see Tarrant 2004, p. 1 (apparatus).

[193] Edition l. 4-28.

[194] Roger Bacon *Opus maius pars secunda*, ed. J. H. Bridges (1900), 3.61. Bacon mentions Augustinus's *De Civitate Dei* Book 8, but I have not found the relevant passage. Chapter 8:4 does, however, treat Pythagoras and the other ancient philosophers.

Philosophia: *naturalis vel artificalis*
  aritificalis: *inliteralis vel literalis*
    literalis: *phisica, logica, ethica*
      phisica: *geometria, arithmetica, musica, astronomia*
      logica: *gramatica, rhetorica, dialectica*
      ethica: *boni et mali mores*

In this taxonomy, the liberal arts have been inserted under the general header *philosophia*. The category *philosophia literalis phisica* equates to the quadrivium and the *logica* the trivium. A similar division is found in a contemporary work by Rupert of Deutz in the chapter *De scientia* (book 7:3) of *De operibus spiritus sancti*.[195]

After having described these and their sub-categories, we get a seemingly unrelated paragraph describing the different modes of writing, an *accessus* topic that Ralph Hexter calls *modus recitandi*.[196] Here we learn that Ovid writes in the mixed mode, which is a mixture of two modes: the dramatic (where characters speak) and exegematic (where only the authors speak). This division is also found as *accessus* 26 in the *Accessus ad auctores*, the *accessus* to *Heroides*, where there is textual corruption at the very place where the mixed mode is described using the same word as in clm 4610, *cinamicticon*.[197] This word, *cinomenticon* in clm 4610, *cinamicticon* in the *Heroides accessus*, is of Greek origin and is probably related to the following passage from Bede's *De arte metrica*:

> *aut commune uel mixtum, quod graeci coenon uel micton uocant.*[198]
>
> Common or mixed, which the Greeks call *coenon* or *micton*.

From this passage, it would appear as though a compound word has been constructed in the *accessus* from the two alternatives suggested by Bede (*coenon* or *micton*). A similar description, but without the Greek words, is found in Servius on the *Bucolica*, and, in the fifth century, the Virgil commentary of Junius Philargyrius, which uses only *micton* in this case.[199]

---

[195] *De sancta Trinitate et operibus eius. Libri 1-9*, ed. R. Haacke (1971).

[196] Hexter 1986, p. 161. Ed. l. 29–33.

[197] *Accessus ad auctores*, p. 90.

[198] Beda Venerabilis *De arte metrica* 25:4, ed. C. B. Kendall (1975).

[199] Thilo-Hagen vol. 3:1, 29 and vol. 3:2, 2. Hexter discusses this passage, but seems to have the wrong reference. He refers to Thilo-Hagen 3.1-2, where I can find nothing relating to this. cf Hexter 1986, p. 162.

After this follows a three-paragraph description of three different schools of philosophers and their compatibility with Christianity, some of which appear to be derived from Macrobius or an intermediary.[200] This section of the text, which begins *quidam philosophi fuerunt*, can be found in all of the manuscripts in the Bavarian B family as well as in the margin of a late twelfth-century *Metamorphoses* manuscript.[201]

The *accessus* in clm 4610 is unique in that the majority of the text is not related directly to Ovid or the *Metamorphoses*. The different *accessus* in the Bavarian B family stay much closer to the typical form of the *accessus* and primarily focus on Ovid and the *Metamorphoses*.[202] This also seems to be the case with all the other *Metamorphoses accessus* from the twelfth and thirteenth centuries.[203] The fact that clm 4610 is the oldest preserved commentary and that the *accessus* mainly discusses different aspects of philosophy may be a sign of what sort of associations the readers made when they read and discussed the *Metamorphoses*.

Function of the Commentary: Categories of Explanation

The following contains a discussion of an inventory of all the explanations in the entire commentary, and what sorting them into different explanatory categories can tell us about what purpose they might have served.

A similar method has also been employed in previous scholarship. The scholar best known for applying a strict set of categories to his material is G. E. Wieland in *The Latin Glosses on Arator and Prudentius*.[204] Wieland has defined five major categories of glosses: glosses on prosody, lexical, grammatical, syntactical and commentary glosses. These categories contain several sub-groups, for example, the category 'commentary glosses' contains seven sub-categories. Wieland's explicit purpose is to 'reach conclusions about *all* the functions of Latin

---

[200] For more on this see chapter 2 The Fate of Ovid Until the Twelfth Century. See also Herren 2004, pp. 221-223. Macrobius, *Commentarii in Somnium Scipionis* 1.2.14, ed. J. Willis (1970). Edition l. 34-50.

[201] Copenhagen, Det kongelige bibliotek, GKS 2008 4:0. The *accessus* is edited by Paule Demats, pp. 179-184.

[202] The *accessus* of the Bavarian B family is also discussed in chapter 5.

[203] For examples of other *accessus* to the *Metamorphoses* see *Accessus ad auctores* and Frank T. Coulson 'Hitherto Unedited Medieval and Renaissance Lives of Ovid' I-II in *Mediaeval Studies* 49 (1987) pp. 152-207; 59 (1997) pp. 111-53.

[204] Gernot R. Wieland, *The Latin glosses on Arator and Prudentius in Cambridge University library, Ms GG.5.35* (Toronto: Pontifical Institute of Mediaeval Studies, 1983).

glosses'.[205] He seeks to do this as a reaction to older research, which, in his opinion, has been overly focused on vernacular or bilingual glossing.

The empirical material in Suzanne Reynolds and her *Medieval Reading: Grammar, Rhetoric and the Classical Text* consists of commentaries on Horace, but the categories she uses as well as her other analytical methods are focused on arguing in favour of her overarching research object, namely medieval reading.[206] Reynolds uses at least seven categories, each of which contains several sub-categories. A third example, and most relevant to research on Ovid, is Ralph Hexter and his work *Ovid and Medieval Schooling*.[207] Hexter explores several different commentaries on three of Ovid's works by using the categories 'replacement', 'identification', and 'expansion'. Each of these then contains at least three sub-categories.

What is evident from the work of these scholars is that nobody uses the same categories. Instead, different categories are used according to the analytical focus they provide and the possibilities offered by the examined texts. Furthermore, of these three scholars, only Hexter treats the *catena* format, the other two only treat marginal and interlinear glossing, which often consists of very short pieces of text keyed to the target text. The latter format, because of its direct relation to the target text, seems to be more attractive to analyse than the *catena* commentary. Even Hexter uses most of his categories when discussing glossed Ovid manuscripts and much fewer when discussing the *catena* commentary.

Inspired by the scholars mentioned above, I have grouped the ten categories I first postulated after having analysed the text under four overarching categories of function into the following scheme:

Background: mythological background explanations
Grammar: grammatical explanations, paraphrase
Lexical: patronymics, lexicon, etymology
Interpretative: Euhemeristic, natural philosophy, narrative, plot

These categories are not absolute, since the commentary contains circa 460 explanations and many of these can belong to more than one category at the same time. In addition, some explanations fall outside these main categories, either because they are a mixture of explanations belonging to different categories or because they are of a unique character that would demand a category of its own. These

---

[205] Wieland 1983, p. 2 (my emphasis).

[206] Reynolds 1996.

[207] Hexter 1986.

explanations are discussed under the headings 'complex explanations' and 'explanations outside the categories'. The purpose of this inventory is to provide the reader with a heuristic aid to the commentary. Each category below is given a general introduction, then discussed with the help of examples from the commentary, and finally provided with a short conclusion with regard to what function they might have filled. A complete list of all explanations belonging to each category is listed at the end of the discussion of each of the four groups.[208]

Background: Mythological Background

With 190 explanations fitting into this category, it is the biggest by far. It would be possible to further subdivide it, but that is not strictly necessary in order to perform this analysis.

The general characteristic of this category is to provide a background or explanation to characters and events that may only be mentioned in passing or alluded to in the *Metamorphoses*. They are written in reasonably clear language and tend to be the longest type of explanation. The basic type consists of just one background story, but quite often the explanation may provide an alternative, which is signalled by a *sed* (but) or *vel* (or) and some type of reference like *quidam dicunt* (some say), *secundum* (according to) + a name of an authority or just a reference to a story, or simply by writing *aliter* (alternatively) or *vel* (or) and then giving the alternative story. These explanations rarely interact with the lemma directly. Usually a name in the lemma functions as a trigger for the explanation. These explanations are also among those where it is possible to find a source and where indeed a source may sometimes even be given.[209]

The first example illustrates a simple and short form of mythological background story:

> 1. *MONICHIOSQVE VOLANS. Monichius fuit gigas et dicitur iuuisse in constructione murorum Athenarum.* (2:709)
>
> AND FLYING [HE LOOKED DOWN ON] THE MUNYCHIAN [FIELDS]. Munychius was a giant and he is said to have aided in the construction of the walls of Athens.

[208] The explanations are identified by the book and line in the *Metamorphoses*, to which they react (these numbers can be found in the left margin in the edition). Sometimes several different explanations are given to the same line, in which case, e.g., the second explanation is given a x:2 to identify it in the inventory.
[209] See the section entitled The Commentary and its Sources.

This explanation simply tells us who Monichius is and gives the reason why the name is used in this instance.

Example 2 shows a typical mythological background story:

> 2. *ANDROMEDAN PENAS. Cepheus rex habuit coniugem Casiope<m>, que dixit se pulcriorem esse Iunone uel deabus marinis. Pro quo peccato belua exiens mare commedebat suum regnum. Iudicauit Iupiter, ut filiam suam Andromedam daret belue ad commedendum, et sic homines ulterius non commederentur.* (4:671)

> THAT ANDROMEDA [SHOULD PAY] THE PENALTY. King Cepheus had a wife, Cassiope, who said she was more beautiful than Juno or the sea goddesses. For this sin a monster came from the sea and devoured his kingdom. Jupiter decided to give his daughter, Andromeda, to the monster to be eaten, and thus the people were no longer eaten.

The explanation is triggered by two words in the lemma and describes who Andromeda is, as well as the background and the nature of her penalty. The phrase *uel deabus marinis* signals that there are two different versions of this story. In one version, Cassiopeia claims that she is more beautiful than Juno and, in the other, more beautiful than some sea-goddesses.

The third example is of a slightly longer explanation:

> 3. *PALLAS ERICTONIVM. Dum Pallas faciebat Athenas, Vulcano complacita est, cum qua dum uellet concumbere, sed Pallade respuente <u>uel renuente</u> cecidit ex Vulcano semen in terram, unde Erictonius creatus est. Sed quidam dicunt, quod Erictonius fuit gigas, qui uoluit cum Pallade concumbere in silua. Illa uero interposuit nubem. Qui existimans se rem habere cum ea iecit semen in terram, uel in nubem, quod illa suscipiens posuit in cista. Vnde creatus est Erictonius, iuxta quem posuit draconem, qui enutriret eum.* (2:553)

> PALLAS [ENCLOSED] ERICHTHONIUS. When Pallas made Athens she was very pleasing to Vulcan, who wanted to sleep with her, but when Pallas rejected or refused him the semen fell from Vulcan on the ground, from which Erichthonius was created. But some say that Erichthonius was a giant, who wanted to sleep with Pallas in the forest. She placed a cloud between them. He, thinking that he was having intercourse with her, ejected his semen on the ground

or into the cloud, which she took up and put in a chest. From this Erichthonius was created, next to whom she placed a snake to nurture him.

Here we yet again see that the explanation reacts to both of the words in the lemma. In this explanation, we are provided with two different versions of the story behind Erichthonius birth. In the first version, he is said to have Vulcan as father and, in the other story, a giant by the same name as himself, Erichthonius. The second version is signalled by the typical vague marker of an alternative source *sed quidam dicunt* (but some say). Both versions also contain one alternative fact each. In the first it says that Pallas rejected Vulcan, or that she refused him (*vel renuente*), which has been written above the line as an alternative. In the second version, we are told that the giant ejected his semen either on the ground or into a cloud.

The longest example of a background story is the explanation to lemma 9:408. This explanation concerns the lines 408-412 in Book 9 of the *Metamorphoses* and it presents the entire Thebes cycle on three pages in the manuscript (by far the longest explanation in the commentary). It is more or less told in the manner of a continuous story, where in simple yet effective and dramatic language, it goes through the Thebes cycle from the birth of Oedipus to the start of the war on Thebes. The story roughly corresponds to the three first books of the Thebaid, ending with a tale of a cursed necklace and the misfortunes that befell its owners, which gives a background to *Met.* 9:411-412.[210]

In some cases, the background explanations display an interpretative characteristic, as in the following example:

> 4. *SAXVM SISIPHON GRAVE VRGET. Antidia dicitur fuisse mater Vlixis. Que ante Leherte nuptias eum ex Sisipho, filio Eoli, concepit. Sed non est uerum, rapta quidem a Sisipho fuit, sed intactam eam reddidit.* (13:26)

> THE HEAVY STONE PRESSES SISYPHOS. Anticlea is said to be Ulysses' mother. She conceived him from Sisyphos, the son of Eolus, before her marriage to Laertes. But this is not true, she was indeed carried off by Sisyphos, but he returned her unviolated.

---

[210] This explanation is also discussed in relationship to other twelfth-century commentaries in chapter 5.

Here the explanation not only provides us with a background to Sisyphus, but also interprets the information for us. In this case, the commentator seems to have access to information from two different sources and decides that one is true and the other false. However, while this example displays an interpretative element, this mainly revolves around interpreting different background stories and not the story in the *Metamorphoses* itself, which is the characteristic of the category Plot.

Function: These background stories appear to be meant to provide the reader with a grasp of 'the big picture' of the Greco-Roman mythological world (as it was available at this period) in its entirety.

Mythological background explanations: 1:10, 81, 106, 188, 231, 313, 563, 580, 624, 690, 694, 763; **2:139**, 239, 247, 247:2, 264, 539, 545, 544, 553, 555, 642, 646, 685, 709, 755; **3:13**, 14, 111, 126, 132, 269, 665; **4:19**, 291, 333, 457, 458, 460, 461, 463, 501, 671, 786; **5: 347**, 352, 407, 424x2, 499; **6:70**, 99, 108, 111, 112, 115, 117, 178, 384, 415, 652; **7:1:2**, 3, 7, 74, 149, 361, 363, 435, 437, 438, 444; **8:179**, 182, 183, 261, 276, 313, 316, 305; **9:67**, 88, 123, 183, 184, 187, 187:2, 188, 189, 190, 192, 197, 232, 233, 294, 397, 403, 404, 405, 408, 647, 693, 690, 694; **10:10**, 13, 65, 68, 90, 91, 151, 168, 196, 206, 224, 240, 450; **11:25**, 46, 69, 106, 211, 214, 279, 393, 413, 583, 745, 763; **12:35**, 109, 112, 401, 606, 610; **13:2**, 26, 39, 46, 53, 56, 98, 99, 217, 386, 399, 444, 626, 628, 629, 631, 635, 690, 693, 710, 714, 715, 716, 717, 720; **14:82:2**, 103, 114, 119, 155, 331, 449, 452, 457, 468, 472, 565, 533, 639, 694:2, 712, 720, 773, 774, 776, 799, 830; **15:13**, 164, 309, 326, 462, 475, 552, 836.

Grammar

This category consists of two sub-categories: grammatical explanations and paraphrase. This is the second biggest category. Together, the two sub-categories occur 172 times in the commentary (grammatical: 112 and paraphrase: 60).

Grammatical Explanations

This sub-category usually consists of short explanations that provide help in construing the sentence or in understanding certain features of the text on a purely linguistic level. This type of explanation sometimes works by simply rearranging the word order of the lemma so as to make the syntactical relationship clearer to the reader. This is the case in the following example, where the rearranged lemma itself constitutes the grammatical explanation and the rest belongs to the natural philosophy category.

> 5. *CIRCVMFLVVS HVMOR POSSEDIT VLTIMA et COHERCVIT SOLIDVM ORBEM, id est terram, quia nisi aqua circumdaret terram, terra esset solubilis et arenosa.* (1:30)
>
> THE FLOWING WATER OCCUPIED THE LAST PLACE and ENCLOSED THE SOLID ORB, that is the earth, since if water did not enclose the earth, the earth would be soluble and sandy.

In the *Metamorphoses*, the passage reads as follows: *circumfluus umor ultima possedit solidumque coercuit orbem*. The explanation has simply moved the verbs so as to make their relation to their objects clearer. The commentary has also removed the enclitic *-que* and replaced it with a normal *et* (and).

The grammatical explanations may also interject words into the lemma to explain how the sentence should be understood. Example 6 shows a more complex example that uses a rearranged lemma, extra words and some other strategies.

> 6. *SERVAT ADHVC SALAMIS. Ordo: Salamis ciuitas seruat illud SIGNVM VENERIS QVOQVE TEMPLVM HABET illud SIGNVM NOMINE, id est sub nomine, hoc est nomen inscriptum ostendat signum fuisse ANAXETES. VENERIS, dico, PROSPICIENTIS, id est uidentis ultionem.* (14:760)
>
> SALAMIS STILL KEEPS. Order: Salamis's city keeps this IMAGE OF VENUS AND THE TEMPLE HAS the SIGN WITH THE NAME, that is under this name, that is an inscribed name shows that the sign was OF ANAXARETES. OF VENUS, I say, LOOKING OUT FOR, that is with her mind set on vengeance.

In this explanation, the lemma preserves the word order from the *Metamorphoses*, then the key word *ordo* (order) signals that what follows is how the sentence should be construed. Demonstrative pronouns are supplied to add clarity to the construction. The word *nomine* is further explained by the prepositional phrase *sub nomine* introduced by *id est*. Following this, yet further explanation is added by a sentence declaring that this refers to Anaxarete, who is mentioned by name in the *Metamorphoses* ten lines before this passage. Finally, *Veneris* and *prospicientis* are declared to belong together by inserting a declarative verb *dico* (I say) between them and then as a last addition, these words are rephrased in the last *id est*-phrase (the last part could be considered as belonging to the next sub-category).

There are a few instances of a more formal grammatical explanation, which often seems to be inspired or taken directly from Servius or Priscian. In example 8, Servius is even called upon by name:

> 7. *RECIDIT IN SOLIDAM. Re- ante consonantem literam, si producitur, non est nisi cum positione, ut 'relique', 'reccido' et etiam 'retineo'. Si produceretur, oportet esse duo tt ibi scripta.* (10:180)
>
> IT FELL AGAIN (*RECIDIT*) TO THE SOLID [GROUND]. Re- before a consonant, if it is lengthened, it can only be by position, such as *relique, reccido* and also *retineo*. If it (*retineo*) were to be lengthened, then there should be two t's there.
>
> 8. *DIXIT ET INSANIS. Seruius dicit 'insanus' pro 'magnus', sicut insana Iuno pro magna.* (12:510)
>
> HE SPOKE AND THROUGH [AUSTER'S] RAGING [POWERS]. Servius says that 'raging' [can be used] for 'great', as in raging Juno for great Juno.

In the final example in this sub-category the commentary mentions the rhetorical figure *pars pro toto*. Discussion of rhetoric and meter is otherwise almost completely absent in this commentary.

> 9. *EXCIPIT ET NVRIBVS. 'Nuribus' ponit pro mulieribus, partem uidelicet pro toto.* (2:366)
>
> IT RECEIVES AND TO THE BRIDES. 'Brides' is used for women, clearly as a part for the whole (*pars pro toto*).

Paraphrasing

This sub-category of explanations explains grammar by paraphrasing the commented-upon passage in the *Metamorphoses*. Generally, the paraphrase is written in the same person as the relevant passage, i.e. if it is a first-person speaker in the *Metamorphoses*, then the paraphrase will also be in the first person. The paraphrases are often signalled by a phrase such as *sic* or *quasi diceret*.

In example 10, we find an explanation that combines a grammatical explanation in the same style as that in example 6 above with a paraphrase explanation.

> 10. *SOLA CONIVNX IOVIS et NON TAM ELOQVITVR, an PROBET, an CVLPET QVAM GAVDET CLADE, hoc est non eloquitur, ut uel culpet uel laudet, sed gaudet.* (3:256)

ONLY JUPITER'S WIFE DID NOT SPEAK SO MUCH TO APPROVE or TO BLAME, AS SHE REJOICED IN THE DISASTER, that is she does not speak so as to blame or praise, but she rejoices.

Example 11 shows an explanation that operates with paraphrase only:

11. *EXCVSAT, sic dicens: O dii omnes uos scitis, quod non potui aliud facere, quin fulmina mitterem.* (2:397)
[JUPITER] EXCUSES, saying thus: O gods, you all know that I could not do anything else but to throw my thunder bolts.

In this example, the single verb *excusat* is expounded in an entire sentence, which states what this excuse might have sounded like.

Function: If the background category was meant to help the reader to grasp the entire world, of which the *Metamorphoses* is an expression, then this category serves the purpose of helping the reader to navigate the text by clearing up textual difficulties. The explanations in this category are the ones closest in style to interlinear glosses.

Grammatical explanations: 1:4, 3, 6, 24, 29, 53, 69, 73, 190, 211, 231, 371, 562, 563, 578, 593, 670, 763; **2:153**, 219, 272, 544, 561, 626, 802, 844; **3:32:2**, 88, 256; **4:33**, 199, 333, 509, 801; **5:19**, 370, 372, 371, 378:2, 450; **6:71**, 90, 233, 237, 393, 506, 538, 539; **7:1**, 3, 121, 438, 444, 759, 794, 759:2; **8:182**, 421, 655; **9:23**, 33, 51, 69, 83, 88, 245, 248, 248:2, 348, 432, 448, 476, 735; **10:25**, 68, 127, 168, 180, 196, 223, 240, 252, 284, 287, 596; **11:3**, 48, 101, 150, 380, 410, 627; **12:401**, 432, 510; **13:187**, 408, 569, 611, 635, 638, 653, 714, 720, 804; **14:233**, 324, 729, 739, 760; **15:39**.

Paraphrasing: 1:190, 470, 563, 587, 615; **2:397**, 533, 566, 596, 626, 802; **3:253**; 4:641; **5:372:2**; 7: 54, 76, 149, 687, 704, 794; **8:131**; 9:23, 83, 182, 248, 248:2, 275, 299, 326, 327, 403, 404, 432, 649, 735, 755; **10:25**, 168, 221:2, 310, 628, 727; **11:150**, 380, 390, 763, 783; **12:399**; 13:141, 187, 408; **14:324**, 331, 337, 657, 722, 724, 725, 729, 827.

Lexical

This category consists of the sub-categories: patronymics, lexicon and etymology. Together they occur 113 times (patronymics: 42, lexicon: 34, etymology: 37).

Patronymics

This sub-category of explanations revolves around family relations and identifying characters. It is often caused by Ovid's poetic phrasing when names of places and characters are concerned. In this category, we may include strict patronymics, but also other explanations that identify family ties.

> 12. *AT REX ODRISIVS. Odrisius fuit rex Tracie. Inde Tracia uocatur Odrisia. Inde reges Odrisii uocantur.* (6:490)
>
> BUT THE ODRYSIAN KING. Odrysius was the king of Thrace. From this Thrace is called Odrysia. From this kings are called Odrysian.

Patronymics sometimes occur on their own, but quite often they are only a part of a bigger explanation. In this category, I have also included other explanations that revolve around kinship and origin of names. Some of these converge with the mythological background category (and are listed doubly in my inventory).

In the following example, only the first sentence explains the patronymic *Belides*. The remainder belongs to the mythological background category.

> 13. *ASIDVE REPETVNT QVAS PERDANT BELIDES VNDAS. De semine Beli natus est Egistus et Danaus. Cuius Danai asensu quinquaginta filie sue acceperunt uiros quinquaginta filios Egisti. Et eos omnes interfecerunt, excepta una, que uirum suum interficere noluit. Pro hoc peccato fas sine fundo de aqua implere debe<n>t.* (4:463)
>
> THE INCESSANT BELIDES SEEK AGAIN THE WATER THAT THEY LOSE. Aegistus and Danaus were born from the seed of Belus. With Danaus's approval his fifty daughters took as their husbands Aegistus's fifty sons. And they murdered them all, except for one [daughter] who did not want to murder her husband. For this sin they must fill a vase without bottom with water.

Lexicon

This small sub-category of explanations consists of either a simple synonym or a slightly longer explanation in a style typical of dictionaries. Here, the object explained is not mythological.

> 14. *Phoce sunt uituli.* (2:267)
> *Phocae* are sea-calves.

This short explanation carries a strong resemblance to an interlinear gloss.

Example 15 shows a longer lexicon explanation:

> 15. *PARS SECRETA DOMVS EBORE ET TESTVDINE CVLTOS. Testudo proprie est quoddam concauum, ubi aliud quoddam continetur, sed hic pro hoc laqueari ponitur.* (2:737)
>
> A SEPARATE PART OF THE HOUSE WERE [CHAMBERS] ADORNED WITH IVORY AND TORTOISE-SHELL. Tortoise-shell is strictly speaking something concave, in which something else may be contained, but here it is used for the panelled ceiling.

Here we are presented with a definition of the relevant word (*testudo*) and then we are told that this is not the intended use in this case, but that it is rather an example of metonymy. This category is related to the etymology type, but it does not contain etymological derivation. Example 15 is also related to the grammatical explanation since what this explanation actually does is to explain the figure metonymy, but without using that term.

Etymological

This sub-category consists of an explanation of the origin of a word, usually by means of connecting it to a Greek word, but sometimes just by explaining the verb from which it is derived. Examples 16 and 17 illustrate the two types:

> 16. '*Centaurus' Grece, Latine equus dicitur.* (2:636)
>
> *Centaur* in Greek. In Latin it is called 'horse'.
>
> 17. *Apricus et Aprilis ab 'aperio' dicuntur. Hic uero dicitur APRICA frondosa.* (4:331)
>
> *Apricus* (sunny, sheltering) and *Aprilis* (April) are named from *aperio* (to open). But here APRICA means leafy.

Many but not all of these etymologies can be traced back to Isidor's *Etymologiae*. Often the explanations have made connections to the wrong Greek words, as witnessed in this section of a longer explanation:

> 18. *Yppocentauri deberent dici. 'Yppo' enim Grece, Latine 'subtus'. 'Centaurus' 'equus', sed Latini breuitate Centaurum pro utroque acceperunt, scilicet pro 'subtus' et 'equo'.* (12:210)

> They should be called Hypocentaurs. Hypo in Greek, 'below'
> in Latin. Centaurus means 'horse', but for the sake of brevity
> the Latins use Centaur for both, namely for 'below' and
> 'horse'.

Here the Greek *hippo* (horse) has been confused with *hypo* (under).

The opposite is true in the following example, where the place name
Taenarius in *Metamorphoses* has been changed (at some point) to
Trenareus and the changed form defended by a rather sound Greek
etymology.

> 19. *ET Trenareus EVROTAS. Trenareus est mons Laconie, ubi est
> descensus ad inferos. 'Trene' Grece, id est lamentationes.* (2:247)

> AND Trenarian EUROTAS. Trenareus is a mountain in
> Laconia, where there is a descent to the underworld. *Trene* in
> Greek, that is 'lamentations'.

Function: These three sub-categories may not, at first glance, have that
much in common, but if we suppose that the function of these
explanations was to generate vocabulary, then we can start to see a
common denominator.[211] In example 12, we can see a chain of
derivation from the name Odrisius, which could teach the student how
to create similar derivations. The sub-category lexicon is cruder and, at
a basic level, works by forcing the student to learn synonyms. Finally,
the etymological sub-category must be understood as teaching the
students a method for how to handle and how to explain strange
words.

As in many other cases, the borders between categories are not
clear-cut. This category also contains elements of the background
explanation, but if the latter serves the purpose of familiarising the
students with the world of the text, then this category is more active
and teaches the student how to extract knowledge from the text.

Patronymics: 1:670; 2:441, 509, 545, 743, 757, 844; **3:126**, 132; **4:291**, 463; **5:363**,
378:2; **6:90**, 112, 113, 176, 117, 176:2, 384, 490; **7:668**, 672, 685; **8:207**, 316; **9:12**,
421, 448; **10:91**, 148, 221, 284, 297; **11:383**, 413; **13:596**, 728; **14:83**, 233, 426, 694.

Lexicon: 1:219, 332, 690; **2:2**, 266, 267, 737, 854, 854:2; **3:132**, 665; **4:501**, 505, 667,
750; **5:450; 6:254; 8:25**, 244, 564, 655; **9:341**, 694; **10:1**, 106, 267, 708; **11:25**, 46, 599;
13:589, 653, 804; **14:720**.

---

[211] Suzanne Reynolds makes this point regarding a bigger group of categories relevant to
her material, Reynolds 1996, p. 79.

Etymology: 1:14, 69, 180, 371, 694; **2:2**, 153, 247:2, 264, 340, 416, 636, 721, 755, 854:2; **3:32**; **4:291**, 331; **5:347**, 499, 555; **6:70**, 395, 587; **7:3**; **9:33**, 690; **10:219**, 223; **11:215**; **12:210**; **13:455**, 569, 619; **14:44**, 90, 457.

Interpretative

This category consists of the sub-categories: Euhemeristic, natural philosophy, narrative and plot. Together they occur 135 times (Euhemeristic: 12, natural philosophy: 30, narrative: 18, plot: 75).

Euhemeristic

Explanations belonging to this sub-category describes mythological phenomena as natural. This type is not very common and does not follow a consistent pattern. Some phenomena are explained euhemeristically, while other similar phenomena are not.

The quintessential Euhemeristic explanation can be found in Book 12:

> 20. *DVXERAT YPODAMMEN coniugem A<VDACI> NATVS YXIONE. Laphite et Centauri, quorum rex Perithous fuit de genere Yxionis, fuerunt forte genus hominum, non tamen gigantes. Centauri uero dicti sunt quidam ex illis ideo, quia quadam die sedentes super e<qu>os ablatis bubus, cum alii insequerentur eos uenientesque ad quandam aquam equos suos potarent, uisi sunt et dicti ab indigenis illius terre capita equorum non uidentibus semihomines et semiequi. Et ex illo tempore apellati sunt Centauri.* (12:210)

> THE SON OF BOLD IXION HAD TAKEN HIPPODAME as a wife. The Laphits and the Centaurs, whose king, Pirithous, descended from Ixion, were a strong tribe of humans, [they were] not, however, giants. Some of them are called Centaurs, since one day - after they had left their cows, since others were coming after them - sitting on their horses, they came to some water and allowed the horses to drink, and they were then seen and named half men and half horse by the inhabitants of this country who had not seen the heads of the horses. From this time onward they were called Centaurs.

Here we see a natural explanation to the origin of the mythological creature the centaur.

In example 21 we find a common marker for the Euhemeristic explanation, the phrase *secundum rei ueritatem* (in reality), which is then followed by the explanation.

> 21. *FIDIBVSQVE MEI COMMISSA MARITI et cetera. Cadmus fecit Thebas. Amphion uero adauxit. Et dicitur etiam mouisse cum suis fidibus lapides ad muros faciendos. Sed secundum rei ueritatem non fuit aliud, nisi quia Amphion fuit homo sapiens et docuit rudes homines facere ciuitatem. Ciuitas enim est collectio hominum ad iure uiuendum.* (6:178)
>
> ENTRUSTED TO MY AND MY HUSBAND'S LYRE et cetera. Cadmus founded Thebes, but Amphion enlarged it. And he is even said to have moved stones for the construction of the walls with his lyre. But in reality this was nothing other than that Amphion, being a learned man, taught the unskilled men to build the city. For a city is an assembly of men with the purpose of living according to the law.

The Euhemeristic explanations do not need to be very elaborate. Example 22 presents a very short explanation in which it is simply stated that this is an exaggeration (this could also be considered to belong to the category of plot). Following that, in example 23, we have a short explanation in which the long list of the Fury's magical ingredients described in the *Metamorphoses* is reduced to *integumenta et inuolucra* (obscure expressions and veiled utterances) and then explained to be a means of simply describing that the characters involved in this story went insane.

> 22. *TRIPLICI STANT ORDINE DENTES. Non stant triplici dentes ordine, sed ideo hoc dicit, ut magnitudinem eius exageret.* (3:34)
>
> THE TEETH STAND IN A TRIPPLE ROW. The teeth do not stand in a triple row, he says this to exaggerate its size.
>
> 23. *ERRORESQVE VAGO<S>. Per talia integumenta et inuolucra nihil aliud nobis dicit, nisi quod fecit eos furere.* (4:502)
>
> AND VAGUE DELUSIONS. By such obscure expressions and veiled utterances he tells us nothing else than that it made them mad.

Natural philosophy

This sub-category consists of explanations taken from the realm of natural philosophy, often cosmography. They do not occur very frequently and are mainly to be found in Books 1, 2 and 15. They tend to revolve around the elements and things that have to do with astrology. Example 24 is probably the most sophisticated of these explanations, while example 25 shows a more typical, short explanation.

> 24. *HEC QVOQVE NON PER<STANT> QVE NOS HELEMENTA VOCAMVS. Hoc dicunt philosophi, ut Plato et ceteri, quod non proprie helementa uocentur hoc, quod uidemus, scilicet terram, aquam et alia, sed ideas quasdam in dei mente. Entes proprie helementa dixerunt, quod numquam mutarentur. Sed hic non dicunt de illis helementis.* (15:237)

> AND NOT EVEN THESE WHICH WE CALL THE ELEMENTS PERSIST. The philosophers, such as Plato and others, say that these things that we see, that is to say the earth, water and other things, should not strictly speaking be called 'elements', but rather ideas in the mind of God. Strictly speaking they called elements entes, since they never change. But here they do not speak about this kind of elements.

> 25. *NAIADES HESPERIE TRIFIDA. Trifida dicit, quia flat, findit, urit. Hec tria fulmen habet.* (2:325)

> THE WESTERN NAIADS BECAUSE OF THE THREE-FORKED. He says three-forked because it blows, cleaves and burns. Lightning has these three properties.

The explanation in example 25 occupies itself with the number three and elemental powers. This type reoccurs here and there in the commentary. Example 26 is the first of this type:

> 26. *AMPHITRIDES dicitur Neptunus, ex amphi, id est circum, et tridente. Tridentem enim habet propter tres aque diuersitates. Aqua est labilis, mobilis, lauilis. Lauat et non lauatur.* (1:14)

> AMPHITRIDES is a name for Neptune, from amphi, that is 'around', and trident. For he has a trident on account of the three characteristics of water. Water is flowing, mobile and has the ability to clean. It cleans and is not cleansed.

As stated above, there are not that many explanations that can be said to belong to this group, but the style of the explanation, calling upon the vocabulary and style of natural philosophy, calls for a separate category.

Narrative

In the narrative sub-category, we find explanations that clarify or even criticise the plot structure or the order of events in the *Metamorphoses*. It is not a very common type of explanation, but it is an important type, because it gives us a glimpse of the style of literary criticism used by the commentator. Frequently, the narrative element may only be a small part of the explanation.

The following example is typical of this sub-category:

> 27. *TVNC ADERAS ELIM. Nota, quod hic dicit Phebum exutum a diuinitate adhuc Esculapio filio suo uiuente. Secundum uero aliam, post mortem Esculapii Phebus diuinitatem dicitur amisisse. Hoc non est mirandum, quia fabule quedam sic commiscentur.* (2:679)

> YOU WERE [NOT] PRESENT [YOU LIVED IN] ELIS. Note that here he says that Phoebus was stripped of his divinity while his son Aesculapius was still alive. According to another version Phoebus is said to have lost his divinity after Aesculapius's death. It is not strange, since these stories are confused in this way.

In example 27, two versions of the event are compared and then a final remark simply states that existing alternatives contribute to the confusion of the stories.

Example 28 makes a direct mention of Ovid. This two-part explanation starts with a grammatical explanation of the lemma and then tells us how we must understand the sentence if we want to keep a working chronology of the stories. The commentator then states the consequence if we do not accept this, namely that Ovid simply did not care about the order of the stories.

> 28. *NVNC QVOQVE, VT ATTONITOS non solum MVTAVIT crines IN IDROS, sed etiam nunc fert idros IN PECTORE ADVERSO. Perseus pro constanti habebat, quod daturus erat Palladi caput Gorgonis. Ideo dicit quod iam ferebat 'in pectore', id est in lorica, que antiquitus tantum in pectore habebatur. Vel Ouidius non curauit ordinem.* (4:801)

AND NOW ALSO TO [SCARE] THE TERRIFIED SHE not only CHANGED her locks INTO SERPENTS, but she also now carries the serpents ON THE FRONT OF HER BREAST. Perseus knew for sure that he was going to give the head of the Gorgon to Pallas. Therefore Ovid says that she already carried it 'on her breast', that is on the cuirass, which in former times was carried on the breast only. Or Ovid did not care about the order of the stories.

In the last example, the explanation states that this part of the story sets the scene for what is to come. This refers to a passage in the *Metamorphoses* circa sixty lines later, where Cyane reappears in the story in the form of the pool where Ceres finds her daughter's girdle.

29. *EST MEDIVM CIANES. Istud ad hoc perstruit, quia ualebit future narrationi, quia ibi Cores post reperit uesti<ment>a filie sue, id est zonam.* (5:409)

THERE IS BETWEEN CYANE [AND PISAEAN ARETHUSA]. That builds up to this, because it will be of importance for the story to come, because this is where Ceres later finds her daughter's clothes, that is the girdle.

As we have seen, this sub-category is concerned with the general narrative structure of the *Metamorphoses*, as well as whether Ovid is presenting the mythological stories correctly and coherently.

Plot

This sub-category shares traits with the background and grammatical categories, but the main criteria for this sub-category is that the explanation is derived from the *Metamorphoses* itself. The plot is explained in a manner that does not draw as much on external knowledge or sources as it performs a reading of the text, in the manner of a more mature and experienced reader who would have already been familiar with the plot of the *Metamorphoses,* explaining to a less mature reader what is happening. Thus, the explanations belonging to this category signify a different hermeneutical method, an interpretation or elucidation instead of an addition of facts as in the mythological background category. This sub-category is also intimately related to the text of the *Metamorphoses*. Whereas a background explanation could be taken from anywhere and applied to a passage that seemed relevant to the commentator, the plot explanation is derived from the *Metamorphoses* and cannot easily be applied to another work.

In examples 30 and 31, the information provided is not background information, but rather a conclusion drawn from the content.

> 30. *TIMVERE DEI PRO VI<N>DICE T<ERRAE>. Merito, quia terram uindicabat Hercules a pluribus monstris. Ideo timuerunt dei, ne eo mortuo monstra contra eos surgerent.* (2:118)
>
> TITAN COMMANDED THE QUICK HOURS TO YOKE HIS HORSES. Justly 'Hours', since hours remain throughout the day or the night and throughout [the orbit of] the sun.

> 31. *NON INTELLECTAM VOCEM, id est Cinara intellexit quod filia talem uellet uirum, in quo plus non ardere quam in se, id est in patre, deberet, scilicet putauit in castitate uelle manere.* (10:365)
>
> THE MISUNDERSTOOD VOICE, that is Cinyras understood that his daughter wanted such a man for whom she would not burn more than for him, that is her father, that is to say he thought she wanted to remain chaste.

Example 32 may look like a typical mythological background explanation. It reacts to *clavigeram* (the club bearing) in the lemma and, without explicitly saying so, it gives the reader the information as to whom this refers. However, all of this information is already available in the *Metamorphoses* and therefore this explanation should rather be considered to belong to the category plot.

> 32. *CLAVIGERAM V<IDIT>. Vulcanus quendam filium pessimum habuit, qui Epidauriam uastabat. Quem Theseus interfecit.* (7:437)
>
> SAW THE CLUB-BEARING. Vulcan had an evil son, who laid Epidaurus to waste. Theseus killed him.

The last two examples are simple explanations of what is happening in these scenes. The first simply recaps a three-line description of a compass, which does not mention the word compass itself. In the second, the commentator has interpreted the verb in the lemma (*variat*) to mean 'to waver' and explains that this has to do with the throwing of spears.

> 33. *ALTERA PARS STARET. Fecit circinum.* (8:249)
>
> ONE PART STOOD STILL. He made a compass.

34. AT MANVS EONIDE VARIAT. Scilicet et in iaculando unam hastam, nunc aliam. (8:414)

AND THE HAND OF THE OENEAN WAVERS. Namely in throwing now one spear and now another.

Function: The name of this category makes its function quite clear; it provides an interpretation of the text in the *Metamorphoses*, either by applying a Euhemeristic or natural philosophical perspective, or by interpreting the structure of the text. These types of explanation bring to mind a lecture-style means of delivering information.

Euhemeristic: 2:11, 850; **3:34**, 34:2, 269; **4:502**; 6:178; **9:233**; 11:208; **12:210**; 13:730; **14:88**.

Natural philosophy: 1:5:2, 5:3, 6, 14, 17, 21, 25, 30, 45, 73, 89, 111, 117, 255, 408; **2:26**, 118, 153, 325, 527, 848; **3:397**; **4:199**; **10:78**, 106?, 206?, 704; **15:237**, 249, 251.

Narrative: 1:3, 32, 78; **2:527**, 679; **3:269**; **4:409**, 750, 801; **5:409**, 499; **7:149**, 687; **8:201**; 9:186; **10:223**; 12:309; **15:622**.

Plot: 1:29, 106:2, 113, 133, 150, 237, 513, 615, 749; **2:272**, 510, 544, 642, 846; **3:101**, 572; **4:509**, 510; **5:378**; **6:72**, 393; **7:306**, 361, 794; **8:171**, 201, 222, 244, 249, 414, 744; **9:123**, 184, 192, 232, 241, 245?, 274, 275, 326, 341, 348, 403, 476, 694; **10:65**, 215, 252, 284, 297, 365, 444, 708; **11:25**, 48, 211, 380, 410, 599, 673; **12:35**, 104, 399, 583; **13:230**, 398, 619, 700; **14:83:2**, 119, 149, 153; **15:5**, 39, 41.

Complex Explanations

It is possible to roughly label almost all explanations in the commentary using the above categories. The fact that an explanation often contains more than just one mode has been touched upon in exploring the individual categories above. In the following, we will continue to explore explanations with a focus on the complex.

The first example includes explanations belonging to three different sub-categories.

35. VISVS ERAT PHINEVS, subaudi 'ab Argonautis'. Fineus fuit quidam diues, qui de uxore iam mortua duos filios habebat, quos instinctu nouerce / illorum, que nouerca Nubes dicebatur, excecauit. Ideo dii irati fuerunt et eum lumine priuauerunt et tres arpias, que uocabantur Aello, Cillerio, Occipete, sibi apposuerunt. Que cibos suos omnes conmacularent ad quem fine[u]m, cum Hercules et Argonaute uenerunt. Ab eo arpias Hercules auertit et iussit filiis Boree, ut illas fugarent. Qui usque ad Strophados insulas eas fugauerunt, qui aureum uellus rapiendum uenerunt. Strophos Grece, Latine dicitur 'conuersio'. (7:3)

PHINEUS HAD BEEN SEEN, supply 'by the Argonauts'. Phineus was a rich man who had two sons from his now dead wife. These he blinded on the instigation of their stepmother, this stepmother was called Nubes. Therefore the gods were angered and deprived him of his sight and placed with him three harpies, called Aello, Celaeno, Ocypete, who were to pollute all his food. When Hercules and the Argonauts came to this Phineus, Hercules took the harpies off him and commanded the sons of Boreas to chase them away. They, who came to snatch the golden fleece, chased the harpies all the way to the Strophades islands.

Here, we first encounter a short grammar explanation in the form of the *subaudi*-phrase. Then a mythological background explanation provides the necessary background, and finally, an etymological explanation is added to explain something in the commentary text itself.

Example 36 contains even more categories:

36. *VIRGINEVSQVE DICON, quia ibi habitabant Muse, ET NONDVM OEAGRIS HEMVS. Adiectiuum pro fixo hic ponitur. OEAGRIVS pater Orphei fuit – sed oe est diptongus. Ideo dicit 'nondum Oeagris', quia Orpheus, filius Oeagri, interfectus fuit a mulieribus in Hemo monte, unde postea dictus est mons Oeagrius consecratus Orpheo. Orpheus licet dicatur Apollinis filius, sicut Hercules Iouis, tamen dicitur filius Oeagrii, ut Hercules Amphitrionis. (2:219)*

AND MAIDENLY HELICON, since the Muses lived there AND NOT YET OEGRIAN HAEMUS. An adjective is used for a noun. OEAGRUS was Orpheus's father – but oe is a diphtong. He says 'not yet Oeagrian', since Orpheus, Oeagrus's son, was killed by women on Mount Haemus, wherefore the mountain was called Oeagrian, consecrated to Orpheus. Even though Orpheus may be called Apollo's son, as Hercules is Jupiter's, he is nevertheless called Oeagrius's son, as Hercules is Amphitryo's.

Example 36 starts with a grammar explanation injected into the lemma. Following this comes a grammatical/patronymic explanation with an oddly placed, brief appendix in the form of the statement that the 'oe' in Oeagrius is a diphthong (this statement may have originally been an interlinear gloss that was adopted into the main text in this copy). We are then provided with a background story about why the mountain is 'not yet Oeagrian'. Finally, Orpheus's double fathers are explained with a parallel to Hercules.

In example 37 from Book 3, among other things, we find one of the few text-critical explanations in the commentary.

> *37. FERT VTERO ET MATER QVOD VIX MIHI CONTIGIT VNI uel VNO. Si dixerimus, quod Iuno dicat 'uix mihi contigit uni' Iunoni, ut essem mater de Ioue, cum alie plures fuerint matres, tunc dicemus, quod Ouidius non caret peruertere fabulas. Vel 'contigit mihi in [i]uno', id est in Vulcano, quem de Ioue habuit, ut esset mater.*
>
> *Dicitur de lactuca comedisse, et inde Hebem genuisse. Hebe dicitur translata in celum, ut Iouis pincerna esset, sed quia, secundum rei u<er>itatem, de aliquo adultero illam Hebem habuit Iuno, ideo a Ioue / expulsa fuit et in loco eius Ganimedes, filius Troili, positus fuit.* (3:269)

SHE CARRIES IN THE WOMB AND [WISHES TO BE MADE] A MOTHER, WHICH HAS BARELY HAPPENED TO ME ALONE (*uni*) or WITH ONE (*uno*). If we say that Juno says 'which has barely happened to me, Juno, alone' (*uni*) that I have been made a mother from Jupiter, although many others have been made mothers - then we will say that Ovid does not abstain from corrupting the stories. Or [Juno says] 'that has happened to me with one' (*uno*), that is with Vulcan, whom she had from Jupiter, so that she is a mother.

She is said to have eaten lettuce and from this to have given birth to Hebe. Hebe is said to have been transferred to heaven, to be Jupiter's cupbearer, but since Juno, according to reality, had Hebe from some sort of adultery, she was banished by Jupiter and Ganymede, Troilus's son, was put in her place.

In this example, the lemma offers two alternatives, *uni* or *uno*. Both are extant in manuscripts of the *Metamorphoses* (although *uno* only as a correction or addition). Here the commentator argues for the plausibility of the different readings by adding further attributes to *uni* and *uno*. In the first case, he adds a noun and then two dependant clauses; in the second, an attribute in the form of an *id est*-clause and then two dependant clauses can be found. The first alternative seems to be ruled out in a conditional clause, which states that, if this alternative is valid, then Ovid has the stories wrong. Here the commentator presents two alternatives, but rules out the first. In contrast, the second alternative is backed up by a mythological background explanation, where we learn about Juno's child Hebe. In this explanation, the basic myth (Juno became pregnant by eating lettuce) is presented first and then, by the use of a Euhemeristic explanation, we learn that in fact Hebe was born from an act of adultery.

Examples 36 and 37 are fairly short but in a way act as a small lecture in themselves. They contain a dialogicity, for instance, in example 36, the passage that states that Oeager is Orpheus's father is thought to raise the question 'but is not Apollo his father?', which is then answered.

In the last, longer example of a complex explanation, we will take a look at a complicated case:

> 38. *EPIRROS REGNATA[T]QVE VATI scilicet Butro. Pirrus,*
> *filius Achillis, accepta Andromache, uxore Hectoris, in coniugium*
> *post Troianam uictoriam Epirum possedit. Postea duxit*
> *Hermionem, filiam Menelai, quam ipse Menelaus apud Troiam sibi*
> *desponsauerat et etiam constituit diem. Heleno uate frustra*
> *deortante eum licet captiuum eum duxisset. Horestes autem, filius*
> *Agamemnonis et Clitemeste, dolens Hermionem desponsatam sibi*
> *ab auo suo Tindareo alii contingere †lateris postquam dea aram†*
> *Pirrum de tosicata sagitta uulnerauit, sed tamen Pirrus uiuus*
> *reuerssus est. Ibique inter cetera, que moriturus disposuit Heleno*
> *uati, quia fideliter eum, ne iret, monuit, Andromachen in*
> *coniugium et partem regni dedit, quam olim quidam uates nomine*
> *Brutus possederat.*
> *Literam sic construe: AB HIS Grecis TENETVR EPIRRVS*
> *QVONDAM REGNATA BRVTO VATI, sed tum regnata*
> *FRIGIO uati, id est Heleno. Et tenetur ab his TROIA*
> *SIMVLATA, que Ericon dicitur. Ideo dicit 'simulata', quia*
> *Helenus omnia edificia in Egipto facit ad similitudinem*
> *Troianorum edificiorum et etiam nomina fluuiorum transtulit*
> *inde. Eneas adueniens patriam se uidere putauit.* (13:720)

> EPIRUS RULED BY AN ORACLE, namely Butros. After Pyrrhus, Achilles' son, had taken as wife Andromache, Hector's wife, and after the Trojan victory, he took possession of Epirus. After this he married Hermione, Menelaus's daughter, whom Menelaus himself had betrothed to him in Troy and even set the day [for the marriage]. The oracle Helenus dissuaded him in vain,

although he (Pyrrhus) had taken him away as a prisoner. Orestes, the son of Agamemnon and Clytemnestra, who grieved that Hermione, who had been engaged to him by her grandfather Tyndareus, would belong to another †lateris postquam dea aram† wounded Pyrrhus with a poisoned arrow, but Pyrrhus nevertheless returned alive. And there among the other things that he had arranged for the oracle Helenus when he was about to die, since Helenus had faithfully advised him not to go, he gave him Andromache's hand in marriage and that part of the kingdom, which once an oracle named Brutus had possessed.

Construe the text thus: EPIRUS IS NOW HELD BY THESE Greeks, ONCE RULED BY THE ORACLE BRUTUS, but then ruled by the PHRYGIAN oracle, that is by Helenus. And the COPIED TROY, which is called Ericon, is held by them. He says 'copied' since Helenus made every building in Egypt in the likeness of the Trojan buildings and he even transferred the names of the rivers from there. When Aeneas arrived he thought that he saw his homeland.

The explanation begins in the grammatical mode by attempting to clarify the lemma by connecting *uati* and *Butro*. The *Metamorphoses* manuscripts have many different readings at this point, none of them Butro, but by matching its case to *uati*, it is clear that the commentary considers the name Butrus to be valid, although it later uses the form Brutus instead. The first part of the explanation consists of a mythological background story concerning Epirus and the fate of Pyrrus, Hermione, Orestes and Helenus. The language in this explanation is complicated and obscure and furthermore seems to contain a corrupt passage (marked by *cruces* in the edition). The explanation is then restarted with the phrase *literam sic construe*, after which the lemma is ordered and made clearer by additional words. Finally, a supplementary explanation follows to explain the word *simulata*.

This explanation reminds us that we cannot always seek to find coherent meaning in the text as it stands. Clm 4610 shows signs of being a copy or assemblage of other texts and it contains errors and distortions. This has to be kept in mind when analysing the text and trying to understand how it operates.

Explanations Outside the Categories

Since the categories described above cannot possibly encompass all the individual features of the commentary, we will, in the following, discuss some unique explanations.

A theological Explanation?

> 39. *HANC LITEM D<EVS> ET M<ELIOR> NATVRA, id est uoluntas Dei, filius Dei, DIREMIT. Et sic quantum ad effectum, id est secundum <eos>, qui uidebant, non quod Deo aliquid accidat, ut sit 'melior'. Dictum est de Ihesu: 'Puer Ihesus proficiebat etate et sapientia apud Deum et homines'.* (1:21)

> THIS STRIFE GOD, AND THE BETTER NATURE, that is the will of God, the son of God, SETTLED. And thus with respect to the effect, that is according to those, who realized that nothing can happen to God, so that he would become 'better'. It is said about Jesus: 'The boy Jesus advanced in wisdom and age and grace with God and men'.

This explanation is unique in that it is the only one containing a Bible quotation, thus relating the *Metamorphoses* explicitly to a Christian context. It concerns the part of the first book of the *Metamorphoses* that treats the creation of the world, and reacts to the fact that the god/God is paired with the phrase *Melior natura* (a better nature), which is said to be the will of God, that is the son of God. The explanation then states that *melior* (better) in no way means that God can be made better, but that this must refer to Jesus, who increased in wisdom as he grew older. Were there more cases like this they would merit a theological category of explanations. This explanation, however, is unique.

Allegory

> 40. *INNICERE ANGVIPEDVM. Gigantes pedes habuisse dicuntur anguineos surgere a terra non ualentes, et significat illos, qui semper adherent terrenis.* (1:184)

> [EACH] OF THE SERPENT-FOOTED [WAS IN ACT] TO LAY. Giants are said to have had snake-legs, not being able to rise from the ground, and this signifies those who always cling to earthly things.

This short example may be one of two allegorical explanations in the commentary. It reacts to the phrase 'each one of the snake-legged ones' (*quisque anquipedum*) in the *Metamorphoses* and first explains that this is said about the giants, a common enough type of explanation, but then it goes on to say that this signifies those who always adhere to earthly things. This is a very short and compact allegorical explanation. In Book 9, we have the second allegorical explanation:

> 41. *QVOQVE CHIMERA IVGO. Chimera est mons, in cuius sumitate habitant leones et ideo dicitur ET HORA ET PECTVS LEENE habere. Et in medio habitant homines cum capris habentes ignem. Et ad radices eius morantur serpentes in lacu. Et metaforice dictum est. Serpens latitando incedit sic et luxuria primum incedit latitando temptans adinuenire, quod uult. Leo fortis est et petulans. Post inceptam delectationem fortitudinem exibet, si necesse. Capra est fetida et inethos tandem nefarium opus fetet.* (9:647)

> AND ON THE RIDGE WHERE CHIMAERA. Chimera is a mountain on whose top lions live, and therefore it is said to have BOTH A LION'S HEAD AND CHEST. And in its middle men, who keep a fire, live with goats. And by its foot snakes dwell in a lake. And this is said metaphorically. The serpent advances by hiding, so also excess first advances by hiding, trying to find what it wants. The lion is strong and wanton. If necessary, it displays strength after a commenced pleasure. The goat is stinking and amoral, as an impious deed stinks in the end.

Here the explanation seems to argue that Chimera is an attribute or apposition to *iugo* (the Chimeran hill, or the hill Chimera) and the passage is interpreted metaphorically. It is said that lions live at the top, which explains 'both a face and chest of a lion'. In the middle of the hill men tending goats live. These men keep fires, which explains 'fire in the middle parts' (*mediis in partibus ignis*) and finally at the bottom serpents dwell, which accounts for 'the tail of a serpent' (*serpentis caudam*). In the *Metamorphoses* this is a direct description of the Chimera (the confusion may be caused because the correlative *iugo* (ablative) is drawn into the relative clause), but the commentary interprets this as a metaphor. What is even more interesting is that it then goes on to interpret the Chimera allegorically. The serpent is associated with *luxuria*, the lion with *fortitudo* and the goat with *nefarium opus*.

An Unidentified Quotation?

> 42. *QVAM SATVS IAPETO. Dii erant et sunt et erunt Prometheus et filius eius, antequam homo fuisset creatus, et hoc secundum philosophos.* (1:81)
>
> [THE EARTH] WHICH THE SON OF IAPETUS. Prometheus and his son were, are and shall be gods before man had been created, and this is according to the philosophers.

This short explanation makes it clear to whom *satus Iapeto* refers, but it does so in a very strange way. It calls Prometheus and his son (Deucalion) gods using the strange phrase *erat et sunt et erunt* (they were, are and will be). It is primarily this phrase that makes this explanation stand out. It could, of course, be used mainly for dramatic effect, but if so, this style is not found anywhere else in the commentary. The vague reference to the philosophers also gives this explanation a twist. The entire explanation looks very much like a quotation, but I have not been able to find anything that resembles it.

The Commentary and its Focus on the *Metamorphoses*

The categories discussed in the previous section allow us to discern the general function of the commentary. However, with a few exceptions, they do not tell us much about the relationship between the commentary and the *Metamorphoses* in its entirety, which is the main focus in this section.

First, we need to consider the entire commentary as a unit to see whether we can justifiably speak about a proper commentary or just a collection of notes. The commentary fills over twenty-three folios and is introduced by an *accessus*, but contains no *explicit,* colophon or other means to signal its end. Instead, after the explanation to *Met.* 15:836, the same hand seamlessly continues with a short commentary on a text related to the Bible.[212] Even though the end of the commentary is not announced, the fact that the explanation is on one of the final lines (line 836 of a total of 876) of the *Metamorphoses*, and the fact that the commentary contains explanations to all fifteen books of the *Metamorphoses*, makes it likely that the text in clm 4610 is a complete text with no substantial parts missing. However, as we will see in the next chapter, commentaries that are extant in different versions often display a great variation between the texts, often in the form of additional information to supplement individual explanations, or even

---

[212] See Part II Manuscript description.

additional explanations. This means that, even though the commentary in clm 4610 may be considered a complete work, this does not mean that another copy of this commentary, if found, would be of the same length.

The fact that commentaries can, in general, possess a highly modular nature in which passages can be added freely from other sources when a new copy of the commentary is made, is reason to be cautious when trying to discern how clm 4610 as a whole relates to the *Metamorphoses*. However, this modular nature does not exclude the possibility that the commentary was composed as a unified text. One indication that this might have been the case is the existence of internal references.

The first reference occurs in the second explanation to *Met.* 7:759 with the words *dixerim superius* (as I said above), which seems to refer to the first explanation to this lemma found only five lines above in clm 4610. The second mention is the explanation to *Met.* 9:186 with the phrase *sicut superius notauimus* (as we have noted above), but in this instance, the place mentioned is not to be found. Just a couple of lines later in the second explanation to *Met.* 9:187, the words *ut superius diximus* refer us all the way back to 7:3. Both explanations are shown here with the latter first and the explanation it refers to below it.

> *VESTRVM STIPHALIDES VNDE. Apud Stiphalides undas, scilicet apud Phineum, Hercules arpias fugauit cum sagittis suis. Et filiis Boree, **ut superius diximus**, iussit eas persequi usque ad Strophados insulas. Dicitur tamen quod apud Stiphalides undas Hercules duos serpentes interficeret. (9:187)*

> YOUR [WORK] THE STYMPHALIAN WAVES. Near the Stymphalian waves, that is to say near Phineus, Hercules chased the harpies away with his arrows. And, **as we have said above**, he commanded the sons of Boreas to follow them all the way to the Strophades islands. However, it is [also] said that Hercules killed two snakes near the Stymphalian waves.

> *VISVS ERAT PHINEVS, subaudi 'ab Argonautis'. Fineus fuit quidam diues, qui de uxore iam mortua duos filios habebat, quos instinctu nouerce illorum, que nouerca Nubes dicebatur, excecauit. Ideo dii irati fuerunt et eum lumine priuauerunt et tres arpias, que uocabantur Aello, Cillerio, Occipete, sibi apposuerunt. Que cibos suos omnes conmacularent ad quem fine[u]m, cum Hercules et Argonaute uenerunt. Ab eo arpias Hercules auertit et iussit filiis Boree, ut illas fugarent. Qui usque ad Strophados insulas eas*

fugauerunt, qui aureum uellus rapiendum uenerunt. Strophos Grece, Latine dicitur 'conuersio'. (7:3)

PHINEUS HAD BEEN SEEN, supply 'by the Argonauts'. Phineus was a rich man who had two sons from his now dead wife. These he blinded on the instigation of their stepmother, this stepmother was called Nubes. Therefore the gods were angered and deprived him of his sight and placed with him three harpies, called Aello, Celaeno, Ocypete, who were to pollute all his food. When Hercules and the Argonauts came to this Phineus, Hercules took the harpies off him and commanded the sons of Boreas to chase them away. They, who came to snatch the golden fleece, chased the harpies all the way to the Strophades islands.

These references could, of course, belong to passages copied from elsewhere, but the fact that the explanations in the last example are quite far apart in the manuscript would seem to indicate some sort of planned composition of the text.

In the explanations to *Met.* 2:527 and 15:326, the commentary uses the phrases *superius etiam dictum est* (it has also been said above) and *in alio loco [...] dicuntur* (in another place [...] they are called). These are references to passages in the *Metamorphoses*, not internal references. These phrases actualise the relationship between the commentary and the target text and its author.

The explicit references to the *Metamorphoses* are not many, but there are a few references directly to Ovid. He is mentioned by name in the *accessus* and nine times in the commentary. Of those, nine times, five of these explanations belong to the narrative sub-category described in the previous section.[213] The four remaining mentions of Ovid are either in Euhemeric explanations, as in the explanations to *Met.* 1:89 and 2:850, or in mythological background explanations, as in the ones to *Met.* 13:635 and 15:836.

Furthermore, the *accessus* in clm 4610 does not contain the topic *vita auctoris*, a short biography of the authors, which is often found in the *accessus*. This topic is treated twice in the *accessus* in clm 14809, which belongs to the Bavarian B family. In clm 4610, the only piece of biographical information on Ovid is one of the final explanations, where it is said:

hoc, quasi proemium, Ouidius ad laudem Augusti Cesaris premittit, ad cuius honorem librum suum scripsit (15:622)

---

[213] Narrative: 1:3, 3:269, 4:801, 7:687, 15:622.

Ovid starts by saying this as an introduction to the praise of Augustus Caesar, in whose honour he wrote his book.

The Euhemeristic explanation to *Met.* 2:850 could also be interpreted as being biographical, since it makes a statement about Ovid's relationship to his contemporaries:

> *INDVITVR FACIEM TAVRI. Hic Ouidius plane Iouem / deridet, non credens illum esse summum deum, sicut et alii philosophi non credebant, sed propter impera[re]tores sic locuti sunt dicentes Iouem esse summum deum (2:850)*

> HE ASSUMED THE FORM OF A BULL. Here Ovid clearly makes fun of Jupiter. He does not believe that Jupiter is the highest god, just as other philosophers did not believe this, but on account of the emperors who said that he was the highest god, they said this.

If we look at how the explanations in the commentary are apportioned in relation to the books of the *Metamorphoses*, we see that, although some books receive a very brief treatment (Book 5 being the briefest with only thirty-four lines of commentary in the edition), overall all books receive almost equal attention from the commentator. However, the number of explanations of the fifteen individual books of the *Metamorphoses* is not symmetric. The commentary on Book 1 contains the most explanations, fifty-nine on 154 lines in the edition, while Book 12 gets the least and only receives thirteen on forty-six lines.[214] The commentary seems to place most focus on Books 1, 2, 9, 10, 13 and 14, all of which contain around forty to sixty explanations each.

In the more commented-upon books, almost every story is covered, and this is also true for some of the less commentated-upon books, but in these cases, some stories may get only a single explanation (e.g. in Book 8). By cross-referencing the inventory of categories of explanations in the previous section to the stories in the *Metamorphoses*, we can draw some conclusions about the focus of the commentary: in Book 1, the creation story receives a significant amount of attention, with twenty explanations to eighty-three lines in the *Metamorphoses*. Of these, the grammatical and natural philosophy categories dominate (nine and ten occurrences each) while the otherwise dominant

---

[214] Most explanations: 1 (59 expl.), 2 (53), 9 (51), 13 (43), 14 (41), 10 (38), 11 (26), 6 (25), 7 (24), 4 (23), 8 (20), 3 (17), 5 (16), 15 (15), 12 (13).
Longest: 9 (272 lines), 13 (168), 2 (160), 1 (154), 14 (122), 10 (105), 7 (94), 4 (77), 11 (73), 8 (67), 6 (64), 3 (57), 15 (54), 12 (46), 5 (34).

mythological background category only appear twice.[215] The short story of Pan and Syrinx on twenty-three lines produces six explanations.

Book 2 is dominated by the story of Phaeton, as is the commentary to this book, but there are also plenty of explanations to the story of the raven, Coronis and the crow and other stories. The story of Phaeton attracts nineteen explanations, with almost every single category of explanation being represented. Here explanations from the etymological and lexicon sub-categories, among others, appear quite frequently, which may indicate that this was a passage with difficult vocabulary that needed to be assimilated. The story of the raven is dominated by background and grammatical explanations.

In Book 3, the commentary focuses on the story of Cadmus, with little attention paid to the other stories. In Book 4, the story of Athamas and Ino receives the most attention, while not a single explanation is given to, for example, Pyramus and Thisbe.

Book 5 is unique in having all of its focus (except for one single explanation) on one story, that of the rape of Proserpine. Of these explanations the grammatical and lexical dominate.

The focus in Book 6 is quite evenly divided, with a main focus on Minerva and Arachne. Book 7 skips several stories and gives priority to Medea and Jason and the story of Cephalus and Procris. Book 8 favours the long story of Meleager and the Calydonian Boar.

The long commentary to Book 9 comments upon every story, but with seventeen explanations dedicated to the story of the death of Hercules (told on 138 lines), of which the background category features most strongly.

The commentary to Book 10 is also evenly divided with explanations for every story. The short stories of Cerastae and the Propoetides receive five explanations for its twenty-two lines, the following story of Pygmalion the same for fifty-five lines, while the story of Myrrha only four explanations for its over 200 lines. The commentary to Book 11 is short, but with the focus evenly divided. The commentary to Book 12 is very short and contains the least amount of explanations, most of which are dedicated to the story of the battle between the Lapiths and Centaurs.

Book 13 is the longest book in the *Metamorphoses* and the second longest book in the commentary. Here almost every story receives several explanations. The story of Scylla and Glaucus is, however, neglected, as is the story of Galatea and Polyphemus.

---

[215] Each explanation can belong to more than one category, thus the total of categories identified will usually be more than the number of explanations.

Book 14 contains many explanations with a discernible emphasis on the latter part of the book. Book 15 is short, with most of its explanations dedicated to the long story about the doctrines of Pythagoras.

Conclusions

By sorting the explanations in the commentary into four categories with sub-categories, a framework for the function of the explanations in the commentary is created. The commentary seems to prioritise familiarising the reader with the world of the *Metamorphoses* by giving background information about the stories contained within. Another prominent function is helping the reader to understand the actual text by giving grammatical help. A lesser function of the commentary is to enable the reader to generate a vocabulary based on the text, which it primarily does by using derivations and etymologies. Finally, the commentary provides a steady stream of interpretations ranging from Euhemeristic to interpretations concerned with the narrative structure of the *Metamorphoses*.

The categories developed here must not hide the fact that these categories often interact and intersect with each other and that not all explanations fit into the framework.

By analysing the function of the commentary through categories, we can also see that some types of explanation, which we might expect to find, are missing. Most noticeable is the almost complete absence of ethical and allegorical explanations, both of which become important in the later tradition of Ovid commentaries. I can see no simple reason for this absence. As remarked above, there are a few rare allegorical explanations, which means that the commentator was not unfamiliar with that mode of explaining, but perhaps simply did not find it relevant here. It could be that the *Metamorphoses* was not yet integrated enough into the curriculum to form a possible threat with its pagan material and thus require a defence in the form of allegorical and ethical explanations.

The second part of this section demonstrated that, by comparing the categorised explanations with the stories in the *Metamorphoses*, we can discern a focus on certain stories in the *Metamorphoses* and the dominance of certain categories of explanations to certain passages. Some stories, for instance the creation of the world in Book 1, receive high levels of attention, but overall, there does not seem to be any evident patterns of preference throughout the commentary. This study could well be broadened to include comparisons to other commentaries, which would then perhaps allow us to see a more general pattern from which we can draw conclusions about the focus

of the twelfth-century text users. For now, however, this study remains
to be done.

The Commentary and its Sources

An anonymous commentary of a composite nature is itself an excellent
example of medieval intertextuality, wherein older texts are
assimilated, borrowed and quoted. This section explores the sources of
clm 4610 and the way the commentaries use its sources.

It goes without saying that the *Metamorphoses* is the most important
source for the commentary. This point would never have to be raised
in a marginal commentary where the commentary is an obvious
paratext. However, in a freestanding commentary it is possible,
although not easy, for the commentary to function on its own,
separated from the text on which it comments. In a more general way,
Virgil and the other ancient authors that were more widely read than
Ovid at this point in time are also important sources. It was through
these authors that the medieval mind encountered the ancient world
and learned 'good' Latin. Virgil has always been first among the
ancients and the medieval reader's familiarity with him could easily be
applied to Ovid, when, for instance, themes or narratives sometimes
overlap with the stories in the *Metamorphoses* (e.g. Book 13 and 14 of
the *Metamorphoses* concerns the adventures of Aeneas). The same could
be said about Statius and Lucan, the other great epic poets. More
important for clm 4610 than Virgil himself is his most famous
commentator, Servius, whose influence on the medieval commentaries
cannot be underestimated. Not only does this incredibly expansive
commentary contain a wealth of material from which the later
commentaries could pick and choose, but Servius also constitutes an
important model for how to comment on ancient Roman literature. He
will be addressed more below. In passing we should also note that
several of the other ancient authors have an older or greater
commentary tradition, from which the Ovid commentator could draw
inspiration or simply extract material. Sadly, the interconnection
between different commentaries is very difficult to identify, but
hopefully this can be done more effectively in the future with the help
of searchable databases.

In second place to Servius as far as a source of material is concerned,
we can safely place Isidore of Seville and his twenty-book *Etymologies*
(*Etymologiarum sive Originum libri xx*), in which the medieval reader
could find information about virtually everything, from grammar to
weapons. Narrower in scope and much later than Isidore, but still
important, are the Latin lexicographers, e.g. the mid-eleventh century

Papias and his *Elementarium*, which gives short, concise definitions of words and is thus perfect for gathering excerpts for a commentary. More specifically relevant to a mythologically themed commentary (which would include commentary on almost all Roman poetry and much of the prose) are the mythographers, such as Hyginus (*Fabulae* and *De astronomia*), Solinus (*Collectanea rerum mirabilium*) and Fulgentius (*Mythologiae*) from the Ancient and Early Medieval era, and later the so-called Vatican Mythographers. The collection of ancient myths, often retold in a brief and simple style in these authors' works, often functioned as a handy reference for the commentators.

As a general source of inspiration for the philosophical or cosmological interest shown in the commentary, it is easy to imagine Martianus Capella, Macrobius, Boethius and Calcidius's translation and commentary on *Timaeus*. The latter was becoming increasingly popular at the end of the eleventh century, while the others had been popular for a long time. Martianus Capella's *De Nuptiis Philologiae et Mercurii* must have been an especially attractive text to match with the *Metamorphoses*, given its framework story populated with mythological beings and the handbook-like nature of the main part of the work. All four of these authors also have a rich commentary tradition of their own, which may have influenced clm 4610.[216]

To this list of general inspiration may be added the grammatical literature, for example, Priscian, inherited from the ancient world and much commented upon throughout the centuries. Besides the pagan literature, there are also the vast amount of biblical, patristic and liturgical commentaries to be reckoned with, such as St Augustine and his *De Civitate Dei* and its long discussion of pagan religion and philosophy.

These are some general suggestions of the type of literature that would have been included in the cultural sphere of clm 4610. These are authors and works that can only be suggested based on their popularity during this period and their relevance for the commentary. As for more concrete evidence of sources used, it would seem as though clm 4610 makes use of what seems to be considered as a sort of intellectual public property, where it is difficult to decide what is more or less a direct copy of older material and what is an adaptation of that

---

[216] For Martianus Capella see Cora E. Lutz's articles in vol. 2 and 3 of *Catalogus Translationum et Commentariorum* (available at: http://catalogustranslationum.org/). For a wide-ranging study of the reception of Martianus see *Carolingian Scholrship and Martianus Capella: Ninth-century Commentary Traditions on De nuptiis in* Context, ed. M. Teeuwen, S. O'Sullivan (Turnhout: Brepols, 2011). For Boethius see *A Companion to Boethius in the Middle Ages*, ed. N. H. Kaylor jr., P. E. Phillips (Leiden: Brill, 2012), https://doi.org/10.1163/9789004225381.

material. However, we can still draw some conclusions. It is possible to discern three categories of sources in the text:
1. Explicit sources (*secundum Manogaldum*).
2. Vague sources (*quidam dicunt*).
3. Implicit sources.

1. Explicit Sources

To this group belong all named sources and direct quotations in the commentary.[217] They appear twenty-two times, with a maximum frequency of four times per book in Books 7 and 11. Thirteen of them appear in mythological explanations, seven in grammar explanations and one each in the sub-categories narrative and natural philosophy.

The mysterious Manegold earns first place with five mentions, followed by Servius with four mentions. Where ancient authors are concerned, Virgil, Statius, Ovid himself and possibly Horace are mentioned by name.[218] There are also several quotations without the authors being mentioned in the text, for instance *libat oscula* in 1:371, which is from Statius (*Theb.* 10:61). Among the grammarians, Priscian is mentioned once. One source is mentioned twice, but with only the first part of the name extant, Teo- or Theo. Two famous Christian *auctores* are referred to: St Jerome in Book 4 and St Augustine in Book 9. In the first case, it is quite possible that we are dealing with a mistake and that Jerome has been confused with Hyginus, who has a passage that fits well with the explanation in the commentary. The reference to Augustine is one of the clearest; both author and work are quoted.

There are also two mentions of a 'history': 'old history' and 'Roman history'. These could be general sources and thus belong to the second category, or they could be references to the *Homerus Latinus* material (*Ilias Latina, Dictys Cretensis* and *Daretis Phrygii de excidio Trojae historia*), since in both instances we are dealing with the Homeric part of the *Metamorphoses*.

When examining how sources are used, the composite nature of the commentary makes it difficult to say if the sources mentioned are collected and reported by the commentator/compiler who created clm 4610, or if they are the result of texts pieced together, that is a quotation within a quotation.

---

[217] These sources are also discussed by Meiser, cf. Meiser 1885, pp. 71-81.

[218] The reference to Horace is uncertain, since the reference only consists of the phrase *dicit or*, where *or* may stand for *oratius*.

Manogaldus—Manegold

The first source that must be addressed in greater depth is Manegold. Five times throughout the commentary, references are made to one Manogaldus. This is significant because it could be the only contemporary name referred to in the commentary. It is even more significant because it refers to a name to which some scholars would like to attribute the entire commentary. The name Manogaldus is believed to refer to Manegold of Lautenbach (c. 1030/40-1112).[219] Manegold was an itinerant teacher in France and later a monk in Rottenbuch in Bavaria and Marbach in Alsace. Of the works attributed to him only two survive, the two polemical texts *Liber contra Wolfhelmum* and *Liber ad Gebehardum*.[220] Through these texts, we get a picture of Manegold as a man opposed to the neo-platonic intellectual environment of his time, but also a man who had expert knowledge of those very texts.

Manegold of Lautenbach has attracted a lot of scholarly attention for an author with only two surviving complete texts. He has been studied by scholars, usually by those interested in the history of philosophy and theology, since the nineteenth century until the present day, with the most recent work known to me being Irene Caiazzo's two articles from 2011.

The association of Manegold with clm 4610 stems from Karl Meiser's article from the late nineteenth century, which has been the main secondary literature on this commentary ever since.[221] Some earlier scholars have assumed that the entire commentary in clm 4610 is the work of Manegold, including E. H. Alton who states: 'his notes on the *Metamorphoses* are disappointing; in criticism he is very often puerile; and he continually tries to substitute the figments of his

---

[219] For a survey of his life and work, see Manitius 1931, pp. 175-180. See also Ziomkowski 2002, which contains a useful introduction and a bio- and bibliographical appendix. The most recent research on Manegold known to me are two articles by Irene Caiazzzo from 2011, of which one contains a good updated bibliography, which should be used together with Ziomkowski. Irene Caiazzo, 'Magister Menegaldus, l'anonyme d'Erfurt et La Consolatio Philosophiae', *Revue d'histoire Des Textes*, N.S., 2011.6, 139–65, https://doi.org/10.1484/J.RHT.5.101218; Irene Caiazzo, 'Manegold: Magister Modernorum Magistrorum', in *Arts Du Langage et Théologie Aux Confins Des XIe-XIIe Siècles*, pp. 317–49, https://doi.org/10.1484/M.SA-EB.3.4872.

[220] *Liber contra Wolfelmum*, ed. W. Hartmann (1972); *Liber ad Geberhardum* in *Monumenta Germaniae Historica: Libelli de lite imperatorum et pontificum saeculis xi et xii vol. 1*, ed. K. Franke (Hannover, 1891), pp. 308-430.

[221] Meiser 1885, pp. 71-72.

imagination for real knowledge'.[222] Michael Herren, in a much more recent article, is very clear about his position that clm 4610 is the product of an anonymous compiler, but that the compiler excerpts from Manegold, which can be seen both in named references and in passages where his name is not mentioned, but that show some similarities to *Liber contra Wolfelmum*.[223] In addition to the five explicit references to Manegold, Herren suggests that the *quidam philosophi* paragraph in the *accessus* and a few other explanations (the *Melior natura* and *Hic Ouidius plane Iouem deridet* explanations)[224] might stem from Manegold, but he wisely concludes with the following statement, with which I fully agree:

> There is not a lot one can do about this kind of compendium. One has neither the right to assume that identified scholia are drawn from complete commentaries (as opposed to lecture notes), nor to assign unassigned scholia to particular authors.[225]

If we turn to clm 4610 itself and investigate how Manegold is used, we find that he is referred to in both grammar explanations and for mythological background. The two grammar explanations are of a quite rudimentary nature.

> *Secundum Manogaldum, qui non uult ullam diptongon Latinam diuidi, aliud nomen est Eneus et aliud Aeneus, et Eripies et Aeripies, et sic etiam in consimilibus.* (7:121)

> According to Manegold, who does not want to divide any Latin diphtong, Eneus and Aeneus, and Eripies and Aeripies are different names, and so also with similar words.

> *CODICE QVI MISSO. Dicit M<anegaldus> quod 'codex' pro 'caudex' fit lapis uel aliquando ramus arboris. Et diptongus mutatur in o.* (12:432)

> HE [CRUSHED] WITH A THROWN TREE-TRUNK. Manegold says that codex for caudex is a stone or sometimes a tree-branch. And the diphtong changes into o.

---

[222] Alton 1960, p. 26.
[223] Herren 2004, p. 223.
[224] Edition l. 92-96, 410-413.
[225] Herren 2004, p. 220.

Here, his authority is called upon for orthographical or phonological matters. In the second example only an initial is used, but since the content again concerns diphthongs, just as in the preceding example, it is reasonable to assume the M. stands for Manegold.

He is also mentioned three times when mythological background is concerned. In the first two instances, he is used to introduce the explanations and in the third, he is used to voice an alternative version.

> *Secundum Manogaldum Diana fecerat quedam carmina ambigua.* (7:759)

> According to Manegold Diana had made some uncertain verses.

> *Secundum Manogaldum quondam Dedalus Theseo ensem et globos piceos consilio Adriagnes dederat.* (8:183)

> According to Manegold Daedalus once gave Theseus a sword and pitched balls following Ariadne's advice.

> *Manogaldus autem dicit Esionem religatam et ab Hercule liberatam et a Telamone ductam fabulosam esse totum.* (11:214)

> However, Manegold says that it is completely fictitious that Hesione was tied up and freed by Hercules and married to Telamon.

The first of these three examples also has a parallel in another commentary, clm 14809.[226] These are, as far as I know, the only explicit mentions of Manegold in the twelfth-century *Metamorphoses* commentaries.

Based on these five references to Manegold we get a glimpse of what looks like a schoolmaster who is concerned with correct use of Latin and who also provides alternative explanations of the ancient myths. Herren and Caiazzo argues convincingly that a few of the more philosophical explanations match quite well with what we believe to be Manegold's position on these matters.

It is interesting and probably significant for the origin and creation of clm 4610 that a contemporary name is mentioned several times, but this does not mean that clm 4610 should be considered Manegold's commentary or necessarily even very closely related to him, just as we would not call it Servius's commentary because of the references to

---

[226] Munich Bayerische Staatsbibliothek clm 14809: *secundum magister manag.* (75r). See next chapter for more information on this.

him.[227] However, Manegold is a contemporary authority and as such important.

Teo/Theo – Theodontius?

> *Vel aliter, secundum Teo- asia fuit mulier* (9:448)
>
> Or differently: according to †Teo† Asia was a woman

> *Vel aliter: Secundum Theo-, quia non conueniebat superos orare pro mortuis, sed infernales.* (11:583)
>
> Or differently: according to †theo-†, since it is not fitting to pray to the gods above for the dead, but to the ones below.

This Teo- or Theo- shows up in two passages; the first time in an explanation from the grammatical and patronymic categories and the second time in a mythological background explanation. In the second case, Theo- functions as an alternative to an explanation that is supported by invoking Servius.

Marianne Pade has argued that this Teo might be the Teodontius mentioned in Boccacio's *De natura gentilium deorum*, but in my opinion the references in clm 4610 are far too short to draw any conclusions regarding this matter.[228]

Servius

In the explicit mentions, Servius is used twice in grammatical explanations and twice in mythological background explanations. Where the grammatical explanations are concerned, the following explanation in Book 12 consists entirely of a reference to Servius:

> *Seruius dicit 'insanus' pro 'magnus', sicut insana Iuno pro magna.* (12:510)
>
> Servius says that 'raging' [can be used] for 'great', as in raging Juno for great Juno.

---

[227] Ascribing the commentary to Manegold only reveals the modern anxiety over handling the anonymous and amorphous texts of which much of medieval literature consists. It is, of course, tempting to use a name, even though a 'pseudo' may have to be inserted in front of it, just for ease of reference. However, in this case it is my opinion that we should refrain from it so as not to create a false image of a 'master's text'.

[228] Marianne Pade 'The Fragments of Theodontius in Boccaccio's *Genealogie Deorum Gentilium Libri'* in *Avignon & Naples. Italy in France - France in Italy in the Fourteenth Century*, (*Analecta Romana Instituti Danici Supplementum* 25) ed. M. Pade and others, 149-182. (Rome: L'Erma di Bretschneider, 1997).

In a reference in Book 9, he is inserted at the very end to provide a solution to the discussion in the explanation.

> *Remedium habemus Seruii, quod dicit: post 're-' communiter poni.*
> (9:51)

> We have Servius's solution that says: *post re communiter poni.*

In the mythological explanations, things are slightly more complicated. In his first appearance in Book 11, I have not been able to trace the source.

> *Seruius dicit, quod non licet alicui sacrificare diis pro mortuo a<li>quo, donec faciens sacrificium purgauerit se aliqua purgatione.* (11:583)

> Servius says that nobody is allowed to sacrifice to the gods for a dead person until the one performing the sacrifice has cleansed himself with some sort of purification.

In the second case, however, a source can be found, but it would seem as though Servius says the exact opposite of what the commentary reports.

> *Mulcifer VREBAT. Seruius dicit quod MVLCIBER est Iupiter, Mulcifer est Vulcanus.* (14:533)

> Mulcifer burned. Servius says that Mulciber is Jupiter; Mulcifer is Vulcan.

This can be compared to the following passage in Servius:

> *MVLCIBER Vulcanus, ab eo quod totum ignis permulcet* (in Aen. 8:724)

> MULCIBER, Vulcan. From the fact that fire tames everything.

These are the only the explicit references to Servius in the commentary, which does not give an accurate picture of his influence. It is, however, interesting to consider what made the commentator decide to refer to Servius by name in these instances and not in others. In the explanations mentioned above there is a reference to authority of a type, which is not needed when only using another text for background material, but there are many other explanations where an authority could be used, but is not. Whether this is only coincidence or because of a choice or a result of the compiling of the text, is almost impossible to say.[229]

2. Vague Sources

> Hoc dicunt philosophi, ut Plato et ceteri (15:237)
>
> The philosophers, such as Plato and others, say

The last explicit source in the commentary is to be found in Book 15. This source functions as a bridge between the two categories of explicit and vague. It is explicit in the sense that it mentions a source by name, i.e. Plato, but it does so in a very general and vague manner. Plato is mentioned as just one of the philosophers who make a certain statement. The vague and unspecific *dicunt philosphi* is typical for this category. There are at least twenty mentions of vague sources, of the type 'some say' or 'according to another story'. In some of these cases, especially when the phrase is *secundum aliam* or *quandam fabulam* it has been possible to find a parallel source.[230]

The majority of vague sources are used in explanations of mythological background and they then serve as introductions to an alternative story.[231]

The vague references are also used in a few instances when grammatical or text critical matters are discussed, for example:

> Quidam dicunt, quod 'Nixi' referatur ad Perseum (8:182)
>
> Some say that 'of the Kneeler' refers to Perseus

This could refer to another commentary or authority of some sort (but to which specific text is unknown). I have chosen to label the types of

---

[229]List of explicit sources: 2:685: *dicit or-* (possibly Or<atius>) (*Odes* I 10, 9-12 according to Meiser); 4:19 *Hoc est quod sanctus Ieronimus testatur* (Not identified, possibly wrong for Hyginus, *De Astronomia* 2:5); 7:121: *Secundum Manogaldum*; 7:363: *hanc fabulam dicit Vergilius*, (*Aeneis* Book 7); 7:687: *in Ovidio epistularum plane inuenitur*, (*Heroides* 4:93); 7:759: *Secundum Manogaldum*; 8:183: *Secundum Manogaldum*; 9:51: *remedium habemus Seruii*; 9:448: *Vel aliter, secundum Teo-*; 9:693: *Hoc de tauro sanctus Augustinus testatur in libro de ciuitate Dei.* (*De civitate Dei*, 18:5); 10:10: *Sicut legitur in quarto libro georicorum*, (*Georgica* 4,485); 11:3: *teste Prisciano*; 11:214: *Manogaldus autem dicit*; 11:583: *Seruius dicit - secundum Theo-*; 12:432: *Dicit M<anegaldus>*; 12:510: *Servius dicit*; 12:610: *ut in ueteri legitur historia*; 13:2: *legitur in statio thebis*; 13:626: *secundum romanam historiam*; 14:533: *servius dicit*; 15:237: *Hoc dicunt philosophi, ut Plato et ceteri*.

[230] cf. 1:10; 1:690; 4;291; 6:117; 13:690; 13:716.

[231] Alternative stories may also be introduced without mentioning a vague source. In those cases, words such as *vel, aliter, tamen dicitur* are used.

references discussed above as 'vague sources'. They could also be regarded as markers for the *variorum*-commentary, which is James Zetzel's position.[232] Clm 4610 is an excellent example of a *variorum*-commentary, a commentary that consist of different layers of previous material, some of which may be conflicting and therefore introduced with the help of phrases such as *quidam dicunt*. Of interest here might be that, according to Zetzel, different phrases can be dated to different periods, for example *aliter* seems to be a product of the Carolingian period.[233] The *variorum*-marker *aliter* only appears six times in clm 4610. Much more common is the listing of alternative explanations with a simple *vel* (forty-one times) and the appeal to authority with the phrases *quidam dicunt* (ten times) and *secundum x* (thirty-five times).[234]

3. Implicit Sources

Explicit and vague sources are found in less than ten percent of all the explanations. The rest of the explanations make no mention of sources at all, although it is obvious that they must have drawn upon some sources in many cases. In a few cases, however, it is actually possible to imagine explanations without external sources. The grammatical explanations as well as the paraphrasing, narrative and plot-based explanations could be written without any other sources.

Finding implicit sources involves sifting through a vast amount of literature. Today this is made a great deal easier by the use of searchable databases.[235] However, it must be pointed out that there is still a certain amount of guesswork involved when it comes to what to look for and where.

Parallels to some of the explanations in the commentary have been found in the works of Servius, Hyginus, Isidore, the Vatican Mythographers and a few others. As far as natural philosophy and the Euhemeristic explanations are concerned, there seem to be some parallels to William of Conches (2:26, 2:527) and possibly to Eriugena (2:2, 2:246 and 15:533) and Remigius of Auxerre (1:255). In Book 1, we also find some explanations that, in part, correspond to Calcidius and an anonymous commentary on Boethius (1:25, 1:117).

---

[232] Zetzel 2005, p. 75-78.

[233] Zetzel 2005, p. 75.

[234] The *quidam dicunt* phrase can also be expressed with the verbs *volunt* and *habent*. The preposition *secundum* can be followed by a name or simply a *quosdam* ('according to some'). The *secundum*-phrase is used frequently in clm 4610. In the much longer commentary in Freiburg 381, one of the manuscripts in the Bavarian B family, the phrase is only used nineteen times.

[235] I have mainly made use of Brepols' Cross Database Search Tool.

Servius

Servius appears both as an explicit source (discussed above) and as an implicit one. I have thus far identified fifteen parallel passages in clm 4610 to Servius's Virgil commentaries.[236] Of these passages, eight are to his commentary on the *Aeneid*, four to the *Georgics* and one to the *Eclogues*. The explanations in clm 4610 using Servius's texts belong to many different categories, but mainly to the mythological background category. At the time the commentary was composed, Servius commentaries were available both in their 'normal' form and in an expanded form, usually referred to as *Servius auctus* or *Servius Danielis*. The expanded Servius, which is believed to have been created in the Carolingian period, contains material from Donatus's lost commentary as well as other sources.[237] All the parallels found thus far are, however, to the shorter, older version of Servius.

Isidore

Isidore of Seville's *Etymologiae* can always be expected to make an appearance in a text like this. I have identified twelve parallel passages to his work.[238] As expected from the title it is frequently used when etymologies are concerned (but not always), and also for other encyclopaedic type facts.

Hyginus

As of yet, I have identified one parallel passage in Hyginus's *De astronomia* (i.e. 4:19 discussed above) and eleven to his *Fabulae*, all of which relate to typical mythological background information.[239] However, the *Fabulae* is highly problematic, since it has only survived in the form of an early printed edition from 1535 by Iacobus Micyllus. Micyllus based his edition on one single Beneventan manuscript, with which he apparently had some difficulties and treated quite freely. Only two damaged fragments of this Benevetan manuscript survive.[240]

The textual problems with the *Fabulae* also make it possible to imagine that the *Fabulae* that survived to this day was composed largely from material from the time of clm 4610 or later, rather than

---

[236] Accessus; 1:14; 1:117; 1:188; 1:580; 1:624; 4:461; 9:51; 9:183; 9:691; 10:90; 13:46; 14:44; 14:103; 14:331; 15:326.

[237] Ziolkowski and Putnam 2008, p. 625.

[238] Accessus l. 18, 20, 21; 1:38; 1:89; 1:332; 1:690; 4:750; 5:347; 5:555; 10:206; 10:223.

[239] 1:10; 1:580; 2:219; 3:665; 4:219; 5:499; 6:117; 9:408; 11:745 12:610 and 13:399.

[240] Cameron 2004, pp. 33-35.

being ancient material. If this were the case, then the parallels to *Fabulae* bears a resemblance to all the parallels that can be found to passages in the thirteenth-century *Fabularius* by Conrad of Mure.[241] In the latter case, I have not reported the parallels in the apparatus, since it is a text of more recent date than clm 4610, but in the former, I have reported parallels, because of the presumed antiquity of the text.

The Vatican Mythographers

I have identified seventeen parallel passages to the so-called Vatican Mythographers. These mythographers are named after the Vatican manuscripts used by their first editor, Angelo Mai, in 1831.[242] They are three in number, with the first two believed to be from the Carolingian period. Of the first, only one twelfth-century manuscript survives but, of the second, at least eleven manuscripts are known. The third mythographer is thought to be from the late twelfth century (at the earliest) and has thus been excluded from this study. The first two mythographers' texts read much like a catalogue or a lexicon of ancient myths organised more or less alphabetically by name. The length of the stories told ranges from a few lines to a page or two. The content consists of prose retelling of the myths, but there is also a distinct commentary element to the texts, with many interpretative comments to be found throughout. Since the mythological background story is the most common form of explanation, a closer study of the treatment of mythography would be valuable. However, I believe that such a study would be better served by having more commentaries, as well as more mythographical material available. The Vatican Mythographers are far from the only mythographers available from this period: another possibly relevant text, the so-called *Liber de Natura Deorum* by an anonymous twelfth-century scribe, is another example.[243]

Of the nine identified parallels (more could probably be found), four are from the first mythographer and five from the second.[244] Virtually all the parallels are found in mythological background explanations.

---

[241] *Conradi de Mure Fabularius*, ed. Tom van de Loo (Turnhout: Brepols, 2006).

[242] The following information is taken from the introduction to Ronald E. Pepin *The Vatican Mythographers* (New York: Fordham University Press, 2008).

[243] Virginia Brown 'An Edition of an Anonymous Twelfth-Century *Liber de Natura Deorum*' in Mediaeval Studies vol. 34, 1972. Toronto: Pontifical Institute of Mediaeval Studies, p. 1-70.

[244] Myt. 1: 1:106; 3:269; 6:652; 7:3; 13:716.

Myt. 2: 1:10; 1:14; 1:690; 4:457; 4:458; 4:460; 4:461; 5:532; 6:384; 6:415; 9,187; 9:647.

Conclusions

In this section, we have briefly discussed the general literary backdrop for the commentary and then analysed the sources using three categories: explicit, vague and implicit sources. As far as the explicit sources are concerned, the most controversial one is that of Manegold, the only contemporary source to be mentioned by name. Although a contemporary authority is interesting, I still maintain that it does not mean that clm 4610 should be considered a Manegold commentary. The vague sources are used to introduce an alternative explanation and also perhaps to confer authority to the commentary by mentioning predecessors, even though they are unnamed. The implicit sources are the most difficult to identify. Not unsurprisingly Servius, Isidore and the compendia of Hyginus and the Vatican Mythographers feature heavily in the text, with the latter leading with seventeen identified parallels; Servius sharing second place with Isidore, both with fifteen parallel passages; and Hyginus last, with twelve. I do not doubt that several more parallels could be found, but the aim here is not to provide a complete catalogue of every single source of the commentary. Rather, it is to suggest possible inspirations as well as to try to find parallels to passages that contain some sort of textual difficulty, which may be resolved with the help of another text.

5. Clm 4610 and the Commentary Tradition

This chapter explores the relationship between clm 4610 and commentary material found in two other types of text; first the marginal commentaries found in *Metamorphoses* manuscripts older than or contemporary with clm 4610, second the other freestanding commentaries from the twelfth century.

Marginal Commentaries in Early *Metamorphoses* Manuscripts: A Prehistory of clm 4610?

As far as we know, the commentary in clm 4610 is the oldest freestanding commentary on the *Metamorphoses*. However, as we have discussed earlier, we know of the metamorphosing relationship between freestanding commentary and marginal commentary. During the late twelfth and thirteenth centuries, for instance, the same commentary could exist both as a freestanding commentary and as a marginal commentary.[245] As far as earlier material is concerned, the tradition of the *Metamorphoses* itself is admittedly of a rather late date, but several of the manuscripts still predate 1100. This naturally invites the question as to whether there are any traces of clm 4610 in the margins of the early *Metamorphoses* manuscripts.

The commentary genre is in many aspects an open one, and even though clm 4610 shows signs of being a copy it is unlikely that we can expect to find a complete exemplar in the margins. The composite nature of commentaries would rather lead us to expect at most a version of the commentary, or, if that is not the case, perhaps material shared by marginal and freestanding commentaries. If we find material in common, and depending on the extent of this material, what can it tell us about the transmission and early reception of the *Metamorphoses*?

The following section will first survey the early *Metamorphoses* manuscript and then examine the marginal commentaries in some of

---

[245] For an example of this see David T. Gura, 'From the Orléanais to Pistoia: The Survival of the Catena Commentary' in *Manuscripta: A Journal for Manuscript Research* 54.2 (Turnhout: Brepols, 2010), https://doi.org/10.1484/J.MSS.1.100987; or Frank T. Coulson 'Ovid's Transformations in Medieval France' in *Metamorphosis: The Changing Face of Ovid in Medieval and Early Modern Europe*, ed. A. Keith and S. Rupp (Toronto: CRRS Publications, 2007).

them. This study is not an in-depth analysis of the relationship between these marginal commentaries; its purpose is rather to investigate the possible relationship between them and clm 4610 as well as the Bavarian B family (discussed in the next section).

Survey[246]

Earliest *Metamorphoses* fragments:
9th century:
Bern, Burgerbibliothek Bern: 363, middle of 9th c., insular scribe.
Leipzig, Universitätsbibliothek Leipzig: Rep. I 74, France (possibly Orléans).[247]
Paris, Bibliothèque nationale de France: lat. 12246, France.[248]
10th century:
Vatican City, Biblioteca Apostolica Vaticana: Vat.Urb.lat. 342, middle of 10th c., France or Germany.

The oldest manuscripts of the *Metamorphoses* are only extant as fragments. They are four in number, but only one of them, lat. 12246, contains a small amount of interlinear gloss. The fragment consists of only two folios and the margins have been cut, which makes it impossible to conclusively state whether it originally included more and longer comments than those on the extant leaves. The glosses that we have are of a simple type, for example, above the word *quadripedes* (*Met.* 2:82) on line 18 on 2ra the word *equos* has been written. Lactantian *tituli* and *narrationes* are also included and have been incorporated with the main text, but marked with a slight indentation.[249] Based on the material we have, there is nothing to suggest a more substantial commentary.

From the late tenth to the early twelfth century, twelve manuscripts survive, which constitute the basis of Tarrant's edition of the

---

[246] The information in this survey is gathered from Tarrant 2004 and Munk Olsen 1985 combined with my own observations.

[247] Digitised copy: https://www.ub.uni-leipzig.de/forschungsbibliothek/digitale-sammlungen/mittelalterliche-handschriften/handschriften-der-rep-signaturenreihe-leihgabe-leipziger-stadtbibliothekw/.

[248] The fragment is bound (upside down) into a manuscript with St. Gregory's *Moralia in Iob*. A reproduction is available at:
http://gallica.bnf.fr/ark:/12148/btv1b10721618t.r=12246.

[249] For a further discussion of the Lactantian material see chapter 4, under the section The Nature of the Commentary.

Metamorphoses. Nine of them contain glosses, of which I have examined all but one:[250]

Florence, Biblioteca Medicea Laurenziana:
Plut. 36.12 (L), 11th/12th c., Germany(?): Main text in pregothic script with a marginal commentary and interlinear gloss also in pregothic script.[251] Much of the marginal commentary is too faded to read. There may be more than one pregothic hand commenting in the margin. There is also a large amount of commentary by a later hand writing in a large and untidy script, which is often too faded to read. The text also contains Lactantian *tituli* in the margins. From 60r (Book 10) the commentary decreases to only scattered words. Size: 27,6x14,8. 72 fol. Contains *Met.* 1-12:298.[252]

San Marco 223 (F), late 11th c., Italy/France/Germany: Main text in pregothic script and marginal commentary and interlinear glosses by a pregothic hand. There is also a second pregothic hand commenting in the margin, but much less frequently than the first one (e.g. on 25r). The occurrence of fusion of the letter combination *pp* may point to these glosses being from the mid to the latter part of the twelfth century.[253] Besides the pregothic hands, there are also some scattered glosses by later hands (also visible on 25r). The text is also supplied with Lactantian *tituli* in both Latin and Italian. The marginal commentary is much less frequent in the latter part of the text. Parts of the text have been lost and replaced by text written by a fifteenth-century humanist hand. The replaced folios (1r-2v, 10r-12v and 14r-15v) carry no commentary

---

[250] Information regarding date and provenance are taken from Tarrant and Munk Olsen 1985. The bracketed letters signify the sigla used by Tarrant and earlier editors. The only manuscript containing glosses, which I have not had the chance to examine, is the following:
London, British Library: Harl.2610 (H), 10th c., Germany.
The three remaining older manuscript (without glossing) are the following:
Copenhagen, Det kongelige Bibliotek: NKS 56 2o, late 11th c., Germany/Speyer.
Munich, Bayerische Staatsbibliothek: Clm 29208, late 11th c., Tegernsee.
Vatican City, Biblioteca Apostolica Vaticana: Pal. lat. 1669, late 11th c., France.
[251] I use the term pregothic for the transitional script of the eleventh and twelfth centuries, which shows characteristics of both the Carolingian and the Gothic scripts. For a further discussion of this see the manuscript description in Part II.
[252] Digitised copy:
http://teca.bmlonline.it/ImageViewer/servlet/ImageViewer?idr=TECA0000423990&keyworks=Plut.36.12#page/1/mode/1up.
[253] Erik Kwakkel 'Decoding the material book: cultural residue in medieval manuscrip' in *The Medieval Manuscript Book: Cultural Approaches*, ed. M. Johnston, M. Van Dussen (Cambridge: Cambridge University Press, 2015), p. 62, https://doi.org/10.1017/CBO9781107588851.004.

except for a few interlinear glosses. Size: 34x23. 66 fol. Contains *Met.* 1-15. (Also contains parts of *Nux, De medicamine faciei* and *Tristia.*)

San Marco 225 (M), late 11th c., Italy: Main text in pregothic script with scattered marginal commentary and occasional interlinear glosses. The more substantial marginal commentaries are found on: 2r-v, 19r, 33r, 51r, 68r, 73r, 81v. Besides these only scattered words or single line notes are to be found. The marginal commentary is written by several different hands, the oldest of which may be contemporary with the main text, but does not seem to be by the same hand. On 1v what may be diagram can be seen in the bottom, left margin, but it is too faded to make out properly. Lactantian *tituli* and *narrationes* are also included and have been incorporated with the main text, but marked with a slight indentation. 119 fol. Contains *Met.* 1-14:830 (Missing some lines in Books 8, 13, and 14.)

London, British Library:
Add. 11967 (E), 10th c., Italy: Main text in Carolingian script with a small amount of marginal commentary and interlinear glossing by a later hand (pregothic script). Lactantian *tituli* and *narrationes* are also included and have been incorporated with the main text. Size: 27,5x18. 29 fol. Contains *Met.* 2-6 (mutilated, also with missing passages in the extant text).

Naples, Biblioteca Nazionale di Napoli:
IV.F.3 (N), 11th/12th c., southern Italy: Main text in beneventan script with Lactantian *narrationes* by the same hand in the margin. The *narrationes* are always enclosed in a red frame. There is marginal commentary by several different hands throughout the text. There is one marginal commentary in pregothic script and interlinear gloss by what looks like a similar or the same hand. Another commentary in a later gothic script by one or several hands (e.g. on 149[v]). This commentary seems to increase in the second half of the manuscript. The manuscript is also richly illuminated (which makes it unique among the manuscripts listed here). Size: 27,5x16,5. 189 fol. Contains *Met.* 1-15. Book 15 is written by a later Gothic hand. (Also contains an excerpt from *Tristia.*)[254]

Paris, Bibliothèque nationale de France:
lat. 8001 (B), 12th c., Germany: The text consists of two parts. The first part has a pregothic main text with a small amount of commentary (c. ten glosses longer than one line) written by at least two hands. Some of the older marginal commentary is either faded or has been erased (e.g. 8[r], 11[r]). The second part has a main text of a later date (early thirteenth century?) with a contemporary commentary. First part: 1[r]-16[v]. Second part: 23[r]-69[r]. Between the first and the

---

[254] Digitised copy: http://www.wdl.org/en/item/4524/.

second parts of the *Metamorphoses* text, on fol. 17-22, a *catena* commentary written by two hands has been inserted. The text contains the *accessus*, parts of the *glosulae* and *Allegoriae* of Arnulf of Orléans. Size: 26,5x19. 69 fol. Contains *Met.* 1-15 (1: 1-6:590; 2: 6:591-15:879). (Also contains an excerpt from *Tristia*.)[255]

St. Gallen, Stiftsbibliothek:
Cod. Sang. 866 (G), 12th c., Sankt Gallen: Pregothic main text with commentary by two different hands. One possibly by the same or a very similar hand as the main text; the other seems to be of a much later date. The commentary text is not very dense, but runs throughout the text. However, it is often too faded to read. Size: 26,5x18,5. 109 fol. Contains *Met.* 1-15 (but with eight folios containing *Met.* 8:548-10:428 missing).[256]

Vatican City, Biblioteca Apostolica Vaticana:
Vat.Urb.lat. 341 (U), late 11th c., southern Italy: Main text in beneventan script, only scattered commentary. Size: 31x19. 176 fol. Contains *Met.* 1-15.[257]

In addition, I have also examined two manuscripts from Tarrant's group of later manuscripts:

Kings 26, early 12th c., Italy: Main text in pregothic script with marginal commentary and interlinear glossing by several hands, the oldest of which may be contemporary with the main text (most of the glossing is found in Books 1-5). Lactantian *tituli* in the margins. Size 25,5x14,5. 134 fol. Contains *Met.* 1-15.
Vat.lat. 11457 (r), late 12th c., German:[258] Pregothic main text with two layers of commentary, one looks to be contemporary with the main text and the other of a later date. Size: 23,5x11,5. 135 fol. Contains *Met.* 1-15. (Also contains excerpts from *Fasti* and *Tristia*.)[259]

The Marginal Commentaries and clm 4610

As mentioned above, the marginal commentaries often consist of strata of commentaries. In this section, I will concentrate on marginal commentary that could be earlier or of the same age as the freestanding commentary. However, it should be kept in mind that the

---

[255] Digitised copy: http://gallica.bnf.fr/ark:/12148/btv1b10724052j.r=8001.

[256] Digitised copy: http://www.e-codices.unifr.ch/de/list/one/csg/0866.

[257] Digitised copy: https://digi.vatlib.it/view/MSS_Urb.lat.341.

[258] Note on selection: From the late twelfth and early thirteenth century we have at least twenty-five preserved manuscripts. Vat. lat. 11457 was chosen because it is believed to be of German origin; it contains glosses and was accessible.

[259] Digitised copy: https://digi.vatlib.it/view/MSS_Vat.lat.11457.

continued addition and accretion of further marginal comments throughout a manuscript's lifetime is evidence of the reception, reaction, and interpretation of Ovid's text and would make an interesting study on its own.

The result of my analysis of the relationship between the commentary in clm 4610 and the marginal comments in the early manuscripts of the *Metamorphoses* is presented here in the form of three categories: close matches, commonplaces, and interpretative focal points.

Close Matches

This category is defined by the primary concern of this section, namely whether any significant parts of clm 4610 can be found in the margins of the early *Metamorphoses* manuscripts. It turns out that only a handful of close matches exist. Our first example revolves around the closest match between clm 4610 and a marginal commentary I have been able to identify thus far, which is found in the manuscript San Marco 223. This manuscript contains some interesting pieces of commentary, which at times seem to be quite close to clm 4610, although comparison is made more difficult by the fact that parts of the original text in San Marco 223 have been lost: for example, the beginning of the text where two folios seem to be missing. These folios have been replaced by a new bifolium with *Met.* 1:1-445 written by a humanist hand.

In *Met.* 2:1 the palace of Apollo is described with the noun *pyropus* (bronze). This word triggers the following explanation in clm 4610:

> **clm 4610**: *Piropos est metallica species ex tribus denariis auri et sex eris. Pyr enim Grece, Latine ignis. Opous Grece, Latine uideo. Vnde piropos quandam similitudinem et uisionem quasi ignis pretendit.* (2:1)
>
> Bronze (*pyropus*) is a sort of metal, [made] from three denars of gold and six of copper. *Pyr* in Greek is fire in Latin. *Opous* in Greek, 'to see' in Latin. Whence bronze presents a similitude and vision of fire.

Almost exactly the same explanation is found in San Marco 223 written by the main glossing hand, which seems to be contemporary to the hand of the main text. The marginal gloss is keyed to the text with the letter A:

> **San Marco 223:** *A. Pyropos metallica species est ex tribus denariis auri et sex eris. Pyr enim grece dicitur ignis, opo uideo. Hinc pyropus, quia similitudinem quandam et uisionem pretendit ignis.* (5va)[260]

This explanation is also present in the Bavarian B manuscripts, but not in the other marginal commentaries. The manuscript Plut. 36.12 comments on this passage but with the following words:

> **Plut. 36.12:** *Pyropus lapis preciosus ignei coloris siue metallum quoddam ignei coloris.* (7^v)
>
> *Pyropus* is a fire coloured precious stone, or it is a fire coloured metal.

In terms of sources, the closest match found so far is a passage from John Scotus Eriugena's commentary on Martianus Capella:[261]

> *Per 'calceos' Apollinis 'ex piropo', repercusio radiorum de terra aut de nube significatur. 01. De sex enim aureis denariis et sex unseis argenteis efficitur piropum. 03. Opo enim uideo dicitur, pir ignis. 03. Sic ergo piropos quasi species ignis dicitur.*[262]

The match between clm 4610 and San Marco 223 concerns only a very short explanation, and also one for which there seems to be a plausible source. However, the close match between the two commentaries at this point would indicate that they either share a source, which would be a different one than the Martianus commentary, or that the one is a copy of the other.

We have a second parallel between clm 4610 and San Marco 223 in the commentary to *Met.* 9:408. This gloss in San Marco 223 is written by a different hand than in the previous example. This hand occurs in only a few places and, judging by the script, seems to be of a later date (see the description of the manuscript above). This parallel includes the longest explanation in clm 4610 which tells the story of Oedipus and the Thebes cycle. It stretches over several pages in clm 4610 and consists of one coherent story, making it unique as regards both length and coherence in style.

---

[260] Glosses/explanations with almost identical content will not be translated.

[261] Although Isidore (*Etymolgiae* 16:20) and later medieval dictionaries such as, for example, Talleur also mentions *pyropus/piropus*.

[262] *Eriugena Glossae in Martiani*, ed. Édouard Jeauneau (1978) I:162: 23. (The paragraph numbering seems to be wrong with 03 appearing twice.)

The text in clm 4610 and San Marco is very similar, but not identical. The two iterations share all the basic facts of the story but differ in such things as verb forms, conjunctions, and spelling. Furthermore, clm 4610 tends to include more details and is slightly longer. The margins in San Marco have been cut, which has resulted in missing words at the beginning of each line of the marginal commentary (marked with a dash in the transcription below).

In the example below we see the beginning and the end of the explanation in both commentaries:

> **clm 4610**: *NATVS ERAT FACTO PIVS ET SCELERATVS EODEM. Laius rex Thebarum, pregnante Iocasta uxore sua, dormiens uidit bestiam unicornem de camera sua egredientem et se ad mensam sedentem interficientem. Hac uisione cognita dixerunt sapientes quod interficeretur ab illo, qui nasceretur de Iocasta. Ideo preceptum est puerum nasciturum uel puellam interfici. Nato puero non est interfectus a matre, quia pulcher uisus est, sed pannis inuolutus bene et in silua proiectus pede forato cum plumbo. (l. 1015) [...] (l. 1114) Et accepto monili aliter quam sperare accidit, quia potius a fratre matris sue Euriphile, qui dicitur Flegias, occisus est. Quare Calliroe, que fuerat coniunx Almeonis, petiit a Ioue, ut infantes, quos ex Almeone habuerat, adultos faceret et confortaret ad hoc, ut patrem suum, uel Almeonem, ulciscentur. Quod donum Iupiter iussit primigenam Hebem dare illi, et factum est.*[263] (9:408)*

> **San Marco 223**: *Lag- rex Thebarum pregnante Iocasta uxore sua dormiens uidit bestiam unicornem de camera sua egredientem et se ad mensam sedentem interficientem. Hac uisione cognita dixerunt sapientes quod interficeretur ab illo, qui nasceretur ex Iocasta, ideo | — puerum nasciturum uel puellam interfici. Nato non est a matre interfectus, quia pulcher uisus est, sed bene pannis inuolutus et in insulam proiectus est pede forato cum plumbo. [...] et accepto munili aliter quam speraret, | quia potius a fratre matris sue qui dicitur Flegias occisus | Cariloe coniunx Alcmeonis peciit a Ioue ut (sup. lin.) in |<fante>s, quos ab Alcmeone habuerat, adultos faceret |-et ut patrem suum Alcmeonem ulciscerentur. | - -um ip- iussit priuigne Hebe dare illi, et factum est.*[264] (31ᵛ)*

The beginning is almost identical, except for the spelling of names, the word position in two cases (*interfectus a matre/a matre interfectus; pannis inuolutus bene/bene pannis inuolutus*) and one preposition (*de/ex*). There

---

[263] For a translation, see edition 9:408.

[264] The dashes in the transcription signifies words or parts of words thar are illegible.

also seems to be a word omitted in San Marco (*nato puero* in clm 4610 and in San Marco just *nato*). On account of the trimmed leaves in San Marco, several words at the beginning of each line are missing at the end of the explanation, which makes comparison more difficult. The same sort of small differences seen here are, however, also present at the end of the selection, namely different prepositions, verb form, and case endings (*ex/ab, ulciscentur/ulciscerentur* and *Hebem/Hebe*), as well as general spelling variations.

To show a more significant difference we need to use a slightly longer example:

> **clm 4610:** *Ethiocles autem, quia maior erat, prior regnauit. / Et interim Pollinices ad Arastrum regem militare iuit. Contigit quod egrediente eo ciuitatem Argon adeo magna inundatio pluuie superuenit. In qua, cum aliquam domum ospitium habere nequiret, tandem ueniens ad quandam porticum Adrastri. Hospitatus est in ea. Tideus uero, quia in uenatione et uolendo non interfecerat fratrem suum Menalippum, exulabat. Consuetudo enim erat, ut exularet quicumque interficeret consanguineum suum, licet nolendo. Accidit, ut eadem pluuia et eadem nocte imminente, licet paulo post, Tideus ingrederetur Argon et ueniret ad eandem porticum, in qua hospitatus est cum Pollinice. Cum quo, quia equi eorum ceperant se inuincem percutere, iurgatus est. Et, quia inuentionem sui gladii Tideus non habuit, non <in>terfecit eum. In ullo enim tam paruo corpore tanta uirtus latuit, quanta in corpore Tidei. Tunc rex Arastus non ualens dormire, tum quia uetus erat, tum quia responsionem Apollinis in animo uoluens, scilicet quod unam filiam marito traderet leoni, aliam apro, audiuit illos rixantes. Et accensis lucernis, dum illos iret uidere et prohiberet, uidit in scuto Pol- / -linices leonem pictum et in Tidei scuto aprum. Consuetudo enim erat, ut, si aliquis magnus aliquam probitatem faceret, omnes consanguinei eius ferrent signum eius probitatis, quod isti duo fecerunt. Hercules interfecerat leonem, quem Pollinices pictum ferebat in scuto, quia de progenie Herculis descenderat. Meneager aprum interfecit, quem Tideus pictum in scuto habebat, quia frater eius erat. Et cognouit Arastus, quod, quia de istis duobus dixerat Apollo, suam filiam Argiam dedit Pollinici, aliam Tideo tradidit.* (Ed. l. 976-999)
> **San Marco:** *Teocles uero, quia maior erat, prior regnavit, Polinices ad |.... -gem iuit Contigit quod ingrediente eo civitatem Argon | .... tio aque supervenit veniens ad domum Arastri hospi | ... Tideus uero quia occiderat fratrem suum Menalippum exu | ...*

deuenit ad domum Arastri et ibi inuenit Pollinicem ha-| -em in scuto et ipse habebat aprum. Tunc rixari ceperunt | .... -ctus est. Tunc Arastrus, non valens dormire, audiuit pu-| -nsis lucernis, uidit illos et somniauerat quia filiam suam le | .... dedit Argiam Pollinici. (31ᵛ)

The most obvious difference, the length, is immediately noticeable. The two manuscripts tell the same basic story but San Marco 223 lacks the dispute between Polynices and Tydeus, the story of Tydeus's exile and of the ornaments on their shields. There are also the same minor differences as have already been noted at the beginning and the end of this story.

However, even with these differences in mind, it seems clear that the two texts here are related somehow. The gloss in San Marco 223 seems to be written by a later hand than clm 4610. Here we must ask ourselves if it is a question of a common source or if San Marco 223 has been influenced by clm 4610. While the short *pyropus* explanation shares an almost word-for-word likeness in the two commentaries, this longer example is not similar enough to suppose a direct copying process. It is more plausible to posit the existence of an intermediary text, perhaps a source text in the shape of a mythological compendium or something similar.[265]

The manuscript Naples IV.F.3 also has a long gloss in the margin to this passage (cf. 118ᵛ). This gloss revolves around the same story, but it focuses on different details and with a different style, which indicates only a common interest but not a textual relationship with clm 4610 and San Marco 223. It does, however, signal an interest in the Thebes material and access to some sort of compendia.

Our next point of comparison is the manuscript Vat. lat. 11457, a twelfth-century manuscript, possibly of German origin. In the beginning of clm 4610, we have two short explanations, both to *Met.* 1:5, which closely match a gloss in Vat. lat. 11457, as seen in the following example.

clm 4610: *ANTE MARE ET, id est antequam istud, quod modo est mare, sic esset diuisum, ut nunc est.*
ET TERRAS. Ideo posuit 'terras' pluraliter et non 'mare', quia notior est nobis diuisio terrarum quam marium, quia tota habitabilis terra in tres diuiditur partes. (1:5)

---

[265] For example, in Hyginus's *Fabulae,* this story is told over several chapters and it partially, but not verbatim, matches the content of explanations above, cf. Hyginus *Fabulae* LXVI-LXXIII, ed. P. K. Marshall (1993).

BEFORE THE SEA AND, that is before this, which is just sea, had been divided as it is now.

AND THE LANDS: He puts 'lands' in the plural and not 'sea' because the division of the lands is more known to us than the division of the seas, since the whole habitable earth is divided into three parts.

vat. lat. 11457: *Ante mare, scilicet quia terra esset diuisum, ut nunc est. Et ... ideo ponit pluraliter ..., quia notior est nobis diuisio terrarum quam maris. Terra enim in tres diuiditur partes*[266] (3ʳ)

Another similarity is found at the end of Book One at the explanation to 1:749:

clm 4610: *PERQVE VRBES IVNCTA PARENTI TEMPLA TENET*, id est ubicumque Iupiter tenet templa et filius suus Epaphus habet capellas. (1:749)

AND THROUGHOUT THE CITIES HAS TEMPLES CONNECTED TO THE PARENT, that is wherever Jupiter holds temples [there] his son Epaphus also has chapels.

vat.lat 11457: *Qui ubicumque habet templum, ibi Epaphus habet capellam.* (11ʳ)

Though not verbatim matches—the explanations in Vat. lat. 11457 are slightly shorter and uses different forms in some cases (e.g. singular *templum* instead of plural *templa*)—these similarities are nevertheless close enough to warrant interest. What makes these examples even more interesting is the fact that these types of explanations are not simple mythological or lexicon-style extracts, but a more direct reaction to the text in the *Metamorphoses* in the shape of an explanation of both grammar and background. Vat.lat. 11457 also contains copious amounts of marginal commentary on 3ʳ, the beginning of the *Metamorphoses*. This text is too faded to be legible, but it is not impossible that it could be an *accessus* or commentary that could prove further connection with clm 4610.

Vat.lat. 11457 is almost certainly of a more recent date than clm 4610. This means that the relationship between these could be a transfer from freestanding to marginal commentary, or a case of a common source. The slight format of Vat.lat. 11457, an oblong manuscript with the dimensions 23,5x11,5 cm (the smallest of those

---

[266] The ... signifies illegible words or parts of words.

studied here), may give support for the idea of a type of school manuscript.[267]

Commonplaces

This category derives from the realisation that many of the explanations in the commentaries provide the reader with information, often mythological, that is so general it could be thought of as a commonplace. This fact, of course, makes it difficult to use these explanations to establish relationships between different manuscripts. This group is considerably larger than the group of close matches.

The following example concerns a typical short mythological explanation to *Met.* 1:690:

> **clm 4610***INTER AMADRIADES. Amadriades sunt dee montium, Nonacrine, possidentes nouem montes, qui sunt in Archaida. Secundum quosdam nonacrine dicuntur dee fontium, naiades dee fluminum, driades dee siluarum.* (1:690)

> AMONG THE HAMADRYADS. The Hamadryads are the goddesses of the mountains, the Nonacrians, inhabiting the nine mountains in Archadia. According to some, the goddesses of the springs are called Nonacrians, the goddesses of rivers Naiads, the goddesses of the forests Dryads.

This can be compared to the following short gloss:

> **Sang. 866:** *Amadriades dee montium, driades siluarum, nonacrine fontium. Naiades nimphe dicuntur.* (Sang. 866, 9[ra])

And the following tidy list found in the upper part of the right margin of **Naples IV.F.3**:

> *Omnia nimpharum sunt hee*
> *Amadriades dicuntur ille dee que cum*
> *arboribus nascuntur et moriuntur*
> *Driades dee siluarum*
> *Oreades dee montium*
> *Napee dee florum*
> *Nereydes dee maris*

---

[267] This format is suitable for handheld use and is close to the format of the holster book thought to have been used in the schoolroom in the eleventh and twelfth centuries. Cf. Erik Kwakkel 2015, pp. 71-73.

> *Humades dee camporum*
> *Naiades dee fontium uel camporum*
> *Potamides dee fluuiorum*
> *Nymphe aquarum dee*
> (Naples IV.F.3 15ʳ)

Both San Marco 223 and Plut. 36.12 have glosses to these lines, but they are not legible. San Marco seems to have three or four short lines, and Plut. 36.12 has five short lines here that seem to be concerned with explaining *syrinx*. Paris lat. 8001 also has a gloss to this passage, but it seems to have been erased.

These glosses on the nymphs can be compared to a passage from Isidore and a longer one from the second Vatican Mythographer:

> *Nymphas quippe montium Oreades dicunt, siluarum Dryades, fontium Hamadryades, camporum Naides, maris Nereides.* (Isid. *Etymol. lib.* 8:11)

> Nymphs of the mountain are called Oreads, of the forest Dryads, of the springs Hamadryads, of the fields Naiads, of the sea Nereids.

> *DE NYMPHIS Nymphe moncium dicuntur Oreades, que inter siluas habitant et arboribus delectantur, Driades, que cum arboribus nascuntur et pereunt, Amadriades, plerumque enim incisa arbore uox erumpit, sanguis emanat, uirgultorum autem et florum Napee, fontium Naides, fluminum Potamides, maris uero Nereides.*[268] (*Vat. Myt.* 2, 64)

> ON NYMPHS. The nymphs of mountains are called Oreads. Those who dwell in forests and delight in trees are Dryads. Those who are born and die in trees are Hamadryads, for very often, when a tree has been cut, a voice bursts forth and blood flows out. The nymphs of wooded vales are Napaeae, those of springs are Naiads, those of rivers are Potamids, and those of the sea are Nereids.

We note that clm 4610 and Sang. 866 both consider the Hamadryads to be mountain goddesses, while Naples IV.F.3 is more in agreement with the Vatican mythographer when it comes to the Hamadryads being tree goddesses. Naples IV.F.3 also uses the phrase *que cum arboribus nascuntur et moriuntur* (who are born and die in trees) which matches the mythographer's *que cum arboribus nascuntur et pereunt*

---

[268] Translation Ronald E. Pepin (2008), p. 126.

(although in the latter case the description is used for the Dryads, not the Hamadryads).

Finally, the Bavarian B family also has this explanation but used for another line in the *Metamorphoses*:

> **clm 14482c:**§*Oreadas NIMPHAS. Oreade nimphe sunt dee montium, driades siluarum, amadriades arborum. Que cum arboribus nascuntur et pereunt. Naiades uel napee foncium, nereides maris.* (1:320)

This example illustrates a typical explanation of the mythological background type. We have two possible sources here and, judging from the phrase *Que cum arboribus nascuntur et pereunt* from the Vatican Mythographer and the almost exact phrasing in Bavarian B and the marginal commentary of Naples IV.F.3, we can see a link between the Mythographer and the commentaries here. Also of interest is that clm 4610 and Sang. 866 share a factual 'error' in describing the Hamadryads as mountain goddesses, a fact not found in any other source. This error could be a lead to a possible common source. The Bavarian B example also serves as an important reminder of the modular nature of the explanations; an explanation can be used wherever the commentator saw fit and not only to one specific passage in the *Metamorphoses*.

Focal Points

This last category, of which I have found only a few examples, explores a phenomenon that could be thought of as focal points in the *Metamorphoses*, that is, lines, phrases, or words that seem to have caused a reaction and hence created a special need for an explanation. None of the early commentaries comment on every single line or even every individual story of the *Metamorphoses*. Why did some passages attract special attention from the commentators? The explanations in this category are not necessarily similar to each other, but the different reactions provide us with an interesting insight into the reception of the *Metamorphoses*.

The following example from clm 4610 consists of two separate explanations to *Met.* 1:562-563, where Apollo is talking about the newly transformed Daphne:

> **clm 4610:** *POSTIBVS AVGVSTIS E<ADEM> F<IDISSIMA> CVSTOS. Ad similitudinem dicitur custos laurus, quia sicut fores custos custodit, sic laurus ante fores erat propter suum bonum odorem.*

MEDIAMQVE TVEBERE QVERCVM. De quercu, qua prius nobiles coronabuntur, pleps a modo coronabitur. De lauro uero tantum nobiles, et ideo dicit 'tuebere quercum mediam', id est communem, quia omnes communiter solebant accipere. 'Tuebere', id est: dignior eris quam quercus. Et est dictum ad similitudinem, quia, qui aliquem tuetur, dignior est illo. (1:562)

BY THE AUGUSTAN DOOR-POSTS THE SAME MOST TRUSTY GUARDIAN. The laurel is said to be a guardian as a simile, since as a guardian guards the doors, so a laurel was placed before the doors on account of its good smell.

AND YOU SHALL WATCH OVER THE MIDDLE OAK. From now on the common people will be crowned with oak, with which first the nobles will be crowned. But only the nobles [are crowned] with laurel, and therefore he says 'you shall watch over the middle oak', that is the common one, since everyone used to receive it together. 'You shall watch over', that is: you shall be more worthy than the oak. And this is said as a simile, since he who watches over someone, is more worthy than he.

Three of the manuscripts with marginal commentary (San Marco 223 is remarkably uninterested in this passage) have reacted to these lines in different ways with both short marginal commentary and interlinear glosses:

Plut. 36.12: *Vel quia postes augusti fient de te uel quia eris plantata ante -tum uiridarii illius.*
Tu eris causa quod quercus non tam sepe incidetur. Que quercus non tam sepe incidetur, que quercus est media, id est communis omnibus, quasi diceret uilis, quia multum habetur de ea.
interlinear glosses: augustis + regalis; eadem + aderis; mediamque tuebere + communem defendes[269] (5ᵛ)

Or since Augustus's door posts will be made from you, or since you will be planted in front of the gate(?) of his tree plantation. You will be the reason that the oak is not so often cut down. The oak is the middle, that is public to all, as though he would say common, since much will be produced from it. /interlinear glosses: augustan + regal; the same + you shall be there; you shall watch over the middle + you will defend the common/public.

---

[269] In the interlinear glosses the first word is the word from the *Metamorphoses*, which is followed by the gloss.

Plut. 36.12 gives two alternatives as to why the laurel is the 'most trusty guardian' and then gives an explanation to why the oak is 'middle' (*mediamque quercum*). These short explanations are completely different from clm 4610. In the interlinear glosses, it uses synonyms to explain *augustis* and *mediamque tuebere*.

Naples IV.F.3 reacts with a very short explanation that gives yet another explanation of why the laurel is a guardian:

> **Naples IV.F.3:** §*Vt fidus custos numquam mouetur a limine.*
> *interlinear glosses: augustis + nobilibus; eadem + tu; tuebere +*
> *defendes; quercum + communem uilem* (13ʳ)

> Just as a trusty guardian you will never move from the threshold. /interlin.: augustan + noble; the same + you; you will watch over + you will defend; oak + public base/cheap.

The interlinear gloss reacts to almost the same words, but in a different way. As does the interlinear gloss in Sang. 866 and Kings ms 26:

> **Sang. 866:** *Ante foris + quia te plantabunt homines S-; mediamque*
> *+ communis scilicet ad coronas faciendas; tuebere quercum + id est*
> *sub potestate tua habe eam* (7ʳ)

> Before the gates + since the men planted you; middle + public, namely for the purpose of making crowns; oak + that is keep it under your power.
> **Kings ms 26:** *Ante foris + q<uasi> d<iceret>: tu laurus stabis in*
> *quercum positam mediam* (11ʳ)

This passage also attracts much attention in the Bavarian B commentary, where each version of the commentary contains an explanation of varying length that focuses on *ante fores*, *quercum*, *mediam* and *tuebere*. An example of this can be found in the edition on lines 413-436.[270]

These extracts show that this particular passage attracted attention from the commentators in various ways, which makes it possible to speculate about the causes and effects here. Do we find explanations in many manuscripts to certain passages in the *Metamorphoses* because of the fact they all go back to one or several older commentaries that commented upon this passage, or do these explanations reveal a more general interest during this time? Would an unsatisfactory

---

[270] See Appendix 1.

explanation, acting as an irritant, give rise to even more new explanations?

Conclusions

The primary aim of this section was to find the answer to whether substantial parts of clm 4610 could be found in the margins of older manuscripts. The result shows that nothing in the marginal commentaries investigated point to them being directly related to clm 4610. Furthermore, all of the *Metamorphoses* manuscripts investigated here are either from the late eleventh century or from the twelfth century and their marginal commentary is sometimes of the same date, but often later. This means that, except for the scattered glosses in the earliest manuscripts, there is no real evidence for a solid commentary tradition on the *Metamorphoses* predating clm 4610.

What did crystallise during this study, however, were some interesting similarities that could be divided into three categories. The first category, the close match, consists of the few examples I have been able to find where passages in clm 4610 and marginal commentaries seem to be the same. Whether these matching explanations were extracted text from an even earlier, possibly freestanding, *Metamorphoses* commentary, or if they derive from some sort of mythological compendium or from a commentary on a different author is at the moment quite impossible to say.

The second category, the commonplace, consists mainly of mythological information, which perhaps does not allow us to establish connections between specific manuscripts. What the commonplace does suggest, however, is the existence and the uses of 'databases' of knowledge/facts/explanations available to the commentators in the form of entries from dictionaries, snippets from grammatical and mythological compendia, *summae* and similar works.

The third category, the focal point, is extrapolated from the fact that many different commentaries often comment on the same passage, but with different explanations. Whether this category is a sign of a fascination for a certain topic in the time period in question or if a convenient tradition of explanations was available to the commentators is difficult to say. Whatever the case, I believe we have the most to gain by investigating this category, if we wish to chart networks of explanations extending over different commentary texts.

Next Steps

As far as the marginal glosses in the eleventh- and twelfth-century *Metamorphoses* manuscripts are concerned there is, I think, more work to be done. I have established that they are not directly related to the freestanding commentary in clm 4610, but it would still be valuable to edit one or several of these marginal commentaries. The problem is often legibility, due to the small script and the often damaged or cut margins of the manuscripts.

A further step would be to investigate the *Metamorphoses* manuscripts from the late twelfth and early thirteenth centuries to establish their possible connection to the twelfth-century freestanding commentaries. It is not practical to do this before the freestanding commentaries have been edited, but to assist future research I will list the manuscripts listed by Munk Olsen as containing glosses.[271]

List of glossed *Metamorphoses* manuscripts from 12th/13th c.:

Erfurt, Wissenschaftliche Allgemeinbibliothek:
Amplon. 2:o 1., late 12th c., German?, Met. 1^r-58^v, with glosses.

Florence, Biblioteca Medicea Laurenziana:
San Marco 238, 12th/13th c., Italy, 3^r-150^v: Met. some glosses.
Strozzi 121, second part of 12th c., Italy, 5^r-139^v: Met. some glosses.

Frankfurt am Main, Stadt- und Universitätsbibliothek:
S. Barthol. 110, c. 1200, unknown, 12^r-90^v: Met. no contemp. glosses.

Heidelberg, Universitätsbibliothek:
Palat. lat. 1661, 12th/13th c., France or Germany, 1^r-116^v: Met. some glosses.

København, Det kongelige Bibliotek:
Gl. kgl. S. 2008 4:0, second part of 12th c., Italy, 4^r-156^r: Met. with glosses.

Lausanne, Bibliothèque cantonale et universitaire:
403, 12th c., France?, 1^r-113^v: Met. with glosses.

Leiden, Bibliothek der Rijksuniversiteit:
Voss. lat. O. 51., second part of 12th c., France, 1^r-148^r: Met. some glosses.

Lucca, Biblioteca Statale:
1417, first part of 12th c., Italy?, 1^r-98^r: Met. with glosses.

Milano, Biblioteca Ambrosiana:
F 102 sup., 12th/13th c. unknown, 1^r-171^r: Met. with glosses.
R 22 sup., end of 12th c., unknown, 1^r-130^v: Met. with glosses.

München, Bayerische Staatsbibliothek:
Clm 23612, end of 12th c., Germany?, 1^r-39^v: Met. with glosses.
Clm 29208, 12th c., Tegernsee, 1^r-41^v: Met. some glosses.

New Haven, Yale Univesity Library:
Marston 47, 12th/13th c., France or Northern Italy?, 1^r-120^v: Met. no info on glosses.

Oxford, Bodleian Library:

---

[271] The list is extracted from Munk Olsen 1985. I have included mentions only of manuscripts that are described as having glosses, or where information about glosses is missing.

Auct. F.4.30., 12th c., England?, 1^r-72^r: Met. some glosses.

Paris, Bibliothèque nationale:

lat. 8000, end of 12th c., France?, 2^r-151^r: Met. with a few glosses.

Savignano di Romagno, Biblioteca Comunlae:

7., 12th c., unknown, 1^r-42^v: Met. no info on glosses.

Tortosa, Bibliotheca catedralica:

134., 12th/13th c., unknown, 1^r-116^v: Met. no info on glosses.

Vatican, Biblioteca Apostolica Vaticana:

Palat. lat. 1669, second part of 11th c., France, 1^r-63^r: Met. no info on glosses.

Vat. lat. 1593, 12th/13th c., Italy, 1^r-146^v: Met. some glosses.

Vat. lat. 1596, 12th/13th c., Italy?, 1^r-152^v.: Met. with glosses.

Wolfenbüttel, Herzog-August Bibliothek:

4.11. Aug. 4:o (2942)-VI, 12th/13th c., Germany, 141^r-199^v: Met. no contemp. Glosses.

Zürich, Zentralbibliothek:

Rheinau 46., 12th c., Germany or Swizerland, 3^r-91^v: Met. with some glosses.

The Twelfth-Century Commentaries on the *Metamorphoses*

In the previous section, it was established that clm 4610 does not have any definite predecessor. In the following section, the aim is to investigate the relationship between clm 4610 and the other *Metamorphoses* commentaries from the twelfth century. The main focus will be on a contemporary commentary extant in four manuscripts. I have named this family Bavarian B (clm 4610 being Bavarian A, but more easily referred to by the name of the only manuscript).

To begin this section, I present a list of all known twelfth-century commentaries on the *Metamorphoses* (none of these commentaries can be dated exactly, so it is not impossible that some of them may be from the early thirteenth century):

Clm 4610
Bavarian B family:
Munich, Bayerische Staatsbibliothek, Clm 14482b and c.
Freiburg im Breisgau, Universitätsbibliothek, 381.
Munich, Bayerische Staatsbibliothek, Clm 14809.
Salzburg, Stiftsbibliothek St. Peter, AV4.
The Franco-German family:
Prague, Státní knihovna CSR, VIII H32.
Berlin, Staatsbibliothek Preussischer Kulturbesitz, lat. oct. 68.
Vatican, Biblioteca Apostolica Vaticana, Reg.lat. 221.[272]
Arnulf of Orléans:
Munich, Bayerische Staatsbibliothek, Clm 7205.
Venice, Biblioteca Nazionale Marciana, Marc. lat. XIV.222 [4007].
Weimar, Herzogin Anna Amalia Bibliothek, Q 91.[273]
Unrelated commentaries/minor families:
Munich, Bayerische Staatsbibliothek, Clm 14482a.
Berlin, Staatsbibliothek Preussischer Kulturbesitz, lat. 4:o 540.

---

[272] Versions of this commentary have also been found in three later manuscripts: Modena, Biblioteca Estense, Est. lat. 306 (W.4.13), fol. 199 (1467); Padua, Biblioteca del Seminario Vescovile, 142, fols. 352r-354r (1456); Verona, Biblioteca Capitolare, CCXLVIII (219), fols. 3r-5r (15th c.). The *accessus* can be found in Vienna, Österreichische Nationalbibliothek, 1757, fols. 104v-105r (s. XII). The accessus to VIII H32 has been edited by F. Coulson as an appendix to the article 'The Catena commentary and its Renaissance Progeny' in Manuscripta: A Journal for Manuscript Research 54.2 (2010).
[273] Arnulf's commentary can also be found in many later manuscripts. For the purpose of this study only clm 7205 has been consulted. For more information see David Gura's forthcoming edition and his articles listed in the bibliography.

San Daniele del Friuli, Biblioteca Guarneriana, Guarner s. n.
Munich, Bayerische Staatsbibliothek, clm 14748.

All of these texts are simple and utilitarian, with almost no decoration besides an occasional coloured initial. Almost all of them are today found in manuscripts of the miscellanea type created during a later period containing many different kinds of texts. The condition of the first and last page, usually faded, damaged and/or darkened, tells us that they were probably originally created and used as simple, unbound booklets. The largest is only a little larger than a modern paperback.[274] In terms of length, the following table presents a simple quantitative comparison of four manuscripts from the four main families:

Comparison of length

Ms.	Fol.	Words
Clm 7205	29	unknown
Clm 4610	23	16,500
Freiburg 381	14	26,000
Prague VIII H32	13	33,300

As we can see, the version of Arnulf's commentary in clm 7205 is the longest as far as manuscript folios are concerned, while the Prague version of the Franco-German family has the shortest commentary. However, if we compare the number of transcribed words, we get a different result. Leaving clm 7205 aside, since I do not have the relevant information available, we can see that clm 4610, which appears to be the second longest, is actually only half the length of Prague VIII H32 in this comparison.[275]

---

[274] Clm 7205: 240x170

Clm 14482: 230x170

Clm 4610: 215x175

Berlin 540: 205x140

Prague VIII H32: 190x125

Freiburg 381: 165x110

Clm 14809: 140x100

Salzburg AV4: 140x100

Berlin 68: c. 210x90

[275] The word count is based on my transcriptions of these manuscripts. The numbers are not exact, since some text-critical information in the transcriptions may have distorted the word count, but the information should hold up on a relative scale. I have not transcribed all of clm 7205, which is why the information on the number of words is lacking.

What follows is a more detailed overview of the Bavarian B family with brief manuscript descriptions, then an analysis of the relationship between the different manuscripts and their versions of the Bavarian B commentary, and finally an analysis of its relationship to clm 4610. After this the remaining groups of commentaries are briefly described and discussed.

Bavarian B—Manuscript Description

Freiburg im Breisgau, Universitätsbibliothek, 381
Provenance unknown
127 fol.
16,5x11
Later part of the 12th century
48 lines/page, 1 column
Content:
1: (paper, dated to 1475-78)
1r-30v: Argumenta to Ovid's *Metamorphoses*
31r-33v: empty
2: (parchment, later part of 12th century)
34r-48v: Commentary on Ovid's *Metamorphoses*
49r-63r: Commentary on Ovid's *Heroides*
63r-71v: Commentary on Cicero's *De amicitia*
72r-98r: Commentary on Ovid's *Epistulae ex Ponto*
98r-107r: Arnulf of Orléans's commentary on Ovid's *Remedia amoris*
107v-125r: Arnulf of Orléans's commentary on Ovid's *Amores*
125v-127v + back pastedown: fragments of commentary on *Metamorphoses*

Remarks: I have not had access to the complete manuscript but to a digital reproduction of 34r-48v and the catalogue. According to the catalogue, the manuscript has a late medieval half-leather binding.
Catalogue: W. Hagenmaier, *Die lateinischen mittelalterlichen Handschriften der Universitätsbibliothek Freiburg im Breisgau* (Wiesbaden: Harrassowitz, 1980)

Munich, Bayerische Staatsbibliothek, clm 14482[276]
Regensburg, Benediktinerkloster St. Emmeram
159 fol
23,1x17,2

[276.] The basic information in the manuscript description is extracted from my own observations, the library catalogues, and Munk Olson 1985. Dating is from Munk Olsen 1985, except in the case of clm 14482c, which has been dated by Dr Teresa Webber, Cambridge. Dating and information about mise-en-page concern the *Metamorphoses* commentary only.

11th/12th century
36 lines/page, 1 column
Content:
1^{rv}: Eberhard of Béthune, verses from *Graecismus* (10:174-240)
2^r–51^r: Three different commentaries on Ovid's *Metamorphoses*:
   2^r-12^r: commentary a
   12^r-26^r: commentary b
   27^r-51^r: commentary c
51^v: illustration of a world map (T-O shape)
52^r–57^v: Ovid, *De remedio amoris* (with marginal commentary)
58^r–80^r: Horace, *Liber epistolarum* (with marginal commentary)
80^v: empty
81^r–117^r: Geoffrey of Vinsauf, *Poetria nova* (with marginal commentary)
117^v: additional notes to *Poetria nova*
118^r–150^v: Cornutus, *Commentum in Persium*
151^r–159^r: Aelius Donatus (Grammaticus), *Vita Vergilii*
159^v: empty

Remarks: Old shelf sign: Em. E 105. Cardboard binding with a leather spine from 18th/19th century (spine possibly older).
14482: http://daten.digitale-sammlungen.de/~db/0004/bsb00046312/images/
Catalogue: Bauer-Eberhardt, Ulrike: *Die illuminierten Handschriften italienischer Herkunft in der Bayerischen Staatsbibliothek. Teil 1: Vom 10. bis zur Mitte des 14. Jahrhunderts* (Wiesbaden: Reichert, 2010)

The oldest example of the Bavarian B commentary seems to be found in the manuscript clm 14482, which consists of eight booklets from different times containing texts by classical authors, commentaries, and grammatical texts. It includes three commentaries on the *Metamorphoses*, of which the longest is found on 27^r-51^r. The first of the two shorter commentaries on 2^r-12^r is not related to the others, and the second one on 12^r-26^r is an abbreviated version of the longer commentary on 27^r-51^r. All three commentaries are written by different hands. The section containing the first two short commentaries is a separate codicological unit to the section containing the longer commentary. These commentaries are referred to as clm 14482a, b and c, according to their order in the manuscript.

Munich, Bayerische Staatsbibliothek, clm 14809
Regensburg, Benediktinerkloster St. Emmeram
114 fol
14,3x10
End of 12th century
32 lines/page, 1 column

Content:

1ʳ-17ʳ: Vergil, *Bucolica*

18ʳ–47ʳ: Horace, *Odes* (Excerpts)

48ʳ–64ᵛ: Ovid, *Remedia amoris* (with marginal commentary)

65ʳ–81ʳ: Commentary on Ovid's *Metamorphoses*

82ʳ–90ᵛ: Vitalis of Blois, *Geta*

91ʳ–99ᵛ: Horace, *Ars poetica* (with marginal commentary)

100ʳ–114ᵛ: Grammatical texts and poems (100ʳ–105ᵛ Donatus, *Ars grammatica* (excerpts); 106r–107ʳ *Te spondee loco primo tunc dactile pono*; 107ᵛ–108ᵛ *Longa fit. a. semper ponenda frequenter*; 109ʳᵛ empty; 110ʳ–112ʳ Serviolus, *Opusculum de primis syllabis* (excerpts); 112ᵛ–114ᵛ on the pronunciation and names of the Greek letters and numbers).

Remarks: Old shelf sign Em. g 10. Leather binding on wooden boards, seems to be medieval.

14809: http://daten.digitale-sammlungen.de/~db/0006/bsb00060108/images/

Catalogue: U. Bauer-Eberhardt, *Die illuminierten Handschriften italienischer Herkunft in der Bayerischen Staatsbibliothek. Teil 1: Vom 10. bis zur Mitte des 14. Jahrhunderts*, (Wiesbaden: Reichert, 2010).

Clm 14809 consists, just as clm 14482, of booklets from different ages containing both works by classical authors and grammatical texts. This *Metamorphoses* commentary is shorter than the others, but contains some unique connections to clm 4610, as will be seen below. The commentary ends with an *explicit* on 79ᵛ (l.13) but is followed on 79ᵛ to 81ᵛ by a new collection of explanations to the *Metamorphoses* written by the same hand. Clm 14809 also shows the most marginal text, which is for the most part faded and often impossible to read, and in some cases even written upside down. The marginal text is found on 65ʳ, 66ʳᵛ, 67ʳ, 71ᵛ, 72ᵛ, 73ʳᵛ, 74ʳ, 76ʳ, 78ᵛ, 79ʳ, 80ᵛ, 81ʳᵛ.

Salzburg, Stiftsbibliothek St. Peter, AV4

Austria

48 fol

14,2x9,8

End of 12ᵗʰ century

23-25 lines/page, 1 column

Content:

Commentary on Ovid's *Metamorphoses*

1ʳ-1ᵛ: *accessus*

2ʳ-5ᵛ: *accessus* with some glosses

5ᵛ-48ᵛ: *accessus* and commentary

Remarks: I have had access only to a microfilm copy of this manuscript. No modern catalogue exists. The type of binding is not visible on reproduction.

The manuscript AV4 is the odd one out, as its sole content is a *Metamorphoses* commentary. It is written in irregular script with many idiosyncrasies. The commentary text has no paragraph markers and sometimes omits the lemma. It has the appearance of being quite hastily copied from another *catena* commentary or perhaps a *Metamorphoses* manuscript with marginal and interlinear commentary. Just like the commentary in clm 14809, this commentary also ends with an *explicit* on 46ʳ and then starts commenting on book one of the *Metamorphoses* again on 46ʳ to 48ᵛ.

It should be noted that the dating of these manuscripts is uncertain. I used the information in the catalogues and the dating given in Munk Olsen vol. 2, which place all of them at the end of the twelfth century, except for clm 14482 which is simply dated to the twelfth century. Dr Teresa Webber dates clm 14482c to the end of the eleventh or beginning of the twelfth century, which makes it contemporary to clm 4610.[277]

Bavarian B: The Other Bavarian Commentary

Before we investigate the relationship between clm 4610 and the Bavarian B family, it is necessary to establish which texts exactly constitute the Bavarian B family. In the four manuscripts described above, we have five representatives of the family. They vary in length to the extent that the longest one (Salzburg AV4) is about double the length of the shortest (clm 14482b).[278] Three of them, clm 14482b, clm 14482c, and Freiburg 381, start with an *accessus* followed by a commentary from Books 1 to 15, while two, clm 14809 and Salzburg AV4, have a small collection of additional glosses at the end of the commentary. Furthermore, Salzburg AV4 has one *accessus* on fol. 1ʳᵛ, another *accessus* and a small separate commentary on Book 1 on 2ʳ-5ʳ, before the proper commentary starts with a third *accessus* and the commentary text. Above the third and last *accessus*, the same hand has written *Incipiunt glose ouidii prologus*. These are the main structural differences. When it comes to content, the five texts need to be studied

[277] Teresa Webber, e-mail message to author, 27 May 2015.
[278] Approximate length of commentaries (number of lines: words per line): Salzburg AV4: 2387:10; clm 14482c: 1740:16; Freiburg 381: 1119:17; clm 14809: 1019:15; clm 14482b: 1007:13. All commentaries have roughly the same number of abbreviated words, but Salzburg AV4 has less text density than the others, so may in the end be about the same length as clm 14482c.

closely and carefully to establish how they relate to each other. In the following, I will analyse them with regard to their *accessus*, Book 1, and Book 6.

To provide a more substantial sample of the Bavarian B commentary than the short examples given in this study and the next, I have edited the *accessus* and Book 1 of the text in 14482c. This edition is found in Appendix 1.

Accessus

The Bavarian B family includes a total of eight *accessus*. As mentioned above, clm 14482c, clm 14809 and Freiburg 381 each have one *accessus*, while clm 14482b has two and Salzburg AV4 three. Of the headings normally included in a medieval *accessus*, which have been discussed above in the chapter Form and Function, the Bavarian B family presents subject matter (*materia*), intention (*intentio*), utility (*utilitas*) and part of philosophy (*cui parti philosophie*). However, these topics are treated in a more or less arbitrary order and number of times, which yet again shows the modular nature of the commentary. They appear to have been rearranged freely by the scribe or commentator, and the same topic might reappear several times, but with a different explanation each time; clm 14482c, for example, covers the topic *intentio* five times.[279] There does not seem to be any apparent order behind these modules of topics, but rather a piling on of yet another possible argument.

Clm 14809 and clm 14482c have the highest number of topics with about eighteen to nineteen each, while Freiburg 381 only has ten. Each *accessus* in the five texts also contains one or several unique topics; clm 14809, for example, has a long *vita*, which is not found in any of the other commentaries. However, except for the first *accessus* in Salzburg AV4, which is unrelated to any of the others, all of the *accessus* share enough material for it to be possible to discern a common base text of some sort. From where this text derives is another question. Perhaps one of these manuscripts could even be that base text, or the text could stem from a different and now lost Ovid commentary.

It is also worth mentioning that the modules in the different *accessus* show that they have, to varying degrees, been adapted to fit into the text. The *accessus* in Freiburg 381 is probably the one that presents the most edited or structured text. It introduces the topics to be examined (although it diverges from them), and it uses connective words or phrases such as *secundum hanc finalis causa est* (according to this the final cause is), clarifying markers such as *sciendum quod materia* (it

---

[279] See Appendix 1, l. 33-80.

should be known that the subject matter), and markers that recognise that the same topic has been covered many times: *intencio est ... uel intencio sua est ... summa intentio est* (the intention is ... or his intention is ... the highest intention is).[280] In comparison, clm 14482c simply piles these topics one upon the other, at most using the phrase *alia intentio* to signal that this topic has been covered before. Freiburg 381 is likely of a later date than clm 14482c, and it is thus possible to speculate about an active scribe/editor in this case, one that has read one or several other *accessus* and decided to structure the text slightly.

Similarities regarding the *accessus* are not significant on their own when it comes to establishing textual relationships between the texts in their entirety, since the *accessus* can have a transmission history quite separate from that of the main text, which is clearly proved in Frank Coulson and Bruno Roy's *Incipitarium ovidianum*.[281] However, since all of the Bavarian B *accessus* have several shared topics, this still speaks of a possible common source at least for these parts.

Book 1

The commentary to Book 1 is the longest portion of the commentary of the texts treated here.[282] Besides a general tendency in most commentaries to comment more heavily in the beginning, the cosmological theme in Book 1 of the *Metamorphoses* seems to have attracted special attention from the commentators.

Directly after the *accessus,* all manuscripts in the Bavarian B family continue with a type of commentary that diverges from the normal style of the commentary, which usually conforms to a strict paragraph marker followed by the lemma and then explanation arrangement. The extent of this irregular section differs from manuscript to manuscript.

In clm 14482c, we find the longest version of this irregular section, almost two pages long in the manuscript and over a hundred lines in the edition.[283] The other manuscripts have shorter versions of this text. The commentary at this point revolves around the first twenty-five lines of Book 1 of the *Metamorphoses*, with special emphasis on the first ten lines. In clm 14482c, the first lines are explained using the rhetorical categories *proponens (propositio)* and *invocatio.* The commentary uses paraphrase and synonyms to explain the first two

---

[280] Freiburg 381, 34^r.

[281] Coulson and Roy 2000.

[282] The *accessus* and commentary to Book 1 are found on the following folios: Freiburg 381: 34^r-36^r; clm 14482b: 12^r-14^v; clm 14482c: 27^r-31^r; clm 14809: 65^r-68^v; Salzburg AV4: 5^v-12^r.

[283] 27^v-28^v, Appendix 1 l. 92-203.

lines and then proceeds to discuss what a transformation is. Then follow lines with more regular lemmatic commentary, but this text is not separated by paragraph markers. After this comes a long explanation of *Met.* 1:25, which centres on the properties of the elements and their numerical counterpart.[284] This seems inspired by Calcidius's *Timaeus,* and almost the same explanation can be found in contemporary commentary on Boethius.[285] After this long explanation, the text reverts to analysing the first lines of the *Metamorphoses* with terminology borrowed from the study of rhetoric, for example, *prologus* and *captatio benevolentiae.*[286] This part of the commentary then ends with a new close reading of the first couple of lines. This time, the commentary even manages to include some Christian interpretation by mentioning that Ovid says 'gods' in plural, but in reality knew that there was only one god.[287]

The other manuscripts have shorter texts at this point, but with the same general content. For example, all of them except for clm 14482b include the long numerological explanation of the elements.

Clm 14482b is an interesting case regarding the beginning of the commentary. Folios 2^r-12^r in the manuscript consist of a short commentary similar to, but not related to the others; then on the second half of 12^r another hand has started a new commentary. The new hand has copied an *accessus* and a short collection of glosses in a style similar to that of the beginning of the other Bavarian B texts. These glosses are then interrupted by another *accessus,* which ends with the cryptic phrase *Vtilitas quod quisquis ex eo intendit negotio commode insequitur Huius sunt partes incolomitas potentia.*[288] The last part of the phrase seems to carry an echo of Cicero's *De inventione,* in which he uses the words *incolumitas* (security) and *potentia* (power) as the two subdivisions of *utilitas* (utility or advantage).[289] The *accessus* is then followed by explanations of *Met.* 1:89, 101, 106, 117, 128 and 313, after which follows an explanation of *Met.* 1:82. From this explanation onwards, the text in 14482b is comparable to the other texts in the family, especially 14482c.

An exceptional aspect of clm 14482b is its inclusion of two Middle High German glosses. On 13^r two words from *Met.* 1:101 are glossed

---

[284] Appendix 1, l. 111-146.

[285] *Saeculi noni auctoris in Boetii Consolationem Philosophiae commentaries,* ed. E. T. Silk (Rome, 1935), p. 160.

[286] Appendix 1, l. 138-140.

[287] See Appendix 1, l. 167-170.

[288] Clm 14482b, 13^r.

[289] *Quare utilitatis duae partes videntur esse, incolumitas et potentia.* Cicero *De Inventione* 2:56, ed. E. Stroebel (1915).

thus: *corna hufen mora brambere*. The first couple is somewhat perplexing; *corna* means cherries, but since *hufen* means 'hoof', it would seem to have been confused with *cornu* (horn or hoof). The second couple is easier: the Latin *mora*, which is mulberries or blackberries, has been glossed with *brambere*, which means blackberry.[290] This is the only appearance of German or any other language besides Latin in the commentary texts and it would seem to suggest that this particular section is a copy of a marginal commentary with interlinear glosses, which have been included in the *catena* commentary.[291]

After this somewhat unorganised first part follows the commentary that is more representative of the structure of the rest of the commentary texts. Our comparison will start by looking at the length of the commentaries. The number of explanations indicates the length of each commentary text:[292]

Clm 14482c:	66
Freiburg 381: C:	63
Salzburg AV4: D:	49
Clm 14482b:	47
Clm 14809:	37

Here we can immediately see that there is a general difference in how much the different commentaries comment on Book 1. Clm 14482c has the longest text with the greatest amount of explanations. Using it as a base, I have compared matching lemmata and explanations between the commentaries and arrived at the following numbers:

	Freiburg 381	AV4	14482b	14809
14482c: 66	63/63	47/49	45/47	32/37

(The figures in the table show the number of explanations shared by clm 14482c and the other manuscripts/the total number of explanations in Book 1 in the manuscripts)

What we can see here is a very close agreement between all the manuscripts when it comes to which lines in the *Metamorphoses* they

---

[290] For a good collection of Middle High German dictionaries see: http://woerterbuchnetz.de.

[291] There are of course also some references to Greek words in the etymological explanations.

[292] This part of the commentary is considered to start with the second *Amphitrites* explanation, which starts on l. 203 in the edition of clm 14482c.

react upon. Another fact that speaks to these five texts being closely related is that the lemma and the explanations are in the same order in the manuscript even when the order is wrong, for example, in all commentary texts (including clm 4610) the explanation to 1:117 has been inserted between those to 1:111 and 1:113. There is no thematic or other obvious connection between 1:111 and 1:117 to justify placing 1:117 before 1:113. This may indicate a common source text or exemplar.

Clm 14482c and Freiburg 381 are the closest match. Clm 14482c comments on two more passages from the *Metamorphoses* than Freiburg 381, but, of the sixty-three passages commented upon that they have in common, only two are significantly different. The first one is the explanation to *Met.* 1:563, where clm 14482c has a much longer explanation than Freiburg 381. The second is the explanation to *Met.* 1:682 where clm 14482c has only a short explanation and Freiburg 381 has extended it with detailed background information. Salzburg AV4 and clm 14482b both frequently omit the lemma and provide only the explanations. They are also the only commentaries that do not use paragraph markers. These two facts may point to them being copies of another *catena* commentary through dictation or from a marginal commentary that perhaps did not use lemma. Except for these two traits, clm 14482b and Salzburg AV4 do not seem to have anything more in common. There are no other significant subgroups that are discernible in Book 1.

The similarities and differences between the manuscripts are either a matter of the number of explanations, that is, one manuscript might have more explanations than another, or a matter of added (or possibly subtracted) information in a particular explanation. There are no instances where the different manuscripts comment on the same passage but do so in completely different ways. The following example gives a good illustration of the small differences that exist in phrasing between the manuscripts:

> **clm 14482c:** *NABATHVS uel Nabath fuit filius Ismahelis filii Abrahe, qui regnauit in oriente, a quo dicta est regio Nabaioht.* (1:61, 29^r)
>
> NABATHUS or Nabath was the son of Ismael, son of Abraham, who ruled in the east. The region is named Nabaioth after him.
>
> **clm 14809:** *NABATHVS uel Nabath uel Nabaioth fuit filius Ysmahelis filii Abrahe, qui regnauit in oriente, a quo dicta est regio Nabaioth.* (67^r)

> **Freiburg 381:** *NABATVS uel Nabant fuit filius Ismahel filii Abrahe, qui regnauit in origente, a quo dicta est regio Nabathon.* (35ʳ)
>
> **Salzburg AV4:** *NABATVS vel Nabath fuit filius Ismaelis filii Abrahe, qui regnavit in oriente, unde dicta est civitas.* (8ᵛ)

Here we see that the texts are virtually the same with the exception of spelling, the inclusion of a third alternative for a name in clm 14809 (*uel nabath uel nabaioth*), and the ending of Salzburg AV4 compared to the others.

The next example shows a grouping of manuscripts:[293]

> **clm 14482c/14809:** *NOMINE PARNASVS. Parnasus mons habet duos uertices, dextrum Heliconem et sinistrum Cytheronem, sed in Helicone est Cirra ciuitas, in Citherone est Nisa, in qua Bachus colitur. Vnde Bachus dicitur Niseus et Venus Citharea <u>in Cirra Apollo et Muse</u>* (1:317, 30ʳ)
>
> [A MOUNTAIN] NAMED PARNASSUS. Mount Parnassus has two peaks, the right one is Helicon, the left Cytheron. But the city Cirrha is on Helicon, on Cytheron is Nysa, where Bacchus is worshipped. Wherefore Bacchus is called Nysean and Venus Cytherean. In Cirrha Apollo and the Muses [are worshipped].
>
> **Freiburg 381/ clm 14482b:** *NOMINE PARNASVS. Parnas habet duos uertices, dextrum Heliconem sinistrum Citherinem, sed in Helico est Cirra ciuitas, <u>in qua colitur Apollo et Muse</u> et in Citherine est Nisa, in qua colitur Bachus. Vnde Bachus dicitur Niseus et Venus Cithereia.* (35ᵛ)

In this example, clm 14482c and clm 14809 agree with each other word for word, except for spelling, and the same with Freiburg 381 and clm 14482b. The interesting thing here is that the first group is united by a common error: they have somehow misplaced the phrase *in Cirra Apollo et Muse* (underlined in the example), which the second group has placed in the more likely position on the second line, directly after *Cirra ciuitas*. This error is significant, but thus far the only one I have found uniting these two manuscripts.

Although clm 14482c has the longest text, it does not mean that it has the 'best' text. In fact, clm 14482c contains many textual errors that

---

[293] When two or more manuscripts agree with each other, I list only the folios for the first manuscript mentioned.

can sometimes be detected with the help of the other manuscripts. The following example shows one such errors:

> **clm 14482c:** *Nam QVA, id est in ut erat illud, quod modo dicitur TELLVS, ILLIC in eodem erat AER.* (1:16, 29ᵛ)
>
> For IN THAT WHICH, that is ?in so that? (381: there where) this   existed   that   recently   is named THE EARTH, THERE in the same place was also AIR.
>
> **Salzburg AV4:** *Nam QVA, id est ibi, ubi erat illud, quod modo dicitur TELLVS, ILLIC, id est in eodem loco, ubi erat AER.* (8ʳ)

Here the nonsensical reading *in ut* (in so that) in clm 14482c can be remedied with the help of Salzburg AV4, where the reading is *ibi ubi* (there where).[294] Perhaps this phrase, abbreviated to only an *i* and an *u*, may have been mistakenly understood as *in ut* by the scribe of 14482c. If this is true, then this would suggest that clm 14482c, although older than the others, is nevertheless a copy of earlier material, or that the other texts have been corrected somewhere in the copying chain. A second example strengthens the argument that clm 14482c is a copy that may have had difficulties with the abbreviations in its exemplar:

> **clm 14482c:** *OMNIA TELLVS. Telluris est numerus terre.* (1:102, 29ᵛ)
>
> EARTH [GAVE] EVERYTHING. Tellurus is a number of the earth.
>
> **Freiburg 381:** *OMNIA TELLVS. Telluris est numen terre.* (35ʳ)

That *numerus* (number) is wrong for *numen* (divinity) can be detected with the help of Freiburg 381. Again, we have reason to suspect a possible misinterpreted abbreviation: *numen*, perhaps abbreviated to *num*, has probably been wrongly interpreted as *numerus*.

Book 6

Since the commentary to Book 1 diverges from the normal pattern of the commentary with its length, extensive individual explanations, and the varying structure of its explanations in the beginning of the text, it may be useful to investigate one of the other books to reach a fuller understanding of the relationship between manuscripts in the Bavarian B family. I have chosen Book 6 because it is short (only about one and a half pages in each manuscript) and contains many brief

---

[294] Freiburg 381 also has a reading similar to Salzburg AV4 in this case.

explanations that are more representative for the commentary in general.[295]

The number of explanations is as follows:

Freiburg 381:	73
Clm 14482c:	60
Salzburg AV4:	55
Clm 14809:	45
Clm 14482b:	19

Comparing the explanations in the same way as above, but this time with Freiburg 381 as a base we get the following result:

	14482c	AV4	14809	14482b
Freiburg 381 (73)	55/60	50/55	42/45	16/19

We see that different texts agree with each other to quite a high degree. What is not shown by this little table is the interesting fact that Freiburg 381 and Salzburg AV4 agree with each other in seventeen unique instances. This subgroup was not discernible in Book 1. The readings of this subgroup are never exactly the same. They can be similar and of almost the same length as in the following example:

> **Freiburg 381:** *Mars idem Gradiuus dicitur, quia gradatim descenditur ad bellum.* (6:427, 40ʳ)
>
> Mars is called Gradivus since he descends to war gradually.
> **Salzburg AV4:** *Mars dicitur Gradiuus gradotim iter ad bellum.* (24ʳ)

Alternatively, they can be an example of one having an expanded explanation where the other has only a short one:

> **Freiburg 381:** *Icarus primum plantauit uineam, cuius filia Erigone, cum in uinea uagaretur, Bachus mutauit se in pulchram uuam, quam, cum illa uellet decerpere, Bachus de uua uersus in homine concubuit cum ea, sed cum rustici bibissent de uino, hinc inebriati putabant se uenenum bibisse et Icarum eis obuiantem interfecerunt et in puteum quandam miserunt. Canidea autem, que semper insequibatur eum, rediens duxit illuc Erigenem filiam eius, que tandiu ibi lamentabant donec Bachus Icarum et filiam et canem transtulit in celum. Et pro tali scelere rusticis imisit corruptum*

---

[295] The commentary to Book 6 is found on the following folios: Freiburg 381: 39ᵛ-40ʳ; clm 14482b: 17ʳ-17ᵛ; clm 14482c: 35ᵛ-36ᵛ; clm 14809: 73ᵛ-74ʳ; Salzburg AV4: 22ᵛ-24ʳ.

aerem, qui responso accepto quod querendo Icarum possent placare Bachum, quem, dum satis quasierant, in terra ligauerunt funes per aerem et ita quarebant eum. (6:125, 40^r)

Salzburg AV4: *Icarus primus cultor uinae Bachi. Filiam Erigonem habuit, quam Bachus mutatus in uuam uiciauit.* (23^v)

Besides this group, the following agreements can be noticed: clm 14482b always appears together with clm 14482c with virtually the same reading every time, with a single exception where clm 14482b instead agrees with Freiburg 381 and Salzburg AV4:

> **clm 14482c/14809:** *NOBILIS est C<ORINTHVS>. Cum Hannibal cepisset Corinthum, omnes statuas aureas, argenteas, ereas in unum rogum congessit et incendit.* (6:416, 37^r)
>
> CORINTH is FAMED. When Hannibal had taken Corinth, he gathered all statues of gold, silver, and bronze on one pyre and set fire to it.
>
> **clm 14482b/Salzburg AV4/Freiburg 381:** *Cum Hannibal cepisset Corinthum, omnes statuas aueras et argenteas et ferreas in unum rogum congessit et incendit, ex qua commixtione preciosa uasa facta sunt.* (17^v)

To conclude this investigation into the relationship in the Bavarian B commentary group we can now state that, although there is variation in terms of the length of the texts in general and the number and extent of explanations, what the different manuscripts have in common is still large enough to allow us to speak of a Bavarian B commentary.

Bavarian B and clm 4610

To investigate the connection between clm 4610 and Bavarian B, I have compared the *accessus*, Books 1, 6, and parts of other books.

When comparing clm 4610 to the Bavarian B family, I will start with the closest match and then move on to the more distant connections. The closest match in this case is the commentary in clm 14809, which has a special connection to clm 4610 not shared with any of the other manuscripts.

The first connection between these two texts is not immediately evident, because the matching passages are not found in the same book. The very last explanation in Book 1 is a long description of the Egyptian gods:

clm 14809: *NVNC DEA LANIGERA. Postquam uenit in Egyptum secundum fabulam humanitate derelicta et in Nilo purgata facta est Ysys dea lanigera, quia cooperuit Osirin mari lana uel lino. Inuenit eum membratim discerptum a fratre Osyris maritus Ysidis siue Io a fratre suo, qui dicitur Absirtus uel Tiphon interfectus fuit, quamdiu Ysis siue Io quesium et tandem inuentum in lineis uel laneis pannis collegit a fratre suo frustratim spersum. / Vnde adhuc Ysis celebrat festum eius in unaquaque noua lunatione pro gaudio illius reperitionis, et tunc exit de Nilo quidam taurus, qui lingua Egyptia apis dicitur, habens in dextro armo maculam ad modum lune factam. Istuc sacerficatur et tamen idem uel eius similis omni anno in alio festo similiter exit de Nilo, qui similiter sacrificatur, et sic fit in quolibet festo. Hoc de tauro testatur secundum Augustinum De Ciuitate Dei. Pingitur aut Ysis cornuta, id est cornua lune habens, et ei seruit sacerdotissa Bubastis et Anubis, id est Mercurius, qui sic apud Egyptios uocatur, et canino ibi depingitur capite et apis et quidam alius famulus, qui famulus dum primum suum os digito omnes alii ministri Ysidis tacent. Cum uero ab ore remouet digitos, tunc ipse et alii omnes cantant. Aspis quoque dicitur Isidem comitari et Osiris suus uir. Et ideo dicitur numquam satis quesitus esse, quia in unaqua noua luna festum eius presentatur ab Yside et ministri eius illum dolorem, quem tunc habuerunt, quando eum quesiuerunt, representant et simulant.* (1:747, 68ʳ)

NOW THE WOOL-BEARING GODDESS. According to the story after Isis came to Egypt her human form was put aside and she was cleansed in the Nile and made into the wool-bearing goddess Isis, since she covered her husband Osiris with wool or linnen. Isis's husband, was killed by his brother Absirtus or Tisiphon. Isis, or Io, searched for him for a long time. Finally she found him dimemembered by the brother and she wrapped him up in linen or woollen cloths and hindered his being dispersed by his brother. Whence they still at every new moon celebrate his feast for the sake of the joy of finding him. And then a bull, which is called apis in the Egyptian tongue, comes from the Nile having on its right shoulder a mark made in the shape of the moon. The bull is then sacrificed, and still the same one, or one similiar to it, comes in the same manner from the Nile every year at every feast, and it is sacrificed in the same manner. And this happens at every feast. In De Civitate Dei St Augustine testifies this about the bull. Isis is portayed with horns, that is having the horns of the moon. A priestess, who is called

Bubastis, belongs to her service. And Anubis, that is
Mercury, who is called thus among the Egyptians, and he is
portrayed there with the head of a dog. And Apis and
someone who then presses his mouth with his finger. All the
other priests of Isis are silent when he removes his finger
from his mouth. Then he and the others sing. There is also a
viper who is said to accompany Isis. And Osiris, who is her
husband. And therefore he is said to never be sought after
enough, since at every new moon his feast is peformed by
Isis, and the attendants perform and imitate the grief they
felt when they searched for Osiris.

Clm 4610 does not react to this passage in the *Metamorphoses* at all, but
the same explanation is instead found almost verbatim in the
explanation to *Met.* 9:693.[296]

As previously mentioned, clm 14809 contains a collection of
explanations placed at the end of the work, after the commentary on
Book 15. These explanations turn out to match those in clm 4610 in
some cases. The following explanation of *Met.* 2:755 shows a match
that even helps to solve a problematic passage in clm 4610:

> **clm 4610:** *Secundum autem quasdam fabulas, dicitur egis esse
> theca, id est †forist lorice Palladis, sed sepe pro lorica illius
> ponitur.* (2:755)
>
> According to other stories, *aegis* is said to be a case, that is
> the †forist of Pallas' cuirass, but it is often used for her
> cuirass.
>
> **clm 14809:** *Alii dicunt egam esse tecam, id est foramen lorice,
> quod ponitur pro lorica.* (80ʳ)
>
> Others say that *aegis* is a case, that is a hole in cuirass, which
> is used for the cuirass.

This parallel shows us a possible emendation to the word *foris* (door;
outside) in clm 4610, which makes no syntactical or lexical sense in the
text. The reading *foramen* (opening) in clm 14809 does make both
syntactical and lexical sense and it is possible to imagine that an
abbreviation of *foramen* was wrongly expanded by the scribe of clm
4610.

---

[296] To identify this type of similarity, every paragraph of two or more texts needs to be
compared. Doubtlessly, more of these matching explanations will be found when more
commentaries are edited.

The next example concerns an explanation of *Met.* 9:432 where the text in clm 14809 can again help us understand the text in clm 4610, but where the reading in clm 4610 is not necessarily erroneous, perhaps only awkward.

> **clm 4610:** *NON AMBITIONE NEC ARMIS. Non sunt isti facti iuuenes 'ambitione', id est honore, scilicet ut Hebe aliquem honorem tamen habeat. 'Nec armis', id est non propter arma illorum iuuenem exercendum ad utilitatem, sed super factum est.* (9:432)

> AND NOT BY AMBITION NOR BY ARMS. They were not made youths because of 'ambition', that is honour, that it to say so that Hebe still would receive some sort of honour [from this]. 'Nor by arms', that is not for the purpose of a youth using their arms for her gain, ?sed super factum est?.

> **clm 14809:** *NON AMBICIONE NEC ARMIS. Non isti facti sunt iuuenes ambitione, id est honore, ut Hebe aliquem honorem inde habeat. 'Nec armis', id est non propter arma illorum iuuenum exercenda ad suam utilitatem, sed secundum fata factum.* (80ᵛ)

The last phrase in clm 4610, *sed super factum est,* is rather obscure as regards meaning, but it is clearly written in the manuscript and leaves no room for an alternative transcription. I have interpreted it as 'but it happened above' with 'above' in the sense of 'as by divine will' or 'by the actions of the gods', or 'above in the text'. Clm 14809 gives us the much more understandable *sed secundum fata factum* ('but it happened according to fate'), which echoes the preceding line in the *Metamorphoses: fatis iuuenescere debent | Calliroe geniti (Met.* 9:431). If we suppose a common source for clm 4610 and clm 14809, it could be imagined how *super* is a mistake for *secundum* with *fata* omitted because of confusion from the following *factum.* On the other hand, this could be the intended although obscure text. Whatever the case might be, clm 14809 gives us a parallel that allows us to better understand the meaning of this passage.

Besides these two instances, the explanations at the end of 14809 also contain parallels to the following explanations in clm 4610 (listed in the order in which they appear in clm 14809): 2:153; 3: 269; 2:239; 2:527; 2:646; 2:566; 5:378; 8:182; 7:444; 8:564; 9:476; 10:90; 10:215; 10:223; 10:240; 1:69; 1:255; 10:206. These are not exact matches to corresponding passages in clm 4610, but similar enough to suggest a common source.

The third connection between clm 4610 and clm 14809 is related to the mysterious Manogaldus (Manegold), who is the only

contemporary authority mentioned by name in clm 4610.[297] Manegold
appears five times in clm 4610, but not once in the Bavarian B texts,
except for clm 14809, which has a parallel passage to clm 4610 in the
commentary of *Met.* 7:759.

After the close matches and parallels in clm 14809, we move on to
more general parallels between clm 4610 and the Bavarian B family.
First, we will consider the *accessus*. Clm 4610 has an overall unique
accessus, but it nevertheless has a few passages in common with the
Bavarian B family.[298] The paragraph beginning with *Quidam philosophi*
is present in all manuscripts, the *intentio Ouidii* in all except for one of
three *accessus* in Salzburg AV4, and the paragraph *Vtilitatem nobis
confert Ouidius* in all except for Freiburg 381.[299]

Turning to Book 1 and examining the quantity of commentary, we
find that out of the fifty-nine explanations in clm 4610 and around
seventy in clm 14482c there are about twenty-one instances of the two
commentaries commenting on the same passage. None of these,
however, are an exact match. Rather, they show different degrees of
likeness in the way they explain the passage. Sometimes, they are quite
close, at others completely different. The following example illustrates
explanations that are very close, but not identical:

> **clm 4610**: *QVOD FACIT AVRATVM EST, quia qui amat,
> pulchrum ei uidetur. Qui uero non amat, amor est PLVMPVM
> scilicet pondus.* (1:470)
>
> THE ONE THAT CAUSES IS GOLDEN, since it seems
> beautiful to him who loves, but for the one who does not
> love, love is LEAD, that is to say a burden.
>
> **clm 14482c/Freiburg 381/Salzburg AV4/clm 14482b**: *QVOD
> factum miratum EST, quia amanti uidetur pulchrum, non amanti
> graue quasi PLVMBVM.* (30ᵛ)

This explanation of *Met.* 1:470 from the two families contain the same
information but expressed in different ways. In clm 4610, the
explanation uses a relative clause (*qui amat/Qui uero non amat*) and in
Bavarian B a participle is used (*amanti/non amanti*), while the final
lemma is explained by providing the synonym *pondus* ('weight') in clm
4610 and by the adjective attribute *graue* ('heavy') in Bavarian B.

---

[297] See chapter 4, section: The Commentary and its Sources for more on Manegold.

[298] These paragraphs are found on lines 34-56 in clm 4610 and lines 33-34, 47-59, and 60-63 in clm 14482c (Appendix 1).

[299] The *quidam philosophi* is also present in the margin of the late twelfth-century *Metamorphoses* manuscript: Copenhagen, Det Kongelige Bibliotek, GKS 2008 4:0.

The next example shows an explanation of the mythological background type:

> **clm 4610:** *ET QVE DECIDERANT. Quercus dicuntur esse sacrate Ioui, quia super illas dabat responsum in Dodona silua, in qua ipse nutritus fuit.* (1:106)
>
> AND [ACORNS] THAT HAD FALLEN. Oaks are said to be sacred to Jupiter, since on top of them he gave an oracle reply in the Dodonian forest, where he was raised.
>
> **clm 14482c/Freiburg 381/Salzburg AV4/clm 14482b:** *IOVIS ARBORE. Quercus dicitur arbor Iouis, uel quia de glandibus suis pascebat homines, uel quia per eam dabat responsa.* (29ᵛ)
>
> JUPITER'S TREE. The oak is called Jupiter's tree either because he fed men with its acorns, or because he gave oracle replies through it.

This explanation of *Met.* 1:106 is identical in four texts of Bavarian B and is partially similar to clm 4610, which offers only one alternative. In the next example, we see a reaction to the same line, *Met.* 1:21, but with completely different content.

> **clm 4610:** *HANC LITEM D<EVS> ET M<ELIOR> NATVRA, id est uoluntas Dei, filius Dei, DIREMIT. Et sic quantum ad effectum, id est secundum <eos>, qui uidebant, non quod Deo aliquid accidat, ut sit 'melior'. Dictum est de Ihesu: 'Puer Ihesus proficiebat etate et sapientia apud Deum et homines'.* (1:21)
>
> THIS STRIFE GOD, AND THE BETTER NATURE, that is the will of God, the son of God, SETTLED. And thus with respect to the effect, that is according to those, who realised that nothing can happen to God, so that he would become 'better'. It is said about Jesus: 'The boy Jesus advanced in wisdom and age and grace with God and men'.
>
> **clm 14482c/Freiburg 381:** *HANC DEVS. Ipsa quidem obstabant, sed deus DIREMIT, id est separauit, illa ligantia et fecit coadunantem naturam ipsorum elementorum, qui post diuisam sunt. NATVRA, dico, que MELIOR, id est efficatior, facta est ad procreationem rerum, postquam erant diuisa, que prius conmixta.* (28ᵛ, AV4 has a different explanation here.)
>
> GOD THIS [STRIFE]. These things did indeed stand against, but God divided, that is separated, those things that were bound together and he made a joined nature of these elements that existed after the division. I say a nature made

> better, that is more efficacious, for the procreation of things
> after those that were previously mingled had been divided.

Here, clm 4610 offers one of its rare theological explanations, while Bavarian B stays closer to the text and explains that this concerns the mingled elements that were then divided. Although the theological mode of explaining things is very rare for clm 4610, this type of difference between clm 4610 and Bavarian B is typical, namely commenting on the same line in the *Metamorphoses*, but with different explanations.

The types of similarities we have found between clm 4610 and Bavarian B thus far seem to remind us of the pattern of similarities between clm 4610 and the marginal glosses.

An analysis of Book 6 gives virtually the same result as for Book 1. There are twenty-one explanations in clm 4610 and, compared with the lemma in Bavarian B, there is a match in sixteen instances. However, as in the case with Book 1, very few of these are matching explanations. The following explanation of *Met.* 6:70 shows the closest match in this book:

> **clm 4610:** *CECROPIA PALLAS. Apollo habet templum Athenis iuxta litus maris. Pallas in medio, Mars in altiori parte arcem, id est templum, habebat. Locus, ubi Mars templum habebat, dicitur Arispagus, id est 'uirtus uille'. Aris enim est uirtus, pagus uilla. Inde sanctus Dionisius dicitur Ariopagita, quia ibi docuit.* (6:70)
>
> PALLAS ON THE CECROPIAN. Apollo has a temple next to the seashore in Athens. Pallas had a castle, that is a temple, in the middle, Mars in a higher place. The place where Mars had his temple is called the Areopagus, that is 'the virtue of the village'. For *aris* is virtue, *pagus* is village. From this St Dionysius is called the Areopagite, since he taught there.
>
> **Salzburg AV4:** *Templum habet Apollo Athenis iuxta litus maris. Pallas in medio, Mars in altiori parte, id est in arce habet templum. Locus uero, ubi Mars habebat t<emplum>, dicebatur Ariopagus. Ares enim uirtus, pagos uilla. Vnde sanctus Dionisius Argiopagita dicebatur et docuit Athenis.* (22ᵛ)

This match is only between clm 4610 and Salzburg AV4. As so often is the case, Salzburg AV4 has left out the lemma and gives only the explanation, which matches clm 4610 almost verbatim. However, this is the only case of a verbatim match; more often the match is only in lemma commented upon and not the explanation itself, as in the following explanation of *Met.* 6:393:

clm 4610: *ET SATIRI FRATRES ET TVNC QVOQVE CLARVS OLIMPVS, id est habitantes iuxta Olimpum. 'Clarum' uocat eum, quia nubes excedit. Ideo omnes isti flebant, quia Marsia multum illos delectauerat suo cantu.* (6:393)

AND THE BROTHER SATYRS AND THEN ALSO THE CLEAR OLYMPUS, that is those living next to Olympus. He calls it 'clear' since it rises above the clouds. All these were crying, since Marsyas had delighted them a lot with his song. **Freiburg 381/clm 14809/Salzburg AV4:** *ET TVNC QVOQVE C<LARVS> O<LYMPVS>, quia postea clarior effectus est propter crebriores mutationes et miracula, que ibi contigerunt. Interpretatur autem Olimpus totus ardens. Quod nomen propter altitudinem suam habet a celo, quod totum est ardens.* (40ʳ)

AND THEN ALSO THE CLEAR OLYMPUS, since later it was made clearer because of more frequent transformations and miracles, which happened there. The Olympus should be interpreted as 'completely burning'. It has this name because of its height from heaven, which is completely burning.

Here clm 4610 explains both *clarus Olympus* and *Satyri fratres* [...] *flerunt* (the verb is on the next line in the *Met.* and not included in the lemma), while Bavarian B is focused solely on *clarus olympus* and gives a more complex explanation of this phrase.

The final example from Book 6 shows yet another occurrence of similar explanations attributed to different passages of Ovid's text:

Salzburg AV4: *Icarus primus cultor uinae Bachi filiam Erigonem habuit, quam Bachus mutatus in uuam uiciauit.* (23ᵛ)
Freiburg 381: *Icarus primum plantauit uineam, cuius filia Erigone, cum in uinea uagaretur, Bachus mutauit se in pulchram uuam, quam, cum illa uellet decerpere, Bachus de uua uersus in homine concubuit cum ea. Sed cum rustici bibissent de uino, hinc inebriati putabant se uenenum bibisse et Icarum eis obuiantem interfecerunt et in puteum quandam miserunt. Canidea autem, que semper insequibatur eum, rediens duxit illuc Erigenem filiam eius, que tandiu ibi lamentabant, donec Bachus Icarum et filiam et canem transtulit in celum. Et pro tali scelere rusticis imisit corruptum aerem, qui responso accepto quod querendo Icarum possent placare Bachum, quem dum satis quasierant in terra ligauerunt funes per aerem et ita quarebant eum.* (40ʳ)

clm 4610: *PRIMVS TEGIS, ICARE, VVLTVS. Bacus per Icarum Atheniensem rusticis Atheniensibus uinum misit. Vnde post quod rustici biberunt putantes se uenenum uel aliam potionem malam bibisse, Ycarum in puteum proiecerunt. Canis autem suus, qui secum iuerat, domum reuersus duxit Erigonem, filiam Icari, ad puteum. Iam vero rusticis tantam Bachus pestem inmisit, ut omnia fere perdedissent, quare, ut a peste posse<n>t liberari, Icarum de puteo extraxerunt. Et statim Icarus et filia et canis in celum translati sunt.* (10:450)

YOU, ICARUS, COVER YOUR FACE FIRST. Bacchus sent wine to the Athenian peasants through Icarus the Athenian. And after they had drunk the wine, they threw Icarus into a pit, thinking that they had been drinking poison or some other bad drink. But his dog, which went with him, returned home and brought Erigone, Icarus's daughter, to the pit. Bacchus sent such a pestilence against the peasants that almost everything died, wherefore the peasants pulled Icarus from the pit, so that they would be freed from the pestilence. And immediately Icarus, his daughter, and the dog were transferred onto heaven.

The first part of this explanation is found in Salzburg AV4 and Freiburg 381; the latter then expands the explanation with a long story about Icarus, which is similar to an explanation in clm 4610, but not to Book 6:125 — rather to Book 10:450. As in the example above with clm 14809 and the explanation of *Met.* 1:747 matching the commentary to *Met.* 9:693 in clm 4610, this is a reminder of the sometimes loose and modular structure of the commentaries.

The Other Twelfth-Century Commentaries

Here follows a brief description of the remaining twelfth-century commentaries.

The Franco-German Family

Manuscript Description

Prague, Státní knihovna CSR, VIII H32
Provenance unknown
91 fol.
19x12,5
1150-1250

53 lines/page, 2 columns
Content:
1^r-53^v: Macrobius's commentary on Somnium Scipionis
54^r-69^r: Adelard of Bath Questiones Naturales
70^r-77^r: (Pseudo-)Seneca, excerpts from letters
77^{r-v}: excerpts from different texts
78^r-91^v: Commentary on Ovid's *Metamorphoses*
91^v: A few verses in Old French

Remarks: Manuscript consists of four different booklets by different hands. Information gathered from my observation from the digitised manuscript and the manuscript information on the website. The manuscript seems to have been brought to the university in Prague in 1370 during the reign of Charles IV.
Available digitised at:
http://www.manuscriptorium.com/apps/index.php?direct=record&pid=AIPDI
G-NKCR__VIII_H_32___4DKIY63-cs#search

Berlin, Staatsbibliothek Preussischer Kulturbesitz, lat. oct. 68
24 fol.
21x9
Twelfth century
54 lines/page, 1 column
Content:
1-22^v: Commentary on Ovid's *Metamorphoses*
23^r: Part of a commentary on something relating to Greco-Roman mythology (inc. Dardanus fuit qui ex ioue et electra filia athlantis)
23^v: Two different texts. Top half: on natural philosophy. Bottom half: rhetorical figures
24^r: Part of a commentary on Lucan
24^v: Part of a commentary on Ovid's Heroides
Remarks: The *Metamorphoses* commentary ends on line 15:535. The commentary in the Prague manuscripts continues until line 15:870. One folio might be missing from Berlin 68.
Available digitised at: https://digital.staatsbibliothek-berlin.de/werkansicht?PPN=PPN768030854&PHYSID=PHYS_0001

Vatican, Biblioteca Apostolica Vaticana, Reg. lat. 221
Vatican, Biblioteca Apostolica Vaticana, Reg.lat. 221
74 fol.
1^r-6^v: Commentary on Ovid's *Metamorphoses*
7^r-8^v: Unidentified text on Roman history
9^r-12^v: Unidentified text (Inc. *presentatur unde frater quantis testimonis remedia*)

13ʳ-33ᵛ: Unidentified text (inc. *eundem - - e peciconibus satisfacere cupiens columbam cuius penne...*)
34ʳ-40ᵛ: Hymns (inc. *Magnificat anima mea*)
41ʳ-74: Augustine Ad Orosium and other texts
Remarks: Commentary starts with 9:284 and ends with 15:870.
Available digitised at: https://digi.vatlib.it/view/MSS_Reg.lat.221

I have given this family the tentative name 'the Franco-German family', since it seems to have divided origin; some evidence suggests a French origin and some a German one. Besides the commentary by Arnulf of Orléans, this is the longest and most complex of the twelfth-century commentaries. It contains a substantial amount of philosophical or cosmological explanations and seems to be quite well structured compared the Bavarian commentaries. The texts in the Prague manuscript and in the Berlin manuscript seem to be fairly closely related. When it comes to its relationship to the other commentaries, this family seems to have some sort of connection to the Bavarian B family. I am currently editing this family and can thus only offer a few preliminary observations here.

> **Freiburg 381**:§*Hemus rex Tracie usurpauit sibi nomen Iouis et Rodope, uxor sua, Iunonis, quare mutati sunt in montes.* (39ᵛ, Met. 6:87)
>
> §Haemus, a king in Thrace, appropriated Jove's name and his wife, Rhodope, Juno's. For this reason they were transformed into mountains.
>
> **Prague VIII H32**:§*Hemus usurpauit sibi nomen Iouis, Rodope regina uxor sua Iunonis, quare in lapideos montes mutati sunt.* (84ʳᵇ)

The first example shows a very close match between the Franco-German family and the Bavarian B family. This is also partially the case in the next example:

> **Freiburg 381**: §*TENVES VMBRE, id est imagines.* (39ᵛ, Met. 6:62)
>
> **Prague VIII H32**: §*TENVES VMBRE, imagines, PARVI DISCRIMINIS, id est parue differentie quantum ad colorem. Talis erat qualitas picture, QVALIS ARCVS SOLET INFICERE L<ONGVM> C<VRVAMINE> cum PERCVSSIS, id est repercussis, SOLIBVS, id est claritati solis, AB IMBRE, id est ab aquosis nubibus.* (84ʳᵇ)

This example illustrates a typical difference between these commentaries. The Franco-German family tends to have longer and more complex explanations compared to the Bavarian B family.

There are also a few similarities with clm 4610:

> **Prague VIII H32:** §*LATOIVS, Phebus. Pallas cantauit fistula in nuptis Iouis, cumque irrisa fuisset propter inflatas buccas, uenit ad Tritonem paludem ibique se aspexit et reiecit. Marsias inuenit a Phebo uictus excoriatus.*
>
> §*Tunc (tum Met.) QUOQUE C<LARVS>, quia postea clarior a ludis habitus est et interpretatur totus ardens, quod nomen propter altitudinem suam habet a celo, quod totum est ardens.*
>
> §*BUCCERA, bouina; caprarius, opilio; subulcus, porcorum; armentarius, equorum.* (84va, Met. 6:384, 393, 395)
>
> **clm 4610:** *QVEM TRITONIACA. Pallas, ut delectaret Iouem patrem suum, tibia canere cepit et fistulis. Quam cum uidissent alii dei genis inflatis ridere ceperunt. Vnde cum uellet uidere utrum dedeceret eam, uenit ad Tritonem paludem ibique cantauit sicut ante Iouem primitus cantauerat. Et uidit se turpem pro bucca inflata. Ideo in Tritonidam paludem tibiam proiecit. Quam postea Marsia accepit et Appolinem ad certamen prouocauit. Et ab Apolline uictus excoriatus est.*
>
> *ET SATIRI FRATRES ET TVNC QVOQVE CLARVS OLIMPVS, id est habitantes iuxta Olimpum. 'Clarum' uocat eum, quia nubes excedit. Ideo omnes isti flebant, quia Marsia multum illos delectauerat suo cantu.*
>
> *LANIGEROSQVE G<REGES> A<RMENTA>QVE BVCERA P<AVIT>, id est omnia illa armenta dicuntur 'bucera', de quorum cornibus bucina potuit fieri, id est cornu.*
>
> WHOM THE TRITONIAN. Pallas began playing on a flute and pipes to delight her father, Jupiter. When the other gods saw this they began to laugh at her inflated cheeks. Whereupon she went to the Tritonian swamp, because she wanted to see if this was unbecoming of her, and there she played just as she had played for Jupiter before. And she saw that she was ugly on account of her inflated cheeks. Therefore she threw the flute in the Tritonian swamp. Marsyas later took this [flute] and challenged Apollo to a contest. And when he was defeated he was flayed by Apollo.
>
> AND THE BROTHER SATYRS AND THEN ALSO THE CLEAR OLYMPUS, THAT IS THOSE LIVING NEXT TO OLYMPUS. He calls it 'clear' since it rises above the clouds.

All these were crying, since Marsyas had delighted them a lot with his song.

AND [WHOEVER] TENDED TO THE WOOL-BEARING HERD AND THE OX-HORNED CATTLE, that is all cattle are called 'ox-horned' (*bucera*), from whose horns a trumpet (bucina), that is a horn, can be made.

This example is interesting because I have thus far not found many instances of these two commentaries reacting to similar passages in the *Metamorphoses*, and here they are reacting to the same three passages. However, just as in several of the previous examples, not exactly in the same way. In the first explanation it is definitively the same background story being told, but the one in clm 4610 contains more details. In the second and third explanations the two commentaries focus on different things. The Bavarian B family also has an explanation very close to the third explanation in the Franco-German commentary here.

The Shorter Commentaries and Fragments: clm 14482a, Berlin 540, Guarner s. n., and clm 14748

Manuscript Description

Munich, Bayerische Staatsbibliothek, clm 14482a: see above under the Bavarian B family.

Berlin, Staatsbibliothek Preussischer Kulturbesitz, lat. 4:o 540
France
15 fol.
20,5x14
End of twelfth century
67-71 lines/page, 1 column
1^{rv}: John of Garland
2^{r}-5ra: Commentary on Juvenal
5rb: Commentary on Virgil (Ecloges)
10^{r}-15^{r}: Commentary on *Metamorphoses*
Remarks: Fragments of three different booklets by different hands from different ages. The *Metamorphoses* commentary is incomplete; it covers Book 1-11:157.
Available digitised at: https://digital.staatsbibliothek-berlin.de/werkansicht/?PPN=PPN768028965

San Daniele del Friuli, Biblioteca Guarneriana, Guarner s. n.

Germany
8 fol.
13x20
Twelfth century
55 lines/page, 2 columns
Content:
1ʳ-5ᵛᵇ: Commentary on *Metamorphoses*
5ᵛᵇ-8ᵛᵇ: Commentary on *Metamorphoses*
Remarks: Same hand in both texts. The first text contains a type of *accessus* focused on transformations and then brief commentary on all fifteen books of the *Metamorphoses*. The second text is incomplete; it starts with an *accessus* and then covers Books 1-8:288.

Munich, Bayerische Staatsbibliothek, clm 14748

Germany/Regensburg
144 fol.
22,5x17
Twelfth century
Remarks: This manuscript contains texts by Sallust and other authors. On 38ʳ the end of a commentary on Sallust is followed directly and in the same hand by a commentary on the *Metamorphoses*, which covers half or 38ʳ and 38ᵛ. This fragment consists of an *accessus* and some commentary on the first lines of Book 1. It seems to be unique; the *accessus* is similar to the other twelfth-century *accessus*. On 38ᵛ Macrobius is mentioned. The text is faded and difficult to make out.
Available digitised at: https://daten.digitale-sammlungen.de/~db/0009/bsb00094604/images/

These four manuscripts do not seem to belong to any of the four larger families, nor is it possible to group them together more than occasionally (see below). Of these four only clm 14482a is complete, but very short compared to the other families. The other three commentaries also seem to be short. I estimate that all of these commentaries are no more than half the length of clm 4610, which is quite interesting in itself. Were they perhaps abridged versions or extracted from marginal notes?

First, we will consider clm 14482a and Berlin 540. The first of the three commentaries in clm 14482 does not show any strong resemblance to the Bavarian B family or clm 4610. However, in the same way as with the relationship between clm 4610 and the Bavarian B family, it does frequently comment on the same passages in *Metamorphoses*, but in a different way. The following example shows three different versions of an explanation to *Met.* 6:90:

clm 4610: *ALTERA PIGMEE, id est Pigmee, id est que fuit mater illorum priorum populorum, qui uocantur Pigmei. Vel proprium nomen regine Pigmearum.* (6:90)

THE OTHER [SHOWS] THE PYGMAEAN, that is 'of the Pygmaean', that is she who was the mother of the earlier people, who are called Pygmies. Or it is the proper name of the queen of the Pygmies.

Bavarian B: *ALTERA PIGMEE, populi. Pigmei, id est cubitales, quia sunt cubiti unius abitudinis. De quibus quedam mulier preferebat se Iunoni. Quam ipsa mutauit in gruem insuperque precepit, ut singulis annis cum aliis gruibus pugnaret contra suos compatriotas.*

THE OTHER [SHOWS] THE PYGMAEAN, a people. Pygmies, that is cubit-long (*cubitales*), since they are one cubit long in appearance. One woman among them favoured herself before Juno, who transformed her into a crane and in addition ordered that every year she had to fight together with other cranes against her own countrymen.

clm 14482a: *Pigmei sunt populi cubitales, quibus grues bellum ingerunt. Et sic exponitur Pigmee matres, id est matres Pigmeorum, vel ut proprium nomen illius mulieris, que fuit regina Pigmeorum dicta Pigmea.* (5ʳ)

The pygmies are a cubit long people, against which the cranes waged war. 'The Pygmean mothers' should be interpreted thus: that is the mother of the Pygmies, or as a proper noun for the woman called Pygmea, who was the queen of the Pygmies.

In another instance, clm 14482a has the same explanation as Berlin 540. This passage is of interest since it helps us make sense of the obscure phrasing of clm 4610 in the explanation of *Met.* 2:11:

clm 4610: *DORIDAQVE ET NATAS. Secundum rei ueritatem Doris quidam rex Grecus fuit, qui in mari cum exercitu submersus fuit. Et ideo secundum fabulam Doris dicitur dea et exercitus dee.* (Ed. l. 224-226)

DORIS AND HER DAUGHTERS. In reality Doris was a Greek king, who was drowned in the sea with his army. Therefore, according to the story, Doris is called a 'goddess' and the army 'goddesses'.

> **clm 14482a:** *DORIDAQVE. Secundum rei ueritatem Doris fuit quidam rex Grecus, qui in mari cum omni suo exercitu perit. Secundum fabulam autem dicitur Doris dea et exercitus filie iii/inde uel Doridis.* (3ʳ)
>
> **Berlin 540:** *Secundum rei ueritatem Doris rex Grecie fuit, qui cum omni exercitu suo mari submersus fingitur. Secundum fabulam in marinam deam conuersus et exercitus filie Doridis uocantur.* (10ᵛ)

When we compare clm 4610 to these two commentaries, it allows us to understand better what clm 4610 probably means with *exercitus dee*, namely, *dee* (*deae* goddesses) as in *filiae* (daughters), and not *dee* as in 'of the goddess', which is also a possible interpretation.

The commentaries in clm 14482a and Berlin 540 seem not to be closely related to each other or clm 4610 or the Bavarian B family, but they nevertheless have some instances of matching content in their explanations.

The third text we must mention is the so-called fragment Guarner. s. n. (*sine numero*). This text is today located at the Biblioteca Guarneriana in San Daniele del Friuli. The library collection is described in an excellent modern catalogue, but, unfortunately, this commentary has been described as a fragment.[300] This is not the case. Instead, we are dealing with a unique case where the commentary text has been preserved in its original booklet form. All other commentaries I have investigated, except possibly for Salzburg AV4, have been bound together with other texts at some point during the middle ages. This little booklet consists of only eight folios comprising two short commentaries on the *Metamorphoses*. Granted, the text is not complete, the second commentary seems to be missing about three folios, but this still does not make it into a fragment. This little booklet may have been the form in which the commentaries were actually used in the twelfth century.

As far as the text of this booklet is concerned, the first commentary may be a version of the *Narrationes*. It is not related to clm 4610 or the Bavarian B commentary. The second commentary, however, seems vaguely related. The *accessus* is definitively a version of the *accessus* found in the Bavarian B commentary. It contains six topics, all of which are found in some form in the Bavarian B commentary. As for the rest of the text, it seems to comment on many of the same passages as both clm 4610 and Bavarian B, but with explanations that are too

---

300 *La Libreria di Guarnerio D'Artegna*, ed. L. Casarsa, M. D'Angelo and C. Scalon (Udine: Casamassima, 1991), p. 462.

different for it to be considered a close relation to the Bavarian commentaries. It is, however, thought to be of German origin.

The following explanation may serve as an example of the two commentaries when the explanations are the most similar:

> **clm 14482c**: *NABATHVS uel Nabath fuit filius Ismahelis, filii Abrahe, qui regnauit in oriente. A quo dicta est regio Nabaioth.* (1:61, 29ʳ)
>
> NABATHUS or Nabath was the son of Ismael, son of Abraham, who ruled in the east. The region is named Nabaioth after him.
>
> **Guarner s. n.:** EVRVS AD AVRORAM N. Q. R., *id est ad regna Nabathi. Nabathus erat filius Ismaelis filii Abrahe, qui regnauit in oriente, de quo tam pagani quam Christiani religionis uiri legunt in historis.* (6rᵃ)
>
> EVRVS AD AVRORAM N. Q. R, that is the kingdoms of Nabathus. Nabathus was the son of Ismael, son of Abraham, who ruled in the east. Both pagan and Christian men have read about him in historical works.

Arnulf of Orléans

Manuscript Description

Munchen, Bayerische Staatsbibliothek, clm 7205
112 fol.
24x17
29ʳ-58ᵛ: Arnulf of Orléans commentary on the *Metamorphoses*
Remarks: I have only been able to consult reproductions on the booklet containing Arnulf's commentary.

The last example of the twelfth-century commentaries is the most famous, and the only one with a name attached to it: the commentary of Arnulf of Orléans. Arnulf's commentary exists in many different manuscripts from several different centuries, of which the manuscript listed above, clm 7205, is probably the oldest and only complete version among the older manuscripts. This is the family about which I must confess I know the least. Instead, we must wait for the forthcoming edition being prepared by David Gura, University of Notre Dame, for Brepols until a proper analysis of the relationship between this family and the other families can be undertaken. For the purpose of this book I have examined only the version of the commentary preserved in clm 7205 and I will limit myself to presenting a few brief examples.

clm 4610:*VIRGINEVSQVE DICON, quia ibi habitabant Muse, ET NONDVM OEAGRIS HEMVS. Adiectiuum pro fixo hic ponitur. OEAGRIVS pater Orphei fuit – sed oe est diptongus. Ideo dicit 'nondum Oeagris', quia Orpheus, filius Oeagri, interfectus fuit a mulieribus in Hemo monte, unde postea dictus est mons Oeagrius consecratus Orpheo. Orpheus licet dicatur Apollinis filius, sicut Hercules Iouis, tamen dicitur filius Oeagrii, ut Hercules Amphitrionis.* (2:219)

AND MAIDENLY HELICON, since the Muses lived there AND NOT YET OEGRIAN HAEMUS. An adjective is used for a noun. OEAGRUS was Orpheus's father – but oe is a diphtong. He says 'not yet Oeagrian', since Orpheus, Oeagrus's son, was killed by women on Mount Haemus, wherefore the mountain was called Oeagrian, consecrated to Orpheus. Even though Orpheus may be called Apollo's son, as Hercules is Jupiter's, he is nevertheless called Oeagrius's son, as Hercules is Amphitryo's.

Freiburg 381: *§DEAIGVS mons, HEMVS est mons, in quo Cicones Trace mulieres Orpheum Oeagri decerpserunt, etiam inde mons post ea dictus est Oeagri.* (36ʳ)

Prague VIII H32: *... Hic NONDVM OEAGRIVS dictus est a patre Orphei (post corr. ex arphei). In hoc Orpheus dilaniatus est, et ideo nomen a patre accepit.* (81va)

clm 7205: *he<mus> non<dum> eagrius mons qui diuidit Macedoniam a Thessalia. Oea<grius> dictus est ab Orpheo ibi a mulieribus dilacerato, sed hoc nondum contigerat, immo futurum erat. Et bene dictus est Oeagrius, quia Oeager pater fuit Orphei putatus, Phebus uero uerus.* (32ᵛᵇ)[301]

Not yet oeagrian Haemus, a mountain that divides Macedonia from Thessaly. Oeagrian, named after Orpheus who was torn to pieces by women there, but this had not yet happened, indeed it was going to happen. And 'Oeagrian' is well said, since Oeager was believed to have been Orpheus's father, but Phoebus was his true father.

Here is a rather rare example of all four major families commenting on the same passage, although none of them are very much alike. All four

[301] All of my examples from Arnulf come from my transcriptions of clm 7205. This manuscript marks lemma by underlining the relevant words (while the other commentaries signal lemma with a paragraph marker), which I have reproduced in the transcription.

commentaries focus on explaining *Oeagrius* in connection with Orpheus. Clm 4610 has the longest explanation, and together with Arnulf explains that Phoebus was Orpheus' real father. The next example also gathers all four families:

> **clm 4610:** *§DVLCE DEDIT TOSTA QVOD TEX<ERAT> ANTE POLENTA[M].* *Tostam uocat polentam panem subcinericium; tostam, qua dulcem liquorem anus cooperuerat.* (5:450)

> §SHE GAVE SOMETHING SWEET, THAT SHE HAD COVERED WITH PEARL-BARLEY ROASTED BEFORE. He calls the bread baked under the ashes parched barley; the parched [barley] with which the old woman had covered the sweet liquid.

> **Freiburg 381:** *§DULCE DEDIT quodam scilicet POLENTA QVOD ANTE, id est prius, COXERAT in TESTA. Quod polenta, indeclinabile. Aliter: dedit quodam dulce, quod coxerat in testa, sed ante dedit polenta, id est prius, quod est genus panis.* (39ʳ)

> §SHE GAVE something SWEET, namely PEARL-BARLEY THAT SHE HAD COOKED BEFORE, that is earlier, in A POT. This pearl-barley, indeclinable. Alternatively: she gave something sweet that she had cooked in a pot, but before that she gave the pearl-barley, that is before, which is a type of bread.

> **Prague VIII H32:** *§DULCE DEDIT, scilicet POLENTA, QVOD COXERAT ANTE, id est prius in TESTA. Vel DEDIT ei quoddam DULCE, id est dulcem potum, quem coxerat cum TOSTA POLENTA, id est subcinericium panem, id est et panem et potum dedit, sed <secundum> priorem lectionem indeclinabile est polenta.* (84ʳᵃ)

> §SHE GAVE THE SWEET, that is the PEARL-BARLEY THAT SHE HAD COOKED BEFORE, that is earlier, in A POT. Or: she gave him something sweet, that is a sweet drink, which she had boiled with roasted pearl-barley, that is bread baked under the ashes, that is she gave both bread and drink, but according to the earlier reading pearl-barley is indeclinable.

> **clm 7205:** <u>dulce</u> *sic construe: dedit quiddam carnes frixe et contuse* <u>polenta</u>, *que dulce* <u>coxerat</u> *in tosta.* (38ᵛᵃ)

> <u>sweet</u>, construe it thus: she gave some roasted meats and some crushed pearl-barley that she had cooked sweetly in a pot.

This is an explanation to a passage in Book 5 in which Proserpina is searching for Persephone and is offered a drink by an old lady. The drink is said to be covered by roasted barley (perhaps in the sense of 'infused with barley', or simply a piece of bread placed in the drink). Clm 4610 is the only commentary that has the reading *texerat* in the lemma, which is found in four of the older *Metamorphoses* manuscripts (and is the one used in modern editions), while the other commentaries have the more common reading *coxerat*. The commentaries seem to be having trouble both with the concept of *tosta polenta* (roasted barley) and the general syntax of the sentence. Freiburg 381 seems to be basing its explanation on a manuscript that besides *coxerat*, also has *testa* (pot or jug) instead of *tosta*. This reading seems fairly rare. The commentator tries to explain the grammar by making *polenta* indeclinable. Freiburg 381 then gives an alternative explanation where *polenta* is described as a type of bread, which is also mentioned by clm 4610. The Franco-German commentary combines explanations from both clm 4610 and Freiburg 381. It is aware of both the readings *testa* and *tosta*, and agrees with Freiburg 381 that *polenta* needs to be indeclinable to work grammatically if the text reads *testa*. It agrees with clm 4610 in mentioning the *subcinericium panem* (ash-baked bread). Finally, Arnulf has a short explanation that is entirely different. Arnulf used the readings *coxerat* and *tosta*, but he also brings roasted meat (*carnes frixe*) into the explanation.[302]

These brief examples illustrate the fact that the commentaries sometimes agree which are the passages that need to be explained, and that the explanations sometimes are close enough to suspect direct contact between the different commentaries. It should also be noted that the examples above do not do justice to Arnulf's commentary, which is usually the most polished, and the most stylistically and pedagogically refined of the twelfth-century commentaries.

Conclusions

This section has considered the other twelfth-century commentaries, especially the Bavarian B family, a commentary family that seems to be from the same geographical area and almost contemporary to or slightly later in time than clm 4610.

I have shown that although individual manuscripts in the Bavarian B family shows many idiosyncrasies, it can convincingly be argued that they constitute a family. The difference between the family

---

[302] It should be pointed out that the text in the manuscript seems to contain some errors. The translation is an interpretation of what the original meaning might have been.

members is largely a matter of added (or possibly omitted) explanations or parts of explanations. As regards the relationship between manuscripts in this family, we also have reason to speculate about what determines the variation between the texts. When the variation is large, it is easy to imagine additions from a third source, but when it is small, just a matter of phrasing, then a third source seems unlikely. In the latter case, we could instead perhaps factor in orality, like dictation or some sort of schoolroom exercise. The Bavarian B family has survived in more copies than the unique commentary in clm 4610. Whether this means that the Bavarian B family was more popular than clm 4610 due to its content or for other reasons, or whether this is just a coincidence is difficult to say. I can see no easy answer to this question based on style or content of the two commentary families. So, I would hazard to guess that it is a coincidence. There could, of course, also exist other, as-yet undiscovered relatives to clm 4610.

As far as the other commentaries are concerned, more work remains to be done. There is a noticeable connection between the Bavarian B family and the Franco-German family, and Arnulf of Orléans's commentary occasionally seems to pick bits and pieces from the other commentaries (or shared sources). The shorter commentaries, which are not as easy to group in families, also share traits with the other commentaries, but I have not as of yet been able to establish any closer connection.

The nature of the relationship between clm 4610 and Bavarian B family reminds us of the relationship with the marginal commentaries in the previous study. There are a few close matches (particularly with the manuscript clm 14809), many cases of commonplaces, and finally a shared number of focal points, where a certain passage in the *Metamorphoses* acts as an irritant on the interpretative eye of the high middle ages and causes a multitude of explanations that warrant further investigation.

Clm 4610 does differ somewhat from the other commentaries by having fewer, but longer explanations. The other commentaries contain long strings of explanations consisting of just one word up to a short sentence, among which are scattered longer explanations. These strings of shorter explanation are gloss-like in appearance and could very well have been copied from a *Metamorphoses* manuscript or other source. In addition, the other commentaries, at least the Bavarian B family, seem to use more material directly excerpted from Servius and Isidore. As an example to support this last point we can compare the commentary to Book in clm 4610 and the Bavarian B family, where I have identified at least fourteen excerpts or parallels to Isidore (many of them verbatim) in Bavarian B and only four in clm 4610. Even though the commentary to Book 1 is almost twice as long in Bavarian B compared to clm 4610 this is still significant. These differences aside, it could be said that in general all of the twelfth-century commentaries are more alike than they are different. None of them adopts a completely different approach to Ovid's text, instead they all seem to focus most of their explanations on providing background information and help with construing the text.

General Conclusions: Clm 4610, Contexts and Connections

This book is first and foremost an edition of a text. As such the first part has aspired to open up the text to the reader by providing it with a context and by analysing its content. The four chapters in the first part of this book have served the function of introducing the commentary in the manuscript clm 4610, and the reception of Ovid leading up to the twelfth century.

Although the commentary is a copy, it has not been possible to find any predecessors or near relatives to it in the marginal glosses transmitted in the early *Metamorphoses* manuscripts or other near-contemporary commentaries, as demonstrated in Chapter 5. This chapter also briefly presented the remaining known twelfth-century commentaries on the *Metamorphoses* and explored some of the connections between the different commentaries. Among these connections are what I call 'common places', which tell us about the shared material all these commentaries built their texts on, and so-called 'focal points'. The latter are the most interesting since it allows us to isolate certain passages in the *Metamorphoses* that attracted attention during the period in question.

The edited text provides the tool for a detailed analysis of the commentary. In Chapter 4 I described its function by sorting its explanations into categories, and by analysing its sources and relationship to the *Metamorphoses*. The commentary makes use of explicit sources and also suggests a number of implicit sources, of which I have traced a number. The function of the commentary proves to be quite heavily oriented towards explaining the mythological background of the *Metamorphoses*, while at the same time providing help with the grammatical understanding of the text, which indicates a text used for teaching. Chapter 4 explored the commentary as a technology by discussing different ways of thinking and talking about a text of this type, but also by dissecting the commentary, and by so doing providing the reader with a heuristic aid to enter into the text.

In Chapter 3, the commentary was situated in the context of a Bavarian monastic or cathedral school. However, the question of what role exactly the commentary played in the schoolroom, also explored in Chapter 3, still remains open. Although attempts at contextualising an anonymous commentary composed at an unknown time at an unknown place may lead to more questions than answers, this chapter, hopefully, provided the reader with some clues to what questions to ask.

The detailed analysis of the commentary also allows us to better understand the place of clm 4610 in the general resurgence of Ovid at the time. Besides the increased copying of the *Metamorphoses* at the end of the eleventh century, a marked interest in Ovid in contemporary literature has been observed, which I explored in Chapter 2. This literature was usually also conceived in the monasteries or cathedral schools. Another important factor of this period, treated in Chapter 2, is the renewed interest in neoplatonic cosmology and transformations of different kind. The *Metamorphoses* and the commentary treat both of these, especially in the *accessus*, which is almost completely dedicated to discussing philosophy. The commentary does not, however, treat neoplatonic material to an extent where it can be considered a philosophical commentary, although it still displays an interest in engaging with the pagan mythological world in a neoplatonic framework, which is also something that can be observed in the poetry of the time.

There remains much work to be done both where the reception of Ovid is concerned and where the more general study of medieval commentary culture is concerned. A single text will never be able to answer all the questions raised in these endeavours, but it is my hope that this text will provide a new piece of the puzzle.

Part II: THE TEXT

In editing a single manuscript tradition of an anonymous high medieval text, we are quite far removed from the classical Lachmannian method of textual criticism as famously described by Martin West and Paul Maas.[303] We are instead much closer to the method employed by Joseph Bédier, although he chose one manuscript among many, while in this case we have no choice. Much more recently, several editors of medieval texts have engaged with the problems of editing single manuscript texts of different kinds in the volume *The Arts of Editing Medieval Greek and Latin: A Casebook*, in which a diverse group of scholars discuss methods for editing a diverse multitude of medieval texts.[304] In this volume, scholars such as Brian M. Jensen and Claes Gejrot discuss the possibilities and difficulties of their specific single manuscript texts.[305] My project fits within this context. Although we each employ different methods of documenting the text, editors of single manuscript texts usually share the goal of carefully documenting their single manuscript, as well as perhaps a slight scepticism towards the traditional philological dream of uncovering the *ur*-text.

Manuscript Description[306]

Munich, Bayerische Staatsbibliothek, clm 4610
Date: 1: Second half of the 11th century; 2: around 1100
Provenance: Benediktbeuren Benedictine monastery
Origin: Germany
Material: Parchment
Size: 21,5x17,5 cm
Writing area: 1: 17x14, 1 column, 25-27 lines; 2: 18x13, 2 columns, 32-33 lines
Folios: 84

---

[303] Martin L. West, *Textual Critcism and Editorial Technique Applicable to Greek and Latin Texts* (Stuttgart: Teubner, 1973) and Paul Maas (transl. B. Flower), *Textual Criticism* (Oxford: Clarendon Press, 1958)

[304] *The Arts of Editing Medieval Greek and Latin: A Casebook,* ed. Elisabet Göransson et al. (Totonto: PIMS, 2016)

[305] Brian M. Jensen 'A Modified Diplomatic Edition of *Lectionarium Placentinum*', pp. 198-218; Claes Gejrot 'Original Value: On Diplomatics and Editorial Work', pp. 122-138 in Göransson 2016.

[306] Based on the information in Glauche's catalogue with some of my own observations from microfilm and on site.

Quires: 1: (V-1) + 3 IV^{32} + (V-2)^{40} + IV^{48} + (IV-1)^{55} + (IV-3)^{60}; 2: IV^{76} + III^{82} + (III-3)^{84}

Binding: Medieval binding. Light brown, undecorated leather, traces of clasp and chain. Three pairs of bands are visible on the spine. Pastedown consists of a page from a ninth-century lectionary.

Contents:

1:

1^r-60^r: Anonymous commentary on Lucan: *Manneus lucanus patrem habuit manneum menelam ex prouincia betica ... est magnus quam pro eius capite debere*

2:

61va-84rb: Anonymous commentary on Ovid's *Metamorphoses*: *Cum multa possint inquiri in capite uniuscuiusque libri ... idcirco iubilet domino circulus uniuerse fabrice mundi*

84rb-84vb: Anonymous text on the quantity of Latin syllables: *Omnia latina in a producuntur ut ama excepto nomninativo ... Omnia in x et i z producuntur*

Remarks on clm 4610[307]

The manuscript clm 4610 consists of two separate booklets. The first booklet (4610:1) is a commentary on Lucan and is dated to the second half of the eleventh century in the catalogue.[308] The second booklet (4610:2) is a commentary on Ovid and is dated to around 1100 in the catalogue (more on dating below).

An owner mark (*iste liber est Monasterii Benedictenpeuren* [sic]) written in a later Gothic script can be found on 1^r, 60^r, 61^{rv} and 84^v. This mark is also found on the back pastedown. The front pastedown carries the text *Commentum in lucanum / Commentum in Ouidium Metamorphoseos* in the same Gothic script. The spine of the manuscripts carries an old library number, 110.

There are also more recent owner's marks on the manuscript. The front pastedown carries a *Biblioteca regia Monacensis* stamp and a sticker with Cod. lat. 4610 on it. The stamp occurs again on fol. 1^r and 84^v.

The microfilm has been digitised and is available at: https://daten.digitale-sammlungen.de/~db/bsb00006777/images/

Catalogue:

G. Glauche, *Katalog der lateinischen Handschriften der Bayerischen Staatsbibliothek München: Die Pergamenthandschriften aus Benediktbeuern: Clm 4510-4663* (Wiesbaden: Harrassowitz, 1994)

---

[307] These remarks are based on examinations of the digitally scanned black-and-white microfilm reproduction of the manuscript as well as my examinations of the manuscript on site in Munich.

[308] This booklet is one of the manuscripts used in the edition *Adnotationes super Lucanum*, ed. J. Endt (Stuttgart: Teubner, 1969).

Detailed Description of clm 4610:2

In the following description I will begin with general features and conclude with a discussion of the script and the text itself, which are most relevant for the editorial principles that follow directly afterwards.

Physical Aspects and Paratextual Observations

The parchment is of a rough quality. The hair side is dark and has a rough structure. There are several holes and tears as well as some faded spots (e.g. on 64rb and 66^{v}), which are not always visible on the black-and-white scan. There are also some blank spaces consisting of clean, unharmed parchment. An example of this can be found before *proprie uocatur* on 66ra (and on 68ra, 69vb and 83vb). I have no explanation for these empty spaces.

The manuscript has been trimmed when bound together, but the pricking from the blind ruling is still visible.

The ink is in two different shades. The main text is written in a dark blackish brown ink, while the additions are written in a lighter brown ink.

The initials are in red, but now almost black from oxidation, and extend over two lines. There are no decorations.

There is no mark for where the commentary ends. Instead (on 84rb, line 3), what looks like the same hand continues seamlessly with fifteen lines of Bible-related commentary.[309] After this, on the rest of 84rb and all of 84^{v}, the same or a similar hand has written on the quantity of syllables in a smaller script. This little text, which I have not been able to identify, seems to treat the Latin alphabet from a to z with regard to quantity.

At each lemma in the commentary, a reference to book and line have been made with a led pencil by a much later hand. This could probably be the work of Karl Meiser, who worked on the manuscript in the late nineteenth century and presented a list of most of the lemmata in a published lecture.[310]

---

[309] *Iurauit et predistinauit /dominator dominus et penitus / nihil penitebat eum Tu es sa-/-cerdos in conspectu illius offerens / libamina in eternum secundum morem / diuinum et iuxta ordinem regis / et sacerdotis Melchisedec Ab- /-scultate omnes ubique fideles /Propagator noster et auctor eternus / dolens male nosmet perisse / a patria longe exulasse Coe- / -ternum sibi filium misit ut eripe- / -ret homines Idcirco iubilet / domino circulus uniuerse fabrice / mundi.*

[310] Meiser 1885.

Mise-en-page and Punctuation

The text has a two-column layout, which makes it unique among the early *Metamorphoses* commentaries. The text clearly marks a new explanation with a paragraph marker, usually followed by a capital letter.[311]

Commentary on each new book is marked by the scribe with the phrase *incipit liber X* or just *liber X*. The only exception is at the start of the commentary to Book 1, which follows upon the *accessus* almost seamlessly.

In two instances the *incipit liber* seems to be wrongly placed. The end of the commentary on Book 4 includes an explanation to 5:19 and in the beginning of the commentary on Book 8 there are two explanations to 7:794 and 7:759.

The scribe uses both different punctuation marks and capital letters to mark a new section. The marks used are the *punctus* (both on the baseline and in the middle, between base and headline) and the *punctus elevatus*. Both marks correspond partially with the comma and full stop in modern syntactic punctuation. Capital letters are used in the four following ways:

- always in the first word of a lemma
- sometimes in the first word after a lemma (especially if the first word is a repetition of a word from the lemma, e.g. NVNC QVOQVE CORALIIS. *Coralii sunt species...*)
- after *punctus*
- sometimes when several alternative explanations are given to one lemma

Marginal and Interlinear Additions and Corrections:

The manuscript contains some additions in the margin which seem to be written by the same hand or by a hand contemporary to that of the rest of the text. These are usually complete explanations, but sometimes just a word or two. On 62va we find an example of a short addition in the form of a correction. A single word (*accidat*) with an insertion mark has been added in the margin next to the line where it is meant to be inserted. On 64ra we find the first longer marginal addition. This one is a short but complete explanation, and the insertion sign places it at the right place in the text. The additions in the margin appear in clusters in the manuscripts. They are found in Book 2 on 64r-65v, Book 6 on 68v and Book 14 on 83r. Book 2 is by far the book with most marginal and interlinear additions. Except for

---

[311] In some cases, for example, 10:127 on 76ra, the paragraph markers are very faint and difficult so see on the microfilm.

these there are only scattered one-word notes in the margins or between lines.

There are also some interlinear additions. Usually, these additions consist of simple corrections, for example on 64[rb] *iunget* is corrected to *iungere* in the normal way by placing a mark under -*t* and adding -*re* above the line. On the same side *uel per noctem* has been added after the words *per diem*, which can be regarded as a correction or as added information. It is not possible to say whether this is a correction of a phrase accidentally omitted by the scribe or an added gloss. Such possible glosses or additions seem partly to coincide with the clusters of marginal additions. Perhaps these were places were the scribe checked the copy against an exemplar or where a second reader or corrector had gone through the text.

On the Scribe and the Script

The catalogue dates clm 4610:2 to around 1100. Earlier scholars have dated it to both the eleventh and the twelfth centuries.[312] The latest editor of *Metamorphoses,* R. J. Tarrant (drawing on both Meiser and Munk Olsen), dates clm 4610 to the end of the eleventh or beginning of the twelfth century.[313]

According to Dr Teresa Webber, the script points to a date at the end of the eleventh century (with the reservation that a long-lived and conservative scribe could have written in such a style at a later date).[314] There is no textual evidence to help with the dating except for the reference to one Manegaldus. If this refers to Manegold of Lautenbach (c. 1030- c. 1103), then it gives us a rough *terminus post quem*, but not much as far as the *terminus ante quem* is concerned.

According to the catalogue the text is written in Carolingian minuscule, but we could perhaps call it a transitional script, or pregothic with Derolez's terminology, simply because of the plausible time frame for the manuscript. As Derolez points out, the term pregothic is relative, and the scripts identified as such are Carolingian scripts that show some new features, which are then fully developed in the gothic script.[315] The script in clm 4610 contains some features that point to an early transitional stage, such as long ascenders and descenders (about twice the length of the x-height), which were not

---

[312] cf. Meiser 1885, p. 48; Haupt 1873, p. 190.

[313] Tarrant 2004, p. xiv.

[314] Teresa Webber, e-mail message to author, 27 May 2015.

[315] Albert Derolez, *The Palaeography of the Gothic Manuscript Books: From the Twelfth to the Early Sixteenth Century* (Cambridge: Cambridge University Press, 2006) p. 57.

common at a later stage. The bodies of the letters are still quite square, compared to the later more rectangular shape, but with some lateral compression of letters such as *h, n,* and *u,* which would suggest later eleventh century rather than the middle.[316] Some other features of the script, which Derolez characterises as pregothic, are the use of both vertical and Uncial *d* (e.g. on fol. 62vb) and double i often marked íí.[317] Some other features of the script that may be worth mention are:

- clubbing on the ascenders
- closed loop *g*
- Carolingian *st-* and *ct-*ligatures
- ampersand is used throughout to represent *et* and *-et-* (e.g. for the *-et* in *ualet* on 71vb)
- *linea nasalis* always drawn as a tilde rather than a straight line.

Abbreviations: In addition to the standard set of abbreviations, the scribe uses some that are rather idiosyncratic. These are the *q* and *h* abbreviations (abbreviations for the relative and demonstrative pronouns), for example as *q* with a line through the descender may stand for either *quod* or *qui*.

The ampersand *et* is leaning in such a way that it may be mistaken for a *quia*-abbreviation. My impression, which has been confirmed by Dr Webber, is that it is unique to this scribe and could perhaps be used to identify the same scribe or perhaps school in other manuscripts.

The spelling of the scribe is quite normal for the time. The scribe makes use of *e-caudata* for the ae and oe diphthong consistently throughout the manuscript and distinguishes clearly between *t* and *c* in most cases when the combination *-ti-/-ci-* is concerned, but with some exceptions (e.g. *penitentia* on fol. 65vb, but *tristicia* on fol. 63rb). As usual with scribes of the period, *h* is sometimes missing and sometimes added where it does not belong (ex. *honerosior* for *onerosior* on 62vb). Somewhat less usual is the fact that the scribe (or a similar hand) also sometimes corrects missing aspiration with a sign above the line. The first of these corrections appears on 63ra in the explanation to 1:117. The scribe often uses *i* for *y* (*phisin* for *physin* on 61va, *Pirra* for *Pyrrha* on 63va), but rarely the other way around. Y is rarely used and almost always in names, and then in a way that does not agree with classical spelling (e.g. *Ypodammen* and *Yxione* for *Hipodamen* and *Ixione* on 78rb). The consonant *b* is sometimes used for *v*. (*acerbo* for *acervo* on 62va), and *p* is sometimes used for *b* (*pleps* for *plebs* on 63vb). In two cases, the scribe uses *f* where *v* would be expected, which may be indicative of a

---

[316] I would like to thank Dr Webber for pointing this out.
[317] Derolez 2006, pp. 60-65.

German speaking scribe (*fas* for *vas* on 67va and *fatem* for *vatem* on 70va).
In many cases, the scribe uses single consonant where classical Latin
would have double (ex. *vacam* for *vaccam* on 64ra and *literas* for *litteras*
on 69rb), and sometimes double consonants where classical Latin
would have single (*peccuniam* for *pecuniam* on 69vb).

The scribe represents numbers either by writing them as a word or
by using Roman numerals (*tres, bis, iii, iiii:or*).

On Errors

There are quite a few scribal errors in the manuscript. I have identified
about 300 in the entire commentary, some of which show a pattern of
difficulties with certain letters/letter combinations, which tell us that
the text is a copy and might even tell us something about the
exemplar.

However, even though these errors tell us that the commentary in
clm 4610 is a copy of some sort, it is still difficult to say whether it is a
copy of another *catena* commentary or an assemblage made from one
or several marginal commentaries, for example.

In the following, I will discuss the errors concerning names, errors
in the lemma, and complex and simple errors in the main text.

When the errors concern names, it is difficult to tell if the errors
were made by the scribe or if they are part of a tradition. The error
ortigianti for *ortigiam* is a clear example of a scribal error where the
scribe has confused the minims. The errors *ciclides* for *eclides* (ci/e) and
euboream for *euboicam* (re/ic) could easily be judged as simple scribal
errors, but they could also be part of a tradition. We have no proof of
the latter, but the type of error is analogous with the error *Antidia* for
Anticlea. The error, *d* for *cl*, is easy to explain on palaeographical
grounds, but the spelling *Antidia* also occurs in the thirteenth-century
Fabularius by Conrad of Mure (Conradus de Mure).[318] If we disregard
the fact that the *Fabularius* could be directly influenced by clm 4610:2,
this would be an indication of a tradition of spelling.

As concerns the spelling *eticina* for *ericina* and *dicon* for *elicon*, the
reason for the errors is equally easy to understand. The interesting
thing here, however, is that the errors occur in the lemma, and the
correct form is found in the explanation. This could either be because
the scribe realised his error, or more likely copied the lemma directly

---

[318] *Conradi de Mure Fabularius*, Lexicon A:Anticlinia, ed. Tom van de Loo (Turnhout:
Brepols, 2006) p. 110.

from an exemplar or a *Metamorphoses* manuscript, which may have been written in a script with difficult letterforms.[319]

The error *herecinthius* for *berecinthius* found in the explanation of 11:106 is an interesting example. Forms of the name appear once in the lemma and three times in the short explanation. In the lemma, the word is spelled *herecinthius* and the first time it appears in the explanation the spelling is *herecinthia*, but it has then been corrected by the scribe or a contemporary hand to *berecinthius*, which is the spelling used in the final two occurrences of the word. This example gives us a glimpse of an active scribe or corrector.

The lemmata involve an extra difficulty since they are often heavily abbreviated; words are often reduced to a single or a couple of letters only. About a sixth of all the errors identified in the text are in the lemma. We do not know if the form of the lemma is the creation of the scribe of this particular manuscript or the form found in an exemplar.

The most extreme error to appear in a lemma is *sed primus natas* for *spinas notatas*. We can draw the conclusion that the *s* in *spinas* has been mistaken for an abbreviated *sed*, *-pinas* has then been interpreted as *primus*, while *notatas* (perhaps abbreviated in the original) dropped the first syllable (*n[ot]atas*).

This type of more complex copying errors is not restricted to the lemma. In the explanations we have the following:
uenam ut for *ueniunt* (a/i, mu/un)
ad buceras for *adhuc erat* (b/h, s/t)
in aurem for *matrem*   (in/m, u/t)
These are essentially two or more errors in one: the words have been mistakenly divided and letters confused. I have found no common denominator for these errors, such as the type of letters confused, for example.

There are also some errors that concern abbreviated conjunctions and adverbs, most notably: *sed* for *secundum* and *non* for *con* (e.g. *non sedere* for *con-sedere*).

Besides these, there are many one-letter errors where we see a tendency to confuse b with h; t with c and c with t; d with the ligature ct; r seems to be problematic in several cases. Some examples:
cum for *eum*
laduca for *lactuca*
aeripiunt for *accipiunt*

---

[319] The Naples manuscript IV.F.3 can serve as an example here. It has no proven connection with the commentary in clm 4610, but it is a *Metamorphoses* manuscript written in a Beneventan script with additional marginal commentary in a pregothic script, which proves that either the manuscript or the scribes travelled and that different scribes and their scripts interacted with each other.

acrocissimo for *atrocissimo*
cantis for *tantis*
fortes for *fontes.*

Besides these errors, there are also many simple scribal errors that consist of missing or misplaced letters or syllables (e.g. *strupata* for *stuprata, uolemque* for *uocalemque*), or sometimes even superfluous words/parts of words (mainly at the end or beginning of a page, e.g. *cre / credentes*). However, it is difficult to judge if some of these errors are scribal errors or errors in the exemplar, as in the case with wrong word forms (e.g. *causa* for *cause; quadam* for *quodam*).

Editorial Principles

The present edition contains the complete text of the commentary of *Metamorphoses* in clm 4610. The edition is accompanied by two sets of apparatus and a translation with notes.

The aim of the edition is to document as many features of the text in clm 4610 as possible, since this commentary exists, as far as we know, only in the manuscript clm 4610. At the same time, the aim is also to interpret (e.g. by way of introducing a syntactical punctuation and correcting perceived errors) the text in a way that makes it accessible to modern readers since the text in the manuscript offers many challenges as far as individual words, syntax, and textual errors are concerned. While the documentary aim of the edition is important, it is important to realise, as William Robins reminds us in 'Toward a Disjunctive Philology', that an edition always emphasises some features of the edited text while at the same time excluding others in order to serve its purpose.[320] Thus the purpose should be clearly stated. While working with the text, I quickly realised that due to its difficulty the interpretative purpose must gain priority over the documentative purpose. This means that I have structured the text in a way I feel gives clarity to the individual explanations in it as well as the interplay between lemma and explanation. This also means that I opted not to document some other features of the text, for example, the original punctuation.

In the following, the different documenting and interpreting procedures of the edition are described.

---

[320] William Robins 'Toward a Disjunctive Philology' in *The Book Unbound: Editing and Reading Medieval Manuscripts and Texts* ed. S. Echard and S. Partridge (Toronto: University of Toronto Press, 2004), pp. 144-158, https://doi.org/10.3138/9781442659933-009.

N.B. At some points in the text the line and word spacing will appear irregular, this is due to the technical constraints involved in presenting the edition with a facing page translation. The irregular spacing is not meant to convey any features of the manuscript.

Errors and Emendations

For the purposes of this edition, I consider such passages or phrases that disagree with the internal logic of the text to be textual errors, or, to borrow Hans Zeller's phrasing: 'The textual fault is an element in the text as documented and transmitted that is contradictory to the structure of the work in question.'[321] This means that I am not interested in possible errors of the author or factual errors.

However, as Eric Cullhed has pointed out in his article 'Editing Byzantine Scholarly Texts in Authorized Manuscripts', the procedure of discovering and handling Zeller's textual faults is a highly subjective and historical event.[322] To put it another way, even though the search for authorial intention is long since dead, the editor is in a sense battling with 'scribal intention'. Through the paleographical arts we have good tools for judging when individual letter forms or words may be erroneous, but, when we encounter words that may be an error or an alternative reading (no matter how obscure), we enter a grey zone in which it is the editor's duty to report and if possible argue the editorial actions taken.

The present edition is based on a sole surviving manuscript, which makes the discovery of errors much more difficult than in the case with two or more manuscripts, since there are no alternative readings to help.

An example of a factual error can be found in the explanation to 10:214/215 where Hercules and his comrades are said to have hidden in the promontory of Sigeum and from this 'to hide' is called *sigere*.[323] There is parallel to this passage in Servius where it is told that the promontory is named after Hercules' quietness, which is *sige* in

---

[321] Hans Zeller 'Record and Interpretation: Analysis and Documentation as Goal and Method of Editing' in *Contemporary German Editorial Theory*, ed. H. W. Gabler, G. Bornstein and G. Borland Pierce (Ann Arbor: The University of Michigan Press, 1995) p. 36.

[322] Eric Cullhed 'Editing Byzantine Scholarly Texts in Authorized Manuscripts' in *The Arts of Editing Medieval Greek and Latin: A Casebook*, ed. E. Göransson et al. (Totonto: PIMS, 2016), p.76.

[323] *Repulsi sunt a Laomedonte et in Sigeo promunctorio latuerunt, unde sigere latere dicitur.*

Greek.[324] From this, we may draw the conclusion that the commentary in clm 4610, or the source it draws upon, has misunderstood Servius's explanation. However, the explanation in the commentary is constructed in such a way that it makes sense linguistically. The word *sigere* has a proper infinitive suffix, which indicates that it was regarded as a verb and thus, even though no dictionary supports the verb itself, it makes sense in its context and is not to be corrected.

Discrepancies in the text, such as variation between single and double consonants in a word, are not judged to be errors as long as they do not affect the understanding of the text. These discrepancies are not corrected but commented upon in the apparatus where needed so that the reader will not think it an error of transcription.

Discrepancies that do affect the understanding of the text are judged to be errors and corrected. I employ a method of correcting errors where the correction is always made visible so that the reader will not confuse the documented text with the interpreted text. I use three methods for representing corrected errors in the edition:

1. When possible, words are corrected in the edition by means of pointed and square brackets to indicate necessary additions or deletions.
Example: con<t>igerat and in the apparatus *correxi*

2. A majority of all the errors consist of simple one-letter/syllable error. The corrected letter or syllable is marked with italics in the text, and the original reading is reported in the apparatus.
Example: *a*gitur and in the apparatus *correxi* igitur *cod.*

3. More complex errors are corrected and the correction marked by showing the entire corrected word in italics and the original reading in the apparatus.
Example: *habentes* and in the apparatus *correxi* hiemes *cod.*

It could be argued that since italics are used in methods two and three, then why not also for the first method of correcting errors. The type of errors corrected by the first method is after all almost the same as the second (i.e. errors consisting of a lacking, surplus, or misplaced letter or syllable). Furthermore, not using the pointed and square brackets would present a more pleasant page for the reader. However, the use of these markers is long since established, and I have thought it a good idea to continue that praxis.

Where names are concerned, I use the same methods as mentioned above, but further justification is needed to correct an error in this case since it is difficult to separate a scribal error from a general tradition of spelling. Proper names are often spelled in ways quite far removed

---

[324] cf. Servius *in Aen.* 2:312, ed. Thilo, Hagen (1881-1902), and *Mytographi Vaticani 2*, 227, ed. P. Kulcsár (1987).

from what we deem the classical spelling. Sometimes, the names might be corrupted in the copying process and sometimes a variant of the classical spelling is given. In these cases, I do not correct, but I give the classical spelling in the apparatus. I correct, however, case endings in names lest the syntax would be faulty (e.g. 2:802: *Herse* for *Herses* and 8:316: *Pollinicem* for *Pollinices*).

In some cases, I make corrections if the same name appears in several different forms in the same passage. Here, a balance must be reached between an internal logic in the text and preserving the variation of the text. I have judged that these errors are minor scribal errors and not part of a tradition of spelling. Examples of these corrections are:

2:555: *Cerope* corrected to *Cecrope* (*Cecrops* in same passage)
4:458: *Pelapis* corrected to *Pelopis* (*Pelopis* in same passage)
4:786: *Pesagon* corrected to *Pegason* (*Pegasus* in same passage).

Besides these corrections, there are also a few instances where I have marked a word with *cruces desperationis* († †) when I cannot make sense of it syntactically. I have also chosen to mark unidentified letters in the lemma with *cruces* (e.g. 4:291). Had these letters occured in the explanations, I may have chosen to delete them, but since we cannot rule out that they are meant to refer to some part of the *Metamorphoses* when they are found in the lemma, I have chosen the *cruces* instead of the square brackets for deletion. Passages marked with the *cruces* are also generally commented upon in the translation.

Apparatus

Apparatus Fontium

The apparatus fontium has four functions. The first is to report explicit sources. However, there are not very many of this type of source in the text. Instead, the main function of the apparatus fontium is to report possible parallels or implicit sources; these are marked with a *cf.(confer)*. The number of implicit sources could potentially be enormous and those reported in the apparatus are best regarded as a sample and not a definite list.

The commentary also contains some cross-references to different parts of the *Metamorphoses*, which are marked in the apparatus wherever I have been able to identify them.

Finally, the commentary also includes some internal cross-references, which have been noted in the apparatus with reference to a page in the edition as well as in the manuscript.

Apparatus Criticus

The apparatus criticus contains details about editorial interventions, clarifying information about medieval spelling, marginal and interlinear additions and corrections, missing or surplus paragraph markers, and about manuscript features that might affect the text.

Corrections made in the main text are always marked in the apparatus, as are the few instances where other scholars have differing readings. To clarify an unusual spelling of names and other words *i.e.* (*id est*) is used. As a general rule, I do not clarify simple medieval spelling (e.g. e for ae, or a missing h), but if two instances of these features occur in one word, thus making it difficult to identify, I make a comment in the apparatus. When variant forms are concerned, I use *pro* to give the standard form of the word (e.g. mare *pro* mari). An erroneous form of a word, most often when names are concerned, is marked with *perperam pro*. The word form may be easily detectable as an error, but that error may be part of a tradition and thus not corrected. *Perperam pro* is also used in a few instances to suggest a possible conjecture, but one not strong enough to have been implemented in the edition. In these cases, the phrase is marked with a question mark (e.g. Inuolucione *perperam pro* motione?). For suppressed words, a note is made in the apparatus preceded by *scil.* (*scilicet*) (e.g. fixo *scil.* fixo nomine). Finally, *cf.* (*confer*) is used to show the reading in Tarrant's *Metamophoses* in a section where the lemma differs (e.g. prebet *cf.* praebebat *Met.*).

Orthography and Punctuation

As a basic principle, I follow the orthography of the manuscript with the exception of the *e-caudata*, which is rendered by a simple *e* in the edition. Following the manuscript, I use *u* to represent both vowel and consonant (when capitals are used, *V* represents both vowel and consonant). Likewise, *i* is used for both vowel and consonant. As a general rule, I have kept the scribe's spelling of names with a note on the classical form in the apparatus (see Errors and emendations above for exceptions). I have also preserved the scribe's way of writing numbers in the edition, although Roman numerals are represented in capitals so as to make them easily distinguishable. Abbreviations are expanded without comments in the apparatus.

I have introduced a syntactic punctuation into the text as well as the use of capital letters at the beginning of a new sentence and for proper names, nationalities, and language names. The text in the manuscript uses a system of punctuation (described above), and it could be argued that the original punctuation should be documented in the edition.

However, to properly interpret the text and to attain a maximum of transparency in that interpretation, I have chosen to adopt strict syntactic punctuation. Furthermore, the medieval punctuation is not consistent.

In addition to the features described above, other interpretative actions/markers employed in the edition are the use of italics, quotation marks, and the special treatment of the lemma.

Single quotation marks are used to mark words in a language other than Latin, usually Greek.

Single quotations marks are also used to denote a meta-word, that is, when the commentary discusses a word that may or may not form a grammatical part of the sentence, for example, 1:5 and 1:6.

Single quotation marks are also used when a word or a phrase from the lemma is repeated in the explanation, for example, 1:24, which is, in fact, the most common function of the meta-word.

Finally, quotation marks (preceded by a colon) are also used for direct quotes, for example, 1:371.

Lemmata from the text of the *Metamorphoses* are given in small capital letters. Words that are found either in the text or in the apparatus of Tarrant's edition are judged to be lemmata. References to Tarrant's edition are given in the margin. Although the lemma may extend over several lines in the *Metamorphoses*, the reference in the margin refers to the first line where the lemma can be identified.

The lemmata have been expanded using pointed brackets and without comments in the apparatus, for example, *Et quod tegit o<mnia> c<elum>* for *Et quod tegit o. c.* (on 62[rb]). The Latin in the expansion strives to conform to the Latin in the commentary. Thus *c<elum>* and not the classical *c<aelum>*.

As mentioned above, the lemmata contain a fairly high number of errors and must therefore be treated carefully. On the other hand, sometimes it is possible to deduce that a word is meant to be part of the lemma even though the reading cannot be found in Tarrant. In these cases, a reference to the corresponding passage in Tarrant is given in the *apparatus criticus*. These readings might be the result of either a mistake when copying the original or a reading from a *Metamorphoses* manuscript not reported in Tarrant. In these instances, it may be tempting to mark these words as lemma as well (as they well might have been intended), but I have thought it wise to mark only words supported by Tarrant's edition.

To complicate the matter further, the lemmata sometimes contains inserted clarifying words, which function as commentary, and it is important not to assume that these were thought to be part of the original *Metamorphoses* text.

Mise-en-page

The edition uses a one-column layout compared to two columns in the manuscript. I have chosen to follow the paragraph division of the manuscript, but add or delete paragraph marks where necessary, always with a comment in the apparatus.

In some cases, where the commentary gives a long explanation, I have made further divisions of the text using new lines and indentations to facilitate reading.

Marginal Additions and Corrections by the Scribe in the Edition

The marginal additions have been incorporated into the main text according to the guidance given by the insertion markers in the manuscript. In the cases where there are no markers, I have inserted the addition where it fits based on content of the comment. In the edition, the marginal additions are marked with a slight indentation. They are also reported in the apparatus. In one unique case (*accidat* on 62va), a single word has been added in the margin. This word is treated as the interlinear additions described below.

The interlinear additions are inserted in the text and marked by being underlined as well as reported in the apparatus. This is not the case with corrections above the line, which are usually just concerned with correcting one letter or syllable. These are simply incorporated and reported in the apparatus with the phrase *post corr. ex* + the form of the word before the correction.

List of Abbreviations and Signs

add.	addidit
cf.	confer
cod.	codex
coni.	coniexit
cum signo inser.	cum signo insertionis
(used to mark marginal additions)	
cum signo h sup. lin.	cum signo h supra lineam
(used by the scribe to mark aspiration)	
del.	delevit
emend.	emendavit
i.e	id est
in marg.	in margine
inter lin.	inter lineas
perp. pro	perperam pro
post corr. ex	post correctione ex

(i.e. the scribe has corrected)

scil.	scilicet
scr.:	scripsit
sugg.	suggerit
sup. lin.	supra lineam
ut vid.	ut videtur
§ adest	presence of paragraph marker where it should not be
§ deest	absence of paragraph marker where it should be

In the edition:

<x>	supplied by editor
[x]	deleted by editor
<u>xxx</u>	text above line in manuscript
/	new column or page (+ number of
fol./column)	
†x†	*cruces desperationis*

in the translation:

[x]	supplied by editor

Principles for the Translation

Some Considerations Regarding the Translation

The aim of the translation is twofold. It is meant to be able to stand on its own and as such provide non-Latinate readers with a version of the commentaries that will give them not only an idea of what the commentary expresses, but also how it expresses it.

A second aim of the translation is to give an extra interpretative dimension to the edition. The transcription, punctuation, emendation, and all other editorial practices make up the first hermeneutical stage; the translation takes the interpretation a step further by rendering my interpretation of the commentary into English. In this interpretation, I have made adaptations, partly to clarify the Latin text (and thus the translation works as an extra apparatus) and partly to provide readable English.

To transfer the commentary into English is no easy task, since Latin and English, in general, offer very different possibilities for authors to express themselves; in the commentaries in particular the ability of the Latin language to be compact is sometimes taken to an extreme. Furthermore, the explanations in the commentary are composite in nature and often consist of several explanations linked together (sometimes in a less obvious way).

When translating shorter extracts of a commentary, it may be attractive to rephrase and reshape the language in it to highlight the effects or message one wants to discuss. However, when dealing with an entire commentary, I feel that this is not the right way to go if we want to get an accurate view of the text. Instead, the style of translation I have chosen to adopt is one that focuses on what Eugene Nida calls 'formal equivalence', which means that the focus is on the message itself in both form and content.[325]

The example below shows the explanation's precise, but a first sight clumsy, way of using prepositional phrases.[326] It would be tempting to translate a sentence like this more freely, but that would not translate the form, only the message, and thus a big part of how the commentary functions would be lost.

> *Ipolitus fuit acusatus Theso patri suo a nouerca Phedra, quia, cum ipse, puer, rogatus esset ab ea, ut iaceret secum, et nollet, illa dixit Theso, quod ex hoc rogata esset ab illo, sed abiecit eum.*
>
> Hippolytos was accused by his mother-in-law Phaedra in front of his father Theseus, since when as a boy he was asked by Phaedra to sleep with her and he refused, she told Theseus that he had asked her about this, but that she had rejected him.

The same is true for the many brief explanations that make use of a short and often tedious way of expressing things. There should be no delighting variation in the English, if none exists in the Latin.

Another challenge when translating the commentary are the explanations that consist of lemma with explanatory words inserted into it, as in the following:

> *CANDIDA PVRPVREVM SIMILIS EDAT. Non ALITER CORPVS Athlante traxit RVBOREM IN PVELLARI CANDORE, QVAM tenuissimum VELVM rubicundum positum SVPER CANDIDA ATRIA, scilicet super parietem album. EDAT, id est ostendit, VMBRAM, que ex repercussione scilicet rubicunda et alba fit.* (10:596)
>
> A SIMILAR BRIGHT [COURT] PRODUCES A PURPLE [AWNING]. Atalanta's BODY catches a REDNESS IN ITS

[325] Eugene A. Nida, *Towards a Science of Translating: With Special Reference to Principles and Procedures Involved in Bible Translating* (Leiden: Brill, 1964), p. 159. | [326] It is also discussed in the chapter 4, section: The Language of the Commentary.

> GIRLISH WHITENESS NOT DIFFERENTLY THAN a very
> fine red AWNING placed OVER A BRIGHT COURT, that is
> to say over a white wall. IT PRODUCES, that is it shows, A
> SHADOW which is red and white from the reflection.

To show what is going on in the Latin here, the translation needs to match the Latin sentence structure quite closely. This type of explanation should not be paraphrased, since that would hide the main strategy in the explanation: that of using the target text (the *Metamorphoses*) mixed with explanatory text.

The reader should be aware that the explanations in the commentaries are of many different sorts. Some will be easy to follow, while others are much more difficult to grasp (both in Latin and English) for a reader with no prior experience of commentary language. For help to understand the peculiarities of the commentary, its language, and explanations I refer the reader to the chapter Form and function.

A caveat: The translation by its very nature solidifies the many potential meanings of the Latin text into one. This is always the nature of a translation, but in this case. I feel it is important to point this out. The reason is that the commentary uses such compact language, sometimes only a simple synonym or small insertions to clarify the syntax, that the 'wrong' choice on the part of the translator might give a faulty perception of the commentary.

Translation Principles

On a sentence level, I strive to follow the Latin as far as the length of the sentence is concerned and to preserve the general structure of dependent clauses. I also strive to match the Latin at word level. This means that I match the use of set phrases in the Latin with the same in English (e.g. *rem habere* is always translated as 'to sleep with') and in general avoid variation if there is none in the Latin.

One noticeable divergence from the principle of reflecting the Latin of the commentary is my treatment of names in the translation. I have chosen to render the names in their English or classical Latin form in the translation rather than using the spelling used in the commentary (e.g. Horace for Horatius, and Ephialtes for Offialtes). The spelling of names during the period and the possible tradition of a certain spelling is interesting, but I have chosen to document that in the Latin text and to use the translation as a way to clarify the spelling in the Latin text. The reader should, however, be aware that this is not the form in which they appear in the Latin.

Square brackets in the translation mark additions. They are most frequently used to make additions to the lemma so as to create a lemma sentence that is on some level understandable. However, it should be understood that the lemmata are not complete sentences and even if they were, the explanations usually react to a much larger portion of the text in the *Metamorphoses* than what is shown in the lemma. Therefore, the commentary should be read together with the *Metamorphoses* for optimal understanding of the text. I do not mark the addition of words commonly left out in Latin, for example, a supplied form of *esse*.

Round brackets are used to supply a Latin or English word when, for example, an etymology is discussed. The principles for etymologies are as follows:

1. In etymologies where the form of the Latin word is important, the Latin is retained in translation and the English translation is put in brackets.

2. In Greek-Latin etymologies, the Greek is retained in italics and not translated and the Latin word translated into English.

3. In all other cases, the words are translated into English and the Latin put in brackets, if needed.

Brackets are sometimes also used to clarify who is doing what to whom, by adding the name of a person or a thing when only pronouns or pure verb forms are used in the Latin (e.g. 13:217).

When Latin words are retained in the translation, they are shown in their dictionary form (i.e. first person singular for verbs and nominative singular for nouns).

Passages marked with *cruces desperationis* in the edition are represented in the original Latin in the translation, with speculation about possible meaning in the notes when possible (e.g. 4:199).

The main function of the notes on the translation is to provide the reader with contextual information. This information could easily turn into a full-length commentary on its own and, for this reason, I have restricted the notes to particularly dense sections in the text.

Edition and Translation of clm 4610

Clm 4610

61va Cum multa possint inquiri in capite uniuscuiusque libri, moderni
quadam gaudentes breuitate tria principaliter inquirenda statuere, id
est materiam, intentionem et cui parti philosophie supponatur.
Cum diximus 'parti', constat philosophiam aliquod totum esse, unde
partes possint procedere. Nunc primo agamus de ethimologia ipsius   5
uocabuli. Olim 'sophi' id est sapientes dicebantur, sed Pithagoras hoc
uidens nimis arrogans apposuit quoddam remedium, id est *'philos'*,
quod est amor. Inde 'philosophus' amator sapientie. Hucusque egimus
de ethimologia ipsius uocabuli. Nunc autem dicamus quod sit ipsa res.

Philosophia est ars uel naturalis uel artificialis. Naturalis est, que   10
omnibus inest, ut ambulare, loqui. Artificialis, que a magistro docetur
et a discipulo discitur. Et hec eadem artificialis diuiditur in duas
partes, scilicet in inliteralem et literalem. Inliteralis est, ut suere, arare.
Literalis, que potest dici uera philosophia, diuiditur in tria, scilicet in
phisicam, logicam, ethicam.   15

'Phisin' Grece, Latine natura. Inde phisica naturalis, que diuiditur in
IIII partes, scilicet geometriam, arithmeticam, musicam, astronomiam.
'Ge' enim Grece, Latine terra. 'Ometria' dicitur mensura. Inde
61vb geometria mensura terre. 'Ares' Grece, / Latine uirtus. 'Methica'
numerus. Inde arithmetica uirtus numeri. 'Mosin' Grece, Hebraice   20
aqua. Inde musica aquatica dicitur, quia omnis uox ab humore et aeris
repercussione conficitur. Astronomia, id est astrorum scientia.

Logica diuiditur in III, scilicet gramaticam, rhetoricam, dialeticam.
'Grama' enim Grece, Latine litera. Inde gramaticus literatus. 'Rethor'
Grece, Latine orator. 'Dia' Grece, Latine duo, 'logos' sermo. Inde   25
dialetica sermo duorum.

Ethica diuiditur in duo, scilicet in bonos mores et malos. 'Ethis'
enim Grece, Latine mores. Inde ethica moralis.

---

4 Cum ... 9 res] *cf. Com. in Boetii Consol.* p. 6: Philosophia est amor sapientiae. Sophia est
sapientia. Sophi enim dicebantur sapientes, sed, quia pernimium mundani sapientes
huic nomini insultabant, temperauit eis Pyt<h>agoras hoc nomen quod est sophi et
uocauit eos philosophos, id est amantes sapientiam.   **18** Ge ... 19 terre] *cf.* Isid. *Etymol.*
3:10: Nam geometria de terra et de mensura nuncupata est. Terra enim Graece γή
uocatur, μέτρα mensura.   **20**   Inde ... numeri] *cf.* Isid. *Etymol.* 3:1: Arithmetica est
disciplina numerorum. Graeci enim numerum ἀριθμόν dicunt. | Hebraice ... 21 aqua]
cf. Eriugena, *Commentarius in euangelium Iohannis*, p. 240: In Ainon, hoc est in aquis;
"enos" enim hebraice aqua dicitur; *cf.* Isid., *Etymol.*, 7,6.: Denique Moyses interpretatur
sumptus ex aqua.

7 philos *correxi*, sophos *cod.*   **13** suere] fuere *scr.* Young   **23** dialeticam *i.e.* dialecticam

Clm 4610

Since many things can be investigated regarding the origin of any book, the moderns - who take delight in a certain brevity - have stated that chiefly three things should be investigated, that is: the subject matter, the author's intention and to which part of philosophy the work belongs.

When we say 'to which part', it is clear that philosophy is something whole, from which parts can be derived. Let us now first treat the etymology of the word itself. Once they were named *sophi*, that is 'the wise ones', but Pythagoras who considered this too arrogant put forth a kind of remedy, that is *philos*, which is love. From this a philosopher is a lover of wisdom. Thus far we have treated the etymology of the word. Let us now say what the thing itself is.

Philosophy is an art that is either natural or artificial. Natural philosophy is that which is present in everybody, such as to walk or to talk. Artificial philsophy is that which is taught by a master and learned by a pupil. And the artifical is divided into two parts: the non-literary and literary. The non-literary is for instance to sew, to plough. The literary, which could be said to be the true philosophy, is divided into three: physics, logic and ethics.

Physin in Greek is nature in Latin. From this natural physics, which is divided into four parts: geometry, arithmethic, music and astronomy. For *Ge* in Greek is earth in Latin. A measuring is called *ometria*. From this geometry is a measuring of the earth. *Ares* in Greek is virtue in Latin. *Methica* is number. From this arithmetic is the virtue of the number. *Mosin* in Greek is water in Hebrew. From this music is called aquatic, since every voice is made from moisture and a repercussion of the air. Astronomy, that is the science of the stars.

Logic is divided into three: grammar, rhetoric and dialectics. *Gramma* in Greek is letter in Latin. Whence *grammaticus* [means] literate. *Rhetor* in Greek is orator in Latin. *Dia* in Greek is two in Latin, *logos* is speech. From this dialectics is speech between two.

Ethics is divided into two: good and bad customs. For *ethis* in Greek is customs in Latin. Whence ethics is moral.

Omnis auctor uel *d*ragmatice uel exegematice uel cinomitice. '*D*ragmaticon' id est fabulosum, et est ubi introducte persone locuntur, ut Terentii. 'Exagematicon' id est enarratiuum, ubi auctor loquitur, <ut> Priscianus. Tercium genus poematis est 'cinomenticon', id est commune, ut Ouidius iste scribit.   30

Quidam philosophi fuerunt, qui mundum de nichilo Deum fecisse crediderunt. Quidam uero alii ex athomis et inanitate, que duo semper   35
fuerunt, dicunt Deum mundum fecisse. Alii autem philosophi, sicut Ouidius et consimiles, tria esse semper dixerunt, scilicet Deum et IIII elementa insimul conmixta et formas omnium rerum in mente Dei
62ra existentes, id est ideas, hoc est diffe-/rentias sicut rationalitatem et caliditatem et frigiditatem et cetera, per que Deus ipse res futuras   40
constituturus erat.

Ista duo genera philosophorum dicentium Deum ex athomis et inanitate mundum fecisse, ex elementis similibus mixtis et ideis, id est differentiis, dicebant Deum artificem non creatorem. Qui uero dicebant de nichilo Deum fecisse mundum, creatorem omnium rerum esse   45
firmiter putabant.

Hii autem omnes philosophi tres personas esse dicebant, scilicet patrem et filium, id est 'togaton' et 'noim', et spiritum sanctum, id est animam mundi, sed filium patre minorem et spiritum sanctum minorem patre et filio. Et in hoc errauerunt.   50
Intentio Ouidii est omniumque fabulas scribentium, utpote Terentii, maxime delectari et delectando tamen mores instruere, quia omnes auctores fere ad ethicam tendunt.
Vtilitatem nobis confert Ouidius, quia, cum fabule in aliis libris tangebantur, ignorabantur, donec iste Ouidius enodauit et enucleauit.   55
Prodest nobis et ad ostendendam pulchram dictionum compositionem.

29   dragmatice … 33 commune] *cf.* Bede *De arte metrica* 25:4: Aut enim actiuum uel imitatiuum est, quod graeci dramaticon uel micticon appellant; aut enarratiuum, quod graeci exegematicon uel apangelticon nuncupant; aut commune uel mixtum, quod graeci coenon uel micton uocant. Dramaticon est uel actiuum in quo personae loquentes introducuntur sine poetae interlocutione, ut se habent tragoediae et fabulae; Serv. *in Buc.* p. 29, 18.   **47**   Hii … 50 errauerunt] *cf. Com. in Boetii Consol.* p. 21: "Qvis spiritvs" ideo dicit, quia hoc tagaton facit, id est Deus Pater uel noys, id est mens diuina, scilicet Filius Dei Patris, sicut dicit Plato.

29   dragmatice *correxi,* pragmatice *cod.*   **30**   Dragmaticon *correxi,* Pragmaticon *cod.* locuntur *i.e.* loquuntur   **32**   ut *suppleui secundum Young* | cinomenticon *i.e.* coeno-
38   mente … 39 est² + *in marg.* Iste liber est monasterii Benedictenpeuren
41 constituturus *post corr. ex* constituturus   **54** Vtilitatem § *adest*   **55** enucleauit *post corr. ex* enuclauit

Every author [writes] in either the dramatic (*dragmatice*), explanatory (*exegematice*) or mixed style (*cinomitice*). *Dragmaticon*, that is in the manner of plays, and it is when the introduced characters, such as those of Terence, speak. *Exagematicon*, that is in the manner of a detailed exposition, where an author, such as Priscian, speaks. The third kind of composition, such as Ovid writes, is *cinomenticon*, that is general.

There were some philosophers who believed that God made the world from nothing. But others say that God made the world from atoms and emptiness, two things that always existed. Other philosophers, such as Ovid and the like, have said that there were always three, namely God and the four elements mixed together at the same time and the forms of all things, which existed in the mind of God, that is the ideas, which are *differentia* (essential properties) like rationality, heat, cold and others, through which God himself would determine things to be.

These two kinds of philosophers - those who say that God made the world from atoms and emptiness [or] from mixed similar elements and ideas, that is from *differentia* - they say that God is a maker not a creator. But they who say that God created the world from nothing, they firmly believe that he is the creator of all things.

But these philosophers all say that there are three persons, namely the father and the son, that is *togaton* and *noim*, and the holy spirit, that is the soul of the world, but that the son is inferior to the father and the holy spirit inferior to the father and the son. And in this they err.

The intention of Ovid and of all writers of stories, as well as that of Terence, is mainly to delight and by delighting to teach morals, since almost all authors strive towards ethics.

Ovid brings us this usefulness, since, although the stories were treated in other books, they were forgotten, until Ovid elucidated and explained. We also benefit by his example of beautiful composition of words.

Quandam uero intentionem possimus dare poeti[u]s, scilicet ut sint Latine lingue correptores et immitatores.

Incipit liber Ouidii Metamorphoseos. 'Meta' id est de. 'Morphoseos' id est transformationum. / 'Morphoseos' est genetiuus Grecus et 'meta' quidem prepositio adiungitur illi et fit ablatiuus. Vtuntur enim Greci genetiuo pro ablatiuo.

PERPETVVM CARMEN. Dicit continuum.

ASPIRATE MEIS CEPTIS, id est aspirare uelitis. Velitis me dicere a principio mundi usque ad tempus Domiciani et Augusti Cesaris fabulas. Ouidius enim fuit in tempore Domiciani et Augusti Cesaris. Non dicit propter hoc 'continuum carmen', quia omnes fabulas ab inicio mundi usque ad tempus suum scribat, sed quia in hoc libro et in aliis suis libris maiorem partem fabularum comprehensurus erat.

ANTE MARE ET, id est antequam istud, quod modo est mare, sic esset diuisum, ut nunc est.

ET TERRAS. Ideo posuit 'terras' pluraliter et non 'mare', quia notior est nobis diuisio terrarum quam marium, quia tota habitabilis terra in tres diuiditur partes.

ET QVOD TEGIT O<MNIA> C<ELVM>. Celum, quod est purus ignis, tegit cetera elementa.

ERAT VNVS VVLTVS qui hodie est IN TOTO ORBE NATVRE, id est totius creature. 'Vultus' bene dixit, quia unumquodque elementum tum co<adu>nari uidebatur.

NVLLVS ADHVC TYTHAN. Tythan, siue Tytanus, gigas dicitur fuisse et cum terra concubuisse et plures tytanes, qui contra deos coniurauerunt, generasse. De quibus Sol fuit et Diana et quia cum aliis fratribus non con- / senserunt, ideo celestes currus meruerunt. Et hoc secundum quandam fabulam, sed secundum alteram fabulam filii Iouis et Latone fuerunt.

---

80   Tythan² ... 85 fuerunt] *cf. Myt. Vat. 2*, 29: Tytan autem dicitur Apollo quasi unus ex Titanibus qui contra deos arma sumpserunt, qui cum in bello contra deos abstinuisset, pro beneficio celum meruisse fingitur, Sol autem dicitur quasi solus ex Titanibus contra deos arma non commouit; Hyg. *Fab.* 33:72: Ex Ioue et Latona, Apollo et Diana.

57   poetis *correxi*   **58**   correptores ... immitatores] correctores et emendatores *emend. Meiser*   **59** Metamorphoseos *post corr. ex* metamorphoseus ut vid.   **63** Perpetuum+ *in marg.* §I   **64** Aspirate § *deest*   **67** quia + quod *sup. lin.*   **68** tempus + -e-/*lin.nas. sup. lin. ut vid.*   **70** antequam] -quam *add. in marg.*   **79** coadunari *correxi*

But we might attribute another intention to the poets, namely that they are the reprovers and imitators of the Latin language.

[Here] starts Ovid's book of Metamorphoses. *Meta*, that is 'about'. *Morphoseos*, that is 'of transformations'. *Morphoseos* is a Greek genitive and *meta* a preposition attached to it, and it should be ablative. For the Greeks use the genitive for the ablative.

CONTINUOUS SONG. He means uninterrupted. 1:4

BREATHE ON MY UNDERTAKINGS, that is may you wish to breath on them. May you wish that I tell the stories from the beginning of the world to the time of Augustus Caesar and Domitian. For Ovid lived in the time of Augustus Caesar and Domitian. He does not say 'continuous song' because he writes all stories from the beginning of the world to his own time, but because in this book and in his other books he intended to include the greater part of the stories. 1:3

BEFORE THE SEA AND, that is before this that is only sea, had been divided as it is now. 1:5

AND THE LANDS. He puts 'lands' in the plural and not 'sea' because the division of the lands is more known to us than the division of the seas, since the whole habitable earth is divided into three parts. 1:5

AND THE SKY THAT COVERS ALL. The sky, which is pure fire, covers the other elements. 1:5

THERE WAS ONE FACE that today is ON THE ENTIRE ORB OF NATURE, that is of the entire creation. '[One] face' is well said, because at that time every element seemed to be joined together. 1:6

YET NO TITAN. Titan, or Titanus, is said to have been a giant and to have slept with earth and engendered many titans, who fought against the gods. Among them were the Sun and Diana and, since they did not agree with their other brothers, they gained the heavenly chariots. This is according to one story, but according to another they were the children of Jupiter and Latona. 1:10

AMPHITRIDES is a name for Neptune, from *amphi*, that is 'around', and trident. For he has a trident on account of the three characteristics of 1:14

1:14   AMPHITRIDES dicitur Neptunus, ex 'amphi', id est circum, et tridente. Tridentem enim habet propter tres aque diuersitates. Aqua est labilis, mobilis, lauilis. Lauat et non lauatur.

1:17   LVCIS EGENS AER, quod per omnem partem sui luce potest perfundi; terram uero et alia non, nisi in superficie sua, et ideo dicit 'aer lucis   90 egens'.

1:21   HANC LITEM D<EVS> ET M<ELIOR> NATVRA, id est uoluntas Dei, filius Dei, DIREMIT. Et sic quantum ad effectum, id est secundum <eos>, qui uidebant, non quod Deo aliquid <u>accidat</u>, ut sit 'melior'. Dictum est de Ihesu: 'Puer Ihesus proficiebat etate et sapientia apud Deum et   95 homines'.

1:24   EXEMIT, id est secreuit, CECO ACERBO. Quantum ad nos dicit 'ceco'.

1:25   DISSOCIATA LOCIS C<ON>C<ORDI> P<ACE> L<IGAVIT>. Ignis est acutus, subtilis, mobilis. Aer subtilis, mobilis, obtunsus. Aqua mobilis, obtunsa, corpulenta. Terra obtunsa, corpolenta, immobilis. Aer habet   100 ab igne, quod est subtilis et mobilis, a terra, quod est obtunsus. Aqua habet a terra, quod est obtunsa et corpolenta, ab igne, quod est mobilis.

1:29   DENSIOR H<IS> T<ELLVS> ELEMENTA G<RANDIA> T<RAXIT>, scilicet truncos, lapides et cetera, que sunt partes terre.

---

86 Amphitrides ... 88 lauatur] *cf.* Serv. *in Aen.* 1:138: [TRIDENTEM ideo tridens Neptuno adsignatur, quia mare a quibusdam dicitur tertia pars mundi, vel quia tria genera aquarum sunt, maris, fluminum, fluviorum, quibus omnibus Neptunum praeesse non nulli dicunt]; *Myt. Vat. 2*, 11: DE NEPTVNO Neptuno deputant mare eum que secunde sortis regnatorem perhibent, quia aqua uicinior est celo quam terra, omne enim quod continet, supra illud est quod continetur. Neptuno autem Amphienam in uxorem deputant, amphienam enim Grece circa dicimus, eo quia tribus elementis aqua conclusa sit. Ideo eum tridentem dicunt habere quod aquarum natura triplici fungatur uirtute, id est liquida, fecunda, potabili.   **95** Ihesus ... 96 homines] *cf.* Luc. 2.52.   **98** Ignis ... 102 mobilis] *cf.* Calcidius, *Commentarius in Platonis Timaeum*, 1:22, p. 72: Si enim uicinum igni elementum quod sit et ex quibus conflatum uoluerimus inquirere, sumemus ignis quidem de proximo duas uirtutes, subtilitatem et mobilitatem, unam uero terrae, id est obtunsitatem, et inuenietur genitura secundi elementi quod est subter ignem, id est aeris; est enim aer obtunsus subtilis mobilis. Rursum que si eius elementi quod est uicinum terrae, id est aquae, genituram consideremus, sumemus duas quidem terrae uirtutes, id est obtunsitatem et corpulentiam, unam uero ignis, id est motum, et exorietur aquae substantia, quae est corpus obtunsum corpulentum mobile.

93   secundum ... 94 uidebant] eos *suppleui;* secundum qui uidebatur *Meiser;* secundum quod uidebatur *Demats*   **94** accidat *in marg. cum signo insert.*   **97** acerbo *i.e.* aceruo

water. Water is flowing, mobile and has the ability to clean. It cleans and is not cleansed.

THE AIR LACKING LIGHT, since it can be imbued from every side by its own light. But it [cannot imbue] the earth and other things, except for their surfaces, and therefore he says 'air lacking light'. 1:17

THIS STRIFE GOD, AND THE BETTER NATURE, that is the will of God, the son of God, SETTLED. And thus with respect to the effect, that is according to those, who realized that nothing can happen to God, so that he would become 'better'. It is said about Jesus: 'The boy Jesus advanced in wisdom and age and grace with God and men'.[1] 1:21

FREED, that is separated, FROM THE BLIND HEAP. With respect to us he says 'from the blind'. 1:24

HE UNITED IN HARMONIOUS PEACE THINGS SEPARATED WITH REGARD TO PLACE. Fire is sharp, fine, mobile. Air is fine, mobile, blunt. Water is mobile, blunt, solid. Earth is blunt, solid and immobile. Air has from fire that which is fine and mobile, from earth that which is blunt. Water has from earth that which is blunt and solid, from fire that which is mobile. 1:25

THE EARTH HEAVIER THAN THESE DRAGGED THE LARGER ELEMENTS ALONG, that is to say: tree trunks, stones and other things that are parts of the earth. 1:29

THE FLOWING WATER OCCUPIED THE LAST PLACE and ENCLOSED THE SOLID ORB, that is the earth, since if water did not enclose the earth, the earth would be soluble and sandy. 1:30

WHEN THE THUS ARRANGED. He repeats, as he adds.[2] 1:32

---

[1] This explanation revolves around 'better nature' (*melior natura*), which is associated with God and the fact that this must be an effect of God, since God cannot be made better.

[2] This phrase refers to the fact that a new description of creation starts here, but it is in part a repetition of the preceding creation story.

1:30 |, | CIRCVMFLVVS HVMOR POSSEDIT VLTIMA et COHER- / CVIT SOLIDVM ORBEM, 105
62vb　id est terram, quia nisi aqua circumdaret terram, terra esset solubilis et
arenosa.

1:32　SIC VBI DISPOSITAM. Repetit, ut addat.

1:38　ADDIDIT ET FONTES ET STAGNA. Stagnum est stans aqua, id est maior
lacus, uel de [a]qua aqua nihil egreditur. Lacus uero *est* locus aque et 110
est minor lacus quam stagnum, uel est aqua, de qua altera aqua ultra
non egreditur.

1:45　VTQVE DVE DEXTRE C<ELVM>, quia in celo considerantur, ideo terre
atribuuntur.

1:53　PONDERE AQVE LEVIOR. Sic fieri debet constructio: QVI AER QVANTO EST 115
LEVIOR PONDERE AQVE, que AQVA est LEVIOR PONDERE TERRE, TANTO EST
HONEROSIOR AER IGNE.

1:69 |　VIX ITA LIMITIBVS. 'Vix' pro mox. Ventis PERMISIT deus deorum. Et NON
1:57　PASSIM, id est non ita, ut unusquisque passus suos dirigeret ad libitum,
scilicet ut 'passim' traherent. Passim dicitur a passu. Et si ita esset, ut 120
ab una parte mundi uel orbis currerent, nihil obstaret.

1:73　STRA TENENT C<ELESTE>, id est animalia scilicet duodecim signa 'tenent
1:73　celeste' SOLVM ET FORME DEORVM. Formas deorum uocat planetas.

1:78　NATVS EST HOMO. Hic uertit se ad fabulas duas dans opiniones,
quomodo in principio post discretionem elementorum sit factus homo. 125

1:81 |　QVAM SATVS IAPETO. / Dii erant et sunt et erunt Prometheus et filius
63ra　eius, antequam homo fuisset creatus, et hoc secundum philosophos.

1:89　AVREA PRIMA ETAS. Sex etates alii philosophi dicunt, que designantur
per aurum, argentum, es, cuprum, stagnum et ferrum. Ouidius
quattuor tantum ponit. 130

109　Stagnum ... 112 egreditur] *cf.* Isid. *Etymol.* 13:19: Nam fontes labuntur in fluuiis;
flumina in freta discurrunt; lacus stat in loco nec profluit. Et dictus lacus quasi aquae
locus. [...] Nam dictus est stagnus ab eo quod illic aqua stet nec decurrat. **128** Sex ... 129
ferrum] *cf.* Isid. *Etymol.* 5:38: Aetas autem proprie duobus modis dicitur: aut enim
hominis, sicut infantia, iuuentus, senectus: aut mundi, cuius prima aetas est ab Adam
usque ad Noe; secunda a Noe usque ad Abraham; tertia ab Abraham usque ad David;
quarta a David usque ad transmigrationem Iuda in Babyloniam; quinta deinde a
transmigratione Babylonis usque ad adventum Salvatoris in carne; sexta, quae nunc
agitur, usque quo mundus iste finiatur.

110 aqua[1] *correxi* | est *correxi*, et *cod.*　**117** honerosior *i.e.* onerosior　**118** Vix[1] ... limitibvs
perperam pro uix nunc obsistitur illis *Met. lin. 58*　**124** Natus § *deest*

HE ADDED BOTH SPRINGS AND POOLS. A pool (*stagnum*) is standing   1:38
water (*stans aqua*), that is quite a large lake, or it is some water from
which water does not flow out. But a lake is also a place of water, and
a lake is smaller than a pool. Or it is water, from which other water
cannot flow further.

AND AS TWO [ZONES] TO THE RIGHT [CUT] THE HEAVEN, since they are   1:45
observed in heaven, they are attributed to earth.[3]

LIGHTER THAN THE WEIGHT OF WATER. The construction should be like   1:53
this: AS MUCH LIGHTER AIR IS THAN THE WEIGHT OF WATER AND WATER
LIGHTER THAN THE WEIGHT OF EARTH, SO MUCH HEAVIER IS AIR THAN
FIRE.[4]

SCARCELY THUS FROM THE BOUNDS.[5] 'Scarcely' (*vix*) for soon (*mox*). The   1:69
god of gods ALLOTED this to the winds. And NOT EVERYWHERE, that is,   1:57
not in such a way that everyone directed their steps at will, that is to
say so that they went 'everywhere'. Everywhere (*passim*) derives from
step (*passus*), and if it were thus that they ran from one part of the
world or the orb, nothing would stand in their way.

THE STARS OCCUPIED THE CELESTIAL, that is the twelve animal signs   1:73
'occupied the celestial' FLOOR, AND THE FORMS OF THE GODS. He calls the
planets 'the forms of the gods'.

MAN WAS BORN. Here he turns to the stories and offers two views on   1:78
how man was created in the beginning after the separation of the
elements.

[THE EARTH] WHICH THE SON OF IAPETUS. Prometheus and his son were,   1:81
are and shall be gods before man had been created, and this is
according to the philosophers.

GOLDEN WAS THE FIRST AGE. Some philosophers say there were six ages,   1:89
defined by gold, silver, copper, bronze, tin and iron. Ovid mentions
only four.

[3] Ovid recounts how the zones on the celestial vault is mirrored on the newly created
earth.
[4] This explanation consists of rearranging the text in *Metamorphoses* and inserting the
weight of air compared to water, where Ovid has only air to fire and water to earth.
[5] Wrong lemma has been entered here. The explanation about the winds belong to
anohter *vix* on line 58.

1:106   ET QVE DECIDERANT. Quercus dicuntur esse sacrate Ioui, quia super illas dabat responsum in Dodona silua, in qua ipse nutritus fuit.

1:106   PATVLA, quia omnibus aperta est ad ingrediendum et respondendum.

1:113   POSTQVAM SATVRNO MISSO a Ioue uel naturaliter ad TARTARA. Ideo non facit mentionem ce*teri*, quia non fuit tam probus sicut Saturnus, 135 saturans homines.

1:111   FLVMINA IAM L<ACTIS> I<AM> F<LVMINA> NECTARIS. Nectar est purum mel et dulce, quo dicuntur frui dii, ideo scilicet, quia eterna dulcedine et leticia utuntur, et hoc est phisica.

1:117   PER HIEMES ET ESTVS. Ideo dicit pluraliter 'hiemes' et 'estus' et 140 'autumnos', quia, cum unumquodque contineat tres menses. Primus mensis ueris dicitur nouum uer, secundum adultum uer, tercium preruptum uer, et sic de omnibus aliis, scilicet primus mensis hiemis noua et sic de ceteris. Per 'auctumnos' accipit uer et auctumnum, quod similes sunt *habentes* utrumque frigus et calorem, sed 'inequales', id est 145

63rb   dissimiles, sunt, quia, cum autumnus sit in principio / sui calidus et in
1:117   fine sui frigidus, contrario modo sit in uere, et ideo dicit INEQVALES AVTVMNOS.

1:133   CARINE QVE STETERANT IN ALTIS MONTIBVS, quantum ad materiem.

1:150   ASTREA, id est Iusticia, quia quamuis homo homini inferat iniuriam, 150 tamen sequitur iusticia, quam modo nullus exhibebat.

1:180   Cesaries est hominum, a cedendo dicta. Come uero mulierum.

1:184   INNICERE ANGVIPEDVM. Gigantes pedes habuisse dicuntur anguineos surgere a terra non ualentes, et significat illos, qui semper adherent terrenis.   155

131   Et … 132 fuit] *cf. Myt. Vat. 1*, suppl. V:227: DE COLVMBIS DODONEIS Dodona ciuitas est Epiri, iuxta quam est silua que etiam Dodona dicitur habundans glandibus, quibus primi pasti dicuntur homines. Iuppiter hic dabat responsa per columbas aereas.
140   Per … 148 avtvmnos] *cf. Com. in Boetii Consol.* p. 21: Ver est in principio frigidum, quia est post hiemem et succedit hiemi et in fine calidum, quia ei succedit aestas, autumnus autem e contrario in principio calidus, quia succedit aestati, in fine frigidus, quia sequitur hiems. Dicitur autem nouus, adultus, praeruptus: in principio nouus in medio adultus in fine praeruptus. Similiter autumnus etc. | Ideo … 145 inequales] *cf.* Serv. *in Georg.* 1:43: ergo 'vere novo' et anni initio accipimus et prima parte veris. nam anni quattuor sunt tempora divisa in ternos menses, qui ipsorum temporum talem faciunt discretionem, ut primo mense veris novum dicatur ver, secundo adultum, tertio praeceps, sicut etiam Sallustius dicit ubique. item nova aestas, adulta, praeceps; sic autumnus novus, adultus, praeceps; item hiems nova, adulta, praeceps vel extrema.

131 Quercus § *adest*   **135** ceteri *correxi* celii *cod.*   **140** hiemes[1] *cum signo* h *sup. lin.*
145 habentes *correxi*, hiemes *cod.*   **150** Astrea *i.e.* Astraea   **152** Cesaries § *deest*
153 Innicere *i.e.* inicere, § *deest*

AND [ACORNS] THAT HAD FALLEN. Oaks are said to be sacred to Jupiter, 1:106
since on top of them he gave an oracle reply in the Dodonian forest,
where he was raised.

SPREADING, since it is open for all to enter and respond. 1:106

AFTER SATURN HAD BEEN SENT to TARTARUS by Jupiter or naturally. He 1:113
does not mention the rest since there was no one as good as Saturn,
satisfying man.

STREAMS NOW OF MILK NOW STREAMS OF NECTAR. Nectar is pure honey 1:111
and sweet, which the gods are said to enjoy, because they are in
possession of eternal sweetness and pleasure, and this is natural
philosophy.

THROUGH WINTERS AND SUMMERS. He says 'winters', 'summers' and 1:117
'autumns' in the plural, because each one contains three months. The
first month of spring is called new spring, the second fullgrown
spring, the third mature spring, and so with all the others, that is to
say, the first month of winter 'new' and in this way with the others. By
'autumns' he understands spring and autumn, since they are similar
holding both cold and warmth, but they are 'unequal', that is
dissimilar, since when autumn is warm in its beginning and cold
toward its end, it is the opposite with spring, and therefore he says
UNEVEN AUTUMNS.

KEELS THAT HAD STOOD UPON THE HIGH MOUNTAINS, with regard to the 1:133
material.[6]

ASTRAEA, that is Justice, since even though man brings injustice to 1:150
man, justice follows, which recently no one showed.

Caesaries (locks), is fitting for men and is said to be from *caedo* (to cut 1:180
off). *Comae* (hair) is fitting for women.

[EACH] OF THE SERPENT-FOOTED [WAS IN ACT] TO LAY. Giants are said to 1:184
have had snake-legs, not being able to rise from the ground, and this
signifies those who always cling to earthly things.

[6] The material from which the keels are made.

1:188 PER FLVMINA IVRO INFERA. Victoria filia Stigie paludis fuit, que quondam superos contra gigantes iuuit. Datum est hoc munus et matri, ne quis periuraret eas. Vel aliter: Ideo timent dii uel quilibet periurare Stigiem, quia timent, cum leticia et tristicia stant contraria, si periurauerint Stigiem ubi est tristicia, ne amissa leticia puniantur a 160 Stigie.

1:190 CVNCTA PRIVS SVNT TEMPTANDA a me, id est: Cuncta prius temptabo et non tantum te<m>ptabo, SED etiam recidam CORPVS INMEDICABILE. Hoc ideo dicit, ut postquam ostenderit, quod ubique fere regnauerit hec
1:241 | ERINIS. PVTES IN FACINVS IVRASSE. Sit constans, quod iurauit 165
1:242 perditionem humani generis.

1:211 CON<T>IGERAT NOSTRAS INFAMIA TEMPORIS. Tempus et mundus sunt
63ᵛᵃ paria, quia / finito uno finietur et aliud, et ideo 'tempus' pro 'mundo' poni potest.

1:219 CVM SERA CREPVSCVLA. Crepusculum, id est dubium inter lucem et 170 tenebras.

1:231 IN DOMINVM DIGNOSQVE ET T<ECTA> PENATES, id est lares familiares dii sunt. Lar, laris pro deo et igne ponitur. Lar, laris rex fuit Telaminorum, quem interfecit Cossus.

1:237 FIT LVPVS. Ista mutatio propinqua est ueritati, quia si umquam posset 175 fieri, taliter mutaretur.

1:255 CONCIPERET ista FLAMMAS L<ONGVS>Q<VE> A<RDESCERET> AXIS, id est linea intellegibilis ab artico polo usque ad antarticum et [de] ab oriente usque ad occidentem, quia omne uolubile, cum in utraque parte possit

156   Per … 161 Stigie] cf. Serv. in Aen. 6:134: STYGIOS LACVS Styx palus quaedam apud inferos dicitur, de qua legimus <324> di cuius iurare timent et fallere numen: quod secundum fabulas ideo est, quia dicitur Victoria, Stygis filia, bello Gigantum Iovi favisse: pro cuius rei remuneratione Iuppiter tribuit ut dii iurantes per eius matrem non audeant fallere. ratio autem haec est: Styx maerorem significat, unde απο του στυγερου, id est a tristitia Styx dicta est. dii autem laeti sunt semper: unde etiam inmortales, quia αφθαρτοι και μακαριοι, [[hoc est sine morte beati]]. hi ergo quia maerorem non sentiunt, iurant per rem suae naturae contrariam, id est tristitiam, quae est aeternitati contraria. ideo iusiurandum per execrationem habent.   177   id … 181 intellegibilem] cf. Remigius Autissiodorensis Commentum Einsidlense in Donati Artem maiorem (libri I-II sec. cod. Einsidlensem 172) p. 226,19: Axis, tribus intelligitur modis; ipsa uidelicet pars, ubi plaustrum uehitur, axis appellatur; est etiam pars caeli, i(dest) septentrio, uel linea intelligibilis a polo usque ad polum, circa quam uoluitur caelum.

156   infera post corr. ex infert ut uid.   157   contra + contra altera manus in marg.
158   periuraret correxi, penetraret cod.   159   periurare correxi, penetrare cod.
160 periurauerint correxi, penetrauerint cod.   163 temptabo correxi   164 fere cf. fera regnat Erinys Met.   165 Erinis i.e. Erinyes   167 Contigerat correxi   173 Lar² § adest   178 de delevi

I SWEAR BY THE INFERNAL STREAMS. Victoria was the daughter of the 1:188
Stygian swamp, who once helped the gods above against the giants.
This gift was given also to her mother, so that no one may swear
falsely by them. Or in another way: the gods or anyone fear to swear
falsely by Styx, since they fear that – since pleasure and sorrow are
opposite – if they should swear falsely by Styx, where sorrow is, they
would be punished by Styx so that pleasure would be lost.

ALL SHOULD FIRST BE TRIED by me, that is: I will first try everything and 1:190
I will not only try, but I will even cut away THE INCURABLE BODY. He
says this so that he later can show that almost everywhere ruled the
FURIE. YOU SHOULD DEEM IT A CONSPIRACY OF CRIME. He must be firm, 1:242
since he swore by the destruction of human kind.

THE INFAMY OF THE TIME HAD REACHED OUR [EARS]. Time and the world 1:211
are the same, since with the end of one the other will also end, and
therefore 'time' can be used instead of 'world'.

WHEN THE LATE TWILIGHTS. Twilight, that is the hesitation between 1:219
light and dark.

THE HOUSE UPON THE MASTER AND THE WORTHY PENATES, that is the 1:231
Lares, they are household gods. *Lar* is used for god and fire. *Lar* was
the king of the Telamonians, whom Cossus killed.

HE BECOMES A WOLF. This transformation is close to the truth, since if it 1:237
could ever happen, he would have transformed in such a way.

This SHOULD CATCH FIRE AND THE LONG AXIS BURN, that is a 1:255
hypothetical line from the North pole all the way to the South, and
from the east all the way to west, because everything that can turn,

uolui, in utraque parte potest habere axem, id est lineam 180
intellegibilem.

1:313   SEPARAT AEONIOS. Aeonia est regio iuxta Thebas. PHOCIS ciuitas est
que separat Thebanos AB ARVIS ACTEIS id est Atheniensibus.

1:332   EXSTANTEM ATQVE hoc MVRICE. Murex est color iuxta litora, uel color,
qui de sanguine fit piscium uidelicet conchilium.   185

1:371   INDE VBI libantes. Libo, id est assumo, id est parum de aliqua re
accipio, unde dictum est: 'libat oscula'. Nota: Sed non est
intelligendum, ut aquam biberet.

1:395   CONIVGIS AVGVRIOque Titanida, id est Pirra, de genere Titanidum nata.
63ᵛᵇ   /   190

1:408   VERSA EST IN CORPORIS VSVM, quia nullum corpus cicius corrumpitur
quam caro.

1:470   QVOD FACIT AVRATVM EST, quia qui amat, pulchrum ei uidetur. Qui
uero non amat, amor est PLVMPVM scilicet pondus.

1:513   NON EGO SVM PASTOR. Hic quattuor, que amori conueniunt - diuicias, 195
nobilitatem, sapientiam, pulchritudinem - tangit tria exponendo, sed
1:525   pulchritudinem non exponit, quia Phebum PLVRA LOCVTVRVM
Da<ph>ne FVGIT.

1:562   POSTIBVS AVGVSTIS E<ADEM> F<IDISSIMA> CVSTOS. Ad similitudinem
dicitur custos laurus, quia sicut fores custos custodit, sic laurus ante 200
fores erat propter suum bonum odorem.

1:563   MEDIAMQVE TVEBERE QVERCVM. De quercu, qua prius nobiles
coronabantur, pleps a modo coronabitur. De lauro uero tantum
nobiles, et ideo dicit 'tuebere quercum mediam', id est communem,
quia omnes communiter solebant accipere. 'Tuebere', id est, dignior 205
eris quam quercus. Et est dictum ad similitudinem, quia, qui aliquem
tuetur, dignior est illo.

1:578   NESCIA GRATENTVR. Gratulor -aris, pro 'gratias ago' hic ponitur, uel pro
'congaudeo', hoc est pro 'gaudere'.

---

184   Murex … 185 conchilium] *cf.* Isid. *Etymol.* 12:6: Murex cochlea est maris, dicta ab
acumine et asperitate, quae alio nomine conchilium nominatur, propter quod circumcisa
ferro lacrimas purpurei coloris emittat, ex quibus purpura tingitur.   **187**   libat oscula] *cf.*
Statius *Thebais* 10:61.

182 Aeonios *i.e.* Aonios   **186** libantes *cf.* libatos *Met.*   **189** Pirra *i.e.* Pyrrha   **193** quia *post*
corr. ex quondam *ut vid.*   **194**   plumpum *i.e.* plumbum   **198**   Daphne *correxi*
203 coronabantur *correxi,* coronabuntur *cod.* | pleps *i.e.* plebs   **204** mediam *post corr. ex* in
mediam *ut vid.*

since it can be turned both ways, can have an axis, that is a hypothetical line, in both directions.

SEPARATES THE AONIAN. Aonia is a region next to Thebes. PHOCIS is a city that separates the Thebans FROM THE ACTAEIAN FIELDS, that is from the Athenians. 1:313

AND RISING UP WITH this MUREX. *Murex* is the colour close to the shore, or the colour that comes from the blood of fish, namely shell-fish. 1:332

FROM THIS WHEN taking a little (*libantes*). *Libo*, that is 'to take', that is to receive a little of something, whence it is said: 'she takes kisses'. Note: But it should not be understood that he drank water. 1:371

BY THE HUSBAND'S PROPHECY and the Titanian, that is Pyrrha, born from the race of titans. 1:395

THEY WERE CHANGED FOR THE USE OF THE BODY, since no body is destroyed quicker than flesh.[7] 1:408

THE ONE THAT CAUSES IS GOLDEN, since it seems beautiful to him who loves, but for the one who does not love, love is LEAD, that is to say a burden. 1:470

I AM NO SHEPHERD. Here, he touches upon four things that go well with love - wealth, nobility, wisdom, beauty - explaining three of them, but he does not explain beauty, since Daphne FLEES from Phoebus who WAS GOING TO SAY MORE. 1:513

BY THE AUGUST DOOR-POSTS THE SAME MOST TRUSTY GUARDIAN. The laurel is said to be a guardian from its similarity, since like a guardian guards the doors, so a laurel was placed before the doors on account of its good smell. 1:562

AND YOU SHALL WATCH OVER THE MIDDLE OAK. From now on the common people will be crowned with oak, with which first the nobles were crowned. But only the nobles [are crowned] with laurel, and therefore he says 'you shall watch over the middle oak', that is the common one, since everyone used to receive it together. 'You shall watch over', that is: you shall be more worthy than the oak. And this is said from the similarity, since he who watches over someone, is more worthy than he. 1:563

NOT KNOWING [WHETHER] TO CONGRATULATE. 'To congratulate' (*gratulor*) is here used instead of 'to thank' (*gratias ago*), or instead of 'to rejoice with' (*congaudeo*), this is instead of 'to be glad' (*gaudeo*). 1:578

---

[7] Regarding rocks that are changed into human beings: The moist and the earthy parts of the rocks transforms into human flesh, which seems to be linked by the commentator to the perishability of flesh.

1:580 ERIDANVS SENEX. In Grecia potest esse fluuius huius nominis, uel iste 210
Eridanus, id est Padus, per Italiam fluens.

1:587 ATQVE ANIMO PEIORA VERETVR, id est quod sit stuprata, quod peius
64ra   esset ei quam si esset /mortua.

1:593 | QVODSI SOLA TIMES. Dico quod futurum est, scilicet TVTA eris DEO
1:594 PRESIDE si SVBIBIS S<ECRETA>.   215

1:615 VT AVCTOR DESINAT INQVIRI cuius sit, quia, si iste nominaret mentiendo
cuius esset, Iuno iret ad eum et quereret ab illo uacam sibi dari.

1:624 SERVANDAM TRADIDIT ARGO, filio Aristoris, quia bonus erat custos.

1:670 PLEIAS ENIXA EST. Pleias proprium coniugis Athlantis habentis septem
filias. Et ponitur primitiuum pro denominatiuo, sed hic est adiectiuum, 220
quia pro Maia accipitur, que Pleiadis filia fuit VII filias habentis.

1:690 INTER AMADRIADES. Amadriades sunt dee montium, Nonacrine,
possidentes nouem montes, qui sunt in Archaida. Secundum quosdam
Nonacrine dicuntur dee fontium, Naiades dee fluminum, Driades dee
siluarum.   225

1:694 RVS HABET ORTIGIAM. Ortigia est insula Delos. Asteria, soror Latone,
mutata in cotornicem et deinde in insulam, que dicitur Delos.
1:691 'Cotornix' Grece, Latine sonat 'ortix', inde Ortigia. SIRIN<GA> Grece,
Latine fistula.

1:749 PERQVE VRBES IVNCTA PARENTI TEMPLA TENET, id est ubicumque Iupiter 230
tenet templa et filius suus Epaphus habet capellas.

1:763 ORAVIT PER CAPVT SVVM ET MEROPIS filii sui. Climene post Phebum
64rb   duxit maritum /quendam Meropem, unde habuit Meropem sic

210 In … 211 fluens] *cf.* Hyg. *Fab.* 154: 2 nam cum esset propius terram uectus, uicino igni omnia conflagrarunt, et fulmine ictus in flumen Padum cecidit; hic amnis a Graecis Eridanus dicitur, quem Pherecydes primus uocauit; Serv. *in Geor.* 4:371: ERIDANVS fluvius Italiae, qui et Padus vocatur.   **223** Secundum … 225 siluarum] *cf.* Isid. *Etymol.* lib. 8:11: Nymphas quippe montium Oreades dicunt, siluarum Dryades, fontium Hamadryades, camporum Naides, maris Nereides; *Myt. Vat.* 2, 64: DE NYMPHIS Nymphe moncium dicuntur Oreades, que inter siluas habitant et arboribus delectantur, Driades, que cum arboribus nascuntur et pereunt, Amadriades, plerumque enim incisa arbore uox erumpit, sanguis emanat, uirgultorum autem et florum Napee, fontium Naides, fluminum Potamides, maris uero Nereides.   **226** Ortigia … 229 fistula] *cf.* Serv. *in Aen.* 3:73: ut autem Delos primo Ortygia diceretur, factum est a coturnice, quae graece ορτυξ vocatur

210 Grecia *post corr. ex* gentia *vel* Ingentia *ut vid.*   **212**   stuprata *correxi,* strupata *cod.*   **217** uacam *i.e.* uaccam   **219** proprium *scil.* proprium nomen   **222** Amadriades[1] *i.e.* Hamadryades   **223**   Archaida *i.e* Archadia   **226**   Ortigiam *correxi,* ortigianti *cod.*   **227** mutata *fortasse post corr. ex* mutatam | cotornicem *i.e.* coturnicem

OLD ERIDANUS. It could be a river in Greece with this name, or it is that 1:580
Eridanus, that is the Po, which flows through Italy.

AND IN HIS SOUL HE FEARS WORSE THINGS, that is that she was violated, 1:587
which would be worse for him than if she were dead.

IF YOU FEAR [TO GO] ALONE. I say that this is the future tense, namely: 1:593
you will be SAFE UNDER A GOD'S PROTECTION if you APPROACH THE
SECRET PLACES.

THAT THE CREATOR MIGHT CEASE TO BE INQUIRED ABOUT whose the cow 1:615
is, because, if he lies and says whose it is, Juno would go to him and
demand that he would give her the cow.

SHE GAVE HER TO ARGUS TO WATCH, to the son of Arestor, since he was 1:624
a good guardian.

PLEIAS BORE. Pleias is a proper noun for the wife of Atlas, who had 1:670
seven daughters. And the root-form is used for a derivative, but here it
is an adjective, since it is taken for Maia, who was the daughter of
Pleias, who had seven daughters.

AMONG THE HAMADRYADS. The Hamadryads are the goddesses of the 1:690
mountains, the Nonacrians, inhabiting the nine mountains in Arcadia.
According to some the spring goddesses are called Nonacrians, the
goddesses of rivers Naiads, the goddesses of the forests Dryads.

THE COUNTRY CONTAINS THE ORTYGIAN. Ortygia is the island Delos. 1:694
Asteria, Latona's sister, was transformed into a quail and then into an
island, which is called Delos. *Cotornix* in Greek, in Latin this signifies
ortyx, whence *Ortygia*. SYRINX in Greek, pipe (*fistula*) in Latin.[8] 1:691

AND THROUGHOUT THE CITIES [EPAPHUS] HAS TEMPLES CONNECTED TO 1:749
THE PARENT, that is wherever Jupiter has temples, his son Epaphus also
has chapels.

HE BEGGED BY HIS OWN LIFE AND THAT OF MEROPS her son's. After 1:763
Phoebus Clymene took herself a husband, a certain Merops, by whom
she had [the boy] called Merops. [BY HER] HEAD AND [THE TORCH] OF

[8] Here something seems to have gone wrong in the etymology. *Ortix* should be the
Greek word explained by *cotornix* (i.e *coturnix*, quail).

uocatum. CAPVTQVE SORORVM. Sororum scilicet Epaphi, quia Epaphi
erant sorores.   235

INCIPIT LIBER II

2:1   REGIA SOL*IS* ERAT.

2:2   Piropos est metallica species ex tribus denariis auri et sex eris. 'Pyr'
       enim Grece, Latine ignis. 'Opous' Grece, Latine uideo. Vnde piropos
       quandam similitudinem et uisionem quasi ignis pretendit.   240

2:11   DORIDAQVE ET NATAS. Secundum rei ueritatem Doris quidam rex
       Grecus fuit, qui in mari cum exercitu <u>sub</u>mersus fuit. Et ideo
       secundum fabulam Doris dicitur dea et exercitus dee.

2:26   SECVLAQVE ET P<OSITE> S<PATIIS> EQVALIBVS HORE. Hora est spatium
       donec dimidium signum oriatur et dimidium occidat.   245

2:118 IVNGERE EQVOS TYTAN V<ELOCIBVS> I<MPERAT> HORIS. Merito horis,
       quia hore per diem <u>uel per noctem</u> et per solem stant.

2:139 NEVE SINESTERIOR P<RESSAM> R<OTA> D<VCAT> AD ARAM. Ara Herculis,
       in qua Ioui sacrificabatur. Que ara in celum translata est, sed quedam
       stella est iuxta antarticum polum, que dicitur Ara, de qua Phebus hic   250
       ait.

2:153 INTEREA VOLVCRES PIROVS, id est splendens, EOVS, id est calens, ETHON
       ardens, FLEGON, id est tepescens. Qui tales equi bene attribuuntur soli,
       quia iste IIII^{or} nature sunt in sole, quia quando oritur est splendens et
       quod sequitur.   255

---

238   Piropos ... 239 ignis] *cf.* Eriugena *Glossae in Martiani,* lib. 1:162: 23. Per 'calceos'
Apollinis 'ex piropo', repercusio radiorum de terra aut de nube significatur. 01. De sex
enim aureis denariis et sex unseis argenteis efficitur piropum. 03. Opo enim uideo
dicitur, pir ignis. 03. Sic ergo piropos quasi species ignis dicitur.   **244**   Hora ... 245
occidat] *cf.* William of Conches *Dragmaticon,* 4:12: Quod ut cognoscas audi: hora est
spatium qua dimidium signum oritur. Horae uero aequinoctialis diei sibi sunt aequales,
horae uero aliarum dierum inequales. Omnis uero dies duodecim habet horas, et omnis
nox duodecim. Omni uero die sex signa oriuntur et omni nocte alia sex.

237 solis *correxi,* solus *ut uid. cod.*   **238** Piropos *i.e.* pyropus, § *deest*   **242** submersus] sub
sup. lin.   **243**   fabulam + dicitur *scr. sed postea del. cod.* | dicitur *sup. lin.* | dee + et
secundum aliam fabulam *scr. sed postea del. cod.*   **244**   Seculaque ... occidat *in marg. cum
signo insert.*   **246** Iungere *post corr. ex* iunget   **247** uel ... noctem *sup. lin.*   **248** sinesterior
post corr. ut uid.   **249**   Ioui *post corr. ex* iouis   **250**   stella *fortasse post corr. ex* stellam
252 Pirous *i.e.* Pyrois | Ethon *i.e.* Aethon

THE SISTERS. That is to say of Epaphus's sisters, since they were Epaphus's sisters.

HERE STARTS BOOK II

THE PALACE OF THE SUN WAS. 2:1

Bronze (*pyropus*) is a sort of metal, [made] of three denars of gold and six of copper. *Pyr* in Greek is fire in Latin. *Opous* in Greek, 'to see' in Latin. Whence bronze offers a similitude and an appearance of fire. 2:2

DORIS AND HER DAUGHTERS. In reality Doris was a Greek king, who was drowned in the sea with his army. Therefore, according to the story, Doris is called a 'goddess' and the army 'goddesses'.[9] 2:11

AND CENTURIES AND THE HOURS PLACED AT EQUAL DISTANCES. An hour is a period during which the half zodiac sign rises and the half sinks.[10] 2:26

TITAN COMMANDED THE QUICK HOURS TO YOKE HIS HORSES. Justly 'Hours', since hours remain throughout the day or the night and throughout [the orbit of] the sun.[11] 2:118

NOR LET THE WHEEL LEAD YOU TOO MUCH TO THE LEFT TOWARDS THE LOWERED ALTAR. Hercules' altar, on which one sacrificed to Jupiter. This altar was transferred to heaven, but there is [also] a star next to the antarctic pole that is named the Altar, of which Phoebus speaks here. 2:139

MEANWHILE THE [SUN'S] SWIFT [HORSES] PYROÏS, that is 'shining', EOÜS that is 'warming', AETHON 'burning', PHLEGON that is 'being tepid'. These kinds of horses are rightly attributed to the sun, since these four 2:153

---

[9] This seems to be an euhemeristic explanation where Doris and her daughters are thought to represent a king and his army, but the explanation is expressed in an obscure manner.

[10] About the divsion of time by the means of the zodiac signs (12 signs for 24 hours, thus half a sign for one hour).

[11] i.e. it is good that Titan assigns the job to the hours since they (as opposed to e.g. the stars) are there all the time.

2:161   SED LEVE PONDVS ERAT. Quasi diceret: Equi uelociter ibant et bene officium suum agebant, sed rector eos male regebat.

2:219   VIRGINEVSQVE DICON, quia ibi / habitabant Muse, ET NONDVM OEAGRIS
64ᵛᵃ   HEMVS. Adiectiuum pro fixo hic ponitur. OEAGRIVS pater Orphei fuit – sed oe est diptongus. Ideo dicit 'nondum Oeagris', quia Orpheus, filius 260 Oeagri, interfectus fuit a mulieribus in Hemo <u>monte</u>, unde postea dictus est mons Oeagrius consecratus Orpheo. Orpheus licet <u>dicatur</u> Apollinis filius, sicut Hercules Iouis, tamen dicitur filius Oeagrii, ut Hercules Amphitrionis.

2:239   QVERIT BOETIA DIRCEN. Licus habuit uxorem Antiopem nomine, quam 265 posuit in carcere persuadente Dirce alia coniuge super eam introducta. Sed dum esset in carcere, Iupiter ab amore eius correptus in ea genuit Amphionem et Zetum. Quibus postea querentibus quare mater illorum esset illic, responsum fuit, quod Dirce nouerca illorum fecerat. Vnde commot*i* corripientes ipsam Dircen indomitis tauris ligauerunt et 270 ita dilacerata est. Et tandem miseratione deorum in fontem uel paludem mutata est.

2:247   MIGDONIVSQVE MELAS. Migdonia et Meonia est regio iuxta Troiam, unde Homerus fuisse dicitur.

2:247   ET Trenareus EVROTAS. Trenareus est mons Laconie, ubi est descensus 275 ad inferos. 'Trene' <u>Grece</u>, id est lamentationes.

2:264   Ciclades sunt insule maris ad modum cir- / culi.
64ᵛᵇ
2:266   <u>DELPHINES, porci marini.</u>

2:267   Phoce sunt uituli.

---

265   Qverit … 272 est] *cf.* Hyg. *Fab.* 8:3: Antiopa Dirce uxori Lyci data erat in cruciatum; ea occasione nacta fugae se mandauit; deuenit ad filios suos, ex quibus Zetus existimans fugitiuam non recepit. in eundem locum Dirce per bacchationem Liberi illuc delata est; ibi Antiopam repertam ad mortem extrahebat. 5 sed ab educatore pastore adulescentes certiores facti eam esse matrem suam, celeriter consecuti matrem eripuerunt, Dircen ad taurum crinibus religatam necant.   **273** Migdonia … 274 dicitur] *cf. Pseudacronis scholia in Horatium* 1:6: MEONII CARMINIS ALITE] Homeri, qui de Meonia fuit.

258 Virgineusque § *deest* | Dicon *i.e.* elicon (Helicon) | Oeagris *i.e.* Oeagrius   **259** pro fixo *scil.* pro fixo nomine   **261** Oeagri -a- *sup. lin.* | monte *sup. lin.*   **262** dicatur *sup. lin.*   **270** commoti *correxi*, commota *cod.*   **275** Trenareus[1] *cf.* Taenarius *Met.* | Laconie *post corr. ex* licaonie | est[2] *sup. lin.*   **276** Trene *post corr. ex* tene | Grece *sup. lin.*   **278** Delphines … marini *sup. lin.*

properties are in the sun, since when it rises it is shining, and the rest follows.

BUT THE WEIGHT WAS LIGHT. As though he would say: The horses went quickly and performed their duty well, but the master steered them badly.

2:161

AND MAIDENLY HELICON, since the Muses lived there AND NOT YET OEGRIAN HAEMUS. An adjective is used for a noun. OEAGRUS was Orpheus's father – but oe is a diphtong. He says 'not yet Oeagrian', since Orpheus, Oeagrus's son, was killed by women on Mount Haemus, wherefore the mountain was called Oeagrian, consecrated to Orpheus. Even though Orpheus may be called Apollo's son, as Hercules is Jupiter's, he is nevertheless called Oeagrius's son, as Hercules is Amphitryo's.

2:219

BOEOTIA SEEKS DIRCE. Lycus had a wife by the name of Antiope, but Dirce, a second wife who had been introduced in place of Antiope, persuaded him to place Antiope in prison. But while in prison, Jupiter, seized by love for her, begot Amphion and Zetus by her. When they thereafter asked why their mother was being kept there, the response was that Dirce, their stepmother, had caused it. Wherefore the enraged sons siezed Dirce and tied her to untamed bulls and so she was torn to pieces. At last because of the compassion of the gods she was transformed into a spring or a swamp.

2:239

AND MYGDONIAN MELAS. Mygdonia and Meonia is a region next to Troy, from which Homeros is said to come.

2:247

AND Trenarian EUROTAS. Trenareus is a mountain in Laconia, where there is a descent to the underworld. *Trene* in Greek, that is 'lamentations'.

2:247

The Cyclades are completely round islands in the sea.

2:264

DOLPHINS, porpoises.

2:266

Phocae are sea-calves.

2:267

EARTH HOWEVER NOURISHING, AS SHE WAS. She has the power, namely to show that Earth can raise herself.

2:272

2:272   ALMA TAMEN T<ELLVS>, V<T> E<RAT>. Hec habet vim, scilicet ut 280
ostendat, quod Tellus potuit se extollere.

2:325   NAIADES HESPERIE TRIFIDA. Trifida dicit, quia flat, findit, urit. Hec tria
fulmen habet.

2:340   ELIADES. 'Elios' Grece, Latine sol.

2:366   EXCIPIT ET NVRIBVS. 'Nuribus' ponit pro mulieribus, partem <u>uidelicet</u> 285
pro toto.

2:397   EXCVSAT, sic dicens: O dii omnes <u>uos</u> scitis, quod non potui aliud
facere, quin fulmina mitterem.

2:416   GRACIOR HAC TRIVIE. Triuia dicitur Diana, quia in triuiis colitur, uel
quia est in celo, secundum hoc, quod dicitur Luna et in terra Diana et 290
in inferno Proserpina.

2:441   ECCE SVO COMITATA. Dictinus est mons, ubi Diana colitur. Inde
dicitur DICTINNA.

2:509   FVLSIT ET AD CANAM D<ESCENDIT> I<N> E<QVORA> THETIN. Occeani
coniugem dicit, cuius Thetidis neptis fuit coniux Pelei, mater Achillis.   295

2:510   QVORVM REVERENTIA MOVIT superos, scilicet maximam reuerentiam
feccerunt Occeano alii dii et The<tidi>.

2:527   AD VOS SI LESE T<ANGIT> C<ONTEMPTVS> ALVMPNE. Bene dicit 'alumne',
quia nutrita est Iuno, id est aer spissus, a Thetide et Occeano. Scilicet
ex humore aer spissus conficitur, et hoc secundum phisicam. Superius 300
etiam dictum est, quod Iris esset Iunonis nuntia, id est spissi aeris.
Scilicet sicut intelligitur hic spissus aer Iuno, ita et superius est
intelligendum, quia quando <u>uel quotiens</u> Iris aparet, spissus aer
designatur.

2:533   TAM NVPER PICTIS C<ESO> P<AVONIBVS> A<RGO>, quod est breuiter 305
65ʳᵃ   dicere: Tam nuper pauones Iunonis erant picti de oculis Argi, quam /
2:535   hoc fuit factum, quod tu, CORRVE, es VERSVS IN NIGRANTES ALAS.

2:539   CEDERET ANSERIBVS. Scilicet nec illi anseri, qui insonuit iuxta templum
Iunonis, *que* postea moneta dicitur, quia monuit Romanos per

---

289 uel … 291 Proserpina] *cf.* Eriugena *Annotationes in Marcianum*, p. 156: 27. 'Celo -que'
mediam terram dimisit quia nullus potest ab initio ad finem peruenire nisi per medium,
ergo Lucina dicitur in caelo, Diana in terris, Prosperpina in inferno.   **299** aer spissus] *cf.*
William of Conches *Dragmaticon*, 5:6; 5:8.   **300** Superius … 301 est¹] *cf. Met.* 1:270.

280 Alma … 281 extollere *in marg. cum signo insert.*   **284** Eliades … *in marg. cum signo
insert.*   **285** partem + p--it *sed postea del.* | uidelicet *sup. lin.*   **287** uos *sup. lin.*   **291** inferno]
in- *sup. lin.*   **292** Dictinus *i.e.* Dictynnaeus   **294** Fulsit, *correxi* fluxit *cod.*   **296** superos *cf.*
saepe deos *Met.*   **303** uel quotiens *sup. lin.*   **309** que *correxi,* quod *cod.*

THE WESTERN NAIADS BECAUSE OF THE THREE-FORKED. He says 2:325
three-forked because it blows, cleaves and burns. Lightning has these
three properties.

THE HELIADS. Helios in Greek, in Latin 'sun'. 2:340

IT RECEIVES AND TO THE BRIDES. 'Brides' is used for women, clearly as a 2:366
part for the whole (*pars pro toto*).

[JUPITER] EXCUSES, saying thus: O gods, you all know that I could not 2:397
do anything else but to throw my thunder bolts.

MORE DEAR TO TRIVIA THAN SHE. Diana is called Trivia (three-ways), 2:416
since she is worshipped at three-way-crossings (*trivium*), or because,
according to the fact that when she is in heaven she is called Luna (the
moon), Diana on earth and Proserpina in the underworld.

SEE, SHE ATTENDED BY HER [CHOIR]. Dictynnaeus is a mountain where 2:441
Diana is worshipped. From this she is called the DICTYNNAEAN.

SHE WAS GLEAMING AND DESCENDED INTO THE WATER TO WHITE TETHYS. 2:509
He means the wife of Oceanus, Tethys, whose granddaughter was the
wife of Peleus, mother of Achilles.

THE REVERENCE FOR THEM MOVED the ones above, that is to say the 2:510
other gods held Oceanus and Thetys in the greatest reverence.

BUT IF THE SCORN AGAINST YOUR WOUNDED FOSTER-DAUGHTER AFFECTS 2:527
YOU. Foster-daughter is well said, since Juno, that is thick air, was
raised by Thetis and Oceanus. That is to say thick air is created from
moisture, and this is according to natural philosophy. It has also been
said above that Iris was the messenger of Juno, that is [messenger] of
thick air. That is to say that just as thick air is understood here as Juno,
so it is also to be understood above, since when or as often as Iris
appears it refers to thick air.

THE PEACOCKS SO RECENTLY ORNAMENTED WITH THE SLAIN ARGUS, 2:533
which is a short way of saying: Just as Juno's peacocks were recently
adorned with Argus's eyes, so it happened that you, RAVEN, WERE
CHANGED INTO BLACK FEATHERS.

WAS [NOT] INFERIOR TO THE GEESE. That is to say neither to the goose 2:539
that sounded next to the temple of Juno, who is thereafter called Juno

anserem, quando Semiones Galli Romam destruebant et Capitolium 310
capere uolebant, nec illi inanimato et de argento facto, qui postea
factus <u>uel positus est in</u> templo Iunonis.

2:545 SENSIT ADVLTERIVM PHEBEIVS. <u>Coruus ideo dicitur Phebeius,</u> id est
Phebo consecratus, quia presignat tempestatem futuram, sicut et
Phebus dicit futura, preterita et presentia.   315

2:544 VEL DVM CASTA FVIT VEL INOBSERVATA, id est corrupta et non obseruata,
quia multe <u>mulieres</u> caste sunt et non tamen obseruate.

2:553 PALLAS ERICTONIVM. Dum Pallas faciebat Athenas, Vulcano complacita
est, cum qua dum uellet concumbere, sed Pallade respuente <u>uel</u>
<u>renuente</u> cecidit ex Vulcano semen in terram, unde Erictonius creatus 320
est. Sed quidam dicunt, quod Erictonius fuit gigas, qui uoluit cum
Pallade concumbere in silua. Illa uero interposuit nubem. Qui
existimans se rem habere cum ea iecit semen in terram uel in nubem,
quod illa suscipiens posuit in cista. Vnde creatus est Erictonius, iuxta
65ʳᵇ   quem posuit draconem, / qui enutriret eum.   325

2:555 GEMINO DE CE<C>ROPE NAT*IS*. Bicorpor Cecrops dicitur ideo, quia duo
regna habuit, scilicet Atheniensium et Lacedemoniorum.

2:561 APORRECTVMQVE DRACONEM. Erictonius ex inferiori parte erat draco et
hoc est, quod dicit 'aporrectumque draconem', id est dimiidietate
corporis Erictonii erat draco coniunctus.   330

2:566 AT, PVTO, NON VLTRA, non tantum, quod dixi, POTEST <u>te</u> ADMONVISSE,
NE QVERAS PERICVLA per vocem tuam, sed PVTO, quod hoc potuit te
ADMONVISSE, ne eas. Scilicet quod IPSA Pallas PETIT, pro PETIIT ME. ME,
dico, NON ROGANTEM VLTRA NEC QVICQVAM TALE, scilicet ut sim in sua
TVTELA. Et, quamuis PETIIT ME et non ego eam, tamen non ideo minus 335
repulit me a se. Solent domini in illos minus seruire, quos in sua
TVTELA esse petunt, quam illos, qui sua sponte caus*a* sue utilitatis eis
adherent. Hoc ideo dicit cornix, quod coruus ei posset obicere: O

---

310 Semiones *i.e.* Senones **312** uel … in *sup. lin.* **313** Sensit § *deest* | Coruus … Phebeius
sup. lin. **317** mulieres *sup. lin.* | mulieres caste *post corr. ex* coste sunt m<ulieres>
318   complacita *sup. lin.* uel -uit (complacuit) **319** uel … **320** renuente *sup. lin.*
320 Vulcano + cecidit *sed postea del. cod.* **326** Cecrope *correxi* | natis *correxi,* nata *cod.*
328 Aporrectumque *i.e.* apporectumque **329** dimiidietate *i.e.* dimidietate **331** te *sup. lin.*
admonvisse] -d- *sup. lin.* **333** admonvisse] -d- *sup. lin.* **337** causa *correxi,* cause *cod.*

Moneta, because, when the Senonic Gauls were destroying Rome and wanted to capture the Capitol, she warned (*moneo*) the Romans through the goose; nor to that inanimate one made of silver, which later was made or placed in Juno's temple.

THE PHOEBEAN [BIRD] SENSED THE ADULTERY. The raven is called   2:545
phoebean, that is consecrated to Phoebus, since it foretells the coming of a storm, just as Phoebus tells the future, the past and the present.

WHEN SHE WAS CHASTE OR UNDETECTED, that is corrupt and not   2:544
watched over, since many women are chaste and still not watched over.

PALLAS [ENCLOSED] ERICHTHONIUS. When Pallas made Athens she was   2:553
very pleasing to Vulcan, who wanted to sleep with her, but when Pallas rejected or refused him the semen fell from Vulcan on the ground, from which Erichthonius was created. But some say that Erichthonius was a giant, who wanted to sleep with Pallas in the forest. She placed a cloud between them. He, thinking that he was having intercourse with her, ejected his semen on the ground or into the cloud, which she took up and put in a chest. From this Erichthonius was created, next to whom she placed a snake to nurture him.

TO THE DAUGHTERS OF TWIN-BORN CECROPS. Cecrops is called   2:555
two-bodied since he had two kingdoms, namely the Athenian and the Lacedaimonian.

A SERPENT STRETCHED OUT. From the waist down Erichthonius was a   2:561
serpent and this is why he says 'a serpent stretched out', that is the serpent was joined with half of Erichthonius's body.

BUT, I BELIEVE, NOT BEYOND. Not only, CAN THIS, which I have said,   2:566
ADVISE you NOT TO SEEK OUT DANGERS with your own voice, but I BELIEVE that this could HAVE ADVISED you not to go. That is to say, the fact that Pallas HERSELF SEEKS – for sought – ME I mean, WHO IS NOT ASKING MORE AND NOT FOR ANY SUCH THING, namely that I should be in her CARE. And even though SHE SOUGHT ME and not I her, she nevertheless rejected me. Lords usually tend less to those whom they ask to be in their care than to those who freely attach themselves to them on account of their usefulness. The crow therefore says this because the raven could reproach it: "O crow, I do not fear that anything bad will come to me through my lord Phoebus, since I am very close to him."

Or, alternatively, the raven could say to it: "You approached her without being asked and therefore she rejected you." And the crow: "I

cornix, ego non timeo aliquid mali mihi fore a domino meo Phebo, quia multum familiaris ego sum ei.   340

Vel aliter posset dicere ei coruus: Tu sine rogatu accessisti et ideo proiecit te. Et cornix: Amputo, id est destituo quod dicis, quia IPSA PETIIT ME NON VLTRA, id est non mea sponte.

65ᵛᵃ   Vel aliter /dicit coruus: Obiecit te et recipiet te. Et cornix: Tu putas, quod recipiat me, sed ego PVTO, QVOD VLTRA NON PETET ME 345 NEQVICQVAM, id est in uanum, ROGANTEM TALE, id est ut recipiat me. Dicit: Si non recipit te, tunc pro infidelitate et pro fidelitate obiecit te. LICET, id est licitum est, tibi, ut QVERAS HOC A PALLADE an pro infidelitate uel fidelitate expulerit me, quia QVAMVIS sit IRATA et cetera.

2:636   'Centaurus' Grece, Latine equus dicitur.   350

2:596   SINT TIBI AIT, id est †m. a. s.† ab aliquo malo futuro te reuocante. Vel sit tibi ad malum.

2:626   VT TAMEN INGRATES, qui quamuis uidet frustra et suas artes tum FVDIT ipsa IN PECTORA O<DORES> ET D<EDIT> AMPLEXVS et PEREGIT IVSTA et INIVSTA et postquam hoc fecit.   355

2:642   ASPICIT INFANTEM. Iste puer Esculapius fuit, filius Apollinis.

2:646   POSSE DARE HOC ITERVM. Iupiter fulmine interfecit Esculapium filium Phebi.

Ipolitus fuit acusatus Theso patri suo a nouerca Phedra, quia, cum ipse puer rogatus esset ab ea, ut iaceret secum, et nollet, illa dixit 360 Theso, quod ex hoc rogata esset ab illo, sed abiecit eum. Hoc audito Theseus rogauit Neptunum, auum suum, ut esset contra Ipolitum filium suum. Ipolito postea eunti per mare Neptunus per mare ostendit phocas, id est uitulos marinos. Pro quibus e<qu>i eius exterriti duxerunt eum ad litus, ubi ipse cadens interfectus est ab eis.   365

Et quia Ipolitus dilexit castitatem, ideo Diana uirgo reducens eius
65ᵛᵇ   animam ab inferno, deprecata est Esculapium, ut suis medicaminibus /

---

339 fore *post corr. ex* forte   343 vltra + uel -o *sup. lin.* (*i.e.* uel ultro)   344 Vel aliter *bis scr. cod. sed postea del. cod.*   346 neqvicqvam *i.e.* nequiquam   349 sit *sup. lin.*   351 Sint ... fecit *in marg.*   353 et *vix legitur* | tum *vix legitur*   354 et² *vix legitur*   356 filius Apollinis *sup. lin.*   363 Ipolito *post corr. ex* ipolitii.   364 equi *correxi*

cut you off," that is, "I disregard what you say, since she personally sought me – no more," that is, "not because I asked for it."

Or alternatively the raven says: "She has reproached you and she will receive you again." And the crow: "You think she will receive me, but I THINK THAT SHE WILL NOT SEEK ME ANYMORE AT ALL," that is "in vain," "ASKING FOR SUCH A THING," that is, "that she will receive me." [The raven] says: "If she does not receive you – she reproached you back then both for infidelity and fidelity." "YOU MAY," that is you are allowed to, "ASK THIS OF PALLAS: whether she expelled me for my infidelity or my fidelity, since ALTHOUGH SHE WAS ANGERED," et cetera.[12]

Centaur in Greek. In Latin it is called 'horse'.   2:636

MAY, HE SAID, [THESE RECALLS] BE ON YOU, that is †m. a. s.† from   2:596
something bad that will happen to you who recall this. Or: may it go
badly for you.[13]

NEVERTHELESS, although he sees her limbs to no purpose, HE then   2:626
POURED THANKLESS PERFUME ON HER BREAST AND GAVE AN EMBRACE and
COMPLETED both THE DUE and UNDUE CEREMONIES and afterwards he
did this.[14]

SHE LOOKED UPON THE INFANT. This boy was Aesculapius, Apollo's son.   2:642

TO BE ABLE TO GIVE THIS A SECOND TIME. Jupiter killed Aesculapius,   2:646
Phoebus's son, with a thunderbolt.

Hippolytos was accused by his mother-in-law Phaedra in front of his father Theseus, since when as a boy he was asked by Phaedra to sleep with her and he refused, she told Theseus that he had asked her about this, but that she had rejected him. When Theseus heard this he asked Neptune, his grandfather, to act against Hippolytus, his son. Later when Hippolytos was going along the sea, Neptune brought forth *phocae*, that is sea-calves, all over the sea. The horses became terrified because of the sea-calves and carried him to the shore, where he fell and was killed by them.

And since Hippolytos loved chastity, Diana, the virgin, brought his spirit back from the underworld, she asked Aesculapius to revive him

---

[12] In this explanation two lines of dialogue between the crow and the raven in Met. is explained by rearranging the sentence in Met. and paraphrasing (the first parahprase starts after the dash, with *sed* (but), which is a synonym for *at* (but). The situation is made more difficult by the fact that the Met. text (and, as it seems, the commentary) has several different readings here, e.g. two different tenses in *petit* and *petiit*. In the second part of this explanation the commentary explores the birds relations to their masters with potential arguments and counter-arguments. In doing so it tries a new reading, namely *amputo* (I curtail) instead of *at puto* (but I think).

[13] This explanation is a marginal addition and it contains three letters (*m. a. s.*), which may be a lemma, but I have not been able to find out what they refer to.

[14] This explanation is a marginal addition and contains three words which are difficult to make out in the manuscripts.

suscitaret eum. Et quia Esculapius hoc fecit cum fulmine interfectus est
a Ioue, licet postea a Diana res<us>citatus dicatur, quia Ipolitum
res<us>citauit. Vnde Phebus iratus occidit ciclopes fabricantes fulmina 370
Iouis et inde Iupiter commotus abstulit sibi currum et exuit eum a
diuinitate et posuit eum ad custodiendos boues in domo Admeti regis
per septem annos pro penitentia. Et hoc intelligendum est *secundum*
aliam fabulam, quia secundum istam fuit ipse in domo Admeti regis
ante mortem Esculapii.   375

2:679   TVNC ADERAS ELIM. Nota, quod hic dicit Phebum exutum a diuinitate
adhuc Esculapio filio suo uiuente. Secundum uero aliam, post mortem
Esculapii Phebus diuinitatem dicitur amisisse. Hoc non est mirandum,
quia fabule quedam sic commiscentur.

2:685   PROCESSISSE BOVES. Dicit †tort† Herculem prius esse furatum sagittas 380
Phebo per nigromantiam, quam Phebus uideret Herculem boues suas
furentem. Quem cognouit, cum uellet *e*um sagitis percutere et cum
sagittas non inueniret.

2:709   MONICHIOSQVE VOLANS. Monichius fuit gigas et dicitur iuuisse in
constructione murorum Athenarum.   385

2:721   CIRCINAT AVRAS. Circ*us* est campus et inde circino, id est et circu<e>o.

2:737   PARS SECRETA DOMVS EBORE ET TESTVDINE CVLTOS. Testudo proprie est
66ra   quoddam conca- / uum, ubi aliud quoddam continetur, sed hic pro hoc
laqueari ponitur.

2:743   PLEIONESQVE NEPOS. Pleione et Pleias eadem est coniunx Athlantis.   390

2:755   EGIDA CONCVTERET. 'Ega' est apellatiuum nomen Grecum, capras
significat. 'Egis', 'egidis', deriuatiuum, id est caprina. Proprie uocatur
capra, que Iouem nutriuit in Creta. Secundum autem quasdam fabulas,
dicitur 'egis' esse theca, id est *foramen* lorice Palladis, sed sepe pro
lorica illius ponitur. Et secundum aliam fabulam, dicitur Iupiter eam in 395
celo habere et cum ea tonare.

2:757   LEMNIACAM STIRPEM. Ideo dicitur Erictonius Lemniaca stirps, quia
pater suus Vulcanus colitur in Lemno insula.

---

380 †tort†] *fortasse* Hor. *Carmen* 1:10.   392 Proprie … 396 tonare] *cf.* clm 14809, 80r: §Ega
est nomen grecum et dicitur capra §Amalctea est proprium nomen capre illius que
nutritur iouem alii dicunt egam esse tecam id est foramen lorice quod ponitur pro lorica.

369 resuscitatus *correxi* 370 resuscitauit *correxi* 373 secundum *correxi,* sed *ut vid. cod.*
376 Elim *i.e.* Elin 380 †tort† *fortasse* Oratius 382 eum *correxi,* cum *cod.* 384 Monichiosque
i.e. Munychiosque 386 auras *correxi,* aures *cod.* | Circus *correxi,* circis *cod.* | circueo
correxi 394 foramen *correxi secundum* clm 14809, foris *cod.*

with his medicines. Since Aesculapius did this Jupiter killed him with a thunderbolt, even though he is later said to have been revived by Diana, since he revived Hippolytos. Enraged by this Phoebus killed the cyclops who made Jupiter's thunderbolts and therefore the enraged Jupiter took from him his chariot and stripped him of his divinity and placed him to guard cattle in the house of King Admetus for seven years as penitence. And this can be understood according to another story since according to this one, he was in the house of King Admetus before the death of Aesculapius.

YOU WERE [NOT] PRESENT [YOU LIVED IN] ELIS. Note that here he says   2:679
that Phoebus was stripped of his divinity while his son Aesculapius was still alive. According to another version Phoebus is said to have lost his divinity after Aesculapius's death. It is not strange, since these stories are confused in this way.

THAT THE CATTLE WENT FORWARD. †ort† he says that Hercules stole the   2:685
arrows from Phoebus through necromancy, before Phoebus saw Hercules stealing his cows. When he recognized Hercules he tried to shoot him with his arrows, but he could not find them.[15]

AND FLYING [HE LOOKED DOWN ON] THE MUNYCHIAN [FIELDS].   2:709
Munychius was a giant and he is said to have aided in the construction of the walls of Athens.

HE FLEW IN CIRCLES IN THE AIR. *Circus* is a field and from this *circino* (to   2:721
round), that is *circueo* (to go around).

A SEPARATE PART OF THE HOUSE WERE [CHAMBERS] ADORNED WITH IVORY   2:737
AND TORTOISE-SHELL. Tortoise-shell is strictly speaking something concave, in which something else may be contained, but here it is used for the panelled ceiling.

GRANDSON OF [ATLAS] AND PLEIONE. Pleione and Pleias is the same,   2:743
Atlas's wife.

SHOOK THE AEGIS. *Ega* is a Greek common noun, it means goats. *Aegis*   2:755
is a derivative, that is 'pertaining to goats'. Strictly speaking the goat that nurtured Jupiter on Crete is called thus. According to other stories, *aegis* is said to be a case, that is the opening of Pallas' cuirass, but it is often used for her cuirass. And according to another story Jupiter is said to have this in heaven and to make thunder with it.

THE LEMNIAN OFFSPRING. Erichthonius is called the Lemnian offspring,   2:757
since his father, Vulcan, is worshipped on the island Lemnos.

---

[15] The word †ort† may refer to Oratius (Horace).

2:802   NEVE MALI CAVSE. 'Cause' uocat presentiam bonorum Herse<s>. Que
        presentia fuit causa, id est cur malum infortunium passa sit Aglauros.   400
2:803   Et, ne presentia illa abesset per longum spatium temporis, ideo posuit
        ANTE OCVLOS.

2:844   VBI MAGNI FILIA REGIS. 'Regis', id est Agenoris, qui rex erat tam Tiri
        quam Sidonis.

2:846   MAIESTAS ET AMOR NON BENE C<ONVENIVNT>. Per hoc, quod sequitur,   405
        manifestum est, quod non bene conueniunt maiestas et amor.

2:848   ILLE PATER RECTORQVE DEVM C<VI> D<EXTRA> T<RISVLCIS>. Ideo fulmen
        dicitur Iouis esse trisulcus ignis, quia habet tres naturas, scilicet urit,
        secat et splendet.

2:850 | INDVITVR FACIEM TAVRI. Hic Ouidius plane Iouem / deridet, non   410
66rb   credens illum esse summum deum, sicut et alii philosophi non
        credebant, sed propter impera[re]tores sic locuti sunt dicentes Iouem
        esse summum deum.

2:854   COLLA TORIS EXSTANT. 'Thoros' uocat neruos circa collum.

2:854   ARMIS PALEARIA PENDENT. Palear est pellis a pendendo dicta.   415

INCIPIT LIBER <III>

3:13   BOETIAQVE ILLA VOCATO. Boetia uocat terram, ubi sunt Thebe.

3:14   VIX inde CASTALIO. Castalis est fons in Parnaso monte.

3:32   MARTIVS ANGVIS ERAT. Omne bellorum subditur Marti et ideo anguis
        iste, bellicosus cum esset, dicitur Martius.   420

3:32   CRISTIS ET AVRO, id est aureis cristis.

3:34   TRESQVE MICANT LINGVE. Ideo serpens tres dicitur linguas habere, quia
        nimis uelocissime emittit et retrahit linguam, uel ideo quia tres habet
        pilos in ea.

3:34   TRIPLICI STANT ORDINE DENTES. Non stant triplici dentes ordine, sed   425
        ideo hoc dicit, ut magnitudinem eius exageret.

3:88   PLAGAMQVE SEDERE, id est manere, uel non sinebat plagam profundam
        esse.

3:101   ECCE VIRI FAVTRIX, id est Pallas ostendit, quod per sapientiam suam
        usque potest sibi consulere positus in timore.   430

---

399 Herses *correxi*   405 Maiestas § *deest*   410 Induitur § *deest*   412 imperatores *correxi*
415 Palear § *adest*   416 III *supplevi*   418 inde *cf.* bene *Met.*   425 ordine[1] *in marg.*

AND SO THAT REASONS FOR GRIEF WOULD NOT. He calls the presence of   2:802
Herse's good fortune 'reasons'. This presence is the reason, that is why
Aglauros suffered bad misfortunes. And lest this presence should be
absent for a long period of time, she placed them BEFORE HER EYES.[16]

WHERE THE GREAT KING'S DAUGHTER. 'The king's', that is Agenor's, who   2:844
was king of Tyre as well as of Sidon.

MAJESTY AND LOVE DO NOT GO WELL TOGETHER. Through what follows it   2:846
is made clear that majesty and love do not go well together.

HE, THE FATHER AND RULER OF THE GODS, IN WHOSE RIGHT HAND A   2:848
THREE-FORKED. Jupiter's lightning is said to be a three-forked fire, since
it has three characteristics, namely it burns, it cuts and it shines.

HE ASSUMED THE FORM OF A BULL. Here Ovid clearly makes fun of   2:850
Jupiter. He does not believe that Jupiter is the highest god, just as other
philosophers did not believe this, but on account of the emperors who
said that he was the highest god, they said this.

THE NECK IS THICK WITH MUSCLES. He calls the tendons around the neck   2:854
'muscles'.

THE DEW-LAP HANGS FROM THE SHOULDERS. The dew-lap (*palear*) is the   2:854
skin (*pellis*), said to derive from 'to hang' (*pendere*).

HERE STARTS BOOK [III]

AND CALL IT BOEOTIA. He calls the land where Thebes is Boeotia.   3:13

BARELY FROM THE CASTALIAN [CAVE]. Castalis is a spring on mount   3:14
Parnassus.

A MARTIAL SNAKE. Everything belonging to wars is subject to Mars and   3:32
therefore this snake, since it is warlike, is called martial.

WITH CRESTS AND WITH GOLD, that is with golden crests.   3:32

THREE TONGUES FLICKED. The serpent is said to have three tongues,   3:34
since it sticks out and retracts the tongue very quickly, or since it has
three hairs on it.

THE TEETH STAND IN A TRIPPLE ROW. The teeth do not stand in a triple   3:34
row, he says this to exaggerate its size.

THE THRUST TO BE SETTLED, that is 'to remain', or it (the serpent) does   3:88
not allow the thrust to be deep.

BEHOLD, THE MAN'S PROTECTRESS, that is Pallas shows that through her   3:101
wisdom he, full of fear, can make provisions for himself.

---

[16] Envy provokes Aglauros to misery with images of her sister Herse's happiness.

3:111   SIC VBI TOLLVNTVR FESTIS AVLEA THEATRIS. Iulius Cesar deuictis
Britannis quosdam captiuos Romam duxit et ad facienda aulea theatri
66ᵛᵃ   illo constituit. Et dum faciebant aulea ibi suas imagines pingebant, / ut
esset signum, quod Britanni ea aulea exhinc pro debito essent facturi.

3:126   QVINQVE SVPERSTITIBVS Q<VORVM> F<VIT> V<NVS> ETHION. Ogigius   435
etiam fuit unus de V superstitibus, qui iuu<i>t facere Thebas, inde
Bachus dicitur Ogigius Thebanus.

3:132   SOCERI TIBI MAR[I]SQVE VENVSQVE. Hermione est. Fuit filia Martis et
Veneris et coniunx Caducei. Caduceus est uirga Mercurii.

[Monichosque. Monichus fuit gigas et dicitur iuuisse in   440
constructionem murorum athenarum.]

3:253   RVMOR EST IN AMBIGVO, id est fama erat de morte Acteonis, sed tamen
dubitatio erat, an bene fecisse an male. Quidam laudabant et quidam
non.

3:256   SOLA CONIVNX IOVIS et NON TAM ELOQVITVR, an PROBET, an CVLPET   445
QVAM GAVDET CLADE, hoc est non eloquitur, ut uel culpet uel laudet,
sed gaudet.

3:269   FERT VTERO ET MATER QVOD VIX MIHI CONTIGIT VNI uel VNO. Si
dixerimus, quod Iuno dicat 'uix mihi contigit uni' Iunoni, ut essem
mater de Ioue, cum alie plures fuerint matres, tunc dicemus, quod   450
Ouidius non caret peruertere fabulas. Vel 'contigit mihi in [i]uno', id
est in Vulcano, quem de Ioue habuit, ut esset mater.

Dicitur de lactuca comedisse, et inde Hebem genuisse. Hebe dicitur
translata in celum, ut Iouis pincerna esset, sed quia, secundum rei
66ᵛᵇ   u<er>itatem, de aliquo adultero illam Hebem habuit Iuno, ideo a Ioue /   455
expulsa fuit et in loco eius Ganimedes, filius Troili, positus fuit.

431   Iulius … 434 facturi] *cf.* Serv. *in Georg. 3:25*: PVRPVREA INTEXTI TOLLANT
AVLAEA BRITANNI hoc secundum historiam est locutus. nam Augustus postquam
vicit Britanniam, plurimos de captivis, quos adduxerat, donavit ad officia theatralia.
dedit etiam aulaea, id est velamina, in quibus depinxerat victorias suas et
quemadmodum Britanni, ab eo donati, eadem vela portarent, quae re vera portare
consueverant: quam rem mira expressit ambiguitate, dicens 'intexti tollant'; nam in velis
ipsi erant picti, qui eadem vela portabant. aulaea autem dicta sunt ab aula Attali regis, in
qua primum inventa sunt vela ingentia, postquam is populum Romanum scripsit
heredem.   **453**   Dicitur … genuisse] *cf. Myt. Vat. 1, 201:55*: Eben genuit Iuno de Ioue,
secundum quosdam de lactuca.

431 theatris *cum signo h sup. lin.*   **435** Ethion *i.e.* Echion   **436** iuuit *correxi*   **438** Marsque
correxi   **439** Caduceus § *adest*   **440** Monichosque … 441 athenarum *delevi (cf. 65ᵛᵇ)*
451 uno *correxi*   **453** lactuca *correxi,* laduca *cod.*   **455** ueritatem *correxi*

SO WHEN THE CURTAINS ARE LIFTED IN THE FESTIVE THEATRES. After the   3:111
Britons had been conquered Julius Caesar brought some prisoners to
Rome and ordered curtains to be made for the theatre. While they
made these curtains they painted their pictures on it, so that it would
be a sign that the Britons were to make these curtains hereafter on
account of their debt.

FOR THE FIVE REMAINING, ONE OF WHICH WAS ECHION. For Ogygius was   3:126
one of the five that had survived, he who helped build Thebes, from
this Bacchus is called the Theban Ogygius.

MARS AND VENUS HAVE BECOME YOUR PARENTS-IN-LAW. This is   3:132
Hermione. She was the daughter of Mars and Venus and the wife of
Caduceus. Caduceus is the staff of Mercury.

<Monychean. Monychus was a giant and he is said to have helped
with the construction of the walls of Athens.[17]>

THE RUMOUR WAS UNCERTAIN, that is there was a rumour about the   3:253
death of Actaeon, but yet there was some hesitation about whether she
had done good or bad. Some praised [her] and some not.

ONLY JUPITER'S WIFE DID NOT SPEAK SO MUCH TO APPROVE or TO BLAME,   3:256
AS SHE REJOICED IN THE DISASTER, that is she does not speak so as to
blame or praise, but she rejoices.

SHE CARRIES IN THE WOMB AND [WISHES TO BE MADE] A MOTHER, WHICH   3:269
HAS BARELY HAPPENED TO ME ALONE (UNI) or WITH ONE (UNO). If we say
that Juno says 'which has barely happened to me, Juno, alone' (uni)
that I have been made a mother from Jupiter, although many others
have been made mothers - then we will say that Ovid does not abstain
from corrupting the stories. Or [Juno says] 'that has happened to me
with one' (uno), that is with Vulcan, whom she had from Jupiter, so
that she is a mother.

She is said to have eaten lettuce and from this to have given birth to
Hebe. Hebe is said to have been transferred to heaven, to be Jupiter's
cupbearer, but since Juno, according to reality, had Hebe from some

---

[17] This explanation appears to be wrongly places. It is an exact copy of the explanation to
II,709 found on 65[vb].

3:397   ADDVCITQVE CVTEM M<ACIES> ET I<N> A<ERA> SVCCVS. [hic] Hic
intelligitur aerem confici ex succo.

3:572   ECCE CRVENTATI REDEVNT. 'Cruentati' dicuntur, quia q<u>osdam ex
Bachi seruis multum tormentauerant.   460

3:665   SERPVNT ET in GRAVIDIS D<ISTINGVVNT> V<ELA> CORIMBI<S>. Corimbi
sunt uue hederarum.

Bachus de India cum suo exercitu regrediens per Libiam rogauit in
Libia sicienti suo exercitu Iouem, patrem suum, ut aquam preberet.
Qui aparens in similitudine arietis fontem filio Bacho ostendit et ideo   465
Bachus templum ei ibi fecit, qui Amon in illa lingua dicitur, in quo
Iupiter cornutus in specie arietis pingitur. Bachus uero pingitur ibi, si
4:19   non cornibus tamen, et ideo VIRGINEVM CAPVT EST TIBI CVM ADSTAS SINE
CORNIBVS. Dicitur Bachus 'cornutus', quando iratus et cum ad pugnam
tendit.   470

Theseus Egei filius fuit et Thetidis, matris Achillis, qui, dum per
sortem missus fuit Minoo regi Corete insule, cepit ei minari iactans se
esse Thetidis filium. Vnde Minos iratus proiecit anulum suum in mare
et dixit Theseo: Nisi eum reddideris mihi, non es filius Thetidis et non
eris inpunitus. His dictis iuit Theseus super litus maris. Rogauit   475
matrem suam, ut anulum regis sibi redderet. Mater uero statim
67ra   reddidit et insuper coronam / ei dedit, quam postea dedit Adriane.
Quam postea coronam Bachus pro honore Adrianes in celum
transtulit. Hoc est <quod> sanctus Ieronimus testatur.

463   Bachus ... 467 pingitur[1]] *cf.* Hyg. *Fab.* 133: HAMMON> Liber in India cum aquam
quaereret nec inuenisset, subito ex harena aries dicitur exiisse, quo duce Liber cum
aquam inuenisset, petit ab Ioue ut eum in astrorum numerum referret, qui adhuc hodie
aequinoctialis aries dicitur. in eo autem loco ubi aquam inuenerat, templum constituit
quod Iouis Hammonis dicitur.   **479**   Hoc ... testatur] *cf.* Hyg. *Astr.* 2:5: Simili de causa
Theseus sine ulla precatione aut religione parentis in mare se proiecit; quem confestim
delphinum magna multitudo mari provoluta lenissimis fluctibus ad Nereidas perduxit, a
quibus anulum Minois et a Thetide coronam quam nuptiis a Venere muneri acceperat
retulit, compluribus lucentem gemmis. Alii autem a Neptuni uxore accepisse dicunt
coronam; quam Ariadne Theseus dono dicitur dedisse, cum ei propter virtutem et animi
magnitudinem uxor esset concessa; hanc autem post Ariadnes mortem Liberum inter
sidera collocasse.

457 hic *delevi, bis scr. cod.* | Hic § *adest*   **459** quosdam *correxi*   **461** corimbis *correxi*
464 sicienti *i.e.* sitienti   **468** adstas *correxi*, actas *cod.*   **471** Theseus § *adest*   **472** Corete *i.e.*
Crete   **477** Adriane *i.e.* Ariadne   **479** quod *addidi*

sort of adultery, she was banished by Jupiter and Ganymede, Troilus's son, was put in her place.

AND THINNESS WRINKLES THE SKIN AND THE MOISTURE [GOES] INTO THE AIR. Here it is to be understood that the air is made from moisture.   3:397

BEHOLD, THE BLOODIED RETURN. They are called 'bloodied', since they had gravely tortured some of Bacchus' servants.   3:572

THEY CREEP UP AND THE SAILS ARE ADORNED WITH HEAVY CLUSTERS. Clusters are the fruits of the ivy.   3:665

When Bacchus returned from India with his army through Libya he asked Jupiter, his father, to provide water for his army, who was thirsting in Libya. Jupiter, appearing in the guise of a ram, showed his son Bacchus a spring and for this reason Bacchus made him a temple there, in which Jupiter, called Hammon in their language, is portrayed with horns in the shape of a ram. Bacchus is portrayed there, but not with horns and therefore YOUR HEAD IS VIRGINLIKE WHEN YOU STAND HERE WITHOUT HORNS. Bacchus is called 'horned' when he is angered and goes to battle.   4:19

Theseus was the son of Egeus and Thetys, Achilles' mother. When he after a drawing of lots was sent to king Minos on the island of Crete, he started to threaten him bragging that he was the son of Thetys. Angered by this Minos threw his ring into the ocean and said to Theseus: 'If you do not retrieve this to me, you are not the son of Thetys and you shall not go unpunished'. After this had been said Theseus went to the seashore. He asked his mother to retrieve the king's ring for him. His mother immediately brought him the ring and furthermore she gave him a crown, which he later gave to Ariadne. This crown Bacchus later transferred to heaven in honour of Ariadne. This is testified by St Jerome.

LIBER IV   480

4:33   INTEMPESTIVA MINERVA. Minuerua quondam est dea lane, ideo ponitur
pro lana. 'Intempestiua', id est non apto tempore uel congruo
adaptata.

4:199   SPECTANDIQVE MORA B<RVMALES> PORRIGIS, id est prolongas, HORAS, id
est noctes significat, unde noctes sint inequales, que prius fuerant 485
equales diebus, †sed quondam diciturt.

4:291   NOMEN QVOQVE †sit† A<B> ILLIS. Filius Mercurii et Veneris dicitur
Hermafraditus. Hermes, id est interpres. Mercurius fuit domini
interpres ferens etiam [in]iussa patris Iouis. 'Afrodis' dicitur spuma.
Quando Saturnus Celei, patris sui, subsecuit uirilia et in mare proiecit, 490
de illa spuma in mare concreta Venus fuit creata. Secundum aliam
fabulam filia Iouis et Dione fuit. Ophion pater fuit Celei, Celeus
Saturni, Saturnus Iouis.

4:331   Apricus et Aprilis ab 'aperio' dicuntur. Hic uero dicitur APRICA
frondosa.   495

4:333   CVM FRVSTRA RESONANT ERA A<VXILIARIA> LVNE. Quedam gentes, cum
uident lunam eclipsin pati, putant Thesalicas mulieres eam incantare,
ut descendens ad terras spuat in herbas, de quibus maleficium faciunt.
Et ideo accipiunt et percutiunt illa, ut luna non audiat incantantionem
67ᵗᵇ   illarum Thesalicarum. Sed 'frustra' hoc / faciunt, cum luna non 500
incantationes illarum paciatur. Vel 'frustra', quia licet percutiuntur
aera, tamen descendit luna ad terram per incantationem, ut spuat in
herbas.

4:409   Ne QVA PERDIDERINT VETEREM. Contra si posset dici, certim dicis
qualiter ista membra sint mutata, sicut de Licaone et quibusdam aliis. 505
Respondit: Ideo, quia in tenebris mutate sunt.

489   Afrodis ... spuma] *cf.* Fulg. *Myt.* 2:1: Unde et Afrodis dicta est - afros enim Grece
spuma dicitur -, siue ergo quod sicut spuma libido momentaliter surgat et in nihilum
ueniat, siue quod concitatio ipsa seminis spumosa sit.   **491**   Secundum ... 492 fuit¹] *cf.*
Hyg. *Fab.* 19:57: Ex Dione et Ioue, Venus.

480   IV *fortasse altera manus add.*   **485**   significat] fing- *ut vid.*   **487**   si *cf.* traxit *Met.*
488   Hermafraditus *i.e.* Hermaphroditus   **489**   iussa *correxi*   **490**   mare *pro* mari
499   accipiunt *correxi*, aeripiunt *ut vid. cod.*, aera capiunt *Meiser, p. 84*   **504**   Ne *cf.* nec *Met.*
Contra *incerte* (cc/tt *ut vid.*)

BOOK IV

UNTIMELY MINERVA. 'Minerva' is sometimes the goddess of wool, therefore she may be used in place of wool. 'Untimely', that is not adapted to a fit or suitable time.   4:33

THROUGH A DELAY TO SEE [HER] YOU STRETCH OUT, that is you prolong, THE WINTRY HOURS, that is it signifies the nights, whence nights, which before were equal to the days, may be uneven, †sed quondam diciturt.[18]   4:199

AND ALSO THE NAME [HE DREW] FROM THEM. The son of Mercury and Venus is called Hermaphroditus. Hermes, that is messenger. Mercury was the messenger of the lord carrying also the commands of his father, Jupiter. *Afrodis* means foam. When Saturn cut off the manhood of Celeus, his father, and threw it in the ocean, Venus was created from this foam that had hardened in the ocean. According to another story she was the daugher of Jupiter and Dione. Ophion was Celeus's father, Celeus Saturn's, Saturn Jupiter's.   4:291

Apricus (sunny, sheltering) and *Aprilis* (April) are named from *aperio* (to open). But here APRICA means leafy.   4:331

THE MOON, WHEN HELPBRINGING COPPER RESOUNDS IN VAIN. When some people see the moon undergo an eclipse, they believe that Thessalian women bewitch it so that when descending to the ground it spits on the grass, from which they make a poison. And therefore the people grab and strike this [copper], so that the moon will not hear the incantations of the Thessalians. But they do this 'in vain', since the moon does not suffer their incantations. Or 'in vain', since they strike the copper and still the moon descends to the earth to spit on the grass because of the the incantations.   4:333

And [THE DARKNESS WILL NOT ALLOW THEM TO KNOW] IN WHAT [WAY] THEY HAVE LOST THEIR OLD [SHAPE]. On the contrary, if this could be told, one would certainly tell how these limbs were transformed just as   4:409

---

[18] The last phrase in this explanation appears corrupted. It reads 'but once it was said' (*sed quondam dicitur*). There could be words missing after this phrase.

4:457   VISCERA prebet TICIVS. Ticius quidam gigas fuit, qui cum Latona concumbere uoluit. Quem per scorpionem Latona interfecit. Qua de causa apud inferos talem patitur penam, quod uultur iecur eius commedit. Vel Phebus interfecit eum, cum esset filius Latone.   510

4:458   TIBI, TANTALE, NVLLE D<EPRENDVNTVR> A<QVE>. Tantalus, filius Iouis et pater Pelopis, inuitauit deos ad conuiuium et filium suum, Pelopem, ad commedendum eis prebuit uolens diuinitatem eorum probare. Pallas preueniens ceteros deos commedit humerum Pelopis. Et, cum omnes uenissent, Iupiter eam carnem humanam esse cognouit et non   515
commederunt. Et pro humero commesto eburneum humerum fecerit. Qua de causa Tantalus in inferno positus est. Habens sub guture furcam, non potuit bibere de aqua, que tangit barbam illius, neque commedere de pomis nasum tangentibus, quia, cum accipere uult illa cum ore, f[i]ugiunt sursum.   520

4:460 | AVT PETIS AVT VRGES R<EDITVRVM>, SISIPHE. Sisyphus cum Dia- / na
67va   concumbere uoluit. Ideo apud inferos saxum uoluit. Vel Sisiphus socerum suum ad conuiuium inuitauit. Quem uenientem, cum oscularetur, in antrum uiuis plenum carbonibus fraudulenter precipitauit. Et ideo saxum uoluit.   525

---

507   Ticius … 510 Latone] *cf. Myt. Vat. 2, 125*: DE TICIONE Ticion Terre filius fuit, qui tante fuit magnitudinis ut amplitudine sui corporis viiii iugera occuparet. Hic amauit Latonam propter quod Apollinis confixus est sagittis et dampnatus hac lege apud inferos ut uultur renascentibus semper fibris eius iecur exedat.   **511**   Tantalus … 520 sursum] *cf. Myt. Vat. 2, 124*: DE TANTALO Tantalus rex Corinthiorum amicus numinibus fuit, que cum frequenter susciperet et quodam tempore defuissent epule, uolens diuinitatem eorum temptare inuitatis filium suum Pelopem occidens epulandum apposuit. Tunc abstinentibus cunctis Ceres humerum eius exedit, quem cum dii per Mercurium reuocare ad superos uellent, eburneus est ei humerus restitutus. Ideo autem sola Ceres dicitur comedisse quia ipsa est terra que corpus resoluit ossa tantum reseruans. Per Mercurium autem fingitur ob hoc reuocatus quod ipse est deus prudentie. Tantalus autem hac lege apud inferos dicitur esse dampnatus ut in Eridano inferorum stans nec undis presentibus nec uicinis eius pomariis fame deficiens perfruatur. **521**   Sisyphus … 525 uoluit] *cf. Myt. Vat. 2, 127*: DE SISIPHO Cum inter duo maria, Sisipheum uidelicet et Lecheum, positum montem Sisiphus crudeli latrocinio occupasset, homines pretereuntes ingens saxum super eos precipitando solitus erat necare, quod scelus luendo dicitur apud inferos contra montis uerticem saxum uoluere quo semper relapso nunquam uoluendi labore quiescere.

507 prebet *cf.* praebebat *Met.* | Ticius *i.e.* Tityos | Latona *post corr. ex* -latona   **514** Pelopis *correxi*, pelapis *cod.*   **520** fugiunt *correxi*   **521** Sisyphus § *adest*   **522** uoluit[2] *correxi* uollut *cod.*

with Lycaon and certain others. He responds: since they were transformed in darkness.

TITYOS offers HIS INNARDS. Tityos was a giant who wanted to sleep with Latona. Latona killed him with a scorpion. For this reason he suffers the punishment in the underworld that a vulture eats his liver. Or Phoebus killed him, since he was the son of Latona. 4:457

NO WATER IS CAUGHT BY YOU, TANTALUS. Tantalus, Jupiter's son and Pelops's father, invited the gods to a feast and offered to them his son Pelops, to eat, because he wanted to test their divinity. Pallas arrived before the others and ate Pelops's shoulder. When everyone had arrived Jupiter realised that it was human flesh and they did not eat. And in place of the eaten shoulder that had been eaten he made an ivory shoulder. For this reason Tantalus was placed in the underworld. Since he had a pole under his throat he could not drink from the water that touched his beard, and he could not eat from the apples touching his nose, since they escaped upwards when he wanted to take them with his mouth. 4:458

YOU EITHER FETCH OR PUSH THE RETURNING [ROCK], SISYPHUS. Sisyphus wanted to sleep with Diana. Therefore he rolls a rock in the underworld. Or Sisyphus invited his father-in-law to a feast. When he came and they kissed, he deceitfully threw him down into a cave full of burning coal. And therefore he rolls the rock. 4:460

4:461   VOLVITVR ISION. Ision sec<r>etarius Iouis fuit, qui uolens cum Iunone
concu<m>bere. Ipsa apposuit ei nubem in speciem sui, in qua ipse
semen suum fundens. Nati sunt qui 'nubigene' uel Yxiones appellati
sunt. Quapropter rote alligatus est.

4:463   ASIDVE REPETVNT QV*AS* PERDANT BELIDES VNDAS. De semine Beli natus   530
est Egistus et Danaus. Cuius Danai asensu quinquaginta filie sue
acceperunt uiros quinquaginta filios Egisti. Et eos omnes interfecerunt,
excepta una, que uirum suum interficere noluit. Pro hoc peccato fas
sine fundo de aqua implere debe<n>t.

4:501   ET VIRVS ECHINNE. Echinna est serpens, que solo a flatu necat.   535

4:502   ERRORESQVE VAGO<S>. Per talia integumenta et inuolucra nihil aliud
nobis dicit, nisi quod fecit eos furere.

4:505   COXERAT ERE CAVO. Que in ere coquuntur, peiora sunt quam que in
alia re.

4:509   CONSEQVITVR MOTOS. Inuolucione consecuta est fax ignis. Vnde   540
intelligendum est, quod eos acce<n>dit ad furorem. Non est
67vb   intelligendum, quod fa- / cem proiecisse[n]t super illos, sed, cum illa
est accensa, accendit illos.

4:510   SIC VICTRIX I<VSSI>QVE P<OTENS> AD INANIA REGNA. Ideo dicit 'inania',
quia umbre sunt ibi sine corporibus.   545

4:641   SIVE ES MIRATOR RERVM, id est qui uelis mira audire, MIRABERE NOSTRAS
res. Ego possum tibi mira referre de Gorgone et aliis rebus.

4:667   MOTIS TALARIBVS. Talaria sunt calciamenta pennata.

4:671   ANDROMEDAN PENAS. Cepheus rex habuit coniugem Casiope<m>, que
dixit se pulcriorem esse Iunone uel deabus marinis. Pro quo peccato   550
belua exiens mare commedebat suum regnum. Iudicauit Iupiter, ut

---

526   Ision² ... 529 est] *cf. Myt. Vat. 2, 128*: DE IXIONE Ixion Phlegie filius imperator
Laphitarum Thessalie gentis amicissimus Ioui cum misericordia eius in celum translatus
fuisset, Iunonem de stupro interpellare ausus est. Que de audacia eius conquesta Ioui
suadente ipso pro se Nubem ei opposuit cum qua Ixion concubuit unde geniti sunt
Centauri. Reuersus autem ad mortales Ixion gloriatus est se cum Iunone concubuisse, ob
quam causam Iuppiter eum fulmine percussit et ad rotam serpentibus circumfusam
apud inferos uoluendum ligauit.   **528**   Nati ... 529 sunt] *cf. Met.* 12:209; *Serv. in Aen.*
8:293: NVBIGENAS de Ixione et Nube procreatos Centauros, ut superius diximus.

526 Ision² *i.e.* Ixion | secretarius *correxi*   **527** concumbere *correxi* | ipse *fortasse post corr.*
ex ipsa   **530** Asidue *i.e.* ass-/adsidue | quas *correxi,* quos *cod.*   **531** asensu *i.e.* assensu
533 fas *pro* vas   **534** debent *correxi*   **535** Echinna *i.e.* Echidna | necat *post corr. ex* neca
536 uagos *correxi*   **540** motos § *adest*   **541** accendit *correxi*   **542** proiecisset *correxi*
549 Casiopem *correxi*   **551** mare *pro* mari

IXION SPINS. Ixion was Jupiter's secretary, who wanted to sleep with   4:461
Juno. She placed a cloud in the shape of herself before him, into which
he poured his seed. And the ones called 'the cloudborn' or Ixiones
were born. For this he was tied to a wheel.

THE INCESSANT BELIDES SEEK AGAIN THE WATER THAT THEY LOSE.   4:463
Aegistus and Danaus were born from the seed of Belus. With Danaus's
approval his fifty daughters took as their husbands Aegistus's fifty
sons. And they murdered them all, except for one [daughter] who did
not want to murder her husband. For this sin they must fill a vase
without bottom with water.

AND THE ECHIDNA'S POISON. Echidna is a serpent that kills with its   4:501
breath alone.

AND VAGUE DELUSIONS. By such obscure expressions and veiled   4:502
utterances he tells us nothing else than that it made them mad.

SHE COOKED IN THE HOLLOW COPPER. Things cooked in copper are   4:505
worse than those cooked in something else.

SHE REACHES MOVING [FIRES]. The firebrand is the result of an allegory.   4:509
From which it should be understood that she kindled their fury. It
should not be understood that she had thrown the torch over them,
but, when she was incited, she incited them.

THUS VICTORIOUS AND SUCCESSFUL WITH [HER] COMMAND [SHE RETURNS]   4:510
TO THE EMPTY KINGDOMS. He says 'empty' because the shadows were
without bodies there.

OR IF YOU ARE AN ADMIRER OF DEEDS, that is one who wishes to listen to   4:641
marvellous things, YOU SHALL MARVEL AT OUR things. I can tell you
wonderous stories about the Gorgon and other things.

WITH MOVING TALARIA. *Talaria* are winged shoes.   4:667

THAT ANDROMEDA [SHOULD PAY] THE PENALTY. King Cepheus had a   4:671
wife, Cassiope, who said she was more beautiful than Juno or the sea
goddesses. For this sin a monster came from the sea and devoured his

filiam suam Andromedam daret belue ad commedendum, et sic homines ulterius non commederentur.

4:750   NVNC QVOQVE CORALIIS. Coralii sunt species, que petra rubea est. Et est gracilis in modo subtilis uirge et iuxta mare inuenitur. Iste autem 555 fabulose dicit, quod sub aqua est uirga, super aqua petra.

4:786   PEGASON ET FRATRES. Pegasus et multi serpentes nati sunt de sanguine Gorgonis.

4:801   NVNC QVOQVE, VT ATTONITOS non solum MVTAVIT crines IN IDROS, sed etiam nunc fert idros IN PECTORE ADVERSO. Perseus pro constanti 560
68ʳᵃ   habebat, quod daturus erat Palladi caput Gorgonis. / Ideo dicit quod iam ferebat 'in pectore', id est in lorica, que antiquitus tantum in pectore habebatur. Vel Ouidius non curauit ordinem.

5:19   EX ILLO TEMPORE RAPTA EST TIBI QVO PERITVRA FVIT, et ideo quiescere debes, NISI ita sis CRVDELIS, ut exigas ID IPSVM, scilicet VT PEREAT et 565 cetera.

INCIPIT LIBER V

5:347   TRINACRIS. Dicitur Sicilia 'Trinacris', quia habet tria acr[i]a, scilicet Sillam, que de animali facta lapis, in quo naues illic dimittuntur, et Caripdis et Ethma. Vel quia habet tria promontoria super tres portus 570 suos, uel a tribus questibus portuum, qui magni ibi esse solent.

5:352   DEGRAVAT ETHMA CAPVT. Encheladus, quidam alius gigas, dicitur esse oppressus sub monte Iranimes.

---

554 Coralii … 556 petra] cf. Isid. Etymol. 16:8: Corallius gignitur in mari, forma ramosus, colore uiridi sed maxime rubens. Bacae eius candidae sub aqua et molles; detractae confestim durantur et rubescunt, tactu que protinus lapidescunt; Lact. Nar. 15:41: Coralium lapis sub aqua mollis est, extra durescit.   568 Trinacris[1] … 571 solent] cf. Isid. Etymol. 14:6: Prius autem Trinacria dicta propter tria ακρα, id est promontoria: pelorum, Pachinum et Lilybaeum. Trinacria enim Graecum est, quod Latine triquetra dicitur, quasi in tres quadras diuisa.   572 Degravat … 573 Iranimes] cf. Myt. Vat. 2, 67:11: Re uera nisi que de Gigantibus legimus, fabulose acceperimus, ratio non procedit, nam cum in Flegra Thessalie loco pugnasse dicantur, quemadmodum in Sicilia Enceladus, Otus in Creta secundum Salustium, unde: Otii campi, Typheus in Campania, ut: Inarime Iouis imperiis imposta Typheo?

557 Pegason correxi, pesagon cod.   559 ut sup. lin. | crines cf. crinem Met.   565 id correxi, ad cod.   568 acra correxi   569 Sillam i.e. Scyllam   570 Caripdis i.e. Charybdis | Ethma i.e Aetna   572 Encheladus i.e. Enceladus   573 Iranimes i.e. Inarimes

kingdom. Jupiter decided to give his daughter, Andromeda, to the monster to be eaten, and thus the people were no longer eaten.

EVEN NOW IN CORALS. Corals are a species that is red stone. It is thin in the manner of a slender stalk and it is found by the sea. But he incredibly says that it is a stalk under water and a stone above.   4:750

PEGASUS AND HIS BROTHERS. Pegasus and many serpents were born from the blood of the Gorgon.   4:786

AND NOW ALSO TO [SCARE] THE TERRIFIED SHE not only CHANGED her locks INTO SERPENTS, but she also now carries the serpents ON THE FRONT OF HER BREAST. Perseus knew for sure that he was going to give the head of the Gorgon to Pallas. Therefore Ovid says that she already carried it 'on her breast', that is on the cuirass, which in former times was carried on the breast only. Or Ovid did not care about the order of the stories.   4:801

SHE WAS SNATCHED FROM YOU at THE MOMENT WHEN SHE WAS GOING TO PERISH, and therefore you should be still, UNLESS you are so CRUEL as to demand THIS, that is to say THAT SHE PERISHES et cetera.[19]   5:19

HERE STARTS BOOK V

TRINACRIAN. Sicily is called 'Trinacrian' since it has three promontories: Scylla - which was made stone from a living being - against which ships break up, and Charybdis and Etna. Or since it has three mountain-ridges above its three ports, or from three trades from the ports, which used to be big there.   5:347

ETNA WEIGHS DOWN THE HEAD. Enceladus, another giant, is said to be pressed down by a mountain on Inarime.   5:352

---

[19] This passage is explained mainly by rearranging the sentence structure and adding a few clarifying words.

5:363   DEPOSITOQVE †et† V<IDET> H<VNC> ERICINA. Erix fuit filius Veneris et
Butes, qui fecit templum in honore matris sue in monte, qui dicitur 575
Ericus. Et a monte dicitur 'Ericina'.

5:370   IPSVMQVE REGIT QVI N<VMINA>. R<egit> Neptunum.

5:372   IMPERIVM PROFERS, id est extendis.

5:371   TARTARA QVID CESSANT, subaudis 'imperium'.

5:372   AGITVR PARS TERTIA MVNDI, id est ego loquor de tertia parte mundi, id 580
est de inferno.

5:378   AC TV PRO SOCIO REGNO, id est pro asociando infernali regno cum
celesti regno.

5:378   SI QVA EST EA GRATIA, id est si Proserpina potest fieri 'ea gratia', id est
68ʳᵇ   ea amicitia coniu<n>gere eam patruo. Pluto frater Iouis / erat.   585

5:407   ET que BACHIADE. Bachiade de Chorinto *ueniunt* in Siciliam.

5:409   EST MEDIVM CIANES. Istud ad hoc perstruit, quia ualebit future
narrationi, quia ibi Cores post reperit uesti<ment>a filie sue, id est
zonam.

5:424   ET PRONOS CVRRVS M<EDIO> CRATERE. †ut† Vertiginem aqua uocat 590
craterem. Que uertig[i]o Caripdis est, per quam Pluto infernum
ingresus est, que iuxta Siciliam.

5:450   DVLCE DEDIT TOSTA QVOD TEX<ERAT> ANTE POLENTA[M]. Tostam uocat
polentam panem subcinericium; tostam, qua dulcem liquorem anus
cooperuerat.   595

5:499   ADVEOR ORTIGIAM. 'Ortigia' Grece, Latine dicitur 'coturnix', id est
Asteria, que fuit mutata in Delo insula iuxta Siciliam, ubi Latona
peperit Apollinem et Dianam. Illa autem Latona cum duobus natis,
priusquam peperit, inde recessit, sicut libro dicit sequenti. Nec dicitur

---

588 quia … 589 zonam] *cf. Met.* 5:464.   **596** Adveor … 603 eam] *cf. expl.* 1:694 (cod. 64ʳᵃ);
Hyg. *Fab.* 53:1: ASTERIE Iouis cum Asterien Titanis filiam amaret, illa eum contempsit; a
quo in auem ortygam commutata est, quam nos coturnicem dicimus, eam que in mare
abiecit, et ex ea insula est enata, quae Ortygia est appellata.   **599** sicut … sequenti] *cf.*
Met. 6:188-191.

574 e *cf.* metu *Met.* | Ericina *correxi*, Eticina *cod.*   **580** Agitur *correxi*, igitur *cod.*   **582** Ac *cf.*
at *Met.* | asociando *i.e.* associando   **584** qua *correxi*, que *cod.*   **585** amicitia *correxi*, amiticia
cod. | coniungere *correxi*   **586** que *cf.* qua *Met.* | Bachiade[1] *i.e.* Bacchiadae | ueniunt
correxi, uenam ut *cod.*   **587** perstruit *correxi*, perstrait *cod.*   **588** Cores *pro* Ceres
uestimenta *correxi*   **591** uertigio *correxi*   **592** ingresus *i.e.* ingressus   **593** tosta *correxi*, testa
ut vid. cod. | polenta *correxi*   **594** qua *correxi*, quo *cod.*   **596** Adueor *i.e.* aduehor
598 peperit *post corr. ex* pereperit

AND WITH [FEAR] PUT ASIDE †et† ERYCINIAN SEES HIM. Eryx was the son of Venus and Butes. He made a temple in honour of his mother on the mountain called Erycus. And from this mountain she is called 'Erycinian'.[20] 5:363

HIM WHO GOVERNS THE DEITIES [OF THE SEA]. He (Jupiter) controls Neptune. 5:370

YOU EXTEND, that is you enlarge, THE DOMINION. 5:372

WHY DOES TARTAROS HOLD BACK, supply 'the dominion'. 5:371

THE THIRD PART OF THE WORLD IS TREATED , that is I speak about the third part of the world, that is about the underworld. 5:372

And YOU FOR THE SAKE OF A UNITED REALM, that is for the sake of uniting the nether realm with the heavenly realm. 5:378

IF THIS FAVOUR IS ANYTHING, that is if Proserpina could become 'this favour', that is to unite her with her uncle through this alliance. Pluto was Jupiter's brother. 5:378

AND THE BACCHIADAE. The Bacchiadae come from Chorint to Sicily. 5:407

THERE IS BETWEEN CYANE [AND PISAEAN ARETHUSA]. That builds up to this, because it will be of importance for the story to come, because this is where Ceres later finds her daughter's clothes, that is the girdle. 5:409

THE CHARIOT TURNED DOWNWARDS [IS RECEIVED] BY THE MIDDLE CRATER. †ut† He calls this whirling in the water a crater. This whirling is Charybdis, through which Pluto entered the underworld, and it is next to Sicily.[21] 5:424

SHE GAVE SOMETHING SWEET, THAT SHE HAD COVERED WITH PEARL-BARLEY ROASTED BEFORE. He calls the bread baked under the ashes parched barley; the parched [barley] with which the old woman had covered the sweet liquid. 5:450

I AM CARRIED TO ORTYGIA. *Ortygia* in Greek, in Latin it is called 'quail', that is Asteria, who was transformed on the island of Delos next to Sicily, where Latona gave birth to Apollo and Diana. But Latona had departed from there with her two children before she gave birth, just as he relates in the following book. And Phoebus is not said to have 5:499

---

[20] The lemma contains the letter e, which does not correspond to any reading in the *Metamorphoses*. It may be an error or a lemma from an undocumented manuscript.

[21] The lemma or the beginning of the explanation contain the letter u. It may be an error or a lemma from an undocumented manuscript.

Phebus dare responsum in illa Delos insula, sed in illa, que est iuxta 600
Parnasum montem et que in medio orbis dicitur esse. Coturnix, id est
Asteria, que fuit soror Latone, cum qua Iupiter uoluit concumbere.
Ideo Delos uocatur Ortigia, quia ortigia est mutata in ea<m>.

5:555 'Siren' Grece, Latine dicitur 'attrahere'. Inde etiam Sirtes dicuntur a
'tractu'. Et sirenes a cantu suo attrahebant naues et postea spoliabant. 605

INCIPIT LIBER SEXTVS

6:1   PREBVERA[N]T DICTIS.

6:70 | CECROPIA PALLAS. Apollo habet templum Athe- / nis iuxta litus maris.
68ᵛᵃ   Pallas in medio, Mars in altiori parte arcem, id est templum, habebat.
        Locus, ubi Mars templum habebat, dicitur Arispagus, id est 'uirtus 610
        uille'. 'Aris' enim est uirtus, 'pagus' uilla. Inde sanctus Dionisius
        dicitur Ariopagita, quia ibi docuit.

6:71   PINGIT ET A<NTI>Q<VAM> D<E> T<ERRAE> N<OMINE> LITEM, que fuit inter
        Palladem et Neptunum de nomine ciuitatis.

6:72   BIS SEX CELESTES, id est ibi duodecim dii fuere iudices inter Palladem et 615
        Neptunum.

6:90   ALTERA PIGMEE, id est Pigmee, id est que fuit mater illorum priorum
        populorum, qui uocantur Pigmei. Vel proprium nomen regine
        Pigmearum.

6:99   ISQVE GRADVS TEMPLI. Filie Cinare, dum in templum Iunonis 620
        prohiberent homines, ne Iunoni sacrificarent, omnes mutate sunt in
        'gradus templi'. Et etiam pater earum in gradus mutatus est.

6:108   FECIT ET ASTERIEN. Iupiter cum Ast<er>ia uoluit concu<m>bere, que
        erat soror Latone, sed ipsa aufugit et facta est coturnix. Et ipse, ut
        aquila, insecutus est eam, donec in rupem mutata est.   625

6:111   Antiopam, filiam Nictei, in specie satyri stuprauit.

---

604   Inde … 605 tractu] *cf.* Isid. *Etymol.* 13:8: Syrtes sunt harenosa in mari loca. Syrtes
autem Sallustius a tractu uocari dicit, quod omnia ad se trahant, et adpropinquanti
uadoso mari haereant.

603 eam *correxi* **604** Siren § *deest* **605** cantu *correxi,* cairtu *ut uid. cod.* **607** Prebuerat
correxi **620** Isque § *deest* | Cinare *i.e.* Cinyrae **623** Asteria *correxi* | concumbere *correxi*
626 Antiopam … *in marg. cum signo insert.*

given oracle reply on this island of Delos, but on the one next to mount Parnassus, which is said to be in the middle of the world. 'Quail', that is Asteria, who was Latona's sister, with whom Jupiter wanted to sleep. Delos is called Ortygian since the quail (*ortygia*) was transformed into the island.

Siren in Greek, in Latin it is called 'to attract' (*attraho*). From this also   5:555
the Syrtes [sand-banks] are named from drawing in (*tractus*). And the Sirens attracted ships through their song and thereafter they plundered them.

HERE STARTS BOOK SIX

SHE HAD OFFERED [HER EARS] TO THE STORIES   6:1

PALLAS ON THE CECROPIAN. Apollo has a temple next to the seashore in   6:70
Athens. Pallas had a castle, that is a temple, in the middle, Mars in a higher place. The place where Mars had his temple is called the Areopagus, that is 'the virtue of the village'. For *aris* is virtue, *pagus* is village. From this St Dionysius is called the Areopagite, since he taught there.

AND SHE PORTRAYS THE ANCIENT DISPUTE REGARDING THE NAME OF THE   6:71
LAND, [the dispute] which existed between Pallas and Neptune regarding the name of the city.

TWO TIMES SIX HEAVENLY, that is the twelve gods were the judges   6:72
between Pallas and Neptune there.

THE OTHER [SHOWS] THE PYGMAEAN, that is 'of the Pygmaean', that is   6:90
she who was the mother of the earlier people, who are called Pygmies. Or it is the proper name of the queen of the Pygmies.

AND HE [EMBRACING] THE STEPS OF THE TEMPLE. When the daughters of   6:99
Cinyras forbade people in the temple of Juno to sacrifice to Juno, they were all transformed into 'the steps of the temple'. And also their father was transformed into steps.

SHE ALSO FORMED ASTERIA. Jupiter wanted to sleep with Asteria, who   6:108
was Latona's sister, but she fled and was made into a quail. He, as an eagle, followed her, until she was transformed into a cliff.

In the shape of a satyr he ravished Antiopa, Nycteus's daughter.   6:111

6:112   AMPHITRION. Alcmena fuit mater Herculis et est coniunx Amphitrionis. In cuius specie Amphitrionis Iupiter aparens per tres noctes continuas, *sed* non die, cum ea Alcmena concubuit. Et a ciuitate Tyrinthia uocatur TYRINTHIA.   630

6:113   ASOPIDA iusserit IGNIS, id est Eginam, filiam Esopii fluuii.

6:176 | IVPPITER pater Tantali. /

68vb
6:115   Neptunus in specie Eniphei fluminis concubuit cum filia Ablii.

6:117   GIGNIS A<L>EIDAS, Zetus et Offialtes. Secundum uulgi opinionem filii Alei fuerunt et Mennoside. Qui singulis mensibus cubitum creuerunt. 635 Et tamen secundum ueritatem Neptuni filii fuerunt.

6:176   SOCERO *QVOQVE*. Iuppiter pater Amphionis, mariti Niobes.

6:178   FIDIBVSQVE MEI COMMISSA MARITI et cetera. Cadmus fecit Thebas. Amphion uero adauxit. Et dicitur etiam mouisse cum suis fidibus lapides ad muros faciendos. Sed secundum rei ueritatem non fuit 640 aliud, nisi quia Amphion fuit homo sapiens et docuit rudes homines facere ciuitatem. Ciuitas enim est collectio hominum ad iure uiuendum.

6:233   CARBASA DIDVCIT, id est expandit, ut cicius fugere possit.

6:237   ILLE VT ERAT PRONVS PER C<RVRA> ADMISSA, id est 'currentia', quia 645 quando equus currit, tunc sepi*us* crura mouendo et pedes ad se recipit.

6:254   AT NON INTONSVM S<IMPLEX>, pueri. Vsque ad XV annos pueri fuerant intonsi.

---

634   Gignis ... 636 fuerunt] *cf.* Hyg. *Fab.* 28:1: XXVIII. 1. OTOS ET EPHIALTES Otos et Ephialtes Aloei et Iphimedes Neptuni filiae filii mira magnitudine dicuntur fuisse; hi singuli singulis mensibus nouem digitis crescebant.   **642**   Ciuitas ... 643 uiuendum] *cf.* Marius Victorinus, *Explanationes in Ciceronis Rhetoricam*, 1:1: MVLTAS VRBES CONSTITVTAS, PLVRIMA BELLA RESTINCTA, FIRMISSIMAS SOCIETATES, SANCTISSIMAS AMICITIAS. Dicendum est hoc loco quid sit ciuitas: est autem ciuitas collecta hominum multitudo ad iure uiuendum.

628   aparens *i.e.* apparens   **629**   sed *correxi*, si *cod.*   **630**   Tyrinthia¹ *i.e.* Tirynthia Tyrinthia² *cum signo h sup. lin.*   **631**   iusserit ignis *cf.* luserit *Met.* | Esopii *i.e.* Asopii **632**   Ivppiter ... Tantali *in marg.*   **633**   Neptunus ... Ablii *in marg.* | Ablii *i.e.* Aloei **634**   aleidas *correxi* | Offialtes *i.e.* Ephialtes   **635**   Alei] *i.e.* Aloei   **637**   Socero ... Niobes *in marg. cum signo insert.* | quoque, *correxi* qui *cod.*   **644**   diducit *i.e.* deducit | cicius *i.e.* citius **646**   sepius *correxi*, sepias *cod.*

AMPHITRYO. Alcmena was the mother of Hercules and the wife of Amphitryo. In the shape of Amphitryo Jupiter appeared three nights in a row, but not during the day, and slept with Alcmena. And she is called TIRYNTHIA from the city Tirynthia.   6:112

AS A FLAME he had commanded THE ASOPID, that is Aegina, daughter of the river Asopus.   6:113

JUPITER, father of Tantalus.   6:176

Neptune in the shape of the river Enipeus slept with the daugther of Aloeus.   6:115

YOU BEGET THE ALOIDS, Zethus and Ephialtes. According to popular belief they were the sons of Aloeus and Mennoside. They grew one cubit each month. However, in reality they were the sons of Neptune.   6:117

ALSO AS FATHER-IN-LAW. Jupiter was the father of Amphion, the husband of Niobe.   6:176

ENTRUSTED TO MY AND MY HUSBAND'S LYRE et cetera. Cadmus founded Thebes, but Amphion enlarged it. And he is even said to have moved stones for the construction of the walls with his lyre. But in reality this was nothing other than that Amphion, being a learned man, taught the unskilled men to build the city. For a city is an assembly of men with the purpose of living according to the law.   6:178

HE SPREADS THE SAILS, that is he expands them so as to be able to flee quicker.   6:233

HE HANGING FORWARD, AS HE WAS, OVER THE FREED LEGS, that is the running [legs], since when a horse runs, then by moving its legs very much it also draws its feet back to itself.[22]   6:237

AND NOT A SIMPLE [WOUND IS INFLICTED ON] THE NOT YET SHAVEN, of a boy. Boys were unshaven until fifteen years of age.   6:254

---

[22] This explanation seems to have been caused by the participle *admissa* (freed), which is explained by a synonym and then in more detail.

6:384   QVEM TRITONIACA. Pallas, ut delectaret Iouem patrem suum, tibia
canere cepit et fistulis. Quam cum uidissent alii dei genis inflatis ridere   650
ceperunt. Vnde cum uellet uidere utrum dedeceret eam, uenit ad
Tritonem paludem ibique cantauit sicut ante Iouem primitus
cantauerat. Et uidit se turpem pro bucca inflata. Ideo in Tritonidam
paludem tibiam proiecit. Quam postea Marsia accepit et Appolinem ad
69ᵃ   cer- / tamen prouocauit. Et ab Apolline uictus excoriatus est.   655

6:393   ET SATIRI FRATRES ET TVNC QVOQVE CLARVS OLIMPVS, id est habitantes
iuxta Olimpum. 'Clarum' uocat eum, quia nubes excedit. Ideo omnes
isti flebant, quia Marsia multum illos delectauerat suo cantu.

6:395   LANIGEROSQVE G<REGES> A<RMENTA>QVE BVCERA P<AVIT>, id est omnia
illa armenta dicuntur 'bucera', de quorum cornibus bucina potuit fieri,   660
id est cornu.

6:415   ET NONDVM TORVE CALIDON INVISA DIANE, sed postea fuit inuisa Diane,
quia rex Calidonie non sibi sacrificauit, cum omnibus aliis diis
sacrificasset. Ideo Diana inmisit aprum terribilem, qui omnia
deuastaret. Et sic primitie frugum, que sibi sacrificate non sunt, aliis   665
sacrificari non potuerunt.

6:490   AT REX ODRISIVS. Odrisius fuit rex Tracie. Inde Tracia uocatur Odrisia.
Inde reges Odrisii uocantur.

6:506   VTQVE FIDEI PIGNVS D<EXTRAS> V<TRIVS>QVE P<OPOSCIT>. Pandion a
Tereo accepit fidem, ut bene illam seruaret et cito illam remitteret. A   670
6:538   Philomela etiam, ut rediret. TV GEMINVS CONIVNX NON HEC MIHI DEBITA
PENA, subaudi 'sit', sed potius me interficiam. Et hoc est quod dicit
6:539   sequens uersus, scilicet QVIN ANIMAM.

649   Pallas … 655 est] *cf. Myt. Vat.* 2, 138: DE MINERVA Minerua aliquando tibiis in
consortio deorum canente dii intuentes buccam eius turpiter inflatam ceperunt ridere.
Illa quid riderent ignorans ad Tritonam paludem uenit ibi que labiorum suorum
turgorem intuita tibias abiecit. Quas Marsia inueniens illis utendo in tantum factus est
peritus ut Apollini se compararet. Cum quo cum diu Apollo contenderet et eum
superare non posset, ei inuertit cytharam et canere cepit. Inuersis autem tibiis cum se
Marsia Apollini equiperare nequiret, Apollo eum ad arborem religauit, uirgis cedendo
ad interitum usque cepit punire, de cuius sanguine fons ortus est eius ornatus nomine.
Cuius turpitudinis memoria Marsia cauda depingitur porcina.   **662**   sed … 666
potuerunt] *cf. Myt. Vat.* 2, 167: DE ENEO Eneus Parthaonis filius rex Etholie, cuius
ciuitas erat Calidon, regni sui statum turbauit negligentia sacrorum. Annua siquidem
uota pro imperii fructibus celebrans numen Diane contempsit. Ea aprum summe
magnitudinis regioni eius inmisit qui uastatis Calidoniis terris Calidonius ab urbe gentis
est appellatus.

649 Quem *correxi,* que ti- *ut uid. cod.*   **654** Marsia *i.e.* Marsya   **671** coniunx *post corr. ex*
coniunix *ut uid.*

WHOM THE TRITONIAN. Pallas began playing on a flute and pipes to delight her father, Jupiter. When the other gods saw this they began to laugh at her inflated cheeks. Whereupon she went to the Tritonian swamp, because she wanted to see if this was unbecoming of her, and there she played just as she had played for Jupiter before. And she saw that she was ugly on account of her inflated cheeks. Therefore she threw the flute in the Tritonian swamp. Marsyas later took this [flute] and challenged Apollo to a contest. And when he was defeated he was flayed by Apollo. 6:384

AND THE BROTHER SATYRS AND THEN ALSO THE CLEAR OLYMPUS, that is those living next to Olympus. He calls it 'clear' since it rises above the clouds. All these were crying, since Marsyas had delighted them a lot with his song. 6:393

AND [WHOEVER] TENDED TO THE WOOL-BEARING HERD AND THE OX-HORNED CATTLE, that is all cattle are called 'ox-horned' (*bucera*), from whose horns a trumpet (*bucina*), that is a horn, can be made. 6:395

AND CALYDON NOT YET HATEFUL TO FIERCE DIANA, but later it was hateful to Diana, since the king of Calydon did not sacrifice to her when he had sacrificed to all the other gods. Therefore Diana sent a terrible wild-boar that laid everything to waste. And thus the first of the new crops, which had not been sacrificed to her, could not be sacrificed to the others. 6:415

BUT THE ODRYSIAN KING. Odrysius was the king of Thrace. From this Thrace is called Odrysia. From this kings are called Odrysian. 6:490

HE ASKED FOR BOTH OF THEIR RIGHT HANDS AS A PLEDGE OF FAITH. Pandion received an oath from Tereus that he would protect her well and send her back soon. Also from Philomela [he recieved an oath] that she would return. YOU, A DOUBLE HUSBAND, THIS PUNISHMENT MUST NOT, supply 'be', FOR ME, but I would rather kill myself. And this is what the following verse says, namely WHY NOT [MY] LIFE. 6:506
6:538

6:587 TEMPVS ERAT, QVO S<ACRA> S<OLENT> TRIATERICA. Triaterica
conponitur ex 'tribus' et 'theron', id est 'sollemne'. Et dicitur 'triateri- / 675
69ʳᵇ ca festiuitas' Bachi et Apollinis fratris sui, uel quia per tres noctes
fiebant, uel ter in anno, uel post tres annos.

6:652 Ithis postquam fuit a patro commestus, uersus est in faxanum, quod
alibi legitur.

INCIPIT LIBER SEPTEM   680

7:1 IAMQVE MINIE. Minie pluralitatem habent tantum. Vel a terra dicitur
'Minie' uel ab actu uel a rubore, quia capillos rubicundos habebant,
sicut est minium. Eodem modo ab actu Phenecei Punicei dicuntur,
quia ipsi primi capitales literas fecerunt cum minio. Et ideo Punicei
dicuntur, id est rubicundi.   685

7:1 PEGASEA a Pegaso opido. Pegasum dicitur opidum, iuxta quod fuit
facta Argo. Vel secundum quosdam Argo dicitur 'Pegasea', quia
Pegasus erat ibi inpictus.

     Eson et Pelias fratres fuerunt, sed Pelias non habens filios sed
tantum filias timuit, ne ipse senex et filie sue dei[e]cerentur suo regno 690
ab Iasone, suo nepote, filio Esonis. Et ideo misit Iasonem nepotem
suum ad aureum uellus adquerendum, ut ibi periret, quia audierat
illud non posse haberi nisi magno discrimine uite.

7:3 VISVS ERAT PHINEVS, subaudi 'ab Argonautis'. Fineus fuit quidam
diues, qui de uxore iam mortua duos filios habebat, quos instinctu 695
69ᵛᵃ nouerce / illorum, que nouerca Nubes dicebatur, excecauit. Ideo dii
irati fuerunt et eum lumine priuauerunt et tres arpias, que uocabantur
Aello, Cillerio, Occipete, sibi apposuerunt, que cibos suos omnes
conmacularent. Ad quem Fineum, cum Hercules et Argonaute
uenerunt, ab eo arpias Hercules auertit et iussit filiis Boree, ut illas 700

---

678   quod ... 679 legitur] cf. Myt. Vat. 1, 4: Qua cognita Progne Ythin filium interemit et
patri epulandum apposuit. Postea omnes in aues mutati sunt: Tereus in upupam, Ithis in
phassam, Progne in hirundinem, Philomela in lusciniam.   700   Boree] cf. Myt. Vat. 1, 27:
Hoc ergo beneficio illecti Argonaute Zetum et Calain filios Boree et Orythie alatos
iuuenes ad pellendas Arpyas miserunt. Quas cum strictis gladiis persequerentur pulsas
de Archadia, peruenerunt ad insulas que appellabantur Plote.

674 Triaterica¹ i.e. Trieterica   683 Phenecei i.e. Phoenicei   684 literas i.e. litteras   689 Eson
§ adest   690   deicerentur correxi + in marg. littera X   691   misit + in marg. littera X
692 adquerendum i.e. adquirendum   695 filios post corr. ex filius ut vid.   697 arpias i.e.
Harpyias   698 Aello ... Occipete i.e. Aello, Celaeno, Ocypete

THERE WAS A TIME, WHEN THEY USED TO [CELEBRATE] THE TRIENNIAL   6:587
RITES. Triennial is composed of 'three' and *theron*, that is 'yearly'. And
it is called the triennial festivity of Bacchus and of his brother Apollo,
either since is takes place during three nights, or three times a year, or
after three years.

After Itys was eaten by his father he was turned into a pheasant, which   6:652
can be read elsewhere.

HERE STARTS BOOK SEVEN

AND NOW THE MINYANS. *Minyae* is a *plurale tantum*. Or 'Minya' is   7:1
named after the land, or from a practice, or from redness, since they
had red hair, just as cinnabar (red lead). In the same way Phoenicians
are called Punics from a practice, since they first made capital letters
with cinnabar. And therefore they are called Punics, that is red ones.

PEGASEAN from the city Pegasum. The city next to which Argo was   7:1
made is named Pegasum. Or according to some Argo is called
'Pegasean', since Pegasus was painted on it.

Aeson and Pelias were brothers, but Pelias, not having any sons just
daughters, feared that as an old man he and his daugthers would be
thrown out of their kingdom by Jason, his nephew and Aeson's son.
And therefore he sent his nephew Jason to get the golden fleece, so
that he would perish there, since he had heard that it could not be
acquired without great danger to one's life.

PHINEUS HAD BEEN SEEN, supply 'by the Argonauts'. Phineus was a rich   7:3
man who had two sons from his now dead wife. These he blinded on
the instigation of their stepmother, this stepmother was called Nubes.
Therefore the gods were angered and deprived him of his sight and
placed with him three harpies, called Aello, Celaeno, Ocypete, who
were to pollute all his food. When Hercules and the Argonauts came to
this Phineus, Hercules took the harpies off him and commanded the

fugarent. Qu*i* usque ad Strophados insulas eas fugauerunt, qu*i* aureum uellus rapiendum uenerunt.

'Strophos' Grece, Latine dicitur 'conuersio'.

7:7   PHRIXEAQVE VELLERA. Athemas de qu*a*dam marina dea habuit Frixum et Hellem. Qui secum manere nequerunt pro afflictione nouerce 705 I[u]nonis. Et cum recedendo uenirent ad mare, mater eorum dedit eis arietem habentem aureum uellus et ualentem tam ire per mare quam per terram, ut in eo sedentes transirent mare, predicens illum esse submersurum, qui retro aspiceret. Et quia Helle retro aspexit, submersa est, unde mare, in quo cecidit, Hellespontiacum dicitur. 710 Phrixus transiens per mare, quod est inter Sexton et Abidon, ad Cholcon insulam iuit et ibi arietem Marti consecrauit uel sacrificauit. Et <eo> sacrificato translatus est signum celeste. Vellus uero positum in

69ᵛᵇ   sumitate cuiusdam arboris costoditur a dracone in ea inuoluto, / ne uellus inde auferatur, quia, si auferet ur, non esset ibi caput mundi, 715 sed locus ille, in quo fuerit uellus.

7:54   STANT M<ECVM> VOTA SORORIS, id est quod idem, quod soror, uolo, et illa, quod ego.

7:74   IBAT AD A<NTIQVAS> HECATES. Cum Perseus iuit interficere Gorgonem, prius Hecatem adorauit, id est Dianam uel Proserpinam. Quo exemplo 720 Iasonis monitus prius eam audiuit.

7:76   ET IAM FORTIS. Confortata erat Medea, ne amaret Iasonem.

7:121   GALEA TVM SVMMIT AENA. Secundum Manogaldum, qui non uult ullam diptongon Latinam diuidi, aliud nomen est Eneus et aliud Aeneus, et Eripies et Aeripies, et sic etiam in consimilibus. 725

7:149   PERVIGILEM SVPEREST HERBIS SOPIRE DRACONEM. Quondam dimisit narrare quomodo draco incantatus esset, cuius dentes seminauerat, ideo nunc explet. Quidam tamen dicunt, quia alius fuit ille, cuius dentes seminauit, et alius, qui custodiebat arborem.

7:306   Atque PETVNT PRECIVM S<INE> F<INE>. Petiit Medeam, ut pacisceretur 730 'precium', quod esset 'sine fine', id est infinitam peccuniam, ut patrem suum faceret iuuenem.

---

701   fugarent *post corr. ex* fugaret | Qui *correxi,* quos *cod.* | qui *correxi,* que *cod.*
704 Phrixeaque *cum signo* h *sup. lin.* | Athemas *i.e.* Athamas | quadam *correxi,* quodam *cod.*   **706** Inonis *correxi*   **709** aspexit *i.e.* aspexit   **711** Sexton *i.e.* Seston   **712** Cholcon *cum signo* h *sup. lin.*   **713** eo *supplevi*   **714** costoditur *i.e.* custoditur   **723** summit *i.e.* sumit
724 diptongon *i.e.* diphthongum   **730** Atque *cf.* idque *Met.*   **731** peccuniam *i.e.* pecuniam

sons of Boreas to chase them away. They, who came to snatch the golden fleece, chased the harpies all the way to the Strophades islands.

Strophos in Greek, in Latin it is called 'a turning'.

THE PHRIXEAN FLEECE. Athamas had Phrixus and Helle from a sea goddess. They could not stay with him because of oppression from their step-mother, Ino. And when they were departing and came to the sea, their mother gave them a ram that had a golden fleece and could walk on water as well as on land, so that they might cross the sea sitting on it and she warned them that the one who looked back would be drowned. Since Helle looked back, she was drowned, wherefore the sea into which she fell is called the Hellespont. Phrixus crossed the sea between Sestos and Abydus and came to the island of Colchis and there he consecrated or sacrificed the ram to Mars. When the ram had been sacrificed it was transformed into a heavenly sign. The fleece was placed in the top of a tree and is guarded by a serpent wrapped around it, so that the fleece cannot be carried away, because, if it were to be carried away, then the centre of the world would not be there, but in the place where the fleece would be. 7:7

MY SISTER'S VOWS STAND WITH ME, that is I want the same as my sister, and she the same as I. 7:54

SHE WENT TO THE ANCIENT [ALTAR] OF HECATE. When Perseus went to kill the Gorgon he first beseeched Hecate, that is Diana or Proserpine. Advised by Jason's example, he listened first to her. 7:74

AND NOW STRONG. Medea was strengthened not to love Jason. 7:76

THEN HE TOOK FROM THE BRONZE (*aena*) HELMET. According to Manegold, who does not want to divide any Latin diphtong, Eneus and Aeneus, and Eripies and Aeripies are different names, and so also with similar words. 7:121

THERE REMAINS TO PUT THE EVER WATCHFUL SERPENT TO SLEEP WITH HERBS. He once omitted to tell how the serpent, whose teeth he had sown, was enchanted, therefore he completes [the story] now. However, some say that the one whose teeth he sowed was one [serpent] and the one who guarded the tree another. 7:149

And THEY BEGGED THE PRICE WITHOUT A LIMIT. She begged Medea to agree to a price that would be without a limit, that is unlimited money, so that she would make her father young. 7:306

7:361   QVA PATER CHORIDI. Choridus iactauerat se quod, quando pater
mor<i>etur, sepelire<t> eum in medio mari. Quod et fecit facto tumulo
de arena, in quo posuit eum.   735

7:363   QVA CEE CORNVA MATRES. Hercules *rediens* despoliato trigemino
70ʳᵃ   Gergione susceptus / est in hospitio Cei regis XII suos labores narrare.
'Cee matres', id est matrone uel puelle. Filie Cei in Iunonem, cuius
inuidioso iussu Hercules hoc paciebatur, ceperunt execrare, unde Iuno
irata capitibus eorum inposuit cornua. Et si non aposuit, uisum est   740
tamen illa habere. Quod factum est Hercule recedente ab ospitio Cei.
Hanc fabulam dicit Virgilius. Vel Hercules inposuit eis cornua, quia
furate sunt sibi boues, uel quia preposuerunt formam suam Veneri.

7:435   QVODQVE SVAM S<ECVRVS> A<RAT> CROMIONA, quia latrones siue
tyrannos, qui terram illam, que Cremion dicitur, non permittebant   745
incoli, Theseus perdidit.

7:437   CLAVIGERAM V<IDIT>. Vulcanus quendam filium pessimum habuit, qui
Epidauriam uastabat. Quem Theseus interfecit.

7:438   VIDIT ET I<MMITEM> CEPHASIAS, illa regio C<ephasias>, PRO<CRVSTEN>.
Procustos fuit quidam pessimus latro uel tyrannus, qui homines   750
commedebat. Quem Theseus interfecit.

7:444   COMPOSITO, id est intefecto, SCHIRONE. Schiron fuit quidam latro
residens in quodam loco *a*trocissimo, ubi erat transitus ad Alcitoen. Et
omnes transeuntes cogebat, ut se quasi deum adorarent. Ad quem
Schironem cum Theseus iuisset et se illum adorare simulasset, accepit   755
eum per crura et de loco excelso, ubi sedebat, obruit.

7:668 | EXCIPIT EACIDES. Peleus et The- / lamon erant de una parte. PHOCVS
70ʳᵇ   solus de alia, scilicet nimphe, que dicitur Salmate, filius erat.

7:672   ASP[ER]ICIT EOLIDEN, id est Cephalum, qui dicitur ex progenie Eoli uel
de terra illa, que uocatur Eolia.   760

---

736 Qva ... 743 Veneri] *cf.* Lact. *Nar.* 7:10:2: Ab his regionibus digressam Eurypyli urbem
contigisse, in qua Coae matronae in cornutas transfiguratae sunt propter effectum quod
Veneri formam suam anteposuerunt dein Telchinas Ialysios transgressam, quos Iuppiter
propter odium coniugis suae Iunonis subiecerat mari quorum regione relicta Ceam
urbem pervenisse, in qua Alcidamantem scribit ex filia vidisse columbam procreatam
esse. **742** Hanc ... Virgilius] *non inveni.*

733 Choridus *i.e.* Corythus **734** morietur *correxi* | sepeliret *correxi* **736** Cee *i.e.* Coae
rediens *correxi,* ridens *cod.* **737** Gergione *i.e.* Geryone | XII *correxi* CII *cod.* **738** cuius
post corr. ex cuus **740** aposuit *i.e.* apposuit **749** Cephasias[1] *i.e.* Cephisias | Cephasias[2]
supplevi **750** Procustos *i.e.* Procrustes **752** Schiron § *adest* **753** atrocissimo *correxi,*
acrocissimo *cod.* | Alcitoen *verbum non inveni* **759** aspicit *correxi*

WHERE THE FATHER OF CORYTHUS. Corythus bragged that, when his father died, he would bury him in the middle of the ocean. This he also did after having made a mound of sand, in which he placed him. 7:361

WHERE THE COAN MOTHERS [WORE] HORNS. Hercules, returning after triform Geryon had been robbed, was received in the hospitality of king Coeus to tell about his twelve labours. 'Coan mothers', that is wifes or girls. Coeus's daughters began to curse Juno, whose hostile command had made Hercules suffer this, wherefore the angered Juno put horns on their heads. And if she did not put [them there], they nevertheless seemed to to have them. This happened when Hercules departed from Coeus's hospitality. Virgil tells this story. Or Hercules placed horns on them, since the cows had been stolen from him, or since they preferred their own looks to that of Venus. 7:363

AND THAT [THE FARMER] SAFELY PLOUGHS HIS CROMYON, since Theseus destroyed the bandits or tyrants who did not permit this land, called Cromyon, to be inhabited. 7:435

SAW THE CLUB-BEARING. Vulcan had an evil son, who laid Epidaurus to waste. Theseus killed him. 7:437

AND CEPHISIAS, the land of Cephisias, SAW THE ROUGH PROCRUSTES. Procrustes was an evil bandit or tyrant who ate people. Theseus killed him. 7:438

SCIRON WAS LAID TO REST, that is killed. Sciron was a bandit who lived in a most terrible place, where there was a passage to Alcicoen. He forced everyone who passed there to worship him like a god. When Theseus came to Sciron and pretended to worship him, he took him by the legs and threw him down from the high place where he sat. 7:444

THE AEACIDE RECEIVES. Peleus and Telamon were from one lot. PHOCUS alone was the son of another, namely a nymph, who is called Psamathe. 7:668

HE SEES THE AEOLIDE, that is Cephalus, who is said to be of Aeolus's lineage, or from the land called Aeolia. 7:672

7:685   TVNC VERO IVVENIS NEREVS. Phocus a matre sua nimpha, scilicet neride, que[m] proprio nomine dicitur Salmate, uocatur Neris.

7:687   QVE PETIT ILLE REFERT. Maledictum est istud: Ea refert Cephalus ubi nullus pudor sibi esset, si refert, scilicet unde iaculum habuisset, id est QVA MERCEDE iaculum TVLERIT, qualiter ab Aurora raptus sit. ET   765 CETERA PVDORE sibi, scilicet quomodo cum Aurora rem habuerit, quia hoc non posset notificari nisi cum pudore. Et tamen ex libro hoc non habemus, quod concubuisset Cephalus cum Aurora, sed in Ouidio epistularum plane inuenitur, quod cum ea concubuerit.

7:704   LICEAT MIHI REFERRE cum PACE DEE, id est ne irascatur mihi de hoc,   770
7:705   quod dicam, id est: istud dicam, quamuis SIT SPECTABILIS, id est, quamuis sit multum pulchra, ego tamen magis amabam pulchram quam eam.

7:759   CARMINA NAIADES. Secundum Manogaldum Diana fecerat quedam
7:763   carmina ambigua: 'ALTERA alteram, scilicet sagita uxorem, alter *non*   775 alteram, canis non feram'. Quondam que uates illius non soluere
70ᵛᵃ   poterant Diane, homines ea carmina non intelligentes iue- / -runt ad Naiades. Que Naiades soluerunt illa. Illam autem uatem, que soluere non potuit, precipitando occiderunt. Vnde Diana irata misit ad illorum exicium quandam feram. Vel ita Naiades soluerunt problema   780 Apollinis, quod uates Diane non potuit interpretari. Vnde Aonii irati precipitauerunt eam. Et ideo Diana irata misit bestiam Thebanis. Vates
7:762 | dicitur THEMIS fuisse. Vel ideo dicitur, quod 'iace[n]t PRECIPITATA',
7:760   quia et non posset soluere, quod Naiades elucidauerunt, derelicta est.

LIBER OCTAVVS   785

7:794   ACTENVS ET TACVIT. Tacuit hic, quia puduit dicere de interfectione, sed Phocus coegit eum narrare.

7:759   CARMINA NAIADES. Quedam uates dicitur fuisse Themis dee. Que uaticinabatur ita obscura uerba, quod non poterant intelligi. Hac de causa populus commotus precipitauit prefatam fatem. Vnde dea   790 Themis, cuius erat illa uate[n]s, ira stimulata in partibus illis, ubi

---

767 ex … **769** concubuerit] *cf. Her.* 4:93.

761 Nereus *i.e.* Nereius   **762** que *correxi* | Salmate *i.e.* Psamathe | Neris *fortasse perperam pro* Nereius   **772** pulchra *cum signo h sup. lin.* | pulchram *correxi,* pulchrim *cod.*   **775** non *correxi,* in *cod.*   **776** Quondam] quoniamque *sugg. Haupt*   **778** Illam *correxi,* illum *cod.*   **783** iacet *correxi, cf.* iacebat *Met.*   **786** Tacuit *correxi,* inacuit *(i+lin.nas.) cod.*   **790** fatem *pro* uatem   **791** uates *correxi*

THEN THE YOUNG NEREIAN. Phocus is called Nereius from his mother, a   7:685
nymph, namely a nereid, whose proper name is Psamathe.

WHAT HE ASKS, HE TELLS. The curse is this: Cephalus tells this, where   7:687
no shame would exist for him if he tells, namely from where he had
gotten the spear, that is FOR WHAT PRICE HE BROUGHT the spear, how he
had been carried off by Aurora. AND OTHER THINGS WITH SHAME for
him, namely how he had intercourse with Aurora, since this cannot be
made known without shame. And still from this book we do not have
it that Cephalus had slept with Aurora, but in Ovid's Letters it can
plainly be found that he slept with her.

MAY I with THE GODDESS'S LEAVE BE ALLOWED TO TELL [THE TRUTH], that   7:704
is so that she may not be angry with me for what I say, that is: I may
say this even though she IS REMARKABLE, that is even though she may
be very beautiful, I still loved one more beautiful than she.

THE NAIADS [SOLVED] THE VERSES. According to Manegold Diana had   7:759
made some uncertain verses: *altera alteram, scilicet sagita uxorem, alter
non alteram, canis non feram*. Once her, Diana's, oracles could not solve
them, so the people who could not understand these verses went to the
Naiads. The Naiads solved them. But they killed that oracle, who
could not solve [the verses], by throwing her headlong. Wherefore the
angered Diana sent a beast to their destruction. Or thus: the Naiads
solved Apollo's problem, which the oracle of Diana could not explain.
Wherefore the angered Aonians threw her headlong. And therefore
the angered Diana sent the beast against the Thebeans. The oracle is
said to have been THEMIS. Or it is said she lies THROWN HEADLONG,
since she could not solve that, which the Naiads had explained, she
was forsaken.

BOOK EIGHT

THUS FAR AND HE WAS SILENT. He was silent, because it shamed him to   7:794
speak about the killing, but Phocus forced him to tell.

THE NAIADS [SOLVED] THE VERSES. An oracle is said to have belonged to   7:759
the goddess Themis. She prophesied words so obscure that they could
not be understood. For this reason the agitated people threw the
aforementioned oracle headlong. Wherefore the goddess Themis,

interfecta est uates, beluam pestilentie inmisit. Et licet, dixerim superius, illam uatem obscure protulisse uaticinia carmina, tamen Naiades uenientes interpretate sunt. CARMINA illius enim INTELLECTA ab INGENIIS populorum PRIORVM interpretatorum, licet male.   795

8:25 CRISTATA CASSIDE PENNIS. Pennas cassidis uocat, uel fil[i]a in
70ᵛᵇ summitate cas- / sidis ligata quasi pennas, uel caudam ibi ligatam.

8:171 TERTIA SORS A[E]NNI[V]S. Hic est intelligendum, quod Minos iam uenisset Athenas et eas deuicisset et illis legem inposuisset, ut semper in tercio anno persoluerent sibi ad opus Minotauri nescio quid 800 corpora.

8:179 INMISIT CELO. Quidam dicunt, quando Theseus duxit Phedram et reliquit Adriagnam in maris litore, cuius auxilio uicerat Minotaurum, quod Bachus mixtus Adriagne[s]. Post amplexus dedit sibi coronam, quam ipse in capite habebat et postea et coronam, quam sibi dederat, 805 et ipsam Adriagnem in celo posuit. Sed quod melius uidetur, quidam dicunt, quod illa corona sumpta fuit de capite Adriagnes, quam Theseus ei dederat.

8:182 QVI MEDIVS NIXIQVE GENV EST. 'Nixi', id est Herculis in genu. Quadam die, dum Hercules esset interfecturus Idram, flexo genu primum 810 suplicauit diis. Et quia tantus homo sic dignatus est humiliari, ideo et [ideo] imaginem suam dii transtulerant in celo. Quidam dicunt, quod 'Nixi' referatur ad Perseum, cuius imago et ideo dicitur esse in celo, quia deos adorauit, quando liberauit Andromaden draconi destinatam.
8:182 ANGVEM TENENTIS, id est Serpentarii, qui uocatur Ophicus.   815

8:183 DEDALVS INTEREA. *Secundum* Manogaldum quondam Dedalus Theseo
71ʳᵃ en- / sem et globos piceos consilio Adriagnes dederat. Per quos globos ille Minotaurus inmoriturus a Theseo interfectus est. Ideo Minos Dedalum in eandem domum consilio eius Adriagnes conclusit. Sed, quia domus coopertorio carebat, per pennas sibi datas a ministris regis, 820 qui uictum ei semper ministrabant, euasit.

8:201 INPOSITA EST G<EMINAS> O<PIFEX> L<IBRAVIT> IN ALAS. Non ideo dicit, ut iam uolaret, *sed* ut equaliter auolare posse[t] uideret<ur>, sicut post *in*
8:212 libro dicit LEVATVS PENNIS ANTE VOLAT.

8:207 AVT ELICEN IVBEO. Elix proprium nomen est Maioris Vrse. Cinosura 825 Minor. Calisto proprium nomen matris Archadis antequam mutata esset.

796 fila *correxi* **798** annis *correxi*   **802** celo *correxi,* celum *cod.*   **803** Adriagnam *i.e.* Ariadnam   **804** Adriagne *correxi*   **812** ideo *delevi*   **813** Nixi *correxi,* nisi *ut vid. cod.* **815** Ophicus *post corr. ex* opicus   **816** Secundum *correxi,* sed *ut vid. cod.* | Theseo *cum signo* h *sup. lin.*   **823** sed *correxi,* si *cod.* | posse uideretur *correxi* | in *correxi* ut *cod.*

whose oracle she was, spurred by anger sent a beast of pestilence to the region where the oracle had been killed. And although, as I have said above, this oracle uttered prophetic verses obscurely, the Naiads nevertheless came and interpreted them. Indeed her VERSES WERE UNDERSTOOD by THE GENIUS OF the people, the PREVIOUS interpreters, although badly.

A HELMET CRESTED WITH FEATHERS. He refers to the feathers of the helmet, or to the threads tied to the top of the helmet like feathers, or to a tail tied there. 8:25

THE THIRD LOT AFTER YEARS. Here it should be understood that Minos had already come to Athens and subdued it and imposed a law, so that every third year they had to offer him a large number of bodies for the need of the Minotaur. 8:171

HE SENT TO HEAVEN. Some say that, when Theseus married Phaedra and left Ariadne - with whose help he had overcome the Minotaur - by the sea shore, Bacchus had intercourse with Ariadne. After the embrace he gave her the crown he wore on his head and that thereafter he placed both the crown he had given her and Ariadne herself in heaven. But some say, which seems better, that this crown was taken from Ariadne's head and that Theseus had given it to her. 8:179

IT IS IN THE MIDDLE OF THE KNEELER. 'Of the kneeler', that is of Hercules kneeling. One day when Hercules was going to kill the Hydra he first kneeled down to the gods and prayed. And since such a great man had deigned to humble himself, the gods transferred also his image to heaven. Some say that 'of the Kneeler' refers to Perseus, whose image is also said to be in heaven, since he prayed to the gods when he freed Andromeda who was promised to the serpent. OF THE SERPENT-HOLDER, that is of the Serpentarius, which is what Ophiuchus is called. 8:182 8:182

MEANWHILE DAEDALUS. According to Manegold Daedalus once gave Theseus a sword and pitched balls following Ariadne's advice. With these balls the immortal Minotaur was killed by Theseus. Therefore Minos confined Daedalus in this house following Ariadne's advice, but since the house lacked a roof he escaped with wings given to him by the king's servants, who always served him his meals. 8:183

[AFTER] IT WAS FITTED, THE ARTISAN BALANCED ON DOUBLE WINGS. He does not say that he flew already, but that it seems that he can fly away in the same manner, just as he says later in the book: LIFTED UP ON WINGS HE FLIES BEFORE. 8:201 8:212

OR HELICE I ORDER. Helice is the proper name for the Great Bear. Cynosura is the Little. Callisto is the proper name of Arcas's mother before she was transformed. 8:207

8:222 DEXTRA LEBINTES ERAT. In Siciliam uolebat Dedalus eam interrogare unde erat.

8:244 ILLE ETIAM MEDIO *SPINAS NOTATAS*. Serram fecit Perdix ad modum 830
spinarum, quas uidit in quibusdam pisci[pi]bus. Serra est illud instrumentum ferreum, cum quo messes secantur.

8:249 ALTERA PARS STARET. Fecit circinum.

8:261 PRO SVPLICE COCALVS ARMIS. Cocalus, rex Sicilie, sumpsit arma contra quendam tyrannum, qui Dedalum de Sicilia expulerat.   835

8:276 | CE[M]PTVS AGRICOLIS. Duobus modis sic potest / dici HONOR, s<c>ilicet
71ʳᵇ   sacrificium ab agricolis siue a rusticis dis fuit inceptum, et sic
peruenerunt ad omnes deos maiores, uel rustici prius illa sacrificia ceperunt, et ideo deus ambiciosus quisque rusticus per inuidiam laborat sacrificia.   840

8:313 PRIMIS ETIAM nunc NESTOR. Nestor uixit per tria secula.

8:316 CILIDES TVTVS, id est Amphiaraus, qui, quia nolens in bello Pollinices, abscondit se. Coniunx uero monili sibi dato patefecit eum.

8:305 ET IAM NON FEMINA CENEVS. Iste femina fuit, et quia de opressione concubentis Neptuni nimis fleuit, Neptunus dixit se illi dare 845
quecumque uellet, si flere desineret. Et quia maluit fieri masculus, femineam naturam amisit.

8:414 AT MANVS EONIDE VARIAT. Scilicet et in iaculando unam hastam, nunc aliam.

8:421 DEXTRA CONIVNGERE DEXTRA<M>. Sicut milites post uictoriam 850
osculantur se ad inuicem pro gaudio, ita et isti. Dextra Medeagri coniungebat sua<m> dextra<m>.

8:564 SVMMA LACVNABANT, id est arcuabant summa domus. CONCHE ad modum lacunaris arcuabant sumitates domus. Illa domus dicitur habere lacunar, que in medio tecti quasi lacum habet, sicut ille domus 855
71ᵛᵃ   quarum trabes et solarium uersus tectum / erecta sunt.

8:655 IN MEDIO THORVS EST DE MOLLIBVS VLVIS. Thorum non accipit de ligno factum, sed quasi massam de mollibus uluis [fac] factam quasi

---

830 spinas notatas *correxi secundum Meiser*, sed primus natat *cod.*   831 piscibus *correxi*
834 Pro § *deest* 836 Ceptus *correxi* | scilicet *correxi* 837 a *sup. lin.* 838 sacrificia *post corr.*
ex sacrifica   841 nunc *cf.* num *Met.*   842 Cilides *perperam pro* eclides (*i.e.* Oeclides)
nolens *correxi*, uolens *cod.* | Pollinices *correxi*, Pollinicem *cod.* 845 fleuit *correxi*, flauant
cod. 848 Eonide *i.e.* Oenidae 850 coniungere *correxi*, contingere *cod.* | dextram *correxi*
851 Medeagri *i.e.* Meleagri 852 coniungebat *correxi*, contingebat *cod.* | suam dextram
correxi 858 fac *delevi*

LEBINTHUS WAS ON THE RIGHT. In Sicily Daedalus wanted to ask her 8:222
where she hailed from.

HE [TOOK] THE BACKBONE, OBSERVED IN THE MIDDLE [OF A FISH]. Perdix 8:244
made a saw (*serra*) in the manner of the back-bone he had seen in
some fishes. Sickle (*serra*) is that iron tool with which crops are cut.

ONE PART STOOD STILL. He made a compass. 8:249

AFTER COCALUS [HAD RAISED] ARMS FOR THE SUPPLIANT. The king of 8:261
Sicily, Cocalus, took up arms against the tyrant, who had expelled
Daedalus from Sicily.

BEGAN WITH THE PEASANTS. HONOUR can be understood in two ways, 8:276
namely as a sacrifice begun by the peasants or by the rural gods, and
so they reached all the greater gods. Or the rural gods first began these
sacrifices and therefore every ambitious rural god strives for sacrifices
on account of envy.

NESTOR STILL IN HIS PRIME. Nestor lived for three centuries. 8:313

THE OECLEAN [STILL] SAFE, that is Amphiaraus, who hid himself since 8:316
he did not want [to participate] in Polynices' war. His wife exposed
him after a necklace had been given her.

AND CAENEUS NOT NOW A WOMAN. He was once a woman, and since 8:305
she cried a lot because of Neptune's violence when sleeping with her,
Neptune said that he would give her whatever she wanted, if she
stopped crying. And since she preferred to become a man, she lost her
female nature.

AND THE HAND OF THE OENEAN WAVERS. Namely in throwing now one 8:414
spear and now another.

TO JOIN RIGHT HAND WITH RIGHT HAND. Just as soldiers after a victory 8:421
kiss each other on account of joy, so too did they. Meleager's right
hand was joined to his right hand.

THEY PANELLED THE TOP, that is they curve the top of the house. SHELL- 8:564
FISH curve the ceiling of the house in the manner of a panel-ceiling.
This house is said to have a panel-ceiling that has something like a lake
in the middle of the roof, just as the houses whose beams and terrace
have been raised towards the roof.

THE BED IS OF SOFT SEDGE IN THE MIDDLE. Do not understand that *torus* 8:655
(the bolster) is made from wood, but rather like a heap made from soft
sedge, like a *culcitra* (bed, mattress), since strictly speaking a bolster

8:656 culcitram, quia proprie dicitur thorus a tortis herbis. Thorus, dico,
INPOSITVS LECTO, subaudi 'ligato constanti ex saligna' SPONDA ET 860
SALIGN[I]IS PEDIBVS.

8:744 MEMORESQVE TABELLE. In tabellis erat scriptum 'quercus ista fecit tale
et tale miraculum', et ideo dicuntur 'memores'.

INCIPIT LIBER VIIII

865

9:1 QVE GEMITVS TRVNCEQVE DEO.

9:12 DIXI PARTHAONE NATE. Parthaon fuit pater Oenei, regis Calidonie.

9:23 NAM et QVOD TE IACTAS ALCMENA MATRE CREATVM. Sic continuatur:
Vere ista, que non sunt in me, o Hercules, sed in te, non mihi debent
nocere sed tibi, quia, quod iactas te esse creatum ab Alcmena matre 870
9:24 per concubitum Iouis, nocebit tibi. Et ideo nocebit, quia IVPITER AVT
FALSVS PATER EST AVT VERVS in CRIMINE, sed si hoc est quod sit in
9:25 crimine, tu PETIS PATREM ADVLTERIO.

9:33 TENVIQVE VARAS MANVS. 'Varis uaricis' uena terre est. Que composita
71ᵛᵇ in cruribus curuat illa, et ideo uaras dicimus [curuos] / curuas. Et inde 875
'auarus' dicitur, quia omnia uult rapere.

9:51 REICERE ALCIDES. Licentia poete producitur 're-', quasi diceremus, ut
sint ibi duo i, ut quidam uolunt, ut primum locus duplicis consonantis
postponatur. Non ualet, quia numquam i pro duplici consonante
accipitur, nisi in simplici dictione, ut 'aio', 'adicio' et 'obicio' et 880
consimilibus. Remedium habemus Seruii, quod dicit: post 're-'
communiter poni.

9:67 CVNARVM LABOR EST. Quando Hercules adhuc erat in cunis, Iuno misit
unum serpentem ad dextrum et alium ad sinistrum latus eius, ut eum
interficerent, sed Hercules ambos strangulauit. 885

---

881 Remedium … 882 poni] cf. Serv. in Georg. 3:389: REICE 're' aut quasi monosyllabum
produxit licenter, aut, ut diximus supra, quia, cum faciat 'reieci', ", 'i' pro duplici habetur
et 're' efficit longam; in Aen. 10:473.

861 salignis correxi **868** Nam § deest **874** Varis i.e. uarix **875** curuos delevi **878** locus
correxi, locum cod.   **881** consimilibus correxi, non similibus cod. | re- correxi, se cod.
883 adhuc erat correxi, ad buceras cod.

(*torus*) is said to be from twisted (*tortis*) grass. A bolster, I say, PLACED 8:656
ON THE BED, supply 'bound from firm sedge ' WITH FRAME AND FEET OF
SEDGE.

MEMORATIVE TABLETS. On tablets it was written: 'this oak performed 8:744
such and such a miracle', and therefore they are called 'memorative'.

HERE STARTS BOOK VIIII

[HE ASKED] THE GOD THE [REASON] FOR THE SIGH AND AND THE 9:1
MUTILATED [FOREHEAD].

I SAID, O SON OF PARTHAON. Parthaon was the father of Oeneus, king of 9:12
Calydon.

FOR even THAT YOU BOAST THAT ALCMENA IS YOUR MOTHER. It could be 9:23
continued thus: Truly these [things] that do not exist in me, o Hercules,
but in you, ought not to hurt me but you, since the fact that you boast
that you are sprung from your mother Alcmena through copulation
with Jupiter will hurt you. And it will hurt you since JUPITER IS EITHER 9:24
YOUR FALSE FATHER OR YOUR TRUE FATHER by CRIME, but if it is true that
it is by crime, then you CLAIM YOUR FATHER THROUGH ADULTERY. 9:25

AND I HELD MY BENT HANDS. A *varix* is a vein in the earth. This vein, 9:33
when formed in the legs, bends them, and therefore we call curved
[hands] *uaras* (bent). And from this *auarus* (a greedy person) is
named, since he wants to take everything.

ALCIDES [WANTED] TO DRIVE BACK (*REICERE*). [The syllable] re- is 9:51
lengthened through poetic license, as though we would say that there
are two i here, just as some would have it, so that first the position of
double consonants is placed after it (re-). This is not valid, since i is
never taken as a double consonant, except for in a non-compund word,
such as *aio*, *adicio* and *obicio* and the like. We have Servius's solution
that says: *post re communiter poni*.[23]

---

[23] This explanations concerns the quantity of the syllable *re*. I have interpreted the phrase
simplex dictio as 'non-compund word', but this would apply only to the first in the short
list. It is unclear what 'Servius's solution' is supposed to mean. In the text given in the
apparatus Servius says that 'i' should be taken as a double consonant and that 're' as a
consequence is long.

9:69   QVOTA PARS LERNEE. Idra est proprium nomen illius serpentis, quem Hercules interfecit in Lerna palude. Sed hic appelatiuum nomen quorumdam serpentium ponit pro Idra, scilicet echinna.

9:83   ADMISSVMQVE TRAHENS. Permitebat parum ante se currere, postea me 'trahens', quia ligatum sequebatur.   890

9:88   SACRARVNT DIVESQVE MEO BONA COPIA CORNV EST. Naiades sacrauerunt cornu Acheloi et posuerunt illud in templo dee copie, que
72ʳᵃ   Bona dicitur Dea. Et nimpha, que ser- / uiebat Theseo in hoc conuiuio,
9:91   cum hoc cornu attulit TOTVM AVTVMNVM, id est omnes fructus, qui
9:92   solent haberi in autumno, et FELICIA POMA, id est mala granata. Que 895
ideo 'felicia' uocantur, quia contra uenenum accipiendum ualent.

9:123   AT PATERNI ORBES, id est rota, in qua Ixion in inferno positus est.

9:182   ERGO EGO FEDANTEM. Quandoquidem anima mea fuit ad hoc nata, ut pateretur labores, ergo passus sum hos labores seculi.

9:183   DOMVI BVSIRIM et cetera. Busiris, rex Egipti. Accepto consilio 900 interficiendi aliquem hospitem, ut pluuia redderetur sue terre, et illo sacrificato consuetum hospites in templo mactare. Hercules uero, cum sic deberet interfici, mortificauit eum.

9:184   NEC ME PASTORIS HABERI, Gerion, rex Hispanie, dicitur pastor, quia multa armenta possederat. Gerion dicitur trigeminus uero, quia tria 905 regna dicitur habuisse.

9:186   VOSNE MANVS. Non dicit quod Hercules istum taurum interfecisset, si transduxit de Creta in Maratona montem, sicut superius notauimus.

9:187   VESTRVM OPVS ELIS HABET. Apud Helidem ciuitatem Her<cules> Enomaum, patrem Athalante, occidit. Qui omnes, <qui> non potuerunt 910

---

900   Busiris ... 903 eum] *cf.* Serv. *in Georg.* 3:5: INLAVDATI NESCIT BVSIRIDIS A(RAS) Busiris rex fuit Aegypti: qui cum susceptos hospites immolaret, ab Hercule interemptus est, cum etiam eum voluisset occidere. **905** Gerion ... 906 habuisse] *cf.* expl. 7:363; 9:197. **908** sicut ... notauimus] *non inveni.*

888   echinna *i.e.* echidnae (*cf.* Met. 9:69) **900** Domvi § *deest* **902** consuetum *scil.* consuetum est **904** Haberi *i.e.* Hiberi **909** Vestrum § *deest* | Helidem *cum signo* h *sup. lin.* | Hercules *correxi,* hor *cod.* **910** qui *supplevi*

IT IS THE LABOUR OF [MY] CRADLE. When Hercules still was in the cradle, Juno sent one snake to his right side and another to his left to kill him, but Hercules strangled both of them.   9:67

WHICH PART OF THE LERNAEAN. Hydra is the proper name for the serpent that Hercules killed in the marsh Lerna. But here an appellative (species name) of a kind of serpent, namely *echidna*, is used instead of Hydra.   9:69

DRAGGING [HE FOLLOWS ME] RUNNING. He allowed me to run only a little ahead of him, thereafter dragging me, since he followed me who is tied to him.   9:83

THEY CONSECRATED IT AND BONA COPIA IS RICH THROUGH MY HORN. The Naiads consecrated the horn of Achelous and placed it in the temple of the goddess of abundance, who is called *bona dea*. And the nymph who served Theseus at this feast brought with this horn EVERYTHING AUTUMNAL, that is all fruits available in autumn and LUCKY APPLES, that is pomegranates. These are called 'lucky', since they are antidotes against poison.   9:88
                                                                            9:91
                                                                            9:92

AND THE PATERNAL RINGS, that is the wheel onto which Ixion is placed in the underworld.   9:123

THEREFORE I [SLEW] THE DEFILING. Since indeed my soul was born to this, to suffer labours, I suffered the labours of this world.[24]   9:182

BUSIRIS I VANQUISHED et cetera. Busiris, the king of Egypt. After he had taken counsel that a guest should be killed in order to restore rain to his land and after a guest had been sacrificed it became the custom to sacrifice guests in the temple. But Hercules killed him, since he (Hercules) was going to be killed in this way.   9:183

AND THE IBERIAN HERDSMAN'S [TRIPPLE FORM] DID NOT [MOVE] ME. Geryon, king of Spain, is called 'herdsman' since he owned a lot of cattle. Geryon is called threefold since he is said to have had three kingdoms.   9:184

HANDS, DID YOU. He does not say that Hercules had killed this bull, if it carried [him] across from Crete to mount Marathon, as we have noted above.   9:186

ELIS KNOWS YOUR LABOUR. Near the city of Elis Hercules killed Atalanta's father Oenomaus, who killed all who could not conquer his   9:187

---

[24] Hercules is dying and at this point starts recounting his labours.

72rb   uincere filiam suam Ipodomiam, interficiebat. / Dicitur tamen quod
         Pelops eum interfecit.

9:187   VESTRVM STIPHALIDES VNDE. Apud Stiphalides undas, scilicet apud
         Phineum, Hercules arpias fugauit cum sagittis suis. Et filiis Boree, ut
         superius diximus, iussit eas persequi usque ad Strophados insulas. 915
         Dicitur tamen quod apud Stiphalides undas Hercules duos serpentes
         interficeret.

9:188   PARTHOMIVMQVE NEMVS. Duos leones legitur Herculem interfecisse,
         unum in Nemea silua, cuius pellem semper gerebat, alium in nemore,
         quod dicitur Parthomium. Huius uero leonis pellem non gessit.   920

9:189   TERMO<DO>NTIACO. Termodoon est omnis fluuius Tracie habens
         auream arenam. Rex Tracie Diomedes pugnauit cum Amazonibus, que
         etiam sunt in Tracia, sed deuictus est ab illis et balteus suus aureus
         ablatus est ei. Quadam uero die, dum Hercules apud illum
         hospitaretur, rogauit eum rex, ut balteum suum, quem habebant 925
         Amazones, sibi redderet. Cuius causa regis Hercules pugnauit cum
         Amazonibus illisque deuictis regi balteum reddidit.

9:190   POMAQVE AB INSOMNI CONCVSTODITA. Poma Hesperidum. Hesperides
         filie Athlantis fuerunt, siue Pleiades. Pleiades filie Athlantis, dicuntur
72va   Hesperides, a quodam fratre Athlantis, qui est dictus Hes- / perus.   930

9:192   ARCHADIE VASTATOR APER, quem Hercules ad suum collum et ante
         pedes sociorum proiecit.

9:197   HIS CACVS ORRENDVM. Hercules de Hispania rediens spoliato
         trigemino Gerione ospitatus est apud Euandrum regem, qui illo in loco
         erat, ubi est modo Roma. Erat quoque ibi filius Vulcani, Cacus, in 935
         quodam antro absconditus, habens pro hostio magnum lapidem.
         Quem postquam firmauerat, ab omnibus tutus erat. Iste pessimus duos
         boues Herculis furatus est. Quos, dum Hercules quereret, in antro eius

---

911 Dicitur ... 912 interfecit] *cf. Myt. Vat.* 2, 169: DE ENOMAO Enomaus rex fuit Elide et
Pisarum.Hic equos habuit uelocissimos utpote uentorum flatu procreatos, qui procos
filie Ypotamie multos necauit sub hac conditione ad curule certamen prouocatos ut aut
uictus traderet filiam aut uictor necaret. Postea cum Pelopen Tantali filium, qui a
Neptuno aptos curuli certamini equos acceperat quorum cursu omnes anteiret, amasset
Ypotamia, corrupit Mirtilum aurigam patris primi coitus pactione. Qui factis axibus
cereis cum uictore Pelope a puella promissum posceret premium, ab eius marito
precipitatus est in mare cui et nomen imposuit, nam ab eo Mirtoum dicitur pelagus.
914 ut ... 915 diximus] *cf.* expl. 7:3 (69va cod.).   **918** Duos ... interfecisse] *non inueni*.

913 Stiphalides[1] *i.e.* Stymphalides   **918** Parthomiumque *i.e.* Partheniumque | Herculem
correxi, hercules *cod.*   **921** Termodontiaco *correxi*   **928** concustodita *correxi,* non custodita
cod.   **929** Athlantis[1] *cum signo* h *sup. lin.*

daughter, Hippodamia. However, it is [also] said that Pelops killed him.

YOUR [WORK] THE STYMPHALIAN WAVES. Near the Stymphalian waves, that is to say near Phineus, Hercules chased the harpies away with his arrows. And, as we have said above, he commanded the sons of Boreas to follow them all the way to the Strophades islands. However, it is [also] said that Hercules killed two snakes near the Stymphalian waves. `9:187`

AND THE PARTHENIAN GROVE. It can be read that Hercules killed two lions, one, whose pelt he always wore, in the Nemean forest and the other in a grove called the Parthenian. He did not wear the pelt of this lion. `9:188`

THERMODONIAN. Thermodon is every river in Thrace that has golden sand. Diomedes, king of Thrace, fought with the Amazons, who also live in Thrace, but he was conquered by them and his golden girdle was taken from him. One day when Hercules stayed with him, the king asked him to return to him his girdle, which the Amazons had. For the sake of the king Hercules fought the Amazons and after they had been conquered he returned the girdle to the king.[25] `9:189`

AND THE APPLES GUARDED BY THE SLEEPLESS [SERPENT]. The apples of the Hesperids. The Hesperids, or the Pleiads, were daughters of Atlantis. The Pleiads, daughters of Atlantis are called Hesperids from a brother of Atlantis, who is called Hesperus. `9:190`

THE RAVAGER OF ARCHADIA, THE WILD-BOAR, that Hercules threw upon his shoulders and before the feet of his comrades. `9:192`

BY THESE [ARMS] CACUS THE TERRIBLE [MONSTER]. When Hercules returned from Spain after threefold Geryon had been robbed, he was the guest of king Evander, who lived in the place where Rome is now. And there also the son of Vulcan, Cacus, hid himself in a cave with a big stone for a door. After he had closed this he was safe from everyone. This evil person stole two of Hercules' cows. When Hercules was looking for the cows he heard them in Cacus's cave. And soon he `9:197`

---

[25] The phrasing *omnis fluuius* (every river) is strange. It may possibly be a mistake for *amnis, fluuius* (a stream, a river), in which case a synonym is given to *amnis*.

audiuit. Moxque antrum eius fodiendo inde eum abstraxit et per crura
eum precipitauit.   940

9:232   REGNAQVE VISSVRAS ITERVM T<ROIANA> S<AGITTAS>. Ideo dicit 'iterum',
quia cum Hercules iuisset cum Iasone propter aureum uellem
hospitari apud Troiam uoluerunt, sed expulsi sunt a litore. Et tunc ibi
eius sagitte fuerunt.

9:233   FERRE IVBES. Scilicet dedit Philotete arcum, pharetram et sagittas 945
Herculis. Et secundum rei ueritatem propter hoc dedit, ut cinerem,
postquam corpus esset conbustum insula, in silua Ethes cumularet.
Fecit eum etiam iurare, quod nulli hominum diceret cinerem suum in
terra manere, sed in celo translatum esse.

9:241 | TIMVERE / DEI PRO VI<N>DICE T<ERRAE>. Merito, quia terram uindicabat 950
72ᵛᵇ   Hercules a pluribus monstris. Ideo timuerunt dei, ne eo mortuo
monstra contra eos surgerent.

9:245   QVOD MEMORIS POPVLI. 'Populum' hic uocat deos memor<abili>um
beneficiorum memores.

9:248   OBLIGOR IPSE TAMEN. Scilicet grates inde debeo uobis. Quando aliquid 955
boni facimus alicui, tunc illum, cui facimus, alligamus, id est
debitorem enim nobis astringimus.

9:248   SED ENIM NEC PECTORA VANO FIDA METV PAVEANT. Ita continuatur: Vos
timetis, si timere debetis. Timor hic iste uanus est, et quia uanus, ideo
fido sit, ut pectora uestra non paueant uana m<etu>.   960

9:274   ODIVM sed [in] IN PROLE PATERNVM. Illud 'odium', quod Euristeus
habebat in Herculem, illud postea habuit in filio eius Iolao.

9:275   AT LONGIS ANXIA CVRIS. Alcmene non habet Iolaum nepotem suum, in
9:276   quo PONAT ANILES QVESTVS, id est de morte Herculis. Ideo non potuit
ponere aniles questus in Iolao, quia fugerat ad templum ignoti dei, 965
9:278   quod erat Athenis, ut posset euadere penas Euristei. At HABET IOLEN.

9:294   LVCINAM NEXVSQVE PARES, id est VOCA<BAM> et alios, qui presunt
par<i>entibus, scilicet qui habent potentiam nectendi uuluam <ne>
73ʳᵃ   partus exeat. †Hostaldes† inuo- / caui, ut mihi essent propicii. Vel
aliter: Secundum quod quidam libri habent NEXASQUE DEAS, possit 970
intelligi tres Gratie, que sunt nexe et que iuuant parientes. Hoc quod

---

941 uissuras *i.e.* uisuras   **945** sagittas *correxi,* sagitte *cod.*   **947** Ethes *i.e.* Oetes
950 uindice *correxi*   **953** hic *correxi,* hoc *cod.* | memorabilium *correxi*   **958** paueant *correxi,*
paueont *ut uid. cod.*   **961** sed *fortasse perperam pro* scilicet | in¹ *delevi*   **962** Iolao *correxi,* ialo
cod.   **968** parientibus *correxi* | ne *supplevi*

dug out his cave, dragged him out of there and hurled him down by his legs.

ARROWS THAT SHALL AGAIN SEE THE TROIAN KINGDOM. He says 'again', 9:232 since when Hercules had gone with Jason because of the golden fleece, they wanted to be guests at Troy, but were expelled from the beach. And at that time his arrows were there.

YOU BID [THE SON OF POEAS] TO CARRY. That is to say he gave 9:233 Philoctetes the bow, quiver and arrows of Hercules. And in reality he gave them so that, after his body had been burned to ashes on the island, he would pile the ashes in the Oete forest. He also made him swear that he would tell no one that his ashes remained on earth, but that they had been transferred to heaven.

THE GODS FEARED FOR THE DEFENDER OF THE EARTH. Justly so, since 9:241 Hercules had freed the earth of many monsters. Therefore the gods feared that with him dead the monsters would rise against them.

THAT [I AM CALLED RULER] OF MINDFUL PEOPLE. Here he calls the gods, 9:245 who are mindful of memorable favours, 'people'.

STILL I MYSELF AM OBLIGED. Namely from this I owe you thanks. When 9:248 we do something good towards someone, then we bind to us the one towards whom we have done good, that is we tie him to us as a debtor.

BUT LET NOT YOUR FAITHFUL HEART TREMBLE WITH GROUNDLESS FEAR. It 9:248 may be continued thus: You fear, if you ought to fear. Here this fear is groundless, and since groundless, it is therefore of a faithful person, so that your heart will not tremble with groundless fear.[26]

THE PATERNAL HATRED but AGAINST THE OFFSPRING. The hatred that 9:274 Eurystheus harboured against Hercules, he later harboured against his son, Iolaus.

BUT TROUBLED BY LENGTHY CONCERNS. Alcmena does not have Iolaus, 9:275 her nephew, to whom SHE DIRECTS HER WOMANISH COMPLAINTS, that is 9:276 regarding the death of Hercules. She could not direct her womanish complaints to Iolaus, because he had fled to the temple of an unknown god, which was in Athens, so that he might escape the punishment of Eurystheus. But SHE HAS IOLE. 9:278

LUCINA AND THE EQUAL JOININGS, that is I CALLED and also others, who 9:294 protect those giving birth, namely those who have the power to bind the womb [so that] the birth [does not] go forth. I invoke the †Hostaldest† so that they will be favourable to me. Or differently: According to the fact that some books have AND THE JOINED GODDESSES, this could be understood as the three Graces, who are joined and who assist those giving birth. That the Graces are joined, that is looking

[26] This is an uncertain translation. The explanation seems to be trying to pars the adjectives *fidus* and *vanus*, and the noun *metus*. *Metus* can be both masculine and feminine. The word is taken as feminine in the last sentence. It is uncertain what *fido* should mean here.

Gratie sunt nexe, id est respicientes ad mediam, signum est secundum ueritatem, quod beneficium duplex reuerti debet.

9:299 PRESSA GENV. Quasi diceret: Quamdiu sic erit leuum genu pressum A DEXTRO POPLITE et digiti mei INTER SE iuncti PECTINE, id est ad modum 975 pectinis, Alchmene parere non possit.

9:326 TE TAMEN, O GENETRIX. Quia uetus erat, genitricem eam uocat uel matrem. Ita continuatur: Licet doleas, tamen non de propinqua, *sicut* de alia doles.

9:327 QVID SI TIBI MIRA. Tu fles pro ministra tua. Quid faceres, si referrem 980 mutationem sororis mee? Certe causa mei multo magis fleres.

9:341 IN SPEM BACARVM. In floribus habemus spem fructuum.

9:348 CONTVLERAT VERSOS SERVATO uel SVBLATO NOMINE. Illa membra non fuerunt seruata uel sublata, quando mutarentur. Nomen uero fuit seruatum uel [uel] sublatum a mutatione, quia idem mansit. 985

9:397 NAM LIMINE CONSTITIT ALTO. Hercules accepit coniugem Heben postquam translatus fuit ad celum. Que potestatem habebat renouandi
73ʳᵇ hominem senem et pue- / rum ad iuuentutem ducendi. Hanc rogauit, ut filium Iolaum, quod puer ad templum Min<eru>e pro euadendis insidiis fugerat Euristei, iuuenem facere[n]t, ut uindictam de Euristeo. 990

9:403 NON EST PASSA THEMIS. Hebe uolebat iurare quod ulterius non mutaret aliquem post Iolaum. Themis uates preuidens futura non est hoc passa. Dixitque Iupiter <quod> erat precepturus, quod filii Almeonis et Calliriores de pueritia mutarentur in firmam etatem et uirtutem. NAM IAM DISCORDIA[M] THEBE. Ita continuatur: Iupiter faciet illos pueros 995 mutari per Heben, suam primigenam, ut interficiant Flegam, auunculum sui patris Almeonis. Et hoc ideo eueniet, quia THEBE MOVENT DISCORDIA BELLA.

9:404 CAPANEVSQVE NISI AB IOVE VINCI. Quod bella sint, potes uidere, quia Capaneus iste rex non poterit interfici nisi ab Ioue. Qui fulminatus est 1000 ideo, quia, cum ipse fortis cepisset quandam Thebanam turrim, non solum in Bachum et Mercurium et ceteros deos sed etiam in ipsum Iouem conuicia inferebat, sic neque Iupiter posset hanc turrim aufferre.

9:405 DEFLENT PARES FRATRES IN VVLNERE, id est Ethiocles et Pollinices.
73ᵛᵃ Pollinices uulnerauit fratrem suum ad mor- / tem et post fleuit super 1005

973 duplex *pro* dupliciter   978 sicut *correxi,* sset *ut vid. cod.*   985 uel² *delevi, bis scr. cod.* 986 Nam § *deest*   989 Minerue *correxi*   990 faceret *correxi*   993 quod¹ *supplevi* | Almeonis *i.e.* Alcmaeonis   994 Calliriores *i.e.* Callirhoes   995 discordia *correxi*   996 Flegam *i.e.* Phegeum   1003 aufferre *i.e.* auferre

towards the middle, is in reality a sign that a favour should be doubly returned.[27]

WITH THE KNEE PRESSED. As though she would say: So long as the left knee will be pressed thus FROM HER RIGHT KNEE and my fingers joined TO EACH OTHER in a comb - that is in the manner of a comb - Alcmene cannot give birth.   9:299

YET YOU, O PARENT. Since she was old she calls her parent or mother. It may be continued thus: Although you grieve, still you do not grieve over a relative as over another.   9:326

WHAT IF [I WOULD TELL] YOU THE WONDEROUS [FATE]. You cry over your servant. What would you do if I told you about the transformation of my sister? Surely then you would cry a lot more for my sake.   9:327

IN HOPE OF FRUITS. In flowers we have the hope of fruits.   9:341

SHE BORE THE CHANGED [FEATURES] WITH THE NAME PRESERVED, or SUSTAINED. These limbs were nor preserved or sustained, when they were transformed. The name, however, was preserved or sustained from the transformation, since it remained the same.   9:348

FOR IN THE DEEP ENTRANCE STOOD. Hercules took Hebe as a wife after he had been transferred to heaven. She had the power to rejuvenate an old man and to lead a boy to his youth. He asked her that they would make his son Iolaus a young man so that [he can take] revenge on Eurystheus, because he had fled to the temple of Minerva as a boy to escape Eurystheus's ambush.   9:397

THEMIS DID NOT PERMIT. Hebe wanted to swear that she would not transform anyone else after Iolaus. Themis, the oracle, who could see the future, did not permit this. And Jupiter said that he would order that the sons of Alcmaeon and Callirhoe would be transformed from childhood to a strong age and virtue. FOR THEBES NOW [PREPARES] DISCORDANT [WARS]. It may be continued thus: Jupiter will make it so that these boys are transformed by Hebe, his firstborn, so that they can kill Phegeus, their father Alcmaeon's uncle. And this will happen, since THEBES PREPARES DISCORDANT WARS.   9:403

AND CAPANEUS [SHALL NOT BE] CONQUERED, EXCEPT BY JUPITER. You can see that there are wars, since king Capaneus cannot be killed, except by Jupiter. He was struck by lightning, since when he, a powerful man, had taken a Theban tower, he insulted not only Bacchus and Mercury and the other gods, but also Jupiter himself, [speaking] in this way that not even Jupiter could take the tower.   9:404

THE EQUAL BROTHERS WEEP OVER THE WOUND, that is Etheocles and Polynices. Polynices mortally wounded his brother and later cried over   9:405

---

[27] It is unclear who or what †Hostaldest† is.

eum. Ille uero clam educens gladium interfecit Pollinicem et sic uterque obiit.

9:408   NATVS ERAT FACTO PIVS ET SCELERATVS EODEM. Laius rex Thebarum, pregnante Iocasta uxore sua, dormiens uidit bestiam unicornem de camera sua egredientem et se ad mensam sedentem interficientem. 1010 Hac uisione cognita dixerunt sapientes quod interficeretur ab illo, qui nasceretur de Iocasta. Ideo preceptum est puerum nasciturum uel puellam interfici. Nato puero non est interfectus a matre, quia pulcher uisus est, sed pannis inuolutus bene et in silua proiectus pede forato cum plumbo. Quem puerum homines Crocali regis uenantes et 1015 inuenientes ad Crocalum regem tulerunt. Et impositum est illi Edippus et factus est adoptiuus filius Crocalo. Eo adulto, cum esset werra inter Crocalum et Laium, Edippus interfecit patrem suum. Et superatis Athenis accepit Iocastam matrem suam coniugem.

Quidam autem dicunt quod Edippus, cum in ludo percuteret 1020 proprium filium suum Crocali, dictus est 'inuenticius' ab eo. Hac de causa interrogauit Crocalum, dicens ita: Sum ego filius tuus uel sum 73ᵛᵇ inuenticius, sicut dicit iste filius tuus? / Post quod respondit ei Crocalus quod non erat suus filius, sed inuenticius. Quod erat, inueniens probum quemque querebat scire, si esset pater suus. 1025 Tandem inueniens Laium non Thebis sed in alio loco interrogauit: Es tu pater meus? Laius superbe dixit: Stulte, neque sum pater tuus, neque uolo esse. Ideo Edippus iratus abstulit sibi caput ense et ciuitatem et coniugem eius accepit, de qua habuit quandam filia<m> et duos filios, Ethioclen et Pollinicen. Sed notum factum est sibi quod 1030 Iocasta, coniunx sua, esset sibi mater. Quadam namque die, cum Edippus egrederetur de balneo uiso pede eius de plumbo signato calido, dixit Iocasta: Tu es filius meus. Et huius rei certitudine habita Edippus excecauit semet ipsum et in carcere omnibus diebus uite sue permansit.   1035

Ethiocles uero et Pollinices eius filii inuidentes eum positum in carcere ante palatium irridebant eum. Et, quia ille commotus fuit hoc dolore, rogauit Eumenides, ut discordes eos facerent. Et adeo discordes facti sunt, quod alter alterum pati non poterant. Vnde constitutum est inter eos, quod per annum totum alter regnaret, alter 1040 exul fieret.

74ʳᵃ   Ethiocles autem, quia maior erat, prior regnauit. / Et interim Pollinices ad Arastrum regem militare iuit. Contigit quod egrediente

1008 Natvs … 1119 est] *cf.* Hyg. *Fab.* 66-73.

1014 forato *correxi,* ferato *cod.*   **1016** Edippus *scil.* nomen Edippus   **1029** filiam *correxi* **1043** Arastrum *i.e.* Adrastum

him. But he (Etheocles) secretly drew his sword and killed Polynices and thus they both died.

THE SON WAS DUTIFUL AND WICKED IN THE SAME ACT. When his wife Jocasta was pregnant, Laius, king of the Thebans, saw a unicorn in his sleep that walked out of his chamber and killed him while he was sitting at his table. After this vision had been made known some wise men said that he would be killed by the one to whom Jocasta would give birth. Therefore it was ordered that the boy or girl who was about to be born should be killed. When the boy was born he was not killed by his mother, because he looked beautiful, but well wrapped in swaddling clothes he was thrown into the forest with his feet pierced with led. Some of king Crocalus's men found this boy when they were hunting and they brought him to king Crocalus. [The name] Oedipus was given him and he was made Crocalus's adopted son. When he was an adult and there was war between Crocalus and Laius, Oedipus killed his father. And after Athens had been overcome he took Jocasta, his mother, as his wife. 9:408

Some say that when Oedipus in play struck Crocalus's own son he called him a 'foundling'. Because of this he asked Crocalus speaking thus: 'Am I your son, or am I a foundling, just as your son says?' After this Crocalus replied to him that he was not his own son, but a foundling. Since this was the case, he tried to find out if every good man he met was his father. Finally he found Laius not in Thebes but in another place and he asked him: 'Are you my father?' Laius arrogantly said: 'Stupid boy, I am not your father, nor do I want to be'. Because of this the enraged Oedipus took his head off with his sword and took both his city and his wife, with whom he had a daughter and two sons, Eteocles and Polynices. But it was made known to him that Iocasta, his wife, was his mother. For one day when Oedipus came out from the bath and Iocasta saw his foot marked by the hot led, she said: 'You are my son'. And when he realised this was true, Oedipus blinded himself and remained in prison for the rest of his life.

His sons Eteocles and Polynices were spiteful and mocked him when he was placed in jail in front of the palace. And since he was provoked by this grief he asked the Eumenids to bring discord among them. They grew discordant to such a degree that one could not suffer the other. Wherefore it was decided between them that for one whole year one would rule and the other would be in exile.

Eteocles ruled first, since he was oldest. Meanwhile Polynices went to king Adrastus to soldier. It happened that when he was leaving the

eo ciuitatem Argon adeo magna inundatio pluuie superuenit. In qua, cum aliquam domum ospitium habere nequiret, tandem ueniens ad 1045 quandam porticum Adrastri hospitatus est in ea. Tideus uero, quia in uenatione et uolendo non interfecerat fratrem suum Menalippum, exulabat. Consuetudo enim erat, ut exularet quicumque interficeret consanguineum suum, licet nolendo. Accidit, ut eadem pluuia et eadem nocte imminente, licet paulo post, Tideus ingrederetur Argon et 1050 ueniret ad eandem porticum, in qua hospitatus est cum Pollinice. Cum quo, quia equi eorum ceperant se inuincem percutere, iurgatus est. Et, quia mentionem sui gladii Tideus non habuit, non <in>terfecit eum. In ullo enim tam paruo corpore tanta uirtus latuit, quanta in corpore Tidei.   1055

Tunc rex Arastus non ualens dormire, tum quia uetus erat, tum quia responsionem Apollinis in animo uoluens, scilicet quod unam filiam marito traderet leoni, aliam apro, audiuit illos rixantes. Et accensis 74ʳᵇ lucernis, dum illos iret uidere et prohiberet, uidit in scuto Pol- / linices leonem pictum et in Tidei scuto aprum. Consuetudo enim erat, ut, si 1060 aliquis magnus aliquam probitatem faceret, omnes consanguinei eius ferrent signum eius probitatis, quod isti duo fecerunt. Hercules interfecerat leonem, quem Pollinices pictum ferebat in scuto, quia de progenie Herculis descenderat. Meneager aprum interfecit, quem Tideus pictum in scuto habebat, quia frater eius erat. Et cognouit 1065 Arastus, quod, quia de istis duobus dixerat Apollo, suam filiam Argiam dedit Pollinici, aliam Tideo tradidit.

Apropinquante uero tempore regiminis Pollinicis, tum rogatu suo tum rogatu Argie, iuit Tideus Thebas ad Ethioclen, ut, sicut constitutum erat [ut], permitteret eum regnare. Et, quia Ethiocles 1070 superbe et inflate denegauit pactum fieri, Tideus, ut audax, et animose et tumide uocauit eum perfidum et fallacem, et egressus est curiam. Ethiocles uero misit quosdam milites per portam unam, quosdam autem per aliam ad quendam constitutum locum, ad quem congregati fuissent. Quinquaginta fuerunt. Existimabat eos uerecundiam pati, si 1075 74ᵛᵃ insimul eos mitteret contra unum uirum. Quos omnes / congregatos lucente luna Tideus inuenit. Quorum unus iaculum sibi misit. Cui Tideus: Quis es? Concurre! Et uidens omnes sibi concurrere et exestimans se non posse omnibus resistere fugit ad saxum, in quo Spinx manserat, quem interfecit Edippus. Cuius saxi partes iaciens 1080 super eos iiii:or interfecit uno ictu et alios fugauit. Quos tandem omnes morti tradidit ferro excepto uno, quem dimisit, ut Ethiocli nunciaret uel *ut* diceret uerbum istud ex sui parte: Qualis ego sum, tales omnes

1047 uolendo non *scil.* nolendo   1053 interfecit *correxi*   1064 Meneager *i.e.* Meleager
1068 suo *sup. lin.*   1070 ut *deleui*   1078 uidens *post corr. ex* uides   1083 ut *correxi, et cod.*

city of Argos a great deluge of rain overtook him. When he could not find lodging in any house in this rain, he came at last to one of Adrastus's colonnades and lodged there. Tydeus was in exile, since he had killed his brother, Menalippus, during a hunt, although not willingly. For the custom was to exile whoever killed a relative, even though unwillingly. It happened that Tydeus, threatened by the same rain the same night, although a bit later, entered Argos and came to the same colonnade where he sheltered with Polynices. He quarrelled with him, because their horses started to fight each other. And since Tydeus did not mention his sword, he did not kill him. For in no body so small did such a great virtue hide itself, as in the body of Tydeus.

When king Adrastus could not sleep, both because he was old and because he thought about a reply from Apollo - namely that he would hand over one of his daughters in marriage to a lion and the other to a wild-boar - he heard them quarreling. And when with lighted lanterns he went to see them and stop them, he saw a lion painted on Polynices' shield and a wild-boar on Tydeus's shield. For the custom was that if a great man had done a great deed, then all of his relatives would carry the sign of his greatness, which these two did. Hercules had killed the lion that Polynices carried painted on his shield, since he stemmed from Hercules' lineage. Meleager had killed the wild-boar that Tydeus had painted on his shield, since Meleager was his brother. And since Apollo had spoken about these two, Adrastus understood that he should give his daughter Argia to Polynices and the other he would hand over to Tydeus.

When the time for Polynices' rule was getting close, Tydeus, on his own accord as well as on Argia's request, went to Thebes to Eteocles, so that just as it had been decided he would permit Polynices to rule. And because Eteocles arrogantly and proudly denied that an agreement existed, Tydeus, being bold, both courageously and haughtily called him dishonest and deceitful and left the hall. Eteocles sent some soldiers through one gate, some others through another to a designated place where they would gather. They were fifty. He thought that they would suffer shame if he sent [all of] them at the same time against a single man. By the light of the moon Tydeus found all of them gathered. One of them trew his spear at him. Tydeus [asked] him: 'Who are you? Attack then!' When he saw all of them attacking him and he realised that he could not resist them all, he fled to a rock, where the Sphinx, whom Oedippus killed, had dwelled. Throwing parts of this cliff over them he killed four with one blow and chased away the others. Finally he had delivered all of them to death with his sword, except for one, whom he sent to tell Eteocles about this, or to say this word on his behalf: 'Such as I am, such will all of us

ueniemus in arma. Qui omnibus his nunciatis, ne uel uideretur
diceretur fugisse timore uite, cultro se interfecit.   1085

Arastus dolens de amissione regni Pollinicis et uulnere Tidei, et
uolens cum magno excercitu obsidere Thebas, ad quendam montem ob
augurio quosdam dimisit. Inter quos erat Amphiaraus rex et sacerdos.
Quod, quia aquilas pugnare uiderat cum cingnis, quorum multi
mortui sunt, significantes Thebanos; aquilarum uix aliqua euasit 1090
significans obsessuros reges, quorum tandem nullus euasit, nisi
Arastus. Reges autem septem fuerunt, et hii Arastus et Pollinices,
74vb   Tideus, Amphiaraus, Capraneus, / Ippomedon, Parthonopheus.

Amphiaraus intelligens se ibi mori in quadam fouea abscondit se, in
qua diu mansit. Sed coniunx eius, scilicet Euriphile, dum Capaneus 1095
minaretur destruere omnes domus, ab Argia petebat monile male
fortunatum. Quod sibi illa daret ea tamen conditione, ut uirum suum
indicaret.

Monile autem sic male fatatum est: Venus rogauit Vulcanum, uirum
suum, ut Hermione[s] coniugi[s] Cadmi, <quam> ipsa habuerat de 1100
Marte, quoddam monile faceret. Fabricato monili factum est, ut
semper sequeretur infortunium, quod post Hermionem peruenit ad
Iocastam. Pollinices adduxit illud secum ueniens ad Arastum regem, et
dedit illud Argie, coniugi sue. Quo accepto ab Euriphile raptus est
Amphiaraus indicio coniugis sue. Et ipse et supradicti reges ad 1105
obsidendas Thebas iuerunt, unde nullus illorum reuersus est, nisi
Arastus, quia mortui sunt ibi. Quocirca, quia Almeon, filius
Amphiarai, patrem suum audierat ibi subuersum, et hac proditione
matris interfecit Euriphilem, matrem suam, et accepit eius monile.
75ra   Moxque Almeon furibundus factus est. Quod uidens coniunx / sua 1110
Calliroe expostulare cepit ab eo monile, quod mater Euriphile abstulit,
existimans eum recepturum sanitatem, quia credebat monile male
fatatum plus nocere et infortunium afferre uiro habenti se quam
femine. Et accepto monili aliter quam sperare accidit, quia potius a
fratre matris sue Euriphile, qui dicitur Flegias, occisus est. Quare 1115
Calliroe, que fuerat coniunx Almeonis, petiit a Ioue, ut infantes, quos
ex Almeone habuerat, adultos faceret et confortaret ad hoc, ut patrem
suum, uel Almeonem, ulciscentur. Quod donum Iupiter iussit
primigenam Hebem dare illi, et factum est.

9:421   PALLANTIAS. Aurora, filia Pallantis, coniugis Thitoi.   1120

1085 fugisse *correxi*, figisse *cod.*   1089 cingnis *i.e.* cygnis/cycnis   1092 Reges *post corr. ex*
regens   1093   Capraneus *i.e.* Capaneus | Parthonopheus *i.e.* Parthonopaeus
1100 Hermione coniugi *correxi* | quam *supplevi* 1108 subuersum *correxi*, submersum *cod.*
post corr. ex submersurum   1113   afferre *i.e.* auferre   1115   Flegias *i.e.* Phegeus
1118 donum *correxi*, domum *cod.*   1120 Pallantias § *deest* | Thitoi *i.e.* Tithoni

come in arms.' After the soldier had told all of this he killed himself with a knife, so as not be seen or said to have fled for fear for his life.

Adrastus, who grieved the loss of Polynices' kingdom and Tydeus's wound and wanted to lay siege to Thebes with a great army, sent some people to a mountain to take augury. Among them was Amphiaraus, both king and priest. The fact that he had seen eagles fighting with swans, many of which were dead, signified the Thebans; that barely anyone of the eagles escaped signified the besieging kings, of whom barely none survived in the end, except for Adrastus. There were seven kings and these were Adrastus and Polynices, Tydeus, Amphiaraus, Capaneus, Hippomedon, Parthenopaeus.

Amphiaraus understood that he would die there and hid himself in a pit, where he remained for a long time. But his wife, that is to say Eriphyle, begged for an ill-fated necklace from Argia, when Capaneus threatened to destroy every house. This she gave her, but on the condition that she would betray her husband.

The necklace was ill-fated in this way: Venus asked her husband Vulcan to make a necklace for Cadmus's wife Harmonia, whom Venus had had with Mars. When the necklace was finished it happened that bad fortune always came with it, which after Harmonia came to Jocasta. Polynices carried it with him when he came to king Adrastus and he gave it to Argia, his wife. After it had been received by Eriphyle, Amphiaraus was dragged away through his wife's betrayal. And he and the above-mentioned kings went to lay siege to Thebes, whence none of them returned, since they all died there, except for Adrastus. Therefore Alcmaeon, Amphiaraus's son, since he had heard that his father had been destroyed there, killed Eriphyle, his mother, because of the mother's betrayal and took her necklace. Soon Alcmaon was made mad. When his wife Callirhoe saw this she started to demand the necklace from him, which his mother Eriphyle had taken, thinking that he would regain his sanity, since she believed that the ill-fated necklace hurt more and brought more misfortune when a man owned it rather than a woman. And after she had received the necklace, things happened contrary to what she had hoped, since he was instead killed by his mother's, Eriphyle's, brother, who is called Phegeus. Therefore Callirhoe, who was the wife of Alcmaeon, begged of Jupiter to make the infants she had had from Alcmaeon adults and to strengthen them so that they would avenge their father, or Alcmaeon. Jupiter ordered his firstborn Hebe to give this gift to her, and it was done.

PALLANTIS. Aurora, daughter of Pallas, the wife of Tithonus.   9:421

9:432   NON AMBITIONE NEC ARMIS. Non sunt isti facti iuuenes 'ambitione', id est honore, scilicet ut Hebe aliquem honorem tamen habeat. 'Nec armis', id est non propter arma illorum iuuenem exercendum ad utilitatem, sed super factum est.

9:448   EGEAS METIRIS AQVAS ET IN ASIDE TERRA. Substantiuum, id est in Asia 1125 terra. Vel aliter: Secundum †Teot† Asia fuit mulier, unde patria est dicta. Asis nomen gentile, sed tamen formam habent patronomicam.

9:476 | ILLE qui EST OCVLVS et FORMOSVS / et INIQVVS. Ille dicitur habere oculos
75rb   iniquos, qui quod uidet et cupere non debet, male cupit habere.

9:647   QVOQVE CHIMERA IVGO. Chimera est mons, in cuius sumitate habitant 1130
9:648   leones et ideo dicitur ET HORA ET PECTVS LEENE habere. Et in medio habitant homines cum capris habentes ignem. Et ad radices eius morantur serpentes in lacu. Et metaforice dictum est. Serpens latitando incedit sic et luxuria primum incedit latitando temptans adinuenire, quod uult. Leo fortis est et petulans. Post inceptam delectationem 1135 fortitudinem exibet, si necesse. Capra est fetida et inethos tandem nefarium opus fetet.

9:649   DEFICIVNT SILVE, id est: o BIBLI, tu CONCIDIS in ea parte iugi, in qua 'silue deficiunt'.

9:693   OSIRIS, maritus Isidis, a fratre suo Absirto uel Tiphone interfectus est. 1140 Quem diu Ysis, siue Iocasta, ques<i>uit. Tandem inuenit eum, in lineis pannis inuolutum collegit, a fratre suo frustrauit sparsum. Vnde adhuc

---

1130   Chimera² … 1137 fetet] *cf. Myt. Vat. 2, 154*: Chimera autem dicta est bestia ore leo, postremis partibus draco, media parte capra. Re uera autem mons est Cilicie cuius hodieque ardet cacumen, iugata quod sunt leones, media autem pascua sunt, ima uero montis serpentibus plena.   **1140**   Osiris … 1160 simulant *cf.* clm 14809 (1:747): Osyris maritus ysidis siue io a fratre suo qui dicitur absirtus uel tiphon interfectus fuit quamdiu ysis siue io quesium et tandem inuentum in lineis uel laneis pannis collegit a fratre suo frustatim spersum / Vnde adhuc ysis celebrat festum eius in unaquaque noua lunatione pro gaudio illius reperitionis et tunc exit de nilo quidam taurus qui lingua egyptia apis dicitur habens in dextro armo maculam ad modum lune factam istuc sacerficatur et tamen idem uel eius similis omni anno in alio festo similiter exit de nilo qui similiter sacrificatur et sic fit in quolibet festo hoc de tauro testatur secundum augustinum de ciuitate dei Pingitur aut ysis cornuta id est cornua lune habens et ei seruit sacerdotissa bubastis et anubis id est mercurius qui sic apud egyptios uocatur et canino ibi depingitur capite et apis et quidam alius famulus qui famulus dum primum suum os digito omnes alii ministri ysidis tacent cum uero ab ore remouet digitos/-tem tunc ipse et alii omnes cantant Aspis quoque dicitur isidem comitari et osiris suus uir et ideo dicitur numquam satis quesitus esse quia in una qua noua luna festum eius presentatur ab yside et ministri eius illum dolorem quem tunc habuerunt quando eum quesiuerunt representant et simulant.

1126   Teo *fortasse* Teodontium   **1131**   leene *i.e.* leonae   **1136**   exibet *i.e.* exhibet
1141 quesiuit *correxi*   **1142** adhuc *cum signo h sup. lin.*

AND NOT BY AMBITION NOR BY ARMS. They were not made youths   9:432
because of 'ambition', that is honour, that it to say so that Hebe still
would receive some sort of honour [from this]. 'Nor by arms', that is
not for the purpose of a youth using their arms for her gain, *sed super
factum est.*[28]

YOU CROSSED THE AEGEAN SEA AND ON ASIAN LAND. A noun, that is in   9:448
the land Asia. Or differently: according to †*Teo*† Asia was a woman,
from whom the land is named. Asis is the name of the people, but it
still has the form of a patronymic.[29]

HE who HAS BOTH A BEAUTIFUL AND UNFAIR EYE. He is said to have   9:476
unfair eyes, who sees something and should not desire it, still badly
desires it.

AND ON THE RIDGE WHERE CHIMAERA. Chimera is a mountain on whose   9:647
top lions live, and therefore it is said to have BOTH A LION'S HEAD AND   9:648
CHEST. And in its middle men, who keep a fire, live with goats. And by
its foot snakes dwell in a lake. And this is said metaphorically. The
serpent advances by hiding, so also excess first advances by hiding,
trying to find what it wants. The lion is strong and wanton. If
necessary, it displays strength after a commenced pleasure. The goat is
stinking and amoral, as an impious deed stinks in the end.

THE FORESTS COME TO AN END, that is: o BYBLIS, you FALL DOWN in this   9:649
part of the hill, where 'the forests come to an end'.

OSIRIS, Isis's husband, was killed by his brother Absirtus or Tisiphon.   9:693
Isis, or Jocasta, searched for him for a long time. Finally she found him
and wrapped him up in linen cloths and hindered his being dispersed

---

[28] The last phrase might possibly refer to the fact that the transformation spoken of here
was made above (*super factum est*) in the sense of 'by fate', which is the way it is
expressed in Met. 9:430.
[29] It is unknown who †*Teo*† is. See chapter Sources for more on this name.

celebrant festum eius in una quoque noua lunatione pro gaudio illius
repertionis. Et tunc exit de Nilo quidam taurus, qui lingua Egiptia
75ᵛᵃ   dicitur APIS, habens in dextro armo maculam admo- / dum lune 1145
factam. Is tunc sacrificatur, et tamen idem siue ei similis omni anno in
omni alio festo similiter exit de Nilo, qui similiter sacrificatus est. Et sic
fit in quolibet festo. Hoc de tauro sanctus Augustinus testatur in libro
de ciuitate Dei.

     Pingitur autem Ysis cornuta, id est cornua lune habens. Cuius ad 1150
9:691   ministerium pertinet esse sacerdotissa, que <u>dicitur</u> BVBASTIS. Et
ANVBIS, id est Mercurius, qui sic apud Egiptios uocatur, et canino ibi
depingitur capite. Et APIS et quidam, qui dum PREMIT suum os DIGITO.
Omnes alii ministri Idsidis tacent, cum uero ab ore digitum remouet.
Tunc ipse et alii cantant. Aspis que dicitur Isidem commitari. Et Osiris, 1155
qui erat suus uir.

     Et ideo dicitur NVMQVAM SATIS QVESITVS esse, quia in una quaque
luna noua festum eius representatur ab Iside, et ministri illum
dolorem, quem tunc habuerunt, quando quesiuerunt Osirim,
representant et simulant.   1160

9:735   NE NON, id est ut TAMEN OMNIA CRETE MONSTRA FERAT. Licet Crete
omnia monstra ferat, tamen Crete non tulit monstrum tale.

9:690   CVM QVA LATRATOR ANVBIS. Mercurius est interpres deorum et
elucidat dicta eorum, ideo dicitur Anubis, id est 'sine obscuritate'.

9:694   SERPENS PEREGRINA, id est aspis peregrina dicitur quantum ad 1165
75ᵛᵇ   Romanos, quia in Affrica et in finiti- / mis regionibus solet inueniri.
SOMNIFERIS VENENIS. Ideo dicit, quia uenenum eius dormire facit.

9:755   NVNC QVOQVE VOTORVM NVLLA EST PARS VNA MEORVM. Omnia uota
mea explere possum, sed non possum explere unam partem meorum
uotorum, scilicet quod utar coniuge. Quam partem si optem, 'nulla 1170
est', id est adnichilatur.

1148 Hoc … 1149 Dei] *cf.* Aug. *De civitate Dei,* 18:5.   **1151** Et … 1153 capite] *cf.* Serv. *in
Aen.* 8:698: LATRATOR ANVBIS quia capite canino pingitur, hunc volunt esse
Mercurium, ideo quia nihil est cane sagacius.

1151 dicitur *sup. lin.*   **1152** canino *correxi,* camino *cod.*   **1154** Idsidis *i.e.* isidis   **1155** Et
correxi, id est *cod.*

by his brother. Whence they still at every new moon celebrate his feast for the sake of the joy of finding him. And then a bull, which is called *apis* in the Egyptian tongue, comes from the Nile having on its right shoulder a mark made in the shape of the moon. The bull is then sacrificed, and still the same one, or one similiar to it, comes in the same manner from the Nile every year at every feast, and it is sacrificed in the same manner. And this happens at every feast. In *De Civitate Dei* St Augustine testifies this about the bull.

Isis is portayed with horns, that is having the horns of the moon. A priestess, who is called BUBASTIS, belongs to her service. And ANUBIS, that is Mercury, who is called thus among the Egyptians, and he is portrayed there with the head of a dog. And APIS and someone who then PRESSES his mouth with his FINGER. All the other priests of Isis are silent when he removes his finger from his mouth. Then he and the others sing. There is also a viper who is said to accompany Isis. And Osiris, who is her husband.

And therefore he is said to NEVER be SOUGHT AFTER ENOUGH, since at every new moon his feast is peformed by Isis, and the attendants perform and imitate the grief they felt when they searched for Osiris.

AND NOT THAT NOT, that is 'so that' CRETE MAY NEVERTHELESS BEAR ALL MONSTROUS THINGS. Although Crete may bear all monstruos things, still Crete does not bear such a monster. 9:735

WITH HER ANUBIS, THE BARKER. Mercury is the messenger of the gods and he elucidates their sayings, therefore he is called Anubis, that is 'without obscurity'.[30] 9:690

THE FOREIGN SNAKE, that is the viper is called 'foreign' in relation to the Romans, since it is usually found in Africa and neighbouring regions. WITH SLEEP-BRINGING VENOM. He says this because its venom makes one sleep. 9:694

AND EVEN NOW NOT ONE PART OF MY PRAYERS. I can fulfil all of my prayers, but I cannot fulfil one part of my prayers - namely that I may have her as a wife. If I wish for this part, 'it is nothing', that is it is destroyed. 9:755

[30] The commentator seems to understand Anubis as *a-nubis,* which could be understood as cloudless.

LIBER X

10:1   Vnde PER INMENSVM CROCEO V<ELATVS> A<MICTV>. Croceus est
unctura, sed coccus unde rubra purpura est.

10:10   OCCIDIT IN TALVM. Sicut legitur in quarto libro Georicorum, Eristeus 1175
insequebatur Euridicen, dum serpens illa pugnauit.

10:13   AD STIGIA TRENARIA. Trenarus est mons in Sicilia, per quem descensus
est ad inferos.

10:25   POSSE PATI uoluit. Subaudis Euri<di>ces, scilicet ne in tanto dolore pro
ea.   1180

10:65   QVAM TRIA QVI TIMIDVS. Quidam rusticus uiso Cerbero in lapidem
mutatus est, dum Hercules traxit Cerberum de infero.

10:68   QVIQVE IN SE CRIMEN TRAXIT. Olenos traxit crimen mentis in carnem,
10:69   quia mutatus fuit. Qui VOLVIT VIDERI ESSE NOCENS in hoc, quod
10:70   prohibebat homines a sacris Iunonis. Et eius coniunx LETEA in 1185
pulcritudine ei Iuno<ni> se pretulit et istud crimen in se traxerunt, quia
ambo in lapidem mutati sunt.

10:78   TERCIVS EQVOREIS I<NCLVSVM> P<ISCIBVS> A<NNVM>. De omnibus signis
76ra   potest dici quod / de uno signo usque ad idem signum sole currente
annus finiatur, id est includatur.   1190

10:90   Nam CHAONIS scilicet NON ABFVIT ARBOR. Chaonia terra illa, que *nunc*
dicitur. *Prius* dicebant 'Melosia<m>', sed Helenus postea uocauit
Chaoniam a fratre suo ibi interfecto. Frater Eleni Chaon fuit sepultus in
illa silua, que habe[n]t nomen ab illo sepulto, et que uocatur Dodona.
Ibi quercuum copia est.   1195

10:91   Hoc NEMVS HELIADVM. Heliades, sorores Phetontis, mutate sunt in
alnos.

1175 Sicut ... Georicorum] *cf. Georg.* 4:437-459.   1177 Ad ... 1178 inferos] *cf.* 2:247 (cod.
64va).   1191   Chaonia ... 1195 est] *cf.* Serv. *in Aen.* 3:293: BVTHROTI VRBEM id est
Buthrotium, ut fontem Timavi. haec autem civitas est in Epiro, cuius pars est Chaonia,
quae ante Molossia dicta est.

1173 Vnde *cf.* inde *Met.*   1175 Georicorum *i.e.* Georgicorum | Eristeus *i.e.* Aristaeus
1177 Ad ... trenaria *cf.* ad Styga Taenaria ... porta *Met.* | trenaria *i.e.* Taenaria   1179 Posse
§ *deest* | uoluit *cf.* uolui *Met.* | Euridices *correxi*   1183 Quique § *deest*   1186 Iunoni *correxi,*
Iuno in *cod.*   1188 Tercius § *deest*   1191 nunc *correxi,* non *cod.*   1192 Prius *correxi,* plus
cod. | Melosiam *correxi* (*i.e.* Molossiam)   1194 habet *correxi*

BOOK X

Whence THROUGH THE BOUNDLESS [AIR HYMEN] CLAD IN A SAFFRON 10:1
MANTLE. *Croceus* (saffron/saffron-coloured) is an ointment, but the
coccus (scarlet oak berry) is that from which we get the colour purple
red.

SHE DIED [BITTEN] IN THE HEEL. As we read in the fourth book of the 10:10
Georgics Aristaeus followed Eurydice when this snake was fighting
[her].

THE TRENARIAN [GATE] TO THE STYGIAN WORLD. Trenarus is a mountain 10:13
in Sicily, through which there is an entrance to the underworld.

HE WANTS TO BE ABLE TO ENDURE. Supply 'Eurydice', namely so as not 10:25
to be in such pain for her sake.

[NOT DIFFERENTLY] THAN THE FRIGHTENED MAN WHO [SAW] THE THREE 10:65
[HEADS OF THE DOG]. A peasant, who had seen Cerberus, was turned
into stone when Hercules dragged Cerberus from the underworld.

AND HE TOOK THE CRIME UPON HIMSELF. Olenos took the crime of the 10:68
mind upon his own flesh, since he was transformed. He WANTED TO
SEEM GUILTY since he forbade people to sacrifice to Juno. And his wife
LETHAEA placed herself before Juno when it came to beauty, and they
took this crime upon themselves, since they both were turned into
stone.

THE THIRD [TITAN HAD ENDED] THE YEAR ENCLOSED BY THE WATERY 10:78
PISCES. It can be said about all the Zodiac signs that the year is
concluded, that is enclosed, from one sign all the way around to the
same while the sun is spinning.

For THE CHAONIAN TREE WAS NOT MISSING. This region is now called 10:90
Chaonia. Earlier they used to call it Molossia, but later Helenus named
it Chaonia after his brother, who died there. Chaon, Helenus's brother,
was buried in the forest that has its name from his grave, it is also
called Dodona. There are many oaks there.

THE HELIADEAN GROVE. The Heliads, Phaeton's sisters, were turned 10:91
into alders.

10:106 AFFVIT HVIC TVRBE METAS I<MITATA> C<VPRESSVS>. Meta est finis
alicuius rei. Et similiter cuppressus meta est finis humane uite, quia
sicut cuppressus truncati umquam reuiuescunt, ita et mortuus ex ea 1200
combustus quantum ad hanc uitam. Et etiam propter hoc in funeribus
mortuorum additur cuppressus, cum sit odorifera, ne odor cadauerum
circumstantes corrumpa[n]t.

10:127 CONCAVA LITOREI F<ERVEBANT> B<RACCHIA> CANCRI. Ideo dicit 'litorei',
quia Cancrus celeste signum ad modum maritimi pingitur cancri.   1205

10:148 Caliope mater fuit Orphei et Apollo pater.

10:151 Pleia est mons, ubi gigantes cum diis pugnabant. Ad cuius radicem est
ciuitas similiter dicta. [caruerunt]

10:168 CARVERVNT DELPHI PRESIDE. Delphos insula uacauit a responsis, quia
76rb | Febus non fu- / it ibi, id est in Asia, ubi Delphos est. DVM DEVS 1210
10:169 FREQVENTAT EVROTAM fluuium ET SPARTEN INMVTATA<M>. Scilicet
tantum Phebus Iacinctum dilexit, ut non dimitteret Sparten, ubi
Iacinctus habitabat.

10:180 RECIDIT IN SOLIDAM. Re- ante consonantem literam, si producitur, non
est nisi cum positione, ut 'relique', 'reccido' et etiam 'retineo'. Si 1215
produceretur, oportet esse duo tt ibi scripta.

10:196 LABERIS, OEBALIDE. 'Ebalide' uocatiuus Grecus est. Ebalida est regio
iuxta Licaoniam.

10:206 FLOSQVE NOVVS. Flos, in quem Iacinctus est mutatus, quasi lilium et in
sumitate eius habet rotunditatem et flores diuisos. In medio uero 1220
florum florem unum, quasi uirgulam, habet, que - si solo intellectu -
reffertur ad omnes flores circumstantes. Sic tamen quod in unaquaque
relatione, quasi inter duos flores, flos ille medius intelligatur, sic esse
habemus. Si autem flos medius deorsum uersus intelligitur,
intelli<g>etur litera que dicitur θ, que scribi solet damnatis in fronte et 1225
nomen etiam Aiacis intelligitur.

10:215 IPSE SVOS GEMITVS. In talem florem Iacinctus mutatus est, ubi Phebus
suum representaret dolorem, scilicet e e. Que uox est signum doloris.

1224   Si ... **1226** intelligitur] cf. Isid. Etymol. 1:3: Quinque autem esse apud Graecos
mysticas litteras. Prima Υ, quae humanam uitam significat, de qua nunc diximus.
Secunda Θ, quae mortem [significat]. Nam iudices eandem litteram Θ adponebant ad
eorum nomina, quos supplicio afficiebant.

1198 cupressus correxi, d ut uid. cod.   **1203** corrumpat correxi   **1204** litorei¹ correxi, litora
cod.   **1206** Caliope ... pater cf. Musa parens Met.   **1208** caruerunt deleui   **1210** Febus i.e.
Phoebus   **1211**   inmutatam correxi   **1217**   uocatiuus sup. lin. post corr. ex nomina
1219 nouus, correxi nautis cod.   **1225** intelligetur correxi   **1228** e e i.e. ai ai

IN THIS CROWD THE CYPRESS, IMITATING THE GOAL POSTS WAS PRESENT. 10:106
Goal post is the boundary of a thing. And similarly the cypress is the
goal post at the end of the human life, since just as cypresses that have
at one point been cut off come to life again, so also the dead burned on
it as far as this life is concerned. And because of this the cypress is also
added to the funerals of the dead, since it is fragrant, so that the smell
of the corpses will not affect the bystanders.

THE CURVED ARMS OF THE SHORE-DWELLING CRAB WERE HOT. He calls it 10:127
'shore-', since the celestial sign Cancer is portrayed in the manner of a
maritime crab.

Caliope was Orpheus's mother and Apollo his father. 10:148

Pleia is a mountain, where the giants fought with the gods. At its foot 10:151
is a town by the same name.

DELPHI LACKED ITS GUARDIAN. The island Delphi was void of the oracle 10:168
responses, since Phoebus was not there, that is in Asia, where Delphi
is. WHILE THE GOD VISITS THE EUROTAN river AND UNCHANGED SPARTA.
That is to say Phoebus loved Hyacinthus so much that he did not
abandon Sparta, where Hyacinthus lived.

IT FELL AGAIN (*RECIDIT*) TO THE SOLID [GROUND]. *Re-* before a consonant, 10:180
if it is lengthened, it can only be by position, such as *relique, reccido*
and also *retineo*. If it (*retineo*) were to be lengthened, then there
should be two t's there.

YOU FALL, O OEBALIDES. *Oebalide* is a Greek vocative. Oebalida is a 10:196
region next to Lycaonia.

A NEW FLOWER. The flower—into which Hyacinthus was 10:206
transformed—is like a lily and it has a a round shape and divided
flowers at the top. In the middle of the flowers it has one single flower,
like a little twig, which refers—even if only in our understanding—to
all surrounding flowers. Nevertheless thus since in every relation, as it
were between two flowers, this flower is understood as the middle
one, *sic esse habemus*. But if the middle flower is understood as turned
downwards, then the letter that is called θ, which used to be written
on the forehead of the condemned, should be understood, it is also
understood as the name of Aiax.[31]

HE [INSCRIBED] HIS SIGHS [ON THE LEAVES]. Hyacintus was turned into 10:215
such a flower, on which Phoebus displayed his grief, namely 'ai ai'.
This sound is a sign of grief.

---

[31] The first part of this explanation is quite obscure. The explanation seems to move
betwen a concrete explanation of the flower and an abstract understanding of the same.
It is unclear what the phrase *sic esse habemus* refers to; θ = theta, which stands for *thanatos*
(death).

10:219   ANNVA PRELATA R<EDEVNT> IACINCTINA P<OMPA>. Ludi facti in honore
         Iacincti dicuntur Iacinctina.   1230

10:221 | AN GENVISSE VELIT / PROPEIDAS, filias Propei.

76ᵛᵃ
         ANNVIT EQVE, id est dicit se eque uelle genuisse illas quam istas.
10:221   Scilicet nec istas nec illas uellet genuisse.

10:223   FRONS ERAT VNDE ETIAM. 'Vnde', scilicet ex illis mutatis a Venere in
         tauros. CERASTE postea traxerunt NOMEN, quia isti idem a Venere facti 1235
         uiri post in cera<s>tas serpentes mutati sunt, sed liber non dicit,
         quamuis in illosce serpentes mutasset. 'Ceron' Grece, Latine dicitur
         'cornu'.

10:224   ANTE FORES HORVM. Qui fuerunt postea mutati in tauros, ideo fuerunt
         mutati, quia mactabant suos hospites.   1240

10:240   CORPORA CVM FORMA. FERVNTVR ille mulieres Propeides VVLGASSE sua
         corpora cum forma, id est manifeste attribuerent sua corpora
         meretritio operi. 'Cum forma', id est cum pulcritudine sua, quia
         Venerem deam negauerunt. Et post quod, PVDOR, id est reuerentia,
10:241   recessit ab eis ET SANGVIS ORIS INDVRVIT, scilicet nullum ruborem, qui 1245
         est signum uerecundie, habuerunt. Deinde in apices a Venere mutate
         sunt.

10:252   ARS ADEO LATET in ARTE, id est in factura, SVA. 'Ars' dicit, quia cum
         uidebatur moueri, tamen non mouebatur.

10:267   CONCHA SYDONIE TINCTIS. Concha est testa, ubi est piscis, qui uocatur 1250
76ᵛᵇ   conchilium. De cuius piscis sanguine fit / tinctura.

10:284   CERA REMOLLESCET HIMETIA. Dicitur ab Himeto monte, ubi copia est
         florum, unde apes faciunt mella.

10:287   DVM STVPET ET in MEDIO, id est in medio stupore, ET GAVDET et VERETVR
         FALLI.   1255

10:297   DE QVO TENET INSVLA NOMEN. Insula tenet nomen illius, non quod ab
         illo acciperet, sed potius iste ab illa. Sed quia iste habet nomen illius,
         ideo illa habuit nomen, quia idem est.

1235   Ceraste … 1238 cornu] *cf.* Isid. *Etymol.* 12:4: Cerastes serpens dictus, eo quod in
capite cornua habeat similia arietum; κερατα enim Graeci cornua uocant: sunt autem illi
quadrigemina cornicula, quorum ostentatione, ueluti esca, inlice sollicitata animalia
perimit.

1229 Iacinctina *i.e.* Hyacinthia **1231** propeidas *i.e.* Propoetidas **1235** traxerunt *cf.* traxere
Met. **1236** cerastas *correxi* **1241** Propeides *i.e.* Propoetides **1245** recessit *cf.* cessit *Met.*
1250 Sydonie *i.e.* Sidonide **1252** remollescet *pro* remollescit (Met.) | Dicitur *correxi,*
dicuntur *cod.* **1254** stupore *correxi,* stupere *cod.*

THE YEARLY HYACINTHIA RETURNS WITH A SOLEMN PROCESSION. The 10:219
games created in honour of Hyacinthus are called the Hyacinthia.

IF SHE WOULD LIKE HAVING BROUGHT FORTH THE PROPOETIDES, the 10:221
daughters of Propeus.

SHE WOULD ASSENT EQUALLY, that is she says that she would have 10:221
brought forth these ones or those ones equally. That is to say she did
not want to bring forth these ones or those ones.

THE FOREHEAD WAS [ROUGH], WHENCE ALSO. 'Whence', namely from 10:223
those transformed into bulls by Venus. Thereafter they acquired the
NAME CERASTAE, since the very same were made men by Venus and
later they were transformed into horned snakes, but the book does not
tell about this, even though they were transformed into such snakes.
Ceron is Greek, in Latin it is called 'horn'.

BEFORE THEIR GATES. They who had thereafter been transformed into 10:224
bulls, were transformed since they slew their guests.

THEIR BODIES WITH THEIR FORM. These women, the Propoetides, ARE 10:240
SAID TO HAVE PROSTITUTED their bodies with their form, that is they
openly assigned their bodies to the work of a prostitute. 'With their
form', that is with their beauty, since they denied that Venus was a
goddess. And after this, DECENCY, that is reverence, WITHDREW from
them AND THE BLOOD OF THEIR FACE HARDENED, namely they had no
blush, which is the sign of modesty. After this they were transformed
into summit-stones by Venus.

ART IS HIDDEN IN HIS ART, that is in his manufacture. He says art since 10:252
when it seemed to be moving still it did not move.

ON [PILLOWS] DYED WITH SIDONIAN SHELL-FISH. Shell-fish is a shell 10:267
where a fish lives, which is called *conchylium*. Dye is made from the
blood of this fish.

THE HYMETTIAN WAX BECOMES SOFT. It is named from mount Hymettus, 10:284
where there is an abundance of flowers, from which the bees make
honey.

THEN HE IS STUNNED AND IN THE MIDDLE, that is in the middle of his 10:287
astonishment, HE BOTH REJOICES and FEARS TO BE DECEIVED.

FROM WHOM THE ISLAND HAS ITS NAME. The island has his name, not 10:297
because it received it from him, but rather he from it. But since he has
its name, it has this name, since it is the same.

10:310 TANTI NOVA NON FVIT ARBOR. Arbor numquam fuit tanti precii, quod
uelim eam esse apud nos, ut per illam arborem sic infames essemus, ut 1260
sunt illi, apud quos fecit Mirra tantum facinus et apud quos mutata in
arborem satis caram.

10:365 NON INTELLECTAM VOCEM, id est Cinara intellexit quod filia talem
uellet uirum, in quo plus non ardere quam in se, id est in patre,
deberet, scilicet putauit in castitate uelle manere. 1265

10:444 PRESAGAQVE corpora MERENT, quia mens presagiebat sibi futurum
malum.

10:450 PRIMVS TEGIS, ICARE, VVLTVS. Bacus per Icarum Atheniensem rusticis
Atheniensibus uinum misit. Vnde post quod rustici biberunt putantes
se uenenum uel aliam potionem malam bibisse, Ycarum in puteum 1270
77ra proiecerunt. Canis autem suus, qui secum / iuerat, domum reuersus
duxit Erigonem, filiam Icari, ad puteum. Iam vero rusticis tantam
Bachus pestem inmisit, ut omnia fere perdedissent, quare, ut a peste
posse<n>t liberari, Icarum de puteo extraxerunt. Et statim Icarus et filia
et canis in celum translati sunt. 1275

10:628 NON ERIT INVIDIE V<ICTORIA> N<OSTRA> FERENDE. Si ego causa eius
mortis fuero, mea uictoria erit inuidie magne et non ferende. Scilicet
tantam inuidiam de tali inuidia habeo, quam ferre non potero.

10:596 CANDIDA PVRPVREVM SIMILIS EDAT. Non ALITER CORPVS Athlante traxit
RVBOREM IN PVELLARI CANDORE, QVAM tenuissimum VELVM 1280
rubicundum positum SVPER CANDIDA ATRIA, scilicet super parietem
album. EDAT, id est ostendit, VMBRAM, que ex repercussione scilicet
rubicunda et alba fit.

10:704 DENTE PREMVNT DOMITO CIBELEIA F<RENA> L<EONES>. Ideo dicuntur
currum Cibeles, id est terre, trahere leones, quia terra nutrit, domat et 1285
adamat omnia.

10:708 IVNCTISQVE PER AERA CIGNIS. Ideo dicuntur cigni trahere currum
Veneris, quia pulcri sunt.

10:727 ANNVA PLANGORIS, id est in unoquoque anno populus representabit
meum dolorem. 1290

1263 Cinara i.e. Cinyras 1266 presagiebat post corr. ex. presagebat 1268 tegis correxi,
regis cod. 1273 perdedissent pro perdidissent 1274 possent correxi 1279 Athlante i.e.
Atalantae 1284 domito correxi, domino (dno) cod. 1287 Iunctisque correxi, iunctasque
cod. | cignis i.e. cycnis

NO NEW TREE WAS WORTH SO MUCH. There never existed a tree worth 10:310 such a price that I would like this tree to be among us, so that we would be so disreputable through this tree, as they are, among whom Myrrha committed such a crime and among whom she was turned into a sufficiently precious tree.

THE MISUNDERSTOOD VOICE, that is Cinyras understood that his 10:365 daughter wanted such a man for whom she would not burn more than for him, that is her father, that is to say he thought she wanted to remain chaste.

AND THE FOREBODING body MOURNED, since the mind foreboded its 10:444 future misfortune.

YOU, ICARUS, COVER YOUR FACE FIRST. Bacchus sent wine to the 10:450 Athenian peasants through Icarus the Athenian. And after they had drunk the wine, they threw Icarus into a pit, thinking that they had been drinking poison, or some other bad drink. But his dog, which went with him, returned home and brought Erigone, Icarus's daughter, to the pit. Bacchus sent such a pestilence against the peasants that almost everything died, wherefore the peasants pulled Icarus from the pit, so that they would be freed from the pestilence. And immediately Icarus, his daughter and the dog were transferred onto heaven.

OUR VICTORY WILL BE ATTENDED BY UNBEARABLE HATRED. If I am the 10:628 cause of his death, then my victory will be of a great evil and not bearable. That is to say from such evil I receive such hatred, which I will not be able to bear.[32]

A SIMILAR BRIGHT [COURT] PRODUCES A PURPLE [AWNING]. Atalanta's 10:596 BODY catches A REDNESS IN ITS GIRLISH WHITENESS NOT DIFFERENTLY THAN a very fine red AWNING placed OVER A BRIGHT COURT, that is to say over a white wall. IT PRODUCES, that is it shows, A SHADOW which is red and white from the reflection.

WITH TAMED TEETH THE LIONS PRESS THE CYBELEIAN BRIDLES. Lions are 10:704 said to pull Cybele's, that is the earth's, wagon, since the earth nurtures, tames and deeply loves everything.

THROUGH THE AIR WITH HARNESSED SWANS. Swans are said to pull 10:708 Venus's wagon, since they are beautiful.

AN ANNUAL [COPY] OF [OUR] GRIEF, that is each year the people will 10:727 represent my pain.

[32] Atalanta is worried that she will suffer unbearable hatred if she is the cause of Hippomenes's death. In the first sentence the explanation is given close to Ovid's phrasing and in the next it is paraphrased.

LIBER XI

11:1   CARMINE DVM TALI.

11:3 | TECTE LIMPHATA, pro 'limphantia', scilicet pret<er>itum / pro presenti,
77ʳᵇ   quod licet fieri teste Prisciano.

11:25   STRVCTO VTRIMQVE THEATRO canum uel hominum. Ante noctem prius 1295
         homines explorant ubi ceruus habitet et mane uad*un*t illuc cum
11:26   canibus et capiunt eum. Et ideo dicitur MATVTINA ARENA, quia ibi
         ceruus in mane capitur. 'Str*u*ctum theatrum' dicitur turba canum
         circuiens ceruum. Ceruus in mane antequam mingat, si preocupatur,
         <u>cito capitur.</u>   1300

11:46   POSITIS TE FRONDIBVS ARBOR. De Hispanis dicitur, quod faciunt sibi
         radere omnes capillos capitis in morte amicorum pre nimio dolore.

11:48   OBSCVRAQVE CARBASA, id est uestes, quas flum<in>a habebant, uel uela
         nauium.

11:69   MATRES EDONIDAS. Edonia est regio in Tracia.   1305

11:101   GAVDENS ALTORE RECEPTO. Altore pro alitore sicut altilia pro alitilia.

11:106   GAVDETQVE MALO *B*ERECINTHIVS HER<OS>. De Frigia fuit, ubi colitur
         Berecinthia. Berecinthia est ciuitas, in qua dea colitur, que dicitur
         Berecinthia.

11:150   NAM FRETA PROSPICIENS. 'Nam', quod <T>molus i*u*dicauit, iste Mida 1310
         *uitu*perauit, et sic dicetur 'nam' refferendo ad sententiam.

11:208   INCLINAVIT AQVAS. Secundum rei ueritatem potuit esse aliquod
         d*il*uuium uel maris refluxio in Troiam.

11:211 | REGIS QVOQVE FILIA MONSTRO. Quia Laome- / d<on> fefellit Apollinem
77ᵛᵃ   et Neptunum, ideo religata est filia sua a nereidibus scopulis marinis 1315
         in an*t*iis, id est capillis, ut a MONSTRO EQVOREO deuoraretur, quia

---

1294 fieri ... Prisciano] *locum specificum non inveni.*   1306 sicut ... alitilia] *cf.* Alcuinus
Ortographia, 297:22: Altilia, quasi alitilia, id est aves saginatae.

1293 preteritum *correxi*   1295 Structo *cf.* structoque *Met.*   1296 uadunt *correxi,* uadit *cod.*
1298   Structum *correxi,* strictum *cod.*   1300   cito capitur *in marg. cum signo insert.*
1303 flumina *correxi*   1307 Berecinthius *correxi,* herecinthivs *cod.* | Frigia *i.e.* Phrygia
1308   Berecinthia¹ *post corr. ex* herecinthia   1310 Tmolus *correxi* | iudicauit *correxi,*
indicauit *ut vid. cod.* | Mida *i.e.* Midas   1311   uituperauit *correxi,* imperauit *cod.*
1313 diluuium *correxi,* deduium *ut vid. cod.*   1314 Laomedon *correxi*   1316 antiis *correxi,*
annis *ut vid. cod.*

BOOK XI

WHILE WITH SUCH A SONG. 11:1

COVERED THEIR MADDENED [BREASTS], [maddened] for 'maddening', 11:3
that is to say past tense for present tense, which is allowed according
to Priscian.

ON BOTH SIDES IN THE ERECTED THEATRE for dogs or men. The night 11:25
before the men first investigate where the deer lives and then they go
there early in the morning with dogs and capture it. It is called
MORNING ARENA, since the deer is caught there in the morning. The
pack of dogs encircling the deer is called 'the erected theatre'. If it is
detected, the deer is quickly captured early in the morning, before it
urinates.

THE TREE WITH SHED LEAVES [MOURNED] YOU. The Spaniards are said to 11:46
shave off all the hair on their heads on account of great grief for dead
friends.

FINE LINEN OBSCURED [WITH DARK GREY], that is garments the rivers 11:48
had, or the sails of ships.

THE EDONIC MOTHERS. Edonia is a region in Thrace. 11:69

REJOICING FOR THE RETURNED FOSTER-FATHER (*altore*). *Altore* for *alitore* 11:101
just as *altilia* for *alitilia*.

AND THE BERECYNTIAN HERO REJOICES IN THE BADNESS. He was from 11:106
Phrygia, where Berecyntia is venerated. Berecyntia is a town, in which
the goddess named Berecyntia is venerated.

FOR LOOKING OUT AT SEA. 'For' Midas disparaged that, which Tmolus 11:150
judged, and thus one should say 'for' referring back to the sentence.[33]

HE TURNED [ALL] THE WATERS. In reality this could be a flood or the 11:208
reflux of the sea to Troy.

AND THE KING'S DAUGHTER TO A MONSTER. Since Laomedon betrayed 11:211
Apollo and Neptune, the Nereids tied his daughter by her forelock,
that is by her hair, to a rock by the sea, so that she would be devoured
BY A WATER MONSTER, since they said that they would not be freed from

---

[33] The commentator seems to be interested in the function of *nam* (for) here, but it is
unclear exactly what is meant.

dixerunt non liberari a diluuio aliter, nisi equoreo monstro filia
Laomedontis exponeretur.

11:214 POSCIT EQVOS TANTIQVE OPERIS. Hercules pepigit equos Laomedontis, si
filiam iussu Neptuni expositam liberaret. Liberata autem illa Hercules 1320
precium, scilicet equos, exegit a Laomedonte. Quos ille denegauit.
Quocirca Hercules et Telamon et alii Greci inuaserunt Troiam et
ceperunt, et Telamoni socio militie Esionem dedit uxorem filiam regis
11:215 Laomedontis, et ideo dicit BIS PERIVRA.

Manogaldus autem dicit Esionem religatam et ab Hercule liberatam 1325
et a Telamone ductam fabulosum esse totum. Secundum enim
historiam Hercules et Iason et Telamon et alii, quando ibant ad
aureum uellus, ad Tr<o>iam uenerunt hospitari uolentes ibi. Repulsi
sunt a Laomedonte et in Sigeo promunctorio latuerunt, unde 'sigere'
latere dicitur. Collectis autem uiribus su*is* Troiam hac de causa 1330
77ᵛᵇ ceperrunt et tunc Tela- / mon Esionem duxit. His actis Greci duxerunt
iter ad Colchos sicut proposuerant.

11:279 VELAMENTA MANV. Ramum oliue coopertum iuncis, ut mos erat, quod
erat signum pacis.

11:380 SED MEMOR ADMISSI, id est sceleris sui, id est de interfection*e* Phoci. 1335
Sciuit Peleus de Salmate nimpha, que fuerat mater Phoci, quod hanc
uindictam †de se pe peleo† accipiebat.

11:383 REX IVBET OETEVS. Ceyx vocatur Oeteus a monte Etha, super quem
pater suus Lucifer multum lucet.

11:390 PLENA EST PROMISSI GRATIA VESTRI, id est tantum est mihi uestrum 1340
promissum, ac si iretis pugnatum.

11:393 FESSIS LOCA GRATA CARINIS. In turri et in loco summe arcis ignis solebat
in nocte ardere, et sic aduenientes naues cognoscebant illum locum
esse portum et ideo sicut desiderantes gratulabantur.

11:410 INTEREA FRATRISQVE SVI FRATREMQVE SECVTI. Ceyx turbatur de 1345
PROD<IG>IIS fratris sui et lupi secuti fratrem suum in hoc, quod
mutatus erat.

1328   Repulsi … 1332 proposuerant] *cf. Serv. in Aen.* 2:312: SIGEA duo sunt Troiae
promunturia, Rhoeteum et Sigeum, quod dictum est propter Herculis taciturnitatem, qui
prohibitus hospitio [[a Laomedonte]] simulavit abscessum, et inde contra Troiam per
silentium venit, quod dicitur σιγη.

1328 Troiam *correxi*   **1330** suis *correxi,* suas *cod.*   **1331** ceperrunt *i.e.* ceperunt
1333 Velamenta *correxi,* uelamina *cod.*   **1335** interfectione *correxi,* interfectionis *cod.*
1336 Salmate *i.e.* Psamathe   **1338** Oeteus *post corr. ex* oteus | Etha *i.e.* Oeta, *cum signo* h
sup. lin. **1345** Interea § *deest* **1346** prodigiis *correxi*

the flood unless Laomedon's daughter was offered to the water monster.

HE DEMANDED THE HORSES AND [THE PRICE] FOR SUCH A WORK. Hercules 11:214 demanded Laomedon's horses, if he were to free his daughter, who had been offered [to the monster] on Neptune's command. When she had been freed Hercules demanded his price, namely the horses, from Laomedon. He refused Hercules them. For this reason Hercules, Telamon and the other Greeks invaded and conquered Troy, and Hercules gave Laomedon's daughter Hesione as a wife to his comrade in arms Telamon, and therefore it says TWICE PERJURED.

However, Manegold says that it is completely fictitious that Hesione was tied up and freed by Hercules and married to Telamon. For according to history, when Hercules, Jason, Telamon and others went for the golden fleece, they came to Troy and wanted to be lodged there. They were turned away by Laomedon and hid in the promontory of Sigeum, from this 'to hide' is called *sigere*.[34] After they had gathered their strength they conquered Troy on account of this and then Telamon married Hesione. Having done this the Greeks took the road to Colchos as they had set out to do.

WITH [SUPPLIANT] HAND [EXTENDING] THE *VELAMENTUM*. An olive 11:279 branch covered with rush, as was the custom, since it was a sign of peace.

BUT REMEMBERING THE WRONGDOING, that is his crime, that is regarding 11:380 the killing of Phocus. Peleus knew that he received this punishment *de se Peleo* from the nymph Psamathe, who was the mother of Phocus.[35]

THE OETAEAN KING COMMANDED. Ceyx is called Oeteus from mount 11:383 Etna, above which his father Lucifer shines greatly.

[MY] GRATITUDE FOR YOUR PROMISE IS GREAT, that is your promise is 11:390 worth as much to me as if you would go to battle [with me].

A PLEASING PLACE FOR TIRED KEELS. At night a fire used to burn at the 11:393 top of a tower or at the highest point of a stronghold, and thus the arriving sailors would know that this place was the harbour and therefore they rejoice just as they have longed for.

MEANWHILE ABOUT HIS BROTHER AND ABOUT WHAT FOLLOWED HIS 11:410 BROTHER. Ceyx is disturbed about the PORTENTS about his brother and about the wolf that followed his brother in the sense that it was changed.

---

[34] This word is not supported by any dictionary. It seems to be meant to be a synonym to *latere* (to hide). In Servius version the place name is said to be derived from the Greek word for silence (sige/σιγη).

[35] It is not entirely clear what is meant by *de se pe peleo*. It might be a prepositional frase meant to modify *uindictam*, i.e. 'this punishment regarding himself, Peleus' (in which case *pe* must be deleted).

11:413 AD CLARIVM rogat IRE DEVM. Claros est insula ubi Apollo colitur, a qua Clarius dicitur.

11:583 AT DEA NON VLTRA. Seruius dicit, quod non licet alicui sacrificare diis 1350 pro mortuo a<li>quo, donec faciens sacrificium purgauerit se aliqua

78ra   purgatione. Vel aliter: *secundum* †theot†, quia non con- / ueniebat superos orare pro mortuis, sed infernales.

11:599 CANIBVSqve SAGATIOR ANSER. Anseres cicius sentiunt, si latrones ueniunt, quam aliud animal.   1355

11:627 HERCVLEA[M] TRACHINE IVBE. Aduerbialiter et est nomen ciuitatis uel
11:628 alicuius loci Ceicis. De una filia Herculis Eolus genuit ALTIONEM.

11:673 GESTVMQVE CEICIS M<ANVS> H<ABEBAT>. Sicut fit dum aliquis mouet manum loquendo.

11:745 PERQVE DIES PLACIDOS. Aues iste dicuntur infra septem dies nidificare, 1360 oua ponere, pullos procreare [et]. Et quando naute eas nidos componere sciunt, per illos septem dies se prosperum iter habere.

11:751 PROXIMVS AVT IDEM.

11:763 GRACILI CONATA, id est gracili luna. Quidam senex de progenie Ceicis et Altiones dixit hoc ad laudem illorum mutatorum, quasi diceret: Non 1365 est mirum, si isti sine peccato mutati sunt, cum etiam filius Priami in mergum mutatus sit sine peccato; a simili.

11:783 DIXIT ET E SCOPVLO Q<VEM> R<AVCA> SVBEDERAT VNDA <D>ECIDIT IN PONTVM, quem rauca unda existens sub scopulo ederat, id est manifestauerat, quia per undam raucam sub illo scopulo esse pontum.   1370

LIBER XII

12:35   ERGO VBI QVA DECVIT LENITA EST CEDE DIAN*A*, quia decentius fuit, ut
78rb   cerua sacrificaretur ei quam Effigenia. Et quia pepercit ei, transtu- / lit

1360   Aues ... 1362 habere] *cf.* Hyg. *Fab. 65*: ALCYONE Ceyx Hesperi siue Luciferi et Philonidis filius cum in naufragio periisset, Alcyone Aeoli et Aegiales filia uxor eius propter amorem ipsa se in mare praecipitauit; qui deorum misericordia ambo in aues sunt mutati quae alcyones dicuntur. hae aues nidum oua pullos in mari septem diebus faciunt hiberno tempore; mare his diebus tranquillum est, quos dies nautae alcyonia appellant.

1348 rogat *cf.* parat *Met.*   **1351** aliquo *correxi*   **1352** secundum *correxi*, sed *ut vid. cod.* theo *fortasse* Theodontium   **1354** Canibusque *cf.* canibusue *Met.*   **1356** Herculea *correxi* **1357** Ceicis *i.e.* Ceycis | Altionem *cf.* Alcyonen *Met.*   **1361** et *delevi*   **1368** scopulo *correxi*, scapulo *cod.* | decidit *correxi*   **1372** diana *correxi*, diane *cod.*   **1373** Effigenia *i.e.* Iphigenia

He asked TO GO TO THE CLARIAN GOD. Claros is an island where Apollo 11:413
is venerated, wherefore he is called 'the Clarian'.

BUT THE GODDESS NO FURTHER. Servius says that nobody is allowed to 11:583
sacrifice to the gods for a dead person until the one performing the
sacrifice has cleansed himself with some sort of purification. Or
differently: according to †theo-†, since it is not fitting to pray to the
gods above for the dead, but to the ones below.[36]

AND THE GOOSE MORE ACUTE THAN DOGS. Geese sense more quickly 11:599
than other animals if thieves are on their way.

TO HERCULEAN THRACIN COMMAND. Used adverbially and it is the 11:627
name of a city or some place belonging to Ceyx. Aeolus had ALCYONE
from one of Hercules' daughters.

HIS HAND HAD THE GESTURE OF CEYX. As happens when someone 11:673
moves their hand when speaking.

FOR [SEVEN] PEACEFUL DAYS. These birds are said to build nests, lay 11:745
their eggs and produce their chicks within seven days. And when
sailors know they are building their nests, they know they will have a
prosperous journey for seven days.

THE NEAREST OR THE SAME. 11:751

THE SLENDER RELATION, that is the slender moon. An old man from the 11:763
lineage of Ceyx and Alcyone said this in praise of their transformation,
as though he would say: It is not a wonder if these were transformed
from no fault of their own, when even Priamus's son was transformed
into a diver from no fault of his own; by comparison.[37]

HE SAID THIS AND FROM THE CLIFF THAT THE HOARSE WAVE HAD EATEN 11:783
AWAY BELOW HE FELL DOWN INTO THE OCEAN, [the cliff] which the
hoarse wave, being under the cliff, had eaten, that is had laid bare,
since the ocean is under this cliff in the hoarse wave.

BOOK XII

WHEN THEREFORE DIANA WAS APPEASED BY THE SLAUGHTER, WHICH WAS 12:35
FITTING, since it was more fitting that the deer rather than Iphigenia

---

[36] See note to 9:448.
[37] 'by comparison' is short for: this is said as a comparison to the previous story.

eam in Tauricam regionem regis Thoantis, ubi Diana colebatur ibique humano sanguine tantum placabatur. Et ibi Effigenia est ministra 1375 Diane.

12:104   PHENICIAS VESTES. Achilles putauit se Cignum uulnerasse et tamen sanguinem manare, sed nunc sentit uestes esse rubicundas et non sanguine, quem traxit, tinct*as*.

12:109   MENIA DEIECI. Omnes ciuitates et loca, que hic enumerat, a Schiro ad 1380 Aulidem dum iret, Achilles dicitur expugnasse, quia transitum ei denegabant.

12:112   BIS SENSIT THELEPHVS. Hunc Achilles negantem sibi transitum uulnerauit. Vulneratus uero non ualens sanari, accepit responsum ab Apolline se non posse sanari, ni [ab] ab [a]eadem Achillis hasta, qua 1385 uulneratus fuit, tangeretur. Hoc audito Thelephus Troiam iuit tactus et sanatus rediit.

12:210   DVXERAT YPODAMMEN coniugem A<VDACI> NATVS YXIONE. Laphite et Centauri, quorum rex Perithous fuit de genere Yxionis, fuerunt forte genus hominum, non tamen gigantes. Centauri uero dicti sunt quidam 1390 ex illis ideo, quia quadam die sedentes super e<qu>os ablatis bubus, cum alii insequerentur eos uenientesque ad quandam aquam equos suos potarent, uisi sunt et dicti ab indigenis illius terre ca- / pita

78ᵛᵃ   equorum non uidentibus semihomines et semiequi. Et ex illo tempore apellati sunt Centauri. Yppocentauri deberent dici. 'Yppo' enim Grece, 1395 Latine subtus. 'Centaurus' equus, sed Latini breuitate Centaurum pro utroque acceperunt, scilicet pro 'subtus' et 'equo'.

12:309   NE FVGE AD HERCVLEOS, I<N>Q<VIT>, S<ERVABERIS> ARCVS. Hic patet quod non est curandus ordo fabularum, ubi dicit Nessum ad arcus Herculis seruandum, cum superius dixisset illum interfectum ab 1400 Hercule. Ergo, si uolumus ordinem seruare in fabulis, non proficiemus sicut in libro Genesis.

12:399   NEC EQVI MENDOSA SVB ILLO. Nulla menda, id est nulla macula erat in parte illa, ubi equus est.

12:401   CASTORE DIGNVS ERAT. 'Dignus erat', ut Castor eum haberet, uel similis 1405 huic. Equus Castoris dicitur fuisse Cillarus. Vocatus est eodem modo, quo iste Centaurus.

1400 cum … 1401 Hercule] *cf. Met.* 9:102

1377 Phenicias *i.e.* poeniceas | Cignum *i.e.* Cycnum   1379 tinctas *correxi,* tinctos *cod.*
1380 Menia *i.e.* moenia | Schiro *i.e.* Scyro   1385 ab¹ *delevi* | eadem *correxi*   1391 equos
correxi   1398 seruaberis] s- *fortasse* f- | arcus *correxi,* orcus *ut vid. cod.*

was sacrificed to her. And since she spared Iphigenia, she transferred her to Taurica, king Thoan's region, where Diana was venerated and where she is satisfied solely by human blood. There Iphigenia is Diana's priestess.

PURPLE-RED CLOTHES. Achilles thought he had wounded Cycnus and the blood was nevertheless flowing, but now he realises that the clothes are red and not coloured by the blood that he has drawn. `12:104`

I THREW DOWN THE WALLS. Achilles is said to have conquered all the cities and places that he enumerates here, when he went from Skyros to Aulis, since they denied him passage. `12:109`

TELAPHUS TWICE FELT. Achilles wounded him when he denied Achilles passage. When wounded he could not recover and he then received a response from Apollo that he could not recover unless he was touched by the same spear of Achilles, with which he had been wounded. When he heard this Thelephus went to Troy, touched the spear and returned cured. `12:112`

THE SON OF BOLD IXION HAD TAKEN HIPPODAME as a wife. The Laphits and the Centaurs, whose king, Pirithous, descended from Ixion, were a strong tribe of humans, [they were] not, however, giants. Some of them are called Centaurs, since one day - after they had left their cows, since others were coming after them - sitting on their horses, they came to some water and allowed the horses to drink, and they were then seen and named half men and half horse by the inhabitants of this country who had not seen the heads of the horses. From this time onward they were called Centaurs. They should be called *Hypocentaurs*. *Hypo* in Greek, 'below' in Latin. *Centaurus* means 'horse', but for the sake of brevity the Latins use Centaur for both, namely for 'below' and 'horse'. `12:210`

DO NOT FLEE, HE SAID, YOU WILL BE SAVED FOR THE HERCULEAN BOW. Here, where he says that Nessus should be saved for Hercules' bow, when he has said above that he was killed by Hercules, it is evident that we cannot trouble ourselves with the order of the stories. Therefore, if we want to keep the order in the stories, we cannot accomplish this as in the book of Genesis. `12:309`

AND THE HORSE [SHAPE] UNDERNEATH IT WAS NOT FAULTY. No defect, that is there was no mark on that part where he was a horse. `12:399`

HE WAS WORTHY OF CASTOR. He was worthy to be owned by Castor, or one similar to him. Castor's horse is said to have been Cillarus. It has the same name as this Centaur. `12:401`

12:432   CODICE QVI MISSO. Dicit M<anogaldus> quod 'codex' pro 'caudex' fit lapis uel aliquando ramus arboris. Et diptongus mutatur in o.

12:510   DIXIT ET INSANIS. Seruius dicit 'insanus' pro 'magnus', sicut insana 1410 Iuno pro magna.

12:583 | EXERCET M<EMORES> PLVS QVAM CIVILITER IRAS. Achilles, / quia filius
78ᵛᵇ   erat Tetides, que est sub potestate Neptuni, ideo Neptunus plus iratus ei interficienti cignum, filium suum, quam ciuis possit indignari de ciue.   1415

12:606   CERTAQVE LETIFERA D<EREXIT>. Secundum rei ueritatem non sic interfecit, sed indicio matris sue in templo Apollinis, ubi ipse Achilles sororem Paridis Pollixinam debuit desponsare, quam pulcherrimam uiderat, ubi Hector auro sibi preponderabatur.

12:610   AT SI FEMINEO. Pentesilea, regina Amazonum, dicitur fuisse in 1420 auxilium Troianorum. A qua potius Achilles uellet interfici, quam a Paride, SI FEMINEO MARTE FVIT CADENDVM ei. Que Pentesilea congressa Achilli ab eo interfecta est, ut in ueteri legitur historia.

INCIPIT LIBER XIII

13:1   *CONSEDERE DVCES.*   1425

13:2   CLIPEI SEPTEMPLICIS AIAX. Legitur in Statio Thebis quod Aiax fecerat scutum suum de septem coriis.

13:26   SAXVM SISIPHON GRAVE VRGET. Antidia dicitur fuisse mater Vlixis. Que ante Leherte nuptias eum ex Sisipho, filio Eoli, concepit. Sed non est uerum, rapta quidem a Sisipho fuit, sed intactam eam reddidit.   1430

13:39   Nauplius, pater Palamedis a Caphareo monte, ubi periclitate sunt naves Vlixis.

1410 Seruius … 1411 magna] *cf.* Serv. *in Aen.* 2:343; 6:135.   **1423** ut … historia] *cf.* Dict. Cret. 4:2; Hyg. *Fab.* 112:4.

1408 Manogaldus *supplevi*   **1414** quam *correxi,* quem *cod.*   **1425** Consedere *correxi,* non sedere *cod.*   **1428** Antidia *i.e.* Anticlea   **1429** Leherte *i.e.* Laertae (Laertes)   **1431** Nauplius … 1432 *in marg. sup. fol. 79r*

HE [CRUSHED] WITH A THROWN TREE-TRUNK. Manegold says that *codex*   12:432
for *caudex* is a stone or sometimes a tree branch. And the diphtong
changes into o.

HE SPOKE AND THROUGH [AUSTER'S] RAGING [POWERS]. Servius says that   12:510
'raging' [can be used] for 'great', as in raging Juno for great Juno.

HE EMPLOYED HIS REMEMBERING RAGE MORE THAN CIVILLY (*civiliter*).   12:583
Since Achilles was the son of Thetis, who was under Neptune's power,
Neptune was more angry with Achilles for killing the swan, his son,
than a citizen (*civis*) might be angry over another citizen.

HE GUIDED THE STEADY [ARROW] WITH A DEATH-DEALING [HAND]. In   12:606
reality he (Paris) did not kill him thus, but [he did it] through
information from his mother in the temple of Apollo, where Achilles
himself was supposed to marry Paris's sister Polyxena, whom he
found very beautiful, and where [the body of] Hector was weighed out
for him in gold.

BUT IF BY FEMALE [WAR]. Penthesilea, the queen of the Amazons, is said   12:610
to have been allied with the Trojans. Achilles would have preferred to
be killed by her rather than by Paris, IF HE SHOULD BE SLAIN BY A FEMALE
MARS. This Penthesilea fought with Achilles and was killed by him, as
can be read in the old history.

HERE STARTS BOOK XIII

THE CHIEFS TOOK THEIR SEATS.   13:1

AJAX [LORD] OF THE SEVENFOLD SHIELD. In Statius's Thebaid we can   13:2
read that Ajax had made his shield from seven strips of leather.

THE HEAVY STONE PRESSES SISYPHOS. Anticlea is said to be Ulysses'   13:26
mother. She conceived him from Sisyphos, the son of Eolus, before her
marriage to Laertes. But this is not true, she was indeed carried off by
Sisyphos, but he returned her unviolated.

Nauplius, Palamedes' father, from mount Caphareus, where Ulysses'   13:39
ships were wrecked.

13:46 | EXPOSITVM LEMNOS. De Auli- / de <in> insula<m> missus fuit Vlixes, ut
79ra   Philotectem quereret propter sagittas Herculis, qui manebat ubi
         sepultus erat Hercules. Et Vlixi querenti Philotectes ostendit cinerem et 1435
         cepit ire cum eo ferens sagittas Herculis, quia fatatum erat quod Troia
         capi non poterat sine sagittis Herculis. Sed, quia iurauerat quod nulli
         indicaret eas, cum ferret illas, una illarum cecidit supra pedem eius,
         qui cepit conputrescere. Ideoque Vlixes dimisit eum in Lemnos insula,
         cum uellet eum ducere ad Troiam. Quidam dicunt quod sagitta non 1440
         cecidit supra pedem, sed ipse pedem ignoranter posuit super eam,
         cum quereret sagittas per montem.

13:53   VELATVRQVE ALITVRQVE. Cooperit se de plumis auium et commedit
         aues, quas cum sagittis Herculis interfecit.

13:56   VELLET ET INFELIX P<ELAMEDES>. Pelamedes Vlixem nolentem ad 1445
         obsidionem Troie ire, et ideo insanum salem seminantem, hoc modo
         probauit: Filium eius ante se arrantem posuit, et quia retraxit aratrum,
         ut bene sapiens, ductus est ad Troiam. A cuius obsidione quadam die
         Vlixes missus ad Misiam regionem pro tritico et, quia reuerssus est
79rb   uacuus, missus est Pelamedes / illuc iterum et multum tritici attulit. Et 1450
         his de causis nimis Vlixes habuit eum odio et ubi breue fecit, in quo
         erat scriptum, quod Pelamedes aurum acceperat a Troianis et ideo
         exercitum eius prodere debebat. Et ficto nuncio suo obuiauit, breue ui
         ablatum exercitui ostendit, et omnes querentes aurum scriptum in
         breui. Vlixes - sicut ille, qui industria aurum absconderat - inuenit 1455
         illud sub lecto Palamedis et ideo, quasi ueritas esset inuenta, ab illis
         interfectus est Pelamedes.

13:98   CONFERAT HIS ITACVS Resus. Resus, rex Misorum, quatuor equos albos
         habebat et, si biberent de Xanto fluuio Troiano, fatatum erat quod
         Troia non caperetur. Qui Rhesus, cum uenisset cum magno exercitu 1460
         rogatu Troianorum, noctu hospitatus est iuxta Troiam. Interim Troiani
         miserunt Dolonem uidere quid Greci facerent. Eadem nocte Diomedes
         et Vlixes Doloni obuiauerunt, et pauore et spe uite *nutantem* interfecit

---

1433 De … 1442 montem] *cf.* Serv. *in Aen.* 3:402: inventus itaque Philoctetes cum negaret
primo se scire ubi esset Hercules, tandem confessus est mortuum esse. inde cum acriter
ad indicandum sepulcrum eius cogeretur, pede locum percussit, cum nollet dicere.
postea pergens ad bellum cum exerceretur sagittis, unius casu vulneratus est pedem,
quo percusserat tumulum. ergo cum putorem insanabilis vulneris Graeci ferre non
possent, diu quidem eum pro oraculi necessitate ductum tandem apud Lemnum sublatis
reliquerunt sagittis. hic postea horrore sui vulneris ad patriam redire neglexit, sed sibi
parvam Petiliam in Calabriae partibus fecit.

1433 in *addidi* | insulam *correxi*   1434 Philotectem *i.e.* Philoctetem   1458 Resus[1] *cf.*
Rhesum *Met.* 1460 Rhesus *cum signo* h *sup. lin.* 1463 nutantem *correxi,* notare *cod.*

LEMNOS [WOULD NOT POSSES YOU] WHO ARE EXPOSED. Ulysses was sent   13:46
from Aulis to the island to find Philoctetes, who stayed where
Hercules was buried, because of the arrows of Hercules. And when
Ulysses asked, Philoctetes showed him the ash and came with him
carrying the arrows of Hercules, since it had been foretold that Troy
could not be taken without the arrows of Hercules. But when he
carried them [concealed], since he had sworn that he would not reveal
them to anybody, one of them fell on his foot, which started to putrefy.
Therefore Ulysses left him on the island of Lemnos, even though
Ulysses wanted to bring him to Troy. Some say that the arrow did not
fall on his foot, but that he stepped on it without knowing, when he
was looking for the arrows on the mountain.

HE IS CLOTHED AND FED [BY BIRDS]. He covered himself with bird   13:53
feathers and ate birds that he had killed with the arrows of Hercules.

AND THE UNLUCKY PALAMEDES WANTED. When Ulysses did not want to   13:56
go to the siege of Troy and therefore, as though insane, sowed salt,
Palamedes tested him in this way: He placed Ulysses' son in front of
him when he plowed and since he retracted the plow as a sane man he
was brought to Troy. One day Ulysses was sent from the siege of Troy
to the region of Mysia for wheat, and since he returned emptyhanded
Palamedes was sent there again and he brought back much wheat. For
these reasons Ulysses hated him and he then wrote a letter where it
said that Palamedes had received gold from the Trojans and therefore
he would betray his army. And he intercepted his false messanger,
snatched away the letter with force and showed it to the army and
everyone looked for the gold written about in the letter. Ulysses, as the
one who had hidden the gold on purpose, found it underneath
Palamedes' bed and therefore, as though the truth had been found out,
Palamedes was killed by them.

ITHACAN Rhesus MAY COMPARE THESE. Rhesus, king of the Mysians,   13:98
had four white horses and it was foretold that Troy would not be
captured if the horses would drink from Xanthus, a river in Troy.
When Rhesus on the Trojans' request had arrived with a large army,
he lodged one night close to Troy. Meanwhile the Trojans sent Dolon
to see what the Greeks were doing. The same night Diomedes and
Ulysses met Dolon, and he wavered between fear and hope for his life,

eum Vlixes. Qui, postquam inuenit Rhesum dormientem, interfecit
eum.   1465

13:99   PRIAMIDENQVE HELENVM. Fatatum erat, nisi caperetur palladium - id
79ᵛᵃ   est figura Palladis, que erat Troie - et Helenus, *suus* sacerdos / filius
         Priami, quod nunquam caperetur Troia. Et ideo Vlixes noctu per
         latrinam ingrediens tam Palladium quam Helenum secum asportauit.

13:141   SED ENIM, QVIA RETVLIT AIAX. VIX VOCO EA NOSTRA, SED tamen dicam 1470
         GENVS. Nisi enim dixero genus, uidebor non habere illud, quia ipse
13:142   Aiax PRONEPOS IOVIS RETVLIT illud, id est suum genus.

13:187   ATQVE IN REGE TAMEN PATER EST. Quamuis rex Agamemnon deberet
         communi rei consulere, 'tamen pater', id est dilectio patris, erat 'in' se
         'rege' adeo, quod nolebat eam interfici.   1475

13:217   REX IVBET INCEPTI. Iupiter iussit Agamemnoni per somnum, ut
         congregaret totum suum exercitum et inuaderet Troiam, quia esset
         uictor. Quo facto male Grecis contigit, quia non congregauerunt
         omnes, cum unum Achillem dimisit. Ideo pene fuit deuictus et
         desperatus uoluit reuerti. Consilio perorantis Vlixis tam ipse quam 1480
         exercitus suus retentus est.

13:230   CONVOCAT ATRIDES, ut promeret eis, quid Iupiter in somnis dixerat et
         quid inde futurum sit.

13:386   ARRIPIT ENSEM. Scilicet et iuit in quandam siluam, que erat iuxta castra,
         ibique multas oues occidit putans se Vlixem et interficere, et postea pre 1485
         nimio dolore et uerecundia se occidit.

13:398 | INSCRIPTA / EST FOLIIS, HEC NOMINIS ILLA QVERELE. Prima uero in
79ᵛᵇ   nomine †† et†.

13:399   VICTOR AD YSIPHILES. Lemniades mulieres ex more omnibus diis
         sacrificium fecerunt, nisi soli Diane, que irata omnes illas h*ir[i]*cino 1490
         fetore infecit, ut uiri earum nullo modo eas pati possent. Ob hoc inito
         consilio in expeditionem profecti sunt et ibi biennio morati. Vxores
         uero suspicantes eos alias sibi duxisse uxores conspirauerunt, ut
         quandoque uiros reuertentes in prima nocte interficerent. Virgines
         uero in patribus uel fratribus idem crudelitates exercerent. Omnes sine 1495
         mora scelerosum facinus impleuerunt, sed sola Ysiphile, filia Thoantis
         regis Lemniadum, expauescens scelus patri pepercit construens

---

1466   Helenum *post corr. ex* helenam *ut vid.*   1467   Helenus *correxi,* helenum *ut vid. cod.*
suus *correxi,* suos *cod.*   1470   nostra *sup lin. post corr ex* terra   1489   Ysiphiles *i.e.*
Hypsipyles 1490 hircino *correxi,* hericino *cod.*

but Ulysses killed him. Ulysses afterwards found Rhesus sleeping and killed him.

AND HELENUS THE PRIAMID. It was foretold that Troy would never be 13:99
captured unless the Palladium, that is a statue of Pallas in Troy, and its priest Helenus, Priam's son, were captured. And therefore Ulysses entered Troy at night through the privy and carried away with him the Palladium as well as Helenus.

BUT, SINCE AIAX RELATED. I BARELY CALL THESE OURS, BUT nevertheless I 13:141
mention my DESCENT. For if I would not mention my descent, then I will seem not to have one, since Ajax himself THE GREAT-GRANDSON OF JUPITER RELATED this, that is his descent.

AND IN THE KING THERE STILL IS A FATHER. Although king Agamemnon 13:187
should be mindful of the common good, still there was a father, that is the love of a father, in him, a king, in as much that he did not want her to be killed.

THE KING COMMANDS [US TO LET GO OF THE WORRY] OF THE [WAR] THAT 13:217
HAD BEEN STARTED. Jupiter commanded Agamemnon through a dream to gather his entire army and invade Troy, since he was going to be the victor. When this was done it went badly for the Greeks, since they had not gathered everyone, when he (Agamemnon) had dismissed Achilles alone. Therefore he was almost conquered and desperately wanted to retreat. He himself and his army remained [in the war] through Ulysses' persuading counsel.

THE ATRIDE ASSEMBLES, to relate to them what Jupiter had told him in 13:230
his dream and what would come to be thereafter.

HE SNATCHED THE SWORD. That is to say and went to some forest that 13:386
was next to the camp, and there he killed a lot of sheep thinking he was also killing Ulysses, and afterwards he killed himself on account of great sorrow and shame.

[LETTERS] INSCRIBED ON THE LEAVES, HERE FROM A NAME, THERE FROM A 13:398
COMPLAINT. The first one in the name †† e††.[38]

THE VICTOR [SETS SAILS] TO [THE LAND] OF HYPSIPYLE. The Lemnian 13:399
women made a sacrifice according to custom to all the gods except for Diana alone, who was enraged and cursed all of them with a goatish stench, so that their husbands could not stand them in any way. After they had discussed this the men set out on a campaign and remained there for two years. The wives, who suspected that the men had taken other wives, conspired to kill the men on the first night of their return and to have the maidens commit the same cruelty against their fathers or brothers. All of them fulfilled this wicked crime without delay, but only Hypsipyle, the daughter of Thoan, king of the Lemnians, feared this crime greatly and spared her father by building a magnificent

---

[38] The end of this sentence seems corrupted. In place of †† e†† one would expect 'Ajax' (the complaint is 'aiai').

magnifice rogum, quasi patre occiso. Vnde eius succedit imperio. In alio tamen loco dicitur a mulieribus eiecta fuisse de regno.

13:408   ILLION ARDEBAT. Videtur quod debeat sic distingui: 'Illion ardebat' 1500
13:407   usque ad eam partem, IN QVA HELLESPONTVS CLAVDITVR IN ANGVSTVM. Situs Troie non patitur hoc. Ideo dicitur, quia 'Illion' uidebatur ardere usque ad eam partem, 'in qua longus Hellespontus clau<ditur> in
80ra   an<gustum>', quia tam remota parte ignis poterat / uideri.

13:444   QVO FERVS INIVSTO. Duas puellas, scilicet Criseidem, filiam Crisis, 1505 sacerdotis Apollinis, et Briseidem, Achilles rapuit capiens Lernesia menia, dum in auxilium Grecorum uenit. Criseiden Agamemnoni dedit, sed tabes et pestilentia pro filia sacerdotis ab Apolline premissa est, unde Agamemnon illam ab Achille coactus est reddere, ut ira dei sedaretur. Mox autem rex Achilli Briseidem abstulit, unde ab eo pene 1510 debuit interfici. Vnde etiam Achilles cum suis a pugnare traxit se, donec Greci satisfacerent ei.

13:455   Vsque NEOPTOLOMVM, id est 'nouum militem'. Quod nomen uidetur, puto, filio Achillis conuenire.

13:569   LOCVS EXTAT. 'Locus', ubi Ecube mutata est, 'exstat', id est manifestus 1515 est pro mutatione. Vel 'exstat', id est *prominet*, et nomen habet ex re aliquo modo, sicut multa loca sortita sunt nomina aliquo euentu. Canis dicitur a canis dentibus.

13:589   NON VT DELVBRA. 'Delubra' proprie uocantur illa loca templi, ubi intestina lauantur. Secundum quosdam tamen 'delubra' dicuntur ille 1520 mense, in quibus imagines deorum ponebantur et ante illas desuper erant hostie.

13:596   PRO PATRVO TVLIT ARMA. Titonus, pater Memnonis, fuit frater Priami.

13:611 | SEDVCVNT CASTRA VOLATV, id est †de castra† / fecerunt.
80rb

1498   In … 1499 regno] *cf.* Hyg. *Fab.* 15:1: LEMNIADES In insula Lemno mulieres Veneri sacra aliquot annos non fecerant, cuius ira uiri earum Thressas uxores duxerunt et priores spreuerunt.at Lemniades eiusdem Veneris impulsu coniuratae genus uirorum omne quod ibi erat interfecerunt, praeter Hypsipylen, quae patrem suum Thoantem clam in nauem imposuit, quem tempestas in insulam Tauricam detulit. [...] 5 Lemniades autem postquam scierunt Hypsipylen patrem suum seruasse, conatae sunt eam interficere; illa fugae se mandauit.

1505 Qvo § *deest*   1506 Lernesia *i.e.* Lyrnesia   1507 menia *i.e.* moenia   1509 Achille *cum signo h sup. lin.*   1513 Vsque *cf.* utque *Met.*   1515 Ecube *i.e.* Hecuba   1516 prominet *correxi,* promitti *cod.*

funeral pile, as though the father had been killed. Wherefore she succeeded his rule. However, in another place it says that she was cast out from the kingdom by the women.

ILION BURNED. It seems that it should be divided thus: Ilion burned all 13:408 the way to that place WHERE THE HELLESPONT IS REDUCED TO A STRAIT. The location of Troy does not allow this. Therefore it is said that 'Ilion' seemed to burn all the way to the part 'where the long Hellespont was reduced to a strait', since the fire could be seen from such a remote part.

WHEN HE WILDLY [ATTACKED] WITH AN UNJUST [SWORD]. When Achilles 13:444 came to the help of the Greeks and took the Lernesian walls he stole two girls, namely Chryseis, daughter of Apollo's priest Chryses, and Briseis. He gave Chryseis to Agamemnon, but plague and pestilence was sent by Apollo for the daughter of his priest, wherefore Agamemnon was forced by Achilles to return her, so that the god's anger would be appeased. But soon the king took Briseis from Achilles, wherefore he almost ought to have been killed by him. Wherefore also Achilles withdrew from the battle with his men, until the Greeks compensated him.

Until NEOPTOLEMUS, that is 'the new soldier'. This name, I think, seems 13:455 to fit Achilles' son.

THE PLACE REMAINS. 'The place' where Hecuba was transformed 13:569 'remains' (exsto), that is the place is known on account of the transformation. Or 'it stands out' (exsto), that is it projects and it has its name from an occurrence in some way, as many places are allotted their names from some event. The river Canis is named from dog's teeth.[39]

NOT SO THAT [YOU GIVE ME] TEMPLES (DELUBRA). Strictly sepaking the 13:589 place in the temple where the intestines are cleaned is called delubra. However, according to some delubra is the name for the tables on which the images of the gods were placed and before which there were sacrifices on top [of the tables].

HE BORE ARMS FOR HIS UNCLE. Tithonus, Memnon's father, was the 13:596 brother of Priam.

AT THE [FOURTH] FLIGHT THE CAMP SEPARATES, that is they made †de 13:611 castra†.[40]

[39] Canis is the name of a tributary to the Po, but it is also the standard word for dog.
[40] It is unclear what the phrase †de castra† is supposed to mean.

13:619 SIGNA[M] PARENTALI. Parentalis dies dicitur a 'parento, parentas', in 1525
13:618 quo aliquis pro parentibus suis fecit diis sacrificium. Et MEMNONIDES
in unoquoque anno, cum pugnabant, moriuntur pro inferiis
Memnonis.

13:626 DE TANTIS OPIBVS. Eneas et Antenor, secundum Romanam historiam,
dicuntur Grecis Troiam tradisse et propter hoc multum auri et argenti 1530
accepisse. Aliud facinus etiam fecit Eneas, quia, quando exiuit Troiam,
coniugem suam Crensam, filiam Priami, dimisit.

13:628 FERTVR AB ANTANDRO. Antandros est insula iuxta Troiam, ubi prius
Eneas fecit naues suas.

13:629 ET POLLIDEREO MANANTEM. Ibi uoluit remanere Eneas et sacrificare. Et 1535
tunc accipiens de ramis, qui erant super tumulum Polidori[s], ad suum
sacrificium et de ramis sanguis exiuit. Tunc clamans Pollidorus dixit se
ibi esse sepultum.

13:631 INTRAT APOLLINEAM, id est Delon, ubi hoc responsum accepit:
'Dardanides duri antiquam exquirite matrem'. Inde Eneas fuit 1540
deceptus, quia, cum responsum accepisset de Italia, unde Dardanus
fuerat, intellexit de Creta, unde Teucer erat. Et ideo iuit in Cretam, ubi
80ᵛᵃ multa passus est, deinde in Affricam, scilicet ad Carta- / -ginem.

13:635 LATONA Q<V>ONDAM STIRPES. Iuno uenit cum Parcis, ubi Latona
peperit, ponens ticiones in ignem eadem fatationibus et pueris dixit, 1545
sed illos titiones de igne rapuit Latona et de Ortigia aduxit illos Delon,
ubi haberet pro reliquiis. Supradictos titiones uocat Ouidius 'stirpes';
uel stirps, pro progenie et pro ligno.

13:638 Hoc tapetum -ti et hoc tapete -tis.

13:653 IN SEGETEM LATICESQVE MERI. Omnis liquor 'latex' uocatur et ideo 1550
determinat, quod accipiat, cum dicit 'meri'.

13:690 SICCATOSQVE QVERI[T] FONTES. Nimphe dicuntur flere pro fontibus
Thebanis, quos Latona siccauerat, quia non cessabat ab odio etiam post
mortem Naiabes. Sed tamen quidam dicunt, quia Liber omnes
Thebanos fontes siccauit, ne Arastus in obsidione manere posset, et 1555
hoc erat in cratere signatum.

1540 Dardanides … matrem] cf. Aen. 3:90.   1554 Sed … 1556 signatum] cf. Theb. 4:670-
696.

1525 Signa correxi   1529 tantis correxi, cantis cod.   1532 Crensam i.e. Creusam
1535 sacrificare correxi, sacrificium cod.   1536 Polidori correxi   1540 matrem correxi, in
aurem cod.   1544 quondam correxi   1552 querit correxi   1554 Naiabes i.e. Niobes
1555 fontes correxi, fortes cod. | Arastus i.e. Adrastus

THE [TWELVE] SIGNS WITH THE PARENTAL [VOICE]. *Parentalis dies* 13:619 (parental day) is named from *parento* ('to sacrifice in honour of deceased parents'), when someone made a sacrifice to the gods for their parents. And THE MEMNOAN BIRDS die when fighting there every year as sacrifices to Memnon.

FROM SUCH RICHES. According to Roman history Aeneas and Antenor 13:626 are said to have betrayed Troy to the Greeks and because of this they received a lot of silver and gold. Aeneas also committed another crime, since he sent away his wife Creusa, daughter of Priam, when he left Troy.

HE IS CARRIED FROM ANTANDROS. Antandros is an island next to Troy 13:628 where Aeneas first made his ships.

AND DRIPPING WITH POLYDOREAN [BLOOD]. Aeneas wanted to remain 13:629 there and to sacrifice. And then when he broke off the branches over the grave of Polydorus for the sacrifice, blood poured forth from the branches. Then Polydoros shouted saying that he was buried there.

HE ENTERED THE APOLLINEAN [CITY], that is Delos, where he received 13:631 this oracle reply: 'Hard Dardanids look for the ancient mother'. Aeneas was deceived by this, since he understood the reply to be about Crete whence Teucer came, when it was about Italy, whence Dardanus came. And therefore he went to Crete where he suffered a lot, thereafter to Africa, namely to Carthago.

THE BRANCHES ONCE [HELD BY] LATONA [WHEN SHE GAVE BIRTH]. Juno 13:635 came with the Fates, when Latona gave birth, placing the firebrands in the fire she predicted the same for the children, but Latona took these firebrands from the fire and she moved them from Ortygia to Delos, where she would keep them as relics. Ovid calls the above mentioned firebrands 'branches'; or branch, both for the progeny and for wood.

Tapetum, -ti (carpet, shroud); and *tapete, -tis* (carpet, tapestry). 13:638

[EVERYTHING WAS TURNED] INTO CORN AND LIQUID OF WINE. Every fluid 13:653 is called liquid and therefore, when he says 'of wine', he determines what it consists of.

[NYMPHS] LAMENT THE DRIED SPRINGS. The nymphs are said to cry for 13:690 the Theban springs that Latona had dried out, since she did not cease with her hatred even after the death of Niobe. But still some say that Arastus could not remain in the siege, since Liber dried out all the Theban springs, and this was portrayed on the cup.

13:693 HANC NON in FEMINEVM. He due sorores sponte sunt mortue pro salute
populi, ut sicut secundum atra pestilentia a Latona et Phebe Thebanis
inmissa. Vel tanta pestilentia fuit Thebe, quod omnes moriebantur.
Acceperunt responsum quod, nisi iste mulieres due sua sponte 1560
morerentur, numquam eos liberari posse.

13:700 | ACTENVS / ANTIQVO. Vsque ad hanc partem erant historie inscripte in
80vb cratere. In summitate vero flos pictus.

13:710 PORTIBVS INFIDIS. In Strophados insula erant Arpie, quarum nomina
hec sunt Aello, Cilleno, Occipete. A quibus Eneas multa mala passus 1565
est in mora. Que propheticabant uenturam famem.

13:714 AMBRACHIAM <C>ERTATAM RITE DEORVM. Secundum hanc literam dices
'rite', id est propter ritum deorum. Que consuetudo erat, ut
transeuntes naute unum de sociis suis sacrificarent ibi. Sed
unusquisque pro sua salute sollicitus timens, ne offerretur, pro se 1570
pugnauit. Ideo dicit 'certatam'. Vel alio modo CERTATA LITE DEORVM,
id est potentum uirorum, scilicet Augusti Cesaris et Antonii, quia iuxta
Ambrachiam erat Actius mons, ubi illi conuenerunt.

13:715 IVDICIS ACCIACI. Acciacus quidam iudex fuit, quem Apollo pro prauo
iudicio suo in saxum conuertit.   1575

13:716 VO<CA>LEMQVE S<VA> T<ERRAM> DODONIDA Q<VERCV>. In Dodona
silua dedit Iupiter responsa per ereas ollas. Vel *secundum* aliam
fabulam per columbas.

13:717 CHAONIOSQVE SINVS. Chaon frater fuit Heleni, quem ipse inscius in
quodam nemore interfecit, unde dictum est Chaonium nemus; etiam 1580
81ra tota regio dicitur Chaonia. /

13:717 VBI NATI REGE Molopsos. Andromache fuit Hectoris coniunx. Quam
captiuam Pirrus fecit sibi uxorem, de qua habuit Melopsum. Qui
Melopsus filios, quos habuit, incendere uoluit, sed miseratione deorum
in aues mutati sunt.   1585

1564 Portibvs ... 1566 famem] *cf. expl.* 7:3 (cod. 69va); 9:187 (cod. 72va).   **1577** Vel ... 1578
columbas] *cf. expl.* 1:106 (cod. 62ra); *cf. Myt. Vat.* 1, suppl. V:227: DE COLVMBIS
DODONEIS Dodona ciuitas est Epiri, iuxta quam est silua que etiam Dodona dicitur
habundans glandibus, quibus primi pasti dicuntur homines. Iuppiter hic dabat responsa
per columbas aereas.   **1579** Chaoniosqve ... 1581 Chaonia] *cf. expl.* 10:90 (cod. 76ra).

1558 populi *correxi,* propter *cod.*   **1562** antiquo *correxi,* antique *cod.*   **1564** infidis *correxi,*
insulis *cod.* | Strophados *i.e.* Strophades   **1565** Cilleno *i.e.* Cellaeno   **1567** certatam
correxi | rite *correxi,* ritu *cod.*   **1574** Acciaci *post corr. ex* acciac *ut vid. cf.* Actiaco *Met.*
1576 Vocalemque *correxi*   **1577** secundum *correxi,* sed *ut vid. cod.*   **1579** Chaoniosque
correxi, chaeniosque *cod.*   **1582** Molopsos *cf.* Molosso *Met.*   **1583** Pirrus *post corr. ex*
pirras *ut vid.*

THIS ONE [GIVES] AN UNWOMANLY [WOUND]. These two sisters died of 13:693
their own free will for the safety of their people, so that, just as in the
other case, a black pestilence was sent against the Thebans by Latona
and Phoebe. Or there was such a pestilence in Thebes that everyone
died. They received an oracle reply that lest these two women died by
their own free will, the others could never be freed.

SO FAR ON THE OLD [BRONZE]. Up to this part the stories were inscribed 13:700
on the cup. At its top a flower was pictured.

THE TREACHEROUS HARBOURS. On the Strophadian islands there were 13:710
Harpies, whose names were these: Aello, Cellaeno, Ocypete. Aeneas
suffered a lot of bad things from them during the delay. They
prophesied about a coming famine.

AMBRACIA CONTESTED BY THE RITE OF THE GODS. According to this text 13:714
one should say 'by the rite', that is because of the rite of the gods. The
custom was that when sailors were crossing the sea they used to
sacrifice one of their own there. But any sailor, who was worried about
his own safety and feared that he would be sacrificed, fought for his
life. Therefore he says 'contested'. Or in a different way CONTESTED BY
THE FIGHT OF THE GODS, that is 'of powerful men', namely Augustus
Caesar and Antony, since the Actian mountain, where they met, is next
to Ambracia.

[THE IMAGE] OF JUDGE ACTIACUS. Actiacus was a judge, whom Apollo 13:715
turned into a stone because of his bad judgment.

THE DODONEAN LAND SOUNDING THROUGH ITS OAK. In the Dodonian 13:716
forest Jupiter gave oracle responses through copper pots. Or according
to another story, through pidgeons.

AND THE CHAONIAN BAY. Chaon was the brother of Helenus, whom he 13:717
unknowingly killed in a grove, wherefore this grove is called
Chaonian; the entire region is also called Chaonia.

WHERE THE SONS OF KING MOLOSSOS. Andromache was Hector's wife. 13:717
But Pyrrhus made her his wife when she was captured and begot
Molossus from her. This Molossus had sons whom he wanted to burn,
but through the pity of the gods they were transformed into birds.

13:720 EPIRROS REGNATA[T]QVE VATI scilicet Butro. Pirrus, filius Achillis, accepta Andromache, uxore Hectoris, *in* coniugium post Troianam uictoriam Epirum possedit. Postea duxit Hermionem, filiam Menelai, quam ipse Menelaus apud Troiam sibi desponsauerat et etiam constituit diem. Heleno uate frustra deortante eum licet captiuum eum 1590 duxisset. Horestes autem, filius Agamemnonis et Clitemeste, dolens Hermionem desponsatam sibi ab auo suo Tindareo alii contingere †lateris postquam dea aram† Pirrum de tosicata sagitta uulnerauit, sed tamen Pirrus uiuus reuerssus est. Ibique inter cetera, que moriturus disposuit Heleno uati, quia fideliter eum, ne iret, monuit, 1595 Andromachen in coniugium et partem regni dedit, <u>quam</u> olim quidam uates nomine Brutus possederat.

81rb   Lite- / -ram *sic* construe: AB HIS Grecis TENETVR EPIRRVS QVONDAM REGNATA BRVTO VATI, sed tum regnata FRIGIO uati, id est Heleno. Et tenetur ab his TROIA SIMVLATA, que Ericon dicitur. Ideo dicit 'simulata', 1600 quia Helenus omnia edificia in Egipto facit ad similitudinem Troianorum edificiorum et etiam nomina fluuiorum transtulit inde. Eneas adueniens patriam se uidere putauit.

13:728 HAC SVBEVNT TEVCRI, id est Troiani de genere Teucri. Et Dardanides sunt dicti a Dardano, qui prius fuit Troie et habitauit <prius>quam 1605 Teucer.

13:730 SCILLA LATVS DEXTRVM. Secundum phisicam nihil aliud fuit Scilla, nisi scopulus in litore maris, ad cuius radicem fluctus multum pulsauit. Vnde fictum est mulierem ab inguine esse mutatam in canes. Silla est in Italia, CHARIBDIS in Sicilia.   1610

13:804 Idrus proprie est aquatica serpens, sed hic pro qualibet ponitur.

LIBER XIIII

14:1   IAMQVE Gigantis.

1603 Eneas ... putauit] *cf. Aen.* 3:302; 3:349.

1586 regnataque *correxi* | Butro *cf.* Buthrotos *Met.* (*sed etiam* bruto post *et* butropus *in app. Tarrant*)   **1587** in *correxi*, et *cod.*   **1590** deortante *i.e.* dehortante   **1591** Clitemeste *i.e.* Clytaemnestrae   **1593** tosicata *i.e.* toxicata   **1596** quam *sup. lin.*   **1598** sic *correxi*, scio *cod.* **1605** habitauit *cum signo* h *sup. lin.* | priusquam *correxi*   **1609** Silla *i.e.* Scylla   **1611** Idrus § *deest*   **1613** Gigantis *cf.* Giganteis *Met.*

EPIRUS RULED BY AN ORACLE, namely Butros. After Pyrrhus, Achilles' 13:720
son, had taken as wife Andromache, Hector's wife, and after the
Trojan victory, he took possession of Epirus. After this he married
Hermione, Menelaus's daughter, whom Menelaus himself had
betrothed to him in Troy and even set the day [for the marriage]. The
oracle Helenus dissuaded him in vain, although he (Pyrrhus) had
taken him away as a prisoner. Orestes, the son of Agamemnon and
Clytemnestra, who grieved that Hermione, who had been engaged to
him by her grandfather Tyndareus, would belong to another †lateris
postquam dea aram† wounded Pyrrhus with a poisoned arrow, but
Pyrrhus nevertheless returned alive. And there among the other things
that he had arranged for the oracle Helenus when he was about to die,
since Helenus had faithfully advised him not to go, he gave him
Andromache's hand in marriage and that part of the kingdom, which
once an oracle named Brutus had possessed.[41]

Construe the text thus: EPIRUS IS NOW HELD BY THESE Greeks, ONCE
RULED BY THE ORACLE BRUTUS, but then ruled by the PHRYGIAN oracle,
that is by Helenus. And the COPIED TROY, which is called Ericon, is
held by them. He says 'copied' since Helenus made every building in
Egypt in the likeness of the Trojan buildings and he even transferred
the names of the rivers from there. When Aeneas arrived he thought
that he saw his homeland.

THIS WAY THE TEUCRI APPROACHED, that is the Trojans of Teucer's 13:728
descent. And the Dardanids are named from Dardanus, who was first
in Troy and lived there before Teucer.

SCYLLA [TROUBLES] THE RIGHT SIDE. According to natural philosophy 13:730
Scylla is nothing else than a rock at the sea-shore against the foot of
which the surge strikes hard. From this it was made up that a woman
was transformed from the groin down into dogs. Scylla is in Italy,
CHARYBDIS in Sicily.

The Hydrus is strictly speaking an aquatic snake, but here it is used for 13:804
any kind of snake.

BOOK XIIII

AND NOW ON the giant's [THROAT].   14:1

---

[41] The passage †lateris postquam dea aram† does not seem to fit in the sentence in any
sensible way. It is hard to tell if any of the words should be changed or if there are words
missing.

14:44   HECCATEIA CARMINA M<ISCET>. Ideo Hecate dea inferni hoc nomine
nuncupatur, quod sit centum potestatum.   1615

14:88 | SIRENVM SCOPVLOS. Dicitur nihil aliud fuisse, nisi quidam / sonus
81ᵛᵃ   undarum scopulos uerb<e>rantium.

14:83   AD SEDES ERICIS. Erix fuit filius Veneris et Butes; quod regnauit.

14:83   FIDVMQVE RELATVS ACCESTEM. Neptunus propter precium, quod sibi
Laomedon peracta Troia negauerat, omnes nobiles puellas Troie ad 1620
suplicium poscebat. Ob hoc quidam Troianus filiam suam in naui
posuit et in Siciliam aplicauit. Ibi Crinisius fluuius cum ea concubuit et
ex ea Acestem genuit. Ideo 'fidum' dicit, quia Troianus erat.

14:90   COLLE PHITETVSAS. [Per] Phitetusa Grece, Latine dicitur Scuma.

14:103   EOLIDE TVMVLVM. Misenus, qui fuit de genere Eoli, erat cum Enea. 1625
Dicitur <u>uero</u> Eneas hunc patri suo sacrificasse et ad opus nigromantie
interfecisse et ideo apud inferos dampnatum fuisse. Qui Misenus
tibicen fuit, ideo dicit CANORI, sed Eneam excusans dicit, quia quadam
die, dum Misenus Tritonem uocaret ad cornicandum, cornicinans in
naui Enee precipitatus a Tritone in mare et sic mortuus est.   1630

14:114   FV<L>GENTEM RAMVM IN S<ILVA>. Nulli licuit adire Proserpinam, nisi
offerret ei aureum ramum.

14:119   QVEQVE NOVIS ESSENT ADE<VNDA> PERICVLA B<ELLIS>. Dicit apud
inferos, quod pugnaturus esset cum Turno.

14:149 | AD MINIMVM ONVS, id est in paruissimum / lapidem.   1635

81ᵛᵇ   VOCE TAMEN NOSCAR. Ideo hoc dicit, quia in antro illo ibi mutata est
14:153   postea dabantur responsa.

1614 Ideo … 1615 potestatum] *cf.* Serv. *in Aen.* 4:510: TER CENTVM TONAT ORE DEOS
non 'tercentum deos', sed tonat ter centum numina Hecates: unde [[et]] Hecate dicta est
ηκατην, id est centum, potestates habens.   **1628** sed … 1630 est] *cf.* Serv. *in Aen.* 6:149:
PRAETEREA ac si diceret: est et alia opportunitas descendendi ad inferos, id est
Proserpinae sacra peragendi. duo autem horum sacrorum genera fuisse dicuntur: unum
necromantiae, quod Lucanus exsequitur, et aliud sciomantiae, quod in Homero, quem
Vergilius sequitur, lectum est. sed secundum Lucanum in necromantia ad levandum
cadaver sanguis est necessarius, ut pectora tunc primum ferventi sanguine supplet, in
sciomantia vero, quia umbrae tantum est evocatio, sufficit solus interitus: unde Misenus
in fluctibus occisus esse inducitur.

1617 uerberantium *correxi*   **1619** relatus *correxi*, redatus *cod.*   **1623** fidum *correxi*, filium
cod. **1624** Phitetusas *i.e.* Pithecusas | Per *delevi* | Scuma *i.e.* Cumae **1626** uero *sup. lin.*
1631 Fulgentem *correxi* | Nulli *correxi*, nulla *cod.* **1636** Voce § *deest*

SHE MIXES HECATEAN SONGS. Hecate, the goddess of the underworld, is known by this name because she is of a hundred powers.[42] 14:44

THE ROCKS OF THE SIRENS. This is said to be nothing else than the sound of the waves hitting the rocks. 14:88

TO THE REALM OF ERYX. Eryx was the son of Venus and Butes; [realm] since he ruled there. 14:83

AND HE RETURNED TO FAITHFUL ACESTES. Because of the price that Laomedon had denied Neptune when [the walls of] Troy had been completed, Neptune demanded as a punishment all the noble girls of Troy. Because of this, one Trojan placed his daughter in a boat and sailed to Sicily. There the river Crinisus slept with her and begot Acestes from her. He calls him 'faithful', since he is a Trojan. 14:83

PHITECUSA [LOCATED] ON A HILL. Phitecusa in Greek, in Latin it is called Cumae. 14:90

THE TOMB OF THE AEOLID. Misenus, who was from the stock of Aeolus, was with Aeneas. Aeneas is said to have sacrificed him for his father and killed him for the purpose of necromancy and therefore he was damned among the people of the underworld. Since Misenus was a piper he (Ovid) says MELODIOUS, but [when] he says this he absolves Aeneas, since one day when Misenus challenged Triton in horn playing, he played the horn in Aeneas's boat and was thrown in the ocean by Triton and thus he died.[43] 14:103

IN THE FOREST A GLEAMING BOUGH. Nobody was allowed to approach Proserpine unless they offered her a golden bough. 14:114

AND WHICH DANGERS MUST BE UNDERTAKEN IN NEW WARS. He says this in the underworld, since Aeneas will fight Turnus. 14:119

TO A MINIMAL WEIGHT, that is into a very small stone. 14:149

I WILL STILL BE KNOWN BY MY VOICE. He says this since the oracle replies were later given in the cave where she was transformed. 14:153

---

[42] Here a connection is made between the name Hecate and *heca/hecaton*, Greek for 100.
[43] Two versions of a story, in the latter Aenas is not a murderer and thus Ovid absolves him.

14:155   SEDIBVS EVBO*I*CAM. Illi, qui fecerunt Cumas, fuerunt de Cholchide ciuitate, que est in Euboica patria Grecie.

14:233   INDE LAMI V<ETEREM> LESTRIGONIS. Lestrigon est nomen appellatiuum 1640
14:234   *populi*, super quem olim regnauit Lamus. Postea ANTIPHATES, qui dicitur filius, regnauit super eundem *populum*.

14:324   NEC ADHVC SPECTASSE TOT ANNOS, id est Picus spectasse non POTERA[N]T, id est uidisse, 'tot annos' quot annos representat eum habere hec imago sua, sed ego poteram eum [L]EDERE, id est ostendere 1645 uel demonstrare, QVATER QVINQVENNEM, id est uiginti annorum, a GRAIA PVGNA, in qua Greci Troiam uicerunt.

14:331   SITHICE STAGNVM NEMORALE DIANE. Quasi diceret: 'Stagnum' quod est in Aricio nemore. In quo nemore simulacrum Diane translatum a Taurica prouincia regis Toantis, que regio est in Sothia. Fuit positum 1650 ab Horeste <et> coniuge sua.

14:337   RARA QVIDEM FACIE, SED R<ARIOR> AR<TE> C<ANENDI>. Quasi diceret: Raro posses tam pulcram inuenire et rarissime tam bene cantantem.

14:426 | TIBRIS a *T*iberino ibi submerso nomen accepit, quod prius Albula [uo] /
82ra   uocabatur.   1655

14:449   FAVNIGENEQVE DOMO. Amata matertera Turni uxor fuit Latini, ex qua filiam nomine Lauinam habuit. Quam Turnus propter consanguinitatem et etiam matre consentiente uoluit ducere, sed Latinus pater per augurium cognouit uirum aliene gentis manere coniugium Lauine. Interim Eneas superuenit. Cui petenti Lauinam in 1660 coniugium Turnus bellum intulit et per bellum sibi desponsatam obtinere uoluit. In quo bello Latinus Turnum contra Eneam iuuit, et in iuuando Turnum ignotum noto postposuit. Tandem interfecto Turno Eneas Lauinam uxorem duxit et regnum Latini soceri dotem possedit.

14:452   CONCVRRIT LATIO TYRRENIA TO<TA>. Mezentius fuit quidam pessimus 1665 tyrannus in Tyrrenia, qui hostes suos turpi more uer<ber>abat, scilicet os mortui ori uiui iungebat et alia membra iungendo tandem occidebat. Qui, quia multa mala Tyrrenis siue Tuscis fecerat, ab eis de

---

1648 Quasi … 1651 sua] *cf.* Serv. *in Aen.* 6:136: Orestes post occisum regem Thoantem in regione Taurica cum sorore Iphigenia, ut supra diximus, fugit et Dianae simulacrum inde sublatum haud longe ab Aricia collocavit.

1638 Euboicam *correxi,* euboream *cod.* **1641** populi *correxi,* propter *cod.* **1642** populum *correxi,* pp *ut uid. cod.* **1644** poterat *correxi* **1645** edere *correxi* **1648** Sithice *i.e.* Scythicae (Met.) | Quasi diceret] quae deinceps *coni. Meiser*   **1649** Aricio *post corr. ex* raricio **1650** Sothia *pro* Scythia **1651** et *suppleui* **1654** Tiberino *correxi,* ciberino *cod.* | *uo deleui* **1657** Lauinam *i.e* Lauiniam **1666** uerberabat *correxi*

FROM THE [STYGIAN] ABODE TO THE EUBOEAN [CITY]. Those who made 14:155
Cumae were from the city of Colchis, which is in the Euboean
homeland in Greece.

FROM THERE [WE CAME TO THE] OLD [CITY] OF LAESTRYGONIAN LAMUS. 14:233
Laestrygon is an appellative for the people, over whom Lamus once
ruled. Later ANTIPHATES, who is said to be his son, ruled over the same
people.

[HE COULD] NOT YET HAVE WATCHED SO MANY YEARS, that is Picus 14:324
COULD not have watched, that is to have seen 'so many years' as his
image purports him to have, but I could RELATE TO him, that is show or
point out FOUR TIMES FIVE YEARS, that is twenty years from the GREEK
BATTLE in which the Greeks conquered Troy.

THE WOODED POOL OF SCYTHIAN DIANA. As though he said: The pool in 14:331
the Arician grove. In this grove there was an image of Diana that had
been brought from king Thoas's province Taurica, which is a region in
Scythia. It was placed there by Orestes and his wife.

SHE WAS OF RARE BEAUTY, BUT EVEN RARER IN HER SINGING SKILL. As 14:337
though he said: Rarely can one find one so beautiful and most rarely
one who sings so well.

THE TIBER, which earlier was called Albula, takes its name from 14:426
Tiberinus who was drowned there.

THE HOME OF THE DESCENDANT OF FAUNUS. Turnus's aunt Amata was 14:449
Latinus's wife, with whom he had a daughter named Lavinia. Turnus
wanted to marry her because of kinship and also with her mother's
consent, but her father Latinus knew through an augury that a man
from a foreign people would marry Lavinia. In the meantime Aeneas
arrived. When he asked for Lavinia's hand in marriage Turnus started
a war and through this war he wanted to win her who had been
engaged to him. Latinus helped Turnus in this war against Aeneas,
and by helping Turnus he neglected an unknown person (Aeneas) for
a known. Finally Turnus was killed and Aeneas married Lavinia and
attained his father-in-law Latinus's kingdom as a dowry.

ALL OF TYRRHENIA CLASHED WITH LATIUM. Mezentius was an evil 14:452
tyrant in Tyrrhenia, who used to torment his enemies in a disgraceful
manner, that is to say he would join a dead man's face to that of a
living man and finally he would kill them by joining the other limbs
too. Since he had done many bad things to the Tyrrhenians or Tuscans,

regno est expulsus. Qui etiam Turnum iuuabat contra Eneam. Et ideo
Tusci iuuabant Eneam contra Turnum, quia Turnus hostem illorum 1670
82ʳᵇ receperat. /

14:457 PROFVGI DIOMEDIS AD VRBEM. Diomedes congressus cum Enea
singulari certamine in sinistro brachio uulnerauit Venerem
defendentem Eneam. Inde Venus irata incendit uxorem Diomedis in
amorem alterius uiri et effecit, quod contempto Diomede publice alii 1675
nupsit, cui etiam bona Diomedis dotem dedit. Quibus ille fretus postea
Diomedem redeuntem a Troiano bello de patria fugauit, et liberos,
uxorem et omnia, que sua fuerunt, possedit. Inde Diomedes uenit in
Iapigiam, que pars est Calabrie in fine Italie, ad Daumum regem et
filiam eius uxorem duxit. Dicitur autem Apulia siue Calabria 1680
I[n]apigia a uento, qui ibi maxime flat, qui Iapis dicitur, uel ab aliquo
duce, qui Iapix diceretur. Iapia uero est Venetia.

14:468 NARICVS HEROS, id est Vlixes. In destructione Troie Aiax Oieleus in
templo Palladis concubuit cum Casandra, filia Priami. Que et sacerdos
Apollinis erat, quam Vlixes inde rapuit.   1685

14:472 CVMVLVMQVE CAPHAREA CLADIS. Nauplus dolens de Palamede filio
suo iniuste interfecto ab Vlixe et aliis Grecis, in Caphareo monte
82ᵛᵃ circumdato syrtibus et scopulis / manentibus sub aqua ignem in nocte
lucentem posuit. Ad hunc Greci reuertentes a Troia uenerunt
existimantes ire ad portum, in quo solitus erat ignis lucere in nocte, et 1690
mu<l>te naues ibi sunt fracte et homines mortui. Et quia cadauera
remanserunt in mari, mare habundans tempestate iterum multas naues
eorum et homines submersit. Consuetudo enim est maris etiam
inplacatissimo tempore feruere nimis, si cadauera sint in eo.

14:565 Alcmei SAXVMQVE I<N>C<RESCERE> LIGNO. Alcinous, rex Pheacum, fuit 1695
in auxilium Grecorum et Troianis mala, que potuit, intulit. Et ideo,
dum nauis eius mutaretur in lapidem, Naiades facte de Troianis
nauibus multum letabantur.

14:533 Mulcifer VREBAT. Seruius dicit quod MVLCIBER est Iupiter; Mulcifer est
Vulcanus.   1700

1699 Seruius ... 1700 Vulcanus] cf. Serv. in Aen. 8:724: MVLCIBER Vulcanus, ab eo quod
totum ignis permulcet: [[aut quod ipse mulcatus pedes sit, sicut quibusdam videtur: aut
quod igni mulceatur]]; Eriugena, Annotationes in Marcianum, 187: 07. 'Lemnius' Uulcanus,
a Lemno insula. 07. 'Mulcifer' mulcens ferrum tantum, uel solum modo significat uel
ualde.

1675 quod correxi, que cod.   **1677** liberos correxi libere cod.   **1679** Daumum i.e. Daunum
1681 Iapigia correxi   **1683** Naricus i.e. Narycius | Oieleus i.e. Oileus   **1686** Nauplus i.e.
Nauplius   **1691** multe correxi   **1695** Alcmei cf. Alcinoi Met. | Alcinous post corr. ex
alcmeus ut vid.   **1698** letabantur correxi, letabuntur cod.

he was banished from his kingdom by them. He also helped Turnus against Aeneas. And the Tuscans helped Aeneas against Turnus since Turnus had received their enemy.

TO THE CITY OF THE FUGITIVE DIOMEDES. Diomede met Aeneas in single combat and wounded him, who was protecting Venus, in his left arm. Enraged by this Venus filled Diomedes' wife with love for another man and made it so that she, shaming Diomedes publicly, married another man, to whom she even gave away Diomedes' fortune as dowry. Relying on these things (the fortune), he chased away Diomedes from his land when he returned from the Trojan war, and he took possession of his children, wife and all the things that had been his. From there Diomedes came to Iapygia, which is the part of Calabria at the far end of Italy, to king Daunus and married his daughter. Apulia or Calabria is called Iapygia from a wind that blows very hard there, which is called Iapis, or from some lord named Iapix. But Iapia is Venice. 14:457

THE NARYCIAN HERO, that is Ulysses. At the destruction of Troy Oilean Ajax slept with Cassandra, daughter of Priam, in the temple of Pallas. She, whom Ulysses snatched away, was also the priestess of Apollo. 14:468

AND CAPHEREUS, THE CROWN OF MISFORTUNE. Nauplius, who grieved for his son Palamedes who had been unjustly killed by Ulysses and the other Greeks, placed a fire that burned in the night on mount Caphareus, which is surrounded by sand-banks and rocks under the water. When the Greeks returned from Troy they came to this fire believing they came to a harbour, where a fire usually burned at night. And many ships were destroyed there and many men died. And since the corpses remained in the sea, the sea became abundant with storms and again sank many of their ships and men. For the nature of the sea was to rage exceedingly with unappeasable weather, if there were corpses in the sea. 14:472

Alcmaeus's [SHIP] CHANGES FROM WOOD INTO STONE. Alcinous, king of the Phaeacs, was an allied of the Greeks, and he brought as much evil as he could against the Trojans. And therefore when his ship was transformed into stone, the Naiads, who were created from the Trojan ships, were much delighted. 14:565

Mulcifer BURNED. Servius says that MULCIBER is Jupiter; Mulcifer is Vulcan. 14:533

14:639   SILENVS discipulus Bachi pre nimia ebrietate semper uisus est iuuenis.

14:657   TANTOQVE POTENTIOR INQVIT. Hoc ideo dicit, quia quanto magis laudauit artes Pemone et studium suum mirabatur, tanto plus potuit eam aptare sibi et tanto magis fecit eam intentam.   1705

14:694   IDALIAM. Idala est quedam silua, in qua Venus colitur, et ideo Idalia
82ᵛᵇ   dicitur. Et ab hac silua habundante / columbis Idales dicuntur columbe.

14:694   TIME RAMNVSIDIS IRAM. Ramnis est ciuitas, in qua colitur Fortuna, a qua sic ipsa nominatur. Ideo dicit Vertumnus Pomone, ut timeat, quia 1710 Fortuna nimis irascitur superbis.

14:712   QVOD NORICVS EXQVOQVIT IGNIS. Norica est quedam regio ultra Anglicam, ubi optimi gladii fiunt.

14:720   ET PEANA VOCA. Peana sunt laudes Apollinis, que exclamantur in triumpho alicuius. Quas sortitus est interfecto Phitone.   1715

14:722   CERTE ALIQVOD LAVDARE MEI. Quasi diceret: Tu laudabis me amantem in morte, quod maxime solent mulieres in uirum.

14:724   NON TAMEN ANTE TVI CVRAM. Dixi, quod gaudeas de morte mea, tamen ego ita te diligo, quod amor tui[s] non recedet a me, priusQVAM VITA, et hoc tu MEMENTO.   1720

14:725   GEMINA LVCE, id est luce diei et presentia tui, quam non minus diligo ipsa luce diei.

14:729   SI TAMEN, O SVPERI. Dixerit licet quod PASCAS tua LVMINA, TAMEN non inpune, et ideo O SVPERI, SI VIDETIS.

14:739   ICTA PEDVM MOTV IANVA, id est ianua EST DEDISSE VISA SONVM pro MOTV 1725
83ʳᵃ   PEDVM. So- / num, quem audientes possent trepidare et multum timere.

14:760   SERVAT ADHVC SALAMIS. Ordo: 'Salamis' ciuitas 'seruat' illud SIGNVM VENERIS QVOQVE TEMPLVM HABET illud SIGNVM NOMINE, id est sub
14:750   nomine, hoc est nomen inscriptum ostendat signum fuisse ANAXETES. 1730 VENERIS, dico, PROSPICIENTIS, id est uidentis ultionem.

14:773   NVMITORQVE SENEX. Amul\<i>us fratrem suum Numitorem de regno pepulit eiusque filiam Iliam sacerdotissam dee Veste fecit. Cum qua

---

1701 Silenvs … 1702 iuuenis *in marg. (fol. 83r)*   **1704** Pemone *i.e.* Pomonae   **1709** Time *correxi,* Tune *ut uid. cod.* | Ramnis *i.e.* Rhamnus   **1712**   exquoquit *i.e.* excoquit   **1715** Phitone *i.e.* Pythone   **1718** tui *correxi,* cui *cod.* | Dixi § *adest*   **1719** tui *correxi*   **1725** Icta *correxi,* Leta *cod.* | motv¹ *correxi,* metu *cod.*   **1730** Anaxetes *i.e.* Anaxaretes   **1732** Amulius *correxi*   **1733** eiusque *correxi,* eosque *cod.*

SILENUS, a disciple of Bacchus, seemed to be always young because of   14:639
his excessive drunkeness.

AND HE SAID 'YOU ARE SO MUCH MORE POWERFUL'. He says this since the   14:657
more he praised the arts of Pomona and was amazed by her
endeavour, the more he could tie her to himself and the more eager he
made her.

THE IDALIAN. Idala is a forest, in which Venus is worshipped and   14:694
therefore she is called the Idalian. And since this forest abounds in
doves the doves are called Idalian.

AND FEAR THE WRATH OF THE RHAMNUSIAN. Rhamnus is a city where   14:694
Fortuna is worshipped and from which she is named thus. Vertumnus
tells Pomona to fear, since Fortuna is greatly angered by the arrogant.

THAT NORIC FIRE HARDENS. Norica is a region beyond Anglia, where   14:712
the best swords are made.

AND SING PAEANS. Paeans are songs of praise to Apollo, which are   14:720
sung when somebody has a triumph. He (Apollo) received them after
he had killed Python.

SURELY [YOU WILL BE FORCED] TO PRAISE SOMETHING OF MY [LOVE]. As   14:722
though he said: You will praise me, who love until death, which
women usually [praise] the most in a man.

HOWEVER [REMEMBER THAT] MY CARE FOR YOU [ENDED] NOT BEFORE. I   14:724
said that you may rejoice over my death, nevertheless I love you in
such a way that my love for you will not leave me BEFORE MY LIFE does,
and this you WILL REMEMBER.

TWIN LIGHTS, that is by the light of day and in your presence, which I   14:725
love no less than the light of day itself.

HOWEVER IF, O GODS ABOVE. Although he said FEAST your EYES, not   14:729
without punishment HOWEVER, and therefore O GODS ABOVE, IF YOU
SEE.

THE DOOR WAS HIT BY THE MOVEMENT OF HIS FEET, that is the door   14:739
SEEMED TO HAVE GIVEN THE SOUND on account of THE MOVEMENT OF HIS
FEET. A sound that would make those who heard it tremble and be
much afraid.

SALAMIS STILL KEEPS. Order: Salamis's city keeps this IMAGE OF VENUS   14:760
AND THE TEMPLE HAS the SIGN WITH THE NAME, that is under this name,
that is an inscribed name shows that the sign was OF ANAXARETES. OF
VENUS, I say, LOOKING OUT FOR, that is with her mind set on vengeance.

AND OLD NUMITOR. Amulius drove his brother Numitor from the   14:773
kingdom and made his daughter Ilia priestess of the goddess Vesta.

Martius dicitur concubuisse et ex ea Remum et Romulum genuisse, sed potius fuit sacerdos dee Veste. Qui pueri adulti eiecto Amulio 1735 auum Numitorem in regno restituerunt.

14:774 FESTIS PALILIBVS VRBIS. Pales dea pabuli, in cuius festo Roma cepit edificari.

Pales dea pabuli, in cuius festis condita sunt menia urbis.

14:776 ARCISQVE VIA TARPEIA RECLVSA. Tarpeia filia constituit cum Sabinis, ut 1740 acceptis ornamentis brachiorum aperiret eis portam. Illi autem ingressi tot clipeos posuerunt super eam, quod ipsa sustinere non ualuit. Romani autem nescientes eam aurea ornamenta brachiorum petisse,

83rb sed [cre] / credentes eam pro defensione suffocatam et †non equiuocatam† templum sibi fecerunt in Capitolio.   1745

14:799 Primus rex Romanorum fuit ROMVLVS. Palatinus uero et Auentinus et alii supradicti Albe regnauerunt. Post Romulum uero regnauit Rome Numma Pompilius. Post illum Tullius, post Tullium Tullus, post eum Tarquinius.

14:827 PVLCRA SVBIT FACIES. Quasi diceret: Ille Romulus exutus mortalitate 1750 longe dignior erit illo Romulo, qui quondam regali trabea indutus dignissimus uidebatur.

14:830 Ersilia prius uxor †Da†, postea u<xor>/uero Romuli.

LIBER XV

15:5 ANIMO MAIORA CAPACI CONCIPIT. Numma Pompilius factus rex iuit ad 1755 Crotonem ciuitatem putans Pitagoram inuenire, ut phisicam addisceret.

15:13 LITORA FELICI T<ENVISSE> LACINIA. In Apulia iuxta †sint† pontum Hercules quendam latronem nomine Lacinium interfecit reuertens ab Hispanis. Et ideo illa littora Lacinia dicuntur.   1760

1739 Pales … urbis *in marg.*   **1740** uia *correxi,* tua *cod.*   **1744** cre *delevi*   **1753** Ersilia … Romuli *in marg.*   **1755** maiora *correxi,* maiara *cod.*   **1759** latronem *post corr. ex* latonem

Mars is said to have lain with her and begot Remus and Romulus from her, but she was more probably the priestess of the goddess Vesta. When these boys had grown up they threw out Amulius and reinstated their uncle Numitor to the kingdom.

THE CITY'S [WALLS ARE FOUNDED] ON THE PALILIAN FEAST. Pales is the goddess of food, at whose feast they began to build Rome. 14:774

Pales the goddess of food, at whose feast the walls of the city were built.

TARPEIA WHO REVEALED THE WAY TO THE CITADEL. The daughter Tarpeia came to an agreement with the Sabines to open the city gates for them in return for the ornaments worn on their arms. But after they had entered [the city] they stacked so many shields on top of her that she could not survive. The Romans, who were unaware that she had sought golden bracelets, but rather thought that she had suffocated for the sake of the defense [of the city] †non equiuocatam†, made a temple to her on the Capitol.[44] 14:776

The first king of the Romans was ROMULUS. Palatinus and Aventinus and others mentioned above ruled Alba. Numa Pompilius ruled in Rome after Romulus. After him Tullius, after Tullius Tullus, after him Tarquinius. 14:799

A BEAUTIFUL FORM ENTERS. As though he said: This Romulus, having cast of his mortality, is much more dignified than the Romulus who once dressed in the royal robe and seemed the most dignified. 14:827

Hersilia first the wife of †Da†, later the wife of Romulus.[45] 14:830

BOOK XV

HE CONCEIVES OF GREATER THINGS IN HIS CAPACIOUS MIND. Numa Pompilius was made king and went to the city of Crotona thinking he would find Pythagoras there so that he would learn natural philosophy. 15:5

TO HAVE REACHED THE LACINIAN SHORES ON A FORTUNATE [VOYAGE]. In Apulia next to the †sin† sea Hercules, when returning from Spain, killed a bandit named Lacinius. And therefore these shores are called Lacinian.[46] 15:13

[44] It is unclear what the words non equiuocatam should mean. By their form and position it would seem to be an attribute to eam (i.e. Tarpeia). From the context one would expect maybe non eque ('not justly', i.e. they did not realise that she died justly).
[45] I have not been able to find any person to which †Da† might refer.
[46] The word †sin† could possibly be the beginning of a name for the sea or maybe for sin<um> (bay) then replaced by pontum (sea).

15:39   O CVIVS CELVM BIS SEX LABORES FECERE. Fecere, id est pinxere, quia
         monstra, que iste domuit in terris, translata sunt in celum, ut Leo et
83va   cetera. /

15:41   MOS ERAT ANTIQVIS. Nigri et albi lapilli in urna ponebantur. Si albi
         prius exirent, absoluere[n]tur, qui reus dictus erat; <si nigri>, 1765
         damnaba[n]tur. Sed, ut iste Micilius damnari posset, nullus in ea
         lapillus albus missus est, sed nigri. Sed auxiliante Hercule ei omnes
         egressi sunt albi.

15:164   NVPER ABANTHEIS. Abas rex Argiuorum fuit ibi, ubi Menelaus
         posuerat clipeum Euphorbi. Vnde, quia Pitagoras accepit eum, 1770
         finxerunt Greci, quod anima Euphorbi eadem esset in Pitagora.

15:237   HEC QVOQVE NON PER<STANT> QVE NOS HELEMENTA VOCAMVS. Hoc
         dicunt philosophi, ut Plato et ceteri, quod non proprie helementa
         uocentur hoc, quod uidemus, scilicet terram, aquam et alia, sed ideas
         quasdam in dei mente. Entes proprie helementa dixerunt, quod 1775
         numquam mutarentur. Sed hic non dicunt de illis helementis.

15:249   IDEMQVE RETEXITVR ORDO, id est sicut aer et ignis descendunt, ita
         postea ascendunt.

15:251   GLOMERATA CO<G>ITVR VNDA. TELLVS tamen fit in aquam, cum aqua fit
         lutulenta et turbida de ipsa terra, et sicut 'tellus cogitur' in 'unda 1780
         glomera<ta>', id est sic retinetur in aliquo uertigine aque.

15:309 | MEDIO TVA COR- / NIGER HAMON. Bacho in Indiam eunti et pontum
83vb   querenti Iupiter in specie arietis aparuit. Et, in quo loco aparuit, ibi
         Bachus fontem inuenit et ibi patri suo templum edificauit, in quo
         uocatur Amon. Vel ideo dicitur corniger, quia, cum Tipheus insecutus 1785
         est, deos Iupiter latuit in ariete.

1765 absolueretur *correxi* | si nigri *supplevi* 1766 damnabatur *correxi* | Micilius *i.e.*
Myscelus   1772 Hec *correxi*, hoc *cod.* | perstant *correxi* | nos *correxi*, non *cod.*
1777 retexitur *correxi*, retexetur *cod.* | descendunt *post corr. ex* scendunt 1779 cogitur
correxi 1781 glomerata *correxi* 1782 Hamon *i.e.* Ammon 1783 arietis *sup. lin.*

O YOU WHOSE HEAVEN TWO TIMES SIX LABOURS MADE. 'Made', that is   15:39
portrayed, since the monsters, such as the Lion and others that he had
conquered on earth, were transferred onto heaven.

IT WAS THE CUSTOM FOR THE ANCIENTS. Black and white pebbles were   15:41
placed in an urn. If the white ones came out first, the accused would be
acquitted; [if the black ones came out], he would be condemned. But
not a single white pebble was placed in the urn, only black ones, so
that Myscelus would be condemned. But with the help of Hercules all
pebbles came out white for him.

RECENTLY IN ABASIAN [ARGOS]. Abas was the king of the Argives in the   15:164
place where Menelaus placed the shield of Euphorbus. Wherefore the
Greeks imagined that Euphorbus's soul and Pythagoras's were the
same, since Pythagoras received it (the shield).

AND NOT EVEN THESE WHICH WE CALL THE ELEMENTS PERSIST. The   15:237
philosophers, such as Plato and others, say that these things that we
see, that is to say the earth, water and other things, should not strictly
speaking be called 'elements', but rather ideas in the mind of God.
Strictly speaking they called elements *entes*, since they never change.
But here they do not speak about this kind of elements.

AND THE SAME ORDER IS REPEATED, that is just as air and fire sink so   15:249
they later rise.

[THE EARTH] IS FORCED TOGETHER BY THE CROWDED WATER. THE EARTH is   15:251
turned into water, when water is made muddy and disordered from
the soil, and just as 'the earth is forced together' in 'the crowded
water', that is it is thus retained in a vortex of water.

IN THE MIDDLE [OF THE DAY], HORNED AMMON, [YOUR STREAM]. When   15:309
Bacchus went to India and was looking for the sea, Jupiter appeared
before him in the shape of a ram. And Bacchus found a spring in the
place where Jupiter had appeared, and there he built a temple to his
father, in which he is called Ammon. Or he is called 'horned' since
Jupiter hid the gods in a ram when Typheus attacked.

15:326 PREDITAS ATTONITAS. Filie, que in alio loco Cee matres dicuntur, inebrietate in sacrifio, quia recepto Hercule ueniente de Hispania maledixerunt Iunoni iniungenti tot labores egre<g>io uiro. Ideo Iuno irata fecit, quod ex nimia ebrietate sibi cornute uidebantur. Has 1790 Melampsus quidam *con*fectionibus et uino contrariis a furore liberauit. Quas confectiones deinde cuidam fonti infudit. Vnde postea natura
15:324 CONTRARIA VINO remansit illi fonti ex herbis positis in confectione.

15:462 NEVE THIESTIS. Thiestes et Atreus fratres fuerunt. Atreus habuit quendam filium de coniuge fratris sui. Ideo Thiestes iratus coxit eum 1795 et patri suo Atreo ad commedendum dedit.

15:475 | NEC FORMIDANTES CERVOS ILLVDITE PENNIS. Ve- / natores pennas super
84ra   retia ponunt, ne cerui uidentes illa paueant, sed potius cum minori impetu ingrediantur, et sic illuduntur pennis. Vel uenatores, cum circumdant saltus cum retibus, pennas incendunt in illis locis, ubi retia 1800 desunt, ut cerui accedentes et odorantes et ibi homines esse credentes, per retia potius egrediantur siluam et ita eludunt eos.

15:552 ET AMAZONE NATVS. Theseus cum amazonibus pugnauit. Quibus deuictis Hypoliten reginam ipsorum captiuam duxit, quam coniugem sibi fecit, de qua genuit Ypolitum. 1805

15:622 PANDITE NVNC, MVSE. †M† hoc, quasi proemium, Ouidius ad laudem Augusti Cesaris premittit, ad cuius honorem librum suum scripsit.

15:836 PROSPICIENS PROLEM sanctam. Liuia fuit coniunx Augusti Octouiani. Que habuit filios Drusum et Neronem et Claudium, qui in prima etate fuit probus, sed postea pessimus. Drusus uero melior fuit iuxtaque 1810 Maguntiam interemptus. Liuia uero ante Augustum Cesarem nupserat Tiberino Neroni, de quo habuit Neronem et Claudium, sed mortuo

---

1787   Filie … 1793 confectione] *cf. expl.* 7:363 (cod. 69ᵛᵇ); Serv. *in. Buc.* 6:48: PROETIDES IMPLERVNT F(ALSIS) M(UGITIBUS) A(GROS) Proetides Proeti et Stheneboeae, sive Antiopae secundum Homerum filiae fuerunt, [[Lysippe, Iphinoe, Iphianassa]]. hae se cum Iunoni in pulchritudine praetulissent - [[vel, ut quidam volunt, cum essent antistites, ausae sunt vesti eius aurum detractum in usum suum convertere -,]] illa irata hunc errorem earum inmisit mentibus, ut se putantes vaccas in saltus abirent et plerumque mugirent et timerent aratra: [[quas Melampus, Amythaonis filius, pacta mercede ut Iphianassam uxorem cum parte regni acciperet, placata Iunone, infecto fonte, ubi solitae erant bibere, purgavit et in pristinum sensum reduxit.

1787   Preditas *i.e.* Proetidas   **1789**   egregio *correxi*   **1791**   confectionibus *correxi,* defectionibus *cod.*   **1794**   Thiestis *cf.* Thyesteis *Met.*   **1797**   Nec … 1802 eos + *in marg.* scilicet Eneas nutricem sepeliuit *cf. Met.* 14,441 | illudite *correxi,* illudide *ut uid. cod.* **1805** Ypolitum *i.e.* Hippolytus

THE ASTONISHED PROETEANS. The daughters, who in another place are   15:326
called 'the Coean mothers', were drunk at a sacrifice, since after they
had received Hercules, who came there from Spain, they cursed Juno
who imposed so many labours on this excellent man. Therefore the
enraged Juno made it so that they thought that they had horns,
because of too much drunkeness. A certain Melampus freed them from
this madness through a preparation also contrary to wine. Thereafter
he poured these preparations in a spring, wherefore later a nature
CONTRARY TO WINE remained in this spring from the herbs put in the
preparation.

AND NOT WITH THYESTEAN [COURSES]. Thyestes and Atreus were   15:462
brothers. Atreus had a son from his brother's wife. Therefore the
enraged Thyestes cooked the son and gave him to the father, Atreus, to
eat.

AND DO NOT TRICK TERRIFIED DEER WITH FEATHERS. Hunters placed   15:475
feathers on top of their nets, so that the deer would not be frightened
when they saw them, but rather advance with less force, and so they
are 'tricked with feathers'. Or the hunters, when they encircle their
pasture with their nets, set fire to feathers in those places where there
are no nets, so that the approaching deer will smell them and think
that there are humans there and then rather come out of the forest
through the nets, and thus they trick them.

THE SON OF THE AMAZON. Theseus fought with the Amazons. After   15:552
they had been conquered he took their queen Hippolyte prisoner and
made her his wife, from whom he begot Hippolytus.

EXPLAIN NOW, O MUSES. Ovid starts by saying this as an introduction to   15:622
the praise of Augustus Caesar, in whose honour he wrote his book.

LOOKING FORWARD [HE SHALL COMMAND] the sacred PROGENY. Livia   15:836
was the wife of Augustus Octavian. She had the sons Drusus, Nero
and Claudius, who in his childhood was good but later very bad.
Drusus however was better and was killed close to Maguntia. Livia
had married Tiberinus Nero before Augustus Caesar, from him she

84rb   Tiberino Nerone nupsit Augusto Cesari. Et isti primigeni, qui Cesares /
        sunt apellati, dicuntur ab Ouidio filii Augusti Octouiani diligentis illos.

                                                                              1815

had Nero and Claudius, but after the death of Tiberinus Nero she married Augustus Caesar. And these two first sons, who are called Caesars, Ovid calls the sons of Augustus Octavian because he loved them.

Appendix:
Edition of Book 1 of clm 14482c

Bavarian B—experimental edition of Book 1 from clm 14482c

This appendix contains an edition and translation of the accessus and Book 1 of the version of the Bavarian B commentary found in the manuscript clm 14482c.

This edition is termed experimental since I have employed a somewhat eclectic method to achieve my goal of interpreting a problematic text, while at the same time documenting the text in the manuscript as much as possible.

The basic principles for editing and translating the text are the same as for clm 4610. However, there are some differences because the text is more problematic than clm 4610 and there are several manuscripts containing versions of the Bavarian B commentary, which gives us an opportunity to use variant readings. In the present edition, I have chosen to incorporate variant readings only where I have judged that the text of 14482c is corrupted or hard to make sense of. A more in-depth discussion of the problems in the text will follow below.

The reason for choosing this part of the commentary to edit are threefold. Besides the simple fact that it is the first part of the text, it is also the book which received the greatest and most varied amount of explanations. Secondly, it is proportionately the longest individual part of the commentary. The commentary comments on all fifteen books of the Metamorphoses, but the accessus and Book 1 equal roughly a fifth of the entire text. Thirdly, because of the varied types of explanations as well as the amount of textual difficulties in Book 1, it is also the most difficult part of the text to edit, which almost demands that a responsible editor meets the challenge.

The reason for choosing clm 14482c is simply the fact that it appears to be the oldest version of the Bavarian B commentary, while at the same time having the longest text (as far as Book 1 is concerned). However, upon working with the text, it turned out that it contains many textual errors and problematic passages. All the other versions of the commentary also seem to contain errors, but clm 14482c would appear to stand out and, for this reason, it is uncertain if it would be wise to edit the entire commentary based on clm 14482c.

For further discussion of the Bavarian B commentary and the relationship between the different manuscripts as well as its relationship to clm 4610 see Case Study 2.

THE MANUSCRIPT

The manuscript is described in chapter 5. The following are some brief additions relevant to this edition.

The booklet 14482c consist of 23,5 folios and is found on fol. 27r-51r (l. 12). The text of the accessus and Book 1 consist of ca four folios and is found on fol. 27r-31r (l. 16).

There are no substantial marginal additions in all of 14482c. On the relevant folios, there is one short addition in margin (28r), one unidentified symbol or letters in margin (30r), three short corrections (27v, 29r, 29v), and the occasional interlinear corrections by the same or a contemporary hand. There is also a hole in the manuscripts on fol. 28, but the text is written around the hole.

THE EDITION

Edition and translation

I employ the same principles as those used for clm 4610 as far as orthography, punctuation, mise-en-page, and translation are concerned. This also holds true for the method employed for marking editorial interventions, with the additions that in this edition I employ asterisks (*) to mark words, phrases, or entire passages I consider suspect. These passages are then provided with alternative readings when available and further elaborated on in the translation, in which the problematic passages are also marked with asterisks.

Apparatus

Besides the system used for clm 4610, this edition employs a third apparatus, which documents alternative readings for problematic passages from the other Bavarian B manuscripts. I have chosen to adopt a third apparatus and thus to separate these variant readings from the apparatus criticus for the purpose of clarity and to emphasise that the variants reported are a selection, not a complete set of variant readings to every passage in the commentary.

The text in the third apparatus is a pure transcription from the manuscripts. Abbreviated words have been expanded, but the text has not been provided with punctuation or expanded lemma. Capital letters are represented in the way they are found in the manuscripts. Unclear readings are marked with questions marks (e.g. on line 35: ?or-o?).

The following manuscripts are used in the apparatus:
Freiburg 381 (Frei381)
Clm 14482b

Clm 14809
Salzburg AV4
(and a single reference to the accessus in the manuscript Haun. 2008,
Det Kongelige Bibliotek, Copenhagen)

Further remarks on errors and emendations

The accessus and Book 1 in 14482c consist of 304 lines on eight and a
half pages. On these 304 lines I have thus far made 96 editorial
interventions. These interventions are mainly corrections of different
sorts, but also include lines or passages marked as problematic
(counted as one intervention) and which may, upon further analysis,
turn out to consist of more errors. This means that almost a third of the
lines contain an error or problematic passage. This can be compared to
clm 4610, where I have made 19 interventions on the approximately
190 lines that make up the accessus and Book 1. With such a high rate
of errors, it is hard to describe clm 14482c as anything else than a
problematic text.

The state of the text must be kept in mind when choosing a method
to edit it. I have not been able to solve every problematic passage in
the text, and even if I had, I am not sure it would be wise to completely
'clean' a text such as this. On the other hand, if we return to what I said
above about documenting the text and the fact that the text is highly
problematic, it is possible to imagine a method where one makes no
corrections at all, but simply marks the problematic passages and then
comments on them in the translation. In this case, however, the
translation would rapidly develop to an outright commentary of its
own.

The method I have chosen seeks a compromise between these two
methods.

The number of errors and the fact that they often seem to be the
result of misunderstood abbreviations and letter forms would suggest
that the scribe had some difficulties with the exemplar. The following
is a small sample of different types of errors:

There are the usual instances of words (or lines) written twice, the
occasional missing word, and also the common scribal error which
results from either a missing or a superfluos linea nasalis. There are
many errors where short abbreviated words are concerned, for
example, *vel* for *ut* or *quam* for *quem*.

There are also many cases of wrong word forms, for example,
promissio for *promissione*, *suadetur* for *suadent*, *imprimum* for
imprimuntur. These errors may be the result of trouble with reading the
script in the exemplar or misunderstood or unrealised abbreviations.

These errors cause confusion since they result in proper words and only after careful analysis can a correction be made.

Another type of error are an error that consists of short forms of words, for example, cu for cupit, fis for fistula, fenda for fecunda, which result in nonsense words. It is unclear whether these are just errors or if they are to be considered as idiosyncratic abbreviations.

Because of the many errors and the many different types of them, it is difficult to speculate about the exemplar. One would need to make a more thorough comparison with the other manuscripts and examine letterforms in texts that may be considered possible exemplars (e.g. investigate if misinterpretations of beneventan scripts may have led to the type of errors found in clm 14482c).

In the following, I will discuss some scenarios where I have employed the method of using asterisks.

Passages marked with an asterisk are generally of three kinds: The word or passage may be suspected of being erroneous, but still present a valid reading; it may be in all likeliness erroneous but for different reasons left uncorrected; and finally it may be erroneous and corrected, but still under suspicion and thus marked with asterisks.

All three scenarios are also marked and commented upon in the translation and also provided with alternative readings from the other manuscripts if there are any.

I have not used cruxes (†) in the edition, but some of the passages marked with asterisks may turn out to be hopeless cases and thus marked with cruxes in the end.

We will start by looking at two instances where I have decided to correct the text and not mark it with asterisk. The text is thus, in a sense, considered 'done' (although the translation still comments on these passages).

Example 1

In the accessus (lines 13-14), clm 14482c has: *hi furcas subire* ('these thieves') and the infinitive *subire* ('to go or come under'), while clm 14809 has: *hic furcas subiere*, which corresponds to Met. 8:700. In this case, I have chosen to correct the error. It could perhaps be argued that the reading in clm 14482c could make sense and thus should not be corrected, but because of the grammatical incongruence together with the witness from another manuscript as well as the passage in the Metamorphoses, it is sensible to correct in this case.

Example 2

The explanation to Met 1:588 found on lines 383-386 is severely corrupted. However, because it is largely based on a passage from Isidore as well as the presence of an almost identical passage in Freiburg 381, it is quite easy to correct. In this passage, the lemma reads *redeuntium inpix* for *redeuntem iupiter*. The first word is at least a real form, while the second would seem to make no sense at all. Next comes the first explanation to the word *flumen* where the text reads *aqua depresso* where in all likeliness it should be *aque depressio*, which is comparable in meaning to Isidore's *aquarum decursus*. Freiburg 381 has garbled *decursus* into something that looks like *de confusa* (by turning *cur-* into a *con*-abbreviation). On line 385, we encounter one of the most severe corruptions in the text. Isidore's *prior aqua quam decursus* has been turned into the unintelligible *priora queque cursus* (the scribe seems to have merged *prior* and *aqua*, then confused a part of *aqua* and *quam* with *queque*, and finally possibly dropped the prefix in *decursus*). The last part of this explanation contains a quotation from Virgil. Here, clm 14482c has *donec flumine curuo* instead of *donec flumine uiuo abluero* (found in Freiburg 381) from Aen. 2:717. Clm 14482c seems to have been thinking of a passage in Met. 3:342: *quam quondam flumine curuo*.

I have corrected all of these errors, except for the quotation from Virgil, which I do not consider an error as such as it renders an intelligible text.

These passages serve as a good example of the possibilities to detect and to correct errors when we have other texts for comparison.

Next follows two examples of instances where I have decided not to correct the text.

Example 3

In the accessus (line 15), we have the obviously erroneous *statuam in de statua Pigmalionis mutata in statuam iuuenis hominis*. Although in all likeliness an error, this reading is present in all the manuscripts that contain this passage.

We would expect a *figuram* or *speciem* here, but since all manuscripts have *statuam* I have chosen to not correct this passage, but to mark it as suspect and comment on it in the translation.

Example 4

In the accessus (lines 59-60), clm 14482c has the following reading: *cum intendat de re de transformatione rerum*

Clm 14809 would seem to have the following: *cum intendit dicere de transformatione rerum*.

It should be noted that the reading in clm 14809 is not entirely certain on account of the text being heavily abbreviated. However, if we assume that we have these two variants to make sense of we have two possibilities:

1. when he pays attention to the thing/the matter, to the transformation of things,
2. when he intends to speak about the transformation of things,

The second alternative is quite straight forward. For the first alternative to make sense we must take the second prepositional phrase as an apposition to the first. This may be the result of the phrase originally being an interlinear gloss that has then been incorporated into the main text. It is not a smooth reading, but the commentary text is not very polished and does seem to contain incorporated interlinear glosses here and there. So, it may still be taken to be a plausible, if awkward reading. For this reason, I have marked it as being perhaps suspect, added an alternative reading in the apparatus and commented on it in the translation.

Example 3 and 4 are examples of passages where I have not corrected since the text in the manuscripts may carry the intended meaning. The final two examples revolve around two passages where I have not been able to achieve a good interpretation through judicious emendation and have thus left the text uncorrected.

Example 5

In the accessus (line 70-74), we find yet another suspect passage. With a little help from Salzburg AV4 we can detect some of the errors, and with the help of the accessus in Haun. 2008 we get some further help. We can draw the conclusion that *uidelicet* must be an error for *utilitas*, *uere* should perhaps be *uero*, a verb is missing in the *cum*-clause, and so on. The problem here is that neither Salzburg AV4 or Haun. 2008 offer perfect matches to clm 14482c. Besides this, the meaning is also quite obscure, which makes the difference between textual error and obscure phrasing difficult to pinpoint. For these reasons I have chosen to mark this entire passage as suspect and then offer some speculations in the translation.

Example 6

The long explanation of Met. 1:563 on lines 359-377 would deserve a case study of its own. It is the most difficult and corrupted individual explanation identified in the commentary thus far. Versions of it are present in all manuscripts, but none of them is the same and only some help can be gained by comparing them to each other. Clm 14482c has the longest explanation by far, and part of the difficulty seems to be the fact that it has incorporated interlinear glosses. This makes attempts to translate the passage into a fluent English difficult and dangerous.

On lines 367-378 *laurus una* anjd *que media* may be the result of interlinear glosses having been incorporated in the main text (*una* was in this scenario originally written above *laurus* to clarify the elementary fact that the word is feminine although it has the masculine *–us* ending).

There also seem to be some superfluous id est-abbreviations in clm 14482c, which makes the text difficult to understand. If we compare the following passage in two manuscripts we see that the id est is either added for some obscure reason, or it may be the result of l for *lauro* having been turned into the typical .i. for *id est*.

Clm 14482c: *quia nobiles quidem id est coronabantur*
Clm 14809: *quia nobiles quidam lauro corobantur*

This passage also contains many other possible errors and for the same reason, as in example 5, I have chosen not to correct, but rather to mark and to comment.

Finally, I should also mention that there are two instances where I have not been able to form a sensible interpretation of the text at all. These are found on lines 277 (*Quod est*) and 365 (*Nam ut inde et cetera*). In these cases, the Latin is preserved in the translation and commented upon in the apparatus.

27ʳ Iste liber intitulatur 'liber Ouidii Nasonis Metamorphos', id est 'de transformatione rerum'. 'Meta' Grece, 'de' Latine. 'Morphosios' 'transformatio'. Et de hac siquidem in hoc libro agit tripliciter: de magica, de spirituali, de naturali.

De naturali, id est de mixtura elementorum. De magica sicut de illis, 5
qui mutabantur corpore et non spiritu, ut Licaon. De spirituali, que tantum mutabantur spiritu, ut mater Penthei et sorores.

Mutatio alia fit in corpore, alia in qualitate, ut in Lycaone. Vel in qualitate et non corpore, ut in cornice. Vel in corpore et non qualitate, ut in saxum draco. Mutatio in qualitate et corpore: Alia de naturali 10
materia, ut de elementis, alia de non naturali sicut de hominibus uel de ceteris corporibus. Mutatio in non naturali materia: Alia de animata ad animatam sicut de Licaone, alia de inanimata ad inanimata, ut hi<c> fur*cas* subi<e>re columpne de domo <u>scilicet</u> Bacidi. Aliter de inanimata ad animatam sicut de statua Pigmalionis mutata in *statuam* iuuenis 15
hominis. Aliter de animata ad inanimata sicut draco, qui mutatus est in saxum.

Que autem de animata ad animatam: Vel fit ad animatam sensibilem, ut Lycaon, qui mutatus est in lupum, uel ad animatam et non sensibilem, ut Daphne in laurum, unde coronabantur homines. Que 20
uero de animata ad animatam sensibilem aut fit de magica aut de spirituali. De magica, ut in Acteone, qui, quando lacerabatur a canibus, erat dicturus 'Acteon ego sum, dominum cognoscite uestrum' si posset. De spirituali, ut in Agaue matre Penthei, que furens lacerauit filium suum, quando sacrificabat Bacho. 25

Materia Ouidii sunt res mutate, de qua non sufficienter agit, nisi ad delectationem et ad institutionem morum. Materia Ouidii est mutatio, non quia in rei ueritatem res essent mutate, sed secundum hoc, quod

---

6 Licaon De] *cf. Met.* 1:163 **7** mater …] *cf. Met.* 3:511 **9** in¹ … Vel] *cf. Met.* 2:531 **13** hic … 14 Aliter] *cf. Met.* 8:700 **15** de … 16 Aliter] *cf. Met.* 10:243 **20** Daphne … unde] *cf. Met.* 1:452 **23** ego … si] *cf. Met.* 3:230

13 de² … 14 Aliter] *cf.* **14809 (65v):** alia de inanimata ad inanimatam ut hic furcas subiere columne scilicet de domo baucidis **15** iuuenis] *sic et ceteri mss*

14 sanctam *cf.* sancta *Met.* furcas … columpne *correxi secundum clm14809* hi fures subire *cod.* | Bacidi *sup. lin.*

Bavarian B, clm 14482c

This book is named 'Ovid Naso's book of Metamorphoses', that is 'about the transformation of things'. *Meta* in Greek, 'about' in Latin. *Morphosios* is 'transformation'. And in this book this is treated threefold: magical, spiritual and natural [transformations].

Natural [transformation], that is about the combination of the elements. Magical, such as about those who are transformed in body but not in spirit, such as Lycaon. Spiritual, those who are only transformed in spirit, such as the mother and sisters of Pentheus.

Some transformations happen with regard to the body, others with regard to property, such as with Lycaon. Or with regard to property and not body, such as with the crow. Or with regard to the body and not property, such as with the serpent into a rock. Transformation with regard to both property and body, some [occur] from natural matter, such as with the elements, others from non-natural, such as with humans or other bodies. Transformation with regard to non-natural matter, some [occur] from living to living, such as with Lycaon, others from non-living to non-living, *as the columns that here took the place of the forked wooden supports from the house, namely from Baucis's house*.[47] Or from non-living to living, such as with Pygmalion's sculpture that transformed into a *statue* of a young person.[48] Or from living to non-living, such as the serpent who was transformed into a rock.

Those that are transformed from living to living matter happen either to living with senses, such as Lycaon who was transformed into a wolf, or to living and not with senses, such as Daphne [who was tranformed] into a laurel, with which men are crowned. Those from living to living with senses are either magical or spiritual. Magical as with Actaeon, who when he was torn to pieces by his dogs was going to say this if he could: 'I am Actaeon, know your master'. Spiritual, as with Agave, Pentheus's mother, who in a fit of rage tore her own son to pieces, when she sacrificed to Bacchus.

Ovid's subject matter is things transformed, regarding which he does not treat sufficiently[49], lest for the purpose of delight and the instruction of habits. Ovid's subject matter is transformation, not because things are transformed in reality, but according to the fact that

---

[47] Here the text of 14482c has been corrupted and emended with the help of clm 14809. Instead of *hic furcas* (here the forked wooden supports) the clm 14482c reads *hi fures* (these thieves) and instead of the perfect *subiere* we have the infinitive *subire*, which does not work gramatically in the sentence.

[48] The latin is the text appears corrupted here (as well as in all the other manuscripts). Instead of *statuam* one would expect *figuram* (form) or *speciem* (shape).

[49] This phrase is not entirely clear. It could be interpreted as though the commentator felt that there were many more important (perhaps theological) things to be said about transformations.

unus quisque erat malis moribus, iudicabatur mutari in eam rem, cui
erat consimilis in moribus.   30

Materia dicitur quasi mater rei, que duobus modis accipitur: ut in
domo lapides; in rebus inuisibilibus, ut in Porphirio genus et species.

Intentio sua est delectari et prodesse mores instruendo, quod fere
omnes, qui hoc modo pertractant, ad ethicam pertinere uidentur, uel
dehortari a terrenis ad gloriam, quam consecutus est Hercules et ceteri   35
tales; utpote ab illis, que sunt temporalia et inutilia et incerta, quod
ostendit permutationes rerum earum, que fuerunt a primordio usque
ad suum tempus.

Intentio etenim est animi effectus circa materiam, *uel oratio que*
maxime intendit animum in libris legendo, ut in Lucano reprehendere   40
ciuile bellum et dissuadere.

Utilitas est talis quod, cum fabule in aliis libris tangentur, que
fortassis ingnorarentur, notiores quoque erant in suo tempore, minus
notas recitando iocundas aperit describens.

Utilitas est quod quisque ex eo negotio consequitur commodum, cui   45
intendit.

Quidam philosophi fuerunt, qui mundum de nihilo deum fecisse
crediderunt. Quidam uero alii athomis et inanitate, que duo semper
fuerunt, deum mundum fecisse dixerunt. Alii autem philosophi, sicut
hic Ouidius et similes eius, semper tria esse dixerunt, scilicet deum et   50
iiii:or elementa similiter confusa et formas omnium rerum in mente dei
existentes, id est ideas, differentias, hanc rationalitatem et caliditatem
et frigiditatem, per quam ipse deus futuras constiturus erat. Ista uero
genera philosophorum dicentium deum ex athomis et inanitate
27ᵛ   mundum fecisse et ex chao / et ideis dicebant deum artificem non   55
creatorem. Quidam uero dicebant deum de nihilo mundum fecisse.
Creatorem illum intellexerunt. Hi autem omnes philosophi personas
tres dicebant patrem, filium, *iii:um spiritum sanctum minorem patre
et filio* crediderunt et in hoc errauerunt.

---

39   etenim ... 41] *cf.* **AV4 (2v):** Item intentio etenim est animi affectus circa materiam uel
?or-o? qua maxime intendit ?tnd? animum in libro legendo ut in lucano reprehendere c.
b. et dissuadere   **57** Hi ... 59 errauerunt] *cf.* **14809 (66r):** Hii autem omnes philiosophi iii
personas dicebant patrem id est togaton et filium id est noyn et spiritum sanctum id est
animam mundi sed filium minorem patre et spiritum sanctum filio minorem crediderunt
et in hoc erraverunt

48 athomis *correxi* athenis *cod.*

everyone was judged to be transformed on account of their bad habits into the thing to which he was similar with regard to habits.

Materia (subject matter) is named just as *mater rei* ('the mother of a thing'), which could be understood in two ways, as in the building blocks of a house; [or as] in invisible things, as *genus* and *species* in Porphyry.

His intention is to delight and to benefit manners by instructing, since almost all those who treat things in this way seem to pertain to ethics, or his intention is to dissuade from earthly things towards eternal glory, which Hercules and others like him obtained; namely [he dissuades us] from these things that are temporal, useless and uncertain, since he reveals the permutation of these things, which existed from the very beginning until his own time.

For his intention is to affect the soul in respect to the subject matter, *or a speech that greatly exites the soul towards the reading of books, as in Lucan, to rebuke and dissuade from civil war*.[50]

The utility is such that, although the stories have been touched upon in other works, he reveals and describes the less known [but] delightful stories by retelling them; these are perhaps unknown [now] even though they were quite known in his time.

The utility is that from this matter each one pursues the reward upon which he is intent.

There were some philosophers who thought that God made the world from nothing. Others said that God made the world from two things that had always existed, atoms and emptiness. Other philosophers, such as Ovid and others like him, said that three things had always existed, namely God, the four elements mingled in the same way, and the shape of all things existing in the mind of God, that is ideas, *differentias*; the rationality, warmness and coldness, through which God was going to decide things to be. These kinds of philosophers, who say that god made the world from atoms and emptiness and from chaos and ideas, they say that God is an artificer not a creator. But others say that God made the world from nothing. They understand him as a creator. But all these philosophers say that there are three persons, the Father, the Son and the third, the Holy Spirit, *but they believe that [the Holy Spirit] is less than the Father and the Son, and in this they err*.[51]

---

[50] This part of the sentence seems corrupted or obscure. The phrase *uel oratio* must be seen as a continuation of *intentio est* that offers an alternative intention, or it could possibly be an error for *ut in Oratio* (as in Horace), which would work as a parallel to the *ut in Lucano* phrase below, but this would require several emendations. The infinitives at the end are also somewhat strangely appended. They could be thought to be governed by *intentio est*. This paragraph is also found, with only small differences, in Salzburg AV4.

[51] A part of this sentence is corrupted, *iii:um* may be a copy error for *noim* (found in most of the other manuscripts). Furthermore, a second *sanctum spiritum* is probably missing in the part of the sentence governed by *crediderunt*. I have supplied it in the translation.

Hic intentio est Ouidii et omnium scribentium de fabulis, utpote   60
Terentii, maxime delectare et delectando mores hominum corrigere.
Ad ethicam spectat, quia omnes fere ad ethicam spectant auctores.

Utilitas est nobis Ouidii, quia fabule in aliis libris introducte
ignorabantur, donec iste Ouidius dilucidauit, et prodesse nobis
ostendendo pulchram compositionem.   65

Alia intentio Ouidii est tractare de mutatione rerum.

Materia est de quibus tractat.

Finalis causa hortari nos ad uirtutem et retrahere a uitiis. Nam, cum
intendat *de re* de transformatione rerum, describit, ut ostendat alias
res pro bonis mutatis mutatas esse in melius; alias autem pro malis in   70
peius.

Materia alia falsa, alia uera. Vera alia historialis, ut Lucani, Salustii
et aliorum, qui de historiis scribunt. Alia moralis, ut Horatii et
Iuuenalis et aliorum, qui ueraciter malos mores hominum
reprehendunt. Et falsa alia, si non fuit factum, tamen fieri potuit, ut   75
Terentii et Plauti et Neuii et aliorum multorum. Alia quod numquam
factum est neque fieri potest per naturam, *ut* isti<u>s Ouidii, qui
loquitur de transmutatione rerum in contrariam naturam, quod est
eius materia.

Intentio est Ouidii dissuadere nocuos affectus, ne per eos   80
incurramus iram deorum, ut de proprio statu mutemur in contrarium.

*Videlicet uere confert nobis talem, ut, cum ipse quidem de maxima
felicitate in maximas miserias, de pace in odium in exilium labores,
materiam suam sumpsit transformationem rerum subaudis ostendens
quasi nihil esse, sed adeo alteratum nos quoque debere materiam   85
nobis sumere habitui nostro competentem.*

---

68 Finalis … 69 rerum] *cf.* **14809 (66r):** Finalis causa est hortari nos ad virtutes et terrere a
viciis Nam cum intendit dicere de transformatione rerum   **76**   Alia … 79 materia] *cf.*
14809 (66r): Alia quod neque factum est nec fieri po- / -tuit ut istius o. quem loquitur de
transformatione rerum quam facta est in contrariam naturam quam est eius materia
82   *Videlicet … 86 competentem*] *cf.* **AV4 (3v):** Utilitas vero talem confert nobis ut cum
ipse quidem a maxima felicitate ad maxima miserias de pace et otio in exilium labores
materiam sibi sumpsit transformationem rerum scilicet quasi ostendens nichil miri esse
sed adeo alternatum nos quoque debere materiam nobis sumere habitui nostro
competentem **Haun. 2008 (1vb):** utilitatem nobis confert ut cum ipse qui de maxima
felicitate in maximas miserias decidit de pace et otio ad exilium et labores materiam sibi
sumpsit transformationem rerum scilicet quod ostendens se adeo alteratum nos quoque
debere materiam nobis sumere habitui nostro competentem

64 dilucidauit *sup. lin. cum sign. inser.*   **65** compositionem + *sup. lin.* ao/do num *ut. vid.*
66 de + *in marg. quiddam signum*   **77** ut *correxi secundum clm14809 a cod.* | istius *correxi*
secundum clm14809

Ovid's intention, and that of all those who write stories, such as Terence, is mainly to delight and by delighting to correct man's habits. He tends towards ethics, since almost all authors tend towards ethics.

The utility of Ovid for us is that since the stories that were introduced in other books were unknown, until Ovid made them clear, he also benefits us by showing us his beautiful composition.

Another intention of Ovid's is to treat the transformation of things.

The subject matter is that which he treats.

The final cause is to urge us towards virtue and to restrain us from sin. For, *when he pays attention to the thing, the transformation of things*[52], he describes them so as to show that some things transform to the better because of good transformations; others transform to worse because of bad transformations.

Some subject matter is false, some true. True subject matter can be historical, as that of Lucan, Salust and other, who write about history. Other can be moral, as that of Horace, Juvenal and others, who truthfully rebuke man's bad habits. Subject matter can be false, even if it did not happen, but nevertheless could have happened, such as the subject matter of Terence, Plautus, Naevius and many others. Other subject matter that never happened and never could happen by its very nature, as is that of Ovid himself, who talks about the transmutation of things into an opposite nature, which is his subject matter.

Ovid's intention is to advise against damaging emotions, so that we will not incur the wrath of the gods through them, so that we are transformed from our own state to one opposite.

*In fact he brings us such an utility, because, although he fell from the greatest happiness to the greatest sorrows, from peace and leisure to exile and labour, he chose the transformation of things as his subject matter, that is to say showing that there is nothing extraordinary, but

---

[52] This part of the sentence could be corrupted. The manuscripts has *intendat de re* (pays attention to the thing), while clm 14809 has the reading *intendit dicere de* ('he intends to speak about'), which may be better.

Verbi gratia ut si aliquando superbum mansuetum nobis reddere uolumus, talia et tam humilia scribamus, que iram eius sint frangentia, non ad manus prouocantia. Sic de ceteris.

Scripsit autem in Ponteroo insula, ut in exilio erat expulsus ab 90 Augusto. In fine quoque operis sui laudat eum sperans per hoc gratiam suam recuperare.

1:1   Proponens: FERT, id est cupit, ANIMVS meus de re formata mutata IN NOVAS FORMAS ET CORPORA mutata, id est noua c<orpora>. Vel FERT, id est cu<pit> animus meus de re formata, mutata in noua corpora, id est 95 corpus mutatum in nouas formas, id est alterata per nouas formas superuenientes.

Mutatio est preteriti habitus uariatio, et iste ostendit realiter corpora et formas esse uariatas, ut de homine in arborem. Non tamen sicut, quod corpus erat, fiat non corpus. Corpus autem dictum eo, quod 100 corruptum perit. Solubile est enim atque mutabile, ut aliquando
1:2 | 1:5 soluendum. DII CEPTIS, inuocatio, ANTE MARE, id est quod uocaretur. *Facta proponere et inuocare explanant.*

1:7   Quod Plato dicit 'ylen', poete CHAOS appellant; RVDIS <in>formis;
1:9   INDIGESTA, id est inseparata inordinata SEMINA RERVM. Res, quod erant 105
1:10   semina futurarum rerum. TYTAN a titane patre; quia non consensit
I,19   cum fratribus, receptus est inter deos. FRIGIDA P<VGNABANT> C<ALIDIS>. Hoc ideo dicit, quia ignis est siccus, leuis, mobilis. Aer humidus, leuis, mobilis. Aqua humida, grauis, mobilis.

1:14   AMPHITRITES. 'Amphi' Grecum, 'circum' Latine. 'Trites' quasi terens, 110 uel Triton, deus marinus.

1:21/25 DEVS CONCORDI PACE, id est meliori tritura adducentur duo fundamenta penitus oppositas qualitates habentia, uidelicet ignem et terram. Ignis est calidus, acutus, mobilis. Terra uero est frigida, optusa,
28ʳ   / non mobilis, corpulenta. Hec duo ita sunt repugnantia, scilicet dum 115 per se uidelicet non possunt coherere, posuit quiddam medium, scilicet aquam, que habet duas affinitates cum terra et terciam cum

---

102   Dii … 103 explanant*] *cf.* **14809 (66v)**: Inuocat §dii ceptis Narrat Ante mare id est quod mare uocatur narratio **AV4 (3v)**: explanat Facta proponere inuocat dii ceptis §Ante mare id est quod mare uocatur Narratio

94 fert *correxi* fere *cod.*   **95** cupit *supplevi*   **104** informis *correxi secundum clm14809*

only changed to that point that we should take a subject matter that agrees with our condition.*[53]

For example, if we at any time want to make an arrogant person gentle towards us, then we can write such things and so humble things that will break his anger and not provoke him to violence. The same with the rest.

He wrote this on the island of Pontus, since he was in exile, banished by Augustus. At the end of his work he praises him hoping by this to regain his grace.

He declares: My SOUL URGES [ME], that is wishes, [to speak] of a formed thing, transformed INTO NEW SHAPES AND transformed BODIES, that is new bodies. Or my soul URGES, that is wishes [to speak] of a formed thing, transformed into new bodies, that is a body transformed into new shapes, that is at thing altered by new shapes that come upon it.

A transformation is a change of a former state and he shows that in reality bodies and shapes are diverse, such as ranging from man to tree. Not, however, in such a way that what was a body becomes a non-body. A body (corpus) is called thus because when corrupted (corruptum) it perishes. For it is dissolvable and changeable so that at some time it is to be dissolved. OH GODS, BY YOUR UNDERTAKINGS, is the invocation, BEFORE THE SEA, that is that which is invoked. *To propose and to invoke explain what has happened*.[54]

That which Plato calls *hyle*, the poets call CHAOS; CRUDE [that is] unformed; CONFUSED that is the unseparated and disordered SEEDS OF THINGS. Things, since they were the seeds of future things. TITAN, [named] from his father Titan; since he did not agree with his brothers, he was received among the gods. COLD THINGS FOUGHT WITH WARM THINGS. He says this since fire is dry, light and mobile. Air is moist, light and mobile. Water moist, heavy and mobile.

AMPHITRITES. *Amphi*, a Greek word, is 'round' in Latin. *Trites* as in *terens* (grinding) or Triton, the sea god.

GOD WITH A HARMONIOUS PEACE, that is *by a good grinding*[55] two foundations with totally opposing qualities, namely fire and earth, are brought together. Fire is warm, keen and mobile. Earth is cold, dull, immobile and corporeal. These two are thus opposed, namely while they cannot stick together by themselves, he placed something as a medium, namely water, which has two affinities with earth and a third

---

[53] This passage is severerly corrupted. Salzburg AV4 and clm 14482b have a slightly better text, but the best reading is found in the accessus to the Metamorphoses manuscripts Haun. 2008, which has the best version of the end of this passage: 'showing that he has changed so mucht that we also should take a subject matter that agrees with our condition.' The translation above is not verbatim.

[54] This phrase could be understod as 'to propose and to invoke explains what has happened/the events', but the text may be corrupted.

[55] This may be an error for *meliori natura* (by a better nature), wich would then refer to Met. 1,21, but *meliori tritura* (a good/better grinding) is also a possible reading in this context.

igne. Aqua namque frigida, mobilis, corpulenta. Cum per hoc medium non possit fieri firma concordia terra propter pondus, posuit aliud medium, scilicet aerem unam proprietatem cum terra habentem et 120 duas cum igne. Aer enim calidus, mobilis, corpulens. Et notandum est, quod sicut ignis habet se ad aerem, et ita aer ad aquam, et sicut aer ad aquam, ita aqua ad terram et eodem modo ascendendo, item sicut se ignis habet ad aquam et aer habet se ad terram eodem modo ascendendo. 125

Et hoc fecit ad exemplum duorum numerorum cubicorum primum perfectum, scilicet bis bini bis et ter terni ter. Cubiti dicuntur, qui habent longitudinem, latitudinem, spissitudinem, hi duo numeri supradicti, cum essent penitus oppositi. Unus enim constabat ex paribus, scilicet bis bini bis. Alter ex partibus in partibus, scilicet ter 130 terni ter. Non poterat firmiter colligari, nisi interpositis duobus mediis, id est bis bini ter et ter terni bis. Bini ter habet duas affinitates cum bis bini <bi>s, sed terciam cum ter terni ter. Ter terni bis habet duas cum ternis ter et unam cum bis bini bis. Quibus mediis interpositis ita per se colligantur, quod unus se habet ad alium, et ita per certos 135 sexqualtera proportio est. 'Sex' igitur Grece, 'totum' Latine. Sexqualter dicitur, qui continet aliquem numerum totum in se et eius dimidiam partem, scilicet sex. Vnde sicut ter terni ter, id est xxuii, continet ter terni bis, xuiii, et eius dimidiam partem, scilicet ix. Eodem modo ter terni bis in se bis bini ter, id est xii et eius dimidia partem, scilicet sex. 140 Iterum bis bini ter continet in se bis bini bis, id est octo, et eius dimidiam partem, id est iiii, et e conuerso. Et notandum est quod sicut xxuii se habet ad xii, ita xuiii ad uiii. Continet enim xxuii xii bis in se et eius iiii partem, scilicet iii. Eodem modo xuiii continet in se bis octo et eius iiii partem, id est duo, et e conuerso. 145

1:25   Et hoc est quod dicit Ouidius CONCORDI PACE LIGAVIT et Boetius: Tu numeris elementa ligas.

1:1   IN NOVA FERT ANIMVS. Ponit Ouidius in principio sui operis quosdam uersus, qui secundum Tullium prologus uocantur, in quibus materiam ostendit et lectores auditores beniuolos et dociles reddit. Et alii poete 150 solent facere in suis prologis.

---

146 Tu … 147 ligas] *cf. Consolatio* 3 verse 9:10

127 Cubiti *post corr. ex* Cobicinio, *i.e.* cubici   **130** paribus *post corr. ex* partibus   **133** bini bis *correxi*   **136** sexqualtera *i.e.* sesquialtera   **137** aliquem *correxi secundum Frei 381* aliquando *cod.*   **146** ligavit et + Boetius est terminum *sed postea del. cod.* | Boetius … 147 ligas *in marg. cum sign. insert.*

with fire. For water is cold, mobile and corporeal. When there still could not be a firm concord with earth through this one medium beacuse of the weight, he placed another medium, namely air, which has one quality in common with earth and two with fire. For air is warm, mobile and corporeal. And note that as fire relates to air, so air relates to water and just as air to water, so water to earth and in the same way when moving upwards, again just as fire relates to water and air relates to earth in the same way when moving upwards.

And he does this as the perfect and primary example of two cubic numbers, namely 2x2x2 and 3x3x3. These two above-mentioned numbers that have a length, width and depth are called cubic, although they are utterly different. For one consisted of pairs, namely 2x2x2, the other from parts in parts, namely 3x3x3. It (the number) could not firmly be bound lest by two inserted middle terms, that is 2x2x3 and 3x3x2. 2x3 has two affinities with 2x2x2, but a third with 3x3x3. 3x3x2 has two affinities with 3x3 and one with 2x2x2. With these middle terms inserted they are bound through them so that one relates to another and so with certain numbers there is a sesquialterate proportion (1,5, 2:3). For *ses* in Greek, means 'the whole' in Latin. That is called *sesquialter* (1,5), which contains a whole number and its half in itself, namely 6. Whence just as 3x3x3, that is 27, contains 3x3x2, 18, and its half, namely 9. In the same way 3x3x2 contains in itself 2x2x3, that is 12, and its half, namely 6. Again 2x2x3 contains in itself 2x2x2, that is 8 and its half, that is 4 and conversely. And it should be noted that just as 27 relates to 12, so 18 relates to 8. For 27 contains 12x2 in itself and its quarter, namely 3. In the same way 18 contains 8x2 in itself and its quarter, that is 2 and conversely.

And this is what Ovid means HE BINDS WITH A CONCORDANT PEACE and Boethius: You bind the elements in numbers.

THE SOUL URGES [ME TO SPEAK OF SHAPES TRANSFORMED] INTO NEW [BODIES]. In the beginning of his work Ovid places some verses that according to Tully are called a prologue. In these he shows the subject matter and he makes the readers and listeners benevolent and docile. Usually other poets also do this in their prologues.

1:1   Materiam ostendit cum dicit FERT ANIMVS meus, id est impatienter et
       grauiter laborat ad hoc, ut ostendat res formatas. Que res mutantur,
       uel ui nature, ut humanum corpus in uermem uel quando *terra motione*
       caloris et humoris in uermem mutantur. Vel animi motione, quando   155
       aliquem ita stultum uidemus, quod asinum uocamus, uel ita crudelem,
       quod leonem esse dicimus. Vel in malorum statu artium, in quo *patet*
       omnia mutabilia esse, quare in terrenis non est confidendus. In hac
       materia beniuolos reddit auditores, quia congruam eis materiam
       proponit in util<itat>em.   160

       Sunt quidam, qui hic faciunt casuum mutationem *dicentes* corpora
       m<utata> in uarias formas, ideo quia dicunt corpus non mutari, nisi
       formas tantum. Contra quos nos dicimus c<orpora> et f<ormas>
       equaliter mutari.

1:2   DII CEPTIS. Materia ostensa facit inuocationem, in qua nos attentos et 165
       beniuolos reddit, non quia leue sit, quod dicturus est, sed graue et
       mult*um* *attend*endum est, cum hoc fit, quod deos ad suum auxilium
       inuocet dicens: O DII ASSPIRATE.

       Dictum est a similitudine cantorum, qui dum similiter spirant, id est
1:3   cantant, clamor uocis au*g*mentatur. Et ita dicit iste ASPIRATE, id est me / 170
28ᵛ   scribentem iuuate in hoc opere incepto, dico, *ut iuuetis*. Et potestis,
1:2   NAM VOS MVTASTIS ET ILLA.

       Primo enim ostensa materia et facta inuocatione *ponit utrumque cum
1:4   auxilio materiam dicens*, ut asspiretis et aspirando DEDVCITE CARMEN
       inceptum AB ORIGINE, id est a creatione rerum. Quo modo non   175

---

152   Materiam ... 164 mutari] *cf.* **Frei381 (34v):** M. ostendit cum dicit fert animus meus et
cetera Res mutantur ut humanum corpus in uermes uel animi mocione quando aliquam
adeo stultum uidemus quem asinum uocamus uel ita crudelem quod leonem dicimus
uel ui malarum arcium In quo patet omnia mutabilia esse in terrenis ut esse
confidendum In hac materia beniuolos reddit quia congruam materie proponit eius
utilitatem Sunt quidam philosophi qui hic faciunt mutationem casuum dicentes corpora
mutata In nouas formas ideo quia dicuntur corpora non mutari nisi forma tantum contra
quos nos dicimus quia corpus et forma equaliter mutantur **14809 (67r):** Fert a. m. Res
formatas dicimus id est mutatas esse in noua corpora id est in alias formas quoniam res
mutantur uel ui nature ut humanum corpus in uermulis quando terra motione caloris
uel humoris in ?uerum? mutatur   **171**   *ut iuuetis*] *sic et ceteri mss (Frei + AV4)*
173 *ponit ... 174 dicens*] *sic et ceeri mss (Frei + AV4)*

154   terra motione *correxi secundum* clm14809 ira more *cod.*   **157**   patet *correxi secundum*
Frei381 patri *cod.*   **160** utilitatem *correxi secundum Frei381*   **161** dicentes *correxi secundum*
Frei381 diuertens *cod.*   **167** multum *correxi secundum Frei381* multia *cod.* | attendendum
correxi secundum Frei381 accudendum *cod.*   **170**   augmentatur *correxi secundum Frei381*
argumentatur *cod.*

He shows the subject matter when he says my SOUL URGES ME, that is it works impatiently and heavily to this end so that he will show the things shaped. These things are transformed either by the force of nature, as when a human body [is transformed] into a worm, or when * the earth by the motion of warmth and moisture is transformed into a worm.*[56] Or by the movement of the soul, when we find someone so stupid that we call him an ass, or so cruel that we say he is a lion. *Or in a state of the wicked arts*[57], in which it is clear that all things are changeable, wherefore one should not trust earthly things. In this subject matter he makes the listeners benevolent, since he proposes a subject matter that is suitable for them with regard to its utility.

There are those who here change the cases[58] saying that bodies are transformed into various shapes, since they say that a body does not transform, lest in shape only. Against these we say that bodies and shapes transform equally.

GODS ON MY UNDERTAKINGS. When he has showed the subject matter he makes an invocation, in which he makes us attentive and benevolent, not because it is a light thing that he is going to say, but grave and much to be heeded, when this happens that he calls the gods to his help saying: O GODS, FAVOUR.

This ('O gods, favour') is said in similarity to singers, who while they similarly breathe, that is sing, the sound of their voice is increased. And so he says FAVOUR, that is help me who write this work that has been begun, I say, *so that you help*.[59] And you can, FOR YOU TRANSFORMED ALSO THESE.

For when he first has shown the subject matter and made the invocation *he then uses both with help naming the subject matter*[60] so that you will favour and by favouring YOU BRING this SONG already begun FROM THE ORIGIN, that is from the creation of all things. In this

[56] Here the text has been corrected with the help of clm 14809. The reading in 14482c *ira more* gives no sensible reading.
[57] This phrase seems odd. Freiburg 381 has the simpler *uel ui malarum arcium* (or by the force of the wicked arts).
[58] I have interpreted this phrase as refering to grammatical cases.
[59] It is unclear exactly what this phrase is supposed to mean. No other alternative readings exist in the other manuscripts.
[60] This phrase is obscure. It could also be understood as 'he then uses both when he names the subject matter with help/support' (the support perhaps being the invocation).

1:4
dicuntur ab aliqua origine, que modo fiat, sed a prima, que mundi fuit constitucione. CARMEN dicit PERPETVVM, id est continuatim ductum per mutationem, que facta est usque AD MEA TEMPORA, ut per illam homines a transitoriis, ne in eis confidant, terreantur.

'Deos' plurales ponit quantum ad uulgi opinionem. Ipse enim sciebat 180 unum deum esse, qui diuersos species diuersis rebus presidentes omnia operari non dubitabit. Sed, quia ipse est poeta, nec ex toto ueritatem dicere debet expresse, sed querentibus uerbis eam satis intelligibilem exprimit nobis.

1:6
1:6
Postquam auditores satis attentos per materiam et inuocationem 185 reddidit ad negotium suum peruenit, dicens: ANTEquam res ita essent distribute, quod his designarentur uocabulis, terram et CELUM tegens OMNIA, ERAT VNVS VVLTVS, id est creature substantia unius uultus, id est cogitationis, id est que indifferens erat in toto illo spatio, quomodo dicitur. Et *b. que* uultum, si quis esset, tunc posset uocare 190 confusionem.

1:7
1:8
1:9
1:10
Vultus eius, dico, MOLES. Molis quidem erat et hec quidem ponderosa, quia non erat in quicquam, id est ulla discretione alia NISI PONDVS INERS esset. Pondus iners tamen erat semen, id est principium, futurarum rerum, sed non bene formatum. Nam ipsa elementa uero 195 SEMINA RERVM IVNCTARVM, sed NON BENE, id est pulchre formata, erant CONGESTA, id est coadunata in eodem loco et non discerni poterant. Nam non uera lux erat tunc et, ut tenebre sunt, nihil discerni poterat, et hoc dicit: N<VLLVS> A<DHVC> T<ITAN>, id est illuminacio P<RE>B<EBAT>.   200

Ipse deberet scribere modo illam confusionem, sed quia tantam proprietatem non posset exprimere, ideo ad has negationes se transfert, ut negando ista ad illa chao<s>, que illa esset, in parte describit.

1:14
AMPHITRITES, id est circum sonans. 'Amphi' Grecum, 'circum' Latine. 205 'Triton' sonans. Mare enim in circuitu terrarum litus percutiens sonat.

---

201 Ipse ... 204 describit] *cf.* **Frei381 (34v):** Ipse modo debet illam confusionem dicere sed quia interpretatem exprimere non posset ad has ideo negationes se transfert ut negando ista ab illa chao que confusio illa esset in parte describat

197 congesta *correxi* mesta *cod.*   **199** nvllvs ... Titan] n. at. *pro* n. a. t.   **203** chaos *correxi*

way, they are not said to be from an origin that happened recently, but from the first, which happened with the constitution of the world. He says PERPETUAL SONG, that is led continuously through a transformation made all the way TO MY TIME, so that through this people would be deterred from earthly things, so as not to trust them.

He puts 'gods' in the plural with respect to common opinion. For he himself knew that there is one god, who will not hesitate to cause different shapes to preside over everything through different things. But since he is a poet he does not have to tell the whole truth explicitly, but with inquiring words he expresses it plainly enough for us.

After he has made the listeners attentive enough through the subject matter and the invocation he arrives at his main matter, saying: BEFORE things were so divided that they could be designated with these words, [before] the earth and HEAVEN covering EVERYTHING, THERE WAS ONE FACE, that is the substance of creation with a single face, that is of thought, that is in which there is no difference in this entire space, whatever it is called. *And 'face' is well said*⁶¹, if any such thing exists, then one could call it a mingling.

Its face, I say, A HEAP. There was a heap and a heavy one at that, since it did not exist in anything, that is through no other separation, except an INERT WEIGHT. The inert weight, however, was the seed, that is the beginning, of things to come, but it was not well formed. For the elements themselves were the SEEDS OF THINGS JOINED, but NOT WELL, that is not beautifully formed, they were PRESSED TOGETHER, that is they were collected into the same place and could not be separated. For there was no true light then and, since it was dark, nothing could be discerned, and he says this: AS YET NO TITAN OFFERED [LIGHT], that is an illumination.

*He should describe merely 'this mingling', but since he cannot express such a great quality, he turns to these negations, as by negating this to that he is partly describing the chaos that existed there.*⁶²

AMPHITRITES, that is 'sounding around'. *Amphi* is a Greek word, 'around' in Latin. *Triton* is 'sounding'. For the sea sounds when beating the shore in its way around the lands.

1:14

---

⁶¹ This passage seems to be corrupted, but it reminds us of line 76 from clm 4610, which reads *uultus bene dixit* and is used in the translation.
⁶² This passage is obscure and may be derrived from the language of logic, cf. Boethius 4:10.

1:15 VTQVE. Bene dicit, quia non erat ibi discrecio ista. Nam erat confusio et
hoc dicit: non erat tunc discretio, ut patet in his. Nam QVA, id est *ibi*,
ubi erat illud, quod modo dicitur TELLVS, ILLIC in eodem erat AER. Et
1:16 SIC, quia omnia ita confusa erant, tellus non erat habitabilis, ut aliquis 210
1:17 <neque> desuper staret neque in unda nataret. Nam NVLLI eorum
MANEBAT tunc FORMA SVA. Ista, qu*e* modo si<bi> a deo data est.
Quamuis notet separatim illud elementum, quod tellus dicitur, hoc
uocabulo, quod est tellus, ideo non hoc facit, quin alia elementa
conmixta illi elemento essent, *sed quia malorum uis ill*o* elemento, 215
quod tellus dicitur, <u>esse</u> a uulgo credebatur. Ideo designatur per se hoc
nomine ita dicens*.

1:18 OBSTABAT. Non erant in hac forma, in qua modo sunt, sed erant
confusa. Ideo obstabat, id est impediebat, unum aliud, quia neque nare
posset aliquis in aqua propter terram neque stare in terra propter 220
aquam admixtam, quia erat confusio.

1:21 HANC DEVS. Ipsa quidem obstabant, sed deus DIREMIT, id est separauit,
illa ligantia et fecit coadunantem naturam ipsorum elementorum, qui
post diuisam sunt. NATVRA, dico, que MELIOR, id est efficatior, facta est
ad procreationem rerum, postquam erant diuisa, que prius conmixta. 225

1:24 QVE POSTQVAM diremit et postquam sic uoluit, id est ex glomeratione
ext*r*axit. Et hoc ita quod illuminatum, quia ex eo, ut a CECO ACERVO in
29ʳ LOCIS suis firmiter posuit, LIGAVIT / CONCORDI PACE, ut dictum, quia in
procreacione conueniunt, quamuis sint inter se DISSOCIATA. Nam
1:29 TELLVS TRAXIT in se, id est retinuit quicquid ponderosi in aliis erat et ita 230
PRESSA EST inferius. Sic deus, dixi, dedit unicuique proprietatem suam,
1:33 quia REDEGIT IN MEMBRIS, id est in diuersitatem, ut sint membra, id est
et diuersitas. Et si non est diuersitas nec membra.

---

207   Vtqve … 217 dicens*] *cf.* **Frei381 (34v):** Vt qua est bene dicit quia non erat ibi
discretio ista nam erat ibi confusio et hoc dicit non erat ibi discretio ut patet in hoc Nam
qua ibi ubi erat illa que modo dicitur tellus illic in eodem loco erat aer et quia omnia ista
confusa erant tellus non erat habitabilis ut aliquis desuper staret nec in unda nataret
Nam nulli eorum manebat tunc sua forma ista que modo a deo sibi data est Quamuis
uocet seperatim illud elementum quod tellus dicitur hoc uocabulo quod est tellus non
ideo hoc facit quin aliqua insint illa elementa Sed quia maior uis illi elemento est quod
dicitur tellus et regnat ibi ideo designatur per se hoc nomine ita de ceteris   **226** uoluit] *cf.*
euoluit *Frei381*

207 Vtqve *correxi* ut quia *cod.*   **208** ibi … 209 ubi *correxi secundum Frei381* in ut *cod.*
211 neque¹ *supplevi*   **212** que *correxi secundum Frei381* quam *cod.* | sibi *correxi*   **215** illi
post corr. ex illa | illo *correxi* illi *cod.*   **216** esse *sup. lin.*   **224** diuisam *perp. pro* diuisionem
227 extraxit *correxi secundum Frei381* extexint *cod.* | illuminatum *scil.* illuminatum est

AND THOUGH. He says this well, since there was no separation there. For there was this mingling and he says this: then there was no separation, as is evident in these [lines]. For IN THAT WHICH, that is there where this existed that recently is named THE EARTH, THERE in the same place was also AIR. And THUS, since everything was so confused, the earth was not habitable, so that nobody could stand upon it nor swim in the water.[63] For ITS SHAPE did not then REMAIN IN ANY of them. This [shape] which recently had been given to it by god. Although he separately marks this element, which is named earth, by this name earth, he does not do this in order for the other elements not to be mixed together in this element, *but because an evil force was thought by the common people to reside in this element named earth. Therefore it is designated by itself by this name in saying it this way.*[64]   1:15

STOOD AGAINST. These were not in the shape in which they are now, but they were mingled. Therefore one stood against, that is hindered, the other, since nobody could swim in the water because of the earth and nobody could stand on the earth because of the water mixed in, since there was a mingling.   1:18

GOD THIS [STRIFE]. These things did indeed stand against, but God DIVIDED, that is separated, those things that were bound together and he made a joined nature of these elements that existed after the division. I say a NATURE made BETTER, that is more efficacious, for the procreation of things after those that were previously mingled had been divided.   1:21

AFTER he divided THEM and after he turned[65] them thus, that is extracted them from the crowd. And this in such a way that it was illuminated, since from it HE BOUND them in A CONCORDANT PEACE, as it is said, so that from THE BLIND HEAP he firmly placed them in their PLACES since they come together in procreation, although they are DISJOINED among themselves. For EARTH DREW to itself, that is it retained whatever was heavy in the others and so it was pressed further down. Thus, I said, God gave to each its quality, since HE REDUCED IN PARTS, that is in diversity, so that there were parts, that is also diversity. And if there is no diversity there are no parts.   1:24

[63] The first part of this explanation contains several errors, which can be detected with the help of the other mss, but this passage is still to be considered unstable and unclear.
[64] This passage is possibly corrupted. The text in Freiburg 381 reads: because a greater force belonged to this element, which is named earth and which ruled there, therefore it is designated by itslef/on its own by this name and so with the others (*Sed quia maior uis illi elemento est quod dicitur tellus et regnat ibi ideo designatur per se hoc nomine ita de ceteris*).
[65] Freiburg 381 has *evolvit* (unfolded or released)

1:35   GLOMERAVIT, id est fecit rotundam temperiem, id est similitudinem
celi, qui magnus orbis dicitur, quia alia in se continet elementa. *TVM*, id   235
est propter quod terram glomerauit, diuisit FRETA.

1:38   Iacent*es* aquas dicit STAGNA a stando. Profundas aquas LACVS.
FLVMINA, id est fluentes aquas, ut currerent, misit in DECLIVIA terre et
RECEPT[I]A ea[m] in spaciosis aquis, que LIBERIORES sunt, quia aliis
1:41   nomen auferunt et suum non amittunt, cadunt per illas IN MARE. Mare   240
est generalis collectio aquarum. Siue sint salse siue dulces abusiue
mare nuncupatur. Proprie autem mare appellatur eo quod quedam
aque eius sunt amare.

1:45   UTQVE DVE. Istud fecit in terra et etiam aliud, quia quasdam partes fecit
habitabiles, quasdam inhabitabiles. Nam ut due zone sunt in celo ex   245
parte septentrionis, que DEXTRA dicitur ad cursum solis, que sunt
frigide, et similiter due ab austro. QVINTA ardens est. [que dextra
dicitur ad cursum solis que sunt frigide et similiter due ab austro
quinta ardens est] SIC, id est EODEM modo, deus DISTINXIT terram, que
1:48   est in medio clausa. Nam inprimu*ntur* terra, T<ELLVRE> P<REMVNTVR>.   250
Non ideo tamen dicit ita in terra esse ut in celo, quod illud ex celo
ueniat, sed sic deus fecit illud in celo et in terra.

1:52   IMMINET. Hanc proprietatem dedit deus telluri, istam autem aeri. Nam
1:54   IVSSIT ILLIC stare NEBVLAS ET TONITRVA, id est aeris ipsius collisiones, et
etiam uentos. Et hoc ita quod quisque uentus suum locum obtineret.   255
Dedit enim eis hec iura, *ut aer usque medium orbis spacium quoque
impellentur et tum ultra comprehendere non posset*. Ideo oppositus
est Zephirus, quia aer occidentalis occidentalem aera repellit et sic in
aliis. Si<c> aer, cuius totum aera usque ad occidentem duceret terra, ex
illa parte succumberet, quia totum aera traxit in se tellus, id est retinuit   260

---

237   Iacentes … 238 aquas] *cf*. Isid. *Etymol*. 13:19+21: Nam dictus est stagnus ab eo quod
illic aqua stet nec decurrat. ; Fluuius est perennis aquarum decursus, a fluendo perpetim
dictus.   **240**   Mare … 243 amare] *cf*. Isid. *Etymol*. 13:14: Mare est aquarum generalis
collectio. Omnis enim congregatio aquarum, siue salsae sint siue dulces, abusiue maria
nuncupantur, iuxta illud: "Et congregationes aquarum uocauit maria". Proprie autem
mare appellatum eo quod aquae eius amarae sint.

234   temperiem] *cf*. speciem *Frei381*   **249**   Sic … 252 terra] *cf*. **Frei381 (35r):** Sic id est
eodem modo deus distrinxit terram que est in medio clausa Nam inprimuntur ut t. p.
Nunc ideo tamen dicit ita in terra esse ut in celo quod illud ex celo ueniat sed sic deus
illud fecit in celo et in terra

235 Tum *correxi* eum *cod*.   **237** Iacentes *correxi* iacentis *cod*.   **239** recepta *correxi* | ea
correxi   **244** Utque due *post corr. ex* ut due *ut vid*.   **247** que … 249 est[1] *delevi bis scr. cod*.
250   inprimuntur *correxi secundum Frei381* inprimum *cod*.   **254**   nebulas *post corr. ex*
nebulans   **256** Dedit *post corr. ex* dendit *ut vid*.   **259** Sic *correxi*, § *adest*

HE FORMED INTO A BALL, that is he made a round mixture, that is in the   1:35
likeness of heaven that is called the great orb, since it contains the
other element in itself. THEN, that is because he formed the earth into a
round ball, he divided THE STRAITS.

He calls still waters STAGNA (standing water) from *stare* (to stand).   1:38
LACUS (lake) is deep waters. He sends FLUMINA (rivers), that is flowing
waters, as they run towards DECLIVITIES in the earth and THEY RECEIVE
it in more spacious waters, which are MORE FREE, since they remove the
name from others and do not lose their own, through these the rivers
fall INTO THE SEA. *Mare* (sea) is a general collection of water. It is
unproperly called *mare* wether it is salt or sweet. But properly *mare* is
named from the fact that some of its water is *amare* (bitter).

AND AS TWO. He made this and also another thing on land, since he   1:45
made some parts habitable, some inhabitable. For just as there are two
cold zones in heaven from the northern part, which is called the RIGHT
POINT with respect to the orbit of the sun, there are similarly two zones
from the south point. THE FIFTH is hot. SO, that is IN THE SAME way,
God DIVIDED the earth, which is enclosed in the middle. For they are
imprinted on the earth, THEY ARE PRESSED ON THE EARTH. However, *he
does not say that* it is the same on earth as in heaven, since this one
comes from heaven, but God made it thus both in heaven and on
earth.[66]

IT HANGS OVER. God gave this quality to earth, that to air. For HE   1:52
COMMANDED CLOUDS AND THUNDER, that is the collisions of air itself,
and also winds, to stand THERE. And this so that each wind had its
own place. He gave them this right, *so that air also will be driven all
the way to the middle space of the orb and then it cannot further be
contained*.[67] Zephyros is opposed, since the western air drives away
western air and so with the others. Thus the air, all of which earth
would bring all the way to the west, would sink down from this part,
since earth dragged all air to itself, that is it retained whatever was

[66] Freiburg 381 has the reading *nunc ideo tamen dicit* (now, however, he says), which may
also be a good reading, depending on how the reader interpreted the relevant passage in
the *Metamorphoses*.
[67] This phrase is obscure and is possible corrupted. The translation is an estimation of
what it might mean.

1:57   quicquid ponderosi erat in aliis et ita pressa est inferius. Nam HIS
PERMISIT HABENDVM AERA, sed NON PASSIM.

1:58   VIX NVNC. Et merito non permisit illis, ut haberent passim aera, quia
tunc nihil obsisteret eis, quod in hoc patet. Nam cum non permittitur
quod ideo fit, quia *differencia, qui fratres sunt*, quia ex commoto aere   265
eant uel uno aere creantur. Et uere, dico, quod quisque regit suam
partem, nam est regnum.

1:61   NABATHVS uel Nabath fuit filius Ismahelis, filii Abrahe, qui regnauit in
oriente. A quo dicta est regio Nabaioht.

1:64   SEPTEMQVE TRIONES. Temes, ut secatur dictio in medio.   270

1:82   QVAM SATVS *a* IAPETO. Gentiles primum Prometheum simulacra
hominum de luto finxisse perhibent et ab eo perfectam artem
simulacra et statuas fingendi. Vnde et poete primum ab eo homines
factos esse confingunt figurate propter effigies. Iapetus duos filios
habuit, Prometheum et Epimetheum. Prometheus hominem fecit. Quo   275
facto dicitur celos ascendisse auxilioque Minerue ad solis rotam
adhibita[m] fac<u>la[m] superis ignem furatus est, quem hominum
prebuit usui. Unde dii indignantes maciem et famem in terram
miserunt. Sed postea in monte Caucaso ad scopulum religatus est, ut
29ᵛ   aquila cor eius exederet, et hoc / factum est per Mercurium.   280

Hoc non est aliud, nisi quid puer fuit uir discretissimus et in
Caucaso monte Asirio residens astrologiam summa calliditate
inuestigauit et primus Assiriis propalauit. Mons est enim altissimus, in
quo bene sidera dinoscere potuit. Et quia magna *incepit*, magnum
tormentum sustulit, quia per prudenciam fecit, per Mercurium deum   285
facundie ad saxum religatur. Qui ignem furatus est, *dicitur*
deprendisse racionem de fulmine. Qua arte quamdiu usi sunt hi
homines, bene successit eis, sepius male contingit eis. Vnde pestis
hominibus inmissa dicitur fuisse. I<apetus> et P<rometheus> ante
homines fuerunt secundum philosophos.   290

268 Nabathvs ... 269 Nabaioht] *cf.* Isid. *Etymol.* 14:3: Nabathea regio a Nabeth filio Ismael nuncupata.

263   vix ... 267 regnum] *cf.* **Frei381 (35r):** uix n. merito non permisit illis ut haberent passim aera quia tunc nichil eis obstiteret quod in hoc patet Nam cum non permittitur quod ideo sit diis ?fra? qui fratres sunt quia eodem aere errant uel quia filii dicuntur aurore et astrei fuisse qui fuit unus ?de-tas? Eurus dico quod quisque regit suam partem Nam est re.

270 Temes *i.e.* tmesis   **271** a *correxi secundum 14809* id est *cod.* | Iapeto *correxi* iapeta *cod.*

heavy in the others and so it was pressed further down. For HE ALLOWED THESE TO HAVE AIR, but NOT EVERYWHERE.

BARELY NOW. And justly he did not allow them to have air everywhere, since then nothing would stand in their way, which is evident here. For he did not allow this to happen, since the *differences who are brothers*[68], since they come from disturbed air or are created from the same air. *And in fact*[69], I say that each and everyone ruled his own part, for it is a kingdom.

NABATHUS or Nabath was the son of Ismael, son of Abraham, who ruled in the east. The region is named Nabaioth after him.

SEPTEMQUE TRIONES. Tmesis, so that the utterance is cut in the middle.

WHICH THE SEED of IAPETUS. The pagans claim that Prometheus first created figures of men out of clay and that from him the art of creating figures and statues was perfected. Whence also the poets invent figuratively that men was first created by him because of the effigies. Iapetus had two sons, Prometheus and Epimetheus. Prometheus made man. Having done this it is said that he ascended to the heavens and with the help of Minerva he held a torch against the disk of the sun and stole fire from the gods, which he offered to the use of men. Wherefore the indignant gods sent poverty and famine to earth. But later he was tied to a rock on mount Caucasus, so that an eagle would eat his heart, and this was done by Mercury.

1:58

1:61

1:64

1:82

This is nothing other than that a boy was a very discerning man and residing on the Assyrian mount Caucasus he investigated astrology with the greatest skill and was the first to divulge this to the Assyrians. For this mountain is very high and at its top he could distinguish the stars well. And since he started great things he suffered a great punishment there, since he did this through prudence, he was tied to a rock by the god of learning, Mercury. He who stole fire is said to have discovered the method from lightning. As long as these men used this art, it went well for them, but more often it went badly. Whence it was said that a pestilence was sent against man. Iapetus and Prometheus existed befor man according to the philosophers.

[68] This passage appears corrupted, but there is no help in the other mss to suggest a better reading.
[69] This part could be corrupted. Freiburg 381 has *Eurus* for *et uere*, which is a lemma to line 1,61.

1:102   OMNIA TELLVS. Telluris est num*en* terre. Tellus autem est profunditas terre, in qua arborum et herbarum radices continentur. Terra autem superficies a terendo dicta. Vel Tellus dea ipsa.

1:106   IOVIS ARBORE. Quercus dicitur arbor Iouis uel quia de glandibus suis pascebat homines uel quia per eam dabat responsa.   295

1:111   NECTARIS IBANT. Nectar proprie dicitur potus deorum confectus ex omni dulci potu, sed potest poni pro quolibet dulci liquore.

1:117   INEQVALES, id est frigore et calore, uel serenitate et tempestate. Vel inequales, id est pestiferos corporibus ex calore preterito et frigore ineunte. Pluraliter ponit, id est E<STVSQVE> A<VTVMNOS>, quia unum   300 quodque habet tres menses et tria tempora, id est nouum, adultumm preruptum.

1:113   POSTQVAM SATVRNO. Afferunt enim coniuratione facta Saturnum a regno suo per filium suum Iouem depulsum, ita pacem tempore Saturni ualentem armis Iouem turbasse. Et ideo aureum seculum in   305 argenteum mutauit. Iouis namque tempore multos sapientes in terrenis constat fuisse substantiis. Quam ob rem dicitur argenteum seculum extitisse.

1:123   CEREALIA SVLCIS. Ceres dea dicitur frugum. Quasi Ceres a creando, cuius proprie sunt cerimonie, sicut orgia Liberi.   310

1:140 | IRRITAMENTA M<ALORVM>, quia aurum est causa belli, QVOD PVGNAT
1:142   VTROQVE, id est cum ferro propter aurum.

1:147   ACONITA N<OVERCE>, id est herbas ueneficas a cau*te* natas.

1:151   NEVE FORET. Apud Flegram ciuitatem uel montem Thessalie dicuntur gigantes cum diis pugnasse, sed Varus dicit aliquos ad montes, cum   315 diluuium fuit, confugisse cum utensilibus. Qui postea lacessiti bello ab his, qui de aliis montibus ueniebant, facile ex locis superioribus uincerent. Unde factum est, ut superiores dii, inferiores uero terrigene dicerentur et, quia de humilibus ad superiora reptabant, dicti sunt pro pedibus habuisse serpentes. *Quod est* Saturno de bello fugato titani,   320 filii fratris Saturni patruique Iouis, uoluerunt eum paterna hereditate

EARTH [GAVE] EVERYTHING. Tellurus is a divinity of the earth. But *tellus* 1:102
(earth) is the inner depth of the earth in which the roots of the trees
and herbs are contained. *Terra* (earth) is the surface and named from
terendo (to rub). Or *Tellus* is the goddess.

JUPITER'S TREE. The oak is called Jupiter's tree, either because it feeds 1:106
men with its acorns, or because he gave oracle replies through it.

[RIVERS] OF NECTAR FLOWED. The drink of the gods is properly called 1:111
nectar, it is made from every sweet drink, but it can be used for any
sweet drink.

UNEVEN, that is concerning cold and heat, or concerning clear weather 1:117
and storminess. Or uneven, that is harmful for bodies because of
preceding heat and subsequent cold. He puts it in the plural, that is
SUMMERS AND AUTUMNS, since each has three months and three
periods, that is new, fullgrown and mature.

AFTER SATURN. They say that after a conspiracy Saturn was driven 1:113
from his kingdom by his son, Jupiter, so that Jupiter disturbed with
arms the peace that was kept in Saturn's time. And therefore the
golden age changed into the silver age. For it is clear that in Jupiter's
time there were many wise men among the earthly persons. For this
reason it is said that there was a silver age.

THE CERES [SEED] IN FURROWS. The goddess of grain is named Ceres. 1:123
Ceres as from *creare* (creating), whose characteristic is ceremonies, as
orgies are Liber's.

INCITEMENTS TO BAD THINGS, since gold is the cause for war, WHICH 1:140
FIGHTS WITH BOTH, that is with iron because of gold.

STEPMOTHERS [MIXES] WOLF'S-BANE, that is poisonous herbs born from a 1:147
stone.

AND THAT [THE UPPER AIR] BE NOT. In the city of Flegra or a mountain in 1:151
Thessaly giants are said to have fought with the gods. But Varus/Varro
says that some fled with their tools to the mountains, when there was a
flood. These were later challenged to war by those who came from
other mountains, and easily defeated them from their superior
position. Whence it happened that the gods are called 'the upper ones'
and the ones on earth 'the lower ones', and since they crawled from
low places to higher ones, they were said to have snakes for legs.
Quod est[70] after Saturn had been chased away from the war, the
titans, sons of Saturn's brother and Jupiter's uncle, wanted to deprive
him of his paternal heritage, but Jupiter subdued them with war
machines. Therefore he is said to have hurled lightning on them and
thus to have kept his heritage.

[70] This phrase does not fit into the sentence. It is found in all mss except for Freiburg 381,
which has *Saturnus est de belo fugatus*, which explains the *est* but not the *quod*.

priuare, sed Iuppiter eos machinis bellicis debellauit. Quare dicitur eos fulminasse paternamque hereditatem ita detinuisse.

1:174 POSVERE P<ENATES>. Quasi 'penes uos nati', seu p<enates>, id est omnia consentientes. 325

1:182 NON EGO PRO M<VNDI>. Mundus dicitur a mouendo, quia omnia elementa sunt mobilia preter terram, sed gratia aliorum terra dicitur mundus. Hic autem positum est siue pro celo solo siue toto mundo. Dicitur et terra mundus per antifrasin quasi minime est munda.

1:184 ANGVIPEDVM C<APTIVO>. Dicuntur habere anguinos pedes propter 330 calliditatem. Est enim anguis animal callidissimum. Pedem pro affectu accipe.

1:193 SVNT FAVNI. Fauni dicuntur quasi fanes a fando. 'Fanes' enim Grece, 'uox sonat' Latine, uel a responsis. SATIRI dicuntur a saturitate uoluptatum. SILVANI a siluis, sed fauni proprie siluarum dii, satiri dii 335 planitierum in siluis siue extra, panes montium, *unde quemlibet
30ʳ eorum / colere dicuntur*.

1:216 MENALA TRANSIERAM. Hic menalus et pluraliter hec menala. Montes Thessalie.

1:219 CREPVSCVLA. Enim creperum, id est dubium, unde crepuscula, id est 340 dubia. Partes noctis sunt uii: Crepusculum, conticinium, intempestum, gallicinium, matutinum, aurora, diluculum. Matutinum est inter umbrarum abscessum et aurore aduentum.

1:221 PIA VOTA L<YCAON>. Lycaonem Archadie principem solitum, quibus poterat, constat nocuisse predonemque uehementem fuisse. *Quem* 345 Iuppiter, rex Crete, cupiens deprehendere hospitis habitu cum paucis apud eum cepit hospitium. [quem] Ille ueniens nocte gladio percutere uoluit Iouem esse deum dissimulantem. Iuppiter itaque reuersus Cretam damnatum consiliis bonorum bonis suis priuauit. Ille ita necessitate coactus siluis se uelut latronem abdidit artesque antiquas 350 sicut lupus exercuit.

1:241 FERA REGNAT ERINIS, id est furia infernalis.

1:185 AB VNO, quia unum agmen solum modo erat ex una origine, scilicet
1:188 una progenies, quibus faciebat. PERDENDVM EST, dico, uulnus inferendum est. Re uera perdam, sed uos dicetis mihi, quod PRIVS 355 TEMPTANDA essent, sed e contra dico uobis, quod est VVLNVS

THEY PLACED [THEIR] *PENATES*. As in *penes vos nati* (born with/in   1:174
presence of you)[71], or *penates*, that is 'granting everything'.

I WAS NOT [MORE WORRIED] FOR THE WORLD. *Mundus* (world) is named   1:182
from *movere* (to move), since every element is mobile except for the
earth, but thanks to the other elements the earth is named *mundus*. But
here it is used for heaven only or for the entire world. The earth is also
named *mundus* through antiphrasis, as it is the least clean.

[THE ARMS] OF THE SERPENT-FOOTED ON THE CAPTIVE [SKY]. The giants   1:184
are said to have snake legs because of their slyness. For the snake is the
slyest animal. Interpret 'foot' as their disposition.[72]

THERE ARE FAUNS. Fauns are named as *fanes* from *fando*. For *fanes* in   1:193
Greek is 'a voice sounding' in Latin, or from replies. SATYRS are named
from *saturitas* (satiety/fulness) of pleasures. SYLVANS from *silvis*
(woods), but the fauns are properly the gods of the forests, the satyrs
are the gods of the plains in the forests or outside, the *panes* are [gods]
of the mountains, *whence they are said to worship anyone of them*[73].

I HAD CROSSED THE MAENALA. Maenalus (masculine) and in plural   1:216
Maenala (neutrum). They are mountains in Thessaly.

CREPUSCULE (TWILIGHT). For *Creperum* (darkness) is a wavering,   1:219
whence *crepuscula*, that is waverings. There are seven parts of the
night: *crepusculum, conticinium, intempestum, gallicinium, matutinum,
aurora, diluculum*. *Matutinum* is between the receding of the shadows
and the arrival of dawn.

LYCAON [MOCKED] THEIR PIOUS PRAYERS. It is a fact that Lycaon, who   1:221
used to be the ruler in Arcadia, hurt those he could and that he was a
violent robber. Jupiter, king of Crete, wishing to catch him took
lodging with him together with a few men in the guise of a guest.
Coming in the night he wanted to strike Jupiter, who hid that he was a
god, with his sword. And so when Jupiter returned to Crete he
deprived the condemned man of his fortune through the council of
some good men. He forced by necessity withdrew to the forests like a
bandit and practised his old arts like a wolf.

WILD ERINYS RULES, that is infernal Furia/fury.   1:241

FROM ONE [BODY], since it was but one single troop from a single   1:185
origin, namely a single race, for whom he did this. IT MUST BE
DESTROYED, I say, a wound must be inflicted. Truly I will destroy them,
but you tell me that they must be tried first, but against that I say to
you that it is an INCURABLE WOUND and therefore they should be killed.

---

[71] Freiburg 381 has *nos* (with us), which seems a better reading
[72] i.e. snake leg equals sly disposition
[73] This appears to be a problematic passage. All manuscripts have different readings and
none of them make good sense.

1:192 INMEDICABILE et ideo interficientur. Que ideo etiam ne pars bonorum exemplo malorum corrumpantur. Vere adhuc habeo bonos. Nam MIHI SEMIDEI, ut sunt heremite et ceteri et cetere. Opus est, ut securas faciam, quia imputatis.   360

1:201 Sic est, dico, quia omnes dii tremuerunt. Et si non patet qualiter dii tremuerunt, pateat uidelicet per hoc simile: Nam SIC, id est similiter, PERHORRVIT, id est timuit, TOTVS ORBIS tunc, cum Iulius Cesar interfectus fuit, sicut dii gemuerunt. Et sicut Augustus letatus est ex hoc, quod orbis ita dolebat de morte auunculi sui, ita Iuppiter ex hoc, 365 quod subditi tantam de eo habuerunt pietatem, quando nequitiam Lycaonis audierunt.

1:241 Tres sunt sorores, que dicuntur furie infernales esse: Megea, Thesiphone, Allecto. ERINIS uero maior lis interpretatur.

1:256 AFFORE dictum TEMPVS a FATIS.   370

1:281 HI REDEVNT. Minoribus properantibus personis non conuenit respondere.

1:283 IPSE TRIDENTE SVO. Neptunus dicitur tridentem ferre propter triplicem uim. Est enim potabilis, mobilis, liquida et fe<cu>nda, quia fe<cu>ndat segetes.   375

     Pluto, Neptunus, Iuppiter tridentes depinguntur habere, quia quisque eorum habet potestatem in regno alterius.

1:289 CVLMEN TAMEN. Culmen dicitur a culmo, quia antiqui domos suas stramine tegebant.

1:317 NOMINE PARNASVS. Parnasus mons habet duos uertices, dextrum 380 Heliconem et sinistrum Cytheronem. Sed in Helicone est Cirra ciuitas, in Citherone est Nisa, in qua Bachus colitur. Unde Bachus dicitur Niseus et Venus Citharea. In Cirra Apollo et Muse.

1:320 Oreadas NIMPHAS. Oreade nimphe sunt dee montium, driades siluarum, amadriades arborum. Que cum arboribus nascuntur et 385 pereunt. Naiades uel napee foncium, nereides maris.

1:336 QVE TVRBINE. Turbinem dicit ipsam tortuositatem.

1:346 POSTQVE DIEM L<ONGAM>. Diem ponit pro tempore.

1:373 AD DELVBRA DEE. Delubra ueteres dicebant templa fontes habentia, quibus ante ingressum diluebantur. Dicta a diluendo.   390

Also so that no part of the good men will be corrupted by the example of the bad men. Truly thus far I have good men. For I HAVE DEMIGODS, as there are hermits and other men and women. It is necessary that I make them safe, since you assign them to me.

I say, it is thus, since all the gods trembled. And if it is not evident how the gods trembled, clearly it will be evident through this comparison: For SO, that is in the same way, THE WHOLE WORLD then TREMBLED GREATLY, that is feared, when Julius Caesar was killed, just as the gods sighed. And just as Augustus was gladdened by the fact that the world so mourned his uncle, so Jupiter [is gladdened] by this that his subjects had such a piety regarding this, when they heard about Lycaon's wickedness.

There were three sisters who were said to be the infernal furies: Megaera, Tisiphone, Alecto. ERINYS is interpreted as 'greater strife'. | 1:241

It was said by THE FATES THAT A TIME WOULD COME. | 1:256

THEY RETURN. It is not fit for the lesser persons, who hasten, to reply. | 1:281

HE HIMSELF WITH HIS TRIDENT. Neptune is said to carry a trident | 1:283
because of his threefold power. For Neptune is drinkable, mobile, liquid and fruitful, since he makes the crops fruitful.[74]

Pluto, Neptune and Jupiter are portrayed as having tridents, since each one of them has power in the realm of the others.

CULMEN. *Culmen* (top, roof) is named from *culmus* (stalk, stem), since | 1:289
the ancients covered their houses with straw.

[A MOUNTAIN] NAMED PARNASSUS. Mount Parnassus has two peaks, | 1:317
the right one is Helicon, the left Cytheron. But the city Cirrha is on Helicon, on Cytheron is Nysa, where Bacchus is worshipped. Wherefore Bacchus is called Nysean and Venus Cytherean. In Cirrha Apollo and the Muses [are worshipped].[75]

The Oread NYMPHS. The Oread nymphs are goddesses of the | 1:320
mountains, dryads of the forests, hamadryads of the trees. They are born and they die with the trees. Naiads or napeas [are goddesses] of the springs, nereids of the sea.

WHICH [GROWS] IN A WHIRL. He calls this twisting 'a whirl'. | 1:336

AND AFTER A LONG DAY. He uses 'day' for a period of time. | 1:346

---

[74] Neptune is here understood as water
[75] This phrase is missplaces. It should be placed right after 'where Bacchus is worshipped'.

1:390   Hic PROMETHIDES. Vel quia filius erat Promethei uel quia primus reparauit homines post diluuium, sicut Prometheus ante diluuium. [deucalionem humore] Phisici autem per Deucalionem humorem, per Pirram calorem accipiunt, ex quibus omnia post diluuium creata sunt.

1:391   An FALLAX, id est si mihi non est SOLLERTIA secundum hoc, quod 395 cogito, tunc ORACVLA SVNT PIA, et tunc legi NOBIS pro mihi. Vel aliter: F<ALLAX S<OLLERTIA> NOBIS, an nos sumus decepti in hoc, quod
30ᵛ   putamus deos semper / pia suadere, aut si nos non sumus decepti,
1:393   tunc et nunc pia suadent istud, scilicet MAGNA PARENS TERRA EST.

1:390   EPIMETHIDA DICTIS, id est filia Epimithei, fratris Promethei.   400

1:395   Titanida MOTA est, quia pater eius fuit de progenie Titani.

1:438   MAXIME PHITON. Phiton, quia Iunone precipiente persecutus est Latonam, dum pareret, ab Apolline occisus est. Cuius corio tecti tripode<s> Apollinis. Instituti sunt ludi insignes sue uictorie, qui dicuntur Phiciaci.   405

1:470   QVOD factum miratum EST, quia amanti uidetur pulchrum, non amanti graue quasi PLVMBVM.

1:492   VTQVE STIPVLE. Stipule sunt folia uel uagine, quibus culmus ambitur atque fulcitur, ne pondere fruges curuentur, que sunt in culmo. Stipula quasi usta uel ustipula, collecta enim messe uritur propter culturam 410 agri.

1:521   INVENTVM Mercurii M<EDICINA>, quia ipse repertor intrumentorum et medicine, ut *sunt et he*.

1:563   ANTE FORES S<TABIS>, quia non solum imperatores inde in theatro coronabantur, sed domusque fores eorum. Vel ideo dicit fores 415 C<VSTOS>, quia sublata, que ante fores eorum erat, saxa fiebat et ideo fores accedere metuebant.

     TVEBERE, id est -ris quercus, unde duces soliti erant coronari, *et fieri propter* mediam ad coronandam uulgalem, quia inde plebs tantum

TO THE GODDESS'S *DELUBRA* (shrine). The ancients called *delubra*   1:373
temples that had springs, in which they washed themselves before
entering. They are named from *diluendo* (to wash away).

Here THE PROMETHEAN. Either because he was the son of Prometheus   1:390
or because he first restored the human race after the flood, just as
Prometheus before the flood. The natural philosophers interpret
Deucalion as humidity, Pyrrha as heat, from which two everything
was created after the flood.

OR DECEPTIVE, that is if I do not have INGENUITY according to what I   1:391
think, then THE ORACLES ARE PIOUS and then read US for me. Or
differently: DECEPTIVE INGENUITY FOR US, whether we are decieved in
thinking that the gods always counsel pious things, or if we are not
deceived, then and now pious [oracles] counsel this, namely that
EARTH IS THE GREAT MOTHER.

THE EPIMETHIAN WITH [REASSURING] WORDS, that is the daughter of   1:390
Epimetheus, brother of Prometheus.

The Titanian IS MOVED, since her father was from Titan's race.   1:395

GREAT PYTHON. Python was killed by Apollo, since on Juno's order it   1:438
pursued Latona when she was giving birth. Apollo's tripods are
covered with its skin. Games called Pythian were instituted to
celebrate his victory.

He wonder at WHAT happened, since what seems beautiful for a lover,   1:470
seems heavy like LEAD for one not in love.

AND AS THE *STIPULE* (STALKS). *Stipule* are leaves or sheaths, which   1:492
surround and support the stalk, so that the fruits on the stalk do not
bend from the weight. *Stipula* as in *usta* or *ustipula*, for that which was
collected during the harvest is burned (*urere*) for the cultivation of the
field.

THE INVENTION OF MEDICINE is Mercury's, since he is the inventor of   1:521
instruments and medicine, *as are also these.*[76]

YOU WILL STAND IN FRONT OF THE GATES,[77] since the emperors where   1:563
not crowned only in the theatre, but also at their houses and gates. Or
he says GUARDIAN [IN FRONT OF] THE GATES, *since when the laurel that
was in front of their gates had been removed it became stone, and
therefore they feared to approach the gates.*[78]

AND YOU WILL LOOK TO (*tuebere*), that is 'you will look to' (<*tuebe*>*ris*)
the oaks, whence the lords used to be crowned, *and because the

---

[76] This phrase is possibly corrupted. Freiburg 381 has *ut sequitur* ('as follows').
[77] The entire following passage seems severaly corrupted and is the most difficult
passage to make sense of in book one. All mss have commented upon these lines in teh
Metamorphoses, but with varying content and length. Clm 14482c has the longest and
most problematic explanation.
[78] clm14809: since an altar was made from the laurel in front of their gates and therefore
they feared the gates of the church

1:560   coronabitur. Tibi TVEBERE defendesque DVCIBVS, ne eam sumant. Illam,   420
          dico, sic factam MEDIAM, id est uilem, propter te et merito, quia semper
          eris uiridis. *Nam ut inde et cetera*.

          *Mos erat antiquorum, ut quercus plantaretur ante fores nobilium,
          quo propere corone uictoribus possent inde acquiri, sed domini in
          lauro. Laurus una, scilicet quam sibi plantabant. Sed exterius ante   425
          dicit. Que media, scilicet inter laurus et fores. Vel mediam, id est
          'corone' subaudi, quia post annum id est et nobiles et ignobiles
          coronabantur quercu, sed postea nobiles tantum lauro, ignobiles uero
          quercu. Unde etiam quidam legit 'mediam', id est 'plebeiam' subaudis
          modo per te factam. Ideoque dicit tuebere, id est defendes, quia   430
          nobiles quidem id est coronabantur ante lauro. Tuebere, respicit ad
          illud idem, quo et istud F<IDISSIMA> C<VSTOS> P<OSTIBVS> A<VGVSTIS> et
          nobilium*.

          Non tamen ibi laurus plantabatur, ut corone inde haberentur, sed
          etiam ideo, quia tante dignitatis erat, quod nullus auderet aliquam uim   435
          inferre domui illi, ante quam plantauerat. POSTIBVS autem posuit pro
          tota domo.

1:574   PENETRALIA MAGNI. *Amnis* est fluuius nemore et frondibus redimitus
          ex ipsa amenitate uocatus.

1:577   NESCIA GRATENTVR, id est an gratulantur de honore filie in tam   440
          pulchram arborem mutate, an CONSOLENTVR de eadem amissa.
          Congratulentur, id est an salutent an consolentur de dolore filie

1:588   REDEVNTEM IUPITER F<LVMINE>. Flumen est perennis aque depress<i>o,
          a fluendo perpetim dictus. Sed proprie ipsa aqua dicitur flumen quam
          fluuius, id est *prior aqua quam* <de>cursus. Duo uero sunt genera   445

middle became common for the purpose of crowning, since the people will be crowned only from this*[79]. YOU WILL LOOK TO yourself and fend off THE LORDS, so that they do not take it. This one (the oak), I say, that was made 'the middle one', that is cheap, because of you and justly since you will always be green. †Nam ut inde et cetera†[80]

It was the custom of the ancients to plant an oak in front of the gates of the nobles, from which crowns for the victorious could quickly be acquired, but the lords [were crowned] with laurel. A laurel, namely the one they planted for themselves. But he means 'in front' (ante) as in 'outside' (exterius). The 'middle one' (que media), namely inbetween the laurel and the gates. Or 'the middle' (mediam) supply 'of the crown', since after a year both nobles and commoners were crowned with the oak, but later only the nobles with the laurel and the commoners with the oak. Whence also some read 'the middle', that is 'plebeian', supply 'recently made by you'. And therefore he says 'you will look to', that is 'you will defend', since some nobles were crowned before with laurel. 'Look to', take heed of the same thing, where also THE MOST FAITHFUL GUARDIAN [WILL STAND] AT THE VENERABLE PORTALS [AND LOOK TO THE OAK] of the nobles[81].

The laurel was not, however, planted there, so that they would have crowns from it, but since it was of such a great dignity that nobody dared to do any violece towards the house in front of which he had planted it. He uses AT THE PORTALS for the entire house.

THE INTERIOR OF THE GREAT [RIVER]. *Amnis* is a river encircled by a grove and its foliage and is named from this delightfulness (*amenitate*). 1:574

NOT KNOWING WHETHER TO CONGRATULATE, that is whether they should be gratulated regarding the honour of their daughter transformed into such a beautiful tree, or CONSOLED for having lost her. Congratulated, that is whether to greet or console them regarding the sorrow for their daughter. 1:577

JUPITER [HAD SEEN] HER RETURNING FROM THE STREAM. *Flumen* (stream) is a perpetual press of water, it is named from constantly flowing (*fluere*). But properly this water is named *flumen* rather than *fluuius*, that is water comes before its course.[82] There are two kinds of streams. 1:588

---

[79] There seems to be interjected phrases and some alternative or erronous words in this passage compared to clm 14809: And look to, whence the lords used to be crowned. The middle, that is common, since from this even the commoners were crowned. Or look to, that is you will defend agains the lords, so that that they do not take it. This, I say, thus made the middle, that is cheap on account of you, because you will always be green. *nam ut et cetera*

[80] This phrase makes no sense, the final *et cetera* implies that it is either a quotation or a repetition of a familiar pattern, but if that is the case it is unknown to what it refers.

[81] This passage is severly problematic and the translation is only an approximation of what it might mean. I suspect several errors (e.g. two superfluous *id est*) and incorporated interlinear glossing (e.g. *una* in *laurus una* and *que* in *que media*).

[82] This section is corrupted and heavily emendated in the edition. The text of Freiburg 381 offers a better text..

fluminum: unum torrens, id est fluens cum impetu, alter uero unde
Virgilius: 'donec flumine curuo'.

1:597 | IAM *PASCVA* L<ERNE>. Lerna est palus, quam Hercules siccauit. Liceum
1:598   est promunctuorium.

1:617   SVOS ADICERE AMORES, id est denegare uel adicere. Veritas [id] est 450
         Iionem stupratam Iunonem pedissequam eam Ioue concedente fecisse,
         ut eius detraheret forme oculosque mariti surriperet, scilicet cuidam
         Argo callidissimo camerario suo custodiendam commisit, quare
         centum oculos dicitur habuisse. Quem per Mercurium dicitur occidisse
         Iupiter, quia facunda promissio<ne> sua eum corruptum gratia 455
         Iunonis priuauit. Eo quod eius nutu uirginem uiciauit, oculos prius in
         caudam pauonis collocasse dicitur. Eo quod cuidam seruienti sic
         uocato eandem custodiendam rursus conmisit, et, quia uerbis et factis
31ʳ   persecuta est, dicitur ei sub cauda oestrum po- / -suisse. Tandem Ioue
         interueniente ueniam meruit assumpto habitu religionis. Unde postea 460
1:747   dicit NVNC DEA NILIGERA COLITVR C<ELEBERRIMA> T<VRBA>.

1:649   LITERA PRO VERBIS, QVAM PVLVERE PES D<VXIT>. Rotunda enim ungula
         pedis faciebat circulum in puluere ad modum o, *scilicet* fissura, id est
         quod sonat Io.

1:668   PHORONIDES VLTRA. A Phorone, patre Inachi, quia Phoronis uocata est 465
         aua Io<nis>, unde ipsa Phoronides. Aut a Phoroneo rege.

1:669   NATVMQVE V<OCAT>, id est Mercuri*um*, filium Maie, filie Athlantis et
1:682   Plenionis, unde etiam dictus est ATHLANTIADES.

1:671   ALAS PEDIBVS. Ale Mercurii proprie dicuntur talaria et uirga sua
         caduceus in modum falcis.   470

1:682?   Tres fuerunt atlantes: Maximus Maurus, alius Italicus, pater Electre,
         tercius Archadicus, pater matris Mercurii.

1:688   FISTVLA NVPER. Fis<tulam> quidam dicunt a Mercurio inuentam, alii a
         Fauno, qu*em* uocant Greci Pan. Fis<tula> autem dicta, quod uocem
         emittat. Nam 'fos' Grece, 'uox' Latine, 'staliam' 'missa' dicitur.   475

1:691   SIRINGA uocabatur. A siringa dicitur, 'sirinu' Grece, 'fistula' Latine
         sonat.

1:694   HORRIGIVM STVDIIS. Affri fuit soror Latone, cum qua Iupiter uoluit
         concumbere, sed ipsa implorata est deorum marinorum auxilium, qui
         mutauerunt eam in coturnicem. Ipse quoque mutans se in aquilam 480

One rushing, that is it flows with force, the other whereof Virgil says: Until in the winding stream.

THE PASTURES OF LERNA. Lerna is a swamp that Hercules dried out.   1:597
Lyrceum is a promontory.

TO SURRENDER HIS LOVE, that is to deny or to sacrifice. The truth is that   1:617
Jupiter yielded Io and Juno made her into her attendant, so that she could disparage her beauty and snatch her husband's eyes away from her, namely she entrusted her to one Argus to keep, a very cunning chamberlain, wherefore he is said to have had a hundred eyes. Jupiter is said to have killed Argus through Mercury, since he through Juno's grace deprived him the debauched of his eloquent promise.[83] She is said to have first placed his eyes on the tail of a peacock for this reason that he violated the maiden on her command. She is said to have placed a horse-fly under her tail for this reason that she again entrusted the same girl to be guarded by some servant called thus, and since she persecuted her in both words and deeds. Finally with Jupiter's intervention she was granted mercy after she had assumed the religious habit. Whence he thereafter says: NOW THE NILE-WEARING GODDESS IS WORSHIPPED BY THE VERY LARGE CROWD.

INSTEAD OF WORDS A LETTER, WHICH HER FOOT DREW IN THE DUST. The   1:649
round nail of the foot made a circle in the dirt in the shape of an o, namely a fissure, that is something that sounds Io.

[NO] LONGER THE PHORONEAN'S. From Phoron, Inachus's father, since   1:668
Io's grandmother is called Phoronis, whence Io the Phoronean. Or from king Phoroneus.

AND HE CALLS HIS SON, that is Mercury, son of Maia, daughter of Atlas   1:669
and Pleione, whence he is also called the ATLANTIAD.

WINGS TO HIS FEET. The wings of Mercury are properly called *talaria*,   1:671
and his staff in the shape of a sickle is called *caduceus*.

There were three Atlants: Maurus was greatest, another one was   1:682?
Italicus, Electra's father, the third was Arcadicus, father of Mercury's mother.

THE PIPE RECENTLY [DISCOVERED]. Some say that the pipe was invented   1:688
by Mercury, others by Faunus, whom the Greek call Pan. It is called *fistula* since it emits a sound. For *fos* in Greek, is 'sound' in Latin, *stalia* is 'sent'.

She was called SYRINX. She was named from *siringa, sirinu* in Greek, in   1:691
Latin it denotes a pipe.

[SHE WORSHIPPED] THE ORTYGIAN IN HER ENDEAVOURS. Asteria was the   1:694
sister of Latona, with whom Jupiter wanted to sleep, but she begged the sea-gods for help and they transformed her into a quail. Jupiter transformed himself into an eagle and pursued her. Exhausted from

[83] The last part of this sentence is uncertain. It is unclear exactly who the subject is and to what *facunda promissione* and *gratia Iunonis* refers.

secutus est eam. Ipsa uero fessa uolitando occidens in mare facta est insula, que uocata est Orcigia. Allegorice. 'Corix' enim Grece, coturnix Latine.

1:747   NVNC DEA LANIGERA. Postquam uenit in Egyptum secundum fabulam humanitate derelicta et in Nilo purgata, facta est Isis. DEA LINIG\<ER>A, 485 quia cooperuit Osirim *maritum* lino, quando inuenit eum membratim a fratre discerptum.

EXPLICIT LIBER I INCIPIT SECUNDUS

—

flying she fell down into the sea and was made into an island, which is called Ortygia. Allegorically.[84] For *ortyx* in Greek is quail in Latin.

NOW THE WOOL-WEARING GODDESS. According to the story: after she came to Egypt, she abandoned her humanity and was purified in the Nile and then she became Isis. THE LINEN-WEARING GODDESS, since she covered her husband Osiris with linen, when she found him torn to pieces and scattered by his brother. 1:747

HERE ENDS BOOK I AND BOOK 2 BEGINS

---

[84] i.e. the association between the place Ortygia and the Greek word *ortyx* means that this story should be interpreted allegorically. However, the names (*orcigia* and *corix* for *ortygia* and *ortyx*) have are so distorted in the manuscripts that this association is difficult to spot.

Bibliography

Manuscripts

Berlin, Staatsbibliothek Preussischer Kulturbesitz:
lat. oct. 68
(https://digital.staatsbibliothek-
berlin.de/werkansicht?PPN=PPN768030854&PHYSID=PHYS_0001)
lat. 4:o 540
(https://digital.staatsbibliothek-berlin.de/werkansicht/?PPN=PPN768028965)
Bern, Burgerbibliothek Bern:
363
Brussels, Bibliothèque royale:
10470-10473
Copenhagen, Det kongelige bibliotek:
GKS 2008 4:0
(http://www5.kb.dk/permalink/2006/manus/331/eng/)
NKS 56 2o
(http://www5.kb.dk/permalink/2006/manus/88/eng/)
Florence, Biblioteca Medicea Laurenziana:
Plut. 36.12
(http://teca.bmlonline.it/ImageViewer/servlet/ImageViewer?idr=TECA0000423990&k
eyworks=Plut.36.12)
San Marco 223
San Marco 225
Freiburg im Breisgau, Universitätsbibliothek:
381
Leipzig, Universitätsbibliothek Leipzig:
Rep. I 74
(https://www.ub.uni-leipzig.de/forschungsbibliothek/digitale-
sammlungen/mittelalterliche-handschriften/handschriften-der-rep-signaturenreihe-
leihgabe-leipziger-stadtbibliothek/)
London, British Library:
Add. 11967
Harl. 2610
Kings 26
Munich, Bayerische Staastsbibliothek:
Clm 4610
(https://daten.digitale-sammlungen.de/~db/bsb00006777/images/)
clm 7205
clm 14436
(https://daten.digitale-sammlungen.de/~db/0003/bsb00033074/images/)
clm 14482

(http://daten.digitale-sammlungen.de/~db/0004/bsb00046312/images/)
clm 14748
(https://daten.digitale-sammlungen.de/~db/0009/bsb00094604/images/)
clm 14809
(http://daten.digitale-sammlungen.de/~db/0006/bsb00060108/images/)
clm 19488
(https://daten.digitale-sammlungen.de/~db/0006/bsb00060111/images/)
Clm 29208
(https://daten.digitale-sammlungen.de/~db/0001/bsb00011851/images/)
Naples, Biblioteca Nazionale di Napoli:
IV.F.3
(http://www.wdl.org/en/item/4524/)
Paris, Bibliothèque nationale de France:
lat. 8001
(http://gallica.bnf.fr/ark:/12148/btv1b10724052j.r=8001)
lat. 12246
(http://gallica.bnf.fr/ark:/12148/btv1b10721618t.r=12246)
Prague, Státní knihovna CSR:
VIII H32
(http://www.manuscriptorium.com/apps/index.php?direct=record&pid=AIPDIG-
NKCR__VIII_H_32___4DKIY63-cs#search)
Salzburg, Stiftsbibliothek St. Peter:
AV4
San Daniele del Friuli, Biblioteca Guarneriana:
Guarner s. n.
Sankt Gallen, Stiftsbibliothek:
Cod. Sang. 866
(http://www.e-codices.unifr.ch/de/list/one/csg/0866)
Cod. Sang. 870
(http://www.e-codices.unifr.ch/de/list/one/csg/0870)
Vatican City, Biblioteca Apostolica Vaticana:
Ottob. lat. 3313
(https://digi.vatlib.it/view/MSS_Ott.lat.3313)
Pal. lat. 1669
(https://digi.vatlib.it/view/MSS_Pal.lat.1669)
Reg. lat. 221
(https://digi.vatlib.it/view/MSS_Reg.lat.221)
Vat.Urb.lat. 341
(https://digi.vatlib.it/view/MSS_Urb.lat.341)
Vat.Urb.lat. 342
(https://digi.vatlib.it/view/MSS_Urb.lat.342)
Vat. lat. 3867
Vat.lat. 11457

(https://digi.vatlib.it/view/MSS_Vat.lat.11457)

N.B. See also end of the section Marginal commentaries in early *Metamorphoses* manuscripts for a list of *Metamorphoses* manuscripts with glosses.

Ancient and Medieval Authors

Abelard, *Historia calamitatum: Consolation to a Friend*, ed. Alexander Andrée. (Toronto: PIMS, 2015).

Accessus ad auctores: medieval introductions to the authors (codex latinus monacensis 19475), ed. S. Wheeler (Kalamazoo: Medieval institute publications, 2015).

Adnotationes super Lucanum, ed. Johannes Endt. (Stuttgart: Teubner, 1969).

Alcuinus, *De ortographia*, in *Grammatici Latini*, VII, ed. H. Keil, 295-312. (Leipzig: Teubner, 1880).

Augustinus, *Sancti Aurelii Augustini De civitate Dei*, ed. Bernhardt Dombart and Alphons Kalb (Corpus Christianorum Series Latina, 47-48). (Turnhout: Brepols, 1955).

Baudri de Bourgueil, *Poèmes*, vol. 1, ed. Jean-Yves Tilliette. (Paris: Les Belles Lettres, 1998).

Baudri de Bourgueil, *Poèmes*, vol. 2, ed. Jean-Yves Tilliette. (Paris: Les Belles Lettres, 2002).

Beda Venerabilis *De arte metrica et de schematibus et tropis*, ed. C. B. Kendall (Corpus Christianorum. Series Latina, 123A). (Turnhout: Brepols, 1975).

Boethius, *Philosophiae consolatio*, ed. Ludwig Bieler (Corpus Christianorum. Series Latina, 94). (Turnhout: Brepols, 1958).

Saeculi noni auctoris in Boetii Consolationem Philosophiae commentaries, ed. Edmund T. Silk (Papers and Monographs of the American Academy in Rome, 9). (Rome: American Academy in Rome, 1935).

Calcidius, *Plato Latinus. IV, Timaeus a Calcidio translatus commentarioque instructus*, ed. P.J. Jensen, J.H. Waszink. (London-Leiden: Warburg Institut-Brill, 1962).

Cicero, Brutus, ed. E. Malcovati. (Stuttgart: Teubner, 1970).

— — —, *Rhetorici libri duo qui uocantur De inuentione*, ed. E. Stroebel. (Stuttgart: Teubner, 1915).

— — —, *De officiis*, ed. Carl Atzert. (Stuttgart: Teubner, 1963).

— — —, *On Duties*. Transl. Walter Miller. Loeb Classical Library 30, (Cambridge, MA: Harvard University Press, 1913).

Conradi de Mure Fabularius, ed. Tom van de Loo (Corpus Christianorum Continuatio Mediaevalis 210). (Turnhout: Brepols, 2006).

Dialogus super auctores, ed. R. B. C. Huygens (Collection Latomus, 17). (Berchem-Bruxelles: Latomus, 1955).

Dictys Cretensis, Ephemeris belli Troiani ex graeco in latinum sermonem uersa atque retractata, ed. Werner Eisenhut. (Leipzig: Teubner 1973).

Eriugena, Iohannes Scotus:

   Homilia et commentarius in Euangelium Iohannis, ed. Édouard Jeauneau (Corpus Christianorum Continuatio Mediaevalis, 166). (Turnhout: Brepols, 2008).

   Glossae in Martiani Librum I de nuptiis, ed. Édouard Jeauneau. (Turnhout: Brepols, 1978).

   Annotationes in Marcianum, ed. Cora Lutz. (Cambridge: The Mediaeval Academy of America, 1939).

Fulg. Fulgentius Mythographus, *Mythologiarum libri tres*, ed. Rudolf Helm. (Stuttgart: Teubner, 1970 (1898)).

Gellius, Aulus, *Noctes Atticae*, ed. F. Serra (Pisa: Giardini, 1993).

Grammatici Latini. Vol. 2, Prisciani : Institutionum grammaticarum libri I-XII, ed. Keil, Heinrich & Hertz, Martin Julius (Teubner: Leipzig, 1855-1880)

Guibert of Nogent, Autobiographie, ed. Edmond-René Labande (Paris: Les Belles Lettres, 1981).

Horatius, *Carmina*, ed. D.R. Shackleton Bailey. (Stuttgart: Teubner, 1995).

Pseudacronis scholia in Horatium vetustiora, vol. I, ed. Otto Keller. (Leipzig: Teubner, 1902).

Hugo of Trimberg, *Registrum multorum auctorum*, ed. Johann Huemer. (Wien: Tempsky, 1888).

Hyg. Hyginus

   Astr.   *De astronomia*, ed. Ghislaine Viré. (Stuttgart: Teubner, 1992).

   Fab.   *Fabulae*, ed. P.K. Marshall. (Stuttgart: Teubner, 1993).

Isid. *Etymol*. Isidorus Hispalensis, *Etymologiarum siue Originum libri XX*, ed. W. M. Lindsay. (Oxford: Clarendon press, 1911).

Lact. *Nar*. Lactantius Placidus (Pseudo) *Narrationes fabularum Ouidianarum*, in *Metamorphoses*, ed. Hugo Magnus. (Berlin: Weidmann, 1914).

Liber de Natura Deorum, ed. V. Brown 'An Edition of an Anonymous Twelfth-Century *Liber de Natura Deorum*' in Mediaeval Studies vol. 34. (Toronto: Pontifical Institute of Mediaeval Studies, 1972), p. 1-70.

Luc. *Evangelium secundum Lucam* in *Biblia sacra iuxta vulgatam versionem*, ed. R. Weber. (Stuttgart: Deutsche Bibelgesellschaft, 1994).

Manegold   *Liber ad Geberhardum* in MGH, *Libelli de lite imperatorum et pontificum saeculis XI et XII*, vol. 1, ed. K. Franke, 308-430. (Hannover: Hahn, 1891).

Manegold von Lautenbach Liber Contra Wolfelmum, ed. Wilfried Hartmann. (Weimar: Böhlau, 1972).

Macrobius, *Commentarii in Somnium Scipionis*, ed. James Willis. (Leipzig: Teubner, 1970).

Marius Victorinus, *Explanationes in Ciceronis Rhetoricam*, ed. A. Ippolito (Corpus Christianorum. Series Latina 132). (Turnhout: Brepols, 2006).

Martianus Capella, *De Nuptiis Philologiae et Mercurii*, ed. James Willis. (Leipzig: Teubner, 1983).

MGH *Monumenta Germaniae Historica* (The volumes can be found digitised on: https://www.dmgh.de/)

MGH *Epistolae Karolini aevi (II)*, *Epistolae 4*, ed. Ernst Dümmler (München: Monumenta Germaniae Historica, 1895).

MGH *Epistolae Karolini aevi (III)*, *Epistolae 5*, ed. Ernst Dümmler and Karl Hampe (München: Monumenta Germaniae Historica, 1899).

MGH *Epistolae Karolini aevi (IV)*, *Epistolae 6*, ed. Ernst Dümmler and Ernst Perels (München: Monumenta Germaniae Historica, 1925).

MGH *Die Tegernseer Briefsammlung Des 12. Jahrhunderts, Die Briefe Der Deutschen Kaiserzeit*, ed. Helmut Plechl and Werner Bergmann (Hannover: Hahn, 2002).

MGH *Die Briefe des Bischofs Rather von Verona, Die Briefe der deutschen Kaiserzeit 1*, ed. Fritz Weigle (München: Monumenta Germaniae Historica, 1949).

MGH *Die Briefsammlung Gerberts von Reims, Die Briefe der deutschen Kaiserzeit 2*, ed. Fritz Weigle (München: Monumenta Germaniae Historica, 1966).

MGH *Die ältere Wormser Briefsammlung, Die Briefe der deutschen Kaiserzeit 3*, ed. Walther Bulst (München: Monumenta Germaniae Historica, 1949).

MGH *Briefsammlungen der Zeit Heinrichs IV, Die Briefe der deutschen Kaiserzeit 5*, ed. Carl Erdmann and Norbert Fickermann (München: Monumenta Germaniae Historica, 1950).

MGH *Poetae Latini aevi Carolini 1, Poetae Latini Medii Aevi 1*, ed. Ernst Dümmler (München: Monumenta Germaniae Historica, 1881).

MGH *Die Ottonenzeit. Poetae Latini medii aevi, 5, Fasc. 1/2*, ed. Karl Strecker (München: Monumenta Germaniae Historica, 1978).

MGH *SS 10 Scriptores in folio 10, Annales et chronica aevi Salici; Vitae eavi Carolini et Saxonici*, ed. Georg Heinrich Pertz (Berlin: Weidmann, 1925).

MGH *SS 11 Scriptores in folio 11, Historiae aevi Salici*, ed. Georg Heinrich Pertz (Berlin: Weidmann, 1994).

MGH *SS 16 Scriptores in folio 16, Annales aevi Suevici*, ed. Georg Heinrich Pertz (Berlin: Weidmann, 1925).

MGH *SS 24 Scriptores in folio 24, Annales aevi Suevici (Supplementa tomorum XVI et XVII).Gesta saec. XII. XIII. (Supplementa tomorum XX-XXIII)*, ed. Georg Waitz (Berlin: Weidmann, 1975).

MGH *Ottonis episcopi Frisingensis Chronica sive Historia de duabus civitatibus, Scriptores Rerum Germanicarum in Usum Scholarum Separatim Editi*, 45, ed. Adolf Hofmeister (München: Monumenta Germaniae Historica, 1912).

MGH *Ecbasis cuiusdam captivi per tropologiam, Scriptores Rerum Germanicarum in Usum Scholarum Separatim Editi*, 24, ed. Karl Strecker (München: Monumenta Germaniae Historica, 1935).

Myt. Vat.   *Mythographi Vaticani I et II*, ed. Peter Kulcsár (Corpus Christianorum. Series Latina 91C). (Turnhoult: Brepols, 1987).

Noct. Att.   Aulus Gellius, *Noctes Atticae*, ed. F. Serra. (Pisa: Giardini, 1993).

Ovid:

Met.   *Metamorphoses*, ed. R. J. Tarrant. (Oxford: Oxford University Press, 2004).

P. Ovidi Nasonis Metamorphoseon libri XV: Lactanti Placidi qui dicitur Narrationes fabularum Ovidianarum, ed. H. Magnus. (Berlin: Weidmann, 1914).

Miller, F. J., rev. G. P. Goold in *Ovid Metamorphoses Books I-VIII*. (Cambridge, Mass.: Harvard University Press, 1977).

Metamorphoses: In Two Volumes, 2: Books IX-XV (Cambridge, Mass.: Harvard Univ. Press, 1984).

Her.   *Heroides* in *P. Ovidi Nasonis Amores: Medicamina faciei femineae; Ars amatoria; Remedia amoris*, ed. E. J. Kenney. (Oxford: Clarendon press, 1961).

Remigius of Auxerre, *Commentum Einsidlense in Donati Artem maiorem*, ed. H. Hagen. (Leipzig: Teubner, 1870).

Roger Bacon, *Opus majus*, ed. John H. Bridges. (Oxford: Clarendon press, 1897).

Rupertus Tuitensis, *De sancta Trinitate et operibus eius*. Libri 1-9, ed. Rhabanus Haacke. Corpus Christianorum. Continuatio Mediaevalis. (Turnhout: Brepols, 1971).

Serv. *in Aen., in Georg., in Buc. Servii Grammatici qui feruntur in Vergilii carmina commentarii, vol. 1-3:2,* ed. Georg Thilo, H. Hagen. (Leipzig: Teubner, 1881-1902).
Sextus Amarcius, *Satires* (transl. R. E. Pepin) & Eupolemius (ed. and transl. J. M. Ziolkowski). (Cambridge: Harvard University Press, 2011).
Statius
    Theb.   *Thebais,* ed. Alfred Klotz and Thomas C. Klinnert. (Leipzig: Teubner, 1973).
Suetonius, *De uita Caesarum,* ed. M. Ihm. (Lepizig: Teubner, 1908).
Vergilius
    Aen.   *Aeneis,* ed. Otto Ribbeck. (Leipzig: Teubner, 1895).
    Georg.   *Georgica,* ed. Otto Ribbeck. (Leipzig: Teubner, 1894).
Victorinus, Marius, *Marii Victorini Explanationes in Ciceronis Rhetoricam,* ed. Antonella Ippolito, Corpus Christianorum. Series Latina (Turnhout: Brepols, 2006).
William of Conches   *Guillelmi de Conchis Opera omnia. T. 1, Dragmaticon philosophiae,* Corpus Christianorum. Continuatio Mediaevalis, ed. Italo Ronca. (Turnhout: Brepols, 1997).

Secondary sources

Alton, E. H., 'Ovid in the Medieval Schoolroom', *Hermathena, 1960.94* (1960), 21–38.
Baker, Craig and others, ed., Ovide moralisé, *Livre I, édition collective* (Paris: Société des anciens textes français, 2018).
Beach, Alison I., *Women as Scribes: Book Production and Monastic Reform in Twelfth-Century Bavaria,* Cambridge Studies in Palaeography and Codicology (Cambridge: Cambridge University Press, 2004).
Becker, Gustav, *Catalogi Bibliothecarum Antiqui.: Collegit Gustavus Becker. 1. Catalogi Sæculo 13. Vetustiores. 2. Catalogus Catalogorum Posterioris Ætatis* (Bonn, 1885).
Biancardi, S. and others, *Ovidius explanatus: Traduire et commenter les 'Métamorphoses' au Moyen Âge,* (Paris: Classiques Garnier, 2018).
Bischoff, Bernhard, Günter Glauche, and Hermann Knaus, *Mittelalterliche Bibliothekskataloge Deutschlands Und Der Schweiz. Bd 4, Bistümer Passau, Regensburg, Freising, Würzburg* (München, 1979).
Bischoff, Bernhard, and Elizabeth Ineichen-Eder, *Mittelalterliche Bibliothekskataloge Deutschlands Und Der Schweiz. Bd 4, Bistümer Passau, Regensburg, Freising, Würzburg* (München, 1977).
Black, Robert, *Humanism and Education in Medieval and Renaissance Italy: Tradition and Innovation in Latin Schools from the Twelfth to the*

Fifteenth Century (Cambridge University Press, 2001), https://doi.org/10.1017/CBO9780511496684

Bond, Gerald A., '"Iocus Amoris": The Poetry of Baudri of Bourgueil and the Formation of the Ovidian Subculture', *Traditio, 1986.42* (1986), 143–93.

———, *The Loving Subject: Desire, Eloquence and Power in Romanesque France* (Philadelphia: University of Pennsylvania Press, 1995).

Bauer-Eberhardt, Ulrike, *Die illuminierten Handschriften italienischer Herkunft in der Bayerischen Staatsbibliothek. Teil 1: Vom 10. bis zur Mitte des 14. Jahrhunderts* (Wiesbaden: Reichert, 2010).

Bulst, W., 'Liebesbriefgedichte Marbods', in *Liber Floridus: Mittellateinische Studien Paul Lehmann Zum 65. Geburtstag Gewidmet*, ed. by B. Bischoff and S. Brechter (St. Ottilien: Eos Verlag der Erzabtei, 1950), pp. 287–301.

Bynum, Caroline W., *Metamorphosis and Identity* (New York: Zone Books, 2001)

Caiazzo, Irene, 'Magister Menegaldus, l'anonyme d'Erfurt et la Consolatio Philosophiæ', *Revue d'Histoire des Textes*, 6 (2011), 139–65, https://doi.org/10.1484/J.RHT.5.101218

———, 'Manegold, Modernorum Magister Magistrorum', in *Arts Du Langage et Théologie Aux Confins Des XIe et XIIe Siècles*, ed. by I. Rosier-Catach (Turnhout: Brepols Publishers, 2011), xxvi, 317–49, https://doi.org/10.1484/M.SA-EB.3.4872

Cameron, Alan, *Greek Mythography in the Roman World*, (Oxford; New York: Oxford University Press, 2004).

Carruthers, Mary J., *The Book of Memory: A Study of Memory in Medieval Culture*, Cambridge Studies in Medieval Literature (Cambridge: Cambridge University Press, 1990).

Casarsa, L., M. D'Angelo, and C. Scalon, *La Libreria Di Guarnerio D'Artegna* (Udine: Casamassima, 1991).

Clark, James G., Frank Thomas Coulson, and Kathryn L. McKinley, *Ovid in the Middle Ages* (Cambridge: Cambridge University Press, 2011).

Cleaver, Laura, *Education in Twelfth-Century Art and Architecture: Images of Learning in Europe, c.1100-1220*, Boydell Studies in Medieval Art and Architecture (Woodbridge, Suffolk, UK; Rochester, NY, USA: The Boydell Press, 2016).

Copeland, Rita, 'Gloss and Commentary' in *Oxford Handbook of Medieval Latin Literature*, ed. by R. Hexter and D. Townsend (Oxford: 2012), https://doi.org/10.1093/oxfordhb/9780195394016.013.0009

Cotts, John D., *Europe's Long Twelfth Century: Order, Anxiety and Adaptation, 1095-1229* (Houndmills, Basingstoke, Hampshire: Palgrave Macmillan, 2013).

Coulson, Frank T., 'Hitherto Unedited Medieval and Renaissance Lives of Ovid I', *Mediaeval Studies*, 1987.49 (1987), 152–207.

———, *The 'Vulgate' Commentary on Ovid's Metamorphoses: The Creation Myth and the Story of Orpheus*, Toronto Medieval Latin Texts (Toronto: 1991).

———, 'Hitherto Unedited Medieval and Renaissance Lives of Ovid II', *Mediaeval Studies*, 1997.59 (1997), 111–53.

———, 'Ovid's Transformations in Medieval France', in *Metamorphosis: The Changing Face of Ovid in Medieval and Early Modern Europe* (Toronto: CRRS Publications, 2007), pp. 33–60.

———, *The Vulgate Commentary on Ovid's Metamorphoses Book 1* (Kalamazoo: Medieval institute publications, 2015).

Coulson, Frank T., and Bruno. Roy, *Incipitarium Ovidianum: A Finding Guide for Texts in Latin Related to the Study of Ovid in the Middle Ages and Renaissance*, Publications of the Journal of Medieval Latin; 3 (Turnhout: Brepols, 2000).

Demats, Paule, *Fabula: Trois Études de Mythographie Antique et Médiévale, Publications Romanes et Françaises* (Genève: Droz, 1973).

Derolez, Albert, *The Palaeography of Gothic Manuscript Books: From the Twelfth to the Early Sixteenth Century, Cambridge Studies in Palaeography and Codicology* (Cambridge: Cambridge University Press, 2003).

Dronke, Peter, *Medieval Latin and the Rise of European Love-Lyric. Vol. 2, Medieval Latin Love-Poetry* (Oxford: Clarendon Press, 1968).

———, *Sacred and Profane Thought in the Early Middle Ages* (Firenze: SISMEL, 2016).

———, *The Spell of Calcidius: Platonic Concepts and Images in the Medieval West* (Firenze: SISMEL, 2008).

Eder, C. E., *Die Schule Des Klosters Tegernsee in Frühen Mittelalter Im Spiegel Der Tegernseer Handschriften* (München: Arbeo-Gesellschaft, 1972).

Ehlers, Joachim, 'Deutsche Scholaren in *Frankreich während des 12. Jahrhunderts'*, *Vorträge und Forschungen*, 30 (1986), 97–120, https://doi.org/10.11588/vuf.1986.0.15809

Engelbrecht, Wilken, *Filologie in de Dertiende Eeuw: de Bursarii super Ovidios van Magister Willem van Orléans. Editie, inleiding en commentaar.* (Olomouc: Vydavatelství Univerzity Palackého, 2003).

Feiss, Fr. Hugh, and Juliet Mousseau, ed., *A Companion to the Abbey of Saint Victor in Paris* (Leiden: Brill, 2018), https://doi.org/10.1163/9789004351691

Ghisalberti, Fausto, 'Arnolfo d'Orleans: Un Cultore Di Ovidio Nel Secolo XII', *Memorie Del R. Istituto Lombardo, Classe Lettere*, 1932.24 (1932), 157–234.

———, Giovanni del Virgilio epositori delle Metamorfosi (Firenze: Olschki, 1933).

García, Irene Salvo, 'Ovidio en la 'General estoria' de Alfonso X' (Unpublished doctoral dissertation, Madrid-Lyon 2012).

———, 'Les sources de l'*Ovide moralisé* I: types et traitement', *Le Moyen Âge. Revue d'histoire et de philologie*, 2018/2, tome CXXIV, 307-336.

Giraud, Cédric, and Ignacio Durán, ed., *A Companion to Twelfth-Century Schools, Brill's Companions to the Christian Tradition, volume 88* (Leiden; Boston: Brill, 2020).

Glauche, Günter, *Schullektüre Im Mittelalter: Entstehung Und Wandlungen Des Lektürekanons Bis 1200 Nach Den Quellen Dargestellt, Münchener Beiträge Zur Mediävistik Und Renaissance-Forschung* (München, 1970).

Glauche, Günter and Knaus, H., ed., *Mittelalterliche Bibliothekskataloge Deutschlands und der Schweiz, 4:2 Bistum Freising & Bistum Würzburg* (München 1979).

Glauche, Günter, *Katalog der lateinischen Handschriften der Bayerischen Staatsbibliothek München: Die Pergamenthandschriften aus Benediktbeuern: Clm 4510- 4663* (Wiesbaden: Harrassowitz, 1994).

Godden, Malcolm, 'Glosses to the Consolation of Philosophy in Late Anglo-Saxon England: Their Origins and Their Uses', in *Rethinking and Recontextualizing Glosses: New Perspectives in the Study of Late Anglo-Saxon Glossography*, ed. by Patrizia Lendinara, Loredana Lazzari, and Claudia Di Sciacca (Turnhout: Brepols Publishers, 2011), 67–92, https://doi.org/10.1484/M.TEMA-EB.4.00835

Grotans, Anna A., *Reading in Medieval ST. Gall* (Cambridge: Cambridge University Press, 2006), https://doi.org/10.1017/CBO9780511483301

Gura, David T., 'From the Orléanais to Pistoia: The Survival of the Catena Commentary', *Manuscripta*, 54.2 (2010), 171–88, https://doi.org/10.1484/J.MSS.1.100987

———, 'A critical edition and study of Arnulf of Orléans' philological commentary to Ovid's Metamorphoses' (unpublished doctoral dissertation, Ohio State University, 2010)

———, 'The Ovidian Allegorical Schoolbook: Arnulf of Orléans and John of Garland Take Over a Thirteenth-Century Manuscript', *Pecia 20* (2017, pub. 2018), 7-43.

Göransson, Elisabet and others, ed. *The Arts of Editing Medieval Greek and Latin: A Casebook* (Toronto: Pontifical Institute of Mediaeval Studies, 2016).

Hagenmaier, W., *Die lateinischen mittelalterlichen Handschriften der Universitätsbibliothek Freiburg im Breisgau* (Wiesbaden: Harrassowitz, 1980).

Haskins, Charles Homer, *The Renaissance of the Twelfth Century* (Cambridge, MA: Harvard University Press, 1926).

Haupt, M., 'Coniectanea', *Hermes: Zeitschrift Für Klassische Philologie*, 1873.7 (1873).

Haverkamp, Alfred, *Medieval Germany, 1056-1273*, (translated by H. Braun and R. Mortimer) (Oxford: Oxford University Press, 1992).

Hemmerle, Josef, *Das Bistum Augsburg. 1, Die Benediktinerabtei Benediktbeuern, Germania Sacra. Neue Folge* (Berlin: de Gruyter, 1991).

Herren, Michael W., 'Manegold of Lautenbach's Scholia on the Metamorphoses – Are There More?', *Notes and Queries*, 51.3 (2004), 218–23, https://doi.org/10.1093/nq/510218

Hexter, Ralph J., *Ovid and Medieval Schooling: Studies in Medieval School Commentaries on Ovid's Ars Amatoria, Epistulae Ex Ponto, and Epistulae Heroidum, Münchener Beiträge Zur Mediävistik Und Renaissance-Forschung* (München: Arbeo-Gesellschaft, 1986).

Hexter, Ralph, and David Townsend, ed., *The Oxford Handbook of Medieval Latin Literature* (Oxford University Press, 2012), https://doi.org/10.1093/oxfordhb/9780195394016.001.0001

Hunt, R. W., 'The Introduction to the "Artes" in the Twelfth Century', in *Studia Mediaevalia in Honorem Admodum Reverendi Patris Raymundi Josephi Martin* (Bruge: De Tempel, 1948).

Jaeger, C. Stephen, *The Envy of Angels: Cathedral Schools and Social Ideals in Medieval Europe, 950-1200* (Philadelphia: University of Pennsylvania Press, 1994).

Kaylor, Noel Harold, and Philip Edward Phillips, ed., *A Companion to Boethius in the Middle Ages* (BRILL, 2012), https://doi.org/10.1163/9789004225381

Kintzinger, Martin, ed., *Schule und Schüler im Mittelalter: Beiträge zur europäischen Bildungsgeschichte des 9. bis 15. Jahrhunderts, Beihefte zum Archiv für Kulturgeschichte*, 42 (Köln: Böhlau, 1996).

Kwakkel, Erik, 'Decoding the Material Book: Cultural Residue in Medieval Manuscripts', in *The Medieval Manuscript Book*, ed. by Michael Johnston and Michael Van Dussen (Cambridge: Cambridge University Press, 2015), pp. 60–76, https://doi.org/10.1017/CBO9781107588851.004

Kyle, J. D., 'The Monastery Library at St. Emmeram (Regensburg)', *The Journal of Library History*, 1980.15:1 (1980), 1–21.

Lapidge, Michael, 'The Study of Latin Texts in Late Anglo-Saxon England, I. The Evidence of Latin Glosses', *Latin and the Vernacular*

Languages in Early Medieval Britain, ed. by N. Brooks (Leicester: University Press 1982), pp. 99-140.

Lendinara, Patrizia, Loredana Lazzari, and Claudia Di Sciacca, ed., *Rethinking and Recontextualizing Glosses: New Perspectives in the Study of Late Anglo-Saxon Glossography, Textes et Etudes Du Moyen Âge* (Turnhout: Brepols   Publishers,   2011), https://doi.org/10.1484/M.TEMA-EB.5.107180

Luscombe, David Edward, and Jonathan Simon Christopher Riley-Smith, *The New Cambridge Medieval History. Vol. 4, c. 1024-c. 1198. P. 1* (Cambridge: Cambridge   University   Press,   2004), https://doi.org/10.1017/CHOL9780521414104

— — —, *The New Cambridge Medieval History. Vol. 4, c. 1024--c. 1198. P. 2* (Cambridge: Cambridge University Press, 2004).

Manitius, Max, *Geschichte Der Lateinischen Literatur Des Mittelalters, Handbuch Der Altertumswissenschaft* (München: C.H. Becksche Verlagsbuchhandlung, 1973).

Maurer, Helmut and others, ed., *Schwaben und Italien im Hochmittelalter, Vorträge und Forschungen, Bd. 52* (Stuttgart: Thorbecke, 2001).

Meiser, Karl, 'Ueber Einen Commentar Zu Den Metamorphosen Des Ovid', *Sitzungs-Berichte Der Königlich Bayerischen Akademie Der Wissenschaften. Philosophisch-Philologische Und Historische Klasse, 1885* (1885), 47–117.

Mihaliuk, Melanie, and Gerlinde Möser-Mersky, *Mittelalterliche Bibliothekskataloge Österreichs. Bd 4, Salzburg* (Wien, 1966).

Minnis, A. J., *Medieval Theory of Authorship: Scholastic Literary Attitudes in the Later Middle Ages*, 2nd ed (Philadelphia: University of Pennsylvania Press, 1988).

Minnis, Alastair J., and Ian Johnson, *The Cambridge History of Literary Criticism. Vol. 2, The Middle Ages* (Cambridge: Cambridge University Press, 2005).

Munk Olsen, Birger, *La Réception de La Littérature Classique Au Moyen Age (IXe-XIIe Siècle)* (Copenhagen: Museum Tusculanum Press, 1995).

— — —, *L'étude Des Auteurs Classiques Latins Aux XIe et XIIe Siècles. T. 1, Catalogue Des Manuscrits Classiques Latins Copiés Du IXe Au XIIe Siècle: Apicius-Juvénal* (Paris: Éd. du CNRS, 1982).

— — —, *L'étude Des Auteurs Classiques Latins Aux XIe et XIIe Siècles. T. 2, Catalogue Des Manuscrits Classiques Latins Copiés Du IXe Au XIIe Siècle: Livius - Vitruvius: Florilèges - Essais de Plume* (Paris: Éd. du CNRS, 1985).

— — —, *L'étude Des Auteurs Classiques Latins Aux XIe et XIIe Siècles. T. 3. P. 1, Les Classiques Dans Les Bibliothèques Médiévales* (Paris: Éd. du CNRS, 1987).

— — —, *L'étude Des Auteurs Classiques Latins Aux XIe et XIIe Siècles. T. 4. P. 1, La Réception de La Littérature Classique, Travaux Philologiques* (Paris: CNRS éd., 2009).

— — —, *L'étude Des Auteurs Classiques Latins Aux XIe et XIIe Siècles. T. 4. P. 2, La Réception de La Littérature Classique, Manuscrits et Textes* (Paris: CNRS, 2014).

Nida, Eugene A., *Toward a Science of Translating: With Special Reference to Principles and Procedures Involved in Bible Translating* (Leiden: Brill, 1964).

Noble, Thomas F. X., and John H. Van Engen, *European Transformations: The Long Twelfth Century* (Notre Dame, Ind.: University of Notre Dame Press, 2012).

Pade, Marianne, 'The Fragments of Theodontius in Boccaccio's *Genealogie Deorum Gentilium Libri*' in *Avignon & Naples. Italy in France - France in Italy in the Fourteenth Century*, ed. by M. Pade and others. (*Analecta Romana Instituti Danici Supplementum* 25) (Rome: L'Erma di Bretschneider, 1997) 149-182.

Possamaï-Pérez, Marylène, *L'Ovide moralisé, essai d'interprétation* (Paris: Honoré Champion, 2006).

Reynolds, L. D., and Peter K. Marshall, ed., *Texts and Transmission: A Survey of the Latin Classics* (Oxford: Clarendon Press, 1983).

Reynolds, Suzanne, *Medieval Reading: Grammar, Rhetoric and the Classical Text* (Cambridge University Press, 1996), https://doi.org/10.1017/CBO9780511470356

Riché, Pierre, *Écoles et enseignement dans le Haut Moyen Age: fin du Ve siècle - milieu du XIe siècle*, 3. éd (Paris: Picard, 1999).

Rigg, A. G., and G. R. Wieland, 'A Canterbury Classbook of the Mid-Eleventh Century (the "Cambridge Songs" Manuscript)', *Anglo-Saxon England*, 4 (1975), 113–30.

Rivero García, Luis, *Book XIII of Ovid's Metamorphoses: A Textual Commentary* (Berlin: De Gruyter, 2018), https://doi.org/10.1515/9783110612493

Robins, William, 'Toward a Disjunctive Philology', in *The Book Unbound*, ed. by Siân Echard and Stephen Partridge (Toronto: University of Toronto Press, 2004), https://doi.org/10.3138/9781442659933-009

Rubenstein, Jay, *Guibert of Nogent: Portrait of a Medieval Mind* (New York: Routledge, 2002).

Ruf, Paul, *Mittelalterliche Bibliothekskataloge Deutschlands Und Der Schweiz. Bd 3:1, Bistum Augsburg* (München: Beck, 1932).

Russell, Paul, *Reading Ovid in Medieval Wales*, Text and Context (Columbus: The Ohio State University Press, 2017).

Schubert, Martin, ed., *Schreiborte Des Deutschen Mittelalters: Skriptorien - Werke - Mäzene* (Berlin: De Gruyter, 2013), https://doi.org/10.1515/9783110217933

Sheffler, David, *Schools and Schooling in Late Medieval Germany: Regensburg, 1250-1500* (Brill, 2008), https://doi.org/10.1163/ej.9789004166646.i-417

Somfai, Anna, 'The Eleventh-Century Shift in the Reception of Plato's "Timaeus" and Calcidius's "Commentary"', *Journal of the Warburg and Courtauld Institutes, 65* (2002), https://doi.org/10.2307/4135103

Stotz, Peter, *Handbuch Zur Lateinischen Sprache Des Mittelalters* (München: Beck, 1996).

Sturlese, Loris, *Storia Della Filosofia Tedesca Nel Medioevo Dagli Inizi Alla Fine Del XII Secolo* (Firenze: Olschki, 1990).

Teeuwen, Mariken, and Sinéad O'Sullivan, ed., *Carolingian Scholarship and Martianus Capella: Ninth-Century Commentary Traditions on 'De Nuptiis' in Context, Cultural Encounters in Late Antiquity and the Middle Ages* (Turnhout: Brepols Publishers, 2011), https://doi.org/10.1484/M.CELAMA-EB.6.09070802050003050301070806

— — —, 'Carolingian Scholarship on Classical Authors: Practice of Reading and Writing' in *Studies in Medieval and Renaissance Book Culture: Manuscripts of the Latin Classics 800-1200*, ed. Erik Kwakkel (Leiden University Press 2015.

Thomson, Rodney, 'The Place of Germany in the Twelfth-Century Renaissance', in *Manuscripts and Monastic Culture*, ed. by Alison I. Beach (Turnhout: Brepols Publishers, 2007) 19–42, https://doi.org/10.1484/M.MCS-EB.3.3543

Thue Kretschmer, Marek, 'The Love Elegy in Medieval Latin Literature (Pseudo-Ovidiana and Ovidian Imitations)', in *The Cambridge Companion to Latin Love Elegy*, ed. by Thea S. Thorsen (Cambridge University Press, 2013) pp. 271–89, https://doi.org/10.1017/CCO9781139028288.024

— — —, 'L'Ovidius moralizatus de Pierre Bersuire: essai de mise au point', *Interfaces: A Journal of Medieval European Literatures 3* (2016), 221-244.

Tilliette, Jean-Yves, 'Le Retour Du Grand Pan: Remarques Sur Une Adaptation En Vers Des Mitologiae de Fulgence à La Fin Du XIe Siècle (Baudri de Bourgueil, c. 154)', *Studi Medievali*, 1996.38 (1996), 65–93.

— — —, 'Savants et poètes du moyen âge face à Ovide: Les débuts de l'aetas Ovidiana (v. 1050 – v. 1200)', in *Ovidius redivivus*, ed. by Michelangelo Picone and Bernhard Zimmermann (Stuttgart: J.B. Metzler, 1994), pp. 63–104.

Traube, Ludwig, Franz Boll, and Paul Lehmann, *Vorlesungen Und Abhandlungen. Bd 2, Einleitung in Die Lateinische Philologie Des Mittelalters* (München: Beck, 1911).

Verbaal, Wim, 'How the West Was Won by Fiction: The Appearance of Fictional Narrative and Leisurely Reading in Western Literature (11th and 12th Century)', in *True Lies Worldwide*, ed. by Anders Cullhed and Lena Rydholm (Berlin, Boston: De Gruyter, 2014), https://doi.org/10.1515/9783110303209.189

Ward, J. O., 'From Marginal Gloss to Catena Commentary: The Eleventh-Century Origins of a Rhetorical Teaching Tradition in the Medieval West', *Parergon*, 1996.13:2 (1996), 109–20.

West, M. L., *Textual Criticism and Editorial Technique Applicable to Greek and Latin Texts* (Stuttgart: Teubner, 1973).

Wetherbee, Winthrop 'Learned Mythography: Plato and Martianus Capella', in *Oxford Handbook of Medieval Latin Literature*, ed. by Ralph J. Hexter and David Townsend (Oxford: Oxford University Press, 2012).

Wheeler, Stephen Michael, *Accessus Ad Auctores: Medieval Introductions to the Authors (Codex Latinus Monacensis 19475)* (Kalamazoo: Medieval institute publications, 2015).

Wieland, Gernot R., 'The Glossed Manuscript: Classbook or Library Book?', *Anglo-Saxon England*, 14 (1985), 153–73.

———, *The Latin Glosses on Arator and Prudentius in Cambridge University Library, Ms GG.5.35, Studies and Texts / Pontifical Institute of Mediaeval Studies* (Toronto, 1983).

Wilson, Nigel G., 'A Chapter in the History of Scholia' *The Classical Quarterly*, vol .17:2 (1967), 252-254.

Witt, Ronald G., *The Two Latin Cultures and the Foundation of Renaissance Humanism in Medieval Italy* (Cambridge: Cambridge University Press, 2012), https://doi.org/10.1017/CBO9780511779299

Young, Karl, 'Chaucer's Appeal to the Platonic Deity', *Speculum*, 1944.19:1 (1944), 1–13.

Zeller, H., 'Record and Interpretation: Analysis and Documentation as Goal and Method of Editing', in *Contemporary German Editorial Theory* (Ann Arbor: University of Michigan Press, 1995), pp. 17–58.

Zetzel, James E. G., *Marginal Scholarship and Textual Deviance: The Commentum Cornuti and the Early Scholia on Persius, Bulletin of the Institute of Classical Studies Supplement, 84* (London: Institute of Classical Studies, School of Advanced Study, University of London, 2005).

Ziolkowski, Jan M., and Michael C. J. Putnam, *The Virgilian Tradition: The First Fifteen Hundred Years* (New Haven, Conn.: Yale University Press, 2008)

Ziomkowski, Robert, *Liber Contra Wolfelmum* (Paris: Peeters, 2002).

Plates

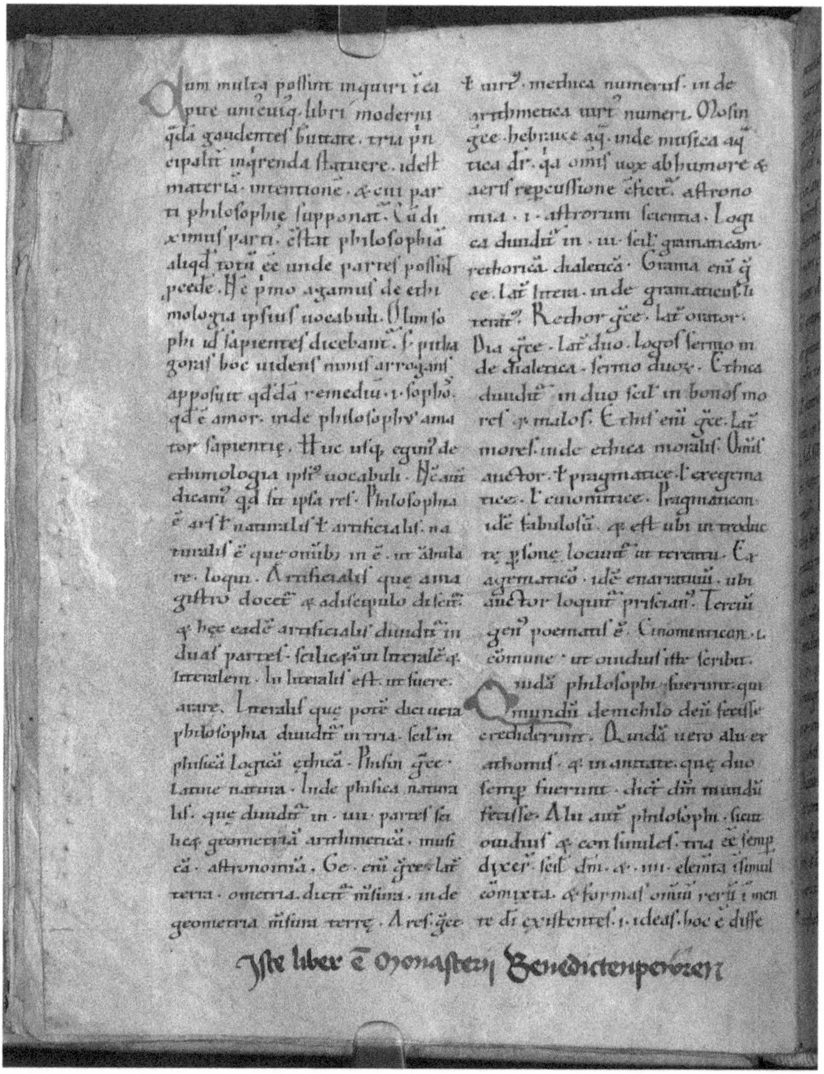

Fig. 1 Bayerische Staatsbibliothek München, Munich, clm4610 61v.

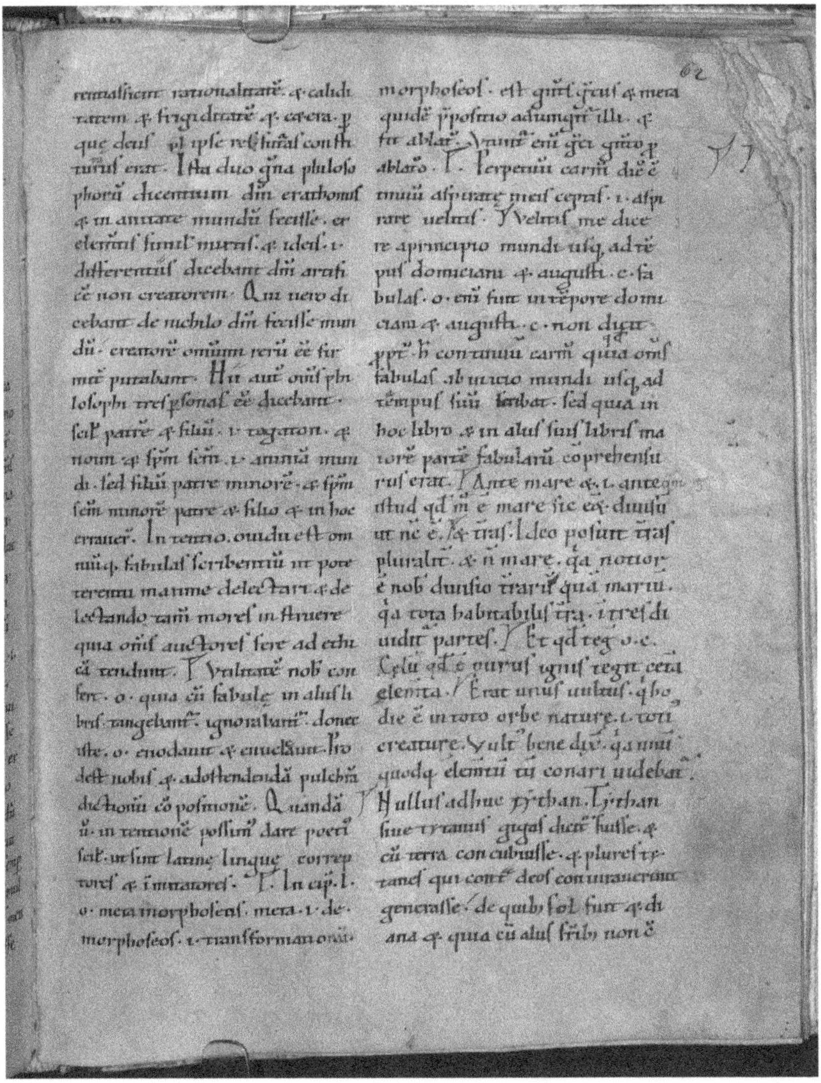

Plates

Fig. 2 Bayerische Staatsbibliothek München, Munich, clm4610 62r.

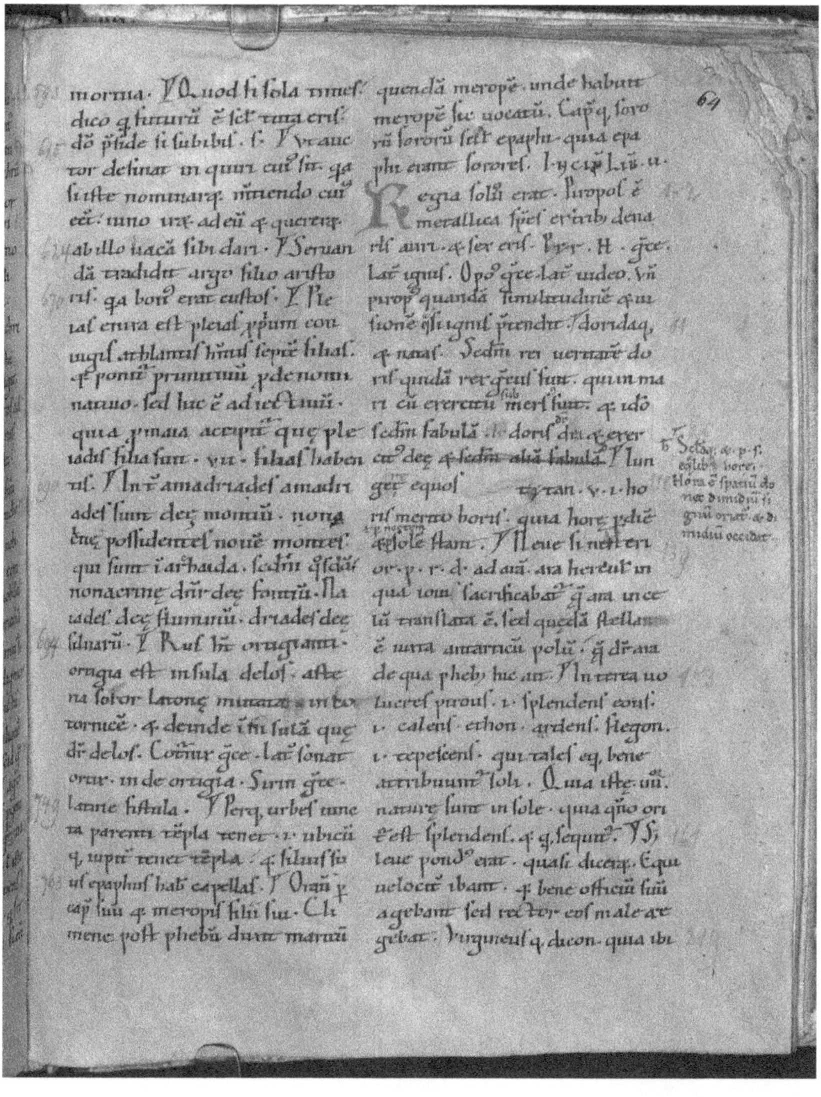

Fig. 3 Bayerische Staatsbibliothek München, Munich, clm4610 64r.

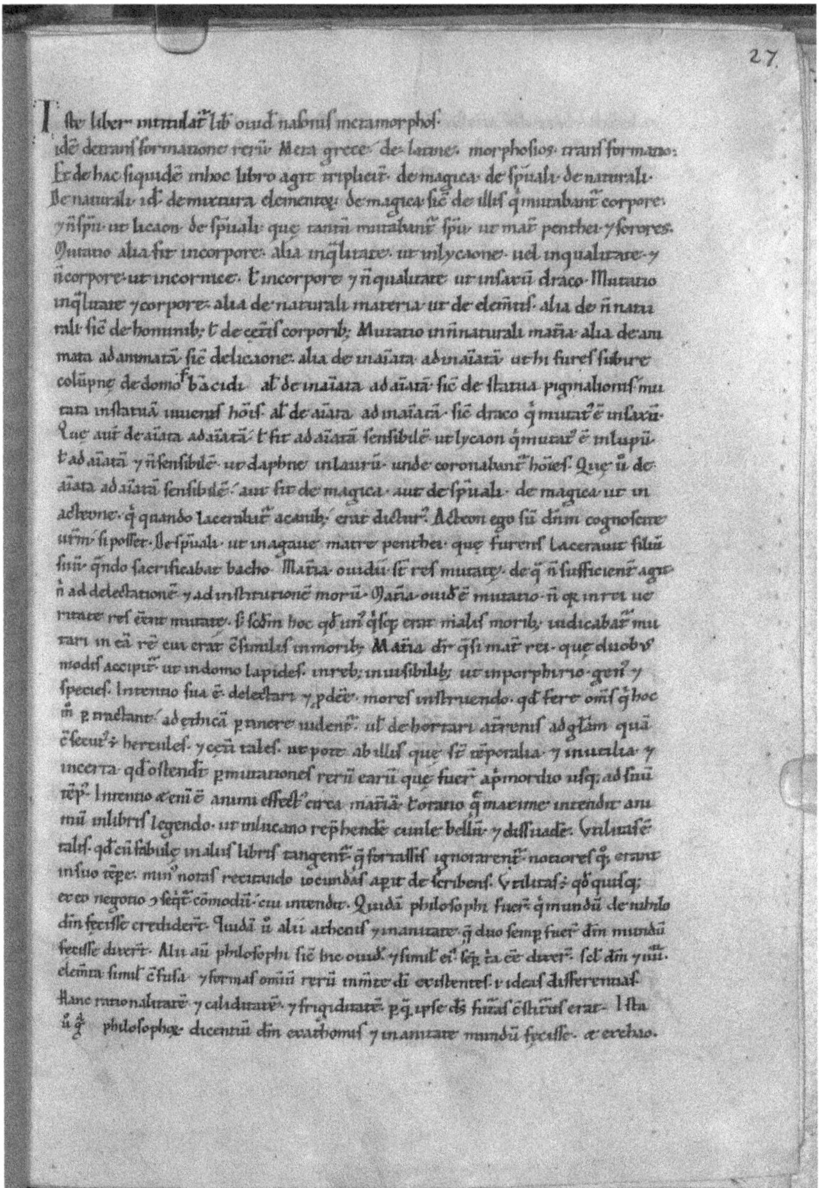

Fig. 4 Bayerische Staatsbibliothek München, Munich, clm14482 27r.

About the Publishing Team

Alessandra Tosi was the managing editor for this book.

Lucy Barnes performed the copy-editing and proofreading.

Anna Gatti designed the cover using InDesign. The cover was produced in InDesign using Fontin (titles) and Calibri (text body) fonts.

Robin Wahlsten Böckerman typeset the book in InDesign. The text font is Palatino Linotype.

This book need not end here…

Share

All our books — including the one you have just read — are free to access online so that students, researchers and members of the public who can't afford a printed edition will have access to the same ideas. This title will be accessed online by hundreds of readers each month across the globe: why not share the link so that someone you know is one of them?

This book and additional content is available at:

https://doi.org/10.11647/OBP.0154

Customise

Personalise your copy of this book or design new books using OBP and third-party material. Take chapters or whole books from our published list and make a special edition, a new anthology or an illuminating coursepack. Each customised edition will be produced as a paperback and a downloadable PDF.

Find out more at:

https://www.openbookpublishers.com/section/59/1

Like Open Book Publishers

Follow @OpenBookPublish

Read more at the Open Book Publishers BLOG

You may also be interested in:

Ovid, Metamorphoses, 3.511-733
Latin Text with Introduction, Commentary, Glossary of
Terms, Vocabulary Aid and Study Questions
Ingo Gildenhard and Andrew Zissos

https://doi.org/10.11647/OBP.0073

Ovid, Amores (Book 1)
William Turpin

https://doi.org/10.11647/OBP.0067

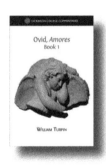

CPSIA information can be obtained
at www.ICGtesting.com
Printed in the USA
JSHW051926051020
8533JS00009B/77

9 781783 745753